Teacher's Book 6

Lynne Robertson

D1740872

OXFORD
UNIVERSITY PRESS

PROPERTY OF
SUMMER BOARDING COURSES LTD

Scope and Sequence

Finn

Sonya

Charlie

April

LISTENING	SPEAKING	WRITING	WRAP UP
New York City Transit People talk about how they use bridges and tunnels to get around **Listening Strategy** Listening for key words	**Correcting Someone** *That bridge is probably used for freight trains. Are you sure?*	**Paragraph Breaks** *Soon they gathered around to study the plans Grandfather drew.* *After that, the strongest men and women of Koi began to dig into the base of Eagle Mountain.* **Writing Practice** Write about a bridge or tunnel you like (Workbook)	• **Writing** Write a persuasive letter (Workbook) • **Presentation** Share your letter with the class • **Review** Units 1 and 2 (Workbook) Big Question 1 Review
Building a Bridge A TV interview with a bridge engineer **Listening Strategy** Listening for sequence	**Describing Steps in a Project** *The first step to making a greeting card is choosing some art supplies.*	**Connectors to Show Support** *The arch itself is what gives the bridge its strength. In fact, even today you can see arch bridges and aqueducts that were built by the ancient Romans.* **Writing Practice** Write about something you wanted to achieve and how you did it (Workbook)	
Exploring Lake Vostok A phone call between a journalist and a scientist **Listening Strategy** Listening for numbers	**Conducting an Interview** *What can you tell us about the new cave you discovered?*	**Parentheses** *The temperature of the inner core (which comprises the metals nickel and iron) can be as high as 5,400 degrees centigrade.* **Writing Practice** Write about a feature of Earth that you think is interesting (WB)	• **Writing** Write a speech (WB) • **Presentation** Share your speech with the class • **Review** Units 3 and 4 (WB) Big Question 2 Review
Volcanoes A student gives a report about different types of volcanoes **Listening Strategy** Listening for time periods	**Offering Suggestions** *We could make a collage for our presentation.*	**Punctuation with Quotation Marks** *Suddenly the lookout cried, "Shallow water and rocks ahead, Admiral!"* **Writing Practice** Write about how you would keep people safe in a big storm (WB)	
Masks in Theater An actor describes the fun and challenge of acting with a mask **Listening Strategy** Listening for instructions	**Finding the Right Word** *What is this thing called? It's used to play a role.*	**Choosing a Good Title** **Writing Practice** Write a story with a title (WB)	• **Writing** Write a personal narrative (WB) • **Presentation** Share your personal narrative with the class • **Review** Units 5 and 6 (WB) Big Question 3 Review 
Fencing An interview with an Olympic fencing champion **Listening Strategy** Listening for advice	**Discussing a Topic** *I think surgeons should have to wear masks. Why do you think so?*	**Using Headings to Organize Your Writing** *Masks for Entertainment* *Masks for Health* *Masks for Safety* **Writing Practice** Write an article with headings (WB)	**Testing Practice 1**
How a Carpenter Uses Symmetry A conversation about the importance of symmetry in making furniture **Listening Strategy** Listening for reasons	**Asking for Clarification** *Look! These pictures are identical.* *I don't know the word "identical." How do you spell it?*	**Writing Numbers as Words** *One side of this butterfly is identical to the other side.* **Writing Practice** Write about an example of symmetry that you like (WB)	• **Writing** Write a personal response (WB) • **Presentation** Share your personal response with the class • **Review** Units 7 and 8 (WB) Big Question 4 Review
Fractals A lecture about fractals and symmetry of scale **Listening Strategy** Listening for gist	**Describing Something You Like** *My favorite example of symmetry is a race car.*	**Prepositional Phrases of Place** *Lia set up her laboratory in the shed at the end of the yard.* **Writing Practice** Write about what you might see in your favorite part of town (WB)	

LISTENING	SPEAKING	WRITING	WRAP UP
Watching a Movie Two people express different emotions while watching a movie **Listening Strategy** Listening for gist	**Expressing Emotions** *Let's go to the museum this weekend!*	**Using Connectors to Show Contrast** *When a language is no longer used we say that it's "dead." However, even after people have stopped speaking a language they sometimes continue to create new words from its roots.* **Writing Practice** Write about something you're good at (WB)	• **Writing** Write a poem (WB) • **Presentation** Perform your poem for the class • **Review** Units 9 and 10 (WB) Big Question 5 Review ▶
Unusual Languages Descriptions of the Silbo Gomera and Hadza languages **Listening Strategy** Listening for similarities and differences	**Expressing Preferences** *Would you rather play soccer or go to the mall? I think I'd prefer to play soccer.*	**Onomatopoeia** *The whistle streamed out of my lungs and carried across the valley.* **Writing Practice** Write a paragraph or poem on a topic you like (WB)	
Recording Memories A son interviews his mom about her memories of growing up in New York **Listening Strategy** Listening for the main idea	**Follow-Up Questions** *I used to go to a school on Kensington Street. Oh, really? Where's Kensington Street?*	**Reflexive Pronouns** *Tenzing dragged himself out beside me.* **Writing Practice** Write about how life today is different from the past (WB)	• **Writing** Write a memoir (WB) • **Presentation** Make a memory wall and retell a classmate's memory • **Review** Units 11 and 12 (WB) Big Question 6 Review ▶
Story Booth A man records his memories of growing up in Italy **Listening Strategy** Listening for facts and opinions	**Telling a Story about Yourself** *My happiest memory is the time my friend and I went camping last summer.*	**Titles in Names** *Mrs. Maggs said I could take some time off.* **Writing Practice** Write about something you've made, written, or drawn (WB)	**Testing Practice 2**
A Poem A poet reads a poem about birds and happiness **Listening Strategy** Listening for reasons	**Expressing Probability** *What will you be doing in five years? I'll be in college. I can't wait!*	**Metaphor** *The albatross is the king of the sky.* **Writing Practice** Write a paragraph about birds (WB)	• **Writing** Write an action plan (WB) • **Presentation** Share your action plan with the class • **Review** Units 13 and 14 (WB) Big Question 7 Review ▶
Bird Song An ornithologist shows how some birds can imitate natural and artificial sounds **Listening Strategy** Listening for examples	**Talking about What You've Learned** *I learned that birds can make tools.*	**Simile** *Like an artist, the bower bird decorates its nest with bright objects in matching colors.* **Writing Practice** Write about why you think birds are special (WB)	
Fears Three people describe things that frighten them **Listening Strategy** Listening for clues	**Suggesting Solutions** *I'm scared of flying. You should try taking a short flight.*	**Connectors to Show Condition** *"People who work in dangerous jobs learn to manage their fear so that they can act quickly and without thinking, even if they're really scared."* **Writing Practice** Write a paragraph to give someone advice (WB)	• **Writing** Write an instructional text (WB) • **Presentation** Share your instructional text with the class • **Review** Units 15 and 16 (WB) Big Question 8 Review ▶
Bungee Jumping An interview with an extreme sportsman **Listening Strategy** Listening for reactions	**Things That Are Scary but Fun** *Have you ever ridden on a roller coaster? Yes! It was really scary but also very exciting!*	**Avoiding Generalizations** *All Aroon could see was an ink-black sky and some tall, creepy objects swaying in the breeze.* **Writing Practice** Write about something that people are afraid of (WB)	
The Boy Who Cried Lynx A folktale that teaches a lesson **Listening Strategy** Listening for the main idea	**Clarifying What You've Said** *That movie wasn't very good. Oh, you didn't like it? What I mean is, it was kind of boring.*	**Reporting Verbs** *"I'm alone too," Martine confided to the giraffe.* **Writing Practice** Write a story of your own (WB)	• **Writing** Write a story (WB) • **Presentation** Share your story with the class • **Review** Units 17 and 18 (WB) Big Question 9 Review ▶
Telling Stories A professional storyteller speaks about her craft **Listening Strategy** Listening for gist	**Talking about Opinions** *Do you think people use smartphones too much? Not really. I think they're great. I use mine for everything.*	**Using Numerals** *Dates: November 19, 1967* *Times: 9:10 p.m.* *Addresses: 72 Barrow Street* *Large numbers: 3 million* **Writing Practice** Write about what you think stories will be like in the future (WB)	**Testing Practice 3**

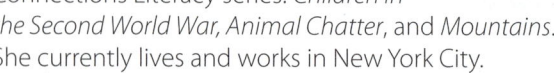

Introduction

Welcome to *Oxford Discover*

Oxford Discover is a six-level course, created to address the evolving needs of young learners of English in the 21st century. Second language acquisition is now much more than an academic pursuit. It has become an essential skill for global cooperation and problem solving. *Oxford Discover* is centered on the belief that language and literacy skills are best taught within a framework of critical thinking and global awareness, and it aims to guide students toward the broader goals of communication.

Oxford Discover creates a positive and motivating learning environment by:

*   providing content that is relevant, informative, and academic.
*   offering multiple perspectives on topics across the curriculum.
*   allowing students to consider key concept questions that they revisit as they gain more information.
*   challenging students to think critically about topics, issues, and questions.
*   developing strategies that help students perform well in tests.
*   fostering a love of reading and writing.

The *Oxford Discover* Author Team

Lesley Koustaff and Susan Rivers

Lesley and Susan are the authors of *Oxford Discover*, levels 1 and 2.

Lesley is a passionate teacher trainer. She has conducted educational workshops all over the world. Lesley lives in New York and writes and edits material to teach students English.

Susan has over 25 years' experience teaching English in Asia and the United States. Susan is the author of *Tiny Talk* and coauthor of *English Time* as well as many other EFL preschool, primary, and secondary teaching materials.

Kathleen Kampa and Charles Vilina

Kathleen and Charles are the authors of *Oxford Discover*, levels 3 and 4. Both Kathleen and Charles have taught Japanese and International School students for over 16 years. They are both active teacher trainers.

Kathleen and Charles are coauthors of *Magic Time* and *Everybody Up*, primary courses published by Oxford University Press.

Kenna Bourke

Kenna Bourke is the author of *Oxford Discover*, levels 5 and 6. Kenna is the author of *The Grammar Lab*, and the *Test it, Fix it* series. Additionally, Kenna has written books for the Oxford Connections Literacy series: *Children in the Second World War, Animal Chatter*, and *Mountains*. She currently lives and works in New York City.

Kindergarten Learning Assumptions

It is assumed that students starting at level 1 of *Oxford Discover* will already have some basic literacy and language skills. The three-level kindergarten course *Show and Tell* gets students ready to learn with *Oxford Discover*. If you use this course or another entry-level course, it is expected that students will know the following:

Literacy and Numeracy

Students will know the alphabet and be able to read words and simple sentences. They will be able to write words and short sentences. Students will know digits and words for numbers 1–29.

Vocabulary

Students will know vocabulary relating to basic classroom objects and greetings, but also some word families:

*   colors
*   shapes
*   toys
*   animals
*   family
*   clothes
*   nature
*   body
*   weather
*   places and things in a house
*   basic verbs and adjectives

Structures

Students will be able to ask and answer basic questions. They will know the present simple, question words, and simple question forms. They will have been introduced to the present continuous for actions happening now.

The Key Principles of *Oxford Discover*

I. Language and Literacy Skills

1. Vocabulary

*   *Oxford Discover*'s rich vocabulary is divided between everyday words and curriculum-based words. Students acquire and retain vocabulary through illustrations and definitions, through context, and through pronunciation and spelling work.

- Students need to encounter new words in different contexts a number of times, before they can recall and recognize the words and autonomously produce them. This is why words are presented and practiced with a focus on meaning before they are highlighted in the reading texts where students encounter them in particular contexts. Vocabulary is then rigorously recycled throughout not only the level, but the entire series, so that students can feel confident when meeting those words again in different situations.

2. Grammar

- *Oxford Discover*'s grammar syllabus is fast-paced, carefully sequenced, and high-level.
- The grammar in *Oxford Discover* comes from the texts in each unit. By providing grammar in context, in an implicit manner, students can be exposed to grammar study with a focus on meaning as well as form. Acquiring a language means developing the ability to use language in natural and communicative situations. Structural input is best when integrated into a meaningful syllabus, utilizing familiar vocabulary and situations. The Student Book takes this approach to teaching grammar, with more explicit grammar practice provided in the Workbook to help students apply it in more contexts and to internalize the rules and forms.
- *Oxford Discover Grammar* is a six-level companion series which provides clear structural grammar input and further practice of the grammatical items presented in the corresponding levels of *Oxford Discover*.

3. Literacy

- *Oxford Discover* introduces words and structures through reading texts in each unit. There is a variety of fiction and nonfiction texts and genre types in each level, which helps students to become familiar with different types of language and language use.
- *Oxford Discover* teaches essential literacy skills through the introduction of reading and writing strategies in each unit. These practical strategies encourage students to read critically and efficiently through a broad range of fiction and nonfiction text types and genres.
- *Oxford Discover Writing and Spelling* is a six-level companion series which provides further literacy input and practice, reviewing the vocabulary and grammatical items, and focusing on the writing strategies presented in the corresponding levels of *Oxford Discover*.

II. 21st Century Skills

We live in an age of rapid change. Advances in communication and information technology continue to create new opportunities and challenges for the future. As our world becomes increasingly interconnected, today's young students must develop strong skills in critical thinking, global communication, collaboration, and creativity. In addition, students must develop life and career skills, information, media, and technology skills, as well as an appreciation and concern for the health of our planet and cross-cultural understanding. *Oxford Discover* strives to help students build each of these skills in order to succeed in the 21st century.

The major 21st Century Skills are addressed in *Oxford Discover*. They build on a broad base of academic subjects presented throughout the course.

1. Critical Thinking

Students in the 21st century need to do more than acquire information. They need to be able to make sense of the information by thinking about it critically. Critical thinking skills help students to determine facts, prioritize information, understand relationships, solve problems, and more. *Oxford Discover* encourages students to think deeply and assess information comprehensively. Students are invited to be curious and questioning and to think beyond their normal perspectives. Throughout every unit, questions labelled *Think* encourage students to apply their own experience and opinions.

2. Communication

As a global course for English in the 21st century, *Oxford Discover* offers students plentiful opportunities to become effective listeners, speakers, readers, and writers. Every unit has two pages devoted comprehensively to communication, but these skills are also utilized in general tasks and exercises. In addition, *Oxford Discover* iTools and Online Practice promote online communication and computer literacy, preparing students for the demands of the new information age.

3. Collaboration

Collaboration requires direct communication between students, which strengthens the personal skills of listening and speaking. Students who work together well not only achieve better results, but also gain a sense of team spirit and pride in the process. *Oxford Discover* offers opportunities for collaboration in every lesson, with students working together in pairs, small groups, or as an entire class.

4. Creativity

Creativity is an essential 21st Century Skill. Students who are able to exercise their creativity are better at making changes, solving new problems, expressing themselves through the arts, and more. *Oxford Discover* encourages creativity throughout each unit by allowing students the freedom to offer ideas and express themselves without judgment. In the lower levels, students complete a project which reflects their learning about the Big Question, after every pair of units. In the higher levels, they learn presentation skills and implement learning through creative processes.

III. Inquiry-based Learning

Inquiry-based learning maximizes student involvement, encourages collaboration and teamwork, and promotes creative thinking. Students employ the four skills of listening, speaking, reading, and writing as they identify questions about the world around them, gather information, and find answers.

Oxford Discover supports an inquiry-based approach to learning English. Each pair of units in *Oxford Discover* revolves around a Big Question on a specific curricular theme. The curricular themes come from school subjects such as social studies (community, history, geography), sciences (life science, physical science, earth science), the arts (music, art) and mathematics. The Big Question is broad, open-ended, and thought-provoking, appealing to students' natural curiosity.

Throughout the process of inquiry-based learning, students play an active role in their own education. Teachers facilitate this learning by guiding students to ask questions, seek information, and find answers. As students work together and share information, they build essential skills in communication and collaboration.

The following guidelines will help teachers create the most effective classroom environment for *Oxford Discover*, ensuring maximum student participation and learning.

1. Facilitate student-centered learning

Student-centered learning gives students an active role in the classroom. The teacher acts as facilitator, guiding the learning and ensuring that everyone has a voice. Students work individually and together to achieve the goals they have set for the lessons. As a result, student participation and dialogue are maximized.

2. Wonder out loud

Curious students are inquirers, ready to look beyond the information on a page. Curiosity can be developed in your students if you are curious, too. As new ideas, stories, or topics encountered, use these sentence starters to help students start wondering:

- *I wonder why these insects are becoming extinct.*
- *I wonder how inventors came up with their first ideas.*
- *I wonder what happens when / if …*

3. Let student inquiry lead the lesson

When students are presented with a topic, invite them to ask their own questions about it. In doing so, they are more motivated to seek answers to those questions. In addition, as students find answers, they take on the added role of teacher to inform others in the class.

4. Explore global values

Students need to understand the importance of values at an early age. Taking an inquiry-based approach means that they are encouraged to think about different situations and the effect that particular behavior has within those situations. *Oxford Discover* promotes global values throughout the series, with texts and activities prompting students to examine values from an outside and a personal perspective. The discussion questions in the teaching notes help to make students aware of their own beliefs and the importance of contributing in a positive way to civil society. There are also nine values worksheets per level, one for each Big Question. The values are drawn from the content of the readings in each pair of units and help students develop a personal and in-depth understanding of the topic. Teachers can use the worksheets flexibly, either while studying the two units, or afterwards.

5. Focus on thinking, not memorizing

Oxford Discover is based on the belief that critical thinking is the key to better learning. While retention of words and structures is important for language development, allowing students to access knowledge on a deeper level is equally important and will further encourage effective learning in the classroom. The critical-thinking activities in *Oxford Discover* help students make sense of the information presented to them, ultimately leading to greater understanding and retention.

6. Build strong student-teacher relationships

While maintaining class discipline, it is important to develop a mutual relationship of trust and open communication with students. In this way, students begin to look at themselves as partners in learning with their teacher. This gives them a sense of shared responsibility, creating a dynamic and highly motivating learning environment.

7. Take time to reflect

Every *Oxford Discover* lesson should begin and end with student reflection. The lesson can begin with the question *What have we learned up to now?* and end with *What have we learned today?* The answers are not limited to content, but can also explore methods, strategies, and processes. As students become more aware of how they learn, they become more confident and efficient in their learning.

8. Make connections

Deep learning occurs when students can connect new knowledge with prior knowledge and personal experiences. Give your students opportunities to make connections. For example:

We learned about the explorer Jacques Cousteau. How is he similar to other explorers we've read about? What qualities do you think explorers have? Could you be an explorer?

Connections can be made between units, too. For example: *How are explorers similar to inventors?*

By making such connections, students will be able to understand new vocabulary and grammar input in a contextualized way and retain language and content knowledge.

9. Cooperate instead of compete

Competitive activities may create temporary motivation, but often leave some students feeling less confident and valued. By contrast, cooperative activities build teamwork and class unity while boosting communication skills. Confident students serve as a support to those who need extra help. All students learn the value of working together. Cooperative activities provide win-win opportunities for the entire class.

Assessment for Learning

Overview of the Assessment Program

The *Oxford Discover* approach to assessment offers teachers and students the tools needed to help shape and improve the students' learning, as well as a means to monitor learning goals, through a shared ongoing and creative process. The *Oxford Discover* assessment program includes five categories of tests for each level of *Oxford Discover*: diagnostic placement tests, progress tests, review tests, achievement tests, four-skill assessments, and portfolio self-assessments. The items in these tests have been reviewed by assessment experts to ensure that each item measures what it is intended to measure. As a result, each test provides an accurate assessment of students' ability in English and their progress in *Oxford Discover*.

Oxford Discover levels 1 – 4 correspond to Cambridge English: Young Learners.

Oxford Discover level 5 corresponds to Cambridge English: Key for Schools.

Oxford Discover level 6 corresponds to Cambridge English: Preliminary for Schools.

The assessment audio is found on the Class Audio CD.

Entry Test and Entry Review Worksheets

- The four-page Entry Test is administered at the beginning of each level and is designed to serve as a diagnostic placement test.
- The test assesses mastery of the key grammar topics from the preceding level that will be reintroduced and expanded on in the new level curriculum. Testing these points on entry can help identify each student's readiness for the new level and thus serve as a baseline for individual student performance as well as class performance.
- There is one Entry Review worksheet for each of the grammar points on the Entry Test.
- The review worksheets can be used to give individualized instruction to students or classes that, based on the Entry Test, have not mastered material from the previous level.
- The worksheets can also be used as additional review and practice throughout the course, even for students or classes that have demonstrated success on the Entry Test.

Unit Tests

- The Unit Tests are grammar and vocabulary progress tests.
- There is one Unit Test after each unit.
- Each test is two pages long.

Review Tests

- The Review Tests are grammar and vocabulary accumulative tests.
- There is a Review Test after Unit 6 and Unit 12.
- Each test focuses on the grammar and vocabulary of the preceding six units.
- Each test is four pages long.

Final Test

- This is a Final Achievement Test for the level.
- It is administered after Unit 18.
- It focuses on the grammar and vocabulary of the entire level.
- This test is four pages long.

Skills Assessments

- The Skills Assessments are contextualized four-skills tests using the vocabulary, grammatical structures, and themes in the Student Book.
- These assessments measure acquisition of listening, reading and writing, and speaking.
- The assessments are based on the style of the Cambridge English: Young Learners (YLE), Cambridge English: Key (KET) for Schools, and Cambridge English Preliminary (PET) for Schools.
- There is a Skills Assessment after Units 6, 12, and 18.
- Each assessment is four pages long.

Portfolio Assessment

- The Portfolio Assessment is a continuous and ongoing formative assessment and self-assessment.
- The purpose is to allow students to be creative, collaborative, communicative, and to be critical thinkers – all 21st Century Skills.
- Portfolio items can include: projects, tests and quizzes, self-assessment worksheets, writing samples, lists of books read, audio or video.

- In addition, the Assessment for Learning CD-ROM contains self-assessment worksheets for students to create their own portfolio cover and to assess their own learning every two units by using can-do statements and responding to Big Question cues.

Answer Keys

- A simple answer key for all tests is provided.

Differentiation

Differentiation helps to ensure that all students find success in the classroom. There are many ways to differentiate instruction. In *Oxford Discover*, differentiation strategies are built into the structure of the course to help you instruct your students in the most effective way possible.

The goal is to:

- Offer a clear pathway for students who are at different levels, with regular checking stages to assess progress against a list of competences at the end of every unit.
- Offer both whole-group work and small-group differentiated activities in the first language tradition to meet the needs of varied teaching styles.

Each lesson spread in the Teacher's Book provides an activity to vary the content difficulty for below-level, at-level, and above-level students. These differentiated activities build upon each other. The below-level activity provides support and scaffolding for less confident students before moving on to a task that is at-level. The at-level task then provides support for students to deal with the greater challenge of above-level. This is a practical way of dealing with classroom management of mixed abilities. Teachers may choose to teach the whole class with one activity, and then continue with the additional activities. Alternatively, three separate simultaneous activities can be set up, as in L1 classrooms.

To help teachers meet the needs of students with varying ability levels, differentiation strategies are found consistently throughout the following strands:

- An Entry Test, taken at the start of the year and useful for diagnostic and placement testing, will result in a level diagnosis (below-level, at-level, and above-level).
- Review worksheets (grammar and reading) are provided for below-level students to bring them up to the level needed.
- Additional differentiation strategies are found throughout the course. The wrap up projects invite students to express their ideas through different learning styles (visual, auditory, kinesthetic). Throughout the course, students have opportunities to work alone, in pairs, and in small groups to support differentiated instruction.

Reading and Writing

Reading

Literacy is the ability to read and write and think critically about the written word. *Oxford Discover* promotes greater literacy through a focus on interesting and engaging texts, both fiction and nonfiction, about a variety of subjects.

The texts have been carefully graded so that they are at an appropriate reading level for students. The word length, vocabulary, and structures used gradually increase in difficulty throughout each level.

Text types

Students need to be exposed to different types of texts. In its broadest form this is a focus on introducing them to both fiction and nonfiction. In *Oxford Discover* each Big Question has two texts to help students find their own answers to the question. One text is nonfiction and corresponds to a school subject such as math, life science, or music. The other one is fiction and is written in a particular genre, encouraging students to relate to and enjoy the content.

The nonfiction texts are presented through different text types such as a brochure, magazine article, or website. This helps students understand not only that writing comes in many forms in daily life, but also that that tone and register (formal and informal language) change depending on the way the information is presented.

The fiction texts come from a variety of genres. This includes fairy tales, fables, historical fiction, and realistic fiction. These genres reflect the types of stories that students are exposed to reading in their native language and provide variety throughout the course.

Authentic texts

In every level of *Oxford Discover* there is a range of authentic texts. These have been carefully chosen to add more information to the Big Question. They come from a variety of sources and from well-respected writers and authors. Authentic texts expose students to real contexts and natural examples of language. The texts chosen are of an appropriate language level and encourage students to read with a focus on meaning and understanding language in context.

Reading Strategies

Reading strategies help students approach a text, improve their comprehension of the text, and learn how to read for specific and detailed information. Strategies such as prediction, compare and contrast, summarizing, and focusing on characters can inspire students to not only master the meaning of unfamiliar concepts but expand their own vocabulary as well.

Reading strategies tie in closely to critical thinking as they encourage students to reflect on what they are reading. As students grow more comfortable using a variety of reading strategies they learn to make conscious decisions about their own learning process.

Multimodality

Multimodal texts help to support students' literacy. Texts which include words, images, and explicit design are a very effective way of engaging students in purposeful interactions with reading and writing.

Multimodal is the use of 'two or more communication modes' to make meaning; for example, image, gesture, music, spoken language, and written language.

In everyday life, texts are becoming increasingly visual or multimodal in nature. Websites, magazines, advertisements, and informational literature are relying more and more upon visual stimulation and clear use of design, in headlines, through different types of fonts, and in stylized images. *Oxford Discover* has included multimodality in its use of DVD and posters to support the Student Book, but even within the texts themselves, the use of words, images and design, and the way they interact with each other helps to keep students stimulated while reading and also helps to exemplify meaning.

Intensive Reading

Intensive reading generally occurs in the classroom and focuses not only upon meaning and strategies used to deduce meaning, but language acquisition in the form of understanding new vocabulary or new grammatical structures. Texts need to be at the correct level and long enough to convey enough information or plot to be interesting, but not so long as to tire the student. *Oxford Discover* takes the approach that intensive reading should be instructional but enjoyable and should encourage students to do more extensive reading.

Extensive Reading

Extensive reading generally occurs outside the classroom and is all about reading for pleasure. Students are encouraged to choose to read about topics that interest them and to employ reading strategies explicitly taught through intensive reading, to help them understand the text more effectively. Reading the different genres and text types in *Oxford Discover* will inspire students to read more in their own time.

Extensive reading is often most effective when students are reading at a level that is appropriate and comfortable for them. If students are reading a book that is too high in level they quickly lose interest. It can be helpful to provide students with access to a collection of graded readers that they can read at their own pace. The recommended readers for use with *Oxford Discover* are the nonfiction selection of *Read and Discover* and the fiction selection of *Read and Imagine*.

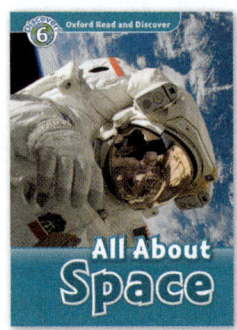

Text Readability

	Level 1	Level 2	Level 3	Level 4	Level 5	Level 6
Flesch Reading Ease Level (F)	85–100	85–95	75–90	70–80	65–80	60–80
Flesch Reading Ease Level (NF)	85–100	80–95	70–85	70–85	60–75	60–75
Flesch-Kincaid Grade Level (F)	0–3	1. 5–3	3–5	3.5–6	4–7	5–7
Flesch-Kincaid Grade Level (NF)	1–3	2–4	3–5	4–6	5–7. 5	6–8
Lexile Measure (F)	75–325	250–450	400–675	500–900	600–750	600–900
Lexile Measure (NF)	125–325	300–550	450–750	725–900	750–950	900–1000

Both sets of readers have been developed with similar themes to those in the Student Book and there is a selection of titles for each level of *Oxford Discover*.

Grading scales

The texts in *Oxford Discover* have been carefully graded to make sure that students understand the texts at their level, and to help students progress in their reading, within one level and from one level to another. In accordance with this, the standards of the Flesch Reading Ease Level, the Flesch-Kincaid Grade Level, and the Lexile Measure, have been taken into account.

The **Flesch Reading Ease Level** is a scale which measures readability. The higher the rating, the easier the text is to understand. There are different scores for fiction and nonfiction texts:

- 100: Very easy to read. Average sentence length is 12 words or fewer. No words of more than two syllables.
- 65: Plain English. Average sentence is 15 to 20 words long. Average word has two syllables.

The **Flesch-Kincaid Grade Level** converts the Flesch Reading Ease Level to a U.S. grade-school level. For example, a score of 5 means that a fifth-grader can understand the text. There are different scores for fiction (F) and nonfiction (NF) texts. It is important to remember that students in any grade will be able to understand a variety of texts around the score.

The **Lexile Measure** gives information about a student's reading ability as well as the difficulty level of a text. Higher Lexile measures represent a higher reading ability. A Lexile reader measure can range from below 200 for beginning readers to above 1600 for advanced readers. There are different scores for fiction (F) and nonfiction (NF) texts. The nonfiction texts can be more challenging than the fiction texts in the same level. Nonfiction texts contain factual content and students are reading to learn.

Writing

Oxford Discover encourages a joy of reading through a variety of texts and text types. However, students also need to be encouraged to produce their own texts and this requires a step-by-step process, helping students to graduate from sentence to text-level output.

Oxford Discover provides many opportunities for students to write. The Word Study and Writing Study sections in the Student Book present the strategies and language focus that help students become more successful writers, and the Workbook provides a four-step writing process (brainstorming, organizing ideas, writing, editing) which helps students to create their own writing output.

Process and Product

Writing tasks are often broken down into process or product from level 3 onwards. The process is all about how students develop and implement writing strategies such as paragraph development, focusing on formal or informal language, and general text layout. The process often includes stages of input, practice, and reflection. The product is the actual writing output that students create. It is often said that the former, process writing, provides a focus on fluency whereas product writing focuses on accuracy. Students need to have both to learn to write confidently and correctly.

Oxford Discover has a process approach with clear and definable product outcomes that can easily be marked against established criteria.

Brainstorming ideas

Too often, teachers expect students to write without giving them adequate time to prepare or strategies to help them develop their ideas. The *Oxford Discover* team believe that encouraging students to plan ideas creatively will create more interest in the process, as well as the final product.

Modelling the writing process

Students are provided with a model text for every writing task. This text is designed to show how topics can be approached, but also how discourse markers, paragraph organization, punctuation, and general textual layout can help to sew a text together.

Personalization

As much as possible, students should be asked to write about things that are of personal relevance to them. This means that although the model in the Student Book or the Workbook may relate to something that is outside their everyday world, the writing task itself will be flexible enough for students to respond using their own ideas and experience. In this way it becomes authentically communicative and a more interesting experience overall.

For a further focus on literacy, *Oxford Writing and Spelling* provides more textual input and encourages students to use the reading strategies they have acquired as they study *Oxford Discover*.

Speaking and Listening

Oxford Discover utilizes an inquiry-led approach to learning English. This means that students are encouraged to ask questions and explore answers for themselves. To do this, they need to develop good oral skills that help them formulate discussions and express opinions confidently, and strong listening skills that help them to understand language of discussion and participate effectively.

Promoting Successful Classroom Discussions

Discussions in the classroom can involve student pairs, small groups, or the entire class.

What makes these class discussions successful? First of all, the questions should be interesting and engaging for students. They should relate to their personal experiences. The teacher needs to act as a moderator, keeping the discussions on track and ensuring that each student is given an opportunity to speak.

There are two kinds of questions that are commonly used in the classroom: close-ended and open-ended questions. Close-ended questions can be answered with one word or with a few words. Yes / No questions and multiple-choice questions are examples of this type of question.

Examples of close-ended questions:

What is the answer to question number three?

What is the name of the explorer in our story?

How do you spell "pineapple"?

Open-ended questions usually require a longer response to answer the question. They prompt more discussion time, allow students to apply new vocabulary, and often lead to more questions.

Examples of open-ended questions:

How do bees help the world?

What plants would you like to grow in your own garden? Why?

What do you think are important qualities of a good student?

Here are some possible open-ended questions you could ask about the topic of healthy eating:

1. *What was the last thing you ate? Describe it.*
2. *Does something have to taste good to be good for you?*
3. *What are some things that you didn't like to eat, but now you like?*
4. *How are healthy foods the same?*
5. *Why is pizza popular?*
6. *What can students do to improve school lunch?*
7. *How do you decide if a food is healthy or not?*

The above questions not only generate strong discussions, but encourage students to ask their own questions and think critically as well.

Here are some discussion starters that can be used to introduce a variety of topics. Don't hesitate to bring in hands-on materials to get students thinking.

What do you think this is, and how would it be used?

What do you think would happen if _____?

How many different ways can you _____?

How are _____ and _____ the same? Different?

How is _____ similar to something that happened in the past?

Why is _____ the way it is?

What should we do to take care of _____?

How do we know this is true?

If you could have a conversation with anyone about _____, who would it be? What would you ask them?

If you could change one thing about _____, what would it be?

Developing a climate of wondering is important in an inquiry-based classroom. While teachers may be accustomed to asking questions and having students take turns to answer, inquiry-based learning invites both students and teachers to ask engaging questions.

Setting up Pairs and Groups

Many activities in this course encourage students to work in pairs or small groups (three or four students). These structures maximize speaking time in a classroom. Students are encouraged to be active rather than passive learners. In groups, they develop collaborative and cooperative skills.

At the beginning of the class year, consider several ways of setting up pairs or small groups. Use one type of grouping for a few classes before changing to a new one. Change groupings throughout the year, so that students interact with many different classmates and have a chance to listen to different vocabulary and structures in different contexts.

Setting up pairs

Side-by-Side Partners

If the classroom is set up with desks in rows, students may work with a partner next to them. If there is an odd number of students, make a group of three.

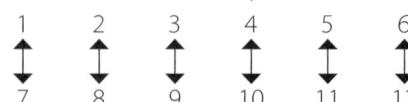

Front and Back Partners

Instead of working with partners next to each other, students work with the partner in front of (or behind) them.

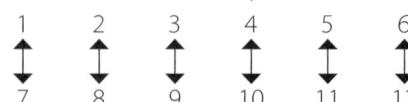

Diagonal Partners

Students work with a partner located diagonally in front of (or behind) them. For ease in discussion, a student may wish to trade seats with the student next to him / her. For example, student 1 and 8 will be partners. Students 1 and 2 might switch seats.

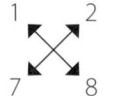 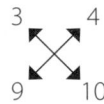 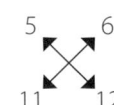

Setting up small groups

Double Partner Groups

Using the partner groups established in pair work above, students form groups of four.

Random Groups

Create random groups of four students by dividing the class size by four, and then having students count off up to that number. For example, if there are 24 students in class, $24 \div 4 = 6$. Students count off from 1 to 6, and then begin again until all have counted off. Point out where each group will have their discussion in the classroom.

Picture Card Groups

Create a set of picture or word cards. Make five of the same card. Pass four out to students and put the fifth card in the location where those students will work. One card per student will be needed. Use topics from the units, such as instruments, colors, biomes, and explorers. Topic cards are fun to use throughout the unit. This grouping is particularly successful with younger students.

Level Groups

Grouping students of similar ability level to work together is a strategy for differentiation. Leveled groups can be reated based on teacher assessments from the Assessment Grid and from your class observations. There are differentiated tasks in the Teacher's Book to allow all students to work at their appropriate level.

Teacher's Role in Setting up Pairs and Groups

1. Explain the task and form groupings. Write the amount of time students will have to complete this task on the board, or set a timer.

2. As students are discussing the prompt or are involved in the activity, walk around the classroom. First of all, be aware of any groups that may have difficulties. If there are personality conflicts or difficulties, deal with this immediately. Secondly, assess student work. Stop and listen to each group. Are students on task? Can errors be corrected individually? Are there any points that need revision with the entire class?

3. On the Assessment Grid, note the level the students are at for this task. Some students may require additional practice.

4. Take note of points for discussion with the entire class.

5. Keep track of the time. Use a signal, such as a raised hand 'quiet signal', to stop small group discussion.

6. Check in with the entire class. Some questions to use:

What was the most interesting thing your partner shared with you?

What was difficult for you, and did you find a solution?

What new questions do you have?

Working in groups may be new for students. The student poster models some effective ways for students to interact. Student "agreements" should be created together with students, but here are some ideas to get started.

Student Agreements

We will . . .

1. Take turns speaking.

2. Listen to our partner or group members.

3. Stay on task.

4. Raise our hand when we see the 'quiet signal' and stop talking.

5. Treat each member of the class with respect. We are a class community.

Functional Language

Students need to learn how to discuss issues and express opinions, but they also need to learn the different elements of functional language. Functional language includes areas such as apologizing, offering and receiving help, transactions, and clarification and explanation.

Learning functional language helps students to understand language 'chunks' and that language often has a very specific purpose. The main function of language is to help students interact and communicate. Dialogues provide models through which students can see and hear authentic communication. Transposition and substitution of vocabulary then allows students to personalize the dialogues through meaningful oral production.

Integrated Component Overview

Student Book
The Student Book contains 18 units. Each pair of units presents students with a different Big Question, encouraging students to examine the world more critically within an inquiry-based learning environment.

Workbook
The Workbook provides students with extra practice of the language and structures taught in class.

Student Online Practice
The Online Practice is a blended approach to learning where students can use online, interactive activities to further practice the language and ideas taught in the Student Book.

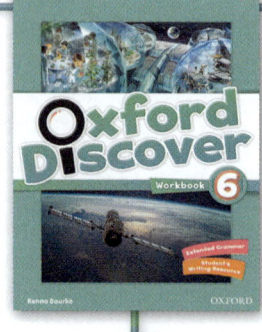

For the Student

Recommended Readers
Oxford Read and Discover is a graded, six-level, nonfiction reading series. *Oxford Read and Imagine* is a graded six-level, fiction reading series. Both draw upon themes and language found in the Student Book.

Dictionaries
Levels 1–4 *Oxford Basic American Dictionary*
Levels 5–6 *Oxford American Dictionary*

Show and Tell
A three-level kindergarten course which introduces students to the 21st Century Skills and prepares students for *Oxford Discover*.

Oxford Discover Grammar
A six-level companion series which follows and supports the grammar syllabus and provides further practice opportunities.

Oxford Discover Writing and Spelling
A six-level companion series which supports students throughout the writing process and introduces them to spelling patterns and strategies.

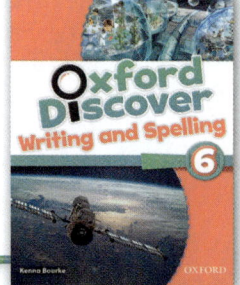

Teacher's Book

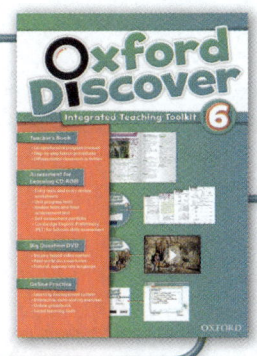

The Teacher's Book is a clear guide for the teacher in all aspects of the course.

Big Question DVD

The Big Question DVD covers each Big Question in the Student Book. Each pair of units has two videos, one with a presenter and one without.

Assessment CD-ROM

Students' progress can be evaluated through continuous assessment, self-assessment, and more formal testing.

Posters

The posters initiate and support classroom discussions and act as visual aids; provide support for learning; and document evidence of learning.

Teacher Online Practice

Teachers have complete access to students' online practice, with a gradebook which enables instant marking.

For the Teacher

Picture Cards

(Levels 1 and 2 only)
The picture cards include all the main unit vocabulary from the Student Book. They can be used to present and recycle vocabulary.

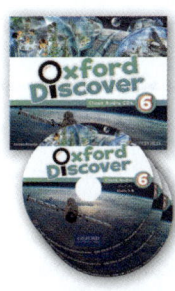

Audio CD

The Class Audio CDs support teaching in class and contain recordings of all the listening texts, reading texts, songs, and speaking dialogues.

iTools

The *Oxford Discover iTools* is a DVD-ROM which contains digital class resources. All the iTools resources can be used either on an Interactive Whiteboard or on a projector.

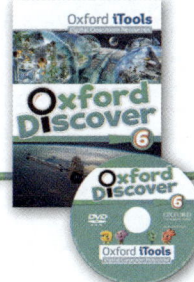

Teacher Website

The Teacher Website provides additional materials for students and teachers to supplement all the other components available.

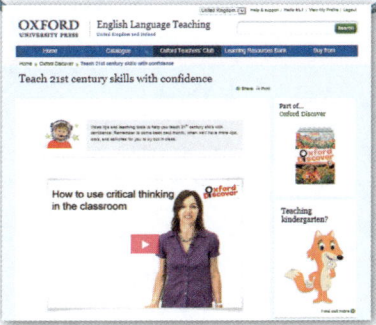

Parent Website

The Parent Website provides support and materials for parents of students studying with *Oxford Discover*.

Tour of Units

Big Question

These pages present the theme and objectives of the following two units. The big picture acts as an introductory visual representation of many of the ideas and language that students will go on to discover in the following pages.

Preview

The preview introduces students to the theme and main objectives of the Big Question. It also gives students information about what they will do and learn throughout the following two units.

In units **9** and **10** you will:

WATCH a video about language.

LEARN about different forms of language.

READ about languages, codes, and how two friends communicate.

88 Big Question 5

A. Big Question DVD

Students watch a DVD about the Big Question in order to stimulate their thinking about the topic. The DVD can be used to elicit vocabulary and to introduce the theme of the following two units. This first viewing of the DVD is silent, as students are encouraged to respond individually to the clips and images. This will also help the teacher determine what students already know and what they want to know.

B. The Big Picture

Students look at the big picture. The big picture helps students to think about what they already know and what they want to know about the topic. It can be used to elicit familiar vocabulary and to motivate students about the theme of the following two units.

WRITE a poem using sounds.

PERFORM your poem for the class.

BIG QUESTION 5

How do we use language?

A Watch the video. Then talk about it with your partner. ▶

B Look at the picture and discuss it with your class.

1 How do you think these people are using language?

2 Why is language important in a train station?

C Think and answer the questions.

1 How do you use language?

2 How many languages do you know?

3 Besides speech, what are some other forms of language?

4 Why do you think people use different languages in other countries?

D Discuss this topic with your class. Fill out the **Big Question Chart**.

What do you know about language? What do you want to know?

89

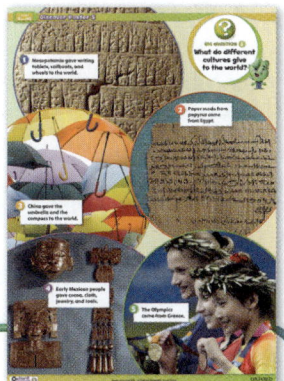

Discover Poster

The Discover Poster should be used to elicit familiar vocabulary and to stimulate interest in the topic.

C. Answer the Questions

Students answer questions that ask about their personal knowledge and life experiences. This starts students interacting personally with the theme of the units and encourages them to make connections to help their learning.

D. The Big Question Chart

Students share what they already know and what they want to know about the Big Question and their ideas are recorded on the Big Question Chart.

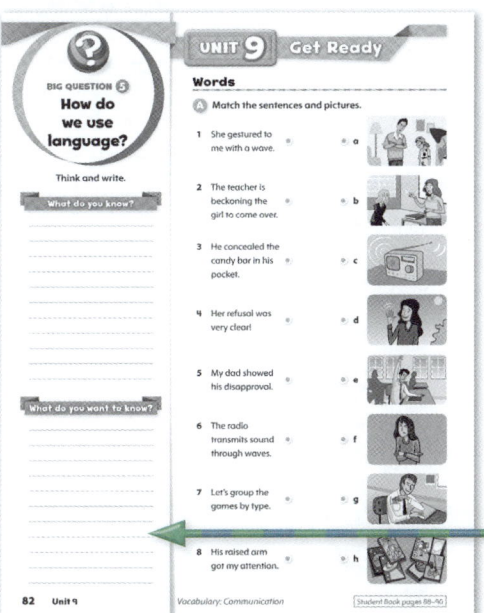

Workbook

Students write about what they know and what they want to know.

Get Ready

This page teaches and helps students practice a vocabulary set. It also encourages students to think critically about the language.

A. Words

Students are introduced to new vocabulary and have the opportunity to connect the words to the pictures and hear them spoken on the Audio CD.

B. Comprehension

Students complete an activity that tests their understanding of the words presented in Exercise A.

C. Critical Thinking

Students complete a critical thinking activity that measures their understanding of some or all of the words.

Workbook

Students complete a variety of activities that build and test their knowledge of the new vocabulary.

UNIT 9 — Get Ready

Words

A Listen and say the words. Then listen and read the sentences. 🔊 2·24

| gesture | beckon | refusal | disapproval | group | lack | raised |

| enable | invaluable | consist | distress | conceal | transmit |

1 I asked the man where the library was, and he **gestured** toward a building.
2 When Maria saw her teacher **beckon**, she knew it was her turn and stepped forward.
3 Nick's **refusal** to help me hurt my feelings.
4 My dad frowned in **disapproval** when he saw the broken plate.
5 I **grouped** the clothing into small and large sizes.
6 The soup **lacked** salt, so I added some more.
7 When I'm cold, I get **raised** bumps on my skin.
8 A cane **enabled** the old man to walk more easily.
9 In my job, a computer is **invaluable**. I couldn't work without one.
10 Our band **consists** of a guitar player and a singer.
11 I felt **distress** when I heard that my brother was sick.
12 We couldn't see the house because it was **concealed** by some trees.
13 There are many ways to **transmit** a message, such as e-mail, text, or letter.

B Circle True (T) or False (F).

1 If someone is beckoning to you, they want you to go away. T F
2 Something that's invaluable is very valuable. T F
3 When you enable something, you stop it from happening. T F
4 If a cake lacked sugar, it would taste great. T F
5 When you conceal something, you hide it from view. T F
6 A refusal is like an agreement. T F
7 If something is raised, it's higher than what's around it. T F

C Work with your partner to answer the questions.

1 If you grouped your classmates into girls and boys, who would the groups consist of?
2 Why would someone transmit a distress message?
3 Make a gesture showing disapproval.

90   Unit 9   *Vocabulary: Communication*

BIG QUESTION 5

How do we use language?

Think and write.

What do you know?

What do you want to know?

UNIT 9   Get Ready

Words

A Match the sentences and pictures.

1 She gestured to me with a wave.
2 The teacher is beckoning the girl to come over.
3 He concealed the candy bar in his pocket.
4 Her refusal was very clear!
5 My dad showed his disapproval.
6 The radio transmits sound through waves.
7 Let's group the games by type.
8 His raised arm got my attention.

B Complete the paragraph with the words from the box.

lack   enable   distress   invaluable   consists

Ships at sea use a signal to show _____ when a ship and its crew and passengers are in danger or in need of help. These signals are _____ because they _____ other ships or rescue services to come to the rescue. There are different types of signals. One of them _____ of orange smoke that goes into the air out of a can. If you _____ the ability to call for help in the usual way (for example, by shouting), it's good to know that there are other ways to get the help you need.

C Circle the correct answer.

1 People who are shy **enable / lack** the confidence to speak in public.
2 When I forgot to do my homework, my mom showed her **disapproval / refusal**.
3 We couldn't see the gifts because they were **transmitted / concealed** behind a curtain.
4 The horse looked as if it were in **distress / disapproval** when it broke its leg.
5 As the play was about to start, the manager **raised / concealed** the curtain.
6 You can **transmit / group** messages all around the world via the Internet.

D Circle the word that doesn't belong.

1 send away   beckon   invite   call
2 distress   upset   comfort   unhappiness
3 show   cover   conceal   hide
4 group   assemble   categorize   separate
5 compliment   criticism   disapproval   blame
6 enable   allow   forbid   permit
7 priceless   cheap   invaluable   precious
8 lack   want   need   own

E Complete the sentences in your own words.

1 _____ enables me to ...
2 I disapprove of ...
3 You can conceal a ...
4 I don't like it when I lack ...

82   Unit 9   *Vocabulary: Communication*   Student Book pages 88–90   Student Book page 90   *Vocabulary: Communication*   Unit 9   83

Before You Read

Students are introduced to a reading strategy which they will then apply to help them understand the text on the following pages. They are also introduced to the text type and information about genre.

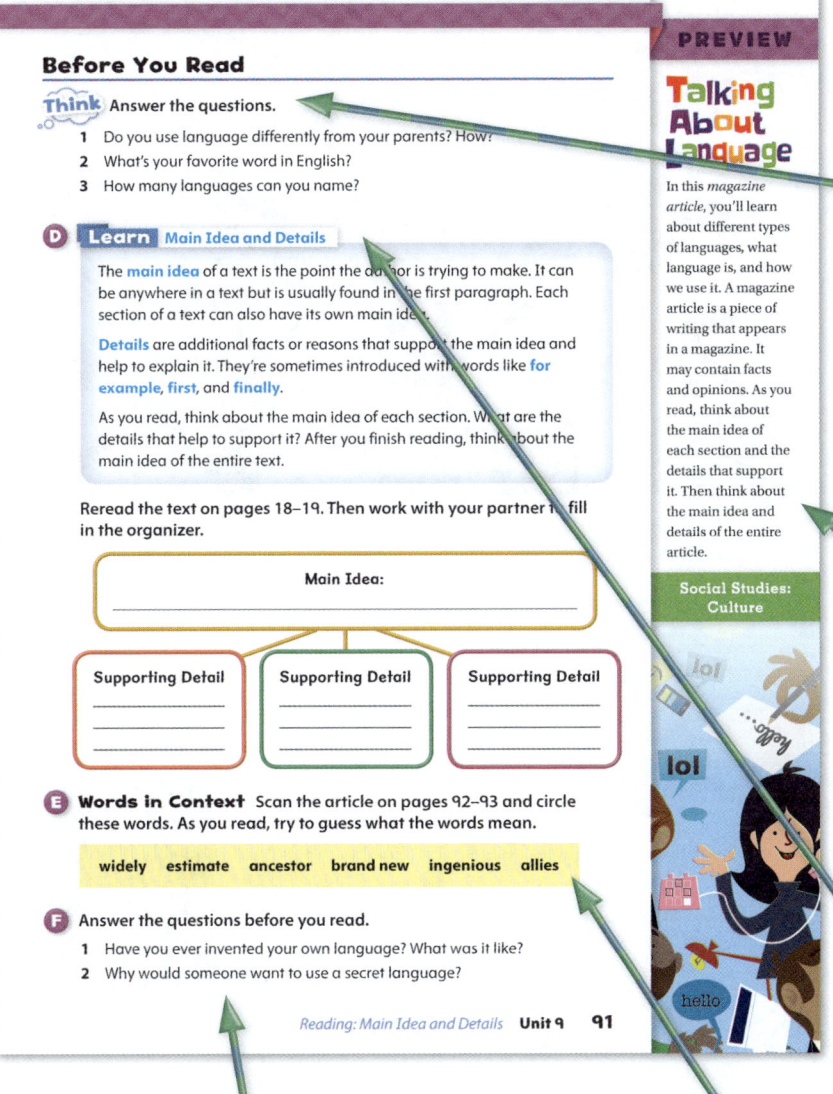

Think: Critical Thinking

These questions act as a lead-in to the reading text. Students use their personal knowledge and life experiences to answer. This activates interest in the topic of the text, and immediately connects it to the students' own lives.

Reading Preview

Students read a preview bar about the upcoming reading. This provides information about the text and helps to build interest. Students are introduced to text genre and understand how texts fulfil different learning needs.

D. Reading Strategy

Students learn and practice a reading strategy that they will apply to the upcoming reading. This helps students develop reading skills which can be applied to any text and to learn how to focus on the micro and macro meanings contained, whether in class or at home.

F. Before Reading

Students answer questions that build interest in the upcoming reading. These questions also activate students' existing knowledge about the text's subject matter which helps overall understanding of the text.

E. Words in Context

Students are encouraged to understand the link between vocabulary and reading by building a greater understanding of how they can approach difficult or unfamiliar words in a meaningful context.

Read

The reading texts are either fiction or nonfiction. Students are encouraged to focus on meaning, before focusing on the reading strategy. This is followed by general comprehension. The vocabulary presented on the *Get Ready* page is highlighted in yellow to help students understand the words in context.

Before Reading

Students are introduced to a text. They engage in before reading activities and examine the reading's features and visuals in order to familiarize themselves with the text before reading it.

During Reading

Students read and listen to the unit's text. Each unit has either a fiction or a nonfiction reading that helps students find answers to the Big Question. The texts are designed to supplement students' learning in different subject areas and to help them make connections between other cultures and their own lives. They are graded to an appropriate vocabulary and grammatical level and meet U.S. readability standards. Students are encouraged to take different approaches to reading the text.

What Is Language?

There are many possible answers to this question, but most people agree that language is a way to communicate ideas or feelings, using signs, gestures, or marks. Since the dawn of time, humans have needed to communicate with each other. We often do this through complex systems, such as speech and writing, but not always. Signs and gestures came before speech, and we still use them to communicate today.

Many gestures are understood and used by people of different cultures. These include beckoning with an arm or hand, as a sign to come closer, nodding the head, as a sign of acceptance, and a smile or hug, as a sign of welcome. Gestures of anger or disapproval, such as shaking the head to show refusal, are also widely recognized.

Think
What's the main idea of this section? What details support it?

92

Languages Around the World

Nobody knows exactly how many languages there are, but experts estimate that there are as many as 7,000. These languages are grouped into families. When languages have a common ancestor, they're part of the same language family. The Indo-European language family, for instance, includes Spanish, English, Hindi, and Russian. When a language is no longer used, such as Latin or Ancient Greek, we say that it's "dead." However, even after people have stopped speaking a language, they sometimes continue to create new words from its roots. The word *astronaut* is an example of this. There were no astronauts in Ancient Greece, of course, but modern people have combined the Ancient Greek word for "star" (*astron*) and "sailor" (*naut*) to form a brand-new word: *astronaut!*

Think Boxes

Think boxes apply the reading strategy that students learned to the reading text and help them focus on the micro skills of reading.

Vocabulary

The vocabulary presented in the *Get Ready* spread is highlighted in yellow throughout the text. This encourages students to focus on the language in context and helps them to understand the meaning of the text.

Codes and Sign Language

Louis Braille

All over the world, people who **lack** the ability to see use a type of code called Braille. Braille was invented in 1824 by a Frenchman named Louis Braille, who lost his sight when he was young. This system of writing allows people to read words through touch. **Raised** dots on a surface **enable** them to feel each letter. Today, entire books are printed in Braille.

A telegraph machine

Another type of code, which is called Morse code, is used to communicate over long distances. When the telegraph was invented in 1832, a man named Samuel Morse created this code to send messages using electricity. This system **consisted** of short signals, called dots, and long signals, called dashes. The code was tapped out, in a series of electrical pulses, and sent over telegraph wires. It was ingenious! The most famous example of Morse code is the **distress** signal used by sailors and pilots: SOS. In Morse code, it looks like this:

· · · — — — · · ·

Unlike Braille and Morse code, sign language is a true language. In fact, there are many different sign languages used around the world, each with its own grammar and vocabulary. Sign language is **invaluable** to people who can't hear. It allows them to communicate by making signs with their hands.

What Do We Use Language For?

As you've seen, we use language for an important human need: to connect with each other. The message we communicate and the way we **transmit** it might be as simple as a smile to say, "I'm happy to see you," or as complex as a book on physics. It might even be a secret, like a message in code that's sent between allies. Each of these types of communication lets us tell another person what we know, how we think, or what we feel. Languages are fascinating. They evolve and change, they're born and they die, and we all use them.

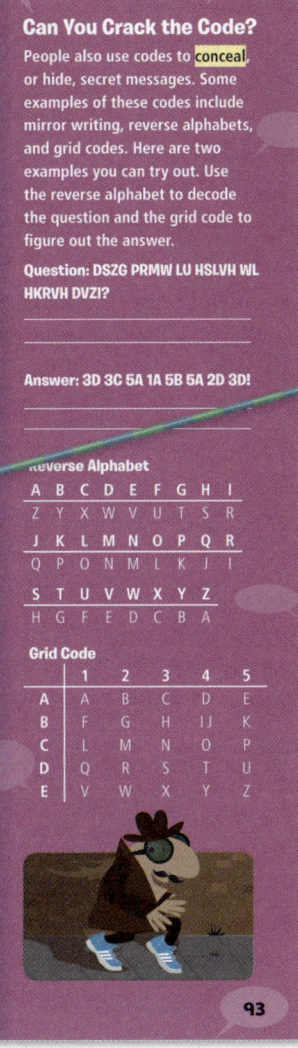

Can You Crack the Code?

People also use codes to **conceal**, or hide, secret messages. Some examples of these codes include mirror writing, reverse alphabets, and grid codes. Here are two examples you can try out. Use the reverse alphabet to decode the question and the grid code to figure out the answer.

Question: DSZG PRMW LU HSLVH WL HKRVH DVZI?

_____

Answer: 3D 3C 5A 1A 5B 5A 2D 3D!

_____

Reverse Alphabet

A	B	C	D	E	F	G	H	I
Z	Y	X	W	V	U	T	S	R
J	K	L	M	N	O	P	Q	R
Q	P	O	N	M	L	K	J	I
S	T	U	V	W	X	Y	Z	
H	G	F	E	D	C	B	A	

Grid Code

	1	2	3	4	5
A	A	B	C	D	E
B	F	G	H	IJ	K
C	L	M	N	O	P
D	Q	R	S	T	U
E	V	W	X	Y	Z

93

The texts are carefully graded to meet U.S. primary grade benchmarks. Some passive vocabulary which has not been explicitly taught has been included. Students need to feel confident dealing with a variety of texts and text types where there are some unfamiliar words. The passive vocabulary has been carefully integrated so that it does not impede understanding of meaning and is often part of collocations or common chunks of language.

Vocabulary

The texts are carefully graded to meet U.S. primary grade benchmarks. Some passive vocabulary which has not been explicitly taught has been included. Students need to feel confident dealing with a variety of texts and text types where there are some unfamiliar words. The passive vocabulary has been carefully integrated so that it does not impede understanding of meaning and is often part of collocations or common chunks of language.

After Reading

Students can work individually or together to complete an activity that relates to the reading. This will exploit the text in regard to meaning as well as form. It helps students have a deeper understanding of the content and to engage more actively with the written word.

Read

(A) Read. What machine do we no longer use?

(B) Read again. Look for the main idea and the details that support it.

New Technology, New Language

Communication between humans is something we don't always think about. You don't even remember saying your first words because you were so young that you've forgotten. But imagine for a moment that you can't speak. You can understand everyone around you, but you can't respond except by **beckoning** with a **gesture**, a smile, or a nod of your head. You can't ask for a snack when you're hungry or a drink when you're thirsty. How would that feel?

Some people really are in that situation, and for them, everyday life is a challenge. For some, it's very **distressing**. Some people are born unable to speak; other people lose the power of speech later in life, perhaps because of an injury or an illness. But advances in modern technology have **enabled** those people to communicate again. They may not speak language in the usual way, but they are communicating in a way that they were not able to do before.

One early form of technology to help people speak was developed in the 1960s. A man named Reg Malin was at a hospital one day when he met a young man who had been badly injured in a waterskiing accident. The young man couldn't move or speak, so when he needed help, he blew on a whistle.

Suddenly, Reg Malin had an idea! He decided to help people who couldn't speak. After various experiments with TVs and lights, he decided to use

Think
Which sentences tell you what the main idea is?

a typewriter. From a typewriter, he made a machine called a POSSUM, which is a Latin word meaning "I can." The POSSUM, which had a mouthpiece, allowed the person using it to suck or blow through the mouthpiece, a bit like you might blow or suck through a drinking straw, and that operated the typewriter. And so a new form of communication began for people who had difficulty communicating.

These days, computers are used instead of typewriters. Some computer programs can be downloaded straight to a cell phone. The ones designed for children often **consist** of pictograms, small pictures that represent a word, a feeling, or an idea.

How does it work? With some systems, the user taps the screen and the program speaks the word or idea for them. But what happens if a person is completely paralyzed and can't move at all? Programmers have thought about this possibility and invented some programs you can operate simply by looking at different parts of the screen. Using a camera, the computer tracks the movement of a part of your eye called the retina and can decode what you want to say. Have you ever heard the expression "talking with your eyes"? Thanks to modern technology, talking with your eyes is now literally possible.

Think
What details support the writer's main idea?

84   Unit 9   Read

Student Book pages 92–93

Workbook

Students read an additional fiction or nonfiction reading featuring vocabulary and the reading strategy from the Student Book reading.

Understand

This page checks students' understanding of the text through personal response, application of the reading strategy, general comprehension, and critical thinking.

Think: Personal Response
Students answer personal response questions that allow them to discuss their opinions and feelings about the reading.

A. Reading Strategy
Students apply the reading strategy that they learned in an activity about the reading, which helps to connect general reading skills with overall comprehension.

B. Reading Comprehension
Students demonstrate their comprehension of the reading through an additional activity. This will show the teacher and the student the level of understanding gained through reading the text. This exercise may also focus further on the reading strategy.

C. Words in Context
Students complete an activity that helps them to work more closely with the words in context and to develop skills of understanding the meaning of vocabulary from the words, phrases, and structures used around it.

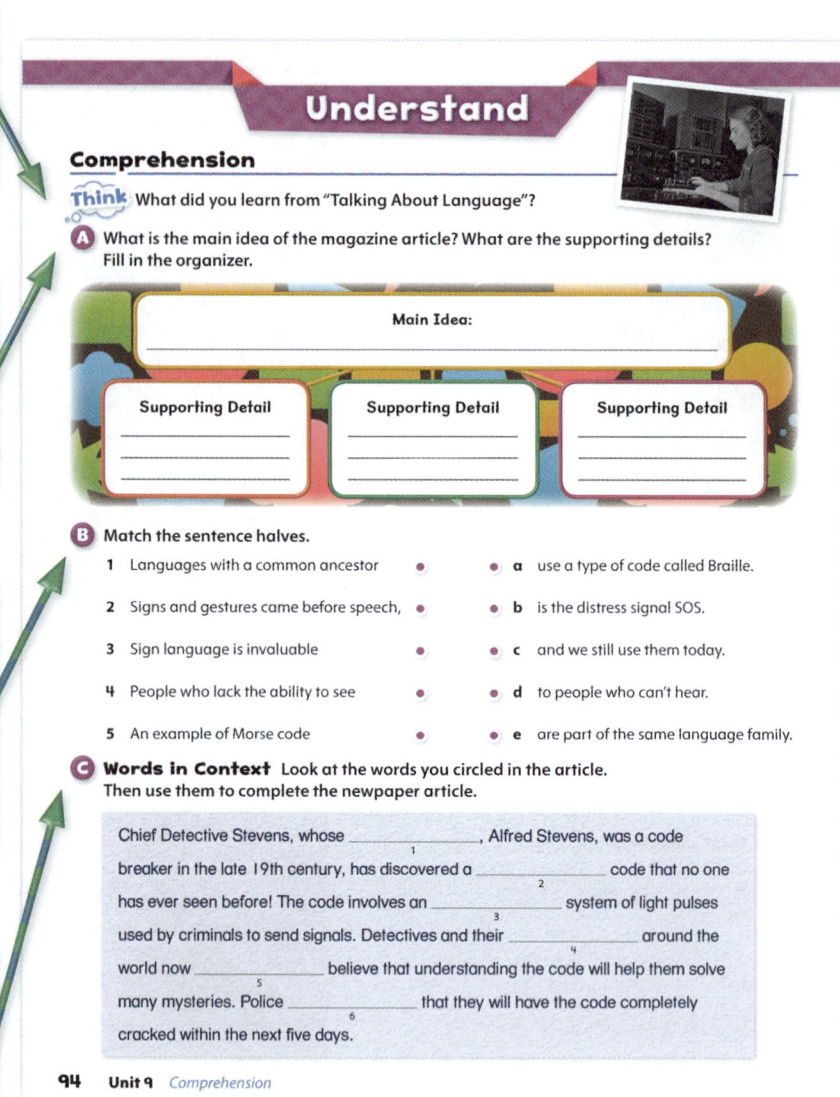

Workbook
Students complete activities that build and test knowledge of the workbook reading and the reading strategy.

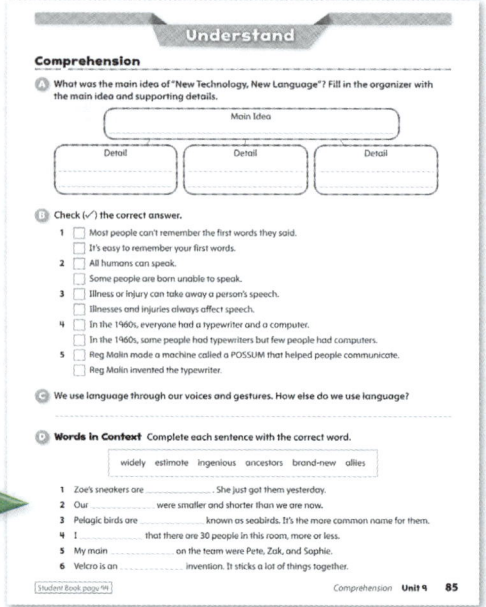

Students are introduced to a grammar structure through the context of cartoon story before working with the structure more closely with a grammar presentation and practice activities that allow them to produce the language in a collaborative situation.

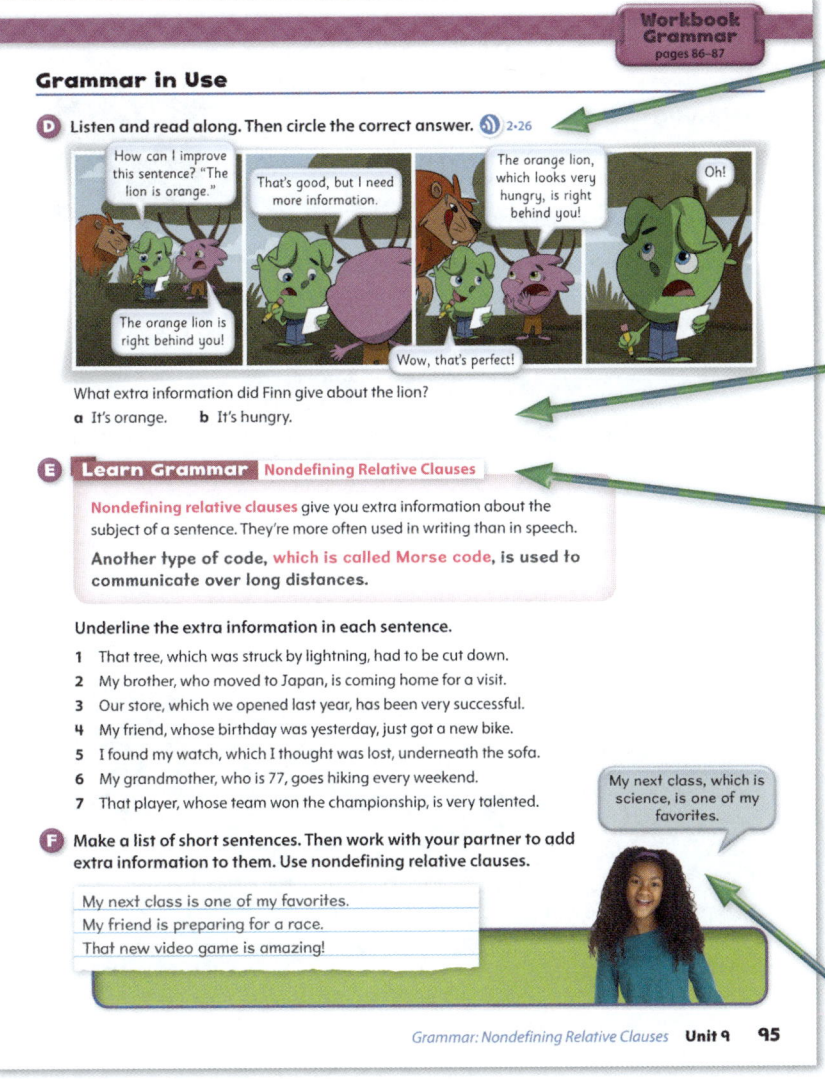

D. Grammar in Context
Students are introduced to the grammar model in a cartoon story. The aim of the story is to present and teach the grammar model through its meaning and its use, and to encourage students to relate to the language in a fun and enjoyable way.

Grammar Comprehension
Students answer simple questions which focus on meaningful comprehension of the story through a focus on the target grammatical structure.

E. Learn Grammar
Students learn about the unit's grammar point. The grammar is explained clearly in a *Learn* box, using examples from the reading when possible. The focus is on the grammar's meaning and use. Students then practice what they have learned in an activity.

F. Practice
Students personalize what they have learned. This activity involves the productive skills of writing and speaking, while using the target language to express ideas in the students own words.

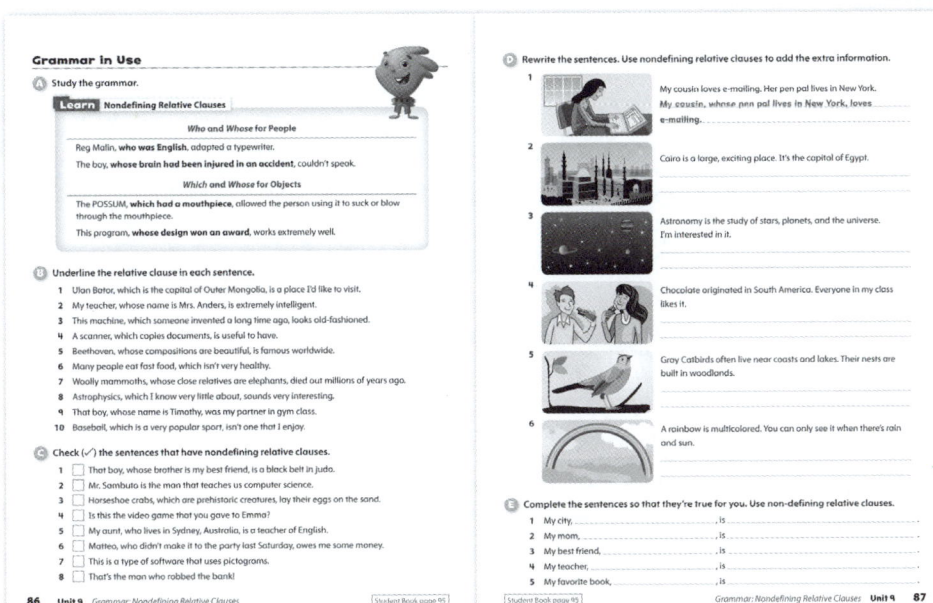

Workbook
Students complete extra grammar practice activities, with a grammar paradigm table to use as reference.

Communicate

This page teaches and helps students implement and practice listening strategies and to practice functional language through spoken production.

Think: Critical Thinking

These questions act as a lead-in to the listening text. Students use their personal knowledge and life experiences to answer. This activates interest in the topic of the text, and immediately connects it to the students' own lives.

A. B. Listening

Students listen to a script that continues to help them find answers to the Big Question. They complete activities which encourage them to listen for detail or specific information, in this way helping them to develop the micro skills of listening.

C. Speaking

Students develop their functional speaking skills in this section. They can read and understand a dialogue which presents useful chunks of language before practicing the dialogue by either choosing substitute words or expressing their own ideas.

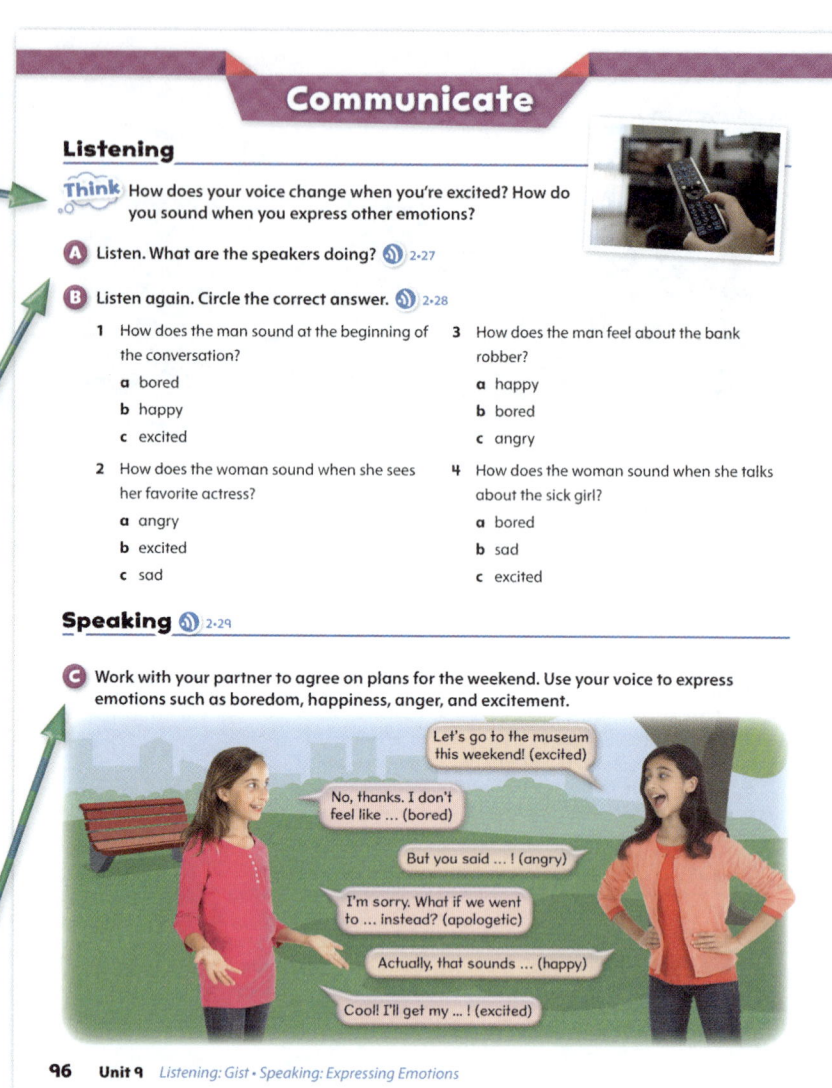

Communicate

Listening

Think How does your voice change when you're excited? How do you sound when you express other emotions?

A Listen. What are the speakers doing? 2·27

B Listen again. Circle the correct answer. 2·28

1 How does the man sound at the beginning of the conversation?
   a bored
   b happy
   c excited

2 How does the woman sound when she sees her favorite actress?
   a angry
   b excited
   c sad

3 How does the man feel about the bank robber?
   a happy
   b bored
   c angry

4 How does the woman sound when she talks about the sick girl?
   a bored
   b sad
   c excited

Speaking 2·29

C Work with your partner to agree on plans for the weekend. Use your voice to express emotions such as boredom, happiness, anger, and excitement.

Let's go to the museum this weekend! (excited)

No, thanks. I don't feel like ... (bored)

But you said ... ! (angry)

I'm sorry. What if we went to ... instead? (apologetic)

Actually, that sounds ... (happy)

Cool! I'll get my ... ! (excited)

96 **Unit 9** *Listening: Gist · Speaking: Expressing Emotions*

Students focus on word patterns and writing strategies in order to build greater fluency and accuracy. They then personalise the learning by writing about something that links back to the Big Question.

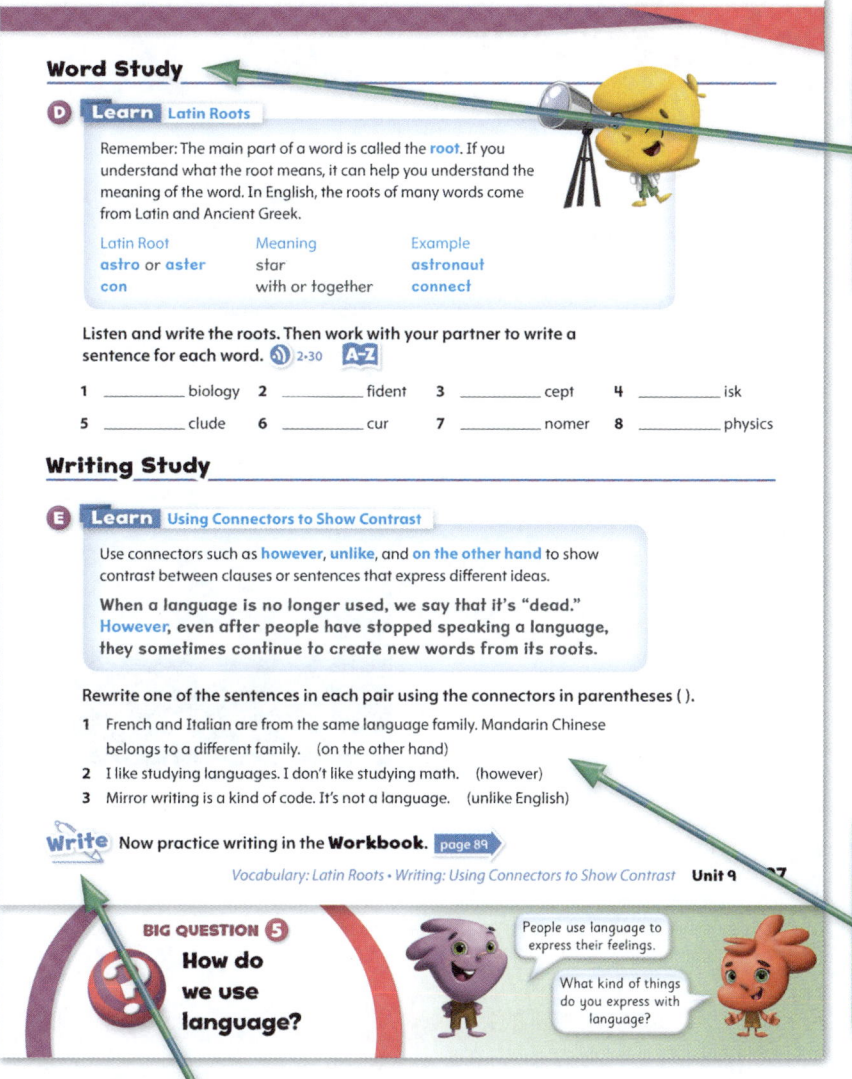

Word Study

D Learn Latin Roots

Remember: The main part of a word is called the **root**. If you understand what the root means, it can help you understand the meaning of the word. In English, the roots of many words come from Latin and Ancient Greek.

Latin Root	Meaning	Example
astro or **aster**	star	**astronaut**
con	with or together	**connect**

Listen and write the roots. Then work with your partner to write a sentence for each word. 🔊 2·30 **A-Z**

1 _____ biology 2 _____ fident 3 _____ cept 4 _____ isk

5 _____ clude 6 _____ cur 7 _____ nomer 8 _____ physics

Writing Study

E Learn Using Connectors to Show Contrast

Use connectors such as **however**, **unlike**, and **on the other hand** to show contrast between clauses or sentences that express different ideas.

When a language is no longer used, we say that it's "dead." **However**, even after people have stopped speaking a language, they sometimes continue to create new words from its roots.

Rewrite one of the sentences in each pair using the connectors in parentheses ( ).

1 French and Italian are from the same language family. Mandarin Chinese belongs to a different family.   (on the other hand)

2 I like studying languages. I don't like studying math.   (however)

3 Mirror writing is a kind of code. It's not a language.   (unlike English)

Write Now practice writing in the **Workbook**. page 89

Vocabulary: Latin Roots • Writing: Using Connectors to Show Contrast **Unit 9**

BIG QUESTION 5

How do we use language?

People use language to express their feelings.

What kind of things do you express with language?

D. Word Study

Each Word Study section focuses on word patterns. This complements and often provides links between vocabulary and grammar learning. Students complete an activity which requires them to utilize their new understanding of the way words work.

E. Writing Study

The Writing Study section helps students learn about different writing strategies and useful language prompts to help them write fluently and accurately.

Write

Students write about one aspect of the Big Question, using vocabulary and structures taught within the unit.

Workbook

Students complete one page of activities that build and test knowledge of the Writing Study. Students then complete activities that focus on writing output.

Communicate

Word Study

A Read the clues. Complete the crossword puzzle.

concept asterisk confident astrophysics
astrobiology concur astronomer
conclude connect

Across
2 scientist of the stars
6 not unsure
8 finalize or finish

Down
1 the study of the physics and chemistry of stars and planets
3 a symbol that looks like a star
4 another word for join
5 the study of the origin and future of life in the universe
6 another word for idea
7 to agree

B Circle the correct answer.
1 Astro or aster before a word means _____.
   a star   b cut in half
2 Con before a word means _____.
   a with or together   b against

C Look at the words in Ⓐ. Complete the sentences.
1 Juan is interested in what stars are made of, so he's going to study _____
2 You think the library should stay open on Sundays, and I _____
3 I like movies that _____ with a very exciting car chase.
4 There's an _____ next to this word, so I'm going to look it up.
5 Eternity is a difficult _____. It's very hard to imagine.
6 I felt very _____ when I went on stage because I knew all the lines of the play.

Writing Study

A Check (✓) the sentences that include a connector that shows contrast. Then underline the connectors.
1 ☐ I'm really good at sports. On the other hand, I'm pretty bad at music and art.
2 ☐ Billy loves swimming and wins a lot of swimming matches.
3 ☐ Some types of fat in food are bad for you. However, the fat in avocados and olive oil is good for you.
4 ☐ Unlike my mom, my dad is very patient.
5 ☐ Both my brother and sister are interested in music. I'm not.
6 ☐ The weather was terrible today. On the other hand, we had a great time.
7 ☐ Johnny and Frank wanted to go out yesterday.
8 ☐ I don't really like carrots. However, I love peas!

B Write. Use the connector in parentheses to show contrast.
1 Running can be good for you. You have to be careful of injury. (on the other hand)

2 My friend Cristina loves singing. She's not very good at it. (however)

3 Eagles are skilled flyers. Chickens aren't good at flying. (unlike eagles)

C Read the paragraph. Circle the connectors that show contrast. Then write a paragraph about something you are good at. Use nondefining relative clauses and connectors to show contrast.

My mom and dad, who are both teachers, are really good at science. Unlike them, I'm not very good at it because I find the concepts hard. However, I'm very skilled at learning languages. When I was very young, I learned Spanish and then Italian. I like to practice speaking languages with other people. Sometimes I make mistakes, but that's OK because you can learn from mistakes. On the other hand, you do need to be careful to correct the mistakes you make.

88 Unit 9   Word Study: Latin Roots

Student Book page 97

Student Book page 97

Writing Study: Using Connectors to Show Contrast   Unit 9   89

Wrap Up - Writing

These pages always come at the end of two units which focus on a Big Question. Students are exposed to vocabulary and grammatical structures learned throughout the previous two units and focus on writing and oral presentations.

A. Text

Students read a particular genre of text in order to focus on the layout, presentation, and writing strategies that this type of text requires.

B. Comprehension

An activity helps students to check their understanding of the meaning of the text, before they are expected to produce a similar type of text themselves.

Workbook

Students are guided through writing a particular text type, with a model text, scaffolded activities, and a writing task.

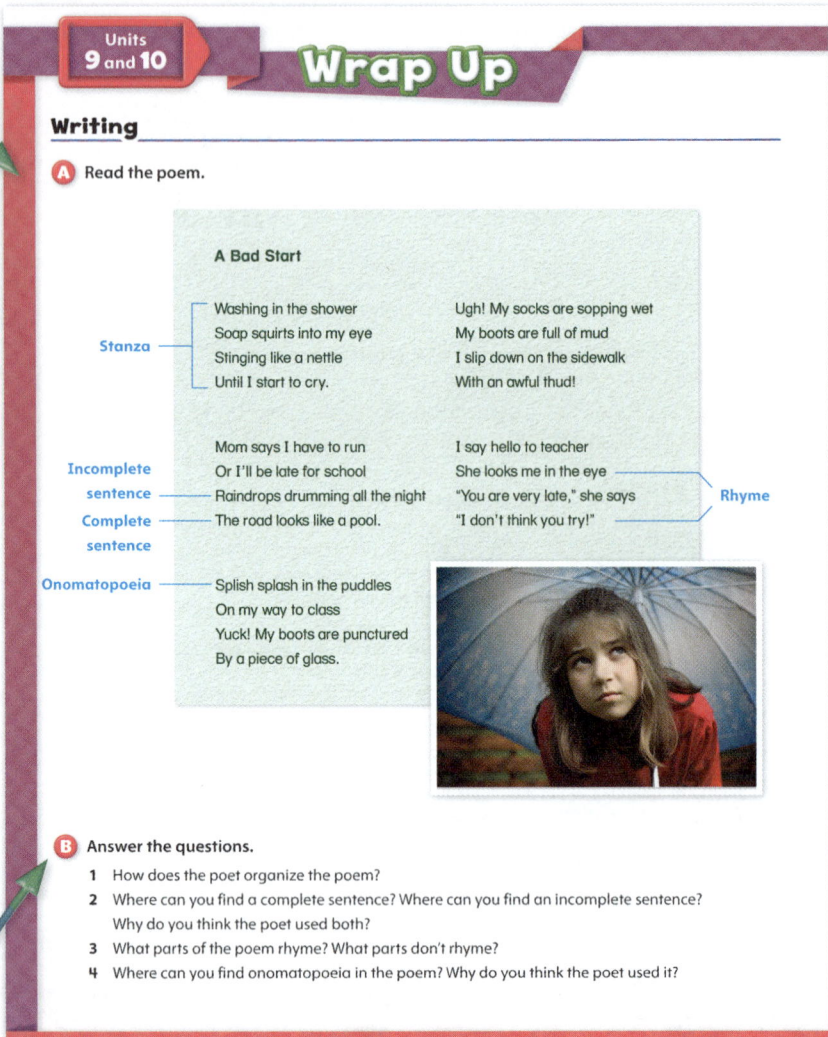

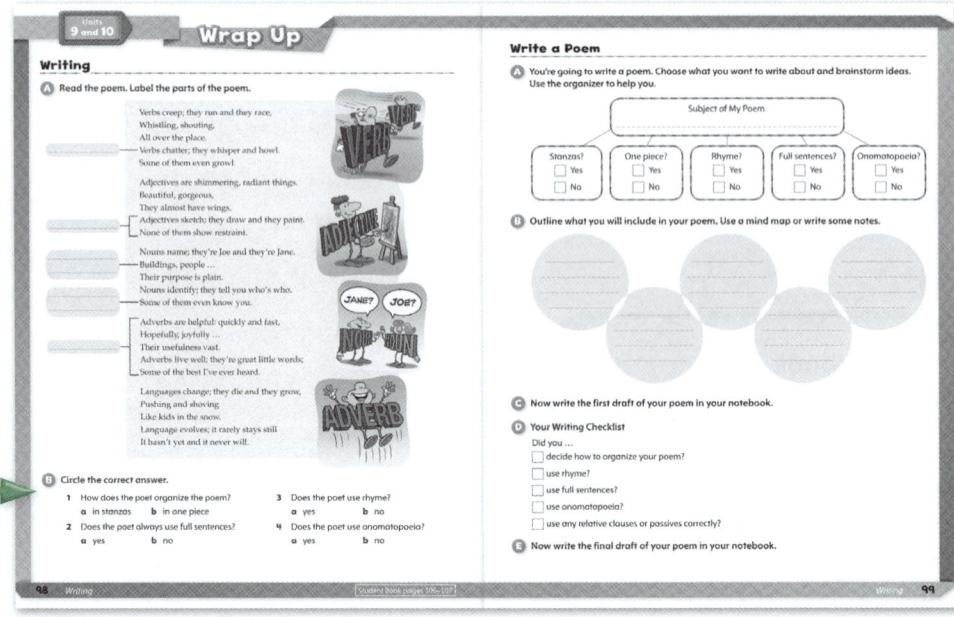

C. Learn
A *Learn* box provides step-by-step guidance for students before they write their own text.

Write
Students are directed to their workbook to plan and write their own text with guided support.

D. Present
Students are encouraged to present their writing to the class. This is supported by tips which help students prepare and reflect upon what they want to say, and how to say it. This focuses on accuracy and fluency and links writing and speaking production.

The Big Question, Big Question Poster, Big Question Chart, and DVD
Students return to the Big Question with new answers in order to describe the images with newly gained knowledge and vocabulary, and they complete the final column in the Big Question Chart with what they have learned. This provides a summing up of learning points throughout the previous units and helps students to critically examine their own learning path.

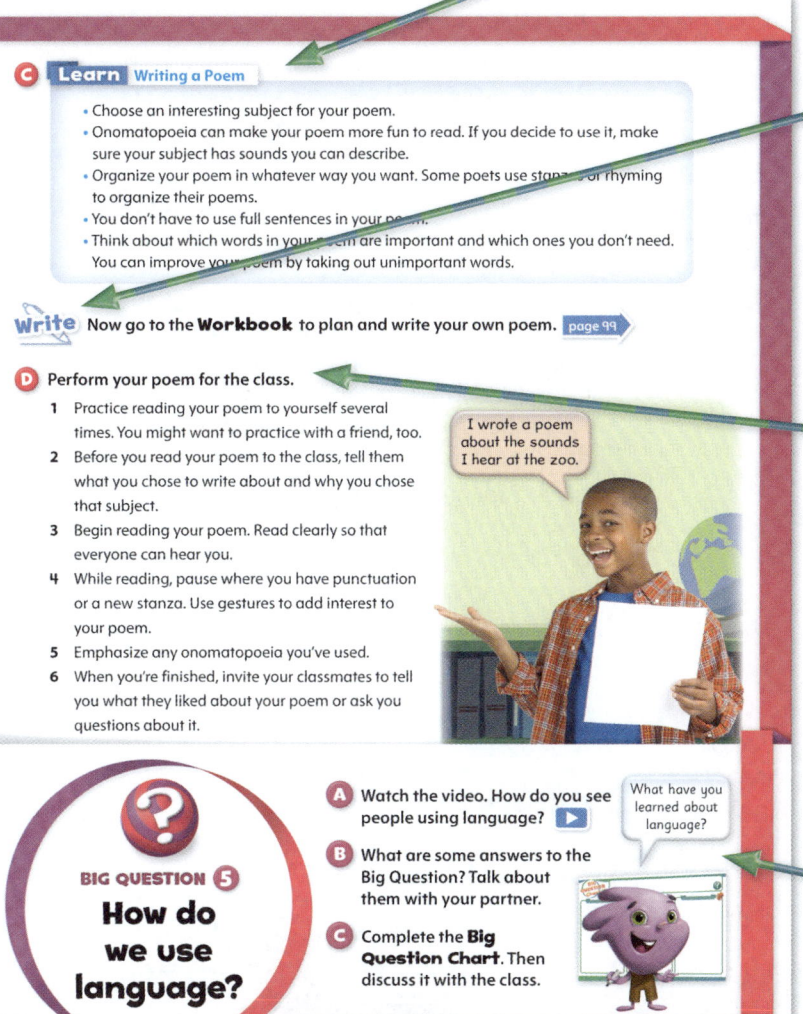

C Learn — Writing a Poem
- Choose an interesting subject for your poem.
- Onomatopoeia can make your poem more fun to read. If you decide to use it, make sure your subject has sounds you can describe.
- Organize your poem in whatever way you want. Some poets use stanzas or rhyming to organize their poems.
- You don't have to use full sentences in your poem.
- Think about which words in your poem are important and which ones you don't need. You can improve your poem by taking out unimportant words.

Write Now go to the **Workbook** to plan and write your own poem. page 99

D Perform your poem for the class.
1 Practice reading your poem to yourself several times. You might want to practice with a friend, too.
2 Before you read your poem to the class, tell them what you chose to write about and why you chose that subject.
3 Begin reading your poem. Read clearly so that everyone can hear you.
4 While reading, pause where you have punctuation or a new stanza. Use gestures to add interest to your poem.
5 Emphasize any onomatopoeia you've used.
6 When you're finished, invite your classmates to tell you what they liked about your poem or ask you questions about it.

I wrote a poem about the sounds I hear at the zoo.

BIG QUESTION 5
How do we use language?

A Watch the video. How do you see people using language?

B What are some answers to the Big Question? Talk about them with your partner.

C Complete the **Big Question Chart**. Then discuss it with the class.

What have you learned about language?

Presentation · Big Question 5 **107**

Workbook
Students do a number of review activities to recycle the language from the previous two units.

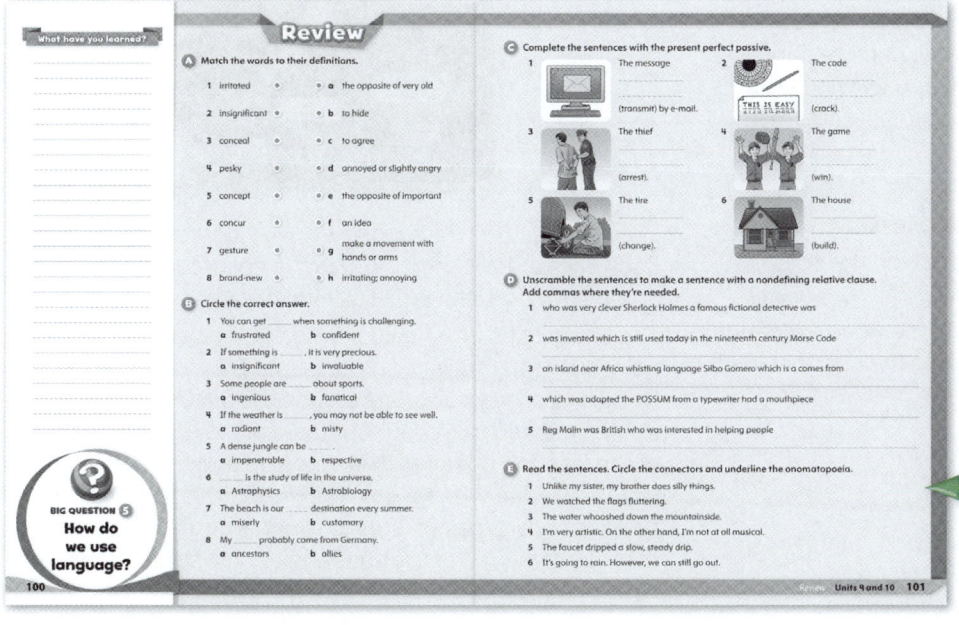

DVD and Posters

The DVD and posters are key to reinforcing the content of the Student Book. They stimulate interest in the Big Question, and they help students to predict, infer, and check the meaning of the main learning points. The learning points are about content not language. Students will think critically and more fully about the process of language when they see interesting and thought-provoking images.

The images on the DVD and posters encourage students to recall, recognize, and acknowledge new concepts and vocabulary. Students analyze the images themselves to understand the meaning. This leads to a greater impact upon the long-term memory as students continue to make associations between pictures and language.

Big Question DVD

Students watch videos about the Big Question in order to stimulate their thinking about the topic and revise what they have learned. This will help the teacher determine what students already know and what they want to know.

The DVD should be used in two places in each pair of units. Play the Big Question video at the beginning of the first unit to activate background knowledge and encourage interest in the topic. Play the Wrap Up video at the end of the second unit to help students summarize their understanding of the topic and to underscore all the learning points which have been studied during the two units.

Suggested Procedure: Beginning of Units

- Explain that students will watch a video about the Big Question, and that it will have pictures but no words. Ask students to write in their notebooks one or more things that they find interesting in the video as they watch it. Explain that words and phrases are acceptable and that full sentences are not necessary.
- Play the video.
- Ask students to compare what they wrote with a partner.
- Elicit some of students' ideas. Write these on the board.
- (Optional) Play the video a second time. Ask students to write down one new thing they see in the video as they watch it. After the video, students talk to their partners and then share their thoughts with the class.

Suggested Procedure: End of Units

- Explain to students that they will now see the video again, this time with a presenter. Play the video. It can be played more than once.
- Ask students to discuss what they learned from the video with a partner.
- Ask students to share what they learned from the video with the whole class.
- Write this information on the **Big Question Chart**.

Expansion Ideas

- Elicit and write useful chunks of language which students can use in discussions about the learning points. Put students into groups and have them make posters with the language and illustrations to help them understand and remember the meaning. Put the posters on the wall and draw students' attention to them before future discussions.
- Have students work in small groups to write a list of their own learning points for the units. Tell them to find or draw pictures to represent the learning points visually. Have each group present their ideas to the class, or create a poster to be put on the wall.
- Make a class DVD based on the *Big Question DVD*, showing images which represent the learning points. Have different students act as the presenter on camera.

Posters

Discover Posters

There is a Discover Poster for every Big Question in the Student Book. They all have the main learning points for two units with accompanying pictures to illustrate the learning points.

The Discover Poster should be used at the beginning of each pair of units to motivate students' interest in the topic and to elicit existing knowledge around the Big Question. It can also be referred to throughout the units to remind students of the learning points as they come up and to build upon the knowledge they are gaining. Finally, it should be used at the end of each pair of units to summarize all of the learning that has come out of the units and to help students prepare to fill in the Big Question Chart.

Suggested Procedure

It is a good idea to have a list of questions which help students to think critically about the images and learning points. Students can answer individually or be encouraged to share their ideas in pairs or small groups before participating in a general class discussion.

General Discussion Questions

- *What can you see in this picture?*
- *How many ... can you see?*
- *Where do you think it is?*
- *What do you think is happening?*
- *What does it mean?*
- *What does this learning point mean?*
- *Can you see the learning point in the picture?*
- *Do you know about this already?*
- *What else would you like to know?*

Big Question Chart

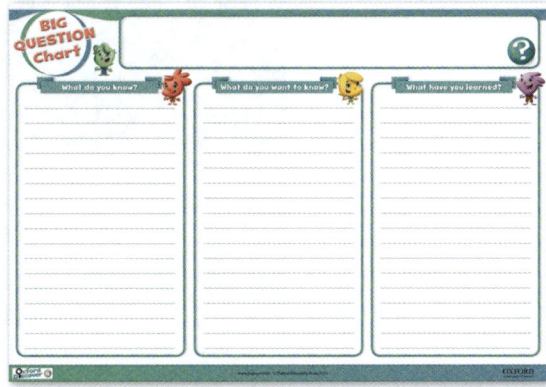

The Big Question Chart has been designed to follow the KWL methodology. K = What do you know about the topic? W = What do you want to know about the topic? L = What did you learn or what have you learned about the topic?

The Big Question Chart can be written on with board pens and then wiped clean so that it can be re-used. If possible, keep it up displayed on the classroom wall.

Suggested Procedure: Beginning of Units

- Have students brainstorm what they already know about the topic surrounding the Big Question. This can be done individually by writing ideas down, or by setting up pair or small group discussions.
- Elicit the ideas and write them on the poster.
- Ask each student to think about something they would like to know about the topic. These could be grouped into categories or headings to help students learn to classify more effectively.
- Write some of the ideas on the chart.
- Don't fill in the final column, as this will be completed once learning has taken place.

Suggested Procedure: End of First Unit

- Look closely at the middle column; *What do you want to know about the topic?* Ask students if they now know the answer to some of those questions. If they do, this information can be moved over to the first column.

- Some ideas can also be elicited to start filling in the third column so that students can see that learning has already taken place around the theme of the Big Question.

Suggested Procedure: End of Units

- Have students look at the middle column and decide if they can answer any more questions they had about the topic. If they have learned about aspects they expressed interest in, this information can be moved over to the column on the right: *What did you learn or what have you learned about the topic?*
- Elicit more information about what they have learned and add it to the third column.

Talk About It! Poster

This poster should be used when students are having a discussion in pairs or groups. If possible, keep it on the wall so that students can refer to it themselves.

In the Student Book it can be used during the Communicate reading pages when students are practicing speaking skills, but also during post-reading discussion tasks and during the Wrap Up project section.

Suggested Procedure

Remind students about the language often and drill the language and practice the intonation. Students begin to acquire authentic process language to then help them express their own ideas and opinions. When introducing it for the first time, elicit possible ways to substitute different opinions while using the sentence frames from the poster. Explain that these prompts can help them to present ideas and to agree and disagree politely with others.

When students are participating in a discussion, point to the sentence frames on the poster and ask them to express their own ideas after using the language indicated.

Dictionary Activities

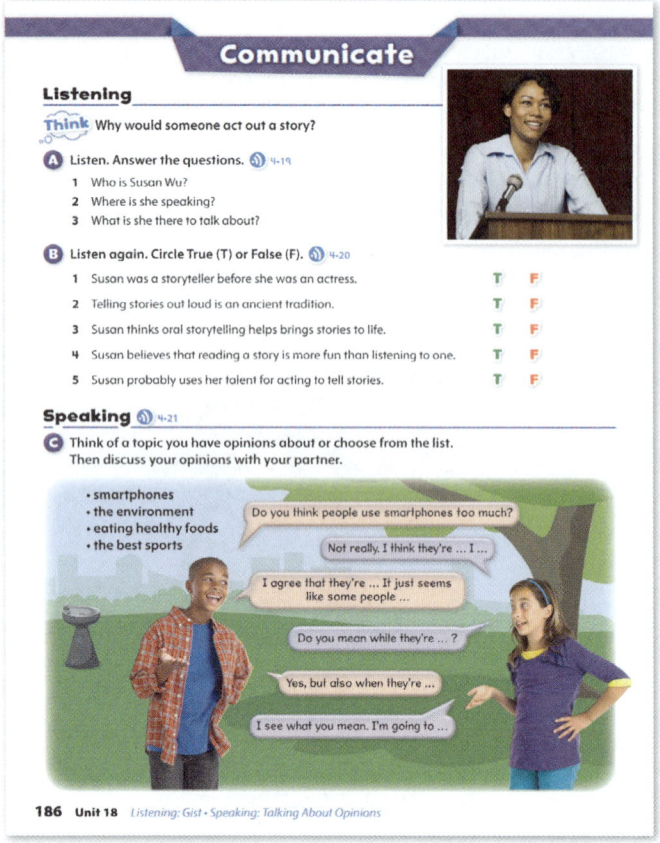

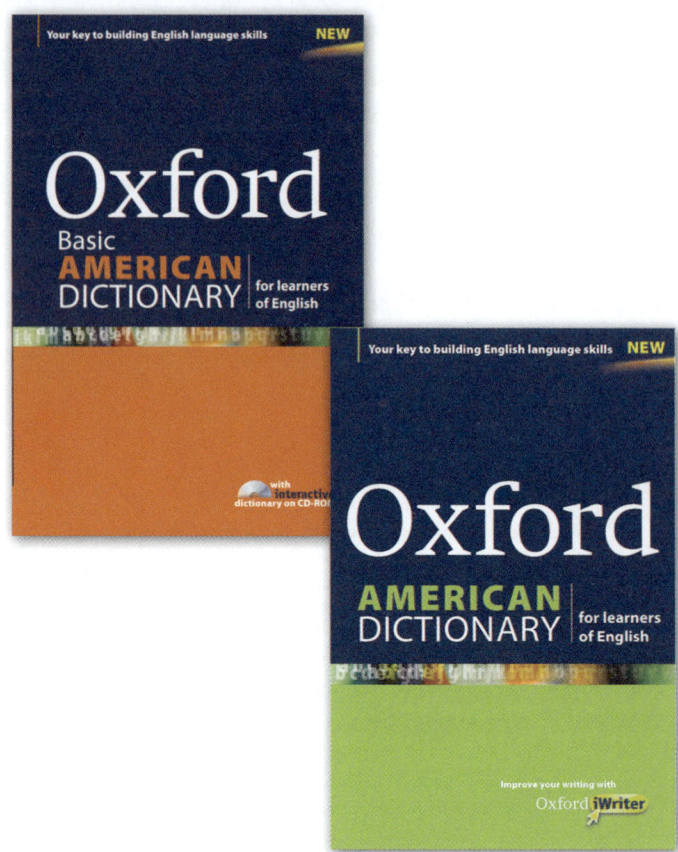

There is an old proverb which is: *Give a man a fish, and feed him for a day. Teach a man to fish and you feed him for a lifetime.*

Dictionary skills need to be mastered by students learning English, even in the primary years. When students have learned how to successfully use a dictionary, they are able to become more independent and autonomous learners, able to increase their own vocabulary and read and write at a higher level.

Dictionary skills are important, not only because the dictionary itself is important but also because it is an introduction into the world of reference materials. Learning how to use common reference materials will help your students' research and writing skills.

A dictionary entry has several parts. It lists the syllabic divisions in a word, the pronunciation, the part of speech, and of course the definition. Students need to learn how to identify and work with all of these components.

Learner training and encouraging the habit of using a monolingual dictionary is an essential element of current classroom practice. Learner training can focus on various aspects, from understanding abbreviations to interpreting symbols, recognizing and understanding syllable indicators and stress marks to effectively finding a particular meaning of an item of vocabulary.

Oxford Basic American Dictionary

This dictionary is suggested for students in levels 1-4 of *Oxford Discover*. It is written specifically for students who want to improve their English language skills and has extra help boxes included with related synonyms, collocations, and word families. It is designed to help students transition from using picture dictionaries by using words that are easy to understand in definitions as well as illustrations. It has a focus on content words from different subject areas such as math, geography and history.

Oxford American Dictionary

This dictionary is suggested for students in levels 5-6 of *Oxford Discover*. It has more than 350,000 words and phrases, with lots of explanatory notes and more than a thousand illustrations. Unlike in more traditional dictionaries, where meanings are ordered chronologically according to the history of the language, each entry plainly shows the principal meaning or meanings of the word, organized by importance in today's English. This makes it relevant and easily understood by primary-aged students.

Student Book Dictionary Activities

The Student Books in levels 3-6 of *Oxford Discover* have dictionary pages referencing the words used throughout the units in the book. This is a good introduction to general dictionary use and students should be encouraged to use these pages as a reference. Additionally there are activities and games which can help students to become more familiar and confident when using the dictionary pages.

Do you know?

- Have students work in pairs and choose a word from the dictionary pages at the back of the Student Book.
- Tell them to write the word and the meaning in their notebook.
- Tell students to write two more meanings which they make up, but which look as if they could also match the word.

- Put pairs together and have them read out their word and the three definitions.
- The other pair must guess the correct definition.
- To exploit the game further, keep moving the pairs around so that they work with everyone in the class.

Put it in a Sentence

- Have students open their Student Books to the dictionary pages at the back.
- Tell them to choose one word from the list of words.
- Have students write a sentence using that word, concentrating on understanding the definition as they do so.
- Ask students to read out their sentence to the class.
- Have the class look up that word in the dictionary pages and decide if the sentence matches the definition and if it is used correctly.

Taboo

- Have students open their Student Books to the dictionary pages at the back.
- Tell them to choose one word from the list of words.
- Make sure that students choose a word where they understand the definition.
- Have students write down four words which describe the word they chose, without using the word itself.
- Put students into groups of four or five.
- Have them take turns to read out the words in their notebook.
- The other students try to guess the dictionary word.
- The first student to guess correctly wins a point.
- The winner is the student in the group with the most points.

Picture Words

- Put students into groups for four or five.
- Give each group a large sheet of clean paper, or a few sheets of smaller paper. Make sure each group also has a pencil.
- Ask one person from each group to come to the front of the class.
- Choose one word from the dictionary at the back of the Student Book and show it (with the definition) to the students at the front of the class. Don't let the rest of the students see or hear the word.
- Each student goes back to their group and draws the word. They cannot speak or write while they are doing this.
- The rest of the group tries to guess the word.
- The first student in the class to guess it correctly wins a point for their team.
- Continue the game by having a different student come out and repeating the activity until each student in the group has had a chance to draw a word.

General Dictionary Activities

General dictionaries are useful to have in the classroom and can be incorporated into many aspects of the lesson.

They can be used when directed by the teacher or kept for reference for students as and when the need arises. Again, it is useful to help students navigate dictionaries with activities and tasks which help them feel comfortable with these reference materials.

Scavenger Hunt

- Write down ten to twelve questions about using a dictionary. Examples can include:

What is the first word in the dictionary?

How many pages of words starting with 'x' are in the dictionary?

Look up the word 'supermarket.' How many syllables does it have?

Find the first adjective in your dictionary which has three syllables.

Find a word which has more than one meaning.

Find a word which can be a verb and a noun.

Word Search

- Put students into pairs and give each pair a dictionary.
- Call out a word (preferably a familiar or recognizable word).
- Each pair of students must try to find the word as quickly as possible.
- The first pair to call out the correct page number where the word can be found is the winner.

Mystery Word

- Choose a word in the dictionary that will be familiar to students.
- Give a dictionary to each pair or small group of students in the class.
- Read out a series of clues to help students find the word. Read the clues out one at a time, as students are following the previous clue. For example:

I begin with the fourth letter of the alphabet.

I have three syllables.

My second letter is 'o.'

I come before 'dog' in the dictionary.

My last letter is 't.'

- Students use the dictionary to follow the clues and find the word.
- The first pair or group of students to find and say the word correctly wins a point.
- Continue with more words.

Words, words, words!

- Give a dictionary to each pair or small group of students in the class.
- Read out (or write on the board) a series of clues at the same time. For example: *A word that begins with 's.' It has to have double letters, be two syllables long and be an adjective.*
- Students use the dictionary to find the word. There may be more than one answer as more than one word may fit the description.
- Have pairs say their words to the class to check if they are correct.

Testing Practice

Why Testing Practice is Important

There are a variety of reasons why students should be encouraged to do testing practice activities.

Testing practice:

- **Provides further language practice** - this ensures that vocabulary and structures that have been taught are recycled, providing more exposure to language.

- **Identifies gaps in knowledge** - testing practice helps students to become aware of their strengths and weaknesses. In this way they can focus on particular areas and allocate further study time effectively.

- **Improves transfer of knowledge to new contexts** - repeated practice helps students to retain facts and also helps to increase the transfer of knowledge to new contexts.

- **Provides feedback for students and teachers** - targeted language practice helps teachers better understand what their students know. In this way they can adjust their teaching and plan future lessons more successfully. But it also often improves the students' own understanding of the learning process. Students will be better able to understand what steps they need to take to close that gap if they are given proper feedback.

- **Provides familiarity with test questions** - students receive better marks on tests when the stress level is decreased. One way of decreasing stress is to make sure that students are familiar with test question types and confident about what is expected. Practice with different test question types, whether formal or informal, should lead to better results in more structured and higher stakes tests.

The testing practice pages can be used as formative and summative assessment. Formative assessment takes place while students are still in the process of learning, and they are used to determine how well that learning is progressing.

When students complete the testing practice pages they can be seen as a "pit stop" on the way to completing the course and this can help guide subsequent teaching and learning. They also provide information about how much students have learned in the preceding units and assess learner achievement and this forms a summative assessment where evidence of learning is required.

How to Use the Testing Practice Pages

- **Make it collaborative:** Put students into pairs or small groups to answer the questions. Set it up as a game or competition so that the process becomes more enjoyable.

- **Review:** You don't necessarily need to have students complete the pages in one sitting. The activities could be integrated into lessons later in the Student Book so they act as a review and help to recycle vocabulary and structures.

- **Peer correction:** Have students correct each other's answers before general class feedback. In this way students can learn from each other. Students tend to be stronger or less confident in different areas, so they can help each other find mistakes. If a discussion stage is built in it is even more useful as students can explain mistakes and corrections to each other and this can be a more meaningful and memorable way of learning and receiving feedback than teacher-centered instruction.

Testing Practice Activities

Test Creation

- Have students work in groups to create more test questions for each section.

- Have groups work together to test each other with their questions.

Group Work

- Photocopy the pages and cut up the different test type sections.

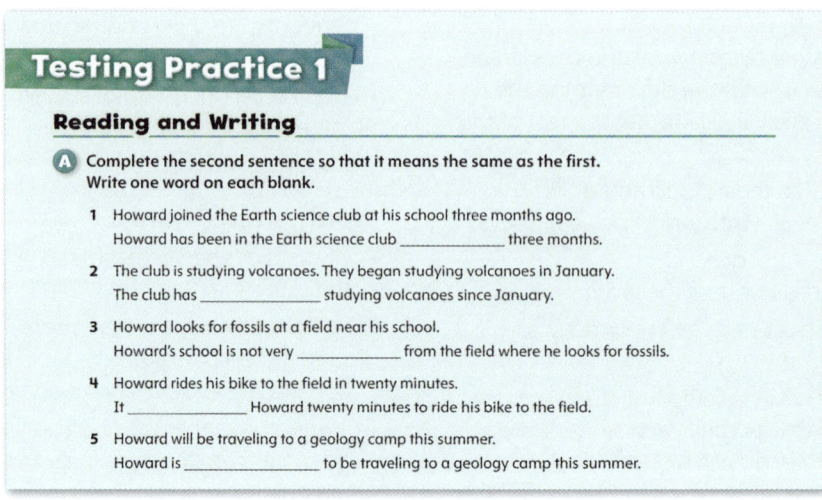

- Put students into groups and hand out the same test part to each group.
- Have groups elect a secretary who will write the answers.
- Give a time limit for answering the questions.
- Once the questions have been answered, each group passes their answers to another group.
- Check the answers together in class.
- Hand out the next section and repeat until the groups have answered all parts of the test.

Test Relay

- Photocopy the page and choose one or two test sections. Make enough copies for a number of teams.
- Cut up each individual question.
- Put students into teams of four or five.
- Put the cut up questions for each team in a particular place in the room, preferably some distance from the team. Make sure each team knows where their questions are located.
- Have each team number themselves from one to four or five.
- Tell them that number ones will go first.
- The first person from each team runs to get a question (it doesn't matter about the order of the questions) and runs back to their group.

- As a group they answer the question and the first person writes the answer on the piece of paper and takes it to the teacher, who then says whether it is correct or not.
- If it is correct, they run back to their team and the next student runs to get the next question and repeats the procedure until all the questions have been answered correctly.
- If it is not correct, they go back to their team and try to answer it again, and do this until they have the correct answer.
- The first team to finish all of the questions correctly is the winner.

Testing Practice Outcomes

- If assessment feedback is to be helpful to students and improve their learning, then the goals and reasons behind the assessment need to be clearly defined. Feedback needs to help students compare their current performance against the target performance and help them to close the gap between them. It also needs to be clear if the results of this assessment are to be included in any mid-year or end-of-year report, or if it is an informal procedure, designed to help them develop their own learning and test-taking techniques.

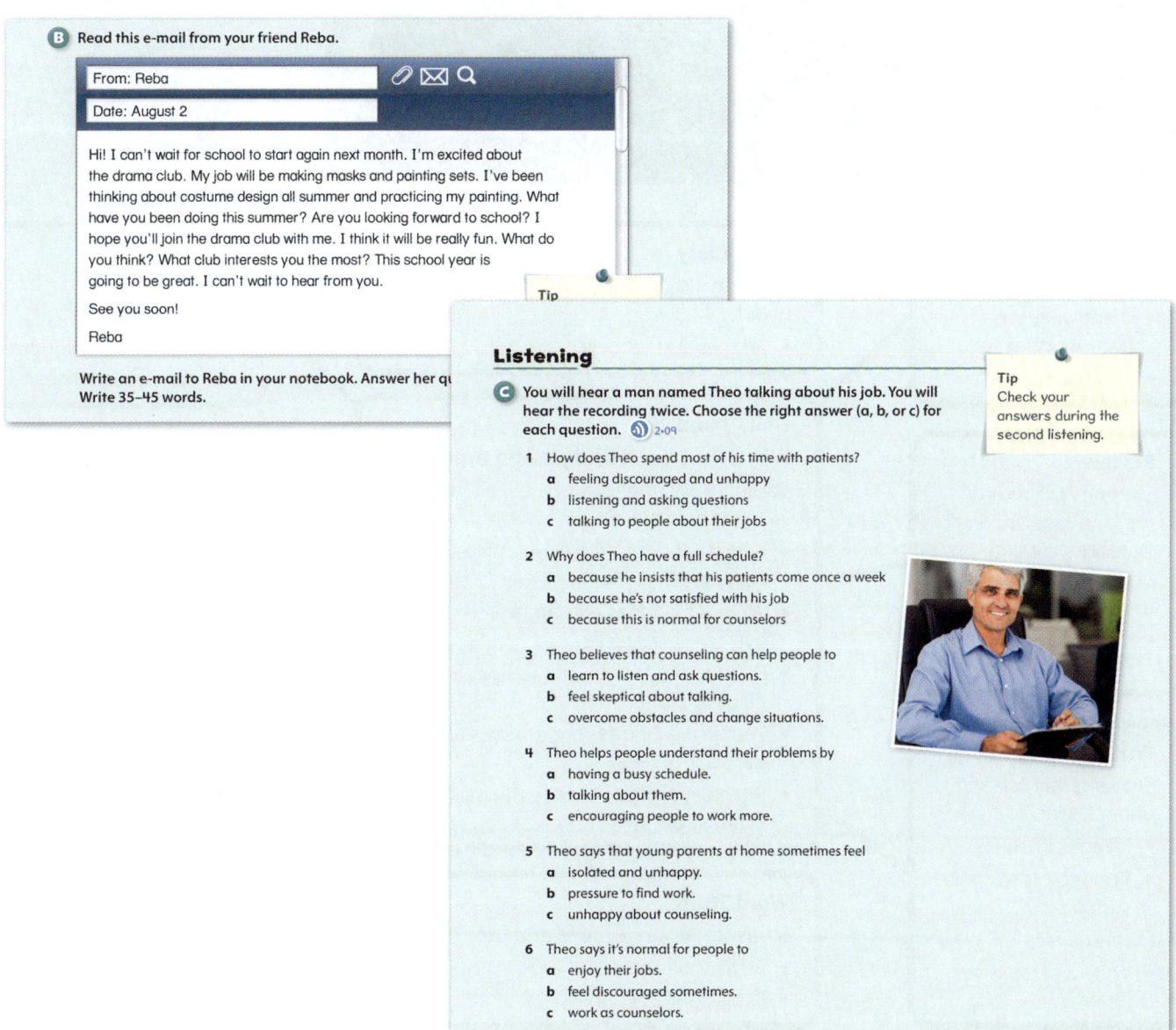

B Read this e-mail from your friend Reba.

From: Reba

Date: August 2

Hi! I can't wait for school to start again next month. I'm excited about the drama club. My job will be making masks and painting sets. I've been thinking about costume design all summer and practicing my painting. What have you been doing this summer? Are you looking forward to school? I hope you'll join the drama club with me. I think it will be really fun. What do you think? What club interests you the most? This school year is going to be great. I can't wait to hear from you.

See you soon!

Reba

Write an e-mail to Reba in your notebook. Answer her qu... Write 35–45 words.

Listening

C You will hear a man named Theo talking about his job. You will hear the recording twice. Choose the right answer (a, b, or c) for each question. 2·09

Tip
Check your answers during the second listening.

1 How does Theo spend most of his time with patients?
  a feeling discouraged and unhappy
  b listening and asking questions
  c talking to people about their jobs

2 Why does Theo have a full schedule?
  a because he insists that his patients come once a week
  b because he's not satisfied with his job
  c because this is normal for counselors

3 Theo believes that counseling can help people to
  a learn to listen and ask questions.
  b feel skeptical about talking.
  c overcome obstacles and change situations.

4 Theo helps people understand their problems by
  a having a busy schedule.
  b talking about them.
  c encouraging people to work more.

5 Theo says that young parents at home sometimes feel
  a isolated and unhappy.
  b pressure to find work.
  c unhappy about counseling.

6 Theo says it's normal for people to
  a enjoy their jobs.
  b feel discouraged sometimes.
  c work as counselors.

Units 1 and 2 — Why do we build bridges and tunnels?

In units 1 and 2 you will:

WATCH a video about bridges and tunnels.

LEARN about how people overcome obstacles.

READ about bridges, tunnels, and a hidden valley.

WRITE a persuasive letter.

PRESENT your letter to the class.

BIG QUESTION 1

Why do we build bridges and tunnels?

A Watch the video. Then talk about it with your partner.

B Look at the picture and discuss it with your class.
1. Why did people build this bridge?
2. Where is the train going?

C Think and answer the questions.
1. What bridges and tunnels are near you?
2. How do people use bridges and tunnels where you live?
3. What are some differences between a bridge and a tunnel?
4. Where do people build bridges and tunnels?

D Discuss this topic with your class. Fill out the **Big Question Chart**.

What do you know about bridges and tunnels? What do you want to know?

6 Big Question 1

7

Reading Strategies
Students will practice:
- Identifying the author's purpose
- Using a mind map

Vocabulary
Students will understand and use words about:
- Bridges and tunnels

Grammar
Students will understand and use:
- The future continuous
- Continuous tenses

Review
Students will review the language and Big Question learning points of Units 1 and 2 through:
- Writing a persuasive letter

Units 1 and 2
Why do we build bridges and tunnels?
Students will understand the Big Question learning points:
- Bridges and tunnels allow us to explore new places.
- We build bridges and tunnels to overcome obstacles.
- Bridges and tunnels help us get from place to place.
- People use bridges and tunnels to transport things.
- We build bridges to carry things like water and cables.

Listening Strategies
Students will practice:
- Listening for key words
- Listening for sequence

Writing Study
Students will use and understand:
- Paragraph breaks
- Connectors to show support

Students will:
- Write a persuasive letter

Word Study
Students will understand and use:
- Prefixes bi- and tri-
- Easily confused words

Speaking
Students will understand and use expressions for:
- Correcting someone
- Describing steps in a project

Units 1 and 2 Big Question page 6

Summary
Objectives: To activate students' existing knowledge of the topic and identify what they would like to learn about the topic.

Materials: Big Question DVD, Discover Poster 1, Big Question Chart

Introducing the topic

- Read out the Big Question. Ask *Why do we build bridges and tunnels?* Write students' ideas on the board and discuss.

A Watch the video. Then talk about it with your partner.

- Play the video and when it is finished ask students to answer the following questions in pairs:
  What do you see in the video?
  What is happening?
  Who do you think the people are?
  What do you like about the video?
- Have individual students share their answers with the class.

B Look at the picture and discuss it with your class.

- Students look at the big picture and talk about it. Ask *What do you see?*
- Ask additional questions:
  Where do you think this picture was taken?
  Have you ever traveled on a train like this?
  Would you like to travel on this train?
  How would you feel if you were on this train?

C Think and answer the questions.

- Have students discuss the questions in small groups, and then with the class.

DIFFERENTIATION
Below level:
- Do a quick review of bridges and tunnels.
- Draw a simple picture of a bridge and a tunnel on the board and elicit sentences about each from the class.

At level:
- Have the class describe how we use bridges and tunnels (e.g. to go over or under things, to transport things and people), and where they occur (water, land, etc.).

Above level:
- Put students into small groups.
- Have each group draw a picture of a bridge or tunnel and label all the parts of it that they can.
- Have each group present their picture and describe the component parts to the class.

CRITICAL THINKING
- Ask students to think about the third question. *What are some differences between a bridge and a tunnel?* Have students say sentences and write them on the board.
- Ask *Who do you think makes bridges and tunnels? How do you think they plan to make them?* Have students say sentences and write them on the board.

Expanding the topic

COLLABORATIVE LEARNING
- Display **Discover Poster 1** and give students enough time to look at the pictures.
- Get students to talk about things you think they will know by pointing to different things in the pictures and asking *What's this? What does this do?*
- Put students into small groups of three or four. Have each group choose a picture that they find interesting.
- Ask each group to say five sentences about their picture.
- Have one person from each group stand up and read out their sentences.
- Ask the class if they can add any more.

DIFFERENTIATION
Below level:
- Encourage students to participate using short sentences.
- Point to details in the big picture and on the poster and ask *What is this?* Write the answers on the board.

At level:
- Elicit complete sentences about what students know about bridges and tunnels.
- Write their sentences on the board.

Above level:
- Elicit more detailed responses.
- Challenge students to write their own sentences on the board.

D Discuss this topic with your class. Fill out the Big Question Chart.

- Display the **Big Question Chart**.
- Ask the class *What do you know about bridges and tunnels? What do you want to know about bridges and tunnels?*
- Ask students to write what they know and what they want to know in their Workbooks.
- Have individual students read out some of their ideas.
- Write a collection of ideas on the **Big Question Chart**.

Discover Poster 1

1 A woman crossing a bridge suspended over a lake; 2 A truck about to enter a tunnel; 3 A train arriving at a subway station in Washington, D.C.; 4 A freight train crossing an arch bridge in the Austrian Alps; 5 An engineer looking at power cables in a tunnel

> **Further Practice**
> **Workbook page 2**
> **Online Practice · Big Question 1**
> **Oxford iTools · Big Question 1**

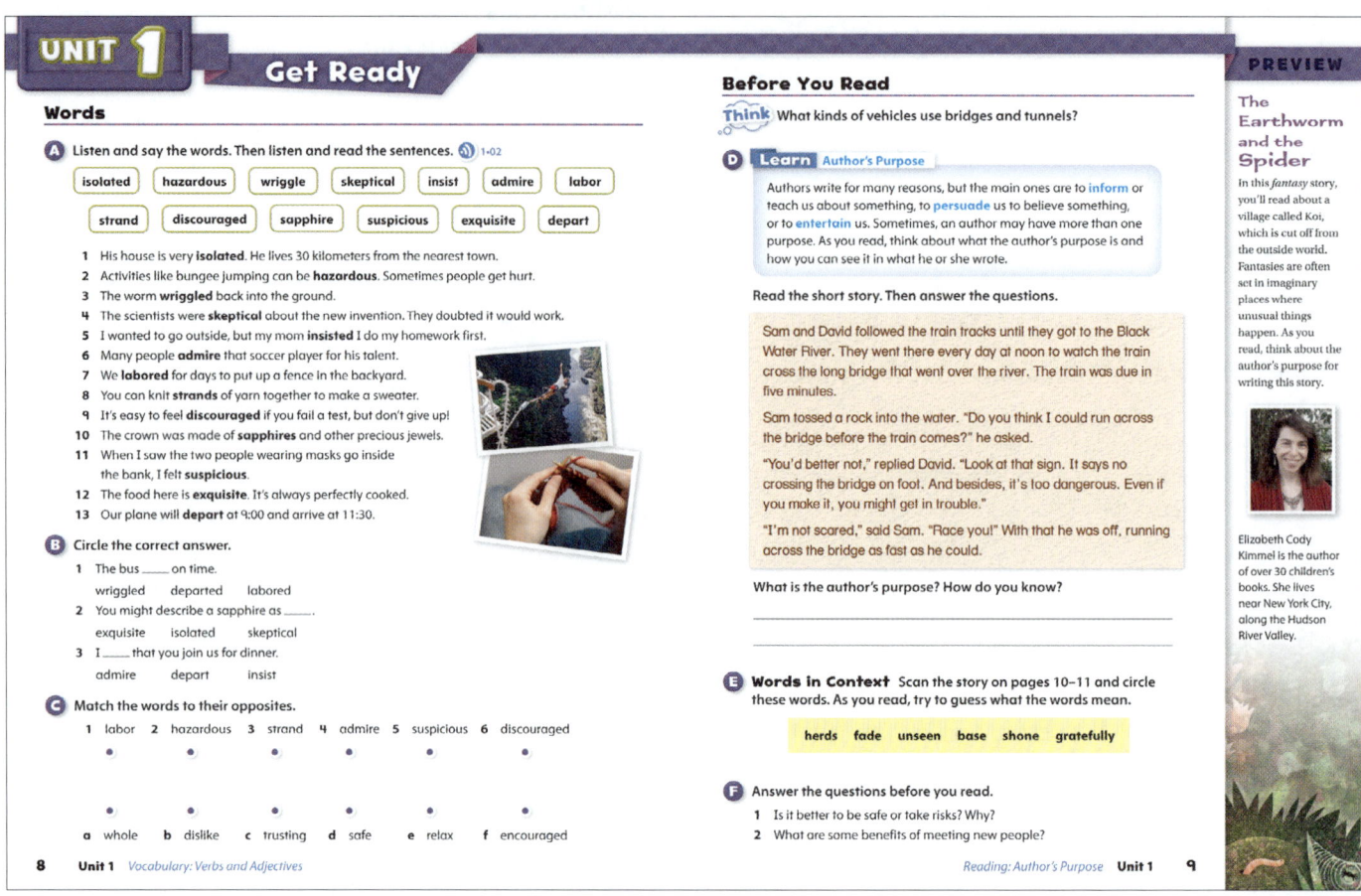

Summary

Objectives: To understand about verbs and adjectives; to apply own experience and a reading strategy to help comprehension of a text.

Vocabulary: *isolated, hazardous, wriggle, skeptical, insist, admire, labor, strand, discouraged, sapphire, suspicious, exquisite, depart, herds, fade, unseen, base, shone, gratefully*

Reading strategy: Author's purpose

Materials: Audio CD

Words

A Listen and say the words. Then listen and read the sentences. 1·02

- Play the audio. Ask students to point to the words and repeat the words when they hear them.
- Then have students listen and read the sentences as they hear them.
- Say the key words out of order and have the class read the sentence aloud.

COLLABORATIVE LEARNING

- Put students into mixed-ability groups. Have groups read through each sentence and discuss the meaning of the new word based on the context of the sentence.
- For any new words the group can't figure out from the sentence's context, have them look up the definition in the dictionary.
- Have groups share their definitions with the class. For each word ask *Is the word a noun, verb, or adjective?*

B Circle the correct answer.

- Tell students to read the sentences and circle the correct word to complete the sentence.
- Have students do the activity on their own.
- Have students compare their answers with a partner.
- Check answers with the class.

ANSWERS

1 departed   **2** exquisite   **3** insist

C Match the words to their opposites.

- Tell students to match the words on the top line with the opposite meaning word on the bottom line.
- Have students do the activity on their own.
- Have students compare their answers with a partner.
- Check answers with the class.

ANSWERS

1 e   **2** d   **3** a   **4** b   **5** c   **6** f

COMMUNICATION

- Put students into pairs. Have pairs write sentences for each other using the new words, e.g. *Some people feel isolated when they go camping.*
- When they have finished, tell the pairs to swap their sentences with another pair.
- Pairs check their work with each other.
- Have pairs read some of their sentences to the class.
- Listen to at least two sentences for each new word.

Below level:

- Give students some simple definitions for the words.
- Say the definitions and have students call out the words together.

At level:

- Books closed. Say the new words in any order and have students write them.
- To check the answers, have individual students stand up and spell the words while a volunteer writes them on the board.

Above level:

- Put students into pairs and have them write sentences using the new words and their opposites from C, e.g. *The ocean waves are hazardous today. Maybe we can swim tomorrow if it is safe.*
- Pairs will write sentences for each of the words from C.
- Then pairs compare their work and correct their sentences.

Before You Read

Think

- Put students into pairs to discuss the question.
- Have pairs share their answers with the class.
- List the answers on the board.
- Ask *Are places different on either side of a tunnel or bridge?* Have the class discuss the answer.

D Learn: Author's Purpose

- Read the *Learn* box together.
- Explain that the author's purpose can tell us something new, influence or change our mind about something, or entertain us. Remind students that sometimes there can be more than one author's purpose.

Read the short story. Then answer the questions.

- Invite a confident student to read the paragraph aloud for the class.
- Ask *Why do you think the boys liked watching the train pass over the bridge every day? Do you think that Sam made it across the bridge in time?*

What is the author's purpose? How do you know?

- Have students work individually to write their answers.
- Have students share their answers in pairs.
- Elicit ideas from the class.

Persuade: The author is trying to persuade us not to do dangerous things.

Entertain: The author entertains us through a story that is suspenseful. We wonder what will happen next.

- Ask the following questions to check understanding about persuasion: *What part of the story is persuasive? Why is the author trying to persuade the readers?*
- Ask the following questions to check understanding about entertainment: *How is the story entertaining? What makes the story entertaining?*

E Words in Context: Scan the story on pages 10–11 and circle these words. As you read, try to guess what the words mean.

- Read each word and have the students follow your pronunciation.
- Have students scan the story on pages 10 and 11 and circle the words. Tell them to guess what the words mean from the context.
- Have the students share their ideas about the words' definitions.

Below level:

- Give students some simple definitions for the words.
- Restate and / or explain the sentences from the story using the definitions, e.g. *Herds are groups of animals like cows, or sheep, or even horses. Why do these kinds of animals need to be kept safe from wolves? Let's say it is a herd of sheep and a herd of cows in this story. We could say "The mountains and rivers keep our herd of sheep and our herd of cows safe from wolves."*

At level:

- Put students into pairs to work out the meaning of the new words from context.
- Tell pairs to look up any words they can't understand from context in the dictionary.
- Have pairs share their answers with the class.

Above level:

- Put students into pairs to restate the sentences with alternate words in place of the words in context.
- Have pairs share their new sentences with the class.

F Answer the questions before you read.

- Put students into small groups to discuss the questions. Tell groups to list the reasons that are their answers for each question.
- Go over the groups' answers and make notes on the board.

Reading Preview

- Read the title of the unit's reading text.
- Have students silently read the content of the preview bar.
- Ask *What type of text is it?* Ask *What does this type of text do?*
- Tell students to think about the author's purpose as they read.
- Read the Author Bio with the class.

Further Practice
Workbook pages 2–3
Online Practice Unit 1 · Get Ready
Oxford **iTools** Unit 1 · Get Ready

The Earthworm and the Spider

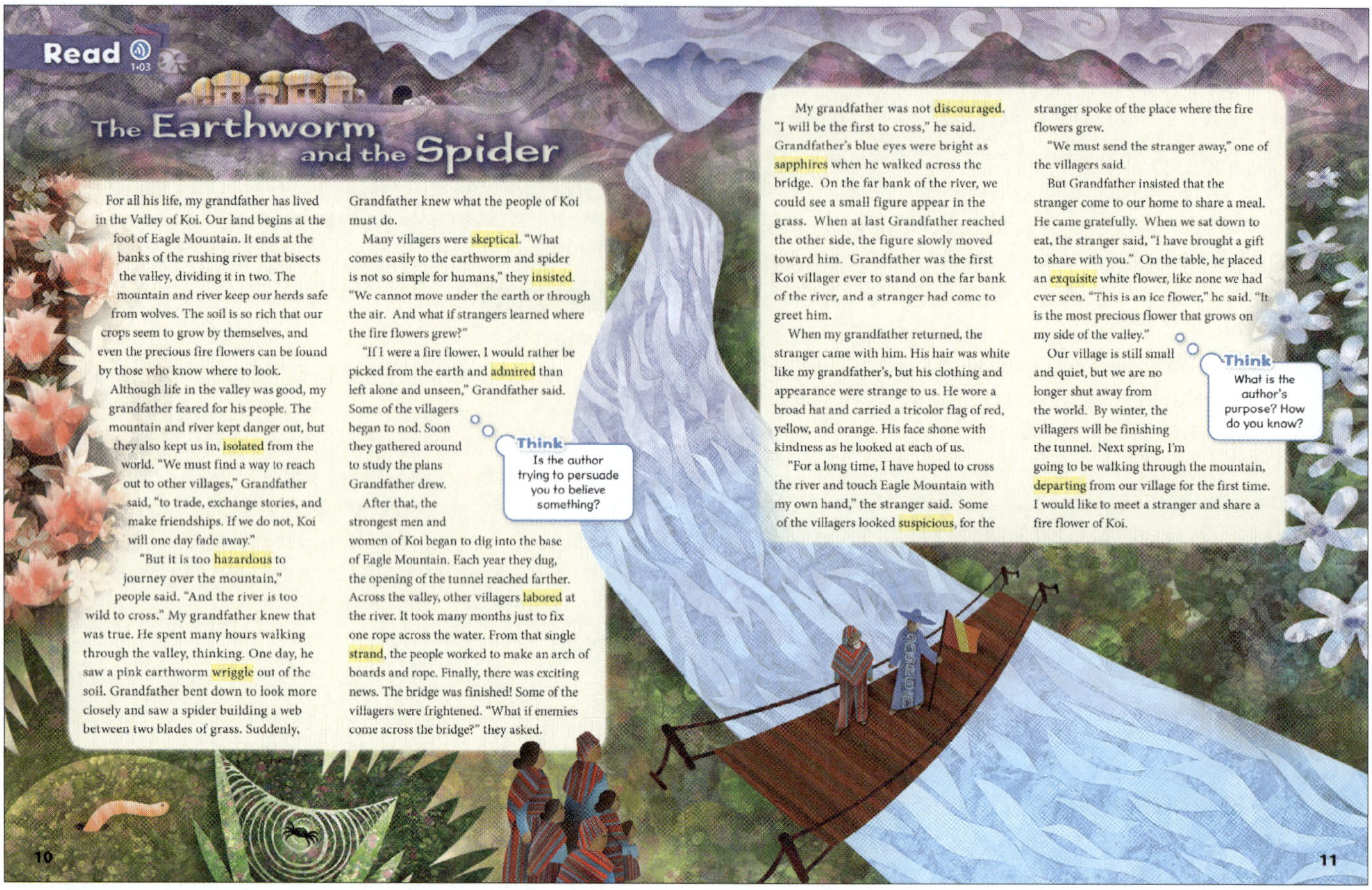

For all his life, my grandfather has lived in the Valley of Koi. Our land begins at the foot of Eagle Mountain. It ends at the banks of the rushing river that bisects the valley, dividing it in two. The mountain and river keep our herds safe from wolves. The soil is so rich that our crops seem to grow by themselves, and even the precious fire flowers can be found by those who know where to look.

Although life in the valley was good, my grandfather feared for his people. The mountain and river kept danger out, but they also kept us in, isolated from the world. "We must find a way to reach out to other villages," Grandfather said, "to trade, exchange stories, and make friendships. If we do not, Koi will one day fade away."

"But it is too hazardous to journey over the mountain," people said. "And the river is too wild to cross." My grandfather knew that was true. He spent many hours walking through the valley, thinking. One day, he saw a pink earthworm wriggle out of the soil. Grandfather bent down to look more closely and saw a spider building a web between two blades of grass. Suddenly,

Grandfather knew what the people of Koi must do.

Many villagers were skeptical. "What comes easily to the earthworm and spider is not so simple for humans," they insisted. "We cannot move under the earth or through the air. And what if strangers learned where the fire flowers grew?"

"If I were a fire flower, I would rather be picked from the earth and admired than left alone and unseen," Grandfather said. Some of the villagers began to nod. Soon they gathered around to study the plans Grandfather drew.

After that, the strongest men and women of Koi began to dig into the base of Eagle Mountain. Each year they dug, the opening of the tunnel reached farther. Across the valley, other villagers labored at the river. It took many months just to fix one rope across the water. From that single strand, the people worked to make an arch of boards and rope. Finally, there was exciting news. The bridge was finished! Some of the villagers were frightened. "What if enemies come across the bridge?" they asked.

Think Is the author trying to persuade you to believe something?

My grandfather was not discouraged. "I will be the first to cross," he said. Grandfather's blue eyes were bright as sapphires when he walked across the bridge. On the far bank of the river, we could see a small figure appear in the grass. When at last Grandfather reached the other side, the figure slowly moved toward him. Grandfather was the first Koi villager ever to stand on the far bank of the river, and a stranger had come to greet him.

When my grandfather returned, the stranger came with him. His hair was white like my grandfather's, but his clothing and appearance were strange to us. He wore a broad hat and carried a tricolor flag of red, yellow, and orange. His face shone with kindness as he looked at each of us.

"For a long time, I have hoped to cross the river and touch Eagle Mountain with my own hand," the stranger said. Some of the villagers looked suspicious, for the

stranger spoke of the place where the fire flowers grew.

"We must send the stranger away," one of the villagers said.

But Grandfather insisted that the stranger come to our home to share a meal. He came gratefully. When we sat down to eat, the stranger said, "I have brought a gift to share with you." On the table, he placed an exquisite white flower, like none we had ever seen. "This is an ice flower," he said. "It is the most precious flower that grows on my side of the valley."

Our village is still small and quiet, but we are no longer shut away from the world. By winter, the villagers will be finishing the tunnel. Next spring, I'm going to be walking through the mountain, departing from our village for the first time. I would like to meet a stranger and share a fire flower of Koi.

Think What is the author's purpose? How do you know?

10   11

Summary

Objectives: To read, understand, and discuss a fantasy story; to apply a reading strategy to improve comprehension.

School subject: Social Studies: Technology

Text type: Fantasy (fiction)

Reading strategy: Author's purpose

Big Question learning points: *Bridges and tunnels allow us to explore new places. We build bridges and tunnels to overcome obstacles. Bridges and tunnels help us get from place to place.*

Materials: Audio CD

Before Reading

- Ask *Why do we build bridges and tunnels?*
- Have students tell you what they see in the pictures.
- Ask students how they know this is a fantasy story.
- Ask students to point to the *Think* boxes. Elicit how students will use the boxes, e.g. read them and think.

During Reading 1·03

- Read the title together.
- Point out the *Think* boxes and explain that students should use these to think about the author's purpose.

DIFFERENTIATION

Below level:

- Have students read along quietly as they listen to the audio.
- Put students into small groups of three or four.

- Have students discuss any unfamiliar or difficult vocabulary or phrases. Ask them to help each other.
- Ask the class to read out any words or phrases that are difficult to understand, despite the context of the word in a sentence.
- Explain the meaning of those words or phrases for the class.
- Have students return to the text and discuss the *Think* boxes in their groups.

At level:

- Put students into mixed-ability pairs.
- Have students read with a partner, taking turns to read the sections of the story.
- Have the students stop and ask each other the meaning of words or phrases that are new or unfamiliar when they come across them in the story.
- Have them stop at each *Think* box to discuss the author's purpose.

Above level:

- Have students read the story independently.
- Put students into pairs.
- Have each pair summarize the story together and discuss the answers for each *Think* box.

COLLABORATIVE LEARNING

Discuss the *Think* boxes as follows:

- *In the first* Think *box, do you think the author is trying to persuade you? Why?*
- *Are you persuaded by what Grandfather says? Why or why not?*

- *Why do we as readers pay attention to what Grandfather says?*
- *In the second* Think *box, what do you think is the author's purpose? How do you know?*
- *What does the next paragraph say about the village?*

After Reading

CRITICAL THINKING

Discussion questions:
- *What are the natural elements surrounding this village?*
- *Where do the bridge and the tunnel go in the story?*
- *What are the fantasy elements of the story?*
- *Why do the villagers want to stay away from strangers?*
- *Why do you think the villagers valued the fire flower so much?*
- *Do you think the different villagers will become friends?*
- *Could this story happen in real life?*

CREATIVITY

- Put students into small groups of three or four.
- Say *Imagine the story has a different ending, what might happen?*
- Have groups spend time brainstorming a different ending to the story.
- Tell each group to nominate or elect a "secretary" who will write down the ending they decide upon.
- Have each group read out their new ending to the class.
- Have the class vote on the most persuasive, entertaining, and interesting endings.

CULTURE NOTE

Famous tunnels

The Seikan Tunnel in Japan is the longest undersea tunnel in the world. It connects the islands of Honshu and Hokkaido and was opened in 1988. It took more than 40 years to be finished and cost a lot of money to build.

The Hoosac Tunnel was the first large tunnel in the United States. It took 20 years to build and was finished in 1876. This was one of the first tunnels to use the power of dynamite to cut through the rock in its construction.

In India, there is a large and complex underground rail system in Delhi. The Yellow Line is 45 kilometers long and there are plans to extend it even further.

Famous bridges

The Millau Viaduct in Southern France is the tallest bridge in the world, as tall as the Eiffel Tower. This bridge spans a valley that was previously slow to travel through on the route from France to Spain.

The Chapel Bridge can be found in Lucerne, Switzerland. It is the oldest covered, wooden bridge in Europe and is one of Switzerland's main tourist attractions. It was constructed in 1333 and was designed to protect the city of Lucerne from invaders.

Sydney Harbour Bridge is one of Australia's most well-known landmarks. It was opened in 1932 and took eight years to build. It is the largest steel arch bridge in the world, with the top of the bridge standing 134 meters above Sydney Harbour. When it is hot or cold the steel expands or contracts and so the bridge is never completely stationary and can rise and fall up to 18 centimeters.

Further Practice
Workbook page 4
Online Practice Unit 1 • Read
Oxford iTools Unit 1 • Read

Understand

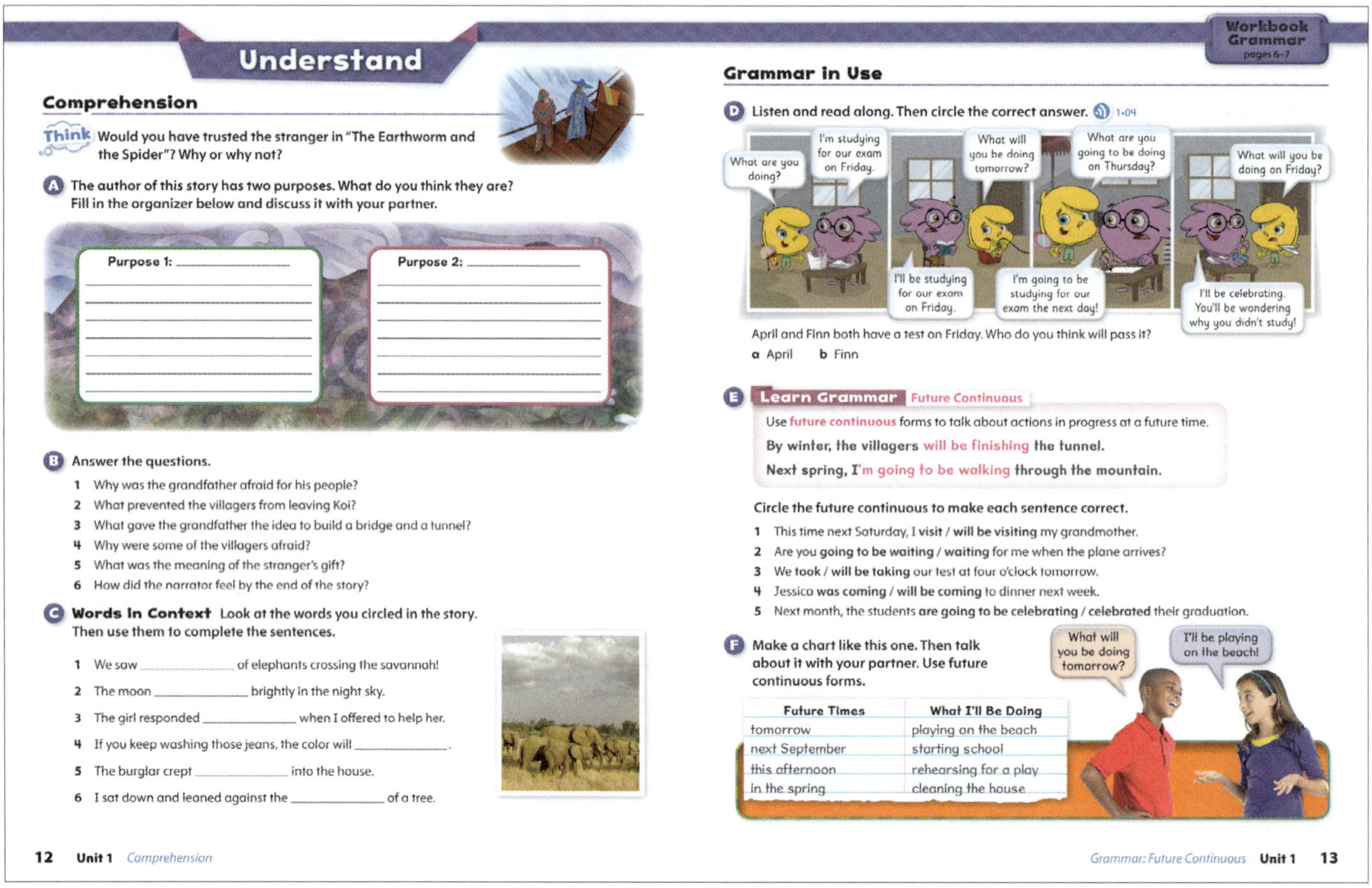

Comprehension

Think Would you have trusted the stranger in "The Earthworm and the Spider"? Why or why not?

A The author of this story has two purposes. What do you think they are? Fill in the organizer below and discuss it with your partner.

Purpose 1: _____

Purpose 2: _____

B Answer the questions.
1 Why was the grandfather afraid for his people?
2 What prevented the villagers from leaving Koi?
3 What gave the grandfather the idea to build a bridge and a tunnel?
4 Why were some of the villagers afraid?
5 What was the meaning of the stranger's gift?
6 How did the narrator feel by the end of the story?

C Words In Context Look at the words you circled in the story. Then use them to complete the sentences.
1 We saw _____ of elephants crossing the savannah!
2 The moon _____ brightly in the night sky.
3 The girl responded _____ when I offered to help her.
4 If you keep washing those jeans, the color will _____.
5 The burglar crept _____ into the house.
6 I sat down and leaned against the _____ of a tree.

12   Unit 1   *Comprehension*

Grammar in Use

Workbook Grammar pages 6–7

D Listen and read along. Then circle the correct answer. 1·04

What are you doing?
I'm studying for our exam on Friday.
What will you be doing tomorrow?
What are you going to be doing on Thursday?
What will you be doing on Friday?
I'll be studying for our exam on Friday.
I'm going to be studying for our exam the next day!
I'll be celebrating. You'll be wondering why you didn't study!

April and Finn both have a test on Friday. Who do you think will pass it?
a April   b Finn

E Learn Grammar Future Continuous

Use future continuous forms to talk about actions in progress at a future time.
By winter, the villagers will be finishing the tunnel.
Next spring, I'm going to be walking through the mountain.

Circle the future continuous to make each sentence correct.
1 This time next Saturday, I visit / will be visiting my grandmother.
2 Are you going to be waiting / waiting for me when the plane arrives?
3 We took / will be taking our test at four o'clock tomorrow.
4 Jessica was coming / will be coming to dinner next week.
5 Next month, the students are going to be celebrating / celebrated their graduation.

F Make a chart like this one. Then talk about it with your partner. Use future continuous forms.

What will you be doing tomorrow?
I'll be playing on the beach!

Future Times	What I'll Be Doing
tomorrow	playing on the beach
next September	starting school
this afternoon	rehearsing for a play
in the spring	cleaning the house

Grammar: Future Continuous   **Unit 1**   13

Summary

Objectives: To demonstrate understanding of a fantasy story; to understand the meaning and form of the grammar structure.

Reading: Comprehension

Grammar input: Future continuous

Grammar practice: Workbook exercises

Grammar production: Talking about what you'll be doing in the future

Materials: Audio CD

Comprehension

Think
- Read the question with the class. Ask students to think about their answer. Put students into groups to discuss their answers.
- Have students put up their hands to show who would or wouldn't trust the stranger and say why or why not.

A The author of this story has two purposes. What do you think they are? Fill in the organizer below and discuss it with your partner.
- After students have read the story, have them fill in the organizer on their own. Go around and help as needed.
- Put students into pairs and tell them to compare their organizers.
- Complete the organizers on the board to check them. Elicit the information to complete them from the class.

Purpose 1: To persuade. The author is trying to persuade us to try new things / meet new people / to not be isolated.
Purpose 2: To entertain. The fantasy story is entertaining. We wonder what will happen when the stranger comes to the village.

DIFFERENTIATION

Below level:
- Review the author's purpose for the short story on page 9.
- Put students into mixed-ability pairs. Have the pairs reread the story together, with the more confident student helping the other student to think about the author's purpose. Go around and help as needed.
- Then pairs complete the organizers together.

At level:
- Students complete the organizers on their own.
- Put students in pairs and ask them to trade books to check each other's work.
- Have pairs work together to rewrite the organizers to present their best version, and then share their revised organizers with the class.

Above level:
- After students have completed the organizers, have them give examples from the story to support the idea of the author's purpose. Say *In the story, find two to three examples that show each of the author's purposes. Take notes or underline them in the story.* Give students a few minutes to find the examples before they compare their answers with a partner.

B Answer the questions.

- For each question, tell students to look back at the story and find details to support their answers:
- Have students work individually and then check their answers with a partner. Elicit answers from the class.

1 He was afraid that because his people were isolated, they might be forgotten and fade away.
2 The people were prevented from leaving Koi because the mountain and the river kept them separate.
3 Seeing the spider build a web between two blades of grass gave him the idea.
4 Some of the villagers were afraid that the bridge would bring enemies. They were afraid when the stranger spoke of their land.
5 The meaning of the stranger's gift was friendship and trust. The stranger brought the most precious gift he could.
6 The narrator is happy at the end of the story. He would like to meet new people.

C Words in Context: Look at the words you circled in the story. Then use them to complete the sentences.

- Have students go back and find the words in the story.
- Tell them to use the context clues to guess at the meaning of each word.

ANSWERS

1 herds   2 shone   3 gratefully   4 fade
5 unseen   6 base

COLLABORATIVE LEARNING

- In small groups, ask students to work together to write new sentences for the words in context.
- As groups write their sentences, encourage them to use the dictionary to help with definitions. Go around and help as necessary.
- Have groups share their sentences with the class.

Grammar in Use

D Listen and read along. Then circle the correct answer. 🔘 1·04

- Listen to the dialogue once and have students read along.
- Have students read the question and circle the correct answer.
- Play the audio again and have students check their answer.

ANSWER
Finn

E Learn Grammar: Future Continuous

- Have a confident student read the *Learn Grammar* box to the class.
- Draw a timeline on the board. Underneath it, evenly spaced, write *spring, summer, fall, winter*. Mark an X on the timeline in the spring section. Say *It is spring today. Today I say, "By winter, the villagers will be finishing the tunnel."* Point to the winter area as you say the sentence. Ask *In spring, when I talk about winter, what time is it? Will the villagers finish the tunnel quickly? Will it take them many days to finish the tunnel? So we can say the future continuous tense means the action will be going on over some time, in the future.*

Circle a section on the timeline in winter as you explain this.

Circle the future continuous to make each sentence correct.

- Read the first sentence together. Identify the choice students have to make: *visit / will be visiting.*
- Complete number 1 together, then have students complete the rest on their own.

ANSWERS

1 will be visiting   2 going to be waiting
3 will be taking   4 will be coming
5 are going to be celebrating

CRITICAL THINKING

Ask follow-up questions and map the class's answers on the board on a simple timeline:

- *How long will this person be visiting his or her grandmother?*
- *How much time does "going to be waiting" mean?*
- *If the test starts at four o'clock, why do we use future continuous?*
- *Did this dinner happen already? How do we know? What verb do we use if the dinner happened? So what verb tense do we use for a dinner that will happen in the future?*
- *Have the students already celebrated the graduation? How do we know?*

F Make a chart like this one. Then talk about it with your partner. Use future continuous forms.

- Have students fill out the chart on their own.
- Put partners in pairs to discuss their charts.
- Have a few pairs say their sentences for the class.

DIFFERENTIATION

Below level:

- Put students into mixed-ability pairs. Have the more confident student help the other student fill out the chart based on his or her real information and plans.
- Have the less confident student read his or her sentences.

At level:

- Have students complete the chart and add two more future times, e.g. next weekend, next summer.
- Have a few pairs say their new dialogues for the class.

Above level:

- Have students add two to three extra future times to the chart as above.
- Put students into small groups. Students try to guess one group member's plans. Going around the circle, students take turns to guess what the other group members will be doing for the specified times, saying, e.g. *Mia will be riding her bike after school tomorrow.* Once a correct guess is made, the group takes turns to guess for the next person.

Workbook Grammar

- Direct students to the Workbook for further practice.

Further practice
Workbook pages 5–7
Online Practice Unit 1 · Understand
Oxford **iTools** Unit 1 · Understand

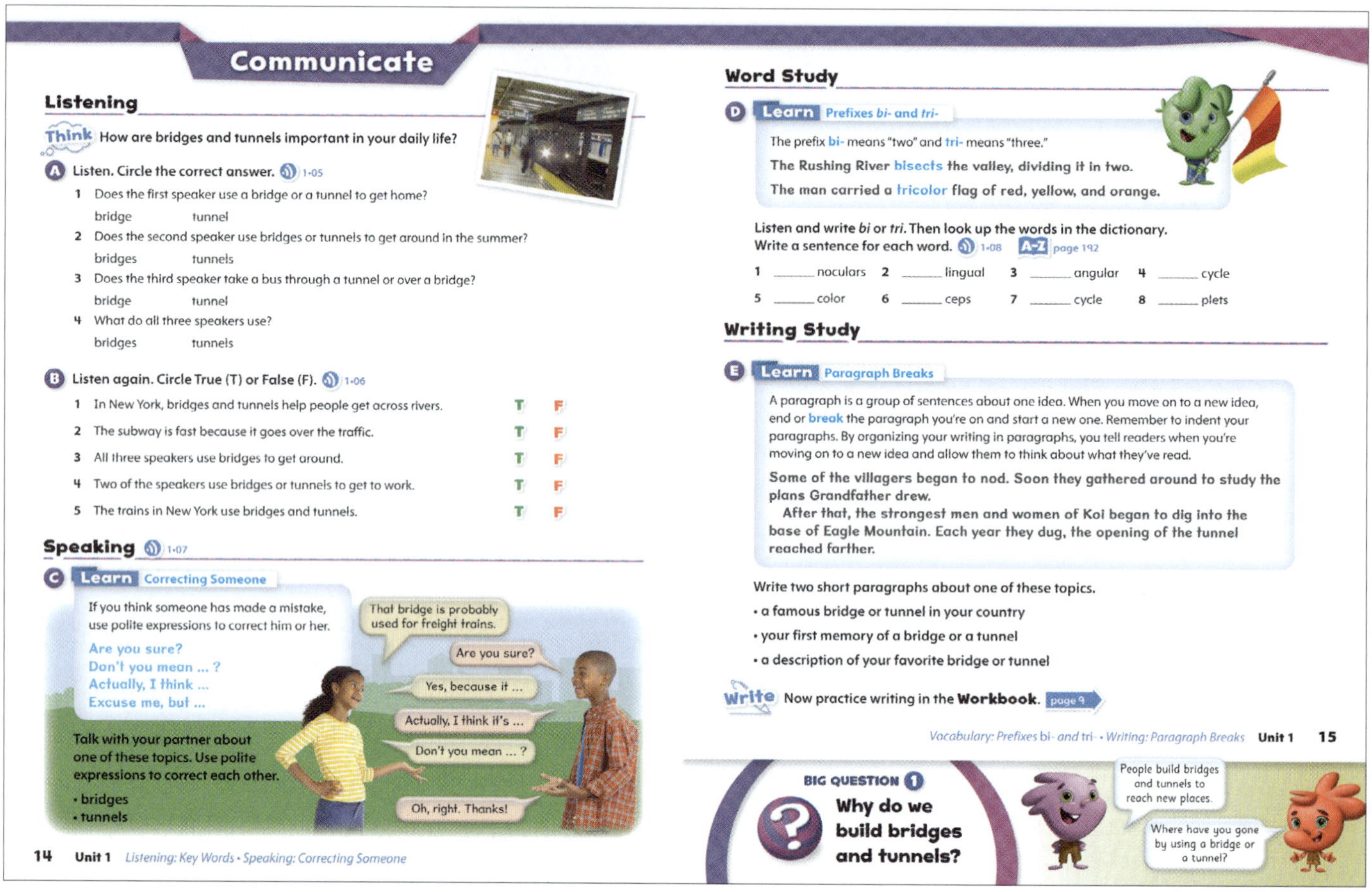

The page reproduces the Student Book spread (pages 14–15):

Communicate

Listening

Think How are bridges and tunnels important in your daily life?

A Listen. Circle the correct answer. 1·05

1 Does the first speaker use a bridge or a tunnel to get home?
   bridge   tunnel
2 Does the second speaker use bridges or tunnels to get around in the summer?
   bridges   tunnels
3 Does the third speaker take a bus through a tunnel or over a bridge?
   bridge   tunnel
4 What do all three speakers use?
   bridges   tunnels

B Listen again. Circle True (T) or False (F). 1·06

1 In New York, bridges and tunnels help people get across rivers.   T   F
2 The subway is fast because it goes over the traffic.   T   F
3 All three speakers use bridges to get around.   T   F
4 Two of the speakers use bridges or tunnels to get to work.   T   F
5 The trains in New York use bridges and tunnels.   T   F

Speaking 1·07

C Learn Correcting Someone

If you think someone has made a mistake, use polite expressions to correct him or her.

Are you sure?
Don't you mean … ?
Actually, I think …
Excuse me, but …

That bridge is probably used for freight trains.
Are you sure?
Yes, because it …
Actually, I think it's …
Don't you mean … ?
Oh, right. Thanks!

Talk with your partner about one of these topics. Use polite expressions to correct each other.
• bridges
• tunnels

14   Unit 1   Listening: Key Words • Speaking: Correcting Someone

Word Study

D Learn Prefixes bi- and tri-

The prefix bi- means "two" and tri- means "three."
The Rushing River bisects the valley, dividing it in two.
The man carried a tricolor flag of red, yellow, and orange.

Listen and write bi or tri. Then look up the words in the dictionary. Write a sentence for each word. 1·08 A-Z page 192

1 _____ noculars   2 _____ lingual   3 _____ angular   4 _____ cycle
5 _____ color   6 _____ ceps   7 _____ cycle   8 _____ plets

Writing Study

E Learn Paragraph Breaks

A paragraph is a group of sentences about one idea. When you move on to a new idea, end or break the paragraph you're on and start a new one. Remember to indent your paragraphs. By organizing your writing in paragraphs, you tell readers when you're moving on to a new idea and allow them to think about what they've read.

Some of the villagers began to nod. Soon they gathered around to study the plans Grandfather drew.
   After that, the strongest men and women of Koi began to dig into the base of Eagle Mountain. Each year they dug, the opening of the tunnel reached farther.

Write two short paragraphs about one of these topics.
• a famous bridge or tunnel in your country
• your first memory of a bridge or a tunnel
• a description of your favorite bridge or tunnel

Write Now practice writing in the Workbook. page 9

Vocabulary: Prefixes bi- and tri- • Writing: Paragraph Breaks   Unit 1   15

BIG QUESTION 1
Why do we build bridges and tunnels?

People build bridges and tunnels to reach new places.
Where have you gone by using a bridge or a tunnel?

Summary

Objectives: To learn and practice listening, speaking, and writing strategies to facilitate effective communication.

Vocabulary: *binoculars, bilingual, triangular, bicycle, tricolor, biceps, tricycle, triplets*

Listening strategy: Listening for key words

Speaking: Correcting someone

Word Study: Prefixes *bi-* and *tri-*

Writing Study: Paragraph breaks

Big Question learning point: *Bridges and tunnels help us get from place to place.*

Materials: Discover Poster 1, Audio CD, Big Question Chart

Listening

Think

• Tell students to think about the question. Then ask the class if they use a bridge or a tunnel or if their parents do.

• If no one uses a bridge or a tunnel, ask if students can think of places or cities where they might find a bridge or a tunnel, e.g. London Bridge in England, Brooklyn Bridge in New York City, the Chunnel (tunnel) from England to France.

A Listen. Circle the correct answer. 1·05

• Have students read the question and answer choices first. Then ask *What are you listening for in this exercise?* (Elicit for sequence.)

• Play the audio once and have students listen.

• Tell students to circle the correct answers. Then play the audio again so they can check their work.

ANSWERS
1 bridge   2 tunnels   3 bridge   4 tunnels

B Listen again. Circle True (T) or False (F). 1·06

• Play the audio so students can complete the exercise.

• Have students compare answers with a partner before checking answers with the class.

ANSWERS
1 T   2 F   3 F   4 F   5 T

Speaking 1·07

C Learn: Correcting Someone

• Read the *Learn* box with the class.

• Play the audio. Say each of the expressions with students echoing as they hear each line.

• Model the dialogue and examples with a confident student in front of the class.

• Ask *Why do we use polite expressions when someone makes a mistake? How do you feel when you make a mistake when you speak? How do you want people to treat you?*

• Put students into pairs and tell them to practice the dialogue, using polite expressions.

Talk with your partner about one of the topics. Use polite expressions to correct each other.

- Put students into pairs.
- Have them create short dialogues using the topics listed (bridges or tunnels).
- Have a few pairs act out their dialogues for the class.

Word Study

D Learn: Prefixes *bi-* and *tri-*

- Read the *Learn* box together.
- Elicit where the prefixes occur in the words (at the beginning). Ask *What does "bisect" mean? How many colors are in the tricolor flag? What are they?*

Listen and write *bi* or *tri*. Then look up the words up in the dictionary. Write a sentence for each word. 🔊 1·08

ANSWERS

1 binoculars   2 bilingual   3 triangular   4 bicycle
5 tricolor   6 biceps   7 tricycle   8 triplets

DIFFERENTIATION

Below level:

- Say the words and have students repeat and spell them.
- Go over the meanings and give examples.

At level:

- Have pairs look up the meanings of the words in the dictionary pages of the Student Book.
- Collect the definitions by having the pairs write them on the board.

Above level:

- Put students into pairs. Have them look up the definitions in the dictionary pages of the Student Book and then write sentences using the new words.
- Have pairs write their sentences on the board and tell the class about them.

Writing Study

E Learn: Paragraph Breaks

- Read the *Learn* box together.
- Have students read the story to themselves. Then have the class point to the paragraph break in their books.
- Ask questions to check understanding:
  What is the idea of the first paragraph?
  What is the idea of the second paragraph?
  Why do we need a paragraph break?

Write two short paragraphs about one of these topics.

CREATIVITY

- Have students read the list of topics. Brainstorm ideas for each topic and write them on the board.
- Then choose one of the ideas and draw a mind map with the topic in the center, and points coming off it for other words associated with the topic that the class says.

- Explain that the points coming off the topic mean different ideas and students would use a paragraph break to write about them.
- Have students write their paragraphs.
- Then put students into pairs to read each other's paragraphs.

CRITICAL THINKING

- Put students into pairs. Have pairs go back through the story on pages 10 and 11.
- Have pairs discuss why the paragraph breaks occur where they do. Tell them to point out the different ideas of each paragraph. Write
- Direct students to the Workbook for further practice.

Big Question 1 Review

Why do we build bridges and tunnels?

- Display **Discover Poster 1**. Discuss what you see.
- Refer to the learning points covered in Unit 1, which are written on the poster and have students explain how they relate to the different pictures.
- Return to the **Big Question Chart**.
- Ask students what they have learned about bridges and tunnels while studying this unit.

> **Further practice**
> **Workbook pages 8–9**
> **Online Practice Unit 1 · Communicate**
> Oxford **iTools** Unit 1 · **Communicate**

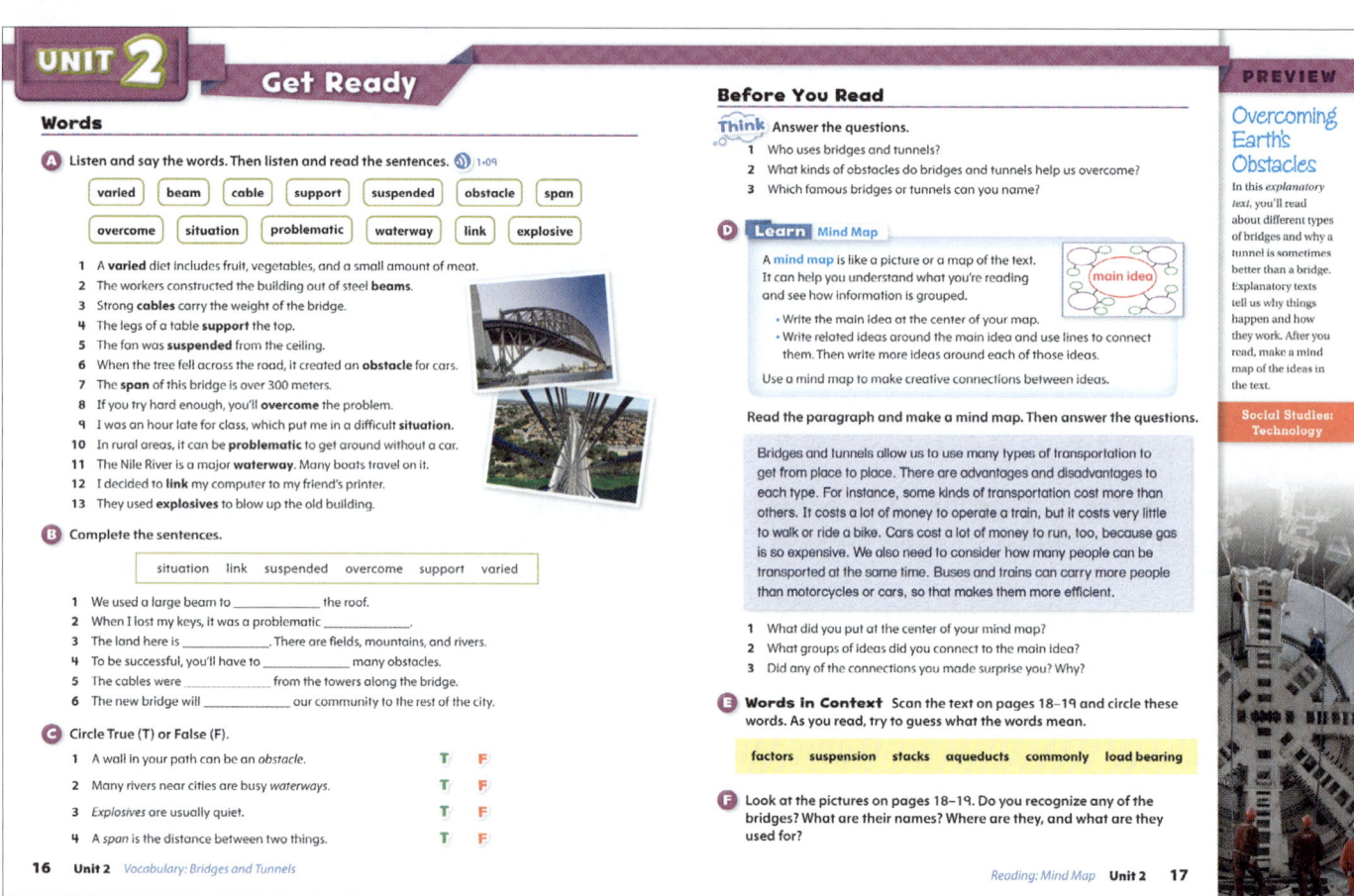

Summary

Objectives: To understand words about bridges and tunnels; to apply own experience and a reading strategy to help comprehension of a text.

Vocabulary: *varied, beam, cable, support, suspended, obstacle, span, overcome, situation, problematic, waterway, link, explosive, factors, suspension, stacks, aqueducts, commonly, load bearing*

Reading strategy: Mind map

Materials: Audio CD

Words

A Listen and say the words. Then listen and read the sentences. 🔘 1•09

- Play the audio. Ask students to point to the words as they hear them.
- Play the audio a second time and have students repeat the words when they hear them.
- Say the words out of order and have students race to point to them on the page.

CRITICAL THINKING

Ask the following questions to check understanding:

- *What two words are parts of a bridge?*
- *Where might you find a bridge?*
- *What do you call the distance of a bridge?*

B Complete the sentences.

- Have the students read the sentences in A again.
- Then have them look at the words in the box and look back at A to see how the words have been used.
- Ask students to complete the sentences with the correct word from the box.
- Have students do the activity on their own and then compare answers with a partner.
- Check answers with the class.

ANSWERS
1 support 2 situation 3 varied 4 overcome
5 suspended 6 link

COLLABORATIVE LEARNING

- Put students into pairs and tell them to use the new words in sentences.
- Go around the room and have pairs say some of their sentences for the class.

C Circle True (T) or False (F).

- Have students read the sentences and circle T for True and F for false.
- Check the answers with the class.
- Have students correct the false sentences so they are true.

ANSWERS
1 T 2 T 3 F 4 T

Before You Read

Think

- Have students read the questions and make notes about their answers individually.
- Ask students to discuss their answers to the questions in small groups.
- Then share some of the answers with the class. List the answers on the board.

D Learn: Mind Map

- Read the *Learn* box with the class.
- Do an example mind map on the board. Write the main idea in the center, e.g. *What kind of people build bridges and tunnels?* and then have students suggest related ideas which you write in the satellite circles off the main idea.

Read the paragraph and make a mind map. Then answer the questions.

- Read the instructions.
- Have students read the text and make their own mind map.
- Put students into pairs to talk about their mind maps and to answer the questions.
- Then go over the three questions with the class. As they answer each question, use their information to draw a mind map for the text on the board.

POSSIBLE ANSWERS

1 Bridges and tunnels allow us to use many types of transportation.
2 The advantages and disadvantages can be connected to the main idea.
3 Answers will vary.

CRITICAL THINKING

Ask the following questions to check understanding about the first text:

- *Is there only one way to make a mind map?*
- *How does the mind map help you to understand this text?*
- *Can you name some other ways we could arrange this mind map?*

DIFFERENTIATION

Below level:

- After students have read the text, model how to make a mind map. Read the first sentence. Ask the students if it is the main idea of the text. Write it in the center circle, saying that this is the main idea.
- Then read the next sentence. Ask if there are any ideas in that sentence that can go in circle. (Elicit *advantages* and *disadvantages*.)
- Have students continue to break down the text in pairs. Go around and help.

At level:

- Have students do their mind maps on their own.
- Then put students into pairs. Each student takes a turn to explain his or her mind map to the other.
- Pairs try to help each other improve their mind maps.

Above level:

- Have students do their mind maps on their own.
- Then put students into small groups to compare and contrast their mind maps.
- Then each group makes one mind map for the text, using as many of their members' ideas as makes sense.
- Students share their mind maps with the class.

E Words in Context: Scan the text on pages 18–19 and circle these words. As you read, try to guess what the words mean.

- Read each word and have students follow your pronunciation.

F Look at the pictures on pages 18–19. Do you recognize any of the bridges? What are their names? Where are they, and what are they used for?

COMMUNICATION

- Have students look at the pictures on pages 18 and 19.
- Ask the questions and have students answer them.

Reading Preview

- Read the title of the unit's reading text.
- Have students silently read the content of the preview bar.
- Ask *What type of text is it?* Ask *What does this type of text do?*
- Tell students to classify and categorize the information in the text. Tell them to use the headings.

Further Practice
Workbook pages 10–11
Online Practice Unit 2 · Get Ready
Oxford **iTools** Unit 2 · Get Ready

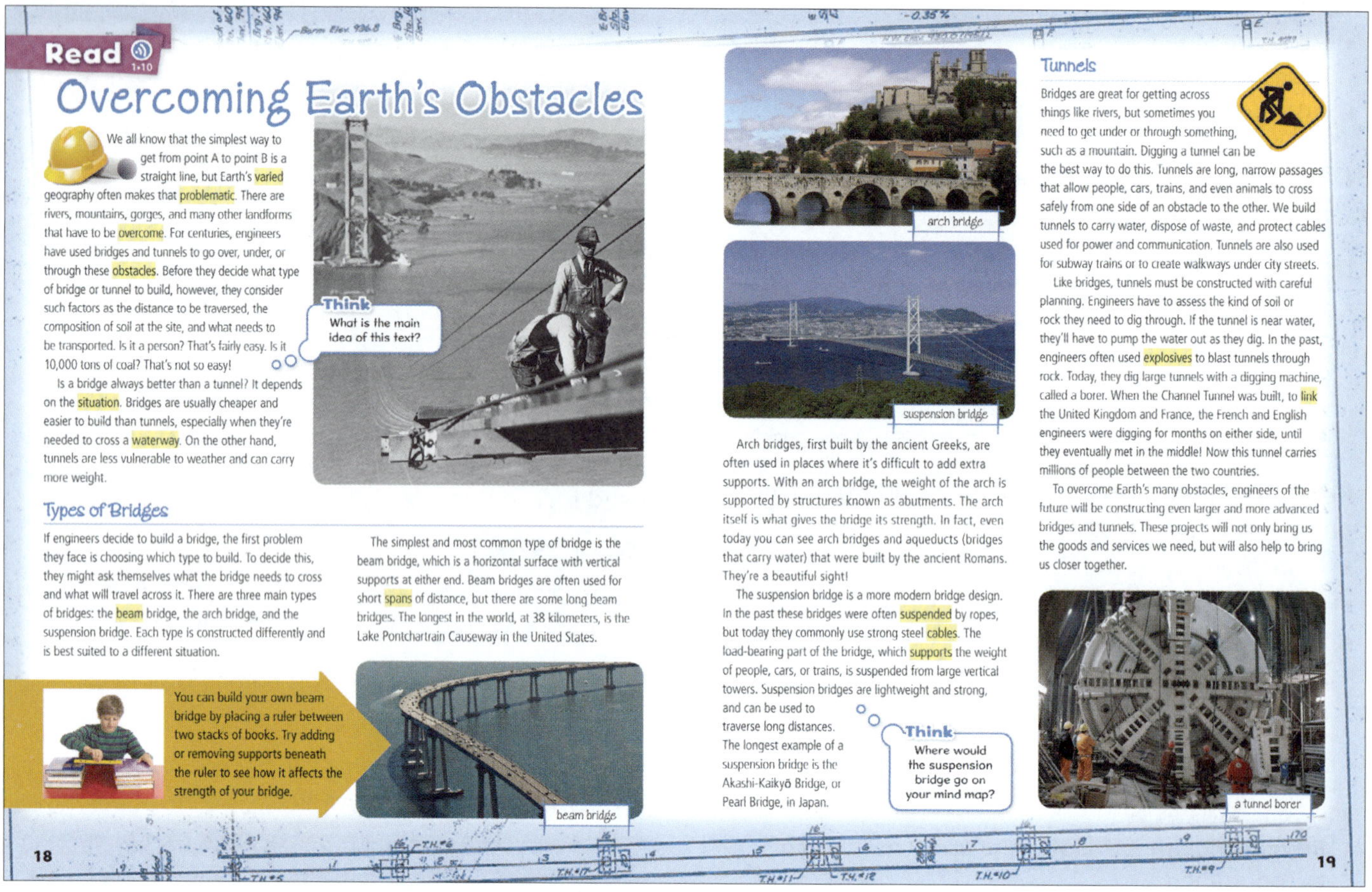

Read 🔊 1·10

Overcoming Earth's Obstacles

We all know that the simplest way to get from point A to point B is a straight line, but Earth's varied geography often makes that problematic. There are rivers, mountains, gorges, and many other landforms that have to be overcome. For centuries, engineers have used bridges and tunnels to go over, under, or through these obstacles. Before they decide what type of bridge or tunnel to build, however, they consider such factors as the distance to be traversed, the composition of soil at the site, and what needs to be transported. Is it a person? That's fairly easy. Is it 10,000 tons of coal? That's not so easy!

Is a bridge always better than a tunnel? It depends on the situation. Bridges are usually cheaper and easier to build than tunnels, especially when they're needed to cross a waterway. On the other hand, tunnels are less vulnerable to weather and can carry more weight.

Think
What is the main idea of this text?

Types of Bridges

If engineers decide to build a bridge, the first problem they face is choosing which type to build. To decide this, they might ask themselves what the bridge needs to cross and what will travel across it. There are three main types of bridges: the beam bridge, the arch bridge, and the suspension bridge. Each type is constructed differently and is best suited to a different situation.

The simplest and most common type of bridge is the beam bridge, which is a horizontal surface with vertical supports at either end. Beam bridges are often used for short spans of distance, but there are some long beam bridges. The longest in the world, at 38 kilometers, is the Lake Pontchartrain Causeway in the United States.

You can build your own beam bridge by placing a ruler between two stacks of books. Try adding or removing supports beneath the ruler to see how it affects the strength of your bridge.

beam bridge

arch bridge

suspension bridge

Arch bridges, first built by the ancient Greeks, are often used in places where it's difficult to add extra supports. With an arch bridge, the weight of the arch is supported by structures known as abutments. The arch itself is what gives the bridge its strength. In fact, even today you can see arch bridges and aqueducts (bridges that carry water) that were built by the ancient Romans. They're a beautiful sight!

The suspension bridge is a more modern bridge design. In the past these bridges were often suspended by ropes, but today they commonly use strong steel cables. The load-bearing part of the bridge, which supports the weight of people, cars, or trains, is suspended from large vertical towers. Suspension bridges are lightweight and strong, and can be used to traverse long distances. The longest example of a suspension bridge is the Akashi-Kaikyō Bridge, or Pearl Bridge, in Japan.

Think
Where would the suspension bridge go on your mind map?

Tunnels

Bridges are great for getting across things like rivers, but sometimes you need to get under or through something, such as a mountain. Digging a tunnel can be the best way to do this. Tunnels are long, narrow passages that allow people, cars, trains, and even animals to cross safely from one side of an obstacle to the other. We build tunnels to carry water, dispose of waste, and protect cables used for power and communication. Tunnels are also used for subway trains or to create walkways under city streets.

Like bridges, tunnels must be constructed with careful planning. Engineers have to assess the kind of soil or rock they need to dig through. If the tunnel is near water, they'll have to pump the water out as they dig. In the past, engineers often used explosives to blast tunnels through rock. Today, they dig large tunnels with a digging machine, called a borer. When the Channel Tunnel was built, to link the United Kingdom and France, the French and English engineers were digging for months on either side, until they eventually met in the middle! Now this tunnel carries millions of people between the two countries.

To overcome Earth's many obstacles, engineers of the future will be constructing even larger and more advanced bridges and tunnels. These projects will not only bring us the goods and services we need, but will also help to bring us closer together.

a tunnel borer

18   19

Summary

Objectives: To read, understand, and discuss an explanatory text; to apply a reading strategy to improve comprehension.

School subject: Social Studies: Technology

Text type: Explanatory text (nonfiction)

Reading strategy: Mind map

Big Question learning point: *We build bridges and tunnels to overcome obstacles. People use bridges and tunnels to transport things. We build bridges to carry things like water and cables. Bridges and tunnels help us get from place to place.*

Materials: Talk About It! Poster, Audio CD

Before Reading

- Read the title of the text. Ask the class for some examples of obstacles.
- Have students point to the pictures and describe what they see.
- Read the headings. Ask the class what kind of text this is. Ask students to explain their thinking.

During Reading 💿 1·10

- Ask a gist question to check overall understanding of the text, and allow students a few minutes to skim the text, e.g. *What is the first part of the text about? What is the second part of the text about?*
- Remind students that they should categorize and classify what they read. Ask *What are two main categories of information in this text?*

- Play the audio. Students listen as they read along. Play the audio a second time if necessary.

DIFFERENTIATION

Below level:

- Have students read the text with you in small groups.
- Explain the illustrations to make sure students understand the words in context.
- Then review the main points of each section of text.

At level:

- Have students read the text silently to themselves once.
- Put students into pairs to read the text to each other. Move throughout the room and provide help as necessary, especially with any unfamiliar words.

Above level:

- Have students read the text individually.
- Put students into pairs and have them summarize the text.

CRITICAL THINKING

Discussion questions:

- *What are the main topics of this text?*
- *What are the three main types of bridge? Have students point to examples of each in their books.*
- *You need to build a bridge over a wide river, but it is difficult to add extra supports. What kind of bridge would you build?*
- *Are bridges better than tunnels?*
- *What do you find interesting about tunnels?*

After Reading

- Put students into pairs.
- Each pair of students will need a ruler and a stack of books.
- Ask the pairs to build the arch bridge, as described on page 19. Remind them to support the bridge.
- Go around and help as needed. Encourage students to add or remove books and supports and see how it affects their bridge.
- Have pairs describe what they discovered in building the bridge.
- Ask *What do you find interesting about bridges? What do you find interesting about tunnels?*

COMMUNICATION

- Display the **Talk About It! Poster** to help students with sentence frames for discussion and expressing personal opinions.
- Put students into pairs to discuss what they find interesting about bridges and tunnels.

CREATIVITY

- Put students into small groups of three or four.
- Have them brainstorm well-known tunnels and bridges in your country.
- Have each group choose a tunnel or bridge and draw it on a large piece of paper.
- Have students label the different components and write sentences saying what they know about it, e.g. when it was built, how long it is, what it carries, how busy it is.
- Have each group choose a speaker to present their picture and knowledge to the class.

> **CULTURE NOTE**
>
> The Lake Pontchartrain Causeway is actually made up of two separate bridges. It can be found in the United States, and links New Orleans and Mandeville in Louisiana. The bridges are supported by 9,500 concrete pilings. After Hurricane Katrina occurred in 2005, the bridge was slightly damaged, however it was one of the only remaining bridges used to transport emergency services after the hurricane was over.
>
> Akashi Kaikyō Suspension Bridge, in Japan, is the longest suspension bridge in the world. It took ten years to construct and was finished in 1998. Two million people worked on it. The steel cable used on the bridge is long enough to circle the world seven times. It links the island of Awaji and Kobe, a city on the mainland.
>
> The Channel Tunnel is the longest international tunnel in the world and connects the United Kingdom and France. It has a passageway that is 50.5 kilometers long. The Eurotunnel Shuttle travels along the tunnel and is the largest vehicle transport in the world. Although the idea of the tunnel existed for hundreds of years, it wasn't constructed until 1988 and finished in 1994.

Further Practice

Workbook page 12
Online Practice Unit 2 · Read
Oxford **iTools** Unit 2 · Read

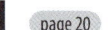
Understand

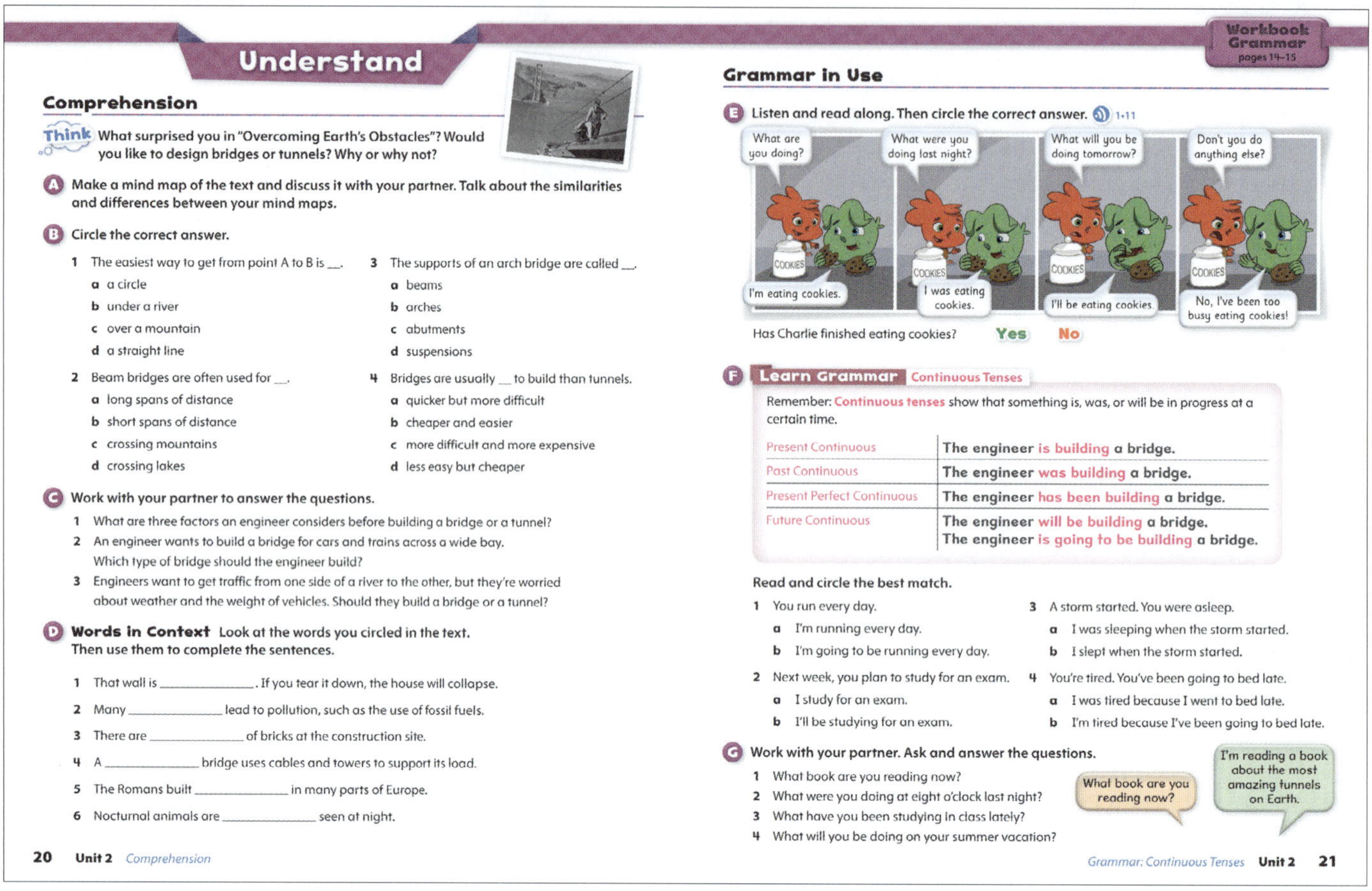

Comprehension

Think What surprised you in "Overcoming Earth's Obstacles"? Would you like to design bridges or tunnels? Why or why not?

A Make a mind map of the text and discuss it with your partner. Talk about the similarities and differences between your mind maps.

B Circle the correct answer.

1 The easiest way to get from point A to B is __.
   a a circle
   b under a river
   c over a mountain
   d a straight line

2 Beam bridges are often used for __.
   a long spans of distance
   b short spans of distance
   c crossing mountains
   d crossing lakes

3 The supports of an arch bridge are called __.
   a beams
   b arches
   c abutments
   d suspensions

4 Bridges are usually __ to build than tunnels.
   a quicker but more difficult
   b cheaper and easier
   c more difficult and more expensive
   d less easy but cheaper

C Work with your partner to answer the questions.

1 What are three factors an engineer considers before building a bridge or a tunnel?
2 An engineer wants to build a bridge for cars and trains across a wide bay. Which type of bridge should the engineer build?
3 Engineers want to get traffic from one side of a river to the other, but they're worried about weather and the weight of vehicles. Should they build a bridge or a tunnel?

D **Words in Context** Look at the words you circled in the text. Then use them to complete the sentences.

1 That wall is _____. If you tear it down, the house will collapse.
2 Many _____ lead to pollution, such as the use of fossil fuels.
3 There are _____ of bricks at the construction site.
4 A _____ bridge uses cables and towers to support its load.
5 The Romans built _____ in many parts of Europe.
6 Nocturnal animals are _____ seen at night.

20　Unit 2　*Comprehension*

Grammar in Use

Workbook Grammar pages 14–15

E Listen and read along. Then circle the correct answer. 1·11

What are you doing? — I'm eating cookies.
What were you doing last night? — I was eating cookies.
What will you be doing tomorrow? — I'll be eating cookies.
Don't you do anything else? — No, I've been too busy eating cookies!

Has Charlie finished eating cookies?　**Yes**　**No**

F **Learn Grammar** Continuous Tenses

Remember: **Continuous tenses** show that something is, was, or will be in progress at a certain time.

Present Continuous	The engineer **is building** a bridge.
Past Continuous	The engineer **was building** a bridge.
Present Perfect Continuous	The engineer **has been building** a bridge.
Future Continuous	The engineer **will be building** a bridge. The engineer **is going to be building** a bridge.

Read and circle the best match.

1 You run every day.
   a I'm running every day.
   b I'm going to be running every day.

2 Next week, you plan to study for an exam.
   a I study for an exam.
   b I'll be studying for an exam.

3 A storm started. You were asleep.
   a I was sleeping when the storm started.
   b I slept when the storm started.

4 You're tired. You've been going to bed late.
   a I was tired because I went to bed late.
   b I'm tired because I've been going to bed late.

G Work with your partner. Ask and answer the questions.

1 What book are you reading now?
2 What were you doing at eight o'clock last night?
3 What have you been studying in class lately?
4 What will you be doing on your summer vacation?

What book are you reading now? — I'm reading a book about the most amazing tunnels on Earth.

Grammar: Continuous Tenses　**Unit 2**　21

Summary

Objectives: To demonstrate understanding of a nonfiction text; to understand the meaning and form of the grammar structure.

Reading: Comprehension

Grammar input: Continuous tenses

Grammar practice: Workbook exercises

Grammar production: Using continuous tenses

Materials: Audio CD

Comprehension

Think

• Have students think about their answers individually first. Then hold a class discussion.

A Make a mind map of the text and discuss it with your partner. Talk about the similarities and differences between your mind maps.

DIFFERENTIATION

Below level:

• Put students into mixed-ability pairs. Have the pair read the text and make a mind map together.

• Put students into groups of four. Have students talk about similarities and differences in their mind maps.

At level:

• Share the mind maps with the class. Put them up where students can see them. Have students walk around and look at all of the mind maps.

• Then have a few students talk about the differences between the mind maps.

Above level:

• Put students into pairs. Students compare and discuss their mind maps and then make suggestions to change or improve each other's mind maps.

• Students revise their mind maps individually.

• Share their work with the class.

B Circle the correct answer.

• If the class has any trouble with the answers, refer back to the appropriate sections on pages 18 and 19.

ANSWERS

1 d　**2** b　**3** c　**4** b

C Work with your partner to answer the questions.

ANSWERS

1 Three factors an engineer considers before building a bridge or a tunnel are: 1) the distance to be traversed, 2) the composition of soil at the site, and 3) what needs to be transported across or through.
2 Suspension bridges are used to cover long distances.
3 They should build a tunnel because it can protect from the weather and carry heavy weights.

CRITICAL THINKING

• Put students into small groups.

• Have groups discuss why a beam bridge might not hold as much weight as a suspension bridge over a long distance.

- Have groups discuss tunnels used in cities and towns for transportation, water, waste, and cables.
- Have groups share their ideas with the class.

D Words in Context: Look at the words you circled in the text. Then use them to complete the sentences.

- Have students go back and find the words in the reading text.
- Tell them to use the context clues to guess the meaning of each word.
- Students complete the sentences.

ANSWERS
1 load bearing   2 factors   3 stacks   4 suspension
5 aqueducts   6 commonly

Grammar in Use

E Listen and read along. Then circle the correct answer. 🔊 1·11

- Listen to the dialogue once and then read it together as a class.
- Have students answer the question individually.
- Check the answers as a class.

ANSWER
No

F Learn Grammar: Continuous Tenses

- Read the *Learn Grammar* box together.
- Brainstorm an example using yourself, e.g. *I'm writing on the board*, or a situation the class is familiar with, e.g. *The gym class is playing soccer.*

Read and circle the best match.

- Complete number 1 together, then have students complete 2 to 4 on their own.
- Check the answers with the class.

ANSWERS
1 a   2 b   3 a   4 b

COLLABORATIVE LEARNING
- Put students into pairs.
- Have pairs think of continuous sentence examples for each of the tenses in the *Learn Grammar* box. Suggest they choose one topic and vary the tense accordingly.
- Have pairs share their example sentences with the class.

G Work with your partner. Ask and answer the questions.

COMMUNICATION
- Put students in pairs. Model how to do the activity.
- Then have students take turns asking and answering the questions.

DIFFERENTIATION
Below level:
- Draw a timeline on the board. (A line with arrows on each end.)
- Read each question with the class and as you do, mark spots along the line and label them: *now, eight o'clock last night, in class lately, summer vacation.* For each question, have the students identify its tense. Then draw a parenthesis under the specific times to label the timeline with the tense, graphically making a map of tenses.
- Then put students into mixed-ability pairs to ask and answer the questions, referring to the timeline.

At level:
- Have students write four questions, one for each tense.
- Students ask a partner their questions.
- Have some pairs share their questions and answers with the class.

Above level:
- Have students write four questions, one for each tense. Tell students they will ask their classmates these questions.
- Students circulate and ask as many classmates as they can in three minutes.
- Have students tell the class about their classmate's responses, e.g. *Kimi was studying ikebana on Saturday.*

Workbook Grammar

- Direct students to the Workbook for further practice.

| **Further practice** |
| Workbook pages 13–15 |
| Online Practice Unit 2 • Understand |
| Oxford **iTools** Unit 2 • Understand |

The reproduced student page (pages 22–23):

Communicate

Listening

Think What's something that you know how to build? What steps do you follow to build it?

A Listen. Number the steps in the correct order. 1•12

_____ Identify the correct place to build the bridge.　　_____ Calculate the length of the bridge.

_____ Begin digging to place the supports.　　_____ Build the bridge.

_____ Determine what kind of bridge is needed.　　_____ Make a computer model of the bridge.

B Listen again. Circle the correct answer. 1•13

1 David King is _____.
  a a computer programmer　b a construction worker　c an engineer

2 He's building _____ bridge across Dolphin Bay.
  a a beam　b a suspension　c an arch

3 He chose this kind of bridge because of the _____ of the bay.
  a depth　b length　c width

4 The bridge will carry _____.
  a traffic　b people on foot　c trains

Speaking 1•14

C Think of a project you've completed or choose one from the list below. What steps are involved in the project? Describe them to your partner.

- making a greeting card
- building a model
- designing a website
- writing a story

> The first step to making a greeting card is choosing some art supplies.
> What do you do after that?
> Next, I draw ...
> Cool. And then what?
> Well, then I add ... Finally I ...
> That sounds ... !

22　Unit 2　_Listening: Sequence • Speaking: Describing Steps in a Project_

Word Study

D **Learn** Easily Confused Words

Some words look or sound similar but have different meanings.
Engineers consider the composition of the earth at the **site**.
The aqueducts, built by the ancient Romans, are a beautiful **sight**!

Look up the words in the dictionary. Then listen to the sentences and number the words. Work with your partner to write two sentences for each pair of words. 1•15　A-Z page 192

_____ knew　_____ desert　_____ site　_____ accept　_____ loose

_____ new　_____ dessert　_____ sight　_____ except　_____ lose

Writing Study

E **Learn** Connectors to Show Support

To show that one idea supports another, use connectors such as **for example, in particular, in fact, similarly,** and **likewise.**
The arch itself is what gives the bridge its strength. **In fact,** even today you can see arch bridges and aqueducts that were built by the ancient Romans.

Write these sentences using the connectors in parentheses ( ).

1 The Millau Viaduct, in France, is very tall. It's one of the tallest bridges in the world. (in fact)

2 Some tunnels are used by many people. The Channel Tunnel, between the UK and France, transports millions of people. (in particular)

3 Bridges can be expensive to build. Tunnels can also be very costly. (similarly)

4 Tunnels have many uses. They can be used for trains or cables, or to carry water. (for example)

5 People have used bridges throughout history. We've used tunnels since ancient times. (likewise)

Write Now practice writing in the **Workbook.** page 17

Vocabulary: Easily Confused Words • Writing: Connectors to Show Support　**Unit 2**　23

Summary

Objectives: To learn and practice listening, speaking, and writing strategies to facilitate effective communication.

Vocabulary: _knew, desert, site, accept, loose, new, dessert, sight, except, lose_

Listening strategy: Listening for sequence

Speaking: Describing steps in a project

Word Study: Easily confused words

Writing Study: Using connectors to show support

Big Question learning point: _We build bridges and tunnels to overcome obstacles._

Materials: Audio CD

Listening

Think

- Tell students to think about something they know how to build, such as a birdhouse or a snowman.
- Then have students make notes on the steps to build it.
- Have students tell a partner how to build something.
- Have a few volunteers tell the class their steps to build something.

A Listen. Number the steps in the correct order. 1•12

- Play the audio once and have students listen. Ask _What is the purpose of this listening text?_ Tell students there are phrases that they can listen for as clues for the order. Ask _How might someone start telling a process?_ Elicit examples such as: _First, then, next, after that, finally, last._ Tell students to listen for phrases such as these.
- Tell students to number the steps in the order they hear them. Then play the audio again so they can check their work.

ANSWERS

2	3
5	6
1	4

CRITICAL THINKING

After checking the answers, go back through and read the answers and have the class supply the phrases to show order: _First, then, next, after that, finally,_ etc.

B Listen again. Circle the correct answer. 1•13

- Play the audio so students can complete the exercise.

ANSWERS

1 c　2 b　3 c　4 a

Speaking ⊙ 1·14

C Think of a project you've completed or choose one from the list below. What steps are involved in the project? Describe them to your partner.

COMMUNICATION

- Read the directions. Model the example with a volunteer. Then model it a second time using a different example.
- Put students into pairs and have them describe the steps in a process to do one of the things on the list or their own thing.
- Have a few volunteers describe their process to the class.

DIFFERENTIATION

Below level:

- Put students into mixed-ability pairs. Have the more confident student help the other student to describe the steps in a project.
- Have pairs share their steps with another pair.

At level:

- Have each student make notes on the steps in one of the projects from the list.
- Then put students into small groups. Have groups compare their steps and choose the best, most orderly process to make one master list of steps to do their project.
- Have groups share their list with the class.

Above level:

- Tell students to make notes about steps in a project that is not one of the examples in the book.
- Tell them to write the steps out of order and not to number them.
- Then students trade papers with a partner. This person will reads the steps and number them in order.
- Students then swap papers to check each other's work.

Word Study

D Learn: Easily Confused Words

- Read the *Learn* box together.
- Point out the homophones *site* and *sight*. Show students how the words sound the same, but by using the context of the sentences, they can understand their different meanings and then know which way to spell the words.

Look up the words in the dictionary. Then listen to the sentences and number the words. Work with your partner to write two sentences for each pair of words. ⊙ 1·15

ANSWERS

1 loose   2 lose   3 dessert   4 desert   5 sight
6 site   7 knew   8 new   9 accept   10 except

COLLABORATIVE LEARNING

- Have partners work in pairs to write sentences for each word. Allow them to use a dictionary to help.
- Have one pair read their sentences to another pair who uses the context to spell each word correctly. Then the second pair reads their sentences for the first pair to spell.
- Have pairs check each other's work.

Writing Study

E Learn: Connectors to Show Support

- Read the *Learn* box together.
- Read the first sentence. Read the second sentence. Explain that the second sentence is a fact supporting the first sentence. It's not a comparison, which would use *similarly* or *likewise*, and it's not a specific example, which would use *for example* or *in particular*.

Write these sentences using the connectors in parentheses ( ).

- Have students complete the exercise on their own. Then go over answers with the class.
- Remind students that these connecting phrases are introductory phrases, so they are followed by a comma.

ANSWERS

1 In fact, it's one of the tallest …
2 In particular, the Channel Tunnel, between …
3 Similarly, tunnels can also be …
4 For example, they can be used for …
5 Likewise, we've used tunnels since …

Write

- Direct students to the Workbook for further writing practice.

Further practice
Workbook pages 16–17
Online Practice Unit 2 · Communicate
Oxford iTools Unit 2 · Communicate

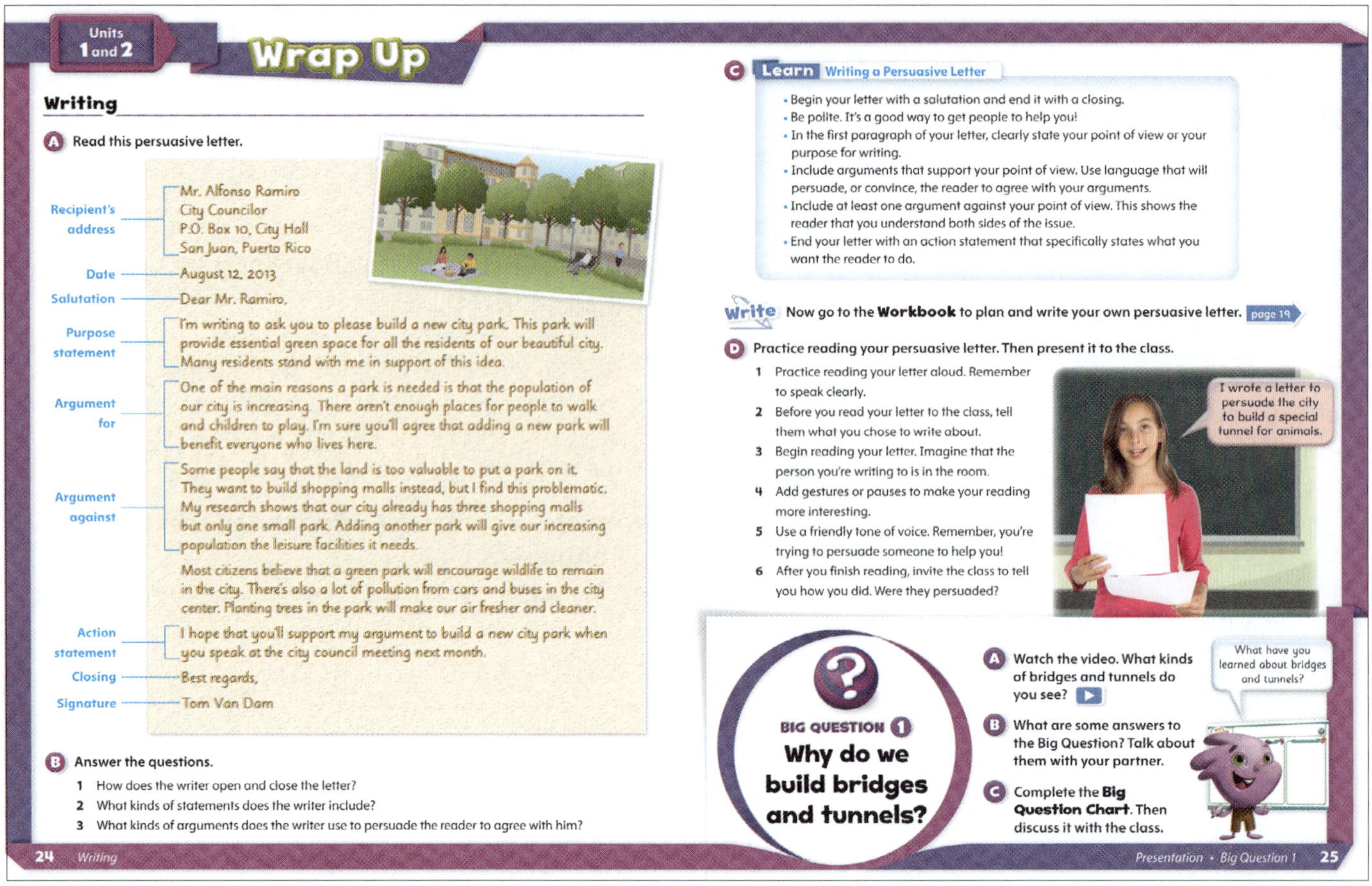

Units 1 and 2 · Wrap Up

Writing

A Read this persuasive letter.

Recipient's address
Mr. Alfonso Ramiro
City Councilor
P.O. Box 10, City Hall
San Juan, Puerto Rico

Date — August 12, 2013
Salutation — Dear Mr. Ramiro

Purpose statement — I'm writing to ask you to please build a new city park. This park will provide essential green space for all the residents of our beautiful city. Many residents stand with me in support of this idea.

Argument for — One of the main reasons a park is needed is that the population of our city is increasing. There aren't enough places for people to walk and children to play. I'm sure you'll agree that adding a new park will benefit everyone who lives here.

Argument against — Some people say that the land is too valuable to put a park on it. They want to build shopping malls instead, but I find this problematic. My research shows that our city already has three shopping malls but only one small park. Adding another park will give our increasing population the leisure facilities it needs.

Most citizens believe that a green park will encourage wildlife to remain in the city. There's also a lot of pollution from cars and buses in the city center. Planting trees in the park will make our air fresher and cleaner.

Action statement — I hope that you'll support my argument to build a new city park when you speak at the city council meeting next month.

Closing — Best regards,
Signature — Tom Van Dam

B Answer the questions.
1 How does the writer open and close the letter?
2 What kinds of statements does the writer include?
3 What kinds of arguments does the writer use to persuade the reader to agree with him?

C Learn | Writing a Persuasive Letter
- Begin your letter with a salutation and end it with a closing.
- Be polite. It's a good way to get people to help you!
- In the first paragraph of your letter, clearly state your point of view or your purpose for writing.
- Include arguments that support your point of view. Use language that will persuade, or convince, the reader to agree with your arguments.
- Include at least one argument against your point of view. This shows the reader that you understand both sides of the issue.
- End your letter with an action statement that specifically states what you want the reader to do.

Write Now go to the **Workbook** to plan and write your own persuasive letter. page 19

D Practice reading your persuasive letter. Then present it to the class.
1 Practice reading your letter aloud. Remember to speak clearly.
2 Before you read your letter to the class, tell them what you chose to write about.
3 Begin reading your letter. Imagine that the person you're writing to is in the room.
4 Add gestures or pauses to make your reading more interesting.
5 Use a friendly tone of voice. Remember, you're trying to persuade someone to help you!
6 After you finish reading, invite the class to tell you how you did. Were they persuaded?

I wrote a letter to persuade the city to build a special tunnel for animals.

What have you learned about bridges and tunnels?

BIG QUESTION 1
Why do we build bridges and tunnels?

A Watch the video. What kinds of bridges and tunnels do you see?
B What are some answers to the Big Question? Talk about them with your partner.
C Complete the **Big Question Chart**. Then discuss it with the class.

Summary

Objectives: To show what students have learned about the language and learning points of Units 1 and 2.

Reading: Comprehension of a persuasive letter

Writing: Writing a persuasive letter

Speaking: Presentation of a persuasive letter

Materials: Big Question DVD, Discover Poster 1, Talk About It! Poster, Big Question Chart

Writing

A Read this persuasive letter.

- Remind students about the Paragraph Breaks they studied in Unit 1, page 15.
- Read aloud the directions and explain that the writer's purpose is to persuade.
- Go over the structure of each section of the letter before reading.
- Point out that in the first sentence, the writer lets you know the purpose of the letter and then makes a statement about it. Then read the section.
- Continue in this way for the rest of the letter.
- After reading the letter with the class, have students read it once independently.

B Answer the questions.

- Have students find the answers in the text.
- Ask a few other questions to check comprehension, e.g. *What is the main reason for a new park?*
What do some people want instead of a park?

ANSWERS
1 The writer opens the letter with a salutation: *Dear Mr. Ramiro* and closes it with a polite closing: *Best regards*.
2 The writer states that the park will provide essential green space and many residents support him.
3 The writer states that some people would prefer to build shopping malls, but adding another park would give the increasing population the leisure facilities it needs.

C Learn: Writing a Persuasive Letter

- Read the directions in the *Learn* box together.
- Explain that students should follow these guidelines when they plan and write their letters.

CRITICAL THINKING

Have students go back to the model to see how the author addressed each requirement. Ask the following questions to check comprehension:

- *What are the salutation and closing?*
- *How is the writer polite?*
- *What is the writer's clear reason for writing?*
- *What is the argument against the writer's point of view?*
- *What are the arguments in support of the writer's point of view?*
- *Does the writer end the letter with an action statement?*

Write

- Direct students to the Workbook to plan and write their own persuasive letter.

CREATIVITY

- Brainstorm some ideas for a persuasive letter topic with the class.
- Put the ideas on the board for students to refer to as they start work on their own persuasive letter.

DIFFERENTIATION

Below level:

- Put students into mixed-ability pairs to brainstorm ideas to write about and statements to support the ideas.
- Have the more confident student make notes that the other student can use as he / she drafts his / her essay.

At level:

- Have small groups brainstorm some fun reasons for writing a persuasive letter, e.g. maybe they want to lower the age for driving a car, or longer school vacations.
- Explain that even if their idea is silly, they should have solid reasons to support it.

Above level:

- Suggest some students write essays with a genuine purpose, e.g. they can draft a letter about an issue they care about, such as more bike lanes, or an endangered animal. They can address it to a local or national politician.
- If several students are interested in the same issue they can work together to draft a group letter and have other students sign it.

D Practice reading your persuasive letter. Then present it to the class.

- Read the list with the class.
- Give students time to practice reading their letters to themselves.
- Have students take turns reading their persuasive letters to the class. Ensure they follow the steps in the direction list.
- After each letter, the class decide if they were persuaded by the letter or not.

COLLABORATIVE LEARNING

- Put students into small groups to practice reading their letters. Invite a more confident student to lead each group.
- Tell students to underline parts of the letter where they will stress what they are saying. They can make marks where pauses go, and add symbols where to use gestures.
- Have students practice their reading in small groups, focusing on tone of voice and gestures.
- Have group members give them constructive feedback on how to improve. Each student should read his or her letter at least once.
- Encourage students to speak clearly and loudly.

Units 1 and 2 Big Question Review

A Watch the video. What kinds of bridges and tunnels do you see? ▷

- Play the video and when it is finished ask students what they know about bridges and tunnels now.
- Have students share ideas with the class.

B What are some answers to the Big Question? Talk about them with your partner.

COMMUNICATION

- Display **Discover Poster 1**. Point to familiar vocabulary items and elicit them from the class. Ask *What is this?*
- Ask students *What do you see?* Ask *What does that mean?*
- Refer to all of the learning points written on the poster and have students explain how they relate to the different pictures.
- Ask *What does this learning point mean*? Elicit answers from individual students.
- Display the **Talk About It! Poster** to help students with sentence frames for discussion of the learning points and for expressing their opinions.

C Complete the Big Question Chart. Then discuss it with the class.

- Ask students what they have learned about bridges and tunnels while studying this unit.
- Put students into pairs or small groups to say two new things they have learned.
- Have students share their ideas with the class and add their ideas to the chart.
- Have students complete the chart in their Workbook.

| Further practice
Workbook pages 18–21
Online Practice • Wrap Up 1
Oxford iTools • Wrap Up 1

What is the Earth made of?

In units **3** and **4** you will:

WATCH a video about the Earth.

LEARN about the layers of the Earth.

READ about the Earth's interior and a volcanic eruption.

WRITE a speech.

PRESENT your speech to the class.

BIG QUESTION 2

What is the Earth made of?

A Watch the video. Then talk about it with your partner.

B Look at the picture and discuss it with your class.

1 Where do you think this person is?
2 What parts of the Earth can you see?

C Think and answer the questions.

1 What is the Earth like where you live?
2 Why do people study the Earth?
3 How do we know what's below the Earth's surface?
4 What things can you name that are inside the Earth?

D Discuss this topic with your class. Fill out the **Big Question Chart**.

What do you know about the Earth? What do you want to know?

26 Big Question 2

27

Reading Strategies

Students will practice:

- Evaluation
- Prediction

Vocabulary

Students will understand and use words about:

- Geology, volcanic eruptions

Grammar

Students will understand and use:

- Modals
- Past perfect

Review

Students will review the language and Big Question learning points of Units 3 and 4 through:

- Writing a speech

Units 3 and 4
What is the Earth made of?

Students will understand the Big Question learning points:

- The Earth is made up of four layers.
- The Earth contains three types of rocks.
- There are frozen lakes beneath parts of the Earth's surface.
- Lava erupts out of the Earth from volcanoes.
- Fossils in the Earth tell us about our planet's history.

Listening Strategies

Students will practice:

- Listening for numbers
- Listening for time periods

Writing Study

Students will use and understand:

- Parentheses
- Punctuation with quotation marks

Students will:

- Write a speech

Word Study

Students will understand and use:

- Homonyms
- Words with *ie* and *ee*

Speaking

Students will understand and use expressions for:

- Conducting an interview
- Offering suggestions

Units 3 and 4 Big Question page 26

Summary

Objectives: To activate students' existing knowledge of the topic and identify what they would like to learn about the topic.

Materials: Big Question DVD, Discover Poster 2, Big Question Chart

Introducing the topic

- Read out the Big Question. Ask *What is the Earth made of?* Write students' ideas on the board and discuss.

A Watch the video. Then talk about it with your partner.

- Play the video and when it is finished, ask students to answer the following questions in pairs:
  What do you see in the video?
  What is happening?
  What is the Earth like?
  What do you like about the video?
- Have individual students share their answers with the class.

B Look at the picture and discuss it with your class.

- Students look at the big picture and talk about it. Ask *What do you see?*
- Ask additional questions:
  Have you ever been in a cave?
  Where do you think the water is coming from?
  Would you like to explore a cave like this one?
  What type of things do you think you would see?

C Think and answer the questions.

- Have students discuss the questions in small groups, and then with the class.

DIFFERENTIATION

Below level:
- Put students into mixed-ability pairs.
- Have the more confident student help the other student to answer the questions.
- Provide clue words that you think students will know and can use to answer each of the questions, e.g. for question 1, about the area where you live: *rocky, dry, sandy.*

At level:
- Put students into small groups to answer the questions.
- Have the class choose the best answers to the questions from each of the groups. Write notes on the board.

Above level:
- Put students into small groups to answer the questions. Allow them to use a dictionary and any resource books available.
- Have groups make a mind map for each question that includes their answer key words.

CRITICAL THINKING

- Ask students to think about the first question. *What is the Earth like where you live?* Have students say sentences and write them on the board.
- Ask *What is the Earth like in other areas?* Refer to a map or globe if available, or name other places and locations students know and elicit what those places are like.
- Have students say sentences and write them on the board.

Expanding the topic

COLLABORATIVE LEARNING

- Display **Discover Poster 2** and give students enough time to look at the pictures.
- Get students to talk about things you think they will know by pointing to different things in the pictures and asking *What's this? Where can you see this?*
- Put students into small groups of three or four. Have each group choose a picture that they find interesting.
- Ask each group to say five sentences about their picture.
- Have one person from each group stand up and read out the sentences they chose for their picture.
- Ask the class if they can add any more.

DIFFERENTIATION

Below level:
- Encourage students to participate using short sentences.
- Point to details in the poster and ask *What is this?* Write the answers on the board.

At level:
- Elicit complete sentences from students on what they know about the Earth.
- Write their sentences on the board.

Above level:
- Elicit more detailed responses.
- Challenge students to write their own sentences on the board.

D Discuss this topic with your class. Fill out the Big Question Chart.

- Display the **Big Question Chart**.
- Ask the class *What do you know about the Earth? What do you want to know about the Earth?*
- Ask students to write what they know and what they want to know in their Workbooks.
- Write a collection of ideas on the **Big Question Chart**.

Discover Poster 2

1 A cross section of the Earth showing its four layers; 2 An illustration of the rock cycle: igneous rock (basalt), sedimentary rock (sandstone), and metamorphic rock (marble); 3 A globe showing the Earth's plates; 4 The active volcano Tungurahua, located in Ecuador; 5 An archaeologist studying fossilized bones

Further Practice

Workbook page 22
Online Practice · Big Question 2
Oxford iTools · Big Question 2

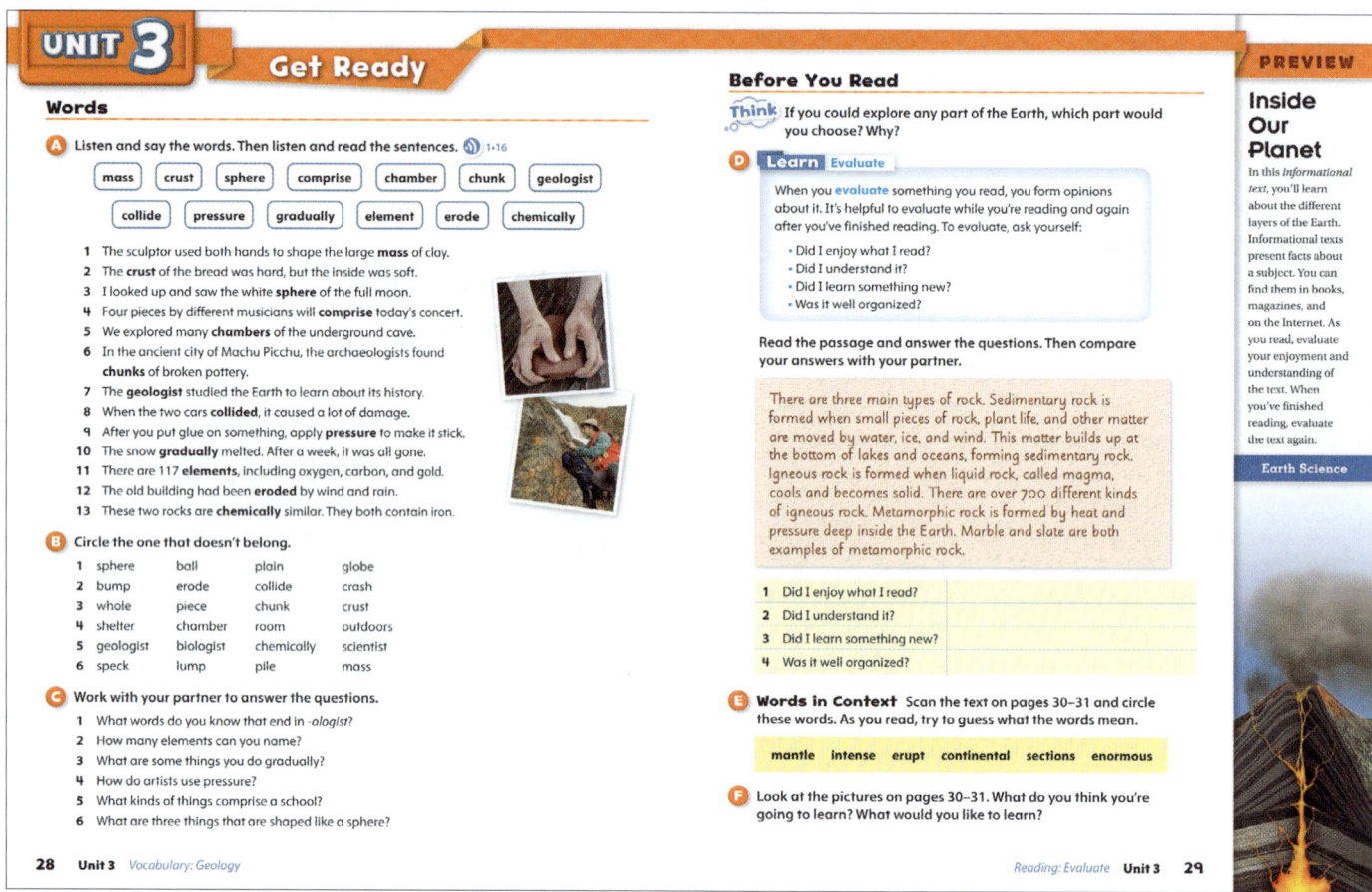

Summary

Objectives: To understand words about geology; to apply own experience and a reading strategy to help comprehension of a text.

Vocabulary: *mass, crust, sphere, comprise, chamber, chunk, geologist, collide, pressure, gradually, element, erode, chemically, mantle, intense, erupt, continental, sections, enormous*

Reading strategy: Evaluation

Materials: Audio CD

Words

A Listen and say the words. Then listen and read the sentences. 1·16

- Play the audio. Ask students to point to the words and repeat the words when they hear them.
- Then have students listen and read the sentences as they hear them.
- Say the sentence numbers out of order and have the class read the sentences aloud.

CRITICAL THINKING

- Put students into pairs.
- Have pairs use the context of the sentences and a dictionary to look up each of the new words and determine if it is a noun, verb, or adverb.
- Check answers with the class.

B Circle the one that doesn't belong.

- Have students do the activity on their own.
- Have them compare their answers with a partner.
- Check answers with the class.

ANSWERS

1 plain   2 erode   3 crust   4 outdoors
5 chemically   6 speck

COLLABORATIVE LEARNING

- Put students into mixed-ability groups.
- Have groups read through each group of words and discuss why the word doesn't belong.

C Work with your partner to answer the questions.

- Put students into pairs to answer the questions.
- Have pairs compare their answers with another pair.
- Check answers with the class.

POSSIBLE ANSWERS

1 Biologist, archaeologist, etc.
2 Helium, hydrogen, iron, bronze, silver, uranium, etc.
3 Learn to play piano / violin, etc.
4 To glue, mold, press things like sculptures, woodblock carvings, or collages, etc.
5 Classrooms, students, teachers, etc.
6 Moon, globe, Earth, etc.

- Put students into pairs. Have pairs write sentences for each other's new words, e.g. *Some people like to eat the crust of the pizza.*
- When they have finished, tell the pairs to swap their sentences with another pair.
- Pairs check each other's sentences.
- Have pairs read some of their sentences to the class. Listen to at least two sentences for each new word.

DIFFERENTIATION

Below level:

- Put students into mixed-ability pairs to write the sentences.

At level:

- Say the new words in any order and have individual students stand up and spell the word, and then use it in a sentence.

Above level:

- Have students write five sentences using any of the five new words they wish, but have them write the sentences leaving a blank where the word should be.
- Students swap papers with another student and fill in the blanks.
- Have the pairs compare their answers and correct their sentences, if necessary.

Before You Read

Think

- Have students think about their answers individually.
- Put students into pairs to discuss their answers.
- List the answers on the board.

D Learn: Evaluate

- Read the *Learn* box together.
- Explain that evaluating a text involves thinking about it from many angles: your reaction, your understanding, any new information, and how it was written.

Read the passage and answer the questions. Then compare your answers with your partner.

- Invite a confident student to read the paragraph aloud for the class.
- Have students answer the questions in the organizer on their own.
- Ask them to compare their answers with a partner.

CRITICAL THINKING

- Put students into pairs. Have pairs think about ways the material could be organized differently. Could it be improved?

E Words in Context: Scan the text on pages 30–31 and circle these words. As you read, try to guess what the words mean.

- Read each word and have the students follow your pronunciation.
- Have students scan the text on pages 30 and 31 and circle the words.

- Tell them to guess what the words mean from the context. Have students share their ideas about the words' definitions.

DIFFERENTIATION

Below level:

- Go through the text with students.
- Have the students find and point to the words, then analyse the text with them to identify the context, e.g. for *mantle*, have students point to the word. Then read the following three sentences and elicit the most important identifying aspect of *mantle*: *the Earths' deepest layer.*
- Continue in this way for the other words.

At level:

- Put students into pairs to figure out the meaning of the new words from context.
- Tell pairs to underline the definitions of the words in context, or clues in the context that indicate the meaning of the words.
- Have pairs share their answers with the class.

Above level:

- Put students into pairs to use the context to provide a definition of each word.
- Have pairs share their definitions with the class.

F Look at the pictures on pages 30–31. What do you think you're going to learn? What would you like to learn?

COMMUNICATION

- Put students into small groups to discuss the questions.
- Tell groups to list the reasons that are their answers for each question.
- Go over each group's answers and make notes on the board.

Reading Preview

- Read the title of the unit's reading text.
- Have students silently read the content of the preview bar.
- Ask *What type of text is it?* Ask *What does this type of text do?*
- Tell students to evaluate as they read, specifically their understanding and enjoyment of the text.

Further Practice

Workbook pages 22–23
Online Practice Unit 3 • Get Ready
Oxford **iTools** Unit 3 • Get Ready

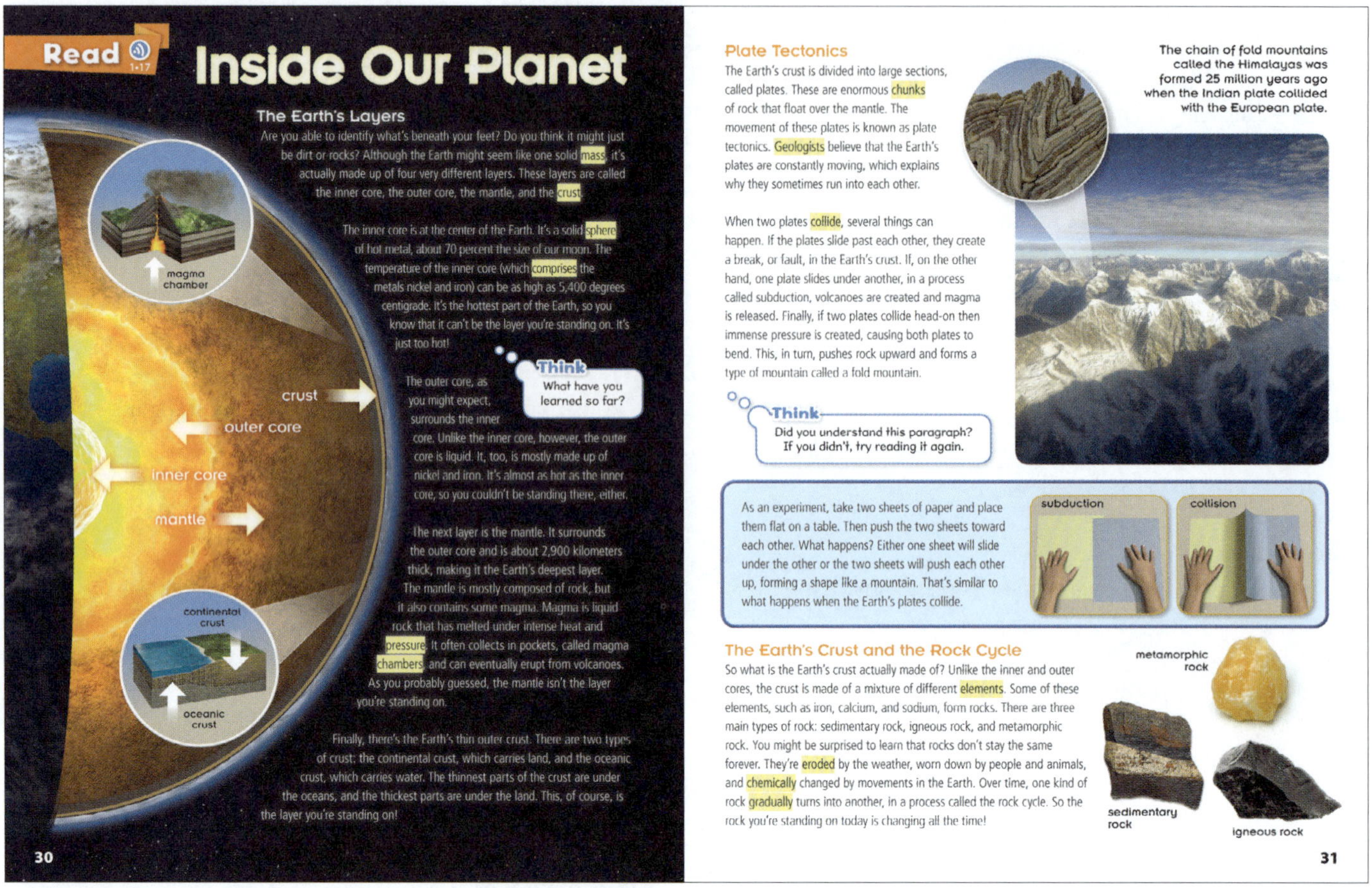

Read 1·17 Inside Our Planet

The Earth's Layers

Are you able to identify what's beneath your feet? Do you think it might just be dirt or rocks? Although the Earth might seem like one solid mass, it's actually made up of four very different layers. These layers are called the inner core, the outer core, the mantle, and the crust.

The inner core is at the center of the Earth. It's a solid sphere of hot metal, about 70 percent the size of our moon. The temperature of the inner core (which comprises the metals nickel and iron) can be as high as 5,400 degrees centigrade. It's the hottest part of the Earth, so you know that it can't be the layer you're standing on. It's just too hot!

The outer core, as you might expect, surrounds the inner core. Unlike the inner core, however, the outer core is liquid. It, too, is mostly made up of nickel and iron. It's almost as hot as the inner core, so you couldn't be standing there, either.

Think
What have you learned so far?

The next layer is the mantle. It surrounds the outer core and is about 2,900 kilometers thick, making it the Earth's deepest layer. The mantle is mostly composed of rock, but it also contains some magma. Magma is liquid rock that has melted under intense heat and pressure. It often collects in pockets, called magma chambers, and can eventually erupt from volcanoes. As you probably guessed, the mantle isn't the layer you're standing on.

Finally, there's the Earth's thin outer crust. There are two types of crust: the continental crust, which carries land, and the oceanic crust, which carries water. The thinnest parts of the crust are under the oceans, and the thickest parts are under the land. This, of course, is the layer you're standing on!

magma chamber
crust
outer core
inner core
mantle
continental crust
oceanic crust

Plate Tectonics

The Earth's crust is divided into large sections, called plates. These are enormous chunks of rock that float over the mantle. The movement of these plates is known as plate tectonics. Geologists believe that the Earth's plates are constantly moving, which explains why they sometimes run into each other.

When two plates collide, several things can happen. If the plates slide past each other, they create a break, or fault, in the Earth's crust. If, on the other hand, one plate slides under another, in a process called subduction, volcanoes are created and magma is released. Finally, if two plates collide head-on then immense pressure is created, causing both plates to bend. This, in turn, pushes rock upward and forms a type of mountain called a fold mountain.

The chain of fold mountains called the Himalayas was formed 25 million years ago when the Indian plate collided with the European plate.

Think
Did you understand this paragraph? If you didn't, try reading it again.

As an experiment, take two sheets of paper and place them flat on a table. Then push the two sheets toward each other. What happens? Either one sheet will slide under the other or the two sheets will push each other up, forming a shape like a mountain. That's similar to what happens when the Earth's plates collide.

subduction
collision

The Earth's Crust and the Rock Cycle

So what is the Earth's crust actually made of? Unlike the inner and outer cores, the crust is made of a mixture of different elements. Some of these elements, such as iron, calcium, and sodium, form rocks. There are three main types of rock: sedimentary rock, igneous rock, and metamorphic rock. You might be surprised to learn that rocks don't stay the same forever. They're eroded by the weather, worn down by people and animals, and chemically changed by movements in the Earth. Over time, one kind of rock gradually turns into another, in a process called the rock cycle. So the rock you're standing on today is changing all the time!

metamorphic rock
sedimentary rock
igneous rock

30

31

Summary

Objectives: To read, understand, and discuss an informational text; to apply a reading strategy to improve comprehension.

School subject: Earth Science

Text type: Informational text (nonfiction)

Reading strategy: Evaluate

Big Question learning points: *The Earth is made up of four layers. The Earth contains three types of rocks.*

Materials: Talk About It! Poster, Audio CD

Before Reading

- Ask *What is the Earth made of?*
- Have students tell you what they see in the pictures.
- Have students read the subtitles.
- Have them say what they already know about what's "Inside Our Planet.": Plate Tectonics; the Earth's Crust and the Rock Cycle.
- Write students' responses on the board so they can be referred back to and checked as the reading progresses.

During Reading 1·17

- Have students read along as they listen to the audio.
- Then have them read through the text again without the audio.
- Remind students to evaluate as they read.

DIFFERENTIATION

Below level:

- Have students read with you in small groups.
- As you read, stop and evaluate each section. Ask students if they've understood what they've read. Help them to restate each section's main ideas. Use the pictures to help with understanding.
- After reading, evaluate the text with students. Ask *What parts did you enjoy reading? What new things did you learn?*

At level:

- Have students read with a partner, taking turns to read the sections of the text.
- Have them stop to evaluate each section as they read, checking for understanding.

Above level:

- Have students read the text independently.
- Then put students into pairs to evaluate what they've read.
- They should take turns telling each other about the sections, to evaluate what they've understood and learned.

Discussion questions:

- *What is beneath your feet right now?*
- *How many layers surround the Earth's inner core?*
- *What other things have crusts?*
- *Are you standing on the thinnest or thickest part of the outer crust? How do you know?*
- *Can you feel the tectonic plates moving right now?*
- *When do you think you can feel them moving?*
- *Have you ever seen a fold mountain?*

After Reading

COLLABORATIVE LEARNING

- Put students into small groups to talk about the text.
- Tell each group that they are going to draw a diagram of something from the text. Tell them that they can choose to draw a sketch of the Earth's layers, plate tectonics, or the rock cycle.
- Have students draw the diagram of their choice and write short descriptions in their own words under the sketch.
- Have each group stand up, present, and explain their sketch to the class.

CRITICAL THINKING

- Put students into pairs. Have pairs read the experiment on page 31. Pairs take two sheets of paper and follow the directions to do the experiment.
- Ask questions to check understanding:
  What do the two sheets of paper represent in this experiment?
  What is it called when one sheet of paper goes under the other?
  What is it called when both sheets of paper bend?

COMMUNICATION

- Display the **Talk About It! Poster** to help students with sentence frames for discussion and expressing personal opinions.
- Put students into pairs to discuss which part of the text is most interesting and what new things they've learned.

CULTURE NOTE

The biggest fault line in the world is the San Andreas Fault. It is 1,300 kilometers long and runs through California in the United States.

It was made because it sits on the tectonic boundary between the North American Plate and the Pacific Plate. There are three main sections, and the oldest sections were formed by the subduction of a spreading ridge 30 million years ago.

There have been a lot of earthquakes along this fault line. The largest occurred in 1857, 1906, 1989, and 2004. The San Andreas Fault Observatory at Depth (SAFOD) is currently drilling into the fault so that they can help to predict future earthquakes and improve recording of tectonic movements.

Further Practice
Workbook page 24
Online Practice Unit 3 • Read
Oxford **iTools** Unit 3 • Read

Understand

Comprehension

Think What are three things you learned from "Inside Our Planet"? Which was the most interesting?

A Evaluate the text and fill in the organizer. Then discuss your opinions with your partner.

> Did I enjoy what I read?
> _____
> _____
> _____

> Did I understand it?
> _____
> _____
> _____

My Opinions

> Did I learn something new?
> _____
> _____
> _____

> Was it well organized?
> _____
> _____
> _____

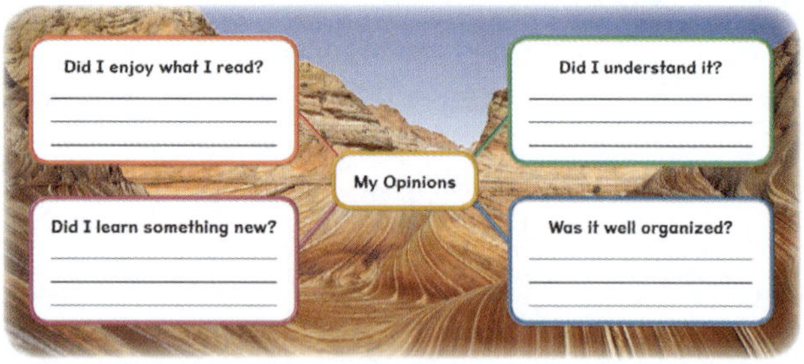

B Answer the questions.

1. How many layers does the Earth have?
2. Which layer surrounds the inner core?
3. Where does magma collect?
4. Which part of the crust is the thickest?
5. How does plate tectonics cause mountains to form?
6. What causes the rock cycle?

C **Words in Context** Look at the words you circled in the text. Then match the sentence halves.

1. Geologists believe that a volcano — a carries land, not water.
2. The continental crust — b new stadium downtown.
3. These sections of the theater — c layer and is mostly composed of rock.
4. They're building an enormous — d could erupt at any time.
5. The mantle is Earth's deepest — e caused a lot of damage.
6. The intense heat from the fire — f can each hold 50 people.

32 **Unit 3** *Comprehension*

Workbook Grammar pages 26–27

Grammar in Use

D Listen and read along. Then circle the correct answer. 1·18

> That can't be right!
> $A \langle m,z,2 \rangle \cdot ? \left(\left(\frac{a \cdot b}{a+b} \right) \right) o_r + \frac{\pi}{3}$ $\sum_{m=1} \cdot ?$
> It must be right!
> It might be right, but I don't think so.
> $A \langle m,z,2 \rangle \cdot ? \left(\left(\frac{a \cdot b}{a+b} \right) \right) o_r + \frac{\pi}{3}$ $\sum_{m=1} \cdot ?$
> We could be wrong!

Are Finn and Charlie sure they have the right answer?   **Yes**   **No**

E **Learn Grammar** Modals

Ability (saying what you are and aren't able to do)	can / can't, could / couldn't, was able to / will be able to
Permission (asking if you're allowed to do something)	can I, may I, could I
Request (asking someone to do something)	can you, could you, would you
Obligation (saying what's necessary)	must, have to / had to / will have to, need to
Possibility (saying what's possible)	may, might, could
Deduction (saying how sure you are about something)	must, can't

Complete each sentence. Then circle the correct answer.

1. _____ you help me with my suitcase? It's heavy.   obligation   request
2. That _____ be an elephant. It doesn't have a trunk!   ability   deduction
3. _____ I sleep over at my friend's house, Dad?   possibility   permission

F Make a chart like this one. Then talk about it with your partner.

Situation	Question
ability	How many languages can you speak?
permission	May I borrow that game?

> How many languages can you speak?
> I can speak three languages.

Grammar: Modals **Unit 3** 33

Summary

Objectives: To demonstrate understanding of an informational text; to understand the meaning and form of the grammar structure.

Reading: Evaluation

Grammar input: Modals

Grammar practice: Workbook exercises

Grammar production: Asking about ability and asking for permission

Materials: Audio CD

Comprehension

Think

- Have students think about three things they learned from the reading text.
- Have them share their favorite parts with the class.

A Evaluate the text and fill in the organizer. Then discuss your opinions with your partner.

- Read the instructions with the class.
- Check understanding of the organizer. Point to the "My Opinions" box in the center and ask *What is this organizer about? What will I put in this box?*
- Tell students that instead of answering *Yes / No* in each box, they should write an example or two, e.g. *I enjoyed reading about plate tectonics and the experiment.*
- After students have read the text again, have them fill in the organizer on their own. Go around and help as needed.

- Complete the organizers on the board to check them. Elicit the information to complete them from the class.

DIFFERENTIATION

Below level:

- Put students into mixed-ability pairs. Have them reread the text in pairs. Tell them to evaluate as they go.
- Help students to fill in the organizer. Read a question from the organizer, e.g. *Did I enjoy what I read?*
- Have pairs discuss their answers and skim the text to find the parts they liked. Then pairs write their individual answers in the organizer. Go around and help as needed.
- Then pairs complete the organizers together.

At level:

- Pairs complete the organizers on their own.
- Then partners compare their organizers and discuss their answers.
- Have pairs share their organizers with the class.

Above level:

- After students have completed the organizers, put them into mixed-ability groups.
- Have groups discuss their answers to the question *Did I understand it?* If anyone didn't understand, have students within each group help clarify information.
- For anything that is still unclear, have the groups share it with the class. Have the class try to explain any answers.
- Finally, you should explain using visual reference for anything that remains unclear.

B Answer the questions.

- For each question, tell students to look back at the reading text to find the answers.

POSSIBLE ANSWERS

1 The Earth has four layers.
2 The inner core is surrounded by the outer core, which is liquid.
3 Magma collects in pockets called magma chambers.
4 The thickest part of the crust is under the land.
5 Plate tectonics is the movement of plates. As the plates collide, they fold upwards to form mountains.
6 The rock cycle is caused by effects on rocks being eroded by weather, worn down by people and animals, and movements in the earth.

C Words in Context: Look at the words you circled in the text. Then match the sentence halves.

- Have students go back and find the words in the text.
- Tell them to use the context clues to guess at the meaning of each word.

ANSWERS

1 d 2 a 3 f 4 b 5 c 6 e

COLLABORATIVE LEARNING

- In small groups, ask students to work together to write new sentences for the words in context.
- As groups write their sentences, encourage them to use the dictionary to help with definitions.
- Have groups share their sentences with the class.

Grammar in Use

D Listen and read along. Then circle the correct answer. 🔘 1·18

- Listen to the dialogue once and have students read along.
- Then have students read the question and circle the correct answer.
- Play the audio again and have students check their answer.
- Check the answer with the class.

ANSWER

No

E Learn Grammar: Modals

- Read the *Learn Grammar* box together. As you do, elicit example sentences for each situation, e.g. *I can play the (piano).* Explain that this means *He / She is able to play the piano.*
- Continue in this way for all of the modals using concrete examples in the classroom.
- Ask permission to borrow a student's pencil. Say *May I …?* Make a request by asking a student to open and close the door, e.g. *Can you / Would you …?* For obligation, tell the class to stand up, e.g. *You must …* .

Complete each sentence. Then circle the correct answer.

- Read number 1 together. Complete the sentence and then identify the choice students have to make: *Can / Could / Would you help me with my suitcase? It's heavy. (request)*
- Then have students complete the rest on their own.

ANSWERS

1 Can / Could / Would (request)   2 can't (deduction)
3 Can / May / Could (permission)

F Make a chart like this one. Then talk about it with your partner.

COMMUNICATION

- Have students fill out the chart on their own.
- Put students in pairs to ask and answer the questions on their charts.
- Have a few pairs say their questions and answers for the class.

DIFFERENTIATION

Below level:

- Put students into mixed-ability pairs.
- Have the more confident student help the other student fill out the chart. Go around and help as needed.
- Have the less confident student read his or her questions for the confident student to answer. Then reverse the roles.

At level:

- Have students complete the chart and add two more questions using modals for different situations, e.g. possibility and obligation.
- Then have a few pairs say their new questions and answers for the class.

Above level:

- Have pairs of students write questions for each modal situation.
- Tell them they can write realistic questions or make up funny questions, as long as they are grammatically correct.
- Have pairs join another pair and take turns asking and answering their questions.

Workbook Grammar

- Direct students to the Workbook for further practice.

Further practice
Workbook pages 25–27
Online Practice Unit 3 · Understand
Oxford iTools Unit 3 · Understand

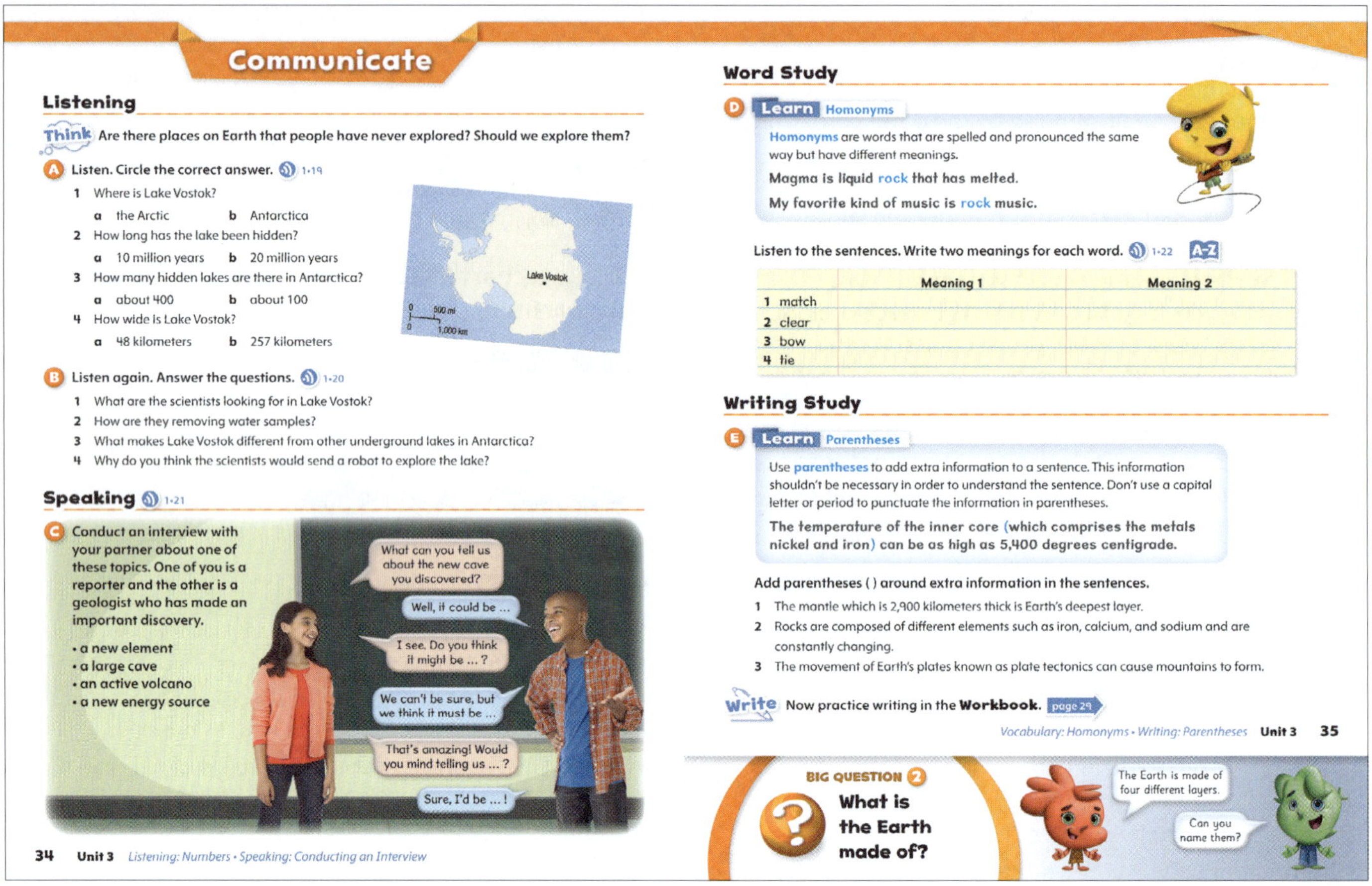

The top portion of the page reproduces the student book pages 34–35:

Communicate

Listening

Think Are there places on Earth that people have never explored? Should we explore them?

A Listen. Circle the correct answer. 1·19

1 Where is Lake Vostok?
   a the Arctic   b Antarctica
2 How long has the lake been hidden?
   a 10 million years   b 20 million years
3 How many hidden lakes are there in Antarctica?
   a about 400   b about 100
4 How wide is Lake Vostok?
   a 48 kilometers   b 257 kilometers

Map showing Lake Vostok, Antarctica. Scale: 500 mi / 1,000 km

B Listen again. Answer the questions. 1·20

1 What are the scientists looking for in Lake Vostok?
2 How are they removing water samples?
3 What makes Lake Vostok different from other underground lakes in Antarctica?
4 Why do you think the scientists would send a robot to explore the lake?

Speaking 1·21

C Conduct an interview with your partner about one of these topics. One of you is a reporter and the other is a geologist who has made an important discovery.

• a new element
• a large cave
• an active volcano
• a new energy source

Speech bubbles:
- What can you tell us about the new cave you discovered?
- Well, it could be …
- I see. Do you think it might be … ?
- We can't be sure, but we think it must be …
- That's amazing! Would you mind telling us … ?
- Sure, I'd be … !

34   Unit 3   *Listening: Numbers • Speaking: Conducting an Interview*

Word Study

D **Learn** Homonyms

Homonyms are words that are spelled and pronounced the same way but have different meanings.
Magma is liquid rock that has melted.
My favorite kind of music is rock music.

Listen to the sentences. Write two meanings for each word. 1·22 A-Z

	Meaning 1	Meaning 2
1 match		
2 clear		
3 bow		
4 tie		

Writing Study

E **Learn** Parentheses

Use parentheses to add extra information to a sentence. This information shouldn't be necessary in order to understand the sentence. Don't use a capital letter or period to punctuate the information in parentheses.
The temperature of the inner core (which comprises the metals nickel and iron) can be as high as 5,400 degrees centigrade.

Add parentheses ( ) around extra information in the sentences.

1 The mantle which is 2,900 kilometers thick is Earth's deepest layer.
2 Rocks are composed of different elements such as iron, calcium, and sodium and are constantly changing.
3 The movement of Earth's plates known as plate tectonics can cause mountains to form.

Write Now practice writing in the **Workbook**. page 29

Vocabulary: Homonyms • Writing: Parentheses   **Unit 3**   **35**

BIG QUESTION 2
What is the Earth made of?

Speech bubbles:
- The Earth is made of four different layers.
- Can you name them?

Summary

Objectives: To learn and practice listening, speaking, and writing strategies to facilitate effective communication.

Vocabulary: *match, clear, bow, tie*

Listening strategy: Listening for numbers

Speaking: Conducting an interview

Word Study: Homonyms

Writing Study: Parentheses

Big Question learning point: *There are frozen lakes beneath parts of the Earth's surface*

Materials: Discover Poster 2, Audio CD, Big Question Chart

Listening

Think

• Tell students to think about the questions individually.
• Have students discuss their answers with a partner. Share the discussions with the class.

A Listen. Circle the correct answer. 1·19

• Have students read the questions and answer choices first.
• Play the audio once and have students listen.
• Tell students to circle the correct answers.
• Play the audio again so they can check their work.

ANSWERS
1 b   2 b   3 a   4 a

B Listen again. Answer the questions. 1·20

• Have students read the questions.
• Play the audio so students can complete the exercise.
• Have students compare answers with a partner before checking answers with the class.

ANSWERS
1 Scientists are looking for ancient bacteria.
2 They are removing water samples by drilling.
3 Lake Vostok is one of the largest lakes on Earth.
4 They would send a robot down to explore because it is one of the coldest places on Earth.

Speaking 1·21

C Conduct an interview with your partner about one of these topics. One of you is a reporter and the other is a geologist who has made an important discovery.

• Read the explanation with the class.
• Say each of the expressions with students echoing the audio as they hear each line.
• Model the dialogue and examples with a confident student in front of the class.
• Ensure the students play along and complete the dialogue, e.g. *What can you tell us about this new volcano? Well, it might be about to explode.*
• Put students into pairs and tell them to practice the dialogue, using polite expressions.

- Have partners use the information from the listening in A about Dr. Kuznetsov and the ancient bacteria to complete the speaking dialogue, e.g.
  A: *What can you tell us about this ancient bacteria?*
  B: *Well, it might be a cure for diseases.*
  A: *I see. So could it possibly help us or harm us?*
  B: *We can't be sure, but we think it must be worth researching in case it is helpful.*
- Have some partners say their dialogues for the class.

Word Study

D Learn: Homonyms

- Read the *Learn* box together.

Listen to the sentences. Write two meanings for each word. 🔊 1·22

1 match: something you use to make a flame; a sports contest (tennis match)
2 clear: empty or free from things; plain and obvious
3 bow: something made of wood and string, used to shoot an arrow; a ribbon tied in a special way
4 tie: a draw in a sports match where both teams get the same number of points; a piece of clothing men wear around their necks

Below level:
- Say the words and have students repeat and spell them.
- Go over the meanings and give examples.

At level:
- Say the meaning of one of the words and have students name the word and spell it.

Above level:
- Put students into pairs. Have them look up the definitions in the dictionary and then write sentences using the new words.
- Have pairs write their sentences on the board and tell the class about them.

Writing Study

E Learn: Parentheses

- Read the *Learn* box together.
- Ask questions to check understanding.
  Is the information in parentheses necessary to understand the sentence? Read the sentence without parentheses.
  What is the purpose of the information in parentheses?
  What does the information in these parentheses tell us?

Add parentheses ( ) around extra information in the sentences.

- Demonstrate how to do the first one. Say *Read the sentence aloud. Then leave out the extra information and read the sentence aloud again to see if it makes sense.*
- Elicit from the class where the parentheses go, in this case before *which* and after *thick*. Ask *Do we need to change the information in the parentheses by adding a capital letter or period?*

- Explain that when we read aloud with parentheses we pause briefly, just like we do when we read a comma aloud, e.g. *The mantle (pause) which is 2,900 kilometers thick (pause) is Earth's deepest layer.*
- Have students complete the rest of the sentences on their own.
- Then put students into pairs to check each other's work.

1 The mantle (which is 2,900 kilometers thick) is Earth's deepest layer.
2 Rocks are composed of different elements (such as iron, calcium, and sodium) and are constantly changing.
3 The movement of Earth's plates (known as plate tectonics) can cause mountains to form.

- Put students into pairs.
- Have pairs go back through the activity and read the sentences without the parenthetical material aloud.
- For each sentence, have pairs discuss what the extra information in the parentheses refers to in each sentence, e.g. *2,900 kilometers thick* refers to the *mantle*.

Write

- Direct the students to the Workbook for further practice.

Big Question 2 Review

What is the Earth made of?

- Display **Discover Poster 2**. Discuss what you see.
- Refer to the learning points covered in Unit 3 that are written on the poster and have students explain how they relate to the different pictures.
- Return to the **Big Question Chart**.
- Ask students what they have learned about the Earth while studying this unit.

Further practice
Workbook pages 28–29
Online Practice Unit 3 · Communicate
Oxford **iTools** Unit 3 · Communicate

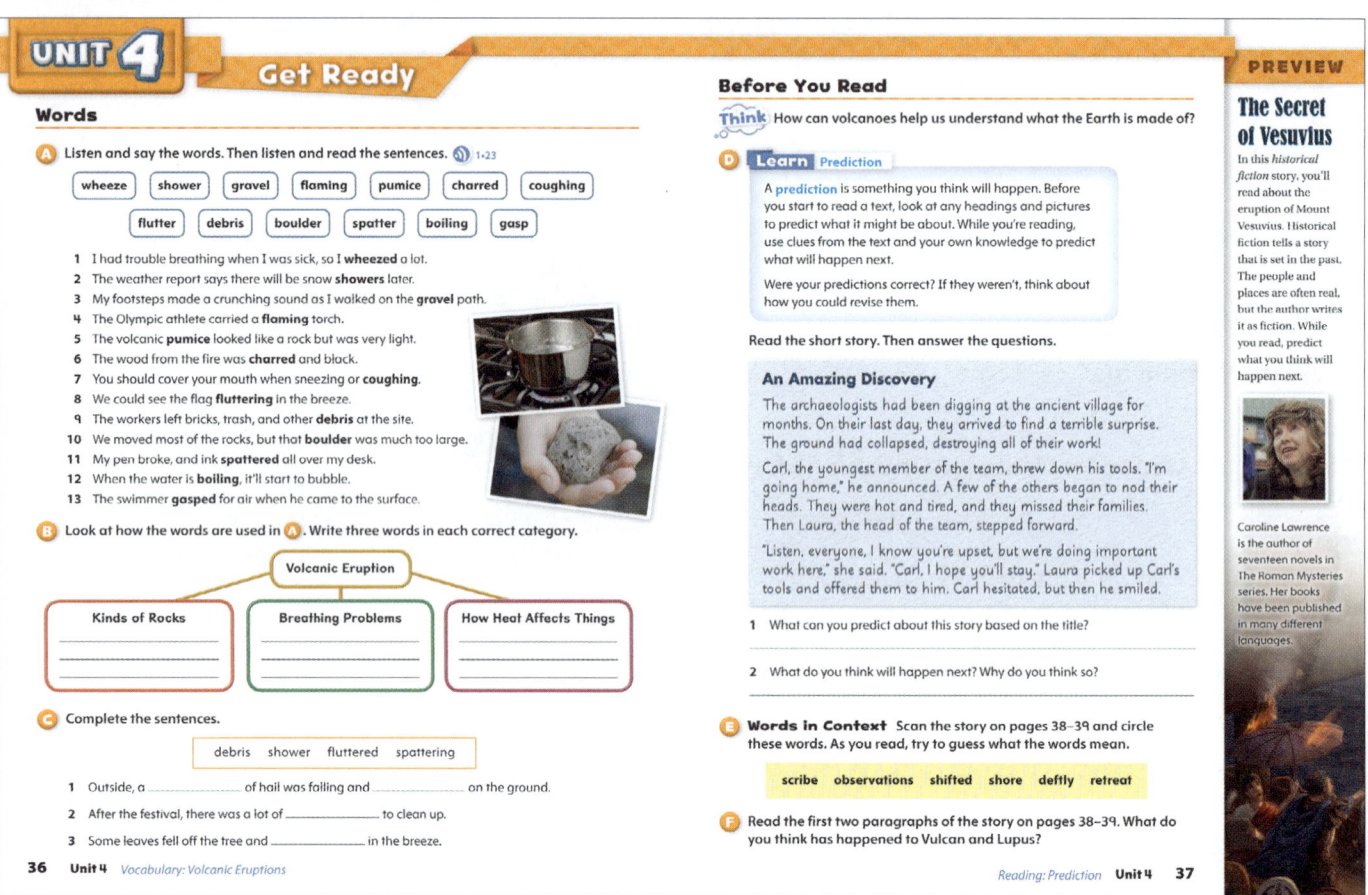

UNIT 4 Get Ready

Words

A Listen and say the words. Then listen and read the sentences. 1·23

wheeze | shower | gravel | flaming | pumice | charred | coughing

flutter | debris | boulder | spatter | boiling | gasp

1 I had trouble breathing when I was sick, so I **wheezed** a lot.
2 The weather report says there will be snow **showers** later.
3 My footsteps made a crunching sound as I walked on the **gravel** path.
4 The Olympic athlete carried a **flaming** torch.
5 The volcanic **pumice** looked like a rock but was very light.
6 The wood from the fire was **charred** and black.
7 You should cover your mouth when sneezing or **coughing**.
8 We could see the flag **fluttering** in the breeze.
9 The workers left bricks, trash, and other **debris** at the site.
10 We moved most of the rocks, but that **boulder** was much too large.
11 My pen broke, and ink **spattered** all over my desk.
12 When the water is **boiling**, it'll start to bubble.
13 The swimmer **gasped** for air when he came to the surface.

B Look at how the words are used in **A**. Write three words in each correct category.

Volcanic Eruption

Kinds of Rocks | Breathing Problems | How Heat Affects Things

C Complete the sentences.

debris   shower   fluttered   spattering

1 Outside, a _____ of hail was falling and _____ on the ground.
2 After the festival, there was a lot of _____ to clean up.
3 Some leaves fell off the tree and _____ in the breeze.

36 **Unit 4** *Vocabulary: Volcanic Eruptions*

Before You Read

Think How can volcanoes help us understand what the Earth is made of?

D **Learn** Prediction

A **prediction** is something you think will happen. Before you start to read a text, look at any headings and pictures to predict what it might be about. While you're reading, use clues from the text and your own knowledge to predict what will happen next.

Were your predictions correct? If they weren't, think about how you could revise them.

Read the short story. Then answer the questions.

An Amazing Discovery

The archaeologists had been digging at the ancient village for months. On their last day, they arrived to find a terrible surprise. The ground had collapsed, destroying all of their work!

Carl, the youngest member of the team, threw down his tools. "I'm going home," he announced. A few of the others began to nod their heads. They were hot and tired, and they missed their families. Then Laura, the head of the team, stepped forward.

"Listen, everyone, I know you're upset, but we're doing important work here," she said. "Carl, I hope you'll stay." Laura picked up Carl's tools and offered them to him. Carl hesitated, but then he smiled.

1 What can you predict about this story based on the title?

2 What do you think will happen next? Why do you think so?

E **Words in Context** Scan the story on pages 38–39 and circle these words. As you read, try to guess what the words mean.

scribe   observations   shifted   shore   deftly   retreat

F Read the first two paragraphs of the story on pages 38–39. What do you think has happened to Vulcan and Lupus?

Reading: Prediction **Unit 4** 37

PREVIEW

The Secret of Vesuvius

In this *historical fiction* story, you'll read about the eruption of Mount Vesuvius. Historical fiction tells a story that is set in the past. The people and places are often real, but the author writes it as fiction. While you read, predict what you think will happen next.

Caroline Lawrence is the author of seventeen novels in The Roman Mysteries series. Her books have been published in many different languages.

Summary

Objectives: To understand words about volcanic eruptions; to apply own experience and a reading strategy to help comprehension of a text.

Vocabulary: *wheeze, shower, gravel, flaming, pumice, charred, coughing, flutter, debris, boulder, spatter, boiling, gasp, scribe, observations, shifted, shore, deftly, retreat*

Reading strategy: Prediction

Materials: Audio CD

Words

A Listen and say the words. Then listen and read the sentences. 1·23

- Play the audio. Ask students to point to the words as they hear them.
- Play the audio a second time and have students repeat the words when they hear them. Pay attention to the pronunciation of the final -er on *shower, flutter, boulder, spatter*.
- Say the words out of order and have students race to point to them on the page.

B Look at how the words are used in A. Write three words in each correct category.

- Read the graphic organizer labels with the class.
- Model how to do the activity by pointing to the organizer as you say *These words all have to do with volcanic eruptions. What is a volcano?* Elicit, e.g. *a mountain that erupts with lava and smoke.* Ask *Which new words in A are types of rocks?*
- Have students do the activity on their own and then compare answers with a partner.
- Check answers with the class.

ANSWERS

Kinds of Rocks: gravel, pumice, boulder
Breathing Problems: wheeze, coughing, gasp
How Heat Affects Things: flaming, charred, boiling

CRITICAL THINKING

- Ask the following questions to check understanding:
Which word is a volcanic rock?
Which rock is big?
Which rock is small?
- Elicit volunteers to demonstrate the noises for the three breathing problems. Then ask *Which word is for hot liquids?*

C Complete the sentences.

- Have students read the sentences and write the words.
- Check the answers with the class.

1 shower, spattering   2 debris   3 fluttered

- Put students into pairs and have them write sentences for the new words, but to leave a blank where the word goes.
- Have pairs trade papers with another pair to complete the sentences.
- Pairs then correct each other's work and discuss any meanings they are not clear about.

Before You Read

Think

- Have students read the question and make notes about their ideas and answers individually.
- Students discuss their ideas to the question in small groups. Then share some of the ideas with the class.
- List the ideas on the board.

D Learn: Prediction

- Read the *Learn* box with the class.
- Ask *As you read, what will predicting what happens next do?*
- Explain that predicting as you read a story doesn't spoil the surprise. It helps you to understand the story.

Read the short story. Then answer the questions.

- Practice predicting with the class. Have students read the title and predict what will happen, e.g. someone will make a discovery. Ask *Who?* and have students skim the story to find the answer. Ask *What do you think the discovery is related to?*
- Have students read the questions before reading the text. Remind students to predict as they read. Then students answer the questions.
- Put students into pairs to talk about their answers.
- Then go over the answers with the class.

1 Archaeologists will make a discovery at an ancient village.
2 Carl will start to dig and discover something.

Ask the following questions to check understanding about the text:

- *What did you predict in the first paragraph?*
- *What did you predict in the second paragraph?*
- *What was confusing in the second paragraph?*
- *What did you predict in the third paragraph?*
- *Who do you think will make the discovery?*

E Words in Context: Scan the story on pages 38–39 and circle these words. As you read, try to guess what the words mean.

- Read each word and have students follow your pronunciation. Elicit meanings for the words to check if students know them.
- Ask questions to help students guess what they think the words could mean before they do the activity.
- Have students circle the words in the story.

F Read the first two paragraphs of the story on pages 38–39. What do you think has happened to Vulcan and Lupus?

Below level:

- Put students into mixed-ability pairs.
- Have students read the first two paragraphs of the story together. Have the more confident student help the less confident student to summarize the two paragraphs.
- Then have the confident student help the other student to identify who Vulcan and Lupus are and what may have happened to them.

At level:

- Have students read the paragraphs on their own.
- Then put students into pairs. Pairs discuss what they think happened to Vulcan and Lupus.

Above level:

- Have students read the paragraphs individually and think about what may have happened to Vulcan and Lupus.
- Then put students into small groups to compare their ideas. Tell students to guess specifically how one person got burned and the other didn't. (They can use the pictures, but without reading ahead.)
- Ask each group to predict what they think will happen to Vulcan and Lupus.

Reading Preview

- Read the title of the unit's reading text.
- Have students silently read the content of the preview bar.
- Ask *What type of text is it?* Ask *What does this type of text do? Is the story true?*
- Tell students to use clues from the story to make predictions.

Further Practice
Workbook pages 30–31
Online Practice Unit 4 • Get Ready
Oxford iTools Unit 4 • Get Ready

The Secret of Vesuvius

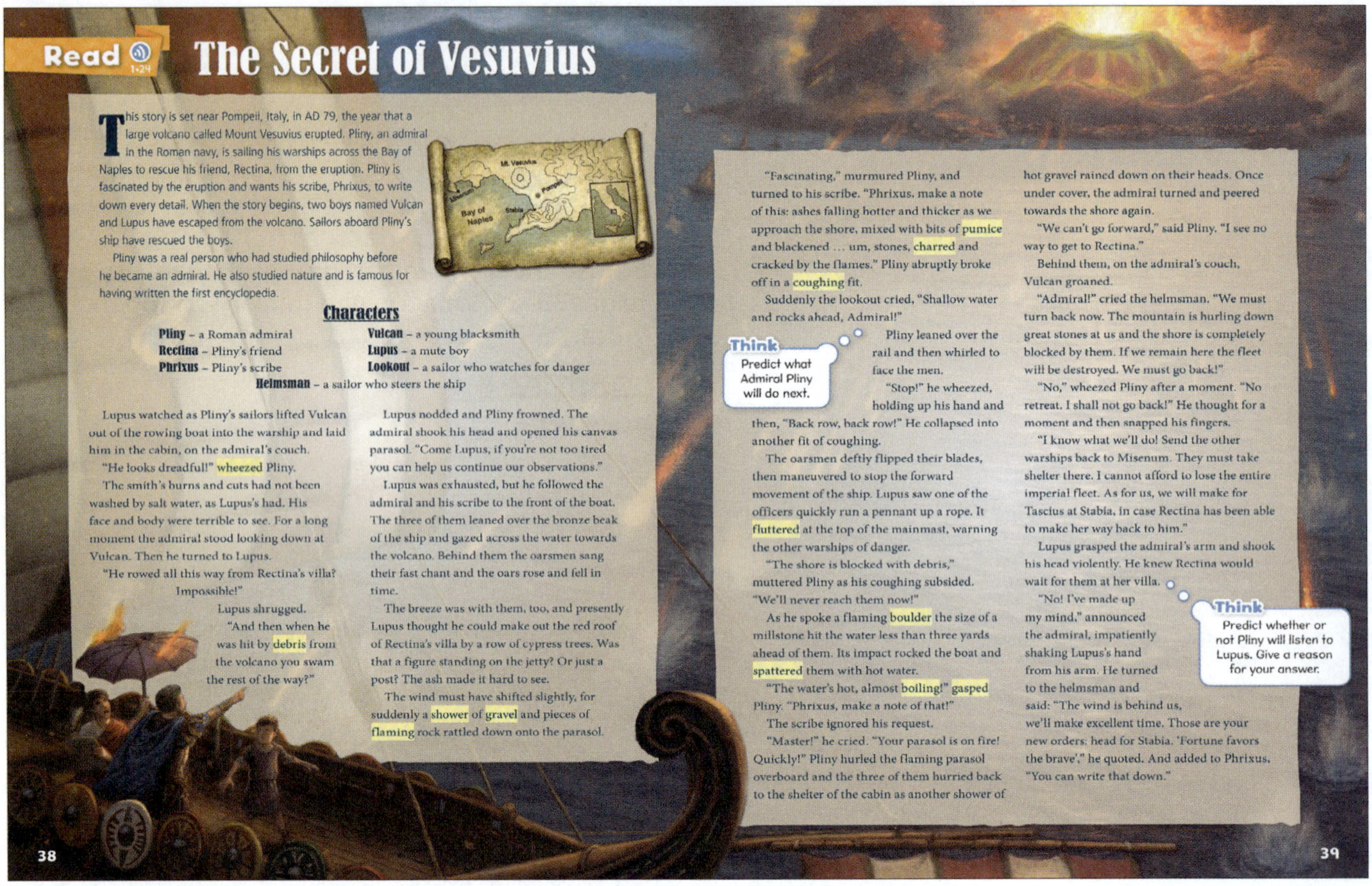

[Reproduction of student book pages 38–39: "The Secret of Vesuvius"]

This story is set near Pompeii, Italy, in AD 79, the year that a large volcano called Mount Vesuvius erupted. Pliny, an admiral in the Roman navy, is sailing his warships across the Bay of Naples to rescue his friend, Rectina, from the eruption. Pliny is fascinated by the eruption and wants his scribe, Phrixus, to write down every detail. When the story begins, two boys named Vulcan and Lupus have escaped from the volcano. Sailors aboard Pliny's ship have rescued the boys.

Pliny was a real person who had studied philosophy before he became an admiral. He also studied nature and is famous for having written the first encyclopedia.

Characters

Pliny – a Roman admiral
Rectina – Pliny's friend
Phrixus – Pliny's scribe
Vulcan – a young blacksmith
Lupus – a mute boy
Lookout – a sailor who watches for danger
Helmsman – a sailor who steers the ship

Lupus watched as Pliny's sailors lifted Vulcan out of the rowing boat into the warship and laid him in the cabin, on the admiral's couch.

"He looks dreadful!" wheezed Pliny.

The smith's burns and cuts had not been washed by salt water, as Lupus's had. His face and body were terrible to see. For a long moment the admiral stood looking down at Vulcan. Then he turned to Lupus.

"He rowed all this way from Rectina's villa? Impossible!"

Lupus shrugged.

"And then when he was hit by debris from the volcano you swam the rest of the way?"

Lupus nodded and Pliny frowned. The admiral shook his head and opened his canvas parasol. "Come Lupus, if you're not too tired you can help us continue our observations."

Lupus was exhausted, but he followed the admiral and his scribe to the front of the boat. The three of them leaned over the bronze beak of the ship and gazed across the water towards the volcano. Behind them the oarsmen sang their fast chant and the oars rose and fell in time.

The breeze was with them, too, and presently Lupus thought he could make out the red roof of Rectina's villa by a row of cypress trees. Was that a figure standing on the jetty? Or just a post? The ash made it hard to see.

The wind must have shifted slightly, for suddenly a shower of gravel and pieces of flaming rock rattled down onto the parasol.

"Fascinating," murmured Pliny, and turned to his scribe. "Phrixus, make a note of this: ashes falling hotter and thicker as we approach the shore, mixed with bits of pumice and blackened … um, stones, charred and cracked by the flames." Pliny abruptly broke off in a coughing fit.

Suddenly the lookout cried, "Shallow water and rocks ahead, Admiral!"

Pliny leaned over the rail and then whirled to face the men.

"Stop!" he wheezed, holding up his hand and then, "Back row, back row!" He collapsed into another fit of coughing.

The oarsmen deftly flipped their blades, then maneuvered to stop the forward movement of the ship. Lupus saw one of the officers quickly run a pennant up a rope. It fluttered at the top of the mainmast, warning the other warships of danger.

"The shore is blocked with debris," muttered Pliny as his coughing subsided. "We'll never reach them now!"

As he spoke a flaming boulder the size of a millstone hit the water less than three yards ahead of them. Its impact rocked the boat and spattered them with hot water.

"The water's hot, almost boiling!" gasped Pliny. "Phrixus, make a note of that!"

The scribe ignored his request.

"Master!" he cried. "Your parasol is on fire! Quickly!" Pliny hurled the flaming parasol overboard and the three of them hurried back to the shelter of the cabin as another shower of hot gravel rained down on their heads. Once under cover, the admiral turned and peered towards the shore again.

"We can't go forward," said Pliny. "I see no way to get to Rectina."

Behind them, on the admiral's couch, Vulcan groaned.

"Admiral!" cried the helmsman. "We must turn back now. The mountain is hurling down great stones at us and the shore is completely blocked by them. If we remain here the fleet will be destroyed. We must go back!"

"No," wheezed Pliny after a moment. "No retreat. I shall not go back!" He thought for a moment and then snapped his fingers.

"I know what we'll do! Send the other warships back to Misenum. They must take shelter there. I cannot afford to lose the entire imperial fleet. As for us, we will make for Tascius at Stabia, in case Rectina has been able to make her way back to him."

Lupus grasped the admiral's arm and shook his head violently. He knew Rectina would wait for them at her villa.

"No! I've made up my mind," announced the admiral, impatiently shaking Lupus's arm from his arm. He turned to the helmsman and said: "The wind is behind us, we'll make excellent time. Those are your new orders: head for Stabia. 'Fortune favors the brave'," he quoted. And added to Phrixus, "You can write that down."

Think Predict what Admiral Pliny will do next.

Think Predict whether or not Pliny will listen to Lupus. Give a reason for your answer.

38 | 39

Summary

Objectives: To read, understand, and discuss historical fiction; to apply a reading strategy to improve comprehension.

School subject: Earth Science

Text type: Historical fiction

Reading strategy: Prediction

Big Question learning point: *Lava erupts out of the Earth from volcanoes.*

Materials: Audio CD

Before Reading

- Read the title. Ask the class what kind of text this is. Ask them to predict what they think the story will be about.
- Have students point to the pictures and describe what they see.
- Have students read the list of characters.

CRITICAL THINKING

- Tell students to skim and use context to elicit meanings for some of the traits and jobs: *admiral* (a person in the navy); *scribe* (a writer); *mute* (unable to speak).

During Reading 1•24

- Tell students to read the summary at the top first. Ask *Who is Pliny?*
- Remind students that they should predict what will happen next as they read.
- Play the audio. Students listen as they read along.
- Play the audio a second time if necessary.

DIFFERENTIATION

Below level:

- Put students into small groups and have them read sections of the text after you. Elicit predictions after the sections.
- Stop at the *Think* boxes and help the group to make predictions about them.

At level:

- Put students into pairs to read the text to each other. Pairs should stop and make predictions as they read.
- Have pairs stop at the *Think* boxes and make predictions.

Above level:

- Have students read the text individually and write down their predictions as they go.
- Put students into pairs to trade their predictions and compare them.

CRITICAL THINKING

Discussion questions:

- *Why does Pliny not believe that Vulcan rowed all the way from the villa?*
- *Why do you think Lupus went to watch the observations even though he was tired? Would you do that?*
- *Why was Pliny constantly coughing and wheezing?*
- *Why do you think Pliny doesn't notice immediately that his parasol was hit by flaming rock?*
- *What kind of person do you think Pliny is?*

After Reading

- Put students into small groups.
- Have students each take a part of a character in the story. One person will need to be the narrator.
- Have them read the story together with students reading their parts.
- Have each group decide how they would act out a small section of the story (one or two paragraphs).
- Have each group stand up and act it out in front of the class.

COLLABORATIVE LEARNING

- Put students into small groups to discuss how much of the story they think is historical (real) and how much is fiction (made up).
- Have groups make two lists: what they think is based in reality and what the author made up.
- Draw a table on the board with two columns. Label them "Real" and "Made up."
- Elicit ideas from the class, writing them into one of the two columns.

CULTURE NOTE

Mount Vesuvius is on the west coast of Italy and is the only active volcano in mainland Europe.

Mount Vesuvius sits over a tear in the African tectonic plate. The African plate is being subducted under the Eurasian plate. This means that heat from the Earth's mantle layer is melting the rock of the African plate. This builds up a lot of pressure that causes explosive eruptions.

The eruption of Mount Vesuvius in 79 AD destroyed the cities of Pompeii and Herculaneum, burying them in ash, mud, and rocks from the eruption. The eruption is estimated to have reached heights of over 20 miles high and said to have been shaped like a pine tree. An estimated 16,000 people were killed.

Mount Vesuvius has erupted many times. The last major event was in 1944. It is still considered a threat to the Naples area of Italy.

Further Practice
Workbook page 32
Online Practice Unit 4 • Read
Oxford **iTools** Unit 4 • Read

Understand

Comprehension

Think Is Pliny brave or foolish for trying to rescue his friend while Mount Vesuvius is erupting? Why do you think so?

A Circle the best prediction.

1 The smoke from the volcano is making Pliny wheeze and cough. What will happen next?
   a Pliny will get better.
   b The eruption will stop, and the air will clear.
   c Pliny will get sicker.

2 Lupus knows that Rectina will stay at her villa. Pliny thinks he will find Rectina at a place called Stabia. What will happen next?
   a They'll find Rectina at her villa.
   b They won't find Rectina.
   c They'll find Rectina at Stabia.

3 The city of Pompeii is only 8 kilometers from Mount Vesuvius. What will happen next?
   a Pompeii will be destroyed.
   b Nothing will change in Pompeii.
   c The volcano will stop erupting.

4 Historians know that Pliny died during the eruption of Mount Vesuvius. What will happen next?
   a Phrixus will stop writing.
   b Phrixus will continue writing.
   c Phrixus will throw his writing away.

B Answer the questions.

1 What's happening to Mount Vesuvius?
2 Why is Pliny sailing across the Bay of Naples?
3 Where are the rocks and debris around Pliny's ship coming from?
4 Why does Pliny want his scribe to write things down?
5 What kind of danger does the lookout see?
6 How does Pliny feel about the eruption?

C **Words in Context** Look at the words you circled in the story. Then use them to complete the sentences.

1 We felt relief at the lion's _____ into the woods.
2 An astronomer makes _____ about the planets, stars, and galaxies.
3 The star player _____ kicked the ball into the goal.
4 I felt uncomfortable and _____ in my seat.
5 The _____ wrote down what people said.
6 We walked along the _____ of the ocean.

40   Unit 4   *Comprehension*

Grammar in Use

Workbook Grammar pages 34–35

D Listen and read along. Then circle the correct answer. 1-25

> Did you get my candy bar?
> Oh, your candy bar. Sorry, I didn't.
> What? Why not?
> It's complicated.
> What do you mean? What happened?
> When I got to the store, it had already closed.
> When did you go?
> When I thought of it, at midnight!

Which thing happened first?
a April went to the store.   b The store closed.

E **Learn Grammar** Past Perfect

Use the **past perfect** to say something happened before another thing happened in the past.

Pliny had studied philosophy before he became an admiral.

(First he studied philosophy. Then he was an admiral.)

Underline the action that happened first.

1 By the time I woke up, my brother had gone to school.
2 After I'd finished my homework, I went to my friend's house.
3 We went to a show after we'd eaten our dinner.
4 When the movie started, I realized I'd seen it before.
5 Lisa had chosen a recipe before she started cooking.
6 The train had just left when we arrived at the station.

F Make a chart like this one. Then talk about it with your partner. Use the past perfect.

> I'd packed a lunch before I went to basketball practice.

Happened Before	Happened After
packed a lunch	went to basketball practice
finished my project	played a game

Grammar: Past Perfect   **Unit 4**   **41**

Summary

Objectives: To demonstrate understanding of a historical fiction text; to understand the meaning and form of the grammar structure.

Reading: Comprehension

Grammar input: Past perfect

Grammar practice: Workbook exercises

Grammar production: Past perfect

Materials: Audio CD

Comprehension

Think

• Have students think about their answers individually first. Then hold a class discussion.

A Circle the best prediction.

• Have students read the questions and possible answers.
• Have them do the exercise on their own.
• Check answers with the class.

POSSIBLE ANSWERS

1 a **2** b **3** a **4** b

DIFFERENTIATION

Below level:

• Put students into mixed-ability pairs. Have the pair read the questions together and circle the best predictions.
• Put students into groups of four. Have students talk about similarities and differences in their predictions.

At level:

• Have students complete the exercise on their own.
• Then check the answers with the class.

Above level:

• Have students complete the exercise on their own.
• Then put students into pairs to compare their answers. Have pairs discuss their reasons for their answers.
• When checking answers with the class, have pairs explain the reasons to the class.

B Answer the questions.

COLLABORATIVE LEARNING

• Put students into small mixed-ability groups.
• Have them work together to answer the questions. Tell students to turn back to the story to find the answers.
• Check the answers with the class.

ANSWERS

1 Mount Vesuvius is erupting. It is spewing ash, gravel, and flaming rock.
2 To rescue his friend, Rectina.
3 They are coming from the eruption of Mount Vesuvius.
4 Pliny is a writer and philosopher. He finds the eruption fascinating.
5 Shallow water and rocks.
6 Pliny is fascinated by the eruption.

C Words in Context: Look at the words you circled in the story. Then use them to complete the sentences.

- Have students go back and find the words in the story.
- Tell them to use the context clues to guess at the meaning of each word. Students complete the sentences.
- Check the answers with the class.

CRITICAL THINKING

- Put students into pairs.
- Have pairs discuss the meaning of the words and write simple definitions for them.
- Then pairs trade papers with another pair and check each other's work. Allow them to use a dictionary.
- Have pairs share their definitions with the class.

Grammar in Use

D Listen and read along. Then circle the correct answer. 🔘 1·25

- Listen to the dialogue once and then read it together as a class.
- Have students circle the correct answer.

ANSWER
b The store closed.

E Learn Grammar: Past Perfect

- Read the *Learn Grammar* box together.
- Using the example in the book, ask *Which verb is the past perfect? Which verb is the simple past? What does the past perfect show?*
- Say an example using yourself, e.g. *I had been a college student before I became a teacher. Which happened first? Which happened second?*

Underline the action that happened first.

- Read the first sentence together. Ask the class to identify which happened first? Elicit which words students will underline.
- Have students complete the rest of the sentences on their own.

ANSWERS
1 had gone   2 'd finished   3 'd eaten   4 'd seen
5 had chosen   6 had just left

COMMUNICATION

- Put students into pairs.
- Have pairs think of four more past perfect sentences.
- Have the pairs share their example sentences with the class. Have the class say the past perfect verb in each.

F Make a chart like this one. Then talk about it with your partner. Use the past perfect.

- Have students individually write the chart out in their notebook.
- Put students into pairs.
- Have pairs make sentences together using the information from the chart, e.g. *He had packed a lunch before he went to basketball practice.*

DIFFERENTIATION

Below level:

- Write four sentence halves on the board: Beginnings: *He jumped into the pool, _____.* / *He had jumped into the pool _____.* Endings: *before he had taken off his shoes / after he took off his shoes.*
- Read the sentence halves with the class. Have the students write the sentences matching the correct halves.
- Have two volunteers come to the board to match the halves. Ask the class to read the correct sentences aloud and check their work.

At level:

- Put students in a circle. One student says the first part of a sentence. It may or may not use the past perfect. He or she turns to the next student in the circle, who must end the sentence using past perfect if required. Then that student says a sentence to the next student in the circle. Continue around the entire circle at least once.

Above level:

- Have half of the students write two sentence starters each on a small piece of paper. Have the other half of the students write two sentence ends each on a small piece of paper.
- Tell students to make one of the beginnings and one of the ends contain the past perfect, while the other doesn't.
- The object is to be the first to get rid of your endings, and complete your beginnings. Students circulate and read their sentence starters and endings to each other to find a matching ending. (It needs to be grammatically correct and possibly make sense.)
- When students find an ending for their beginning, they keep the ending slip of paper.
- Ask students who have successfully completed the activity to read their sentences to the class.

Workbook Grammar

- Direct students to the Workbook for further practice.

Further practice
Workbook pages 33–35
Online Practice Unit 4 · Understand
Oxford iTools Unit 4 · Understand

Unit 4 Communicate

page 42

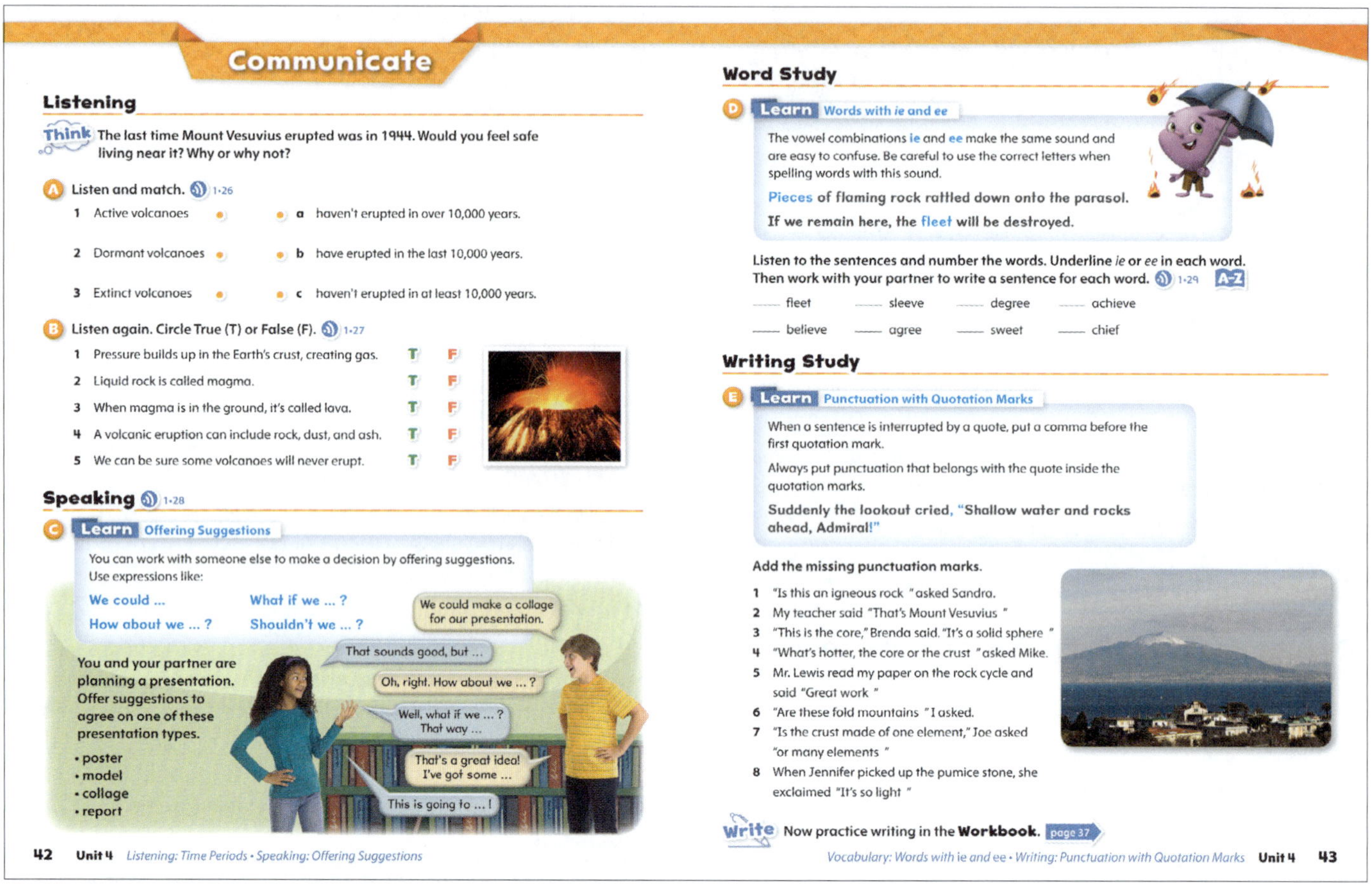

Communicate

Listening

Think The last time Mount Vesuvius erupted was in 1944. Would you feel safe living near it? Why or why not?

A Listen and match. 1•26

1 Active volcanoes • • a haven't erupted in over 10,000 years.

2 Dormant volcanoes • • b have erupted in the last 10,000 years.

3 Extinct volcanoes • • c haven't erupted in at least 10,000 years.

B Listen again. Circle True (T) or False (F). 1•27

1 Pressure builds up in the Earth's crust, creating gas. T F

2 Liquid rock is called magma. T F

3 When magma is in the ground, it's called lava. T F

4 A volcanic eruption can include rock, dust, and ash. T F

5 We can be sure some volcanoes will never erupt. T F

Speaking 1•28

C **Learn** Offering Suggestions

You can work with someone else to make a decision by offering suggestions. Use expressions like:

We could ... What if we ... ?

How about we ... ? Shouldn't we ... ?

You and your partner are planning a presentation. Offer suggestions to agree on one of these presentation types.

- poster
- model
- collage
- report

We could make a collage for our presentation.
That sounds good, but ...
Oh, right. How about we ... ?
Well, what if we ... ? That way ...
That's a great idea! I've got some ...
This is going to ... !

42 Unit 4 *Listening: Time Periods • Speaking: Offering Suggestions*

Word Study

D **Learn** Words with *ie* and *ee*

The vowel combinations ie and ee make the same sound and are easy to confuse. Be careful to use the correct letters when spelling words with this sound.

Pieces of flaming rock rattled down onto the parasol.

If we remain here, the fleet will be destroyed.

Listen to the sentences and number the words. Underline *ie* or *ee* in each word. Then work with your partner to write a sentence for each word. 1•29 A-Z

___ fleet ___ sleeve ___ degree ___ achieve

___ believe ___ agree ___ sweet ___ chief

Writing Study

E **Learn** Punctuation with Quotation Marks

When a sentence is interrupted by a quote, put a comma before the first quotation mark.

Always put punctuation that belongs with the quote inside the quotation marks.

Suddenly the lookout cried, "Shallow water and rocks ahead, Admiral!"

Add the missing punctuation marks.

1 "Is this an igneous rock " asked Sandra.

2 My teacher said "That's Mount Vesuvius "

3 "This is the core," Brenda said. "It's a solid sphere "

4 "What's hotter, the core or the crust " asked Mike.

5 Mr. Lewis read my paper on the rock cycle and said "Great work "

6 "Are these fold mountains " I asked.

7 "Is the crust made of one element," Joe asked "or many elements "

8 When Jennifer picked up the pumice stone, she exclaimed "It's so light "

Write Now practice writing in the **Workbook**. page 37

Vocabulary: Words with ie and ee • Writing: Punctuation with Quotation Marks Unit 4 43

Summary

Objectives: To learn and practice listening, speaking, and writing strategies to facilitate effective communication.

Vocabulary: *fleet, sleeve, degree, achieve, believe, agree, sweet, chief*

Listening strategy: Listening for time periods

Speaking: Offering suggestions

Word Study: Words with *ie* and *ee*

Writing Study: Punctuation with quotation marks

Big Question learning point: *Lava erupts out of the Earth from volcanoes.*

Materials: Audio CD

Listening

Think

- Tell students to think about their answers to the questions.
- Have students tell a partner how they would feel about living near Mount Vesuvius.
- Have students put up their hands to show who would and wouldn't mind living near Vesuvius.
- Ask a few volunteers to tell the class their thoughts on why or why not.

A Listen and match. 1•26

- Have students read the sentence beginnings and answer options. Ask *What will you listen for?*
- Play the audio once and have students listen.
- Tell students to match the phrases. Then play the audio again so they can check their work.

ANSWERS

1 b 2 c 3 a

B Listen again. Circle True (T) or False (F). 1•27

- Play the audio so students can complete the exercise.
- Have students work individually to circle T for True and F for False.
- Put students into pairs to check their answers.
- Check the answers with the whole class.

ANSWERS

1 T 2 T 3 F 4 T 5 F

Speaking 1•28

C Learn: Offering Suggestions

- Read the *Learn* box and the examples.
- Play the audio through one time.
- Play the audio a second time for students to take parts and read along with it.
- Put students into pairs and ask them to read the dialogue.

You and your partner are planning a presentation. Offer suggestions to agree on one of these presentation types.

- Put students into pairs.
- Have them create short dialogues using the topics listed (poster, model, collage, report).
- Ask a few pairs to act out their dialogues for the class.

Word Study

D Learn: Words with *ie* and *ee*

- Read the *Learn* box together.

Listen to the sentences and number the words. Underline *ie* or *ee* in each word. Then work with your partner to write a sentence for each word. 🔘 1·29

- Say one of the words in random order and have students spell it.
- Check the answers with the class.

ANSWERS

1 sweet 2 achieve 3 fleet 4 agree 5 believe
6 sleeve 7 chief 8 degree

Writing Study

E Learn: Punctuation with Quotation Marks

- Read the *Learn* box together.
- Read the example with dramatic emphasis.
- Ask questions to check understanding.
  Which words did the lookout say? How do you know?
  What comes before the quotation marks?
  Where does the punctuation for the quote go?

Add the missing punctuation marks.

- Have students complete the exercise on their own.
- Then have students compare answers with a partner.
- Ask students to come to the board to write the sentences to check the answers.

ANSWERS

1 "Is this an example of igneous rock?" asked Sandra.
2 My teacher said, "That's Mount Vesuvius."
3 "This is the core," Brenda said. "It's a solid sphere."
4 "What's hotter, the core or the crust?" asked Mike.
5 Mr. Lewis read my paper on the rock cycle and said, "Great work!"
6 "Are these fold mountains?" I asked.
7 "Is the crust made of one element," Joe asked "or many elements?"
8 When Jennifer picked up the pumice stone, she exclaimed, "It's so light!"

Below level:

- Put students into mixed-ability pairs.
- Have the more confident student help the other student to decide what punctuation to use and where it goes.
- Have pairs share their answers with another pair.

At level:

- Have students go back to the story and find three examples of punctuation with quotation marks.
- Then put students into pairs.
- Students take turns to read the sentences they found to their partner who writes them down, dictation-style. Then it is the other partner's turn to listen and write.
- Pairs turn back to the story to check their work.

Above level:

- Tell students to write three sentences, without the punctuation. The sentences should be one each for a period, question mark, and a split sentence like number 7.
- Then students trade papers with a partner, who reads them and fills in the punctuation.
- Ask students to swap papers to check each other's work.

Write.

- Direct students to the Workbook for further writing practice.

> **Further practice**
> **Workbook pages 36–37**
> **Online Practice Unit 4 • Communicate**
> **Oxford iTools Unit 4 • Communicate**

Summary

Objectives: To show what students have learned about the language and learning points of Units 3 and 4.

Reading: Reading an informational speech

Writing: Writing a speech

Speaking: Giving an informational speech

Big Question learning point: *Fossils in the Earth tell us about our planet's history.*

Materials: Big Question DVD, Discover Poster 2, Talk About It! Poster, Big Question Chart

Writing

A Read this speech.

- Read aloud the directions and explain that the writer's purpose is to inform.
- Go over the structure of the speech before reading.
- Elicit what the opening statements are and the conclusion. Ask students to predict what they think the speech will be about.
- Read the letter with the class one time. Then have students read it one time on their own.

B Answer the questions.

- Ask a few questions to check comprehension.
  What are fossils?
  Do bone fossils have actual bone in them?
  What is fossilized bone similar to?
  How are fossils formed?
- Have students find the answers in the text.

ANSWERS

1 The writer starts the speech with three questions.
2 The writer uses pictures, too.
3 The writer organizes the speech by paragraphs.

C Learn: Writing a Speech

- Read the *Learn* box together.
- Explain that students should follow these guidelines when they plan and write their essays.

CRITICAL THINKING

- Have students go back to the model to see how the author addressed each requirement.
- Ask *How does the writer get the audience's attention? Does the writer use background information? Does the author use visuals?*
- Ask *What would be a good poster idea for this speech?* e.g. a picture showing how fossils are formed.

Write.

- Direct the students to the Workbook to plan and write their own speech.

- Brainstorm some ideas for a speech with the class.
- Write topics on the board. Then group together students who choose similar topics.

Below level:

- Put students into small mixed-ability groups, preferably with the same topic, to brainstorm topics and details to write a speech about.
- Have the more confident student help the other student to make notes that he or she can use as he / she drafts his / her speech.

At level:

- Have students complete their speeches themselves.
- Then have students read their speeches to a partner.
- The partner should use the checklist to check if the speech meets all of the requirements. If it doesn't, the partner should offer suggestions to make it do so.
- Ask students to revise their speeches.

Above level:

- Have students write their speeches themselves, following the steps in the Workbook.
- Then have a partner read the written speech aloud so the student can hear it fresh. The partner should then offer suggestions to improve the speech. Ask them to switch roles.
- Finally, both students revise their speeches.

D Present your speech to the class.

- Read the list of suggestions with the class.
- Give students time to practice reading their speeches themselves.
- Have students try to memorize as much of the speech as possible. Suggest that they do this in chunks, repeating each chunk several times as they work through the entire speech.
- For points 3 and 4, if possible, have students practice giving their speech in front of a mirror.
- A helpful tip is to imagine they are talking to a friend.

- Put students into small groups to practice giving their speeches. Invite a more confident student to lead each group.
- Tell students to underline parts of the speech where they will stress what they are saying. They can make marks where pauses go, and add symbols where to use gestures.
- Have students practice giving their speech to the group before they present it to the whole class.

Units 3 and 4 Big Question Review

A Watch the video. What parts of the Earth do you see? ▷

- Play the video and when it is finished, ask students what they know about the Earth now.
- Have students share ideas with the class.

B What are some answers to the Big Question? Talk about them with your partner.

- Display **Discover Poster 2**. Point to familiar vocabulary items and elicit them from the class. Ask *What is this?*
- Ask students *What do you see?* Ask *What does that mean?*
- Refer to all of the learning points written on the poster and have students explain how they relate to the different pictures.
- Ask *What does this learning point mean?* Elicit answers from individual students.
- Display the **Talk About It! Poster** to help students with sentence frames for discussion of the learning points and for expressing their opinions.

C Complete the Big Question Chart. Then discuss it with the class.

- Ask students what they have learned about the Earth while studying this unit.
- Put students into pairs or small groups to say two new things they have learned.
- Have them share their ideas with the class and add their ideas to the chart.
- Have students complete the chart in their Workbook.

Further practice
Workbook pages 38–40
Online Practice • Wrap Up 2
Oxford **iTools** • Wrap Up 2

Units 5 and 6 · Why do we wear masks?

In units **5 and 6** you will:

WATCH a video about masks.

LEARN about different uses for masks.

READ a play and a website about masks.

WRITE a personal narrative.

PRESENT your personal narrative.

BIG QUESTION 3

Why do we wear masks?

A Watch the video. Then talk about it with your partner.

B Look at the picture and discuss it with your class.

1 Why is the person in front wearing a bird mask?
2 Why is the boy wearing a mask?

C Think and answer the questions.

1 What is a mask?
2 Have you ever worn a mask? What was it for?
3 What kinds of people wear masks?
4 Where have you seen people wearing masks?

D Discuss this topic with your class. Fill out the **Big Question Chart**.

What do you know about masks? What do you want to know?

46 · Big Question 3

47

Reading Strategies

Students will practice:

- Internal and external conflict
- Identifying facts and opinions

Review

Students will review the language and Big Question learning points of Units 5 and 6 through:

- Writing a personal narrative

Writing Study

Students will use and understand:

- Choosing a good title
- Using headings to organize writing

Students will:

- Write a personal narrative

Vocabulary

Students will understand and use words about:

- Seasonal change, masks

Units 5 and 6
Why do we wear masks?

Students will understand the Big Question learning points:

- Actors wear masks to play characters.
- Many people wear masks for health and safety reasons.
- People around the world use masks for celebrations and ceremonies.
- Fencers wear masks to protect themselves.
- A mask can be part of a costume or disguise.

Word Study

Students will understand and use:

- Suffixes -er and -or
- Suffix -ness

Grammar

Students will understand and use:

- Past perfect continuous
- Defining relative clauses for people

Listening Strategies

Students will practice:

- Listening for instructions
- Listening for advice

Speaking

Students will understand and use expressions for:

- Finding the right word
- Discussing a topic

Units 5 and 6 Big Question page 46

Summary

Objectives: To activate students' existing knowledge of the topic and identify what they would like to learn about the topic.

Materials: Big Question DVD, Discover Poster 3, Big Question Chart

Introducing the topic

- Read out the Big Question. Ask *Why do we wear masks?*
- Write students' ideas on the board and discuss.

A Watch the video. Then talk about it with your partner.

- Play the video and when it is finished ask students to answer the following questions in pairs:
  What do you see in the video?
  What is happening?
  Who do you think the people are?
  What do you like about the video?
- Have individual students share their answers with the class.

Below level:
- After watching, have students describe the masks they saw in the video.
- Have students name holidays, events, or situations where people wear masks.

At level:
- After watching, have students list all of the masks they saw in the video. Write the list on the board.
- For each mask, have the class say why they think someone was wearing it.

Above level:
- After watching, have students write sentences to describe the masks they saw in the video. For each mask they should write what it is used for.
- Have students share their writing with the class.

B Look at the picture and discuss it with your class.

- Students look at the big picture and talk about it. Ask *What do you see?*
- Ask additional questions:
  What sport do you think they are playing?
  What are the people watching doing?
  What country do you think this is?
  Have you ever played this sport?

C Think and answer the questions.

- Have students discuss the questions in small groups, and then with the class.

- Ask students to think about the second question. Have students come to the board and write sentences.
- Ask students to think about the fourth question. Have students come to the board and write sentences.

Expanding the topic

- Display **Discover Poster 3** and give students enough time to look at the pictures.
- Get students to talk about things you think they will know by pointing to different things in the pictures and asking *What's this? What does this do?*
- Put students into small groups of three or four. Have each group choose a picture that they find interesting.
- Ask each group to say five sentences about their picture.
- Have one person from each group stand up and read out the sentences they chose for their picture.
- Ask the class if they can add any more.

Below level:
- Encourage students to participate using short sentences.
- Point to details in the big picture and on the poster and ask *What's this?* Write the answers on the board.

At level:
- Elicit complete sentences about what students know about wearing masks.
- Write their sentences on the board.

Above level:
- Elicit more detailed responses.
- Challenge students to write their own sentences on the board.

D Discuss this topic with your class. Fill out the Big Question Chart.

- Display the **Big Question Chart**.
- Ask the class *What do you know about wearing masks? What do you want to know?*
- Ask students to write what they know and what they want to know in their Workbooks.
- Write a collection of ideas on the **Big Question Chart**.

Discover Poster 3

1 A group of actors wearing masks; 2 A doctor putting on a surgical mask; 3 People wearing masks for the International Mask Festival in Melnik, Bulgaria; 4 Two fencers wearing masks for protection; 5 A display of different masks in Tokyo, Japan

Further Practice
Workbook page 42
Online Practice · Big Question 3
Oxford **iTools** · **Big Question 3**

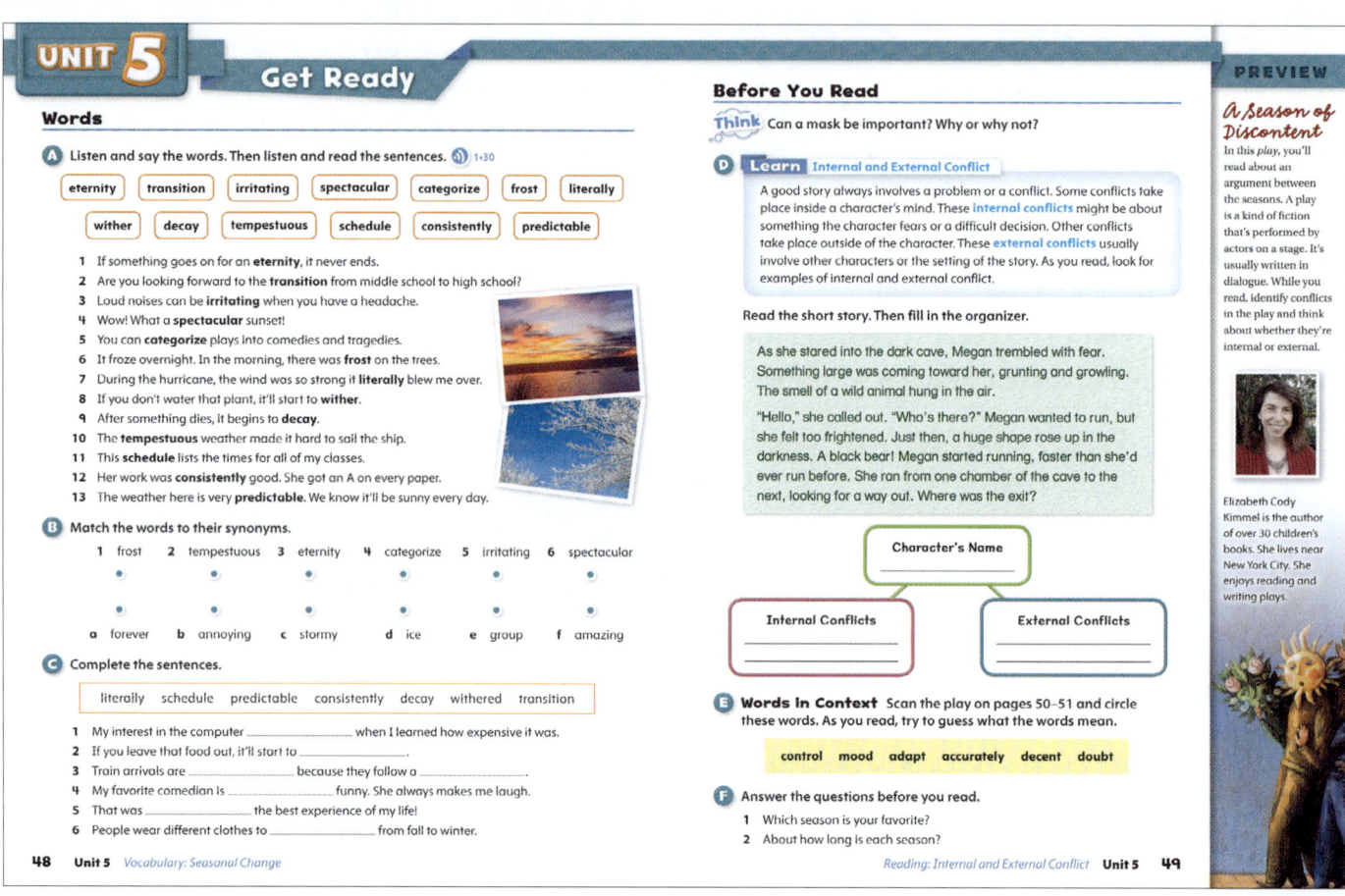

Summary

Objectives: To understand words about seasonal change; to apply own experience and a reading strategy to help comprehension of a text.

Vocabulary: *eternity, transition, irritating, spectacular, categorize, frost, literally, wither, decay, tempestuous, schedule, consistently, predictable, control, mood, adapt, accurately, decent, doubt*

Reading strategy: Internal and external conflict

Materials: Audio CD

Words

A Listen and say the words. Then listen and read the sentences. 🔘 1·30

- Play the audio. Ask students to point to the words and repeat the words when they hear them.
- Then have students listen and read the sentences as they hear them.
- Say the sentence numbers out of order and have the class read the sentences aloud.

B Match the words to their synonyms.

- Tell students to match a word on the top line with its synonym on the bottom line.
- Elicit the meaning of *synonym:* a word that has the same meaning. Have students do the activity on their own.
- Have students compare their answers with a partner.
- Check answers with the class.

ANSWERS
1 d 2 c 3 a 4 e 5 b 6 f

C Complete the sentences.

- Have students do the activity on their own.
- Have them compare their answers with a partner.
- Check answers with the class.

ANSWERS
1 withered
2 decay
3 predictable, schedule
4 consistently
5 literally
6 transition

COLLABORATIVE LEARNING

- Put students into pairs. Have pairs write sentences for each of the new words, e.g. *He is so slow it will take him an eternity to finish the race.*
- When they have finished, tell the pairs to swap their sentences with another pair.
- Pairs check their work with each other.
- Have pairs read some of their sentences to the class.

Before You Read

Think
- Put students into pairs to discuss the questions.
- Have pairs share their answers with the class.
- List the answers on the board.

D Learn: Internal and External Conflict
- Read the *Learn* box together.
- Give examples of internal and external conflict using stories or movies that students are familiar with, e.g. *An external conflict for Harry Potter involves Voldemort. An internal conflict is how he feels about being a wizard.*
- Then elicit other examples from the class.

Read the short story. Then fill in the organizer.
- Invite a confident student to read the paragraph aloud for the class.
- Together with the class fill in the organizer.

Character's Name: Megan
Internal Conflicts: wants to run, but too frightened
External Conflicts: a black bear coming for her; she can't find the exit

CRITICAL THINKING

Ask the following questions to check understanding about conflict:
- *Why is feeling frightened an internal conflict?*
- *What are the two external conflicts?*
- *Why is being lost an external conflict and not an internal one?*

E Words in Context: Scan the play on pages 50–51 and circle these words. As you read, try to guess what the words mean.
- Read each word and have the students follow your pronunciation.
- Ask the students to scan the play on pages 50 and 51 and circle the words. Tell them to guess what the words mean from the context.
- Have students share their ideas about the words' definitions.

DIFFERENTIATION

Below level:
- Give students some simple definitions for the words.
- Restate and / or explain the sentences from the play using the definitions, e.g. *This spring is taking an eternity.* Eternity means *forever, a really long time.* Reread the sentence with the new meaning: *This spring is taking forever.*
- Put students into mixed-ability pairs. Have students reread the sentences using the new definitions.

At level:
- Put students into pairs to figure out the meaning of the new words from context.
- Tell pairs to look up any words they don't recognize in the dictionary.
- Have pairs share their answers with the class.

Above level:
- Put students into pairs to restate the sentences with alternate words in place of the words in context.
- Have pairs share their new sentences with the class.

F Answer the questions before you read.

COMMUNICATION

- Put students into small groups to discuss the questions.
- Tell groups to list the reasons that are their answers for each question.
- Go over the groups' answers and make notes on the board.

Reading Preview
- Read the title of the unit's reading text.
- Have students silently read the content of the preview bar.
- Ask *What type of text is it?* Ask *What is this type of text like?*
- Tell students to think about the internal and external conflicts of the characters as they read.
- Read the Author Bio with the class.

Further Practice
Workbook pages 42–43
Online Practice Unit 5 · Get Ready
Oxford **iTools Unit 5 · Get Ready**

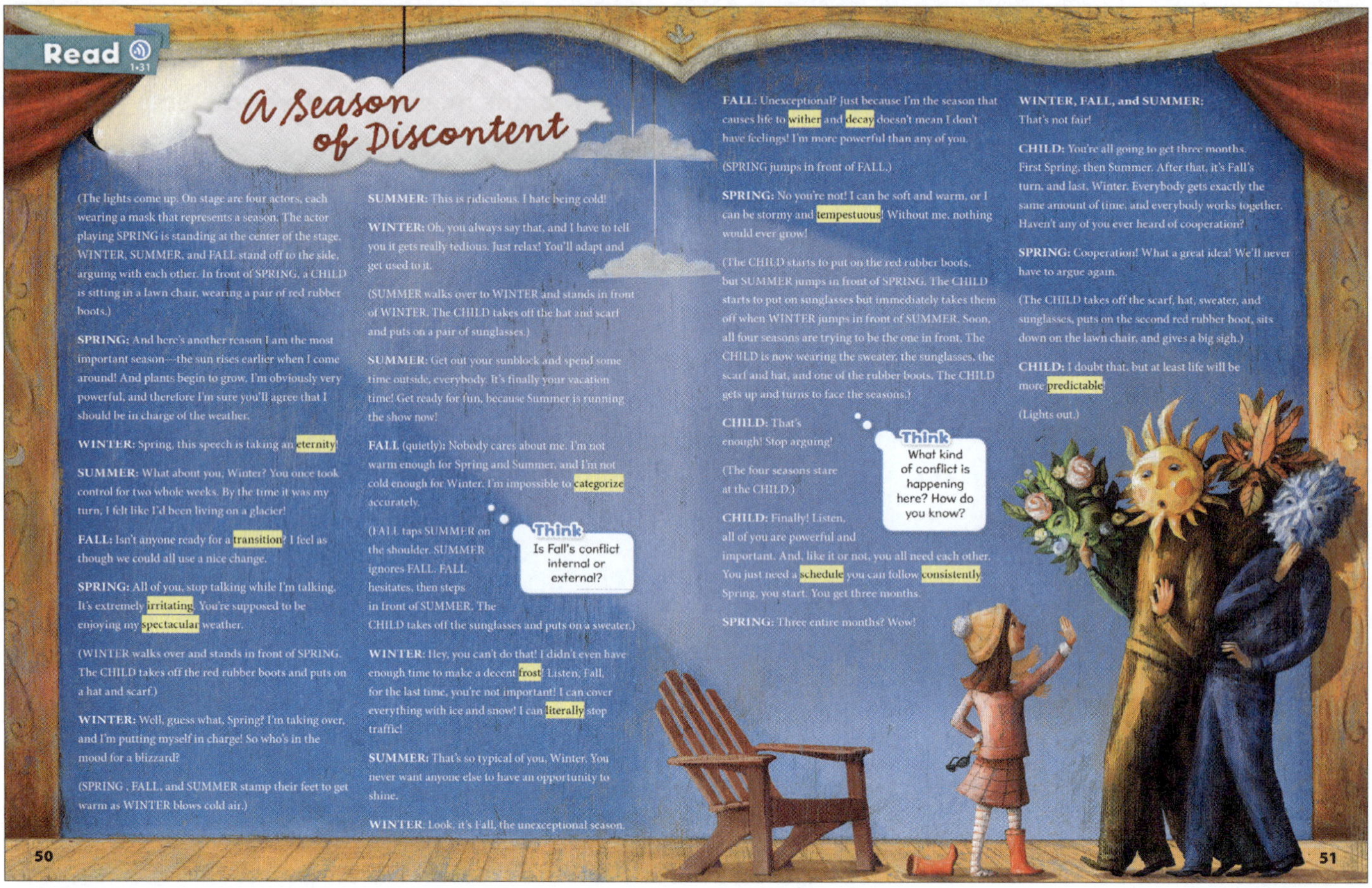

(The play page illustration "A Season of Discontent" appears here, pages 50–51.)

Summary

Objectives: To read, understand, and discuss a play; to apply a reading strategy to improve comprehension.

School subject: Social Studies: Society

Text type: Play (fiction)

Reading strategy: Internal and external conflict

Big Question learning point: *Actors wear masks to play characters.*

Materials: Talk About It! Poster, Audio CD

Before Reading

- Ask *Why do we wear masks?*
- Have students tell you what they see in the pictures.
- Ask students how they know this is a play.
- Ask them to point to and identify each of the characters in the play. Ask *How do their masks represent the season?*

During Reading ◎ 1·31

- Read the title and opening notes together.
- Explain that the stage directions in a play are in parentheses. The stage directions explain the action that the actors perform.
- Explain that students should use the stage directions and the speech to think about the characters' conflicts.
- Play the audio and have the class read along.

Below level:

- Have students read with you in groups of five. Assign one of the seasons and the child role to each student. You read the stage directions and prompt students to read their parts.
- While reading, stop at the *Think* boxes to summarize the action and elicit the character's internal and external conflicts.

At level:

- Have students read in groups of six. Assign one of the seasons and the child role to each student. One student reads the stage directions in parentheses.
- Have students read the play one time, pausing at the *Think* boxes to discuss. Then go back and discuss their characters.

Above level:

- Have students read the story in groups of six. Each student is a season or the child, and one student reads the stage directions in parentheses.
- Have students act out the stage directions as they read.
- Groups should stop and talk about the *Think* boxes.
- Then the groups summarize the internal and external conflicts of the characters.

Discussion questions:

- *In the first* Think *box, is Fall's conflict internal or external?*
- *In the next scene Fall steps in front of Summer and then Winter tells Fall it's not important. What is the conflict now?*
- *In the second* Think *box, is the conflict internal or external? How do you know?*
- *Why does Fall feel so overlooked?*
- *Which season do you think has the loudest voice in the play?*
- *Why does the child think the seasons won't stop arguing, even though there is now a solution to the conflict?*
- *Which season do you think is the most important? Why?*

After Reading

CRITICAL THINKING

- Put students into small groups. Say *Imagine the story has different conflicts. What might happen?*
- Brainstorm some possible conflicts with the class, e.g. *Winter is so cold that the ground is too hard and cold for things to grow when Spring comes along. Summer is so hot that there are forest fires, which ruin the cycle of life for the rest of the seasons.*
- Have groups come up with their different play.
- Then have groups share their plays with the class.

CREATIVITY

- Put students into small groups.
- Have them look back at the previous texts in the Student Book. Ask each group to choose a set of characters from one of the texts. They could be people or things (even tunnels and bridges).
- Hand out plain pieces of paper, scissors, and markers.
- Have each group make a mask for each member of the group, representing a different character in the text they have chosen to represent.
- Once students have finished making their masks, ask each group to stand up and present their "play", explaining the characters to the rest of the class.

COMMUNICATION

- Display the **Talk About It! Poster** to help students with sentence frames for discussion and expressing personal opinions.
- Put students into pairs to discuss which part of the play is most interesting.
- Elicit ideas from the class.

CULTURE NOTE

Many cultures wear masks during plays. In ancient Greek theater (circa BC 550–BC 220), tragedy and comedy were dominant theatrical genres. The mask for tragedy is a sad face and the mask for comedy is a smiling face. These two masks have become symbols for drama and the theater.

In the Middle Ages, masks were very popular in mystery plays. These masks were made very complicated and were made by skilled artisans. Sometimes they belched smoke and fire from hidden devices.

Noh masks are used in dramas in Japan. They became popular in the 14th century and are used to characterize different traits, e.g. a white mask is used to characterize a corrupt ruler and a black mask is used by the villain. These masks are so beautifully carved that when the mask is slightly moved by the actor's hand, the expression on the mask appears to change.

Further Practice
Workbook page 44
Online Practice Unit 5 • Read
Oxford **iTools** Unit 5 • Read

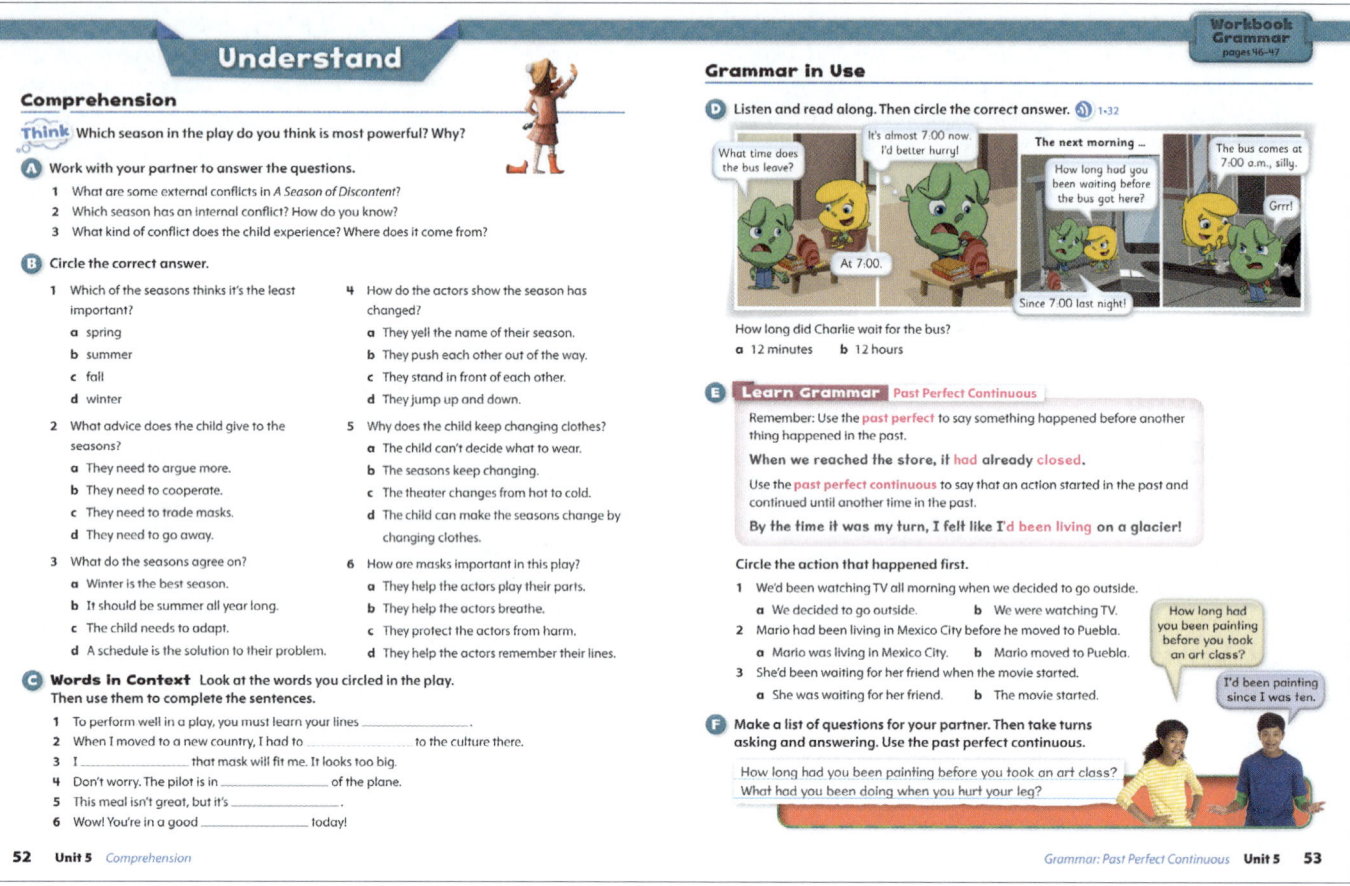

Summary

Objectives: To demonstrate understanding of a play; to understand the meaning and form of the grammar structure.

Reading: Comprehension

Grammar input: Past perfect continuous

Grammar practice: Workbook exercises

Grammar production: Talking about something that happened before another thing happened

Materials: Audio CD

Comprehension

Think

- Read the questions with the class. Ask students to think about their answers.
- Put students into groups to discuss their answers.
- Have groups share their answers. Mark the class's answers on the board to determine which season the class thinks is more powerful.

A Work with your partner to answer the questions.

- Read the instructions with the class. Have students read through the questions.
- Have students do the activity individually. Remind them to turn to the play on pages 50 and 51 to look up answers if they need to.
- Put students into pairs and tell them to compare their answers.
- Check the answers with the class.

POSSIBLE ANSWERS

1 The external conflicts in the play are between the seasons as each season thinks it is the most important.
2 Fall has an internal conflict. We know because Fall speaks to itself.
3 The child experiences an external conflict from the seasons because they keep changing. Also from the setting, because she has to change clothes every time the season changes.

B Circle the correct answer.

- Have the students read through the questions and the answer options.
- Ask the students to work individually.
- Check the answers with the class.

ANSWERS

1 c   2 b   3 d   4 c   5 b   6 a

DIFFERENTIATION

Below level:

- Put students into mixed-ability pairs.
- Have the more confident student help the other student to answer the questions. The students should turn back to pages 50 and 51 where the confident student helps to find the answers.

At level:

- Have students discuss the questions in pairs.
- Then have a few pairs tell the class their answers. Does the class agree?

Above level:

- Have pairs of students discuss the questions and then write answers.
- Put pairs into small groups to read and compare each other's answers.

C Words in Context: Look at the words you circled in the play. Then use them to complete the sentences.

- Have students go back and find the circled words in the play.
- Tell them to use the words and context clues to complete the sentences.
- Check the answers with the class.

ANSWERS

1 accurately   2 adapt   3 doubt   4 control
5 decent   6 mood

Grammar in Use

D Listen and read along. Then circle the correct answer. ◎ 1·32

- Listen to the dialogue once and have students read along.
- Then have students read the question and circle the correct answer.
- Play the dialogue again and have students check their answer.
- Check the answer with the class.

ANSWER

b 12 hours

E Learn Grammar: Past Perfect Continuous

- Read the *Learn Grammar* box together.
- Draw a timeline (line with arrows on each end) on the board. Point to the left side of the line and say *This is the past*. Point to the right side and say *This is the future*.
- Read the example sentence and mark X on the timeline slightly to the right and say *This is "When we reached the store."* Then ask *Where do I mark "it had already closed"?*
- Elicit *to the left,* or *before "it had already closed".* Draw an oval or circle on the spot to the left and say *It had already closed.*
- Explain that you used the oval to indicate "some time" in the past. Do the same procedure to present the second example using a new timeline. This time draw an X slightly to the right of *"By the time it was my turn"* for *"I felt like I'd been living on a glacier!"*
- Elicit, e.g. some time in the past up to and including the X and draw an oval along that space on the timeline to indicate the action from the past continued to the present.

Circle the action that happened first.

- Read the first sentence together. Have the class identify the action that came first: *We were watching TV.*
- Draw a timeline to illustrate the sentence if students are unclear about which action came first.
- Then have students complete the rest on their own.

ANSWERS

1 b   2 a   3 a

CRITICAL THINKING

- In pairs, ask students to compare and contrast the past perfect versus the past perfect continuous verb tense.
- Have pairs use the examples in the *Learn Grammar* box to talk about the form of the verb tenses.
- As students discuss write on the board: *Past perfect = had + _____. Past perfect continuous = had + been + _____.*
- Have pairs fill in the blanks with the appropriate verb tense.

F Make a list of questions for your partner. Then take turns asking and answering. Use the past perfect continuous.

COMMUNICATION

- Read the example questions and model the dialogue with a student.

COLLABORATIVE LEARNING

- Put partners in pairs to ask and answer questions.
- Have a few pairs say their dialogues for the class.
- In pairs, ask students to collaborate to write two new questions using the past perfect continuous.
- Then put students into small groups to ask and answer their questions to other members of the group.
- Be sure everyone has a chance to ask and answer.
- Have some students say their dialogues for the class.

Workbook Grammar

- Direct students to the Workbook for further practice.

Further practice
Workbook pages 45–47
Online Practice Unit 5 • Understand
Oxford **iTools** Unit 5 • Understand

Page 54 content:

Communicate

Listening

Think How would acting with a mask be different from acting without one?

A Listen. Circle the correct answer. 1·33

1 Actors must **never / always** put the mask on while facing away from the audience.
2 Actors must never take the mask off while **facing / facing away from** the audience.
3 You need to make sure the mask is comfortable **before / after** you turn around.
4 You must **sometimes / never** touch the mask while you're wearing it.
5 Never act as **your character / yourself** while you're wearing the mask.

B Listen again. Circle the correct answer. 1·34

1 Mitch is _____ with the West City Theater Group. a an actor b a director
2 _____ of the main actors in the play wear masks. a Some b All
3 Mitch _____ the challenge of wearing a mask while acting. a likes b doesn't like

Speaking 1·35

C Learn Finding the Right Word

When you can't think of what something is called, describe it to someone else so they can help you. Use expressions like:
It's used to …
It looks like …
It's one of those things that …
What do you call … ?

Choose one of these objects and describe it to your partner. Ask him or her to help you name it in English.
• a mask
• an umbrella
• a calendar

What is this thing called? It's used to play a role.
Oh, Is it a … ?
No, that's not it. It's something …
Hmm, it must be a …
Sorry, that's not it either. It's one of those things that …
Ah-hah! I know. It's a … !

54 Unit 5 Listening: Instructions • Speaking: Finding the Right Word

Word Study

D Learn Suffixes -er and -or

The suffixes **-er** and **-or** are used in many job titles. You can often use these suffixes to turn a verb into a noun.

When people **act** in this play, they wear masks.
Each **actor** wears a mask that represents a season.

Listen and say the words. Underline the verb in each word and circle the suffix. 1·36 A-Z

1 actor   2 counselor   3 builder   4 painter
5 plumber 6 surveyor   7 inventor   8 trainer

Writing Study

E Learn Choosing a Good Title

Whether you're writing a report, a story, or a poem, it's important to choose a **good title**. A good title will get your readers' attention and make them want to keep reading. It will also help them to remember what you wrote.

Read the story and give it a title. Then compare your title with your partner's.

A terrible noise woke Jake from his sleep. What had happened? Had the roof fallen in? He leaped out of bed and ran to the window. As he looked out into the darkness, he saw a strange, green light in the distance. Was it a plane crash? Maybe it was an asteroid, he thought. Just then, another massive crash rang out across the night, causing Jake to jump back into his bed and hide under the covers.

Write Now practice writing in the **Workbook.** page 49

Vocabulary: Suffixes -er and -or • Writing: Choosing a Good Title Unit 5 55

BIG QUESTION 3
Why do we wear masks?

Some actors wear masks to play roles.
Have you ever seen masks in a play? What was it like?

Summary

Objectives: To learn and practice listening, speaking, and writing strategies to facilitate effective communication.

Vocabulary: *actor, counselor, builder, painter, plumber, surveyor, inventor, trainer*

Listening strategy: Listening for instructions

Speaking: Finding the right word

Word Study: Suffixes *-er* and *-or*

Writing Study: Choosing a good title

Big Question learning point: *Actors wear masks to play characters.*

Materials: Discover Poster 3, Audio CD, Big Question Chart

Listening

Think

- Ask students to think about the question. Tell them to think about how it would feel to wear a mask. Ask *Would your facial expressions be the same or different? How might it affect how you speak? How would it look to the audience?* etc.
- After students have thought about the question on their own, put them into pairs to compare answers.
- Then hold a class discussion about wearing masks.

A Listen. Circle the correct answer. 1·33

- Have students read the sentences. Then ask *What are you listening for in this exercise?* Elicit *(for advice)*.
- Play the audio once and have students listen.
- Tell them to circle the correct answers.
- Play the audio again so they can check their work.

ANSWERS
1 always   2 facing   3 before   4 never   5 yourself

CRITICAL THINKING

- For each of the statements have students think about reasons why. Some of the reasons were stated in the audio, but some must be inferred.
- Put students into small groups to find a reason for each of the statements.

POSSIBLE ANSWERS
1 and 2 This helps the audience believe the character you become when the mask is on.
3, 4, and 5 You have to pretend the mask is your own face.

B Listen again. Circle the correct answer. 1·34

- Play the audio so students can complete the exercise.
- Have students compare answers with a partner before checking answers with the class.

ANSWERS
1 a   2 b   3 a

Speaking 🔘 1·35

C Learn: Finding the Right Word

- Read the *Learn* box with the class.
- Play the audio one time as students listen.
- Model the dialogue with a confident student in front of the class.
- Ask *What are the expressions we use when we can't remember what something is called?*
- Put students into pairs and tell them to describe an object to their partner.

Choose one of these objects and describe it to your partner. Ask him or her to help you name it in English.

COMMUNICATION

- Put students into pairs.
- Have them create short dialogues using the objects listed (a mask, an umbrella, a calendar).
- Have a few pairs act out their dialogues for the class.

Word Study

D Learn: Suffixes -er and -or

- Read the *Learn* box together.
- Elicit where suffixes occur in the words. Ask *Where do we find -er and -or suffixes? What do these suffixes do?*

Listen and say the words. Underline the verb in each word and circle the suffix. 🔘 1·36

ANSWERS

1 act(or) 2 counsel(or) 3 build(er) 4 paint(er)
5 plumb(er) 6 survey(or) 7 invent(or) 8 train(er)

DIFFERENTIATION

Below level:

- Say the words and have students repeat them.
- Go over the meanings of the words. Then elicit the verb in each and have students underline it before circling the ending.

At level:

- Have students do the activity individually. Then ask some students write the answers on the board.

Above level:

- Have students do the activity in pairs. One student says the word, and without looking at the book, the partner spells the word and says what to underline and what to circle. Then they switch roles.

Writing Study

E Learn: Choosing a Good Title

- Read the *Learn* box together.
- Ask *What does a good title do?*

CRITICAL THINKING

- Hold a class discussion about titles.
- Have students say some of their favorite titles of books, poems, songs, and movies. Write them on the board.
- Then ask the class to describe why these titles are appealing and what makes a title good.

Read the story and give it a title. Then compare your title with your partner's.

CREATIVITY

- Have students read the short story individually and think of a title.
- Have them write their titles. Then compare with a partner.
- Ask students to say their titles and write them on the board. Have the class choose the best title and say why it is good.

Write

- Direct students to the Workbook for further writing practice.

Big Question 3 Review

Why do we wear masks?

- Display **Discover Poster 3**. Discuss what you see.
- Refer to the learning points covered in Unit 5 that are written on the poster and have students explain how they relate to the different pictures.
- Return to the **Big Question Chart**.
- Ask students what they have learned about wearing masks while studying this unit.

> **Further practice**
> **Workbook pages 48–49**
> **Online Practice Unit 5 · Communicate**
> **Oxford iTools Unit 5 · Communicate**

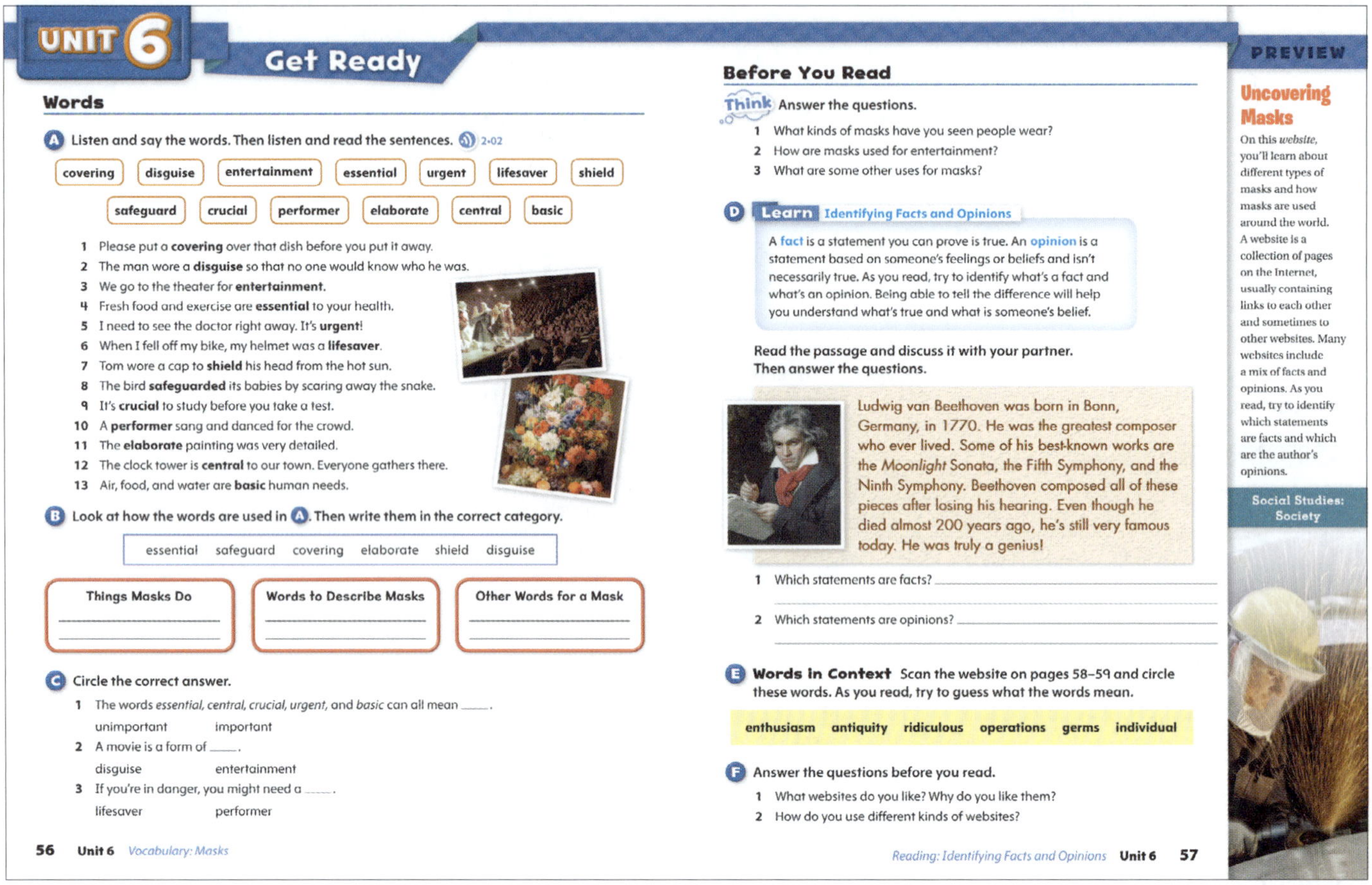

UNIT 6 Get Ready

Words

A Listen and say the words. Then listen and read the sentences. 2•02

covering | disguise | entertainment | essential | urgent | lifesaver | shield

safeguard | crucial | performer | elaborate | central | basic

1 Please put a **covering** over that dish before you put it away.
2 The man wore a **disguise** so that no one would know who he was.
3 We go to the theater for **entertainment**.
4 Fresh food and exercise are **essential** to your health.
5 I need to see the doctor right away. It's **urgent**!
6 When I fell off my bike, my helmet was a **lifesaver**.
7 Tom wore a cap to **shield** his head from the hot sun.
8 The bird **safeguarded** its babies by scaring away the snake.
9 It's **crucial** to study before you take a test.
10 A **performer** sang and danced for the crowd.
11 The **elaborate** painting was very detailed.
12 The clock tower is **central** to our town. Everyone gathers there.
13 Air, food, and water are **basic** human needs.

B Look at how the words are used in A. Then write them in the correct category.

essential   safeguard   covering   elaborate   shield   disguise

Things Masks Do	Words to Describe Masks	Other Words for a Mask

C Circle the correct answer.

1 The words *essential, central, crucial, urgent,* and *basic* can all mean _____.
    unimportant   important
2 A movie is a form of _____.
    disguise   entertainment
3 If you're in danger, you might need a _____.
    lifesaver   performer

56   Unit 6   *Vocabulary: Masks*

Before You Read

Think Answer the questions.
1 What kinds of masks have you seen people wear?
2 How are masks used for entertainment?
3 What are some other uses for masks?

D **Learn** Identifying Facts and Opinions

A **fact** is a statement you can prove is true. An **opinion** is a statement based on someone's feelings or beliefs and isn't necessarily true. As you read, try to identify what's a fact and what's an opinion. Being able to tell the difference will help you understand what's true and what is someone's belief.

Read the passage and discuss it with your partner. Then answer the questions.

> Ludwig van Beethoven was born in Bonn, Germany, in 1770. He was the greatest composer who ever lived. Some of his best-known works are the *Moonlight* Sonata, the Fifth Symphony, and the Ninth Symphony. Beethoven composed all of these pieces after losing his hearing. Even though he died almost 200 years ago, he's still very famous today. He was truly a genius!

1 Which statements are facts? _____
2 Which statements are opinions? _____

E **Words in Context** Scan the website on pages 58–59 and circle these words. As you read, try to guess what the words mean.

enthusiasm   antiquity   ridiculous   operations   germs   individual

F Answer the questions before you read.
1 What websites do you like? Why do you like them?
2 How do you use different kinds of websites?

Reading: Identifying Facts and Opinions   **Unit 6**   57

PREVIEW

Uncovering Masks

On this *website*, you'll learn about different types of masks and how masks are used around the world. A website is a collection of pages on the Internet, usually containing links to each other and sometimes to other websites. Many websites include a mix of facts and opinions. As you read, try to identify which statements are facts and which are the author's opinions.

Social Studies: Society

Summary

Objectives: To understand words about masks; to apply own experience and a reading strategy to help comprehension of a text.

Vocabulary: *covering, disguise, entertainment, essential, urgent, lifesaver, shield, safeguard, crucial, performer, elaborate, central, basic, enthusiasm, antiquity, ridiculous, operations, germs, individual*

Reading strategy: Identifying facts and opinions

Materials: Audio CD

Words

A Listen and say the words. Then listen and read the sentences. 2•02

- Play the audio. Ask students to point to the words as they hear them.
- Play the audio a second time and have students repeat the words when they hear them.
- Say the words out of order and have students race to point to them on the page.

B Look at how the words are used in A. Then write them in the correct category.

- Have students do the activity on their own and then compare answers with a partner.
- Check answers with the class.

ANSWERS
Things Masks Do: shield, safeguard
Words to Describe Masks: elaborate, essential
Other Words for a Mask: covering, disguise

COLLABORATIVE LEARNING

- Put students into pairs and tell them to use the new words in sentences.
- Go around the room and have pairs say some of their sentences for the class.

C Circle the correct answer.

- Have students read the part sentences and answer options.
- Put students into pairs and have them do the exercise.
- Check the answers with the class.

ANSWERS
1 important   2 entertainment   3 lifesaver

Before You Read

Think

- Have students read the questions and make notes about their answers individually.
- Ask the students to discuss their answers to the questions in small groups.
- Then share some of the answers with the class. List the answers on the board.

D Learn: Identifying Facts and Opinions

- Read the *Learn* box with the class.
- Go over an example to check understanding. Say *I was born in (name of town). I live in (name of current town). I am now the best teacher in the whole world!* Ask *What are the two facts? What is the opinion? Why isn't that true?*

Read the passage and discuss it with your partner. Then answer the questions.

- Have students read the text individually. Tell them to underline the facts and circle the opinions.
- Put students into pairs to talk about their answers.
- Then go over the answers with the class.

Facts: was born in Bonn, Germany in 1770; best-known works are *Moonlight* Sonata, Fifth Symphony, and Ninth Symphony; composed after losing all his hearing; died almost 200 years ago; still very famous today
Opinions: greatest composer who ever lived; truly a genius

CRITICAL THINKING

Ask the following questions to check understanding about the opinions:

- *Why isn't "greatest composer who ever lived" a fact?*
- *If Beethoven accomplished so much, why isn't calling him "a genius" a fact?*
- *If I don't believe Beethoven was born in 1770, does that make it is an opinion? Why or why not?*

E Words in Context: Scan the website on pages 58–59 and circle these words. As you read, try to guess what the words mean.

- Read each word and have the students follow your pronunciation.

DIFFERENTIATION

Below level:

- Have students read the text and find the words.
- For each word, go over the context with students and ask questions to help them arrive at the meaning, e.g. *"… started this site to share my enthusiasm with you." What does the writer want to do with enthusiasm?*
- Elicit an answer and then say *We know then enthusiasm is something we can share. What else does the writer say around the word?*
- Elicit *I've been collecting masks for years. I like decorative masks.* Ask *Is that something you can share? Collecting things and liking them? Ok, so what do you think "enthusiasm" could mean?*
- Put students into pairs and continue to go over the words in context in this way.

At level:

- Have students do the activity on their own.
- Then put students into pairs. Pairs go over the words together and talk about what they think the words mean.

Above level:

- Have students find the words on their own. Tell them to write simple definitions of what they think the words mean.
- Then put students into pairs to compare their definitions. See if students can substitute the words in context for their own definitions of other words.
- Students share some of their replacements with the class.

F Answer the questions before you read.

COMMUNICATION

- Have students think about their answers to the questions on their own.
- Have students ask and answer the questions in pairs.
- Then write the students' answers on the board.

Reading Preview

- Read the title of the unit's reading text.
- Have students silently read the content of the preview bar.
- Ask *What type of text is it?* Ask *Do websites have fact, opinion, or both?*
- Tell students to try to categorize the information in the text as fact or opinion as they read.

Further Practice
Workbook pages 50–51
Online Practice Unit 6 • Get Ready
Oxford iTools Unit 6 • Get Ready

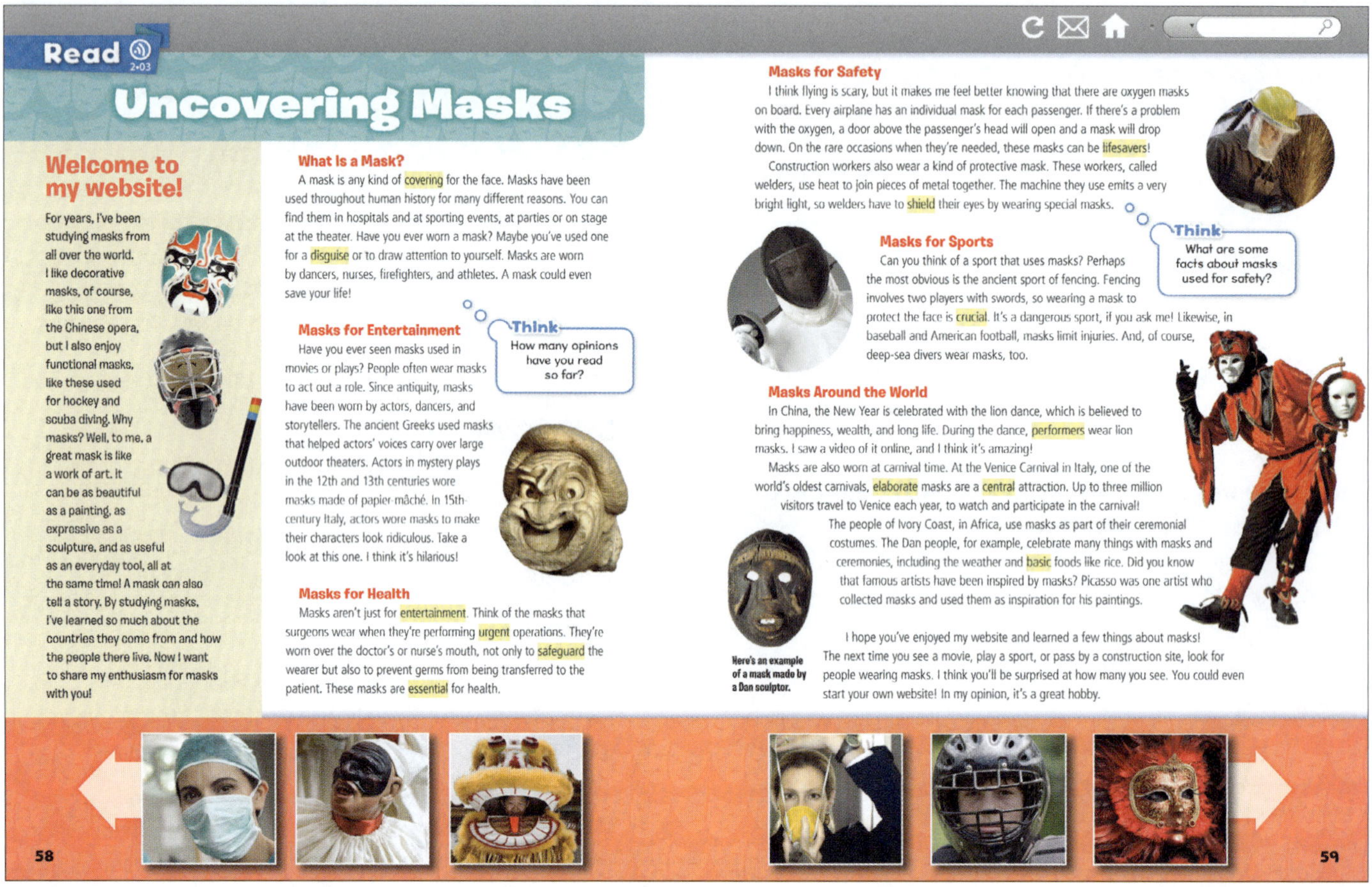

Read 2·03

Uncovering Masks

Welcome to my website!

For years, I've been studying masks from all over the world. I like decorative masks, of course, like this one from the Chinese opera, but I also enjoy functional masks, like these used for hockey and scuba diving. Why masks? Well, to me, a great mask is like a work of art. It can be as beautiful as a painting, as expressive as a sculpture, and as useful as an everyday tool, all at the same time! A mask can also tell a story. By studying masks, I've learned so much about the countries they come from and how the people there live. Now I want to share my enthusiasm for masks with you!

What Is a Mask?

A mask is any kind of covering for the face. Masks have been used throughout human history for many different reasons. You can find them in hospitals and at sporting events, at parties or on stage at the theater. Have you ever worn a mask? Maybe you've used one for a disguise or to draw attention to yourself. Masks are worn by dancers, nurses, firefighters, and athletes. A mask could even save your life!

Masks for Entertainment

Have you ever seen masks used in movies or plays? People often wear masks to act out a role. Since antiquity, masks have been worn by actors, dancers, and storytellers. The ancient Greeks used masks that helped actors' voices carry over large outdoor theaters. Actors in mystery plays in the 12th and 13th centuries wore masks made of papier-mâché. In 15th-century Italy, actors wore masks to make their characters look ridiculous. Take a look at this one. I think it's hilarious!

Think
How many opinions have you read so far?

Masks for Health

Masks aren't just for entertainment. Think of the masks that surgeons wear when they're performing urgent operations. They're worn over the doctor's or nurse's mouth, not only to safeguard the wearer but also to prevent germs from being transferred to the patient. These masks are essential for health.

Masks for Safety

I think flying is scary, but it makes me feel better knowing that there are oxygen masks on board. Every airplane has an individual mask for each passenger. If there's a problem with the oxygen, a door above the passenger's head will open and a mask will drop down. On the rare occasions when they're needed, these masks can be lifesavers!

Construction workers also wear a kind of protective mask. These workers, called welders, use heat to join pieces of metal together. The machine they use emits a very bright light, so welders have to shield their eyes by wearing special masks.

Think
What are some facts about masks used for safety?

Masks for Sports

Can you think of a sport that uses masks? Perhaps the most obvious is the ancient sport of fencing. Fencing involves two players with swords, so wearing a mask to protect the face is crucial. It's a dangerous sport, if you ask me! Likewise, in baseball and American football, masks limit injuries. And, of course, deep-sea divers wear masks, too.

Masks Around the World

In China, the New Year is celebrated with the lion dance, which is believed to bring happiness, wealth, and long life. During the dance, performers wear lion masks. I saw a video of it online, and I think it's amazing!

Masks are also worn at carnival time. At the Venice Carnival in Italy, one of the world's oldest carnivals, elaborate masks are a central attraction. Up to three million visitors travel to Venice each year, to watch and participate in the carnival!

The people of Ivory Coast, in Africa, use masks as part of their ceremonial costumes. The Dan people, for example, celebrate many things with masks and ceremonies, including the weather and basic foods like rice. Did you know that famous artists have been inspired by masks? Picasso was one artist who collected masks and used them as inspiration for his paintings.

Here's an example of a mask made by a Dan sculptor.

I hope you've enjoyed my website and learned a few things about masks! The next time you see a movie, play a sport, or pass by a construction site, look for people wearing masks. I think you'll be surprised at how many you see. You could even start your own website! In my opinion, it's a great hobby.

58　59

Summary

Objectives: To read, understand, and discuss a website; to apply a reading strategy to improve comprehension.

School subject: Social Studies: Society

Text type: Website text (nonfiction)

Reading strategy: Identifying facts and opinions

Big Question learning points: *Many people wear masks for health and safety reasons. Fencers wear masks to protect themselves. People around the world use masks for celebrations and ceremonies.*

Materials: Talk About It! Poster, Audio CD

Before Reading

- Read the title. Ask the class what they think it means to "uncover" masks.
- Have students point to the pictures and describe what they see.
- Read the headings. Ask the class what kind of text this is. Ask *What are two main categories of information in this text?*

CRITICAL THINKING

- With the class, go through the pictures and predict which ones belong to which subhead, e.g. the top photo of a Chinese opera mask is a mask for entertainment.

During Reading 2·03

- Ask a gist question to check overall understanding of the text, and allow students a few minutes to skim the text, e.g. *What is this website about?*
- Remind students that they should identify facts and opinions while they read and think about the *Think* boxes.
- Play the audio. Students listen as they read along.
- Play the audio a second time if necessary.

DIFFERENTIATION

Below level:

- Have students repeat after you as you read sections of the text aloud.
- Pause after each section to discuss the facts and opinions.

At level:

- Have students read the text silently to themselves as they listen to the audio.
- Then have pairs take turns reading different paragraphs aloud to each other.

Above level:

- Conduct a jigsaw reading. Copy the page and cut up each separate paragraph of text.
- Create the same amount of student groups as there are text paragraphs.
- Give each group of students a different paragraph.
- Tell each group to select a "secretary" who will write notes.
- Tell the group to summarize their paragraph in a few bullet points to help them remember the contents.

- Number off the students so that new groups can be formed with a representative student from each of the original groups.
- Tell the new groups that students will take turns summarizing the information in their text (not reading it aloud, but in their own words).
- Students write notes about each other's summaries.
- Disband the groups and have students work individually to read the text and compare their written notes with the paragraphs on the page.

CRITICAL THINKING

Discussion questions:
- *What are the main topics of this text?*
- *Where do you find masks?*
- *Can you name any additional masks for each category?*
- *What do you find interesting about masks?*
- *Which mask do think is the most useful or important? Why?*

After Reading

- Go over the *Think* boxes with the class.
- Read out the first *Think* box and ask students how many opinions they can find. Then ask *What is the opinion?*
- Ask the second *Think* box question and elicit answers.

COLLABORATIVE LEARNING

- Display the **Talk About It! Poster** to help students with sentence frames for discussion and expressing personal opinions.
- Put students into pairs to discuss what they find interesting about wearing masks.
- Ask students if they think differently about masks now. What did they think about masks before reading? What do they think now?

CULTURE NOTE

One more reason that people can wear masks is for intimidation. Masks cover the face, taking away from personal recognition. They can be made or decorated in such a way that they appear scary or threatening to others. A good example of this occurs in some sports. In American hockey and football, some players wear masks that not only have elaborate wire or grids added, but can also be painted into animal faces or with wild designs.

The same thing has occurred throughout history in warfare. Masks are often used on the battlefield. Where helmets cover the head, masks cover the face. From ancient times armies have worn masks that try to scare their opponents into losing their nerve before the battle even commences.

Further Practice
Workbook page 52
Online Practice Unit 6 • Read
Oxford **iTools** Unit 6 • Read

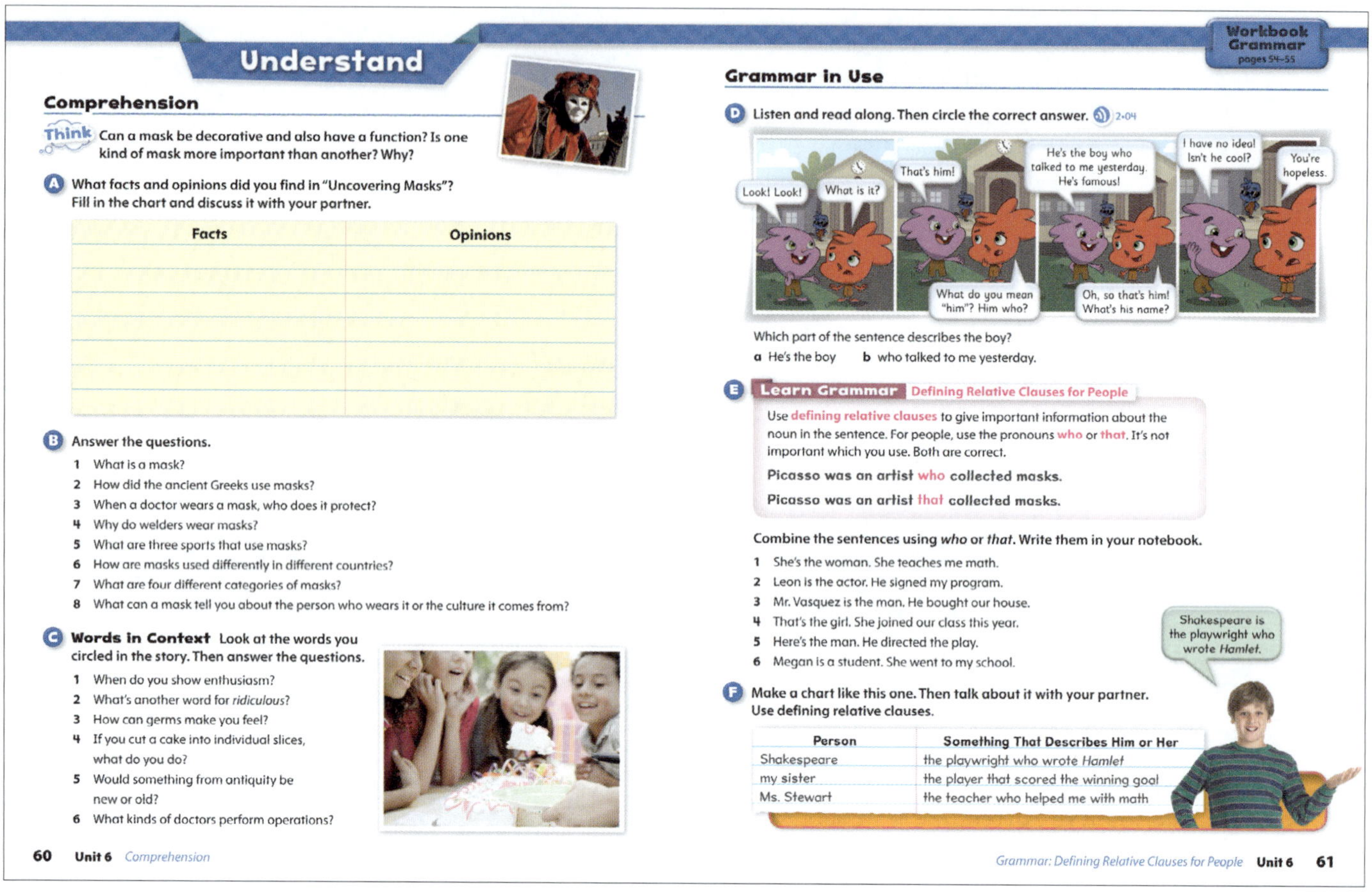

Understand

Comprehension

Think Can a mask be decorative and also have a function? Is one kind of mask more important than another? Why?

A What facts and opinions did you find in "Uncovering Masks"? Fill in the chart and discuss it with your partner.

Facts	Opinions

B Answer the questions.

1 What is a mask?
2 How did the ancient Greeks use masks?
3 When a doctor wears a mask, who does it protect?
4 Why do welders wear masks?
5 What are three sports that use masks?
6 How are masks used differently in different countries?
7 What are four different categories of masks?
8 What can a mask tell you about the person who wears it or the culture it comes from?

C **Words in Context** Look at the words you circled in the story. Then answer the questions.

1 When do you show enthusiasm?
2 What's another word for *ridiculous*?
3 How can germs make you feel?
4 If you cut a cake into individual slices, what do you do?
5 Would something from antiquity be new or old?
6 What kinds of doctors perform operations?

Grammar in Use

Workbook Grammar pages 54–55

D Listen and read along. Then circle the correct answer. 2•04

Look! Look! What is it? That's him! He's the boy who talked to me yesterday. He's famous! I have no idea! Isn't he cool? You're hopeless.

What do you mean "him"? Him who? Oh, so that's him! What's his name?

Which part of the sentence describes the boy?
a He's the boy   b who talked to me yesterday.

E **Learn Grammar** Defining Relative Clauses for People

Use **defining relative clauses** to give important information about the noun in the sentence. For people, use the pronouns **who** or **that**. It's not important which you use. Both are correct.

Picasso was an artist **who** collected masks.
Picasso was an artist **that** collected masks.

Combine the sentences using *who* or *that*. Write them in your notebook.

1 She's the woman. She teaches me math.
2 Leon is the actor. He signed my program.
3 Mr. Vasquez is the man. He bought our house.
4 That's the girl. She joined our class this year.
5 Here's the man. He directed the play.
6 Megan is a student. She went to my school.

Shakespeare is the playwright who wrote *Hamlet*.

F Make a chart like this one. Then talk about it with your partner. Use defining relative clauses.

Person	Something That Describes Him or Her
Shakespeare	the playwright who wrote *Hamlet*
my sister	the player that scored the winning goal
Ms. Stewart	the teacher who helped me with math

Summary

Objectives: To demonstrate understanding of a website; to understand the meaning and form of the grammar structure.

Reading: Comprehension

Grammar input: Defining relative clauses for people

Grammar practice: Workbook exercises

Grammar production: Defining relative clauses with *who* and *that*

Materials: Audio CD

Comprehension

Think

- Have students think about their answers individually first. Then hold a class discussion. Ask students for examples to support their opinions.

A What facts and opinions did you find in "Uncovering Masks"? Fill in the chart and discuss it with your partner.

- Ask students to reread the text on pages 58 and 59 on their own.
- Put them in pairs and ask them to fill in the chart together.

DIFFERENTIATION

Below level:

- Put students into mixed-ability pairs. Have the pairs read the text together and fill in the chart.
- Put students into groups of four. Have them compare and discuss their charts.

At level:

- Have students fill in their charts individually.
- Then have them discuss the charts with a partner.
- Have pairs tell the class about any facts or opinions they disagree on.

Above level:

- Have students fill in their charts individually.
- Then have them discuss their charts with a partner.
- Invite a few students to the board to complete the chart for the class to use to check their work.
- As the class checks the work together, have the students explain why facts and opinions are categorized as they are.

B Answer the questions.

- Have students refer back to the website text on pages 58 and 59 to answer the questions on their own.
- Then have students compare answers with a partner.

POSSIBLE ANSWERS

1 A mask is any kind of covering for the face.
2 The ancient Greeks used masks to help carry actors' voices out over the stage.
3 When a doctor wears a mask, it protects the doctor and the patient.

4 Welders wear masks to shield their eyes from bright light.

5 Three sports that use masks are: fencing, baseball, and American football.

6 Ceremonial masks are used in different countries in different ways: celebrating the weather and rice in Africa, celebrating the New Year in China, and at the Venice Carnival in Italy.

7 The four different categories of masks are: in hospitals, at sporting events, parties, and the theater.

8 A mask can tell you about a person's job, sports they play, or about the history and celebrations of a culture.

COLLABORATIVE LEARNING

- Put students into small groups.
- Have groups choose three of the mask pictures from pages 58 and 59. The masks should be from at least two different categories.
- Have groups discuss the uses of the three masks they chose and offer interpretations for what they think the masks say about the people and culture that use them, e.g. *Surgeons use masks with their patients. I think this shows that they are concerned for their patients. It also shows they are educated because they are aware of how germs spread.*
- Have groups present their ideas to the class.

C Words in Context: Look at the words you circled in the story. Then answer the questions.

- Have students use the words to complete the sentences. Tell them to go back and find the words in the text and to use the context clues to help them figure out the answers.
- Students compare answers with a partner.
- Check the answers with the class.

ANSWERS

1 You show enthusiasm when you like something.
2 *Hilarious* can be another word for *ridiculous.*
3 Germs can make you feel sick.
4 Cut it so that each person will get a slice.
5 It would be old.
6 Surgeons perform operations.

Grammar in Use

D Listen and read along. Then circle the correct answer. 2·04

- Listen to the dialogue once and then read it together as a class.
- Play the audio a second time if necessary.
- Check the answer with the class.

ANSWER

b who talked to me yesterday.

E Learn Grammar: Defining Relative Clauses for People

- Read the *Learn Grammar* box together.
- Read the first example sentence. Ask questions to check understanding:
  What does a defining relative clause do?
  What is the defining relative clause in the first sentence?
  Who does this clause define?
  Can we replace "who" with "that"?
- Then have the class read the sentence with *that.*

Combine the sentences using *who* or *that.* Write them in your notebook.

- Read the first sentence together. Have the class identify the defining relative clause. Elicit how to combine the sentences, e.g. *She's the woman who / that teaches me math.*
- Then have students complete the rest on their own.

ANSWERS

1 She's the woman who / that teaches me math.
2 Leon is the actor who / that signed my program.
3 Mr. Vasquez is the man who / that bought our house.
4 That's the girl who / that joined our class this year.
5 Here's the man who / that directed the play.
6 Megan is a student who / that went to my school.

CRITICAL THINKING

- Put students into pairs.
- Ask them what pronoun they would use if they were writing a relative defining clause about a noun that wasn't a person. How would they combine, e.g. *These are Picasso's paintings. They were inspired by masks.*
- Have pairs share their answers with the class. *These are Picasso's paintings that were inspired by masks.* Explain that we wouldn't use the pronoun *who* with a non-human.

F Make a chart like this one. Then talk about it with your partner. Use defining relative clauses.

- Put students into pairs. Model how to do the activity.
- Then have students take turns asking and answering the questions.

DIFFERENTIATION

Below level:

- Help students think of people to write about and facts to write about them. Brainstorm and write ideas on the board.
- Put students into mixed-ability pairs to fill out the chart and then talk about it with a partner. Have students share their sentences with the class.

At level:

- Have students write their charts.
- Then have students tell their partner their sentences. The partner writes the sentences down.
- Then pairs check each other's work.

Above level:

- Brainstorm four famous people with the students and write them on the board. Have all the students write something about any or all of the four people.
- Then students circulate and say their sentences to as many classmates as they can in three minutes. Students try to find as many classmates as they can who have similar descriptions of the same person.
- Ask students to tell the class some of their sentences.

Workbook Grammar

- Direct students to the Workbook for further practice.

Further practice
Workbook pages 53–55
Online Practice Unit 6 • Understand
Oxford **iTools** Unit 6 • Understand

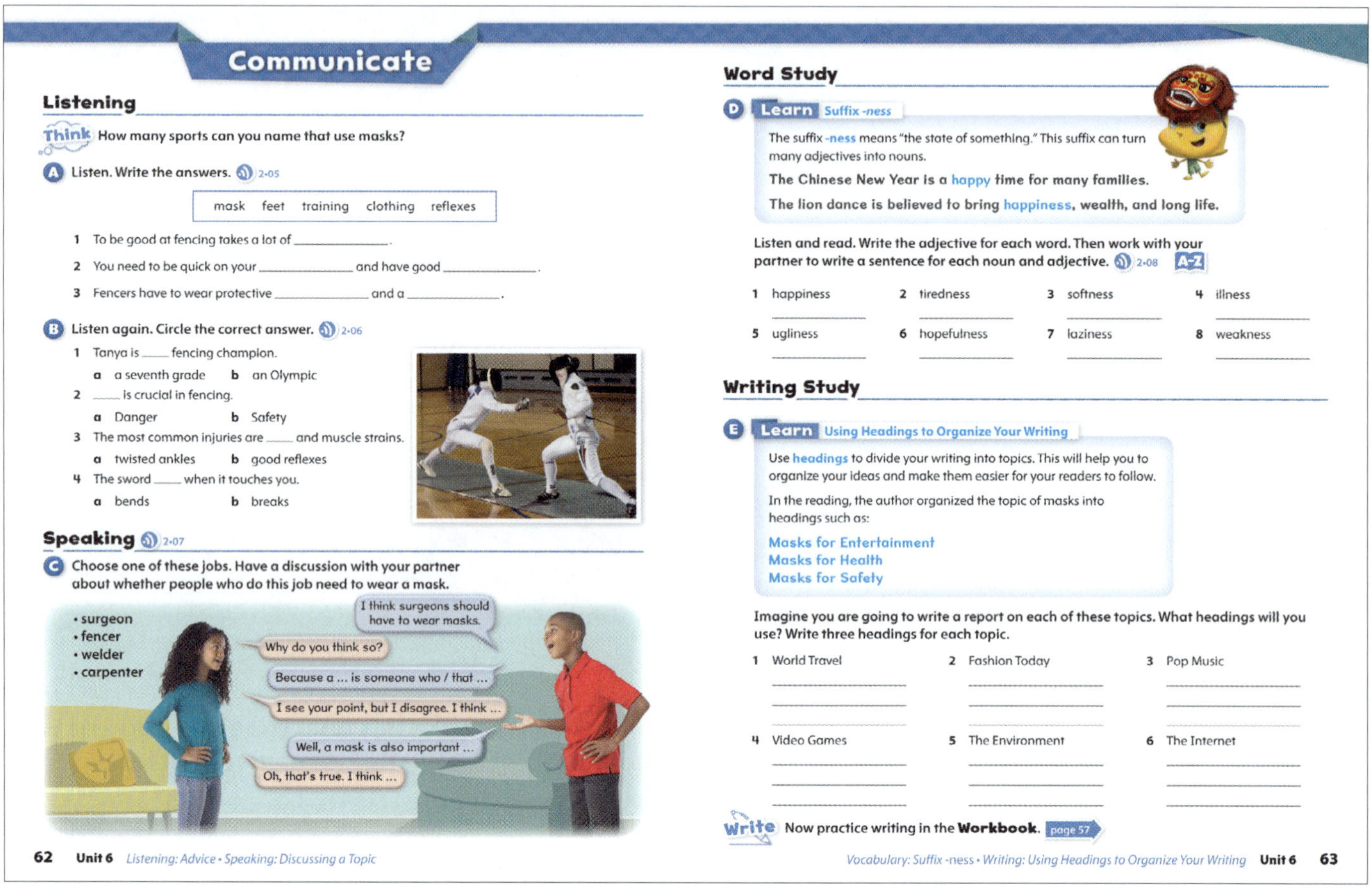

Communicate

Listening

Think How many sports can you name that use masks?

A Listen. Write the answers. 2·05

> mask   feet   training   clothing   reflexes

1 To be good at fencing takes a lot of _____.
2 You need to be quick on your _____ and have good _____.
3 Fencers have to wear protective _____ and a _____.

B Listen again. Circle the correct answer. 2·06
1 Tanya is ____ fencing champion.
  a a seventh grade b an Olympic
2 ____ is crucial in fencing.
  a Danger b Safety
3 The most common injuries are ____ and muscle strains.
  a twisted ankles b good reflexes
4 The sword ____ when it touches you.
  a bends b breaks

Speaking 2·07

C Choose one of these jobs. Have a discussion with your partner about whether people who do this job need to wear a mask.

- surgeon
- fencer
- welder
- carpenter

I think surgeons should have to wear masks.
Why do you think so?
Because a ... is someone who / that ...
I see your point, but I disagree. I think ...
Well, a mask is also important ...
Oh, that's true. I think ...

62 Unit 6 *Listening: Advice • Speaking: Discussing a Topic*

Word Study

D Learn **Suffix -ness**

The suffix **-ness** means "the state of something." This suffix can turn many adjectives into nouns.
The Chinese New Year is a **happy** time for many families.
The lion dance is believed to bring **happiness**, wealth, and long life.

Listen and read. Write the adjective for each word. Then work with your partner to write a sentence for each noun and adjective. 2·08 **A–Z**

1 happiness   2 tiredness   3 softness   4 illness
5 ugliness   6 hopefulness   7 laziness   8 weakness

Writing Study

E Learn **Using Headings to Organize Your Writing**

Use **headings** to divide your writing into topics. This will help you to organize your ideas and make them easier for your readers to follow.
In the reading, the author organized the topic of masks into headings such as:

Masks for Entertainment
Masks for Health
Masks for Safety

Imagine you are going to write a report on each of these topics. What headings will you use? Write three headings for each topic.

1 World Travel   2 Fashion Today   3 Pop Music
4 Video Games   5 The Environment   6 The Internet

Write Now practice writing in the **Workbook**. page 57

Vocabulary: Suffix -ness • Writing: Using Headings to Organize Your Writing Unit 6 63

Summary

Objectives: To learn and practice listening, speaking, and writing strategies to facilitate effective communication.

Vocabulary: *happy, happiness, tired, tiredness, soft, softness, ill, illness, ugly, ugliness, hopeful, hopefulness, lazy, laziness, weak, weakness*

Listening strategy: Listening for advice

Speaking: Discussing a topic

Word Study: Suffix *-ness*

Writing Study: Using headings to organize your writing

Big Question learning point: *Fencers wear masks to protect themselves.*

Materials: Audio CD

Listening

Think

- Tell students to think individually about how many sports they can think of where masks are used.
- Have students share their ideas with a partner.
- Have students tell the class their sports and write them on the board.

A Listen. Write the answers. 2·05

- Have students read the words in the box and then listen for them.
- Play the audio once and have students listen. Ask *What is the purpose of this selection?*
- Have students complete the activity.
- Then play the audio again so they can check their work.

ANSWERS
1 training 2 feet, reflexes 3 clothing, mask

B Listen again. Circle the correct answer. 2·06

- Play the audio so students can complete the exercise.
- Check the answers with the class.

ANSWERS
1 b 2 b 3 a 4 a

CRITICAL THINKING

After checking the answers, ask additional questions:
- *What sport did Tanya mention she wasn't good at?*
- *When did she see the sign to join the fencing team?*
- *How does Tanya say you'd feel after a lot of training?*
- *What does the sword feel like when it touches you?*
- *Would you like to try fencing?*

Speaking 🔘 2·07

C Choose one of these jobs. Have a discussion with your partner about whether people who do this job need to wear a mask.

COMMUNICATION

- Read the directions. Then play the audio and have students listen.
- Divide the class in half and assign a role to each half. Play the audio again and pause so students can repeat their parts. Then switch roles.
- Model the example with a volunteer (*I think surgeons …*). Then model it a second time using a different example (*I think welders …*) and a different student.
- Put students into pairs to have a discussion. Tell them to switch topics and roles and discuss again. Go around and help as needed.
- Have a few pairs discuss for the class.

Word Study

D Learn: Suffix -ness

- Read the *Learn* box together.
- Read the examples. Then say *Happiness is the state of being happy.* So, we could say the second sentence as: *The Lion Dance is believed to bring the state of being happy, wealth, and long life.*

Listen and read. Write the adjective for each word. Then work with your partner to write a sentence for each noun and adjective. 🔘 2·08

- Play the audio and have students read the words.
- Play the audio again and have students repeat.
- Then students write the words.

ANSWERS
1 happy / happiness   2 tired / tiredness
3 soft / softness   4 ill / illness   5 ugly / ugliness
6 hopeful / hopefulness   7 lazy / laziness
8 weak / weakness

COLLABORATIVE LEARNING

- Have partners work in pairs to write sentences for each noun and adjective. Allow them to use a dictionary to help.
- Have pairs check each other's work.
- Then have some pairs say their sentences and write them on the board.

Writing Study

E Learn: Using Headings to Organize Your Writing

- Read the *Learn* box together.
- Read the headings. Draw a graphic organizer on the board. Draw a box at the top labeled *Masks*. Under it, draw three separate boxes, labeled: *Masks for Entertainment, Masks for Health, Masks for Safety.* Explain *These are the headings. Under them you would write the details, such as "Ancient Greek."*

Imagine you are going to write a report on each of these topics. What headings will you use? Write three headings for each topic.

- Go over the first one with the class. Say *What topics would you include on a paper on world travel?*
- Brainstorm and elicit answers from the class, e.g. *Places to go; when to go; getting there.*
- Have students complete the exercise on their own. Then go over answers with the class and write examples on the board.

POSSIBLE ANSWERS
1 World Travel: Places to go, when to go, getting there
2 Fashion Today: Top designers, current trends, street fashion
3 Pop Music: hit songs, hot bands, popular festivals
4 Video Games: multi-player, exciting action, games for girls
5 The Environment: Earth, water, air
6 The Internet: invention of, websites, social media revolution

DIFFERENTIATION

Below level:

- Put students into small mixed-ability groups.
- Have groups discuss and brainstorm headings for each topic.
- Then have students help each other to fill out the charts.
- Have students say their ideas as you write them on the board.

At level:

- Have students fill out the charts in pairs.
- Then put students into small groups. Have pairs compare their charts with the group. Then pairs make any revisions to their charts.
- Have pairs share some of their charts with the class.

Above level:

- Have students fill out the charts individually.
- Ask them to discuss their ideas with a partner. Then students add two to three examples for each heading.
- Have students write them on the board.

Write

- Direct students to the Workbook for further writing practice.

Further practice
Workbook pages 56–57
Online Practice Unit 6 · Communicate
Oxford **iTools** Unit 6 · Communicate

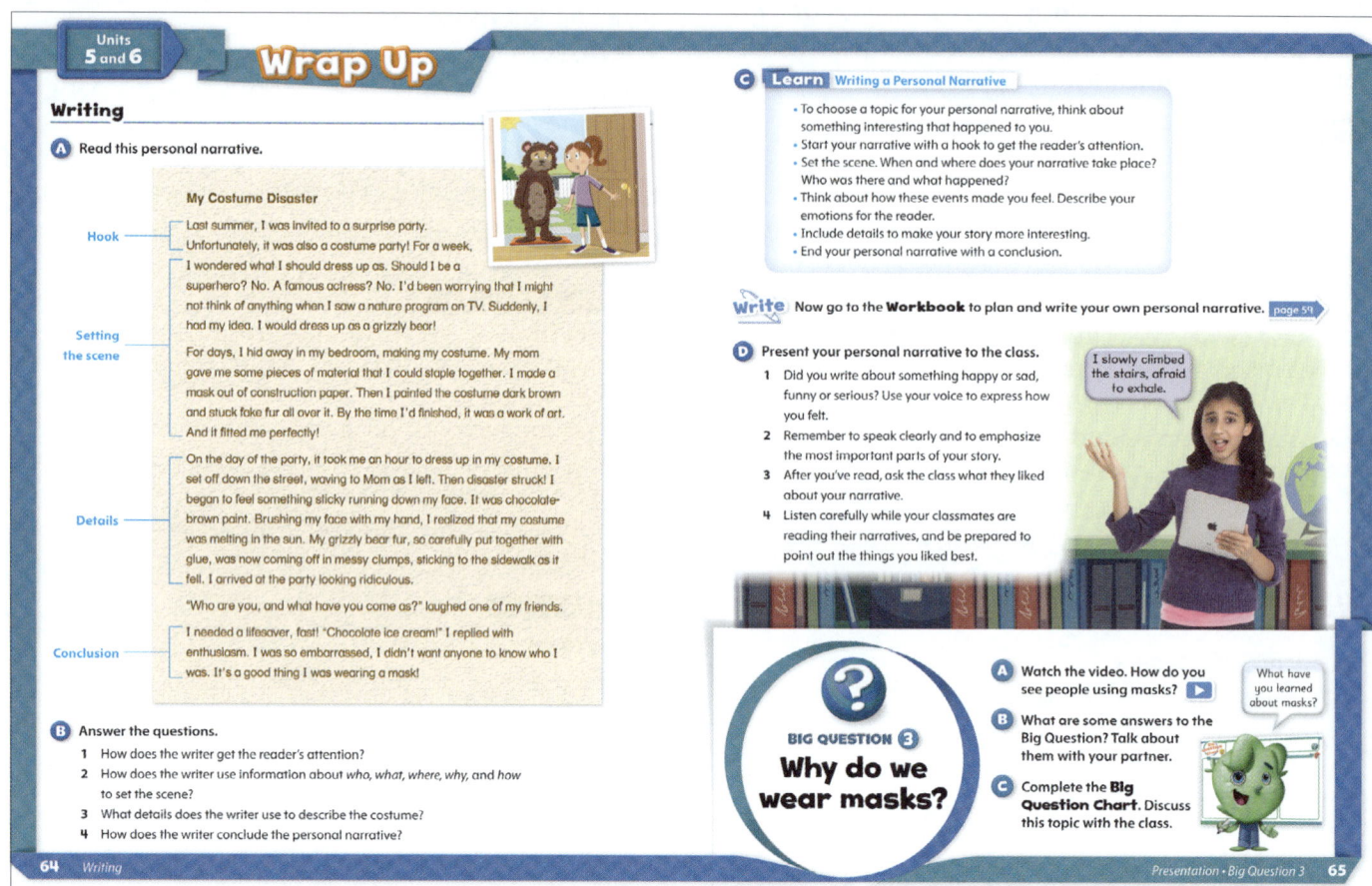

Summary

Objectives: To show what students have learned about the language and learning points of Units 5 and 6.

Reading: Comprehension of a personal narrative

Writing: Writing a personal narrative

Speaking: Sharing a personal narrative

Big Question learning point: *A mask can be part of a costume or disguise.*

Materials: Big Question DVD, Discover Poster 3, Talk About It! Poster, Big Question Chart

Writing

A Read this personal narrative.

- Ask *What is a personal narrative?* Elicit answers, e.g. "*Personal" means it is about a person, told from their point of view. "Narrative" means a story. So it's a person's story.*
- Go over the structure of each section of the narrative before reading. Say *A "hook" is an interesting opening, something that will catch the reader's attention and "hook" them in to reading more.*
- Explain *The setting is where the story takes place and when it happens. The scene is what happens, who is there, how you feel, and why you feel like that. This helps the reader imagine the world of the story.*
- Say *"Details" are specific information that makes the story alive. Finally the conclusion completes the story.*
- Read the narrative with the class one time. Then have students read it one time on their own.

B Answer the questions.

- Have students find the answers in the text.
- Ask this question to check comprehension *Why did the writer say the costume was chocolate ice cream?*
- Check answers with the class.

ANSWERS

1 The writer catches the reader's attention by using a "hook". The title is interesting and makes us wonder what the story will be about.
2 The writer tells us: who (I), when (last summer), what and how (working hard to make a costume).
3 The details are: what it is made of (material stapled together and a construction paper mask), how it is made: (painted and with fur stuck to it) and how it fits: perfectly.
4 The writer concludes the narrative by explaining he or she was so embarrassed it was good to be wearing a mask.

C Learn: Writing a Personal Narrative

- Read the *Learn* box together.
- Explain that students should follow these guidelines when they plan and write their personal narratives.

CRITICAL THINKING

Have students go back to the model to see how the writer addressed each requirement. Ask:

- *How does a hook catch the reader's attention?*
- *What details at the end explain why the writer feels a certain way?*
- *Do you think calling the costume "chocolate ice cream" was a good idea?*

Write

- Direct students to the Workbook to plan and write their own personal narrative.

CREATIVITY

- Elicit some ideas from the class about personal stories they can write about, e.g. the time they got a new baby brother or sister, a new pet, the first day of school, etc.
- Write some examples on the board.

DIFFERENTIATION

Below level:

- Go over the Workbook (page 59), part A organizer step by step with the students.
- Go around and help students work individually to craft a good hook, including important elements to set the scene. Remind students to list three details that are rich in setting and emotion, and finally a clever conclusion. Share successful examples to model what to do for other students.
- Then put students into mixed-ability pairs to discuss their organizers.

At level:

- Have students work on their Workbook organizers individually.
- Then have students discuss their organizers with a partner. Partners should offer helpful suggestions to improve the story. Students then revise their organizers.
- Share a few organizers with the class.

Above level:

- Have students complete their Workbook organizer individually. Then students share their organizers with a partner who gives suggestions.
- Have students continue to through steps B–C. For step D, have students read each other's narrative and apply the Writing Checklist.

D Present your personal narrative to the class.

- Read the Writing Checklist with the class.
- Give students time to practice reading their narratives to themselves.
- Have students take turns presenting their narratives to the class. Ensure they follow the tips list.
- After each narrative, the class points out things they like best.

COLLABORATIVE LEARNING

- Put students into small groups.
- Explain that they will read each other's narratives, not their own, aloud. This will help the student who wrote the narrative hear it from a different perspective and it will help students practice reading dramatically without feeling nervous about what they wrote.
- Have students trade narratives with another student. They should read the narrative to themselves, and ask the author any questions.
- Then have students practice their reading, focusing on tone of voice and gestures in small groups. Have the group say what they liked.
- This can also be done where the narratives are handed out anonymously and the group guesses who the author is. In that case, any questions during preparation should be asked to the teacher, not the author.

Units 5 and 6 Big Question Review

A Watch the video. How do you see people using masks? ▷

- Play the video and when it is finished ask students what they know about wearing masks now.
- Have students share ideas with the class.

B What are some answers to the Big Question? Talk about them with your partner.

COMMUNICATION

- Display **Discover Poster 3**. Point to familiar vocabulary items and elicit them from the class. Ask *What is this?*
- Ask students *What do you see?* Ask *What does that mean?*
- Refer to all of the learning points written on the poster and have students explain how they relate to the different pictures.
- Ask *What does this learning point mean?* Elicit answers from individual students.
- Display the **Talk About It! Poster** to help students with sentence frames for discussion of the learning points and for expressing their opinions.

C Complete the Big Question Chart. Discuss this topic with the class.

- Ask students what they have learned about wearing masks while studying this unit.
- Put students into pairs or small groups to say two new things they have learned.
- Have students share their ideas with the class and add their ideas to the chart.
- Have students complete the chart in their Workbook.

Further practice
Workbook pages 58–60
Online Practice • Wrap Up 3
Oxford **iTools** • Wrap Up 3

Testing Practice

Testing Practice 1 pages 66–67

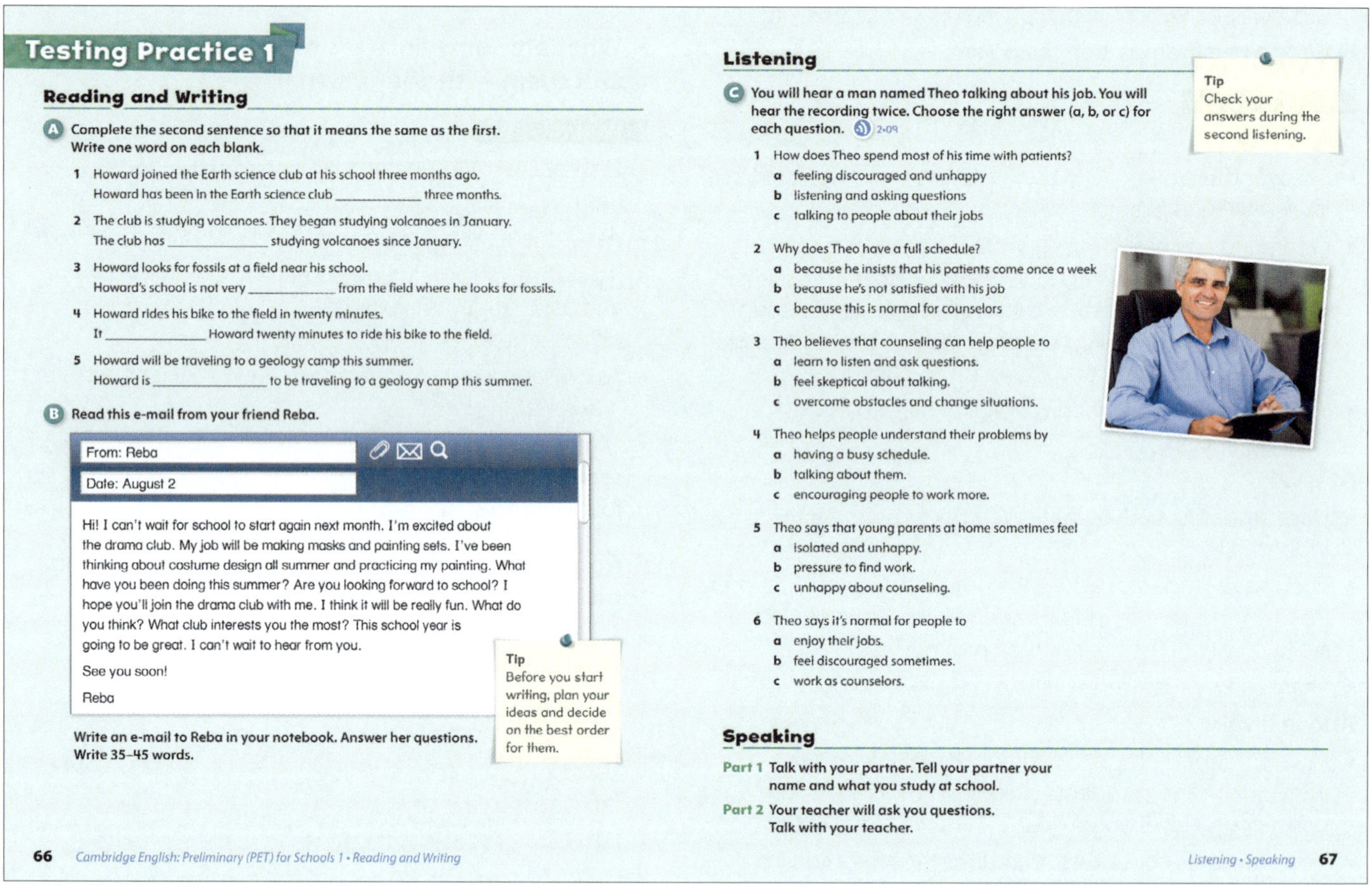

Reading and Writing

A Complete the second sentence so that it means the same as the first. Write one word on each blank.

- Read the instructions with the class and then read the sentences.
- Explain that students will choose a word so that the second sentence will have the same meaning as the first sentence.
- Remind students these words will be words that they have studied.

ANSWERS

1 for   2 been   3 far   4 takes   5 going

B Read this e-mail from your friend Reba.

- Have students read the e-mail individually.
- Ask *What questions did Reba ask you in the e-mail?*

Write an e-mail to Reba in your notebook. Answer her questions. Write 35–45 words.

COMMUNICATION

- Explain that students should write an e-mail to Reba.
- Read the *Tip* box with the class.
- Ask *What will you write about?* Elicit (*answer Reba's questions*).
- Ask *How does an e-mail start and end?* Elicit (*date, salutation, closing, your name*).

SAMPLE ANSWER

Date: August 3
Hi Reba! I have been swimming all summer. I'm looking forward to school, too. I might join the drama club with you. I'd like to try acting. I like the idea of the film club. Maybe we can join that together?
Bye!
(Name)

Listening

C You will hear a man named Theo talking about his job. You will hear the recording twice. Choose the right answer (a, b, or c) for each question. 🔘 2·09

- Have students discuss the questions in small groups, and then with the class.
- Read the *Tip* box with the class. Ask students *When will you mark your answers? The first or second listening? When will you check your answers?*
- After the listening is finished, discuss with students why they decided upon the answers they marked and what information they used to help them decide.
- Check the answers with the class.

ANSWERS

1 b 2 a 3 c 4 b 5 a 6 b

Speaking

Part 1 Talk with your partner. Tell your partner your name and what you study at school.

- Read the instructions with the class.
- Model a conversation with a confident student:
  T: *Hello, My name is (name). What is your name?*
  S: *My name is (name).*
  T: *How do you spell that?* Student spells name.
  S: *How do you spell your name?*
  T: *My name is spelled* (Spell name).
- Put students into pairs to talk about their names and how to spell them.
- Go around and check that students are following the instructions correctly.

DIFFERENTIATION

Below level:

- Write sentence frames on the board for students to use to do the activity:
  Q: *What is your name?*
  A: *My name is _____.*
  Q: *How do you spell that?*
  A: *It's spelled (_ _ _ _).*
  Q: *How do you spell your name?*
  A: *My name is spelled (_ _ _ _ _).*

At level:

- Have students do the activity.

Above level:

- Tell students to ask more questions, such as *Where do you live? What do you like to do?*

Part 2 Your teacher will ask you questions. Talk with your teacher.

COMMUNICATION

- Speak with students individually. Ask them how they spell their names. Ask questions like these:
  How do you make a greeting card / model / ice cream sundae / write a story?
- Have the student describe the steps to you.
- Tell the students you will describe something and they will help you remember what it's called in English, e.g. *What is that thing called? It looks like a mountain.* (a hill? a cliff?) *No, it's not that. It's more like a mountain, but it's very hot inside …* (a volcano?) *That's it!*
- Ask a question and have the students answer and support his or her opinion. Ask *Do you think a sick person should have to wear a face mask? Why do you think that?*

Units 7 and 8

Why do we like symmetry?

In units 7 and 8 you will:

WATCH a video about symmetry.

LEARN how symmetry can be beautiful and useful.

READ about types of symmetry and a girl who studies them.

WRITE a response to a story.

PRESENT your response to the class.

BIG QUESTION 4

Why do we like symmetry?

A Watch the video. Then talk about it with your partner. ▶

B Look at the picture and discuss it with your class.

1 Where can you see symmetry?
2 Why do you think this building is symmetrical?

C Think and answer the questions.

1 What is symmetry?
2 Where can you see symmetry?
3 Do you like the way symmetrical things look? Why or why not?
4 How is symmetry useful?

D Discuss this topic with your class. Fill out the **Big Question Chart**.

What do you know about symmetry? What do you want to know?

68 *Big Question 4*

69

Reading Strategies
Students will practice:
- Classifying and categorizing
- Paraphrasing

Review
Students will review the language and Big Question learning points of Units 7 and 8 through:
- Writing a personal response

Writing Study
Students will use and understand:
- Writing numbers as words
- Prepositional phrases of place

Students will:
- Write a personal response

Vocabulary
Students will understand and use words about:
- Symmetry, scientific study

Units 7 and 8
Why do we like symmetry?
Students will understand the Big Question learning points:
- Repetition makes symmetry both beautiful and practical.
- Symmetrical things are more balanced and easier to use.
- Things that are symmetrical can have a special beauty.
- Symmetry helps us understand how the world works.

Word Study
Students will understand and use:
- Latin roots
- Adjectives with *-ed* and *-ing*

Grammar
Students will understand and use:
- Defining relative clauses for objects and places
- Defining relative clauses with *whose*

Listening Strategies
Students will practice:
- Listening for reasons
- Listening for gist

Speaking
Students will understand and use expressions for:
- Asking for clarification
- Describing something you like

Units 7 and 8 Big Question page 68

Summary

Objectives: To activate students' existing knowledge of the topic and identify what they would like to learn about the topic.

Materials: Big Question DVD, Discover Poster 4, Big Question Chart

Introducing the topic

- Read out the Big Question. Ask *Why do we like symmetry?*
- Write students' ideas on the board and discuss.

A Watch the video. Then talk about it with your partner. ▷

- Play the video and when it is finished ask students to answer the following questions in pairs:
  What do you see in the video?
  What is happening?
  Who do you think the people are?
  What do you like about the video?
- Have individual students share their answers with the class.

B Look at the picture and discuss it with your class.

COMMUNICATION

- Students look at the big picture and talk about it. Ask *What do you see?*
- Ask additional questions:
  Do you know where this building is?
  Would you like to look around this building?
  Why or why not?
  What do you like or dislike about the looking of the building?

C Think and answer the questions.

- Have students discuss the questions in small groups, and then with the class.

DIFFERENTIATION

Below level:

- Go over the questions with the class, leading the discussion. Elicit examples for each question.
- Write a definition for *symmetry* on the board. List places where symmetry can be found.
- Elicit examples of things that are symmetrical and things that aren't. Elicit examples of how symmetry is useful, e.g. making furniture the same on both sides.

At level:

- Put students into small groups.
- Have groups make notes about their answers to the questions.
- Groups should think of two examples to support each of their answers. Then share the answers with the class.

Above level:

- Put students into small groups to list as many examples of things that are symmetrical as they can think of.
- Have groups share their lists with the class. Make notes on the board.

Expanding the topic

COLLABORATIVE LEARNING

- Display **Discover Poster 4** and give students enough time to look at the pictures.
- Get students to talk about things you think they will know by pointing to different things in the pictures and asking *What's this? What does this do?*
- Put students into small groups of three or four. Have each group choose a picture that they find interesting.
- Ask each group to say five sentences about their picture.
- Have one person from each group stand up and read out the sentences they chose for their picture.
- Ask the class if they can add any more.

CRITICAL THINKING

- Keep students in their groups. Ask each group to think about one question for each picture on the poster. Ask *What do you want to know about each picture? What are you curious about?*
- Have students say their questions and write them on the board.

D Discuss this topic with your class. Fill out the Big Question Chart.

- Display the **Big Question Chart**.
- Ask the class *What do you know about symmetry? What do you want to know about symmetry?*
- Ask students to write what they know and what they want to know in their Workbooks.
- Write a collection of ideas on the **Big Question Chart**.

Discover Poster 4

1 A view of the Brooklyn Bridge in New York City; 2 A man lifting a symmetrical barbell; 3 A cross section of a nautilus shell, showing rotational symmetry; 4 A girl examining a sugar crystal under a microscope

> **Further Practice**
> **Workbook page 62**
> **Online Practice • Big Question 4**
> **Oxford iTools • Big Question 4**

Student Page

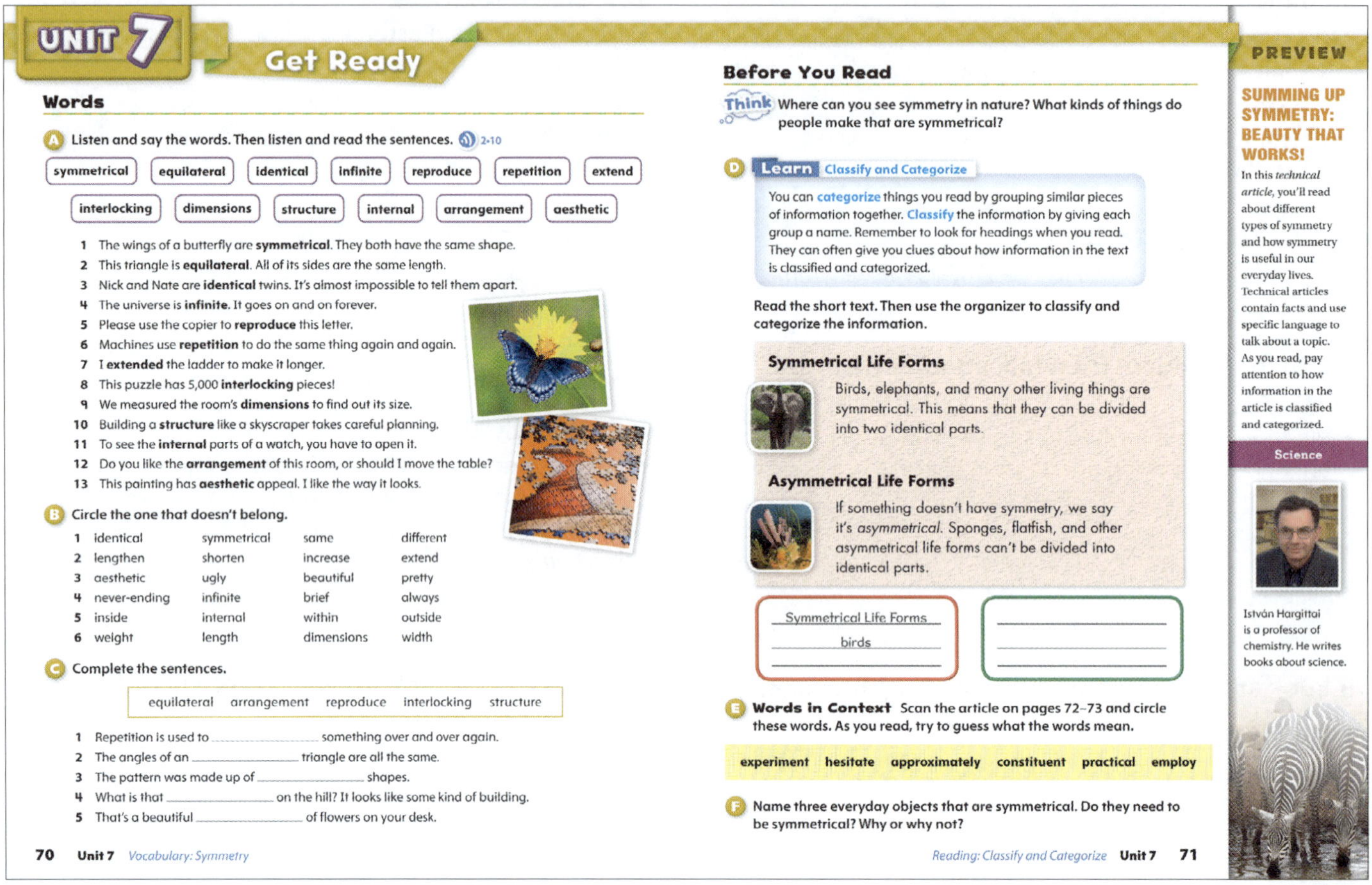

UNIT 7 Get Ready

Words

A Listen and say the words. Then listen and read the sentences. 2·10

symmetrical | equilateral | identical | infinite | reproduce | repetition | extend
interlocking | dimensions | structure | internal | arrangement | aesthetic

1 The wings of a butterfly are **symmetrical**. They both have the same shape.
2 This triangle is **equilateral**. All of its sides are the same length.
3 Nick and Nate are **identical** twins. It's almost impossible to tell them apart.
4 The universe is **infinite**. It goes on and on forever.
5 Please use the copier to **reproduce** this letter.
6 Machines use **repetition** to do the same thing again and again.
7 I **extended** the ladder to make it longer.
8 This puzzle has 5,000 **interlocking** pieces!
9 We measured the room's **dimensions** to find out its size.
10 Building a **structure** like a skyscraper takes careful planning.
11 To see the **internal** parts of a watch, you have to open it.
12 Do you like the **arrangement** of this room, or should I move the table?
13 This painting has **aesthetic** appeal. I like the way it looks.

B Circle the one that doesn't belong.

1 identical | symmetrical | same | different
2 lengthen | shorten | increase | extend
3 aesthetic | ugly | beautiful | pretty
4 never-ending | infinite | brief | always
5 inside | internal | within | outside
6 weight | length | dimensions | width

C Complete the sentences.

equilateral arrangement reproduce interlocking structure

1 Repetition is used to _____ something over and over again.
2 The angles of an _____ triangle are all the same.
3 The pattern was made up of _____ shapes.
4 What is that _____ on the hill? It looks like some kind of building.
5 That's a beautiful _____ of flowers on your desk.

70 Unit 7 *Vocabulary: Symmetry*

Before You Read

Think Where can you see symmetry in nature? What kinds of things do people make that are symmetrical?

D Learn Classify and Categorize

You can **categorize** things you read by grouping similar pieces of information together. **Classify** the information by giving each group a name. Remember to look for headings when you read. They can often give you clues about how information in the text is classified and categorized.

Read the short text. Then use the organizer to classify and categorize the information.

Symmetrical Life Forms
Birds, elephants, and many other living things are symmetrical. This means that they can be divided into two identical parts.

Asymmetrical Life Forms
If something doesn't have symmetry, we say it's *asymmetrical*. Sponges, flatfish, and other asymmetrical life forms can't be divided into identical parts.

Symmetrical Life Forms
birds
_____

_____

E Words in Context Scan the article on pages 72–73 and circle these words. As you read, try to guess what the words mean.

experiment hesitate approximately constituent practical employ

F Name three everyday objects that are symmetrical. Do they need to be symmetrical? Why or why not?

Reading: Classify and Categorize Unit 7 71

PREVIEW

SUMMING UP SYMMETRY: BEAUTY THAT WORKS!

In this *technical article*, you'll read about different types of symmetry and how symmetry is useful in our everyday lives. Technical articles contain facts and use specific language to talk about a topic. As you read, pay attention to how information in the article is classified and categorized.

Science

István Hargittai is a professor of chemistry. He writes books about science.

Summary

Objectives: To understand words about symmetry; to apply own experience and a reading strategy to help comprehension of a text.

Vocabulary: *symmetrical, equilateral, identical, infinite, reproduce, repetition, extend, interlocking, dimensions, structure, internal, arrangement, aesthetic, experiment, hesitate, approximately, constituent, practical, employ*

Reading strategy: Classifying and categorizing

Materials: Audio CD

Words

A Listen and say the words. Then listen and read the sentences. 2·10

- Play the audio. Ask students to point to the words and repeat the words when they hear them.
- Have students listen and read the sentences as they hear them.
- Say the sentence numbers out of order and have the class read the sentences aloud.

CRITICAL THINKING

- Put students into mixed-ability groups.
- Have groups read through each sentence and discuss the meaning of the new words based on the context of the sentences.
- Have students categorize each word as a noun, verb, or adjective.

- For any new words the group can't figure out from the context of the sentences, have them look up the definition in the dictionary.
- For each word, have groups say the definition and category.

B Circle the one that doesn't belong.

- Have students do the activity on their own.
- Have students compare their answers with a partner.
- Check answers with the class.

ANSWERS
1 different 2 shorten 3 ugly 4 brief 5 outside
6 weight

C Complete the sentences.

- Have students do the activity on their own.
- Have students compare their answers with a partner.
- Check answers with the class.

ANSWERS
1 reproduce 2 equilateral 3 interlocking
4 structure 5 arrangement

COLLABORATIVE LEARNING

- Put students into pairs. Have pairs write sentences for all of the new words, e.g. *The pattern on the butterfly's wings are symmetrical.*
- When they have finished, tell the pairs to swap their sentences with another pair.
- Pairs check their work with each other.

- Have pairs read some of their sentences to the class. Listen to at least two sentences for each new word.

Below level:

- Have students close their books. Say the new words in any order and have students write them.
- To check the answers, have individual students stand up and spell the words while a volunteer writes them on the board.

At level:

- Give students a simple definition for one of the words.
- Say the definition and have students call out the word and spell it.
- Repeat for all of the words.

Above level:

- Put students into pairs and have them write sentences using the new words, e.g. *An equilateral triangle does not have a right angle.*
- Have pairs compare their papers and correct their sentences.

Before You Read

Think

- Put students into pairs to discuss the questions.
- Have pairs share their answers with the class.
- After all pairs have shared their answers to each question, have the class add any new ideas to the discussion.

D Learn: Classify and Categorize

- Have a confident student read the *Learn* box to the class.
- Ask *Why do headings help us as we read?*

Read the short text. Then use the organizer to classify and categorize the information.

- Have students read the text to themselves. Then invite two students to read a paragraph each as the class reads along.

- Draw an organizer on the board with one main box and two boxes below it. Tell students to copy it in their notebooks at the top of the page.
- Fill in the organizer together as a class. Ask *What is the main topic of the text?* (*Symmetry in Nature*). Write it in the top box.
- Ask *What are the two categories of information in the text? Complete the two boxes in the organizer.* Have students complete the organizer on their own. Elicit the answers for the two boxes.
- Ask *How many examples are mentioned as symmetrical life forms?* Draw two lines under the Symmetrical Life Forms box. Say *Draw two lines under this box and write the examples in your notebook.*
- Then ask *How many examples are mentioned as asymmetrical life forms?* Draw two lines under the Asymmetrical Life Forms box. Say *Draw two lines under this box and write the examples in your notebook.*
- Have students compare their organizers with a partner and then check answers with the whole class.

E Words in Context: Scan the article on pages 72–73 and circle these words. As you read, try to guess what the words mean.

- Read each word and have the students follow your pronunciation.
- Have students scan the article on pages 72 and 73 and circle the words. Tell them to guess what the words mean from the context.
- Have students share their ideas about the words' definitions.

Below level:

- Put students into mixed-ability pairs.
- Have the more confident student help the other student to work out the meaning from context and take notes on a definition.
- Then put pairs into groups to compare definitions. Share definitions with the class.

At level:

- Put students into pairs to figure out the meaning of the new words from context.
- Tell pairs to look up any words they don't recognize in the dictionary.
- Have pairs share their answers with the class.

Above level:

- Put students into pairs to restate the sentences with alternate words in place of the words in context.
- Have pairs share their new sentences with the class.

F Name three everyday objects that are symmetrical. Do they need to be symmetrical? Why or why not?

- Put students into small groups to discuss the questions.
- Tell groups to name their objects and list their reasons for each question.
- Go over the groups' answers and make notes on the board.

Reading Preview

- Read the title of the unit's reading text.
- Have students silently read the content of the preview bar.
- Ask *What type of text is it?* Ask *What does this type of text do?*
- Tell students to think about the author's purpose as they read.
- Read the Author Bio with the class.

Further Practice
Workbook pages 62–63
Online Practice Unit 7 • Get Ready
Oxford iTools Unit 7 • Get Ready

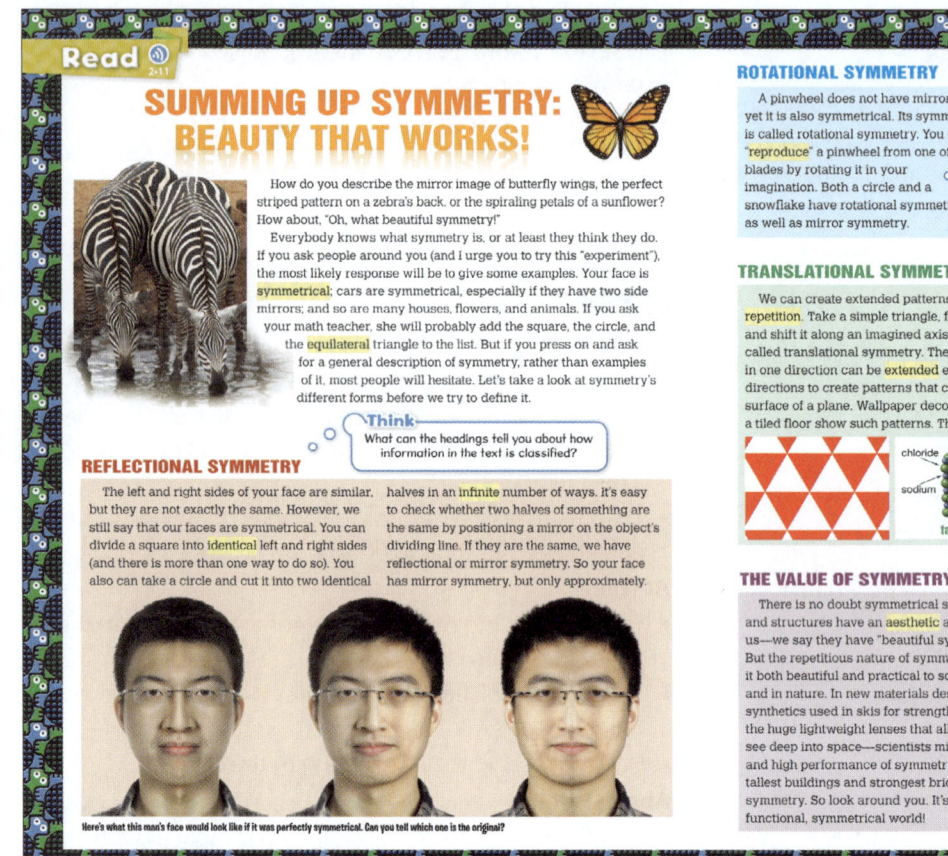

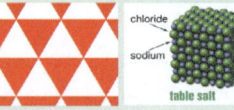

Read 2•11

SUMMING UP SYMMETRY: BEAUTY THAT WORKS!

How do you describe the mirror image of butterfly wings, the perfect striped pattern on a zebra's back, or the spiraling petals of a sunflower? How about, "Oh, what beautiful symmetry!"

Everybody knows what symmetry is, or at least they think they do. If you ask people around you (and I urge you to try this "experiment"), the most likely response will be to give some examples. Your face is **symmetrical**; cars are symmetrical, especially if they have two side mirrors; and so are many houses, flowers, and animals. If you ask your math teacher, she will probably add the square, the circle, and the **equilateral** triangle to the list. But if you press on and ask for a general description of symmetry, rather than examples of it, most people will hesitate. Let's take a look at symmetry's different forms before we try to define it.

Think
What can the headings tell you about how information in the text is classified?

REFLECTIONAL SYMMETRY

The left and right sides of your face are similar, but they are not exactly the same. However, we still say that our faces are symmetrical. You can divide a square into **identical** left and right sides (and there is more than one way to do so). You also can take a circle and cut it into two identical halves in an **infinite** number of ways. It's easy to check whether two halves of something are the same by positioning a mirror on the object's dividing line. If they are the same, we have reflectional or mirror symmetry. So your face has mirror symmetry, but only approximately.

Here's what this man's face would look like if it was perfectly symmetrical. Can you tell which one is the original?

ROTATIONAL SYMMETRY

A pinwheel does not have mirror symmetry, yet it is also symmetrical. Its symmetry is called rotational symmetry. You can "**reproduce**" a pinwheel from one of its four blades by rotating it in your imagination. Both a circle and a snowflake have rotational symmetry as well as mirror symmetry.

Think
Would you categorize a face and a pinwheel together? How would you classify them?

TRANSLATIONAL SYMMETRY

We can create extended patterns by simple **repetition**. Take a simple triangle, for example, and shift it along an imagined axis. This is called translational symmetry. The repetition in one direction can be **extended** easily in two directions to create patterns that cover a whole surface of a plane. Wallpaper decorations or a tiled floor show such patterns. The Dutch graphic artist M.C. Escher is famous for his intriguing patterns of **interlocking** fish, birds, and reptiles.

Now let's imagine that the repetition is extended into the third **dimension** of space. Think of a huge office building in which identical offices divide every floor, and every floor is identical with the floor below and above. There are more such **structures** around us than you may think. Here's one that might not come to mind—tiny table salt crystals. Each crystal has such an **internal arrangement** of its constituent elements, sodium and chloride ions. In fact, so do sugar crystals.

chloride
sodium
table salt

THE VALUE OF SYMMETRY

There is no doubt symmetrical shapes and structures have an **aesthetic** appeal for us—we say they have "beautiful symmetry." But the repetitious nature of symmetry makes it both beautiful and practical to scientists and in nature. In new materials design—from super synthetics used in skis for strength and speed, to the huge lightweight lenses that allow telescopes to see deep into space—scientists mimic the economy and high performance of symmetry in nature. Our tallest buildings and strongest bridges also employ symmetry. So look around you. It's a beautiful, functional, symmetrical world!

72 · 73

Summary

Objectives: To read, understand, and discuss a technical article; to apply a reading strategy to improve comprehension.

School subject: Math

Text type: Technical article (nonfiction)

Reading strategy: Classifying and categorizing

Big Question learning points: *Repetition makes symmetry both beautiful and practical. Things that are symmetrical can have a special beauty.*

Materials: Talk About It! Poster, Audio CD

Before Reading

- Have students tell you what they see in the pictures.
- Ask the students to read the headings. Ask *What do the headings help us to do? What categories of information does this text include? What do you want to know about those types of symmetry?*

During Reading 2•11

- Read the title and introductory text together.
- Point out the *Think* boxes and explain that students should use these to think about the author's purpose.

Below level:

- Have students read with you in small groups.
- During reading, pause and ask students questions, such as *How would you categorize this information? How would you classify this example?*
- Stop and discuss the *Think* box questions when you come to them.

At level:

- Have students read with a partner, taking turns to read the sections of the text.
- Ask the students to stop at each *Think* box to discuss the questions.

Above level:

- Have students read the text independently.
- Then put students into pairs to summarize the text for each other and to discuss the *Think* boxes.

Discussion questions:

- *What other animals have symmetry?*
- *Do you think your face is symmetrical?*
- *Look at the first "Think" box. Would you categorize a face and a pinwheel together?*
- *Do you know a building that has translational symmetry? Does this building have transactional symmetry?*
- *What are the three types of symmetry in the text?*
- *Can you think of other examples for each type of symmetry?*

After Reading

- Put students into small groups.
- Have groups think of two additional examples for each type of symmetry, using things in the classroom or school.
- Then have groups share their ideas with the class.

CRITICAL THINKING

- Keep students in their small groups to discuss the different types of symmetry.
- Have groups make notes to answer these questions:
  Can something have rotational symmetry and mirror symmetry too?
  Can an office building have rotational and mirror symmetry in addition to translational symmetry? Explain.
- Have groups share their ideas with the class. Invite students to the board to make sketches to support their ideas if helpful.

COMMUNICATION

- Display the **Talk About It! Poster** to help students with sentence frames for discussing and expressing personal opinions.
- Put students into pairs to discuss which part of the text is most interesting.

CULTURE NOTE

Symmetry has long been a device employed by architects to give buildings importance and beauty. Some of the outstanding examples of architecture through the ages have relied on symmetry: the pyramids of Egypt, the Parthenon in Greece, the Taj Mahal in India, and Angkor Wat in Cambodia. Even formal French gardens were organized in symmetrical designs in 17th century.

Further Practice
Workbook page 64
Online Practice Unit 7 • Read
Oxford **iTools** Unit 7 • Read

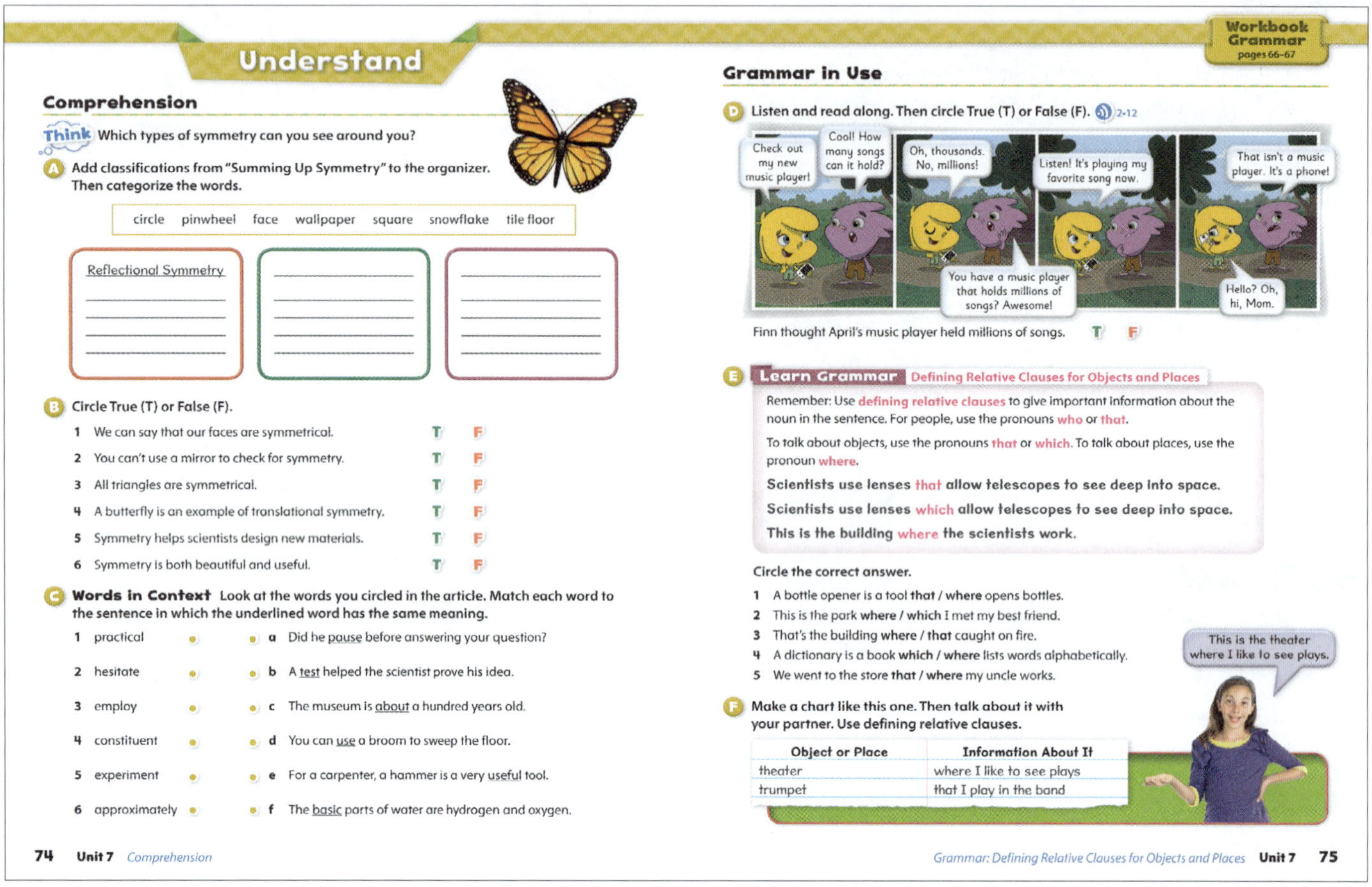

Understand

Comprehension

Think Which types of symmetry can you see around you?

A Add classifications from "Summing Up Symmetry" to the organizer. Then categorize the words.

circle   pinwheel   face   wallpaper   square   snowflake   tile floor

Reflectional Symmetry
_____
_____
_____
_____

_____
_____
_____
_____
_____

_____
_____
_____
_____
_____

B Circle True (T) or False (F).

1 We can say that our faces are symmetrical.   T   F
2 You can't use a mirror to check for symmetry.   T   F
3 All triangles are symmetrical.   T   F
4 A butterfly is an example of translational symmetry.   T   F
5 Symmetry helps scientists design new materials.   T   F
6 Symmetry is both beautiful and useful.   T   F

C **Words in Context** Look at the words you circled in the article. Match each word to the sentence in which the underlined word has the same meaning.

1 practical
2 hesitate
3 employ
4 constituent
5 experiment
6 approximately

a Did he <u>pause</u> before answering your question?
b A <u>test</u> helped the scientist prove his idea.
c The museum is <u>about</u> a hundred years old.
d You can <u>use</u> a broom to sweep the floor.
e For a carpenter, a hammer is a very <u>useful</u> tool.
f The <u>basic</u> parts of water are hydrogen and oxygen.

74   Unit 7   *Comprehension*

Grammar in Use

Workbook Grammar pages 66–67

D Listen and read along. Then circle True (T) or False (F).   2-12

Check out my new music player!
Cool! How many songs can it hold?
Oh, thousands. No, millions!
You have a music player that holds millions of songs? Awesome!
Listen! It's playing my favorite song now.
That isn't a music player. It's a phone!
Hello? Oh, hi, Mom.

Finn thought April's music player held millions of songs.   T   F

E **Learn Grammar** Defining Relative Clauses for Objects and Places

Remember: Use **defining relative clauses** to give important information about the noun in the sentence. For people, use the pronouns *who* or *that*.

To talk about objects, use the pronouns *that* or *which*. To talk about places, use the pronoun *where*.

Scientists use lenses **that** allow telescopes to see deep into space.
Scientists use lenses **which** allow telescopes to see deep into space.
This is the building where the scientists work.

Circle the correct answer.

1 A bottle opener is a tool that / where opens bottles.
2 This is the park where / which I met my best friend.
3 That's the building where / that caught on fire.
4 A dictionary is a book which / where lists words alphabetically.
5 We went to the store that / where my uncle works.

F Make a chart like this one. Then talk about it with your partner. Use defining relative clauses.

This is the theater where I like to see plays.

Object or Place	Information About It
theater	where I like to see plays
trumpet	that I play in the band

Grammar: Defining Relative Clauses for Objects and Places   **Unit 7**   75

Summary

Objectives: To demonstrate understanding of a technical article; to understand the meaning and form of the grammar structure.

Reading: Comprehension

Grammar input: Defining relative clauses for objects and places

Grammar practice: Workbook exercises

Grammar production: Talking about objects using relative clauses

Materials: Audio CD

Comprehension

Think

- Read the question with the class. Ask students to think about their answer.
- Put students into groups to discuss their answers.
- Have groups share their answers.

A Add classifications from "Summing Up Symmetry" to the organizer. Then categorize the words.

- Read the instructions with the class. Have students turn to the article on pages 72 and 73.
- Ask students to read the text again themselves and to think about the classifications and categories. Remind students to reread the *Think* boxes, too.
- After students have read the text, have them fill in the organizer on their own. Go around and help as needed.

- Put students into pairs and tell them to compare their organizers.
- Check answers with the class.

POSSIBLE ANSWERS
Reflectional Symmetry: square, circle, face
Rotational Symmetry: pinwheel, circle, snowflake
Translational Symmetry: wallpaper, tile floor

DIFFERENTIATION

Below level:
- Put students into mixed-ability pairs.
- Have the pairs reread the text together, with the more confident student helping the other student to fill in the organizer. Go around and help as needed.

At level:
- Pairs complete the organizers on their own.
- Then partners compare organizers to check each other's work.
- Have pairs share their organizers with the class.

Above level:
- After students have completed the organizers, have them create an additional organizer for the Value of Symmetry on their own.
- Give students a few minutes to do the activity.
- Then have students compare their Value organizer with a partner. Elicit ideas from the class.

B Circle True (T) or False (F).

- Have students do the activity on their own, looking back to pages 72–73 for answers.
- Have students compare their answers with a partner and correct the false answers.
- Check the answers with the class.

C Words in Context: Look at the words you circled in the article. Match each word to the sentence in which the underlined word has the same meaning.

- Have students go back and find the words in the text.
- Tell them to use the context clues to guess at the meaning of each word.
- Check answers with the class.

COLLABORATIVE LEARNING

- In pairs, ask students to collaborate to write new sentences for the words in context. Tell pairs to write the sentences, but to leave a blank where the word in context goes.
- As pairs write their sentences, encourage them to use the dictionary to help with definitions. Go around and help as necessary.
- Have pairs trade papers with another pair who fills in the blanks. Then pairs check each other's work.

Grammar in Use

D Listen and read along. Then circle True (T) or False (F). 🔘 2•12

- Listen to the dialogue once and have students read along and circle the correct answer.
- Play the dialogue again and have students check their answer.
- Check the answer with the class.

E Learn Grammar: Defining Relative Clauses for Objects and Places

- Read the *Learn Grammar* box together.
- Write the first example sentence on the board and then read it aloud. Underline *that*.
- Ask *What is the defining relative clause? What does "that" refer to? Could we use "who" instead of that? Why not?*

Circle the correct answer.

- Read the first sentence together. Ask students to identify the clause. Ask *What does the clause refer to? What word will you use to combine the sentences? Why?*
- Complete number 1 together. Then have students complete the rest on their own.

F Make a chart like this one. Then talk about it with your partner. Use defining relative clauses.

- Have students create a chart in their notebook.
- Have them copy the first two examples from the Student Book and add three more examples of their own.
- Put students in pairs to say their sentences.
- Ask individual students to say the sentences their partner told them to the class.

DIFFERENTIATION

Below level:

- Put students into mixed-ability pairs.
- Have the more confident student help the other student write three sentence starters. Go around and help as needed.
- Have the less confident student read his or her sentence starters and have the more confident student finish the sentences.
- Then have the less confident student read his or her sentences to the class.

At level:

- Have students write three sentence starters about objects or places individually.
- Have students circulate and say a sentence to a classmate who completes it. The student writes down the answers. Then it is the other student's turn.
- After all the students have completed their sentences, they return to their seats.
- Have students share their sentences with the class.

Above level:

- Have students write three complete sentences about objects that include defining relative clauses.
- Put students into small groups and have them sit in a circle if possible.
- Students take turns to read the first part of their sentence, stopping before the pronoun at the beginning of the relative clause. The group members try to guess the defining clause the student wrote.
- After all sentences have been correctly guessed, have groups choose some of their sentence starters to say for the class to guess.

Workbook Grammar

- Direct students to the Workbook for further practice.

Further practice
Workbook pages 65–67
Online Practice Unit 7 • Understand
Oxford **iTools** Unit 7 • Understand

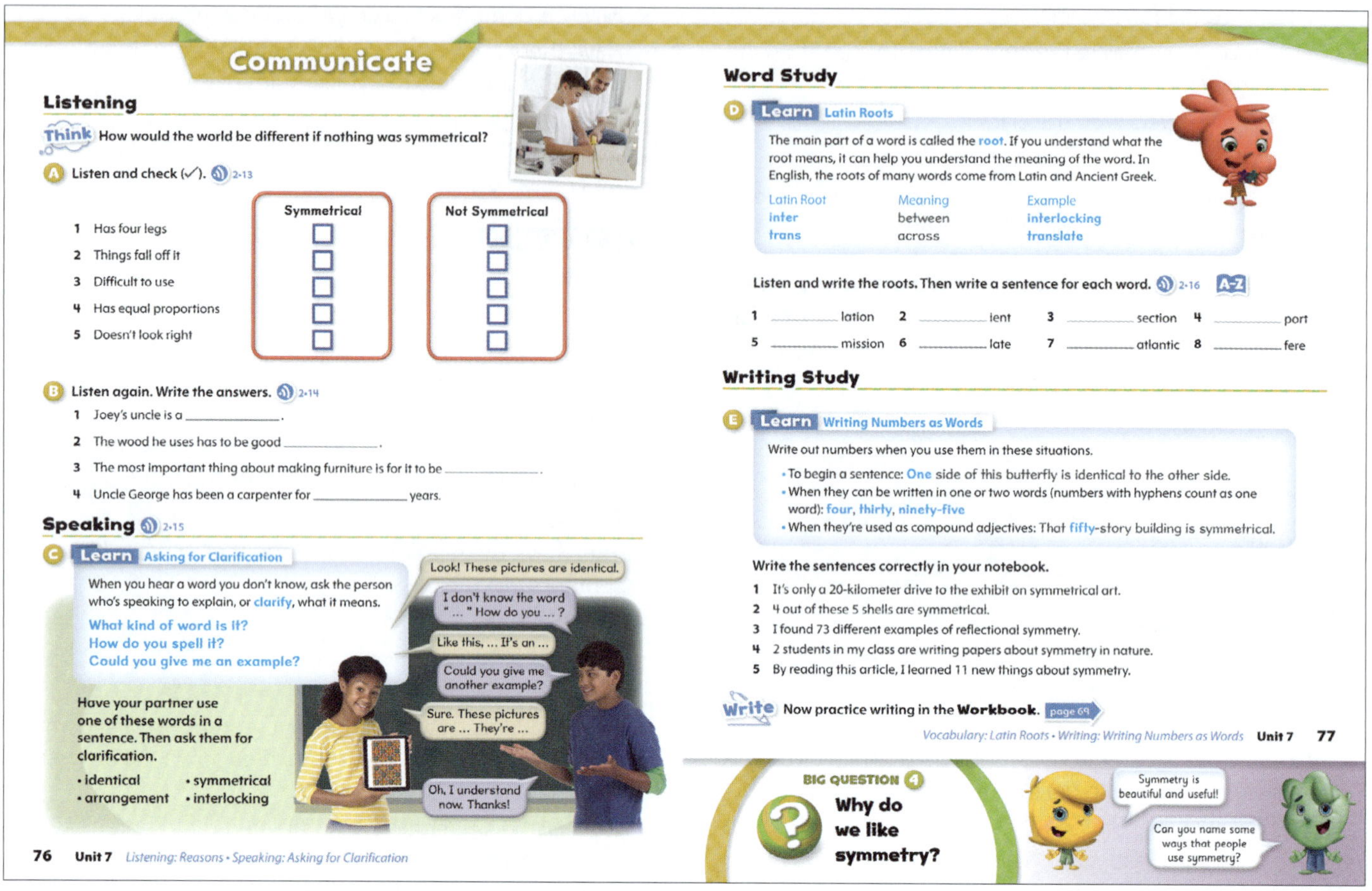
Communicate

Listening

Think How would the world be different if nothing was symmetrical?

A Listen and check (✓). 2-13

	Symmetrical	Not Symmetrical
1 Has four legs	☐	☐
2 Things fall off it	☐	☐
3 Difficult to use	☐	☐
4 Has equal proportions	☐	☐
5 Doesn't look right	☐	☐

B Listen again. Write the answers. 2-14

1 Joey's uncle is a ___________.
2 The wood he uses has to be good ___________.
3 The most important thing about making furniture is for it to be ___________.
4 Uncle George has been a carpenter for ___________ years.

Speaking 2-15

C Learn Asking for Clarification

When you hear a word you don't know, ask the person who's speaking to explain, or clarify, what it means.

What kind of word is it?
How do you spell it?
Could you give me an example?

Have your partner use one of these words in a sentence. Then ask them for clarification.

• identical • symmetrical
• arrangement • interlocking

76 Unit 7 Listening: Reasons • Speaking: Asking for Clarification

Word Study

D Learn Latin Roots

The main part of a word is called the root. If you understand what the root means, it can help you understand the meaning of the word. In English, the roots of many words come from Latin and Ancient Greek.

Latin Root	Meaning	Example
inter	between	interlocking
trans	across	translate

Listen and write the roots. Then write a sentence for each word. 2-16 A-Z

1 ______lation 2 ______ient 3 ______section 4 ______port
5 ______mission 6 ______late 7 ______atlantic 8 ______fere

Writing Study

E Learn Writing Numbers as Words

Write out numbers when you use them in these situations.

• To begin a sentence: One side of this butterfly is identical to the other side.
• When they can be written in one or two words (numbers with hyphens count as one word): four, thirty, ninety-five
• When they're used as compound adjectives: That fifty-story building is symmetrical.

Write the sentences correctly in your notebook.

1 It's only a 20-kilometer drive to the exhibit on symmetrical art.
2 4 out of these 5 shells are symmetrical.
3 I found 73 different examples of reflectional symmetry.
4 2 students in my class are writing papers about symmetry in nature.
5 By reading this article, I learned 11 new things about symmetry.

Write Now practice writing in the Workbook. page 69

Vocabulary: Latin Roots • Writing: Writing Numbers as Words Unit 7 77

BIG QUESTION 4 Why do we like symmetry?

Summary

Objectives: To learn and practice listening, speaking, and writing strategies to facilitate effective communication.

Vocabulary: *translation, translate, intersection, transport, intermission, transient, transatlantic, interfere*

Listening strategy: Listening for reasons

Speaking: Asking for clarification

Word Study: Latin roots

Writing Study: Writing numbers as words

Big Question learning point: *Symmetrical things are more balanced and easier to use.*

Materials: Discover Poster 4, Audio CD, Big Question Chart

Listening

Think

- Ask students to think about the question on their own.
- Tell them to think of examples of what the world would be like if nothing was symmetrical.
- Put students into pairs to discuss the question. Tell them to think of their three best examples of how the world would be different if nothing was symmetrical.
- Have pairs share their best ideas with the class.

A Listen and check (✓). 2•13

- Have students look at the charts first.
- Play the audio once and have students listen.
- Tell students to check the correct answers.
- Play the audio again for students to check their work.

ANSWERS

Symmetrical: Checked are: 1, 4
Not symmetrical: Checked are: 2, 3, 5

B Listen again. Write the answers. 2•14

- Have students read the sentences first.
- Play the audio once and have students listen and write the correct answers. Give students time to complete the activity.
- Play the audio again for students to check their work.

ANSWERS

1 carpenter 2 quality 3 symmetrical 4 22

Speaking 2•15

C Learn: Asking for Clarification

- Read the *Learn* box with the class.
- Play the audio and have students listen.
- Model the dialogue and examples with a confident student in front of the class.
- Put students into pairs and tell them to practice the dialogue.

Have your partner use one of these words in a sentence. Then ask them for clarification.

- Put students into pairs.
- Have them create short dialogues using the words listed (*identical, arrangement, symmetrical, interlocking*).
- Have a few pairs act out their dialogues for the class.

Word Study

D Learn: Latin Roots

- Have a confident student read the *Learn* box to the class.
- Write *interlocking* and *translational* on the board. Invite students to come up and underline the Latin root in each.
- Ask the class to define the root.

Listen and write the roots. Then write a sentence for each word. ⊚ 2·16

- Play the audio and have students write the root words they hear.
- Then play the audio again for students to check their answers.

ANSWERS
1 translation   2 transient   3 intersection   4 transport
5 transmission   6 translate   7 transatlantic   8 interfere

Below level:

- Say the words and have students repeat and spell them.
- Go over the meanings and give examples.

At level:

- Have pairs look up the meanings of the words in a dictionary.
- Collect the definitions by having the pairs write them on the board.

Above level:

- Put students into pairs. Have them look up the definitions in a dictionary and then write sentences using the new words.
- Have pairs write their sentences on the board and tell the class about them.

- Have students look in a dictionary to find other examples of words that have the Latin roots *inter-* and *trans-*.
- Write the words on the board and elicit their meanings.

Writing Study

E Learn: Writing Numbers as Words

- Read the *Learn* box together.
- Say some numbers to check understanding.

Write the sentences correctly in your notebook.

- Have students do the activity on their own.
- Then put the students into pairs to read each other's sentences.
- Check the answers with the class.

ANSWERS
1 twenty-kilometer   2 Four out of five   3 seventy-three
4 Two   5 eleven

Write

- Direct students to the Workbook for further practice.

Big Question 4 Review

Why do we like symmetry?

- Display **Discover Poster 4**. Discuss what you see.
- Refer to the learning points covered in Unit 7 that are written on the poster and have students explain how they relate to the different pictures.
- Return to the **Big Question Chart**.
- Ask students what they have learned about symmetry while studying this unit.

Further practice
Workbook pages 68–69
Online Practice Unit 7 · Communicate
Oxford **iTools** Unit 7 · Communicate

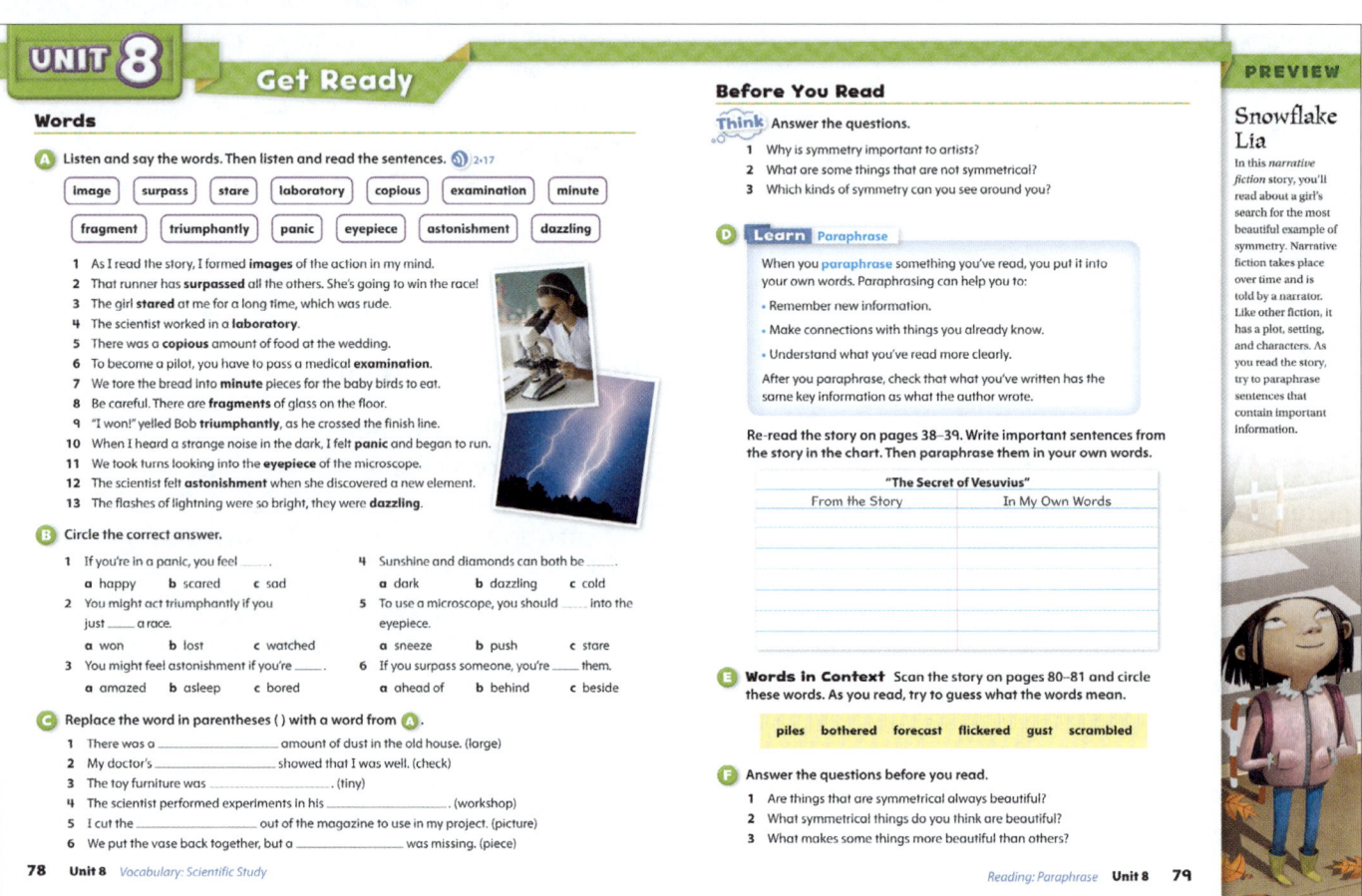

Summary

Objectives: To understand words about scientific study; to apply own experience and a reading strategy to help comprehension of a text.

Vocabulary: *image, surpass, stare, laboratory, copious, examination, minute, fragment, triumphantly, panic, eyepiece, astonishment, dazzling, piles, bothered, forecast, flickered, guest, scrambled*

Reading strategy: Paraphrasing

Materials: Audio CD

Words

A Listen and say the words. Then listen and read the sentences. 2·17

- Play the audio. Ask students to point to the words and repeat the words when they hear them.
- Then have students listen and read the sentences as they hear them.
- Say the sentence numbers out of order and have the class read the sentences aloud.

CRITICAL THINKING

Ask the following questions to check understanding:
- *Which words have to do with sight?*
- *Which word means tiny?*
- *Which word means a lot?*
- *Where do scientists do experiments?*
- *What word would you use to describe fireworks?*
- *Which two words are emotions that you feel?*

B Circle the correct answer.

- Have students do the activity on their own and then compare answers with a partner.
- Check answers with the class.

ANSWERS
1 b   2 a   3 a   4 b   5 c   6 a

COLLABORATIVE LEARNING
- Put students into pairs and tell them to use the new words in sentences.
- Go around the room and have pairs say some of their sentences for the class.

C Replace the word in parentheses ( ) with a word from A.

- Have students do the activity on their own.
- Check the answers with the class.

ANSWERS
1 copious   2 examination   3 minute   4 laboratory
5 images   6 fragment

Before You Read

Think

- Have students read the questions and make notes about their answers individually.
- Students discuss their answers to the questions in small groups.
- Then share some of the answers with the class. List the answers on the board.

D Learn: Paraphrase

- Read the *Learn* box with the class.
- Ask questions to check understanding: *What should you do after you've paraphrased a text? What can paraphrasing help you do?*

Reread the story on pages 38–39. Write important sentences from the story in the chart. Then paraphrase them in your own words.

- Read the instructions.
- Have students reread the story on pages 38 and 39, *The Secret of Vesuvius,* and write their own important sentences.
- Put students into pairs to paraphrase their sentences. Explain that they should compare the paraphrasing to the written sentence to ensure it is accurate.
- Then have students share their paraphrased sentences with the class.

POSSIBLE ANSWERS

1 *The smith's burns and cuts had not been washed by salt water, as Lupus's had.* – Lupus's cuts had been washed by the sea, but Vulcan's wounds weren't.
2 *Pliny hurled the flaming parasol overboard and the three of them hurried back to the shelter of the cabin as another shower of hot gravel rained down on their heads.* – Pliny's umbrella was burning, so he threw it overboard and the men took cover in the cabin from other burning rocks that were flying through the air.
3 *As for us, we will make for Tascius at Stabia, in case Rectina has been able to make her way back to him.* – We will go to Stabia in case Retina has gone there to meet Tasicus.

CRITICAL THINKING

Ask the following questions to check understanding about the text:

- *How does paraphrasing help you to understand the text?*
- *Is there only one way to paraphrase?*
- *Can you think of some other ways to paraphrase your or your partner's sentences?*

DIFFERENTIATION

Below level:

- Have students choose a sentence from the story to paraphrase (or choose one for them), e.g. *Behind them the oarsmen sang their fast chant and the oars rose and fell in time.*
- Then work with the students to paraphrase it. Start by them reading the sentence and then telling you what the sentence says.

- Encourage them to use different words, and possibly to revise the order, e.g. *As the rowers rowed, their oars matched the speed of their chant.*
- Ask the students to work in pairs to paraphrase two more sentences.

At level:

- Have students do their paraphrasing on their own.
- Then put students into pairs. Each student takes a turn to explain his or her paraphrased sentences to the other. Pairs try to help each other improve their paraphrasing.
- Have some pairs share their sentences with the class.

Above level:

- Have students do the activity on their own.
- Then put students into small groups. One student reads only his or her own paraphrased sentence. The rest of the students in the group try to find the original sentence in the story.
- Have a few students share their paraphrased sentences for the class to find the original.

E Words in Context: Scan the story on pages 80–81 and circle these words. As you read, try to guess what the words mean.

- Read each word and have students follow your pronunciation.
- Have students do the activity on their own. Then have them discuss the words with a partner.
- Have a few pairs share their meanings with the class.

F Answer the questions before you read.

COMMUNICATION

- Have students answer the questions on their own.
- Have a class discussion about each question. Elicit examples to support the students' ideas and write them on the board.

Reading Preview

- Read the title of the unit's reading text.
- Have students silently read the content of the preview bar.
- Ask *What type of text is it?* Ask *What does this type of text do? How is it the same as other fiction? How is it different?*

Further Practice
Workbook pages 70–71
Online Practice Unit 8 • Get Ready
Oxford **iTools** Unit 8 • Get Ready

Snowflake Lia

As Lia Bentley walked home from school on a crisp October afternoon, she saw images of symmetry all around her: in the faces of people and the clothes they wore, in the buildings she passed, and in the cars that went by. The birds in the sky were symmetrical, even the autumn leaves that covered the sidewalk and crunched beneath her feet. A butterfly landed on a branch above her, and Lia suddenly stopped. She held her breath and smiled, watching as it opened and closed its perfectly symmetrical wings.

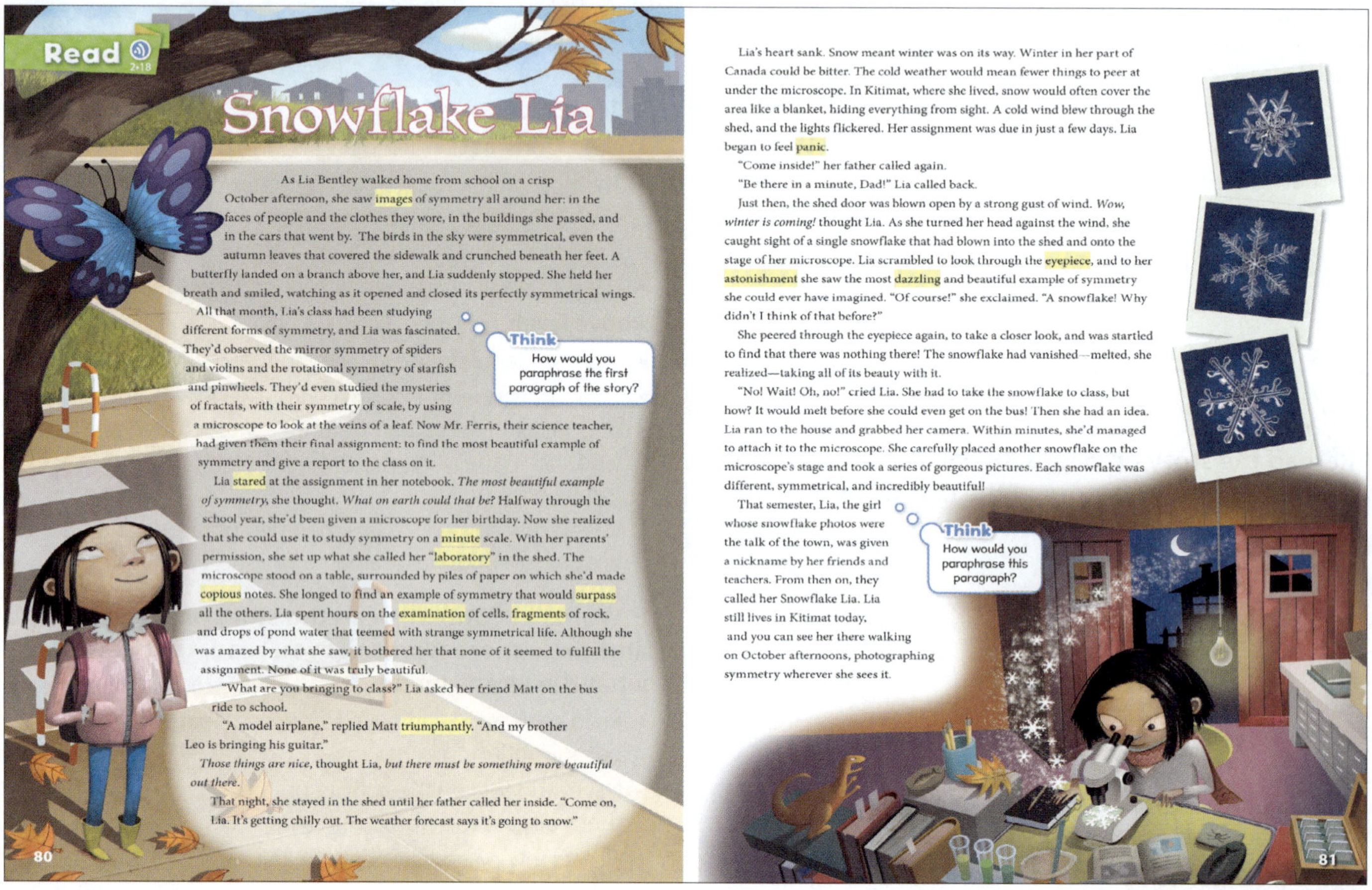

All that month, Lia's class had been studying different forms of symmetry, and Lia was fascinated. They'd observed the mirror symmetry of spiders and violins and the rotational symmetry of starfish and pinwheels. They'd even studied the mysteries of fractals, with their symmetry of scale, by using a microscope to look at the veins of a leaf. Now Mr. Ferris, their science teacher, had given them their final assignment: to find the most beautiful example of symmetry and give a report to the class on it.

Lia stared at the assignment in her notebook. *The most beautiful example of symmetry,* she thought. *What on earth could that be?* Halfway through the school year, she'd been given a microscope for her birthday. Now she realized that she could use it to study symmetry on a minute scale. With her parents' permission, she set up what she called her "laboratory" in the shed. The microscope stood on a table, surrounded by piles of paper on which she'd made copious notes. She longed to find an example of symmetry that would surpass all the others. Lia spent hours on the examination of cells, fragments of rock, and drops of pond water that teemed with strange symmetrical life. Although she was amazed by what she saw, it bothered her that none of it seemed to fulfill the assignment. None of it was truly beautiful.

"What are you bringing to class?" Lia asked her friend Matt on the bus ride to school.

"A model airplane," replied Matt triumphantly. "And my brother Leo is bringing his guitar."

Those things are nice, thought Lia, *but there must be something more beautiful out there.*

That night, she stayed in the shed until her father called her inside. "Come on, Lia. It's getting chilly out. The weather forecast says it's going to snow."

Think
How would you paraphrase the first paragraph of the story?

Lia's heart sank. Snow meant winter was on its way. Winter in her part of Canada could be bitter. The cold weather would mean fewer things to peer at under the microscope. In Kitimat, where she lived, snow would often cover the area like a blanket, hiding everything from sight. A cold wind blew through the shed, and the lights flickered. Her assignment was due in just a few days. Lia began to feel panic.

"Come inside!" her father called again.

"Be inside in a minute, Dad!" Lia called back.

Just then, the shed door was blown open by a strong gust of wind. *Wow, winter is coming!* thought Lia. As she turned her head against the wind, she caught sight of a single snowflake that had blown into the shed and onto the stage of her microscope. Lia scrambled to look through the eyepiece, and to her astonishment she saw the most dazzling and beautiful example of symmetry she could ever have imagined. "Of course!" she exclaimed. "A snowflake! Why didn't I think of that before?"

She peered through the eyepiece again, to take a closer look, and was startled to find that there was nothing there! The snowflake had vanished—melted, she realized—taking all of its beauty with it.

"No! Wait! Oh, no!" cried Lia. She had to take the snowflake to class, but how? It would melt before she could even get on the bus! Then she had an idea. Lia ran to the house and grabbed her camera. Within minutes, she'd managed to attach it to the microscope. She carefully placed another snowflake on the microscope's stage and took a series of gorgeous pictures. Each snowflake was different, symmetrical, and incredibly beautiful!

That semester, Lia, the girl whose snowflake photos were the talk of the town, was given a nickname by her friends and teachers. From then on, they called her Snowflake Lia. Lia still lives in Kitimat today, and you can see her there walking on October afternoons, photographing symmetry wherever she sees it.

Think
How would you paraphrase this paragraph?

80 / 81

Summary

Objectives: To read, understand, and discuss a narrative fiction story; to apply a reading strategy to improve comprehension.

School subject: Math

Text type: Narrative fiction

Reading strategy: Paraphrasing

Big Question learning point: *Things that are symmetrical can have a special beauty.*

Materials: Talk About It! Poster, Audio CD

Before Reading

- Read the title. Ask the class for some examples of symmetry.
- Have students point to the pictures and describe what they see.
- Ask the class:
  What kind of text is this?
  What is the title?
  What do you want to find out about the story? (e.g. *Why does it have that title.*)

During Reading 2·18

- Do the first *Think* box together. Have students read the first paragraph and then paraphrase it.
- Have some students share their ideas, e.g. *One afternoon a girl called Lia was walking home. She saw examples of symmetry everywhere she looked: buildings, cars, birds, leaves, and a butterfly.*
- Remind students that they should paraphrase as they read.

- Play the audio. Students listen as they read along.
- Play the audio a second time if necessary.

Below level:

- Have students read with you in small groups, repeating chunks of text after you.
- Then pause to paraphrase each section of text.

At level:

- Have students read the text silently to themselves one time.
- Put students into pairs to take turns paraphrasing the text to each other. Move throughout the room and provide help as necessary.

Above level:

- Have students read the text individually.
- Put students into pairs and have them paraphrase the text. Explain that students should revise their ideas to improve their paraphrasing.

Discussion questions:

- *What class was Lia's assignment for?*
- *How does Lia bring her two interests (symmetry and science) together?*
- *How does the setting (Canada) contribute to the story of Lia finding a beautiful example of symmetry (snowflake)?*
- *Why is the story titled Snowflake Lia?*

- Put students in pairs.
- Have pairs discuss the *Think* boxes. Go around and help as needed.
- Then have pairs paraphrase the first paragraph (again).
- For the second *Think* box, elicit several examples from different pairs. Then have the class work together to dictate a final version of the paragraph that you (or they) write on the board.

After Reading

CREATIVITY

- Put students into pairs (mixed ability if appropriate).
- Have pairs come up with a brief paraphrase for the whole story. It should be at least five lines long. Explain that it should have a beginning, a middle with about three steps, and an end.
- Ask pairs to make notes on their paraphrased story.
- Go around and help as needed.
- Have pairs read their paraphrased story to the class.
- Then have the class work together to dictate a final version of the paragraph that you (or they) write on the board.

COLLABORATIVE LEARNING

- Display the **Talk About It! Poster** to help students with sentence frames for discussion and expressing personal opinions.
- Put students into pairs to discuss what they find interesting about the story.

CULTURE NOTE

This story is about a girl who photographed snowflakes, and it is fictional. But in reality there was a man, called Wilson Bentley who became famous for doing the same thing.

Wilson Bentley was born in 1865, and he became interested in snowflakes when he was a teenager living on the family farm. He looked at snowflakes through his microscope (just like Lia) and tried to draw what he saw. However, the snowflakes melted too quickly so he attached a camera to the microscope and photographed them instead.

He took over 5,000 photos of snowflakes, and in doing so, found a way of catching them on black velvet so that they didn't melt before he could capture their likeness.

Wilson "Snowflake" Bentley also photographed other forms of ice and natural water formations, such as raindrops, fog, and even clouds.

Further Practice
Workbook page 72
Online Practice Unit 8 • Read
Oxford iTools Unit 8 • Read

Understand

Comprehension

Think If you had Lia's assignment, what would you choose as the most beautiful example of symmetry?

A Choose the paragraph in "Snowflake Lia" that you think is most important, and paraphrase it in your notebook. Discuss what you wrote with your partner.

B Circle the correct answer.

1 Why did Lia hold her breath when she saw the butterfly?
   a It was ugly.
   b It was hurt.
   c It was symmetrical.
   d It wasn't symmetrical.

2 Which kind of symmetry did Lia's class *not* study?
   a rotational symmetry
   b translational symmetry
   c mirror symmetry
   d symmetry of scale

3 What was Lia's friend Matt bringing to class?
   a a microscope
   b a guitar
   c a model airplane
   d a snowflake

4 What two devices did Lia use to finish her assignment?
   a a microscope and a violin
   b a guitar and a pinwheel
   c a bus and a camera
   d a camera and a microscope

C Answer the questions.

1 Was the cold weather a good or a bad thing for Lia? Why?
2 Why couldn't Lia take a snowflake to class?
3 Did people like Lia's photos of snowflakes? How do you know?
4 What do you think Lia will be interested in next?

D **Words in Context** Look at the words you circled in the story. Then use them to complete the sentences.

1 A big _____ of wind turned my umbrella inside out!
2 Could you please pick up those _____ of clothes on the floor?
3 The _____ says it's going to be hot tomorrow.
4 A campfire _____ in the distance.
5 Were you _____ when you didn't win the competition?
6 I _____ to catch the bus before it left.

Grammar in Use

Workbook Grammar pages 74–75

E Listen and read along. Then circle True (T) or False (F). 2·19

> Oh, look! That's the girl!
> Which girl are you talking about?
> It's the girl whose umbrella I borrowed yesterday! Can't you see?
> How am I supposed to know which girl you mean?
> She's the one who doesn't have an umbrella!

The umbrella that Sonya is holding belongs to the girl. **T** **F**

F **Learn Grammar** Defining Relative Clauses with *Whose*

Remember: Use **defining relative clauses** to give important information about the noun in a sentence.

Begin a relative clause with the pronoun **whose** to show possession.

Lia was the girl **whose** snowflake pictures were the talk of the town. (The pictures belong to Lia.)

Combine the sentences using *whose*. Write them in your notebook.

1 Picasso is the artist. His paintings are famous.
2 That's the man. His car was stolen.
3 Do you know the girl? Her mother is a doctor.
4 That's the boy. His website won an award.
5 Mrs. Murray is the teacher. Her son goes to our school.
6 He's the writer. His book is popular.

G Make a chart like this one. Then talk about it with your partner. Use defining relative clauses.

Person	Information About Him or Her
Kevin	whose book I borrowed
Beethoven	whose music I like
Ms. Williams	whose class I'm taking

> Kevin is the student whose book I borrowed.

Summary

Objectives: To demonstrate understanding of a narrative fiction text; to understand the meaning and form of the grammar structure.

Reading: Comprehension

Grammar input: Defining relative clauses with *whose*

Grammar practice: Workbook exercises

Grammar production: Defining relative clauses with *whose*

Materials: Audio CD

Comprehension

Think

- Have students think about their answers individually first. Tell them to take notes. Make sure students think of what they would have chosen.
- Then hold a class discussion.

A Choose the paragraph in "Snowflake Lia" that you think is most important, and paraphrase it in your notebook. Discuss what you wrote with your partner.

- Read the instructions with the class.
- Have students complete the exercise on their own.
- Put students in pairs and ask them to discuss with their partner what they wrote.

Below level:

- Put students into mixed-ability pairs.
- Have the pair read the text together and choose the most important paragraph and paraphrase it together.
- Then have pairs work to paraphrase the last paragraph together.
- Put students into groups of four. Have students compare their work.

At level:

- Have students write paraphrased versions of the most important paragraph and the last paragraph.
- Share the writing with the class. Put their work up where students can see them. Have students walk around and read all of the work.
- Then have a few students talk about the differences between other students' versions of paraphrasing. Does the class agree on the most important paragraph?

Above level:

- Students do the activity individually.
- Put students into pairs. Have them compare and discuss their writing and then make suggestions to change or improve each other's paraphrased text.
- Students revise their writing individually.
- Have students share their work with the class.

B Circle the correct answer.

- Ask the students to look at the sentences and the answer options.
- If the class has any trouble with the answers, refer back to the appropriate sections on pages 80 and 81.
- Check the answers with the class.

1 c 2 b 3 c 4 d

C Answer the questions.

- Have students do the activity individually. Then ask them to compare their answers with a partner.
- Check the answers with the class.

1 The cold weather was a good thing for Lia because she found the most beautiful example of symmetry: a snowflake.
2 Because a snowflake would melt.
3 People loved Lia's snowflake photos. They were the talk of the town.
4 Next, she will be interested in photographing other examples of symmetry. The last sentence says so.

CRITICAL THINKING

- Put students into small groups.
- Read the following sentences: *Lia thinks a snowflake is the most beautiful example of symmetry. But Matt thinks a model airplane is the most beautiful example of symmetry and his brother thinks a guitar is.* Who is right? What is the most beautiful example of symmetry? Can there be one? What do their choices say about them?
- Have groups discuss the questions and then share their ideas with the class.

D Words in Context: Look at the words you circled in the story. Then use them to complete the sentences.

- Have students go back and find the words in the story.
- Tell them to use the context clues to figure out the meaning of each word.
- Have students complete the sentences.
- Check the answers with the class.

1 gust 2 piles 3 forecast 4 flickered 5 bothered
6 scrambled

COLLABORATIVE LEARNING

- Put students into pairs.
- Have pairs think of sentences for each of the words in context.
- Have pairs share their sentences with the class.

Grammar in Use

E Listen and read along. Then circle True (T) or False (F). 2·19

- Listen to the dialogue once and then read it together as a class.
- Play the audio again if necessary.
- Check the answer with the class.

T

F Learn Grammar: Defining Relative Clauses with *Whose*

- Read the *Learn Grammar* box together.
- Write the example sentence on the board and then read it aloud. Underline *whose*.
- Ask *What is the defining relative clause? What does* whose *refer to? Why do we use* whose *instead of* who?

Combine the sentences using *whose*. Write them in your notebook.

- Have students do the activity on their own.
- Ask follow-up questions. In their notebooks as you go over these questions, have students underline the pronoun, circle the clause, and draw a line from the clause to the defined noun:
  What is the clause? Who do the pictures belong to?
  What is the clause? Who did the car belong to?
  What is the clause? Whose mother is a doctor?
  What is the clause? Who has a website?
  What is the clause? Whose son goes to our school?
  What is the clause? Whose book is popular?
- Check answers with the class.

1 Picasso is the artist whose paintings are famous.
2 That's the man whose car was stolen.
3 Do you know the girl whose mother is a doctor?
4 That's the boy whose website won an award.
5 Mrs. Murray is the teacher whose son goes to our school.
6 He's the writer whose book is popular.

G Make a chart like this one. Then talk about it with your partner. Use defining relative clauses.

COMMUNICATION

- Have students create a chart in their notebook.
- Have them copy the examples from the Student Book and add three more examples of their own.
- Put students in pairs to say their sentences. Then put each pair with another pair of students.
- Ask each student to read out their sentences to the group, and have the rest of the group decide if the sentences are correct.

Workbook Grammar

- Direct students to the Workbook for further practice.

Further practice
Workbook pages 73–75
Online Practice Unit 8 · Understand
Oxford iTools Unit 8 · Understand

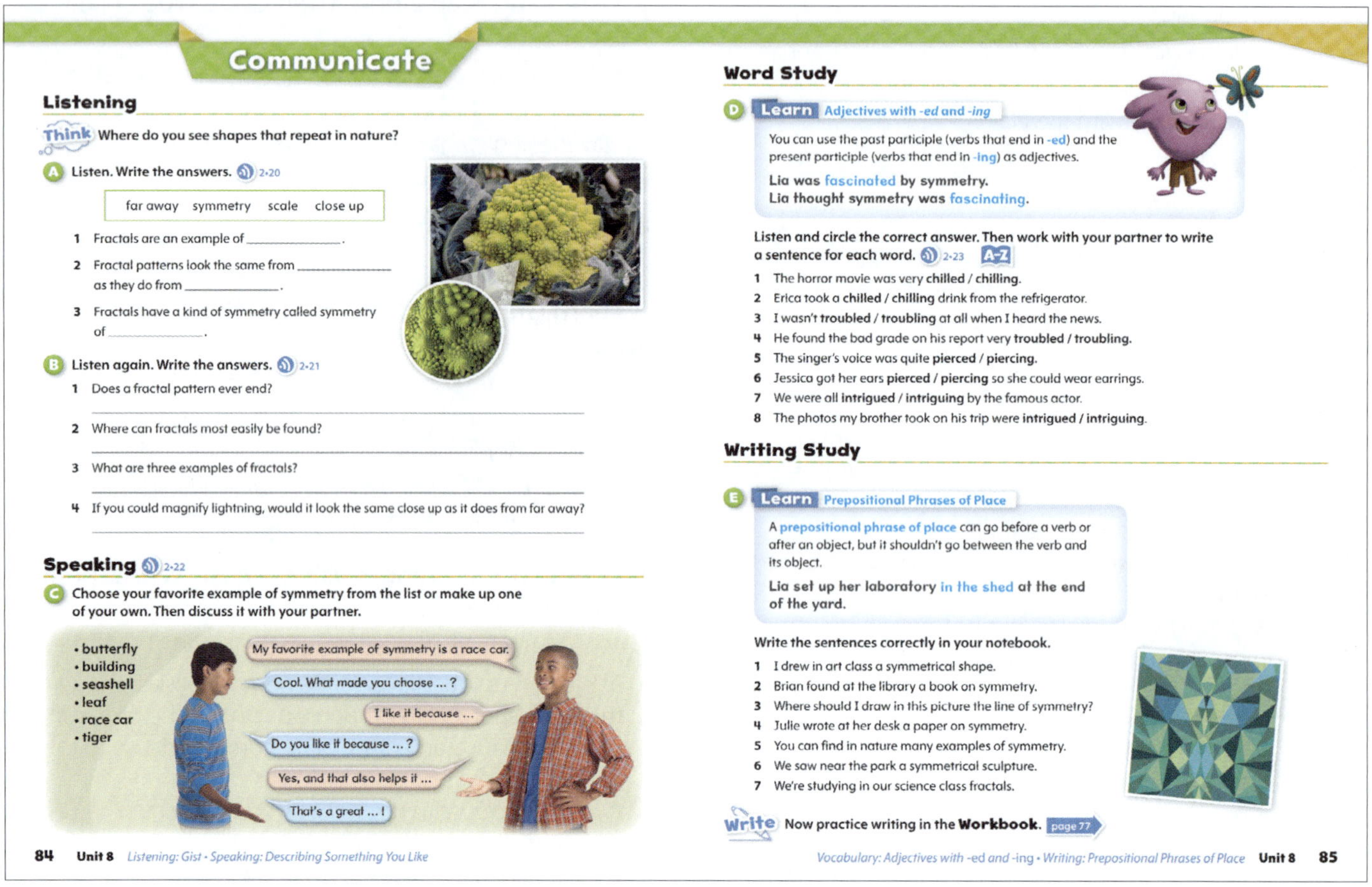

Communicate

Listening

Think Where do you see shapes that repeat in nature?

A Listen. Write the answers. 2-20

far away   symmetry   scale   close up

1 Fractals are an example of _____.
2 Fractal patterns look the same from _____ as they do from _____.
3 Fractals have a kind of symmetry called symmetry of _____.

B Listen again. Write the answers. 2-21

1 Does a fractal pattern ever end?
2 Where can fractals most easily be found?
3 What are three examples of fractals?
4 If you could magnify lightning, would it look the same close up as it does from far away?

Speaking 2-22

C Choose your favorite example of symmetry from the list or make up one of your own. Then discuss it with your partner.

- butterfly
- building
- seashell
- leaf
- race car
- tiger

My favorite example of symmetry is a race car.
Cool. What made you choose ... ?
I like it because ...
Do you like it because ... ?
Yes, and that also helps it ...
That's a great ... !

84   Unit 8   *Listening: Gist • Speaking: Describing Something You Like*

Word Study

D **Learn** Adjectives with *-ed* and *-ing*

You can use the past participle (verbs that end in *-ed*) and the present participle (verbs that end in *-ing*) as adjectives.

Lia was **fascinated** by symmetry.
Lia thought symmetry was **fascinating**.

Listen and circle the correct answer. Then work with your partner to write a sentence for each word. 2-23 **A-Z**

1 The horror movie was very **chilled / chilling**.
2 Erica took a **chilled / chilling** drink from the refrigerator.
3 I wasn't **troubled / troubling** at all when I heard the news.
4 He found the bad grade on his report very **troubled / troubling**.
5 The singer's voice was quite **pierced / piercing**.
6 Jessica got her ears **pierced / piercing** so she could wear earrings.
7 We were all **intrigued / intriguing** by the famous actor.
8 The photos my brother took on his trip were **intrigued / intriguing**.

Writing Study

E **Learn** Prepositional Phrases of Place

A **prepositional phrase of place** can go before a verb or after an object, but it shouldn't go between the verb and its object.

Lia set up her laboratory **in the shed** at the end of the yard.

Write the sentences correctly in your notebook.

1 I drew in art class a symmetrical shape.
2 Brian found at the library a book on symmetry.
3 Where should I draw in this picture the line of symmetry?
4 Julie wrote at her desk a paper on symmetry.
5 You can find in nature many examples of symmetry.
6 We saw near the park a symmetrical sculpture.
7 We're studying in our science class fractals.

Write Now practice writing in the **Workbook**. page 77

Vocabulary: Adjectives with -ed and -ing • Writing: Prepositional Phrases of Place   **Unit 8**   85

Summary

Objectives: To learn and practice listening, speaking, and writing strategies to facilitate effective communication.

Vocabulary: *chilling, chilled, troubling, troubled, piercing, pierced, intriguing, intrigued*

Listening strategy: Listening for gist

Speaking: Describing something you like

Word Study: Adjectives with *-ed* and *-ing*

Writing Study: Prepositional phrases of place

Big Question learning point: *Symmetry helps us understand how the world works.*

Materials: Audio CD

Listening

Think

- Have students think about the question.
- Have them tell a partner their ideas.
- Ask a few volunteers to tell the class where they see shapes repeat in nature.

A Listen. Write the answers. 2·20

- Play the audio once and have students listen.
- Tell students to write the answers.
- Play the audio again so they can check their work.

ANSWERS
1 symmetry   2 close up, far away   3 scale

CRITICAL THINKING

- After checking the answers, put students into small groups.
- Have students paraphrase the listening text.
- Then have them talk about the pictures of fractals. Ask them to explain how the pictures are examples of symmetry of scale.
- Have groups share their paraphrasing and discussion with the class.

B Listen again. Write the answers. 2·21

- Play the audio so students can complete the exercise.
- Check the answers with the class.

ANSWERS
1 no   2 in nature   3 veins in a leaf, lightning bolts, seashells, clouds, trees, rivers, vegetables like broccoli and cauliflower   4 yes; the pattern is identical

Speaking 🔘 2·22

C Choose your favorite example of symmetry from the list or make up one of your own. Then discuss it with your partner.

- Read the presentation box with the class.
- Play the audio and have students listen.
- Model the dialogue using one of the examples from the list with a confident student in front of the class.
- Put students into pairs and tell them to practice the dialogue using one of the examples from the list, or using their own idea of something with symmetry.
- Have a few pairs act out their dialogues in front of the class.

Below level:

- Put students into mixed-ability pairs.
- Have the more confident student help the other student to practice the dialogue.
- Have pairs share their dialogues with another pair.

At level:

- Put students into small groups with even numbers and have them sit in a circle, if possible.
- Have students in the group take turns speaking in pairs around the circle. Each student practices with the partner on his or her right using the first item in the list on page 84 (*butterfly*).
- Then everyone turns to the person on the left and practices the next item. They continue to alternate as they practice the dialogue and go down the items in the list.

Above level:

- Tell students to think of an example of symmetry.
- Ask students to practice the dialogue with a partner, without saying the name of the example. When they finish the dialogue, the partner tries to guess.

Word Study

D Learn: Adjectives with -ed and -ing

- Read the *Learn* box together.
- Check understanding. Ask *In the first sentence, who or what is fascinated? In the second sentence, who or what is fascinating?*

Listen and circle the correct answer. Then work with your partner to write a sentence for each word. 🔘 2·23

- Play the audio for students to complete the exercise.
- Play the audio again if necessary.
- Check the answers with the class.

ANSWERS
1 chilling   2 chilled   3 troubled   4 troubling
5 piercing   6 pierced   7 intrigued   8 intriguing

- Have partners work in pairs to draw a line from the adjective to the noun it modifies in each sentence.

Writing Study

E Learn: Prepositional Phrases of Place

- Read the *Learn* box together.
- Read the example sentence. Ask *What is the verb? What is the object? Where else could the phrase "in the shed" go?*

Write the sentences correctly in your notebook.

- Have students complete the exercise on their own. Then go over answers with the class.

ANSWERS
1 I drew a symmetrical shape in art class.
2 Brian found a book on symmetry at the library.
3 Where should I draw the line of symmetry in this picture?
4 Julie wrote a paper on symmetry at her desk.
5 You can find many examples of symmetry in nature.
6 We saw a symmetrical sculpture near the park.
7 We're studying fractals in our science class.

Write

- Direct students to the Workbook for further writing practice.

Further practice
Workbook pages 76–77
Online Practice Unit 8 · Communicate
Oxford iTools Unit 8 · Communicate

Summary

Objectives: To show what students have learned about the language and learning points of Units 7 and 8.

Reading: Reading a personal response to a story

Writing: Writing a a personal response

Speaking: Sharing a personal response

Materials: Big Question DVD, Discover Poster 4, Talk About It! Poster, Big Question Chart

Writing

A Read this personal response to "Snowflake Lia."

- Read aloud the directions and explain that a personal response is someone's opinion and review of a story.
- Go over the structure of each section of the response before reading. Then read the response.
- After reading the response with the class. Have students read it one time on their own.

B Answer the questions.

- Have students find the answers in the text.
- Check the answers with the class.

ANSWERS

1 The writer paraphrases the story. The label reads "Story summary"; also he / she doesn't use quotes.
2 The comparisons that the writer makes are that he / she can relate to Lia, because he / she wants to learn more about what he / she doesn't know.
3 The writer includes the fact that he / she likes getting birthday presents and also that he / she likes reading

about new discoveries. The writer says he / she didn't like the setting very much because it was hard for him / her to relate to where Lia lives.
4 The writer concludes by saying that there were many similarities between Lia's experience and the writer's life. Lia showed determination and creativity – the writer hopes he / she can always be like her.

CRITICAL THINKING

Ask questions for discussion.

- *Why was the story fun to read for the writer?*
- *Where does the writer live?*
- *Can you enjoy a story if it is not familiar to you? Why or why not?*

C Learn: Writing a Personal Response

- Read the *Learn* box together.
- Explain that students should follow these guidelines when they plan and write their personal response.

Write

- Direct students to the Workbook to plan and write their own personal response.

CREATIVITY

- Elicit spoken personal responses from the class about "Snowflake Lia."
- Write down a list of things students like and don't like on the board.
- Put students into pairs and have them orally explain their final thoughts about the story.

Below level:

- Read the story from the Workbook with the group and have students paraphrase it.
- Put students into mixed-ability pairs to discuss their ideas and opinions.
- Explain that students should use the structure in the *Learn* presentation box and the model response.
- Have the more confident student make notes that the less confident student can use as he / she drafts his / her personal response.

At level:

- After students have read the story, have them go through the structure of the response and discuss their ideas with a partner.
- Have students write their personal response on their own.
- After writing, have partners read each other's response and check if it followed the criteria in the *Learn* box.

Above level:

- Have students do the activity individually.
- Then put students into pairs. Have them read each other's personal response and make comments to improve it.
- Students revise their writing.

D Present your personal response to the class.

- Read the list with the class. Give students time to practice reading their responses aloud.
- Have students take turns reading their personal responses to the class. Ensure they follow the steps in the direction list.
- After each response, the class asks questions and says how the reading went.

COLLABORATIVE LEARNING

- Put students into small groups to practice reading their personal responses.
- Tell them to underline parts of the response where they will stress what they are saying. They can make marks where pauses go.
- Have students practice their reading slowly and in a clear voice.
- Have group members give them considerate feedback on how to improve it. Each student should read his or her response at least once.

Units 7 and 8 Big Question Review

A Watch the video. What kinds of symmetry do you see? ▷

- Play the video and when it is finished ask students what they now know about symmetry.
- Have students share ideas with the class.

B What are some answers to the Big Question? Talk about them with your partner.

COMMUNICATION

- Display **Discover Poster 4**. Point to familiar vocabulary items and elicit them from the class. Ask *What is this?*
- Ask students *What do you see?* Ask *What does that mean?*
- Refer to all of the learning points written on the poster and have students explain how they relate to the different pictures.
- Ask *What does this learning point mean*? Elicit answers from individual students.
- Display the **Talk About It! Poster** to help students with sentence frames for discussion of the learning points and for expressing their opinions.

C Complete the Big Question Chart. Then discuss it with the class.

- Ask students what they have learned about symmetry while studying this unit.
- Put students into pairs or small groups to say two new things they have learned.
- Have them share their ideas with the class and add their ideas to the chart.
- Have students complete the chart in their Workbook.

Further practice
Workbook pages 78–81
Online Practice • Wrap Up 4
Oxford **iTools** • Wrap Up 4

Units 9 and 10
How do we use language?

Reading Strategies
Students will learn about:
- Main ideas and details
- Setting

Vocabulary
Students will understand and use words about:
- Communication

Grammar
Students will understand and use:
- Nondefining relative clauses
- Passive statements (present perfect)

Review
Students will review the language and Big Question learning points of Units 9 and 10 through:
- Writing a poem

Units 9 and 10
How do we use language?
Students will understand the Big Question learning points:
- People use language to communicate with each other.
- We express our emotions through language.
- Language helps us to overcome obstacles.
- We use language to make friends and connect with others.
- Language gives us a way to describe the world around us.

Listening Strategies
Students will practice:
- Listening for gist
- Listening for similarities and differences

Writing Study
Students will use and understand:
- Using connectors to show contrast
- Onomatopoeia
Students will:
- Write a poem

Word Study
Students will understand and use:
- Latin roots
- Connotation

Speaking
Students will understand and use expressions for:
- Expressing emotions
- Expressing preferences

Units 9 and 10 Big Question page 88

Summary

Objectives: To activate students' existing knowledge of the topic and identify what they would like to learn about the topic.

Materials: Big Question DVD, Discover Poster 5, Big Question Chart

Introducing the topic

- Read out the Big Question. Ask *How do we use language?*
- Write students' ideas on the board and discuss.

A Watch the video. Then talk about it with your partner.

- Play the video and when it is finished, ask students to answer the following questions in pairs:
  What do you see in the video?
  What is happening?
  How is language used in the video?
  What do you like about the video?
- Have individual students share their answers with the class.

B Look at the picture and discuss it with your class.

- Students look at the big picture and talk about it. Ask *What do you see?*
- Ask additional questions:
  Where is this picture taken?
  How do you know?
  Have you been in a place like this?
  What are all the people doing?

C Think and answer the questions.

- Have students discuss the questions in small groups, and then with the class.

Below level:

- Put students into mixed-ability pairs.
- Have the more confident student help the other student to answer the questions.
- Go around and help as needed.

At level:

- Have pairs make notes together on their answers.
- Then have pairs compare their answers with another pair.
- Finally, discuss the questions with the class and write notes about their answers on the board.

Above level:

- Put students into small groups to answer the questions.
- For question 3, have groups list as many other forms of language as they can think of. For question 4, they list as many different languages as they think of.
- Compile the answers on the board.

- Ask students to think individually about: *What do we use language for?*
- Then put students into pairs to discuss the question.
- Have pairs share their ideas with the class.

Expanding the topic

- Display **Discover Poster 5** and give students enough time to look at the pictures.
- Get students to talk about things you think they will know by pointing to different things in the pictures and asking *What's this? Where can you see this?*
- Put students into small groups of three or four. Have each group choose a picture that they find interesting.
- Have each group say five sentences about their picture.
- Ask one person from each group to stand up and read out the sentences they chose for their picture.
- Ask the class if they can add any more.

Below level:

- Encourage students to participate using short sentences.
- Point to details in the big picture and on the poster and ask *What is this?* Write the answers on the board.

At level:

- Elicit complete sentences about what students know about language.
- Write their sentences on the board.

Above level:

- Elicit more detailed responses.
- Challenge students to write their own sentences on the board.

D Discuss this topic with your class. Fill out the Big Question Chart.

- Display the **Big Question Chart**.
- Ask the class *What do you know about language? What do you want to know about language?*
- Ask students to write what they know and what they want to know in their Workbooks.
- Write a collection of ideas on the **Big Question Chart**.

Discover Poster 5

1 A woman talking on a cellphone; 2 A soccer player arguing with a referee; 3 A police officer helping two tourists with directions; 4 Two girls having a friendly conversation; 5 A teacher and her students studying sign language

Further Practice

Workbook page 82
Online Practice · Big Question 5
Oxford iTools · Big Question 5

UNIT 9 Get Ready

PREVIEW

Words

A Listen and say the words. Then listen and read the sentences. 2·24

| gesture | beckon | refusal | disapproval | group | lack | raised |

| enable | invaluable | consist | distress | conceal | transmit |

1 I asked the man where the library was, and he **gestured** toward a building.
2 When Maria saw her teacher **beckon**, she knew it was her turn and stepped forward.
3 Nick's **refusal** to help me hurt my feelings.
4 My dad frowned in **disapproval** when he saw the broken plate.
5 I **grouped** the clothing into small and large sizes.
6 The soup **lacked** salt, so I added some more.
7 When I'm cold, I get **raised** bumps on my skin.
8 A cane **enabled** the old man to walk more easily.
9 In my job, a computer is **invaluable**. I couldn't work without one.
10 Our band **consists** of a guitar player and a singer.
11 I felt **distress** when I heard that my brother was sick.
12 We couldn't see the house because it was **concealed** by some trees.
13 There are many ways to **transmit** a message, such as e-mail, text, or letter.

B Circle True (T) or False (F).

1 If someone is beckoning to you, they want you to go away. T F
2 Something that's invaluable is very valuable. T F
3 When you enable something, you stop it from happening. T F
4 If a cake lacked sugar, it would taste great. T F
5 When you conceal something, you hide it from view. T F
6 A refusal is like an agreement. T F
7 If something is raised, it's higher than what's around it. T F

C Work with your partner to answer the questions.

1 If you grouped your classmates into girls and boys, who would the groups consist of?
2 Why would someone transmit a distress message?
3 Make a gesture showing disapproval.

90 Unit 9 *Vocabulary: Communication*

Before You Read

Think Answer the questions.

1 Do you use language differently from your parents? How?
2 What's your favorite word in English?
3 How many languages can you name?

D **Learn** Main Idea and Details

The **main idea** of a text is the point the author is trying to make. It can be anywhere in a text but is usually found in the first paragraph. Each section of a text can also have its own main idea.

Details are additional facts or reasons that support the main idea and help to explain it. They're sometimes introduced with words like **for example**, **first**, and **finally**.

As you read, think about the main idea of each section. What are the details that help to support it? After you finish reading, think about the main idea of the entire text.

Reread the text on pages 18–19. Then work with your partner to fill in the organizer.

| Main Idea: |
| _____ |

| Supporting Detail | Supporting Detail | Supporting Detail |
| _____ | _____ | _____ |

E **Words in Context** Scan the article on pages 92–93 and circle these words. As you read, try to guess what the words mean.

widely   estimate   ancestor   brand new   ingenious   allies

F Answer the questions before you read.

1 Have you ever invented your own language? What was it like?
2 Why would someone want to use a secret language?

Reading: Main Idea and Details Unit 9 91

Talking About Language

In this *magazine article*, you'll learn about different types of languages, what language is, and how we use it. A magazine article is a piece of writing that appears in a magazine. It may contain facts and opinions. As you read, think about the main idea of each section and the details that support it. Then think about the main idea and details of the entire article.

Social Studies: Culture

Summary

Objectives: To understand words about communication; to apply own experience and a reading strategy to help comprehension of a text.

Vocabulary: *gesture, beckon, refusal, disapproval, group, lack, raised, enable, invaluable, consist, distress, conceal, transmit, widely, estimate, ancestor, brand new, ingenious, allies*

Reading strategy: Main idea and details

Materials: Audio CD

Words

A Listen and say the words. Then listen and read the sentences. 2·24

- Play the audio. Ask students to point to the words and repeat the words when they hear them.
- Then have students listen and read the sentences as they hear them.
- Say the sentence numbers out of order and have the class read the sentences aloud.

CRITICAL THINKING

- Put students into pairs. Have pairs focus on the context of the sentences and use a dictionary to look up each of the new words and determine if it is a noun, verb, or adverb.

ANSWERS

Nouns: refusal, disapproval, distress
Verbs: gesture, beckon, group, lack, enable, consist, conceal, transmit
Adjectives: raised, invaluable

B Circle True (T) or False (F).

- Have students do the activity on their own.
- Have them compare their answers with a partner.
- Check answers with the class.

ANSWERS

1 F   2 T   3 F   4 F   5 T   6 F   7 T

COLLABORATIVE LEARNING

- Put students into mixed-ability pairs. Have pairs correct the false sentences.

C Work with your partner to answer the questions.

- Put students into pairs to answer the questions.
- Have pairs compare their answers with another pair.
- Check answers with the class.

POSSIBLE ANSWERS

1 Have students name and count the boys and girls in each group.
2 Because they were in distress, in trouble, e.g. lost at sea, lost in the woods, or trapped somewhere.
3 Answers will vary, especially based on culture, e.g. shaking head side to side, wagging finger back and forth, sucking in breath and turning head, head down and arms crossed.

Below level:

- Put students into mixed-ability pairs to answer the questions.

At level:

- Have pairs answer the questions.
- Ask them to compare their answers with another pair.

Above level:

- Have students answer the questions on their own first and then swap papers with another student to compare answers.
- Ask pairs to think of a gesture for beckon, refusal, and distress.

Before You Read

Think

- Have students think about their answers individually.
- Put students into pairs to discuss their answers.
- Hold a class discussion and list the answers on the board.

D Learn: Main Ideas and Details

- Read the *Learn* box together.
- Ask questions to check understanding:
  What is the point an author is trying to make?
  How many main ideas does the whole text have?
  What do details do?
  What words introduce details?

Reread the text on pages 18–19. Then work with your partner to fill in the organizer.

- Read the directions. Then have students reread the article individually.
- Ask pairs to fill in the organizer together.
- Check the answers with the class.

Main Idea: Bridges and tunnels help us overcome obstacles.
Supporting Detail: Factors such as distance, soil, and transportation needs determine if we build a bridge or a tunnel.
Supporting Detail: Types of bridges: beam bridge, arch bridge, and suspension bridge.
Supporting Detail: What tunnels carry, how they are constructed, the Channel Tunnel.

- Keep students in their pairs.
- Have pairs name the main idea for each of the three types of bridge paragraphs, and for the two tunnel paragraphs.

Beam bridge: for short distances; Arch bridge: strong; Suspension bridge: for long distances
Tunnels carry various things; Tunnels are constructed with careful planning

E Words in Context: Scan the article on pages 92–93 and circle these words. As you read, try to guess what the words mean.

- Read the instructions with the class.
- Read each word and have students follow your pronunciation.
- Have students scan the article on pages 92 and 93 and circle the words. Tell them to guess what the words mean from the context.
- Have the students share their ideas about the words' definitions.

Below level:

- Go through the text with students. Have the them find and point to the words.
- Analyse the text with students to identify the context, e.g. for *gesture*, ask a student to point to the first instance of the word. Say *The context does not reveal much. Find the next instance.* Students read that gestures are understood and then there is an example of a gesture. Ask *You read a gesture is beckoning with the arm. What do you think a gesture is?* Elicit answers and continue for the other words.

At level:

- Put students into pairs to figure out the meaning of the new words from context.
- Tell pairs to underline the definitions of the words in context, or underline clues in the context that indicate the meaning of the words.
- Have pairs share their answers with the class.

Above level:

- Put students into pairs to use the context to provide a definition of each word.
- Have pairs share their definitions with the class. Ask pairs to paraphrase the sentences using their definitions.

F Answer the questions before you read.

- Put students into small groups to discuss the questions.
- Tell groups to give examples that support their answers.
- Go over the groups' answers. Ask if anyone has words that they used as babies or small children that their family still uses today.

Reading Preview

- Read the title of the unit's reading text.
- Have students silently read the content of the preview bar.
- Ask *What type of text is it?* Ask *What does this type of text do?*
- Tell students to think about the main idea and details as they read each section. Then, at the end, to think about the main idea and details of the entire article.

Further Practice
Workbook pages 82–83
Online Practice Unit 9 · Get Ready
Oxford iTools Unit 9 · Get Ready

Read 2·25

Talking About Language

What Is Language?

There are many possible answers to this question, but most people agree that language is a way to communicate ideas or feelings, using signs, gestures, or marks. Since the dawn of time, humans have needed to communicate with each other. We often do this through complex systems, such as speech and writing, but not always. Signs and gestures came before speech, and we still use them to communicate today.

Many gestures are understood and used by people of different cultures. These include beckoning with an arm or hand, as a sign to come closer, nodding the head, as a sign of acceptance, and a smile or hug, as a sign of welcome. Gestures of anger or disapproval, such as shaking the head to show refusal, are also widely recognized.

Think
What's the main idea of this section? What details support it?

Languages Around the World

Nobody knows exactly how many languages there are, but experts estimate that there are as many as 7,000. These languages are grouped into families. When languages have a common ancestor, they're part of the same language family. The Indo-European language family, for instance, includes Spanish, English, Hindi, and Russian. When a language is no longer used, such as Latin or Ancient Greek, we say that it's "dead." However, even after people have stopped speaking a language, they sometimes continue to create new words from its roots. The word *astronaut* is an example of this. There were no astronauts in Ancient Greece, of course, but modern people have combined the Ancient Greek word for "star" (*astron*) and "sailor" (*naut*) to form a brand-new word: *astronaut!*

Codes and Sign Language

Louis Braille

All over the world, people who lack the ability to see use a type of code called Braille. Braille was invented in 1824 by a Frenchman named Louis Braille, who lost his sight when he was young. This system of writing allows people to read words through touch. Raised dots on a surface enable them to feel each letter. Today, entire books are printed in Braille.

A telegraph machine

Another type of code, which is called Morse code, is used to communicate over long distances. When the telegraph was invented in 1832, a man named Samuel Morse created this code to send messages using electricity. This system consisted of short signals, called dots, and long signals, called dashes. The code was tapped out, in a series of electrical pulses, and sent over telegraph wires. It was ingenious! The most famous example of Morse code is the distress signal used by sailors and pilots: SOS. In Morse code, it looks like this:

· · · — — — · · ·

Unlike Braille and Morse code, sign language is a true language. In fact, there are many different sign languages used around the world, each with its own grammar and vocabulary. Sign language is invaluable to people who can't hear. It allows them to communicate by making signs with their hands.

What Do We Use Language For?

As you've seen, we use language for an important human need: to connect with each other. The message we communicate and the way we transmit it might be as simple as a smile to say, "I'm happy to see you," or as complex as a book on physics. It might even be a secret, like a message in code that's sent between allies. Each of these types of communication lets us tell another person what we know, how we think, or what we feel. Languages are fascinating. They evolve and change, they're born and they die, and we all use them.

Can You Crack the Code?

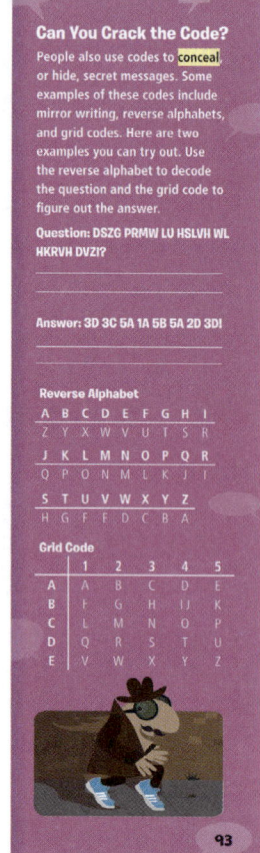

People also use codes to conceal, or hide, secret messages. Some examples of these codes include mirror writing, reverse alphabets, and grid codes. Here are two examples you can try out. Use the reverse alphabet to decode the question and the grid code to figure out the answer.

Question: DSZG PRMW LU HSLVH WL HKRVH DVZI?

_____

Answer: 3D 3C 5A 1A 5B 5A 2D 3D!

Reverse Alphabet

A	B	C	D	E	F	G	H	I
Z	Y	X	W	V	U	T	S	R

J	K	L	M	N	O	P	Q	R
Q	P	O	N	M	L	K	J	I

S	T	U	V	W	X	Y	Z
H	G	F	F	D	C	B	A

Grid Code

	1	2	3	4	5
A	A	B	C	D	E
B	F	G	H	I	J
C	L	M	N	O	P
D	Q	R	S	T	U
E	V	W	X	Y	Z

92

93

Summary

Objectives: To read, understand, and discuss a magazine article; to apply a reading strategy to improve comprehension.

School subject: Social Studies: Culture

Text type: Magazine article (nonfiction)

Reading strategy: Main idea and details

Big Question learning points: *People use language to communicate with each other. Language helps us to overcome obstacles.*

Materials: Talk About It! Poster, Audio CD

Before Reading

- Have students tell you what they see in the pictures.
- Ask them to read the headings.
- Have students say what they already know about languages around the world and what we use language for.

During Reading 🔊 2·25

- Play the audio and have students read along once.
- Then have students read one time individually. Remind them to think about the main idea and details as they read.
- Ask students to stop and answer the *Think* box.

DIFFERENTIATION

Below level:

- Have students read the article with you in small groups.
- As you read, stop and discuss the main idea and details of each section.

- After reading, evaluate the text with students. Ask *What was the main idea of the whole article? What were the details?*

At level:

- Have students read with a partner, taking turns to read the sections of the article.
- Have them stop to evaluate each section as they read, identifying the main idea and details.

Above level:

- Have students read the article independently.
- Put students into pairs to evaluate what they've read. They should take turns telling each other about the main idea and details of each section.
- Together they decide on the main idea and main details of the whole article.

After Reading

CRITICAL THINKING

Discussion questions:

- *What do you think language is after reading this article?*
- *What are some common gestures used in your culture?*
- *Why do you think Morse code was such an ingenious idea to use for communication over long distances?*
- *When do you think it would be useful to use a secret code?*
- *Do you think languages are fascinating? Why or why not?*

- Put students into pairs to decode the message in the box.
- Have pairs work together to decode the message.
- Check the answers with the class. Then have pairs use the code to write a message for another pair to decode.

ANSWERS

Question: What kind of shoes do spies wear?
Answer: Sneakers!

COMMUNICATION

- Display the **Talk About It! Poster** to help students with sentence frames for discussion and expressing personal opinions.
- Put students into pairs to discuss which part of the article is most interesting and what new things they've learned.

CULTURE NOTE

Sign Language

It is often believed that there is a universal sign language, but this is not the case. Just like spoken languages, different countries and cultures have their own sign languages and even dialects.

People also believe that sign languages have some kind of relationship to the spoken language of that country. Again, this is not really the case. The sign languages of Spain and Mexico are very different, even though Spanish is the national language in each country. American Sign Language, used in the United States and in parts of Canada, actually comes from French Sign Language. British Sign Language and American Sign Language are so different that deaf people from the United States have a lot of trouble understanding someone signing from Britain.

Secret Codes

Codes are a method used in cryptography to put a message into an obscured form so it cannot be read by anyone other than the intended recipient. There is often a code book, which helps a person to decipher the code.

One of the most helpful codes for use in battle is called the "idiot code." It is called this because it is impossible to crack. It is created only by the people using it, e.g. any sentence that has the words "dark" and "light" means "attack." And then the place that is mentioned in the following sentence specifies the location.

We moved through the streets at first light and continued until dark. Brigham is a big town. This means, attack Brigham.

Another common way of sending codes was to choose a book and underline certain words or letters. The person deciphering it knows what the letters or words relate to and can decipher it. This could be dangerous in wartime because sometimes the books fell into the hands of the enemy. Then the "code breakers" would do their work and try to crack the code so that they could understand the enemy's communication. Today, most code breaking is done by computers.

Further Practice

Workbook page 84
Online Practice Unit 9 • Read
Oxford **iTools** Unit 9 • Read

Understand

Comprehension

Think What did you learn from "Talking About Language"?

A What is the main idea of the magazine article? What are the supporting details? Fill in the organizer.

Main Idea:
_____

Supporting Detail	Supporting Detail	Supporting Detail
_____	_____	_____
_____	_____	_____

B Match the sentence halves.

1 Languages with a common ancestor   •   • a use a type of code called Braille.
2 Signs and gestures came before speech,   •   • b is the distress signal SOS.
3 Sign language is invaluable   •   • c and we still use them today.
4 People who lack the ability to see   •   • d to people who can't hear.
5 An example of Morse code   •   • e are part of the same language family.

C Words in Context Look at the words you circled in the article. Then use them to complete the newpaper article.

Chief Detective Stevens, whose _____₁, Alfred Stevens, was a code breaker in the late 19th century, has discovered a _____₂ code that no one has ever seen before! The code involves an _____₃ system of light pulses used by criminals to send signals. Detectives and their _____₄ around the world now _____₅ believe that understanding the code will help them solve many mysteries. Police _____₆ that they will have the code completely cracked within the next five days.

94   Unit 9   *Comprehension*

Grammar in Use

Workbook Grammar pages 86–87

D Listen and read along. Then circle the correct answer. 2·26

> How can I improve this sentence? "The lion is orange."
>
> That's good, but I need more information.
>
> The orange lion, which looks very hungry, is right behind you!
>
> Oh!
>
> The orange lion is right behind you!
>
> Wow, that's perfect!

What extra information did Finn give about the lion?
a It's orange.   b It's hungry.

E Learn Grammar Nondefining Relative Clauses

Nondefining relative clauses give you extra information about the subject of a sentence. They're more often used in writing than in speech.

Another type of code, which is called Morse code, is used to communicate over long distances.

Underline the extra information in each sentence.

1 That tree, which was struck by lightning, had to be cut down.
2 My brother, who moved to Japan, is coming home for a visit.
3 Our store, which we opened last year, has been very successful.
4 My friend, whose birthday was yesterday, just got a new bike.
5 I found my watch, which I thought was lost, underneath the sofa.
6 My grandmother, who is 77, goes hiking every weekend.
7 That player, whose team won the championship, is very talented.

> My next class, which is science, is one of my favorites.

F Make a list of short sentences. Then work with your partner to add extra information to them. Use nondefining relative clauses.

My next class is one of my favorites.
My friend is preparing for a race.
That new video game is amazing!

Grammar: Nondefining Relative Clauses   **Unit 9**   95

Summary

Objectives: To demonstrate understanding of a magazine article; to understand the meaning and form of the grammar structure.

Reading: Comprehension

Grammar input: Non-defining relative clauses

Grammar practice: Workbook exercises

Grammar production: Using non-defining relative clauses

Materials: Audio CD

Comprehension

Think

• Read the questions with the class. Ask students to think about their answers individually.

• Then put students into pairs to discuss their answers.

• Have pairs share their discussions with the class.

COLLABORATIVE LEARNING

• In small groups, ask students to collaborate to answer any questions they had during the *Think* exercise.

• Have groups use a dictionary and any other available resources to find answers to their questions about language from the article.

• If students didn't have any specific questions, assign some:
What is the language-family of your native language?
How many people speak your language?
Where in the world do people speak your language?
What languages are spoken in the countries nearest you?

• Have groups share their answers with the class.

A What is the main idea of the magazine article? What are the supporting details? Fill in the organizer.

• Read the instructions with the class.

• Have students turn to the article on pages 92 and 93. Ask students to read the text again themselves and to evaluate it using the organizer as they read.

• Help students to fill in the organizer. Have a few students paraphrase the first paragraph to find the main idea. Ask *What does the heading say? What do you think the main idea will be if that is the heading?*

• Have them fill in the organizer on their own. Go around and help as needed. Tell students to underline the information they are using to complete their organizers.

• Put students into pairs and tell them to compare their organizers.

• Complete the organizers on the board to check them. Elicit the information to complete them from the class.

POSSIBLE ANSWERS

Main Idea: Language is a way to communicate feelings and ideas using signs, gestures, or marks.
Supporting Detail: Languages are grouped into families.
Supporting Detail: Codes like Braille and Morse Code are not languages.
Supporting Detail: Sign language for the deaf is a true language.

Below level:
- Put students into mixed-ability pairs. Have students reread the text in pairs and discuss the main idea and details as they read.
- Then have students paraphrase and use the headings of each paragraph to find the main idea and details.

At level:
- Pairs complete the organizers on their own.
- Have partners compare organizers and discuss their answers. Ask pairs to discuss their organizers with the class.

Above level:
- After students have completed the organizers, put them into pairs.
- Have pairs compare their organizers.
- Then have pairs list additional supporting details for the main idea of each of the three original supporting details.
- Ask pairs to explain the structure of the article to the class.

B Match the sentence halves.
- Students complete the activity individually.
- Check the answers with the class.

ANSWERS
1 e   2 c   3 d   4 a   5 b

CRITICAL THINKING

Ask students additional questions to check understanding:
- *What are some Indo-European languages?*
- *Why are some languages called "dead?"*
- *How does Braille work?*
- *Why do you think Braille is the same everywhere, but there are different sign languages?*

C Words in Context: Look at the words you circled in the article. Then use them to complete the newspaper article.
- Have students go back and find the words in the magazine article.
- Tell them to use the context clues to guess at the meaning of each word and use it to complete the sentences in the newspaper article.
- Check answers with the class.

ANSWERS
1 ancestor   2 brand new   3 ingenious   4 allies
5 widely   6 estimate

Grammar in Use

D Listen and read along. Then circle the correct answer. ⊚ 2·26
- Listen to the dialogue once and have students read along.
- Have students read the question and then circle the correct answer.
- Play the audio again and have students check their answer.
- Check the answer with the class.

ANSWER
b It's hungry.

E Learn Grammar: Nondefining Relative Clauses
- Read the *Learn Grammar* box and example together.
- Ask questions to check understanding:
  What is the nondefining relative clause?
  What does a nondefining relative clause do?
  What is the connecting word?
- Explain to the class: *A non-defining relative clause is different from a defining relative clause because the sentence still makes sense without it, and it uses pronouns like* which *or* who, *but not that.*

Underline the extra information in each sentence.
- Have students complete the activity on their own.

ANSWERS
The following should be underlined:
1 which was struck by lightning   2 who moved to Japan   3 which we opened last year   4 whose birthday was yesterday   5 which I thought was lost   6 who is 77
7 whose team won the championship

F Make a list of short sentences. Then work with your partner to add extra information to them. Use nondefining relative clauses.
- Read the explanation and examples. Have students think of two short sentences on their own.
- Put students into pairs to take turns saying their sentences and then having the partner repeat the sentence with extra information in it.
- Ask a few pairs to say their sentences and clause sentences for the class.

DIFFERENTIATION

Below level:
- Put students into mixed-ability pairs. Have the more confident student help the other student to write two simple sentences.
- Have the more confident student add a nondefining relative clause to the sentences. After which, the other student will explain how the clause gives extra information, but does not change the sentence.
- Then they reverse roles, with the more confident student helping the other student to insert a clause.

At level:
- Have pairs think of two additional sentences, one for an object, and one for a person. Have pairs think of at least three different clauses for each sentence.
- Ask them to notice if the different nondefining relative clauses change the meaning of the original sentences or not.

Above level:
- Have students write three sentences with nondefining relative clauses in them.
- Students give their paper to a partner. The partner changes the nondefining clause.

Workbook Grammar
- Direct students to the Workbook for further practice.

Further practice
Workbook pages 85–87
Online Practice Unit 9 • Understand
Oxford **iTools** Unit 9 • Understand

Communicate

Listening

Think How does your voice change when you're excited? How do you sound when you express other emotions?

A Listen. What are the speakers doing? 2·27

B Listen again. Circle the correct answer. 2·28

1 How does the man sound at the beginning of the conversation?
   a bored
   b happy
   c excited

2 How does the woman sound when she sees her favorite actress?
   a angry
   b excited
   c sad

3 How does the man feel about the bank robber?
   a happy
   b bored
   c angry

4 How does the woman sound when she talks about the sick girl?
   a bored
   b sad
   c excited

Speaking 2·29

C Work with your partner to agree on plans for the weekend. Use your voice to express emotions such as boredom, happiness, anger, and excitement.

Let's go to the museum this weekend! (excited)

No, thanks. I don't feel like ... (bored)

But you said ...! (angry)

I'm sorry. What if we went to ... instead? (apologetic)

Actually, that sounds ... (happy)

Cool! I'll get my ...! (excited)

96 Unit 9 *Listening: Gist • Speaking: Expressing Emotions*

Word Study

D **Learn** **Latin Roots**

Remember: The main part of a word is called the **root**. If you understand what the root means, it can help you understand the meaning of the word. In English, the roots of many words come from Latin and Ancient Greek.

Latin Root	Meaning	Example
astro or **aster**	star	**astronaut**
con	with or together	**connect**

Listen and write the roots. Then work with your partner to write a sentence for each word. 2·30 **A-Z**

1 _____ biology 2 _____ fident 3 _____ cept 4 _____ isk
5 _____ clude 6 _____ cur 7 _____ nomer 8 _____ physics

Writing Study

E **Learn** **Using Connectors to Show Contrast**

Use connectors such as **however**, **unlike**, and **on the other hand** to show contrast between clauses or sentences that express different ideas.

When a language is no longer used, we say that it's "dead." **However**, even after people have stopped speaking a language, they sometimes continue to create new words from its roots.

Rewrite one of the sentences in each pair using the connectors in parentheses ( ).

1 French and Italian are from the same language family. Mandarin Chinese belongs to a different family. (on the other hand)
2 I like studying languages. I don't like studying math. (however)
3 Mirror writing is a kind of code. It's not a language. (unlike English)

Write Now practice writing in the **Workbook.** page 89

Vocabulary: Latin Roots • Writing: Using Connectors to Show Contrast **Unit 9** **97**

BIG QUESTION 5

How do we use language?

People use language to express their feelings.

What kind of things do you express with language?

Summary

Objectives: To learn and practice listening, speaking, and writing strategies to facilitate effective communication.

Vocabulary: *astrobiology, confident, concept, asterisk, conclude, concur, astronomer, astrophysics*

Listening strategy: Listening for gist

Speaking: Expressing emotions

Word Study: Latin roots

Writing Study: Using connectors to show contrast

Big Question learning points: *We express our emotions through language. People use language to communicate with each other.*

Materials: Discover Poster 5, Audio CD, Big Question Chart

Listening

Think

- Tell students to think about the questions individually.
- Have them discuss their answers with a partner.
- Share the discussions with the class.
- Have students model the changes in their voice. Have fun with it.

A Listen. What are the speakers doing? 2·27

- Play the audio once and have students listen.
- Then play the audio again. Ask *What are the speakers doing?* Have the class discuss what they heard.

ANSWERS
The people are watching a movie on TV.

B Listen again. Circle the correct answer. 2·28

- Have students read the questions.
- Play the audio so students can complete the exercise.
- Have students compare answers with a partner before checking answers with the class.

ANSWERS
1 bored 2 excited 3 angry 4 sad

Speaking 2·29

C Work with your partner to agree on plans for the weekend. Use your voice to express emotions such as boredom, happiness, anger, and excitement.

- Read the explanation with the class.
- Have students listen to the audio and read along.
- Say each of the expressions with students echoing as they hear each line. Exaggerate the emotion.
- Elicit explanations for how the voice changes with different emotions. Ask *How does your voice sound when you're excited? How does your voice sound when you're bored? Angry? Happy?*
- Play the audio a second time if necessary.
- Put students into pairs and tell them to practice the dialogue, using polite expressions and including their own ideas for what they want to do on the weekend.
- Have some pairs act out their dialogues for the class.

- Keep students in pairs. Have each student write a simple sentence, e.g. *I'm studying English.*
- Have students swap their sentence with their partner. The other student has to read the same sentence using the five different emotions used in C. Model each of the emotions using your example sentence *I'm studying English.* Point out that the emphasis on certain words changes as does your tone.
- Pairs practice reading the sentence.
- Ask some pairs to say their sentences for the class.

Word Study

D Learn: Latin Roots

- Read the *Learn* box and examples together. Elicit definitions for both example words.

Listen and write the roots. Then work with your partner to write a sentence for each word. ⊚ 2·30

- Play the audio for students to listen one time.
- Ask them to write the root of each word.
- Put students into pairs and ask them to write a sentence for each word.
- Check answers with the class.

1 astrobiology 2 confident 3 concept 4 asterisk
5 conclude 6 concur 7 astronomer 8 astrophysics

Below level:

- Say the words and spell them. Ask the students to write the words.
- Go over the meanings and give examples.

At level:

- Say the meaning of one of the words and have students name the word and spell it.

Above level:

- Put students into pairs. Have them look up the definitions in the dictionary and then write sentences using the new words.
- Have pairs write their sentences on the board and tell the class about them.

Writing Study

E Learn: Using Connectors to Show Contrast

- Read the *Learn* box together.
- Ask questions to check understanding:
  What do connector words do?
  What are some connector words?

Rewrite one of the sentences in each pair using the connectors in parentheses ( ).

- Have students do the activity individually.
- Then put students into pairs to check each other's work before checking answers with the class.

1 French and Italian are from the same language family. On the other hand, Mandarin Chinese belongs to a different family.
2 I like studying languages. However, I don't like studying math.
3 Mirror writing is a kind of code. Unlike English, it's not a language.

- Put students into pairs. Have them go back through the sentences and use different connecting phrases.
- Mention that some connectors will make better sense than others, so students should choose carefully.
- Check the answers with the class.

Write

- Direct students to the Workbook for further writing practice.

Big Question 5 Review

How do we use language?

- Display **Discover Poster 5**. Discuss what you see.
- Refer to the learning points covered in Unit 9 that are written on the poster and have students explain how they relate to the different pictures.
- Return to the **Big Question Chart**.
- Ask students what they have learned about language while studying this unit.

Further practice
Workbook pages 88–89
Online Practice Unit 9 • Communicate
Oxford iTools Unit 9 • Communicate

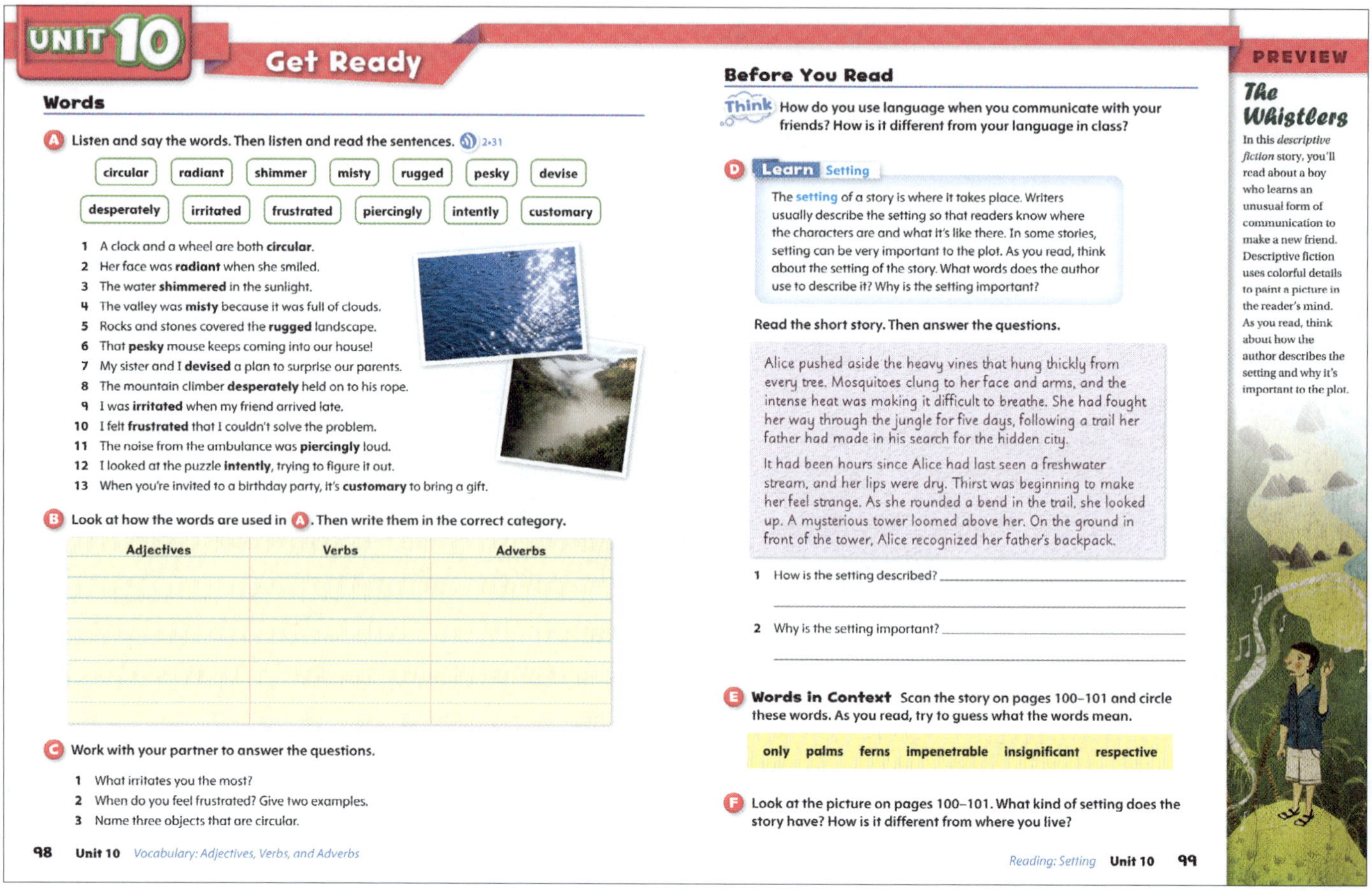

UNIT 10 — Get Ready

Words

A Listen and say the words. Then listen and read the sentences. 2·31

circular	radiant	shimmer	misty	rugged	pesky	devise

desperately	irritated	frustrated	piercingly	intently	customary

1 A clock and a wheel are both **circular**.
2 Her face was **radiant** when she smiled.
3 The water **shimmered** in the sunlight.
4 The valley was **misty** because it was full of clouds.
5 Rocks and stones covered the **rugged** landscape.
6 That **pesky** mouse keeps coming into our house!
7 My sister and I **devised** a plan to surprise our parents.
8 The mountain climber **desperately** held on to his rope.
9 I was **irritated** when my friend arrived late.
10 I felt **frustrated** that I couldn't solve the problem.
11 The noise from the ambulance was **piercingly** loud.
12 I looked at the puzzle **intently**, trying to figure it out.
13 When you're invited to a birthday party, it's **customary** to bring a gift.

B Look at how the words are used in **A**. Then write them in the correct category.

Adjectives	Verbs	Adverbs

C Work with your partner to answer the questions.

1 What irritates you the most?
2 When do you feel frustrated? Give two examples.
3 Name three objects that are circular.

98 Unit 10 *Vocabulary: Adjectives, Verbs, and Adverbs*

Before You Read

Think How do you use language when you communicate with your friends? How is it different from your language in class?

D **Learn** Setting

The **setting** of a story is where it takes place. Writers usually describe the setting so that readers know where the characters are and what it's like there. In some stories, setting can be very important to the plot. As you read, think about the setting of the story. What words does the author use to describe it? Why is the setting important?

Read the short story. Then answer the questions.

> Alice pushed aside the heavy vines that hung thickly from every tree. Mosquitoes clung to her face and arms, and the intense heat was making it difficult to breathe. She had fought her way through the jungle for five days, following a trail her father had made in his search for the hidden city.
>
> It had been hours since Alice had last seen a freshwater stream, and her lips were dry. Thirst was beginning to make her feel strange. As she rounded a bend in the trail, she looked up. A mysterious tower loomed above her. On the ground in front of the tower, Alice recognized her father's backpack.

1 How is the setting described? _____
_____

2 Why is the setting important? _____

E **Words in Context** Scan the story on pages 100–101 and circle these words. As you read, try to guess what the words mean.

only	palms	ferns	impenetrable	insignificant	respective

F Look at the picture on pages 100–101. What kind of setting does the story have? How is it different from where you live?

Reading: Setting **Unit 10** 99

PREVIEW

The Whistlers

In this *descriptive fiction* story, you'll read about a boy who learns an unusual form of communication to make a new friend. Descriptive fiction uses colorful details to paint a picture in the reader's mind. As you read, think about how the author describes the setting and why it's important to the plot.

Summary

Objectives: To understand about adjectives, verbs, and adverbs; to apply own experience and a reading strategy to help comprehension of a text.

Vocabulary: *circular, radiant, shimmer, misty, rugged, pesky, devise, desperately, irritated, frustrated, piercingly, intently, customary, only, palms, ferns impenetrable, insignificant, respective*

Reading strategy: Setting

Materials: Audio CD

Words

A Listen and say the words. Then listen and read the sentences. 2·31

- Play the audio. Ask students to point to the words and repeat the words when they hear them.
- Then have students listen and read the sentences as they hear them.
- Say the sentence numbers out of order and have the class read the sentences aloud.

B Look at how the words are used in A. Then write them in the correct category.

- Read the organizer labels with the class.
- Model how to do the activity with the first example. Point to the organizer as you ask *What kind of word is circular?* Show students where to write it on the organizer.
- Have students do the activity on their own and then compare answers with a partner.
- Check answers with the class.

ANSWERS

Adjectives: circular, radiant, misty, rugged, pesky, irritated, frustrated, customary
Verbs: shimmer, devise
Adverbs: desperately, piercingly, intently

CRITICAL THINKING

Ask the following questions to check understanding:

- *Which words might you use to describe a landscape?*
- *Which words are feelings?*

C Work with your partner to answer the questions.

- Have pairs read the questions and answer them together.
- Check the answers with the class.

POSSIBLE ANSWERS

1 Loud noises irritate me the most.
2 I feel frustrated when I don't get my way. I feel frustrated when my brother is right about something.
3 A watch face, a coin, a round tabletop are all circular.

- Put students into pairs and have them write sentences for the new words, but tell them to leave a blank where the word goes.
- Have pairs trade papers with another pair to complete the sentences.
- Ask them to correct each other's work and discuss any meanings they are not clear about.
- Share some sentences with the class by having pairs write them on the board.

Before You Read

Think

- Have students read the questions and make notes about their ideas and answers individually.
- Students discuss their ideas to the questions in small groups.
- Ask them to share some of the ideas with the class. List the ideas on the board.

D Learn: Setting

- Read the *Learn* box with the class.
- Ask *What is "setting?" What do authors describe in the setting?*

Read the short story. Then answer the questions.

- Students read the short story individually. Then they answer the questions.
- Put students into pairs to compare their answers.
- Then go over the answers with the class.

1 The setting: heavy vines, trees, mosquitoes clinging to her face and arms, intense heat, no freshwater, mysterious tower.
2 Important: the heat makes it difficult to breathe; we get the feeling she is trapped (pushing aside vines); and uncomfortable (thirsty).

Ask the following questions to check understanding about the text:

- *What do the details of the setting's description make you feel?*
- *Would this story be different if it were in a different setting? How?*

E Words in Context: Scan the story on pages 100–101, and circle these words. As you read, try to guess what the words mean.

- Read each word and have students follow your pronunciation.
- Elicit meanings for the words to check if students know them.
- Then ask questions to help students guess what they think the words could mean before they do the activity.
- Tell students to think about the words as they read the story.

F Look at the picture on pages 100–101. What kind of setting does the story have? How is it different from where you live?

- Have students look at the picture in the Student Book
- Ask them to tell you what kind of setting the story has and how it is different from where the students live.

Below level:

- Put students into mixed-ability pairs.
- Have pairs discuss the picture. Then have pairs compare and contrast the picture to where they live.
- Have a few pairs share their ideas with the class.

At level:

- Put students into pairs.
- Have pairs discuss the picture and make a list of phrases to describe them.
- Ask pairs to make a list of phrases to describe and contrast where they live.
- Have pairs read their lists to the class.

Above level:

- Have students list descriptions for the picture and the place they live individually.
- Then put students into small groups to compare their lists.
- Have each group come up with a master list.
- Have groups share their lists and make notes on the board.

Reading Preview

- Read the title of the unit's reading text.
- Have students silently read the content of the preview bar.
- Ask *What type of text is it?* Ask *What does this type of text do? Is the story true?*
- Tell students to think about how the author describes the setting and why it is important to the story as they read.

| **Further Practice**
Workbook pages 90–91
Online Practice Unit 10 · Get Ready
Oxford **iTools** Unit 10 · Get Ready

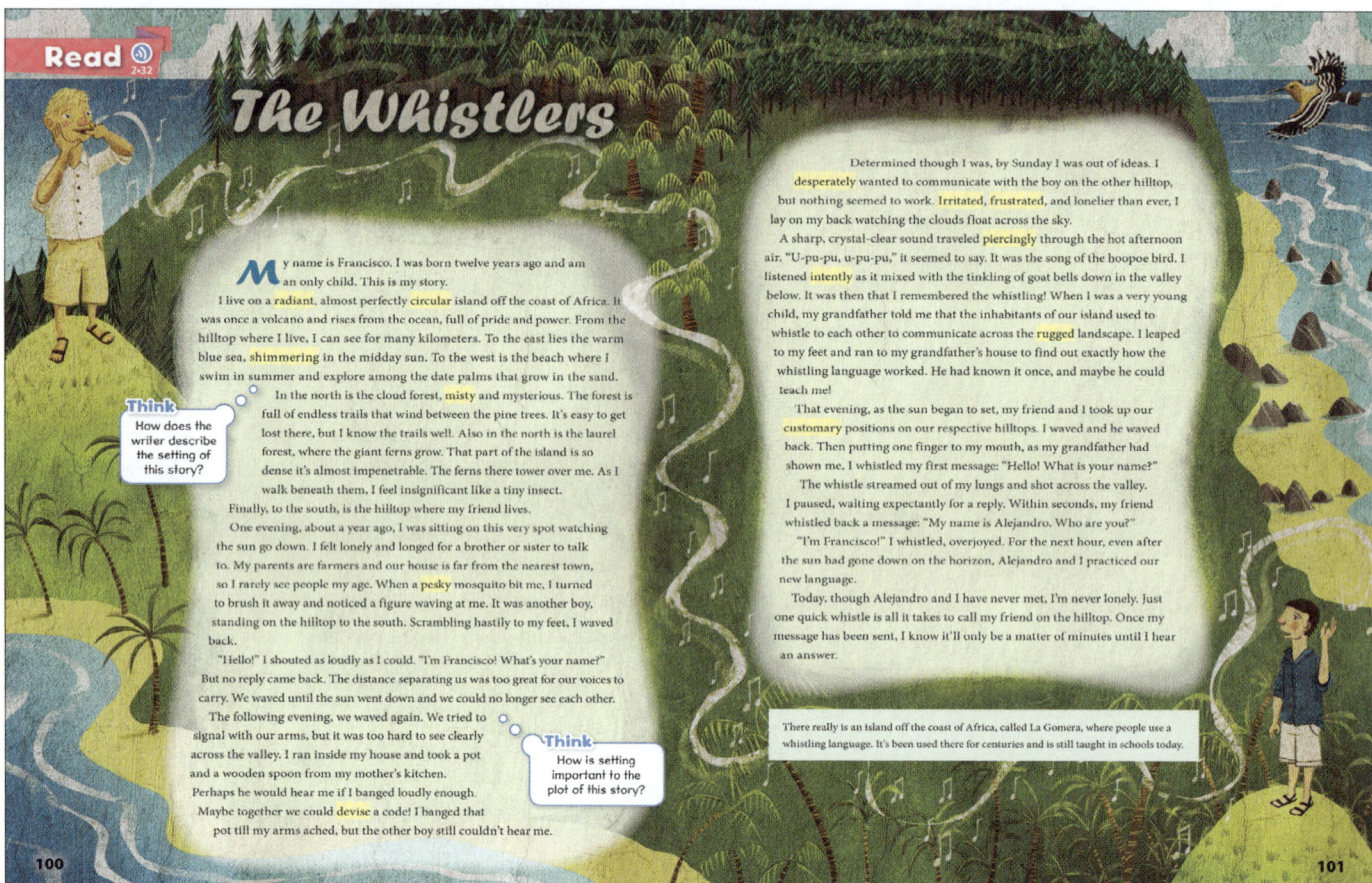

The Whistlers

My name is Francisco. I was born twelve years ago and am an only child. This is my story.

I live on a radiant, almost perfectly circular island off the coast of Africa. It was once a volcano and rises from the ocean, full of pride and power. From the hilltop where I live, I can see for many kilometers. To the east lies the warm blue sea, shimmering in the midday sun. To the west is the beach where I swim in summer and explore among the date palms that grow in the sand.

In the north is the cloud forest, misty and mysterious. The forest is full of endless trails that wind between the pine trees. It's easy to get lost there, but I know the trails well. Also in the north is the laurel forest, where the giant ferns grow. That part of the island is so dense it's almost impenetrable. The ferns there tower over me. As I walk beneath them, I feel insignificant like a tiny insect.

Finally, to the south, is the hilltop where my friend lives.

One evening, about a year ago, I was sitting on this very spot watching the sun go down. I felt lonely and longed for a brother or sister to talk to. My parents are farmers and our house is far from the nearest town, so I rarely see people my age. When a pesky mosquito bit me, I turned to brush it away and noticed a figure waving at me. It was another boy, standing on the hilltop to the south. Scrambling hastily to my feet, I waved back.

"Hello!" I shouted as loudly as I could. "I'm Francisco! What's your name?" But no reply came back. The distance separating us was too great for our voices to carry. We waved until the sun went down and we could no longer see each other.

The following evening, we waved again. We tried to signal with our arms, but it was too hard to see clearly across the valley. I ran inside my house and took a pot and a wooden spoon from my mother's kitchen. Perhaps he would hear me if I banged loudly enough. Maybe together we could devise a code! I banged that pot till my arms ached, but the other boy still couldn't hear me.

Think How does the writer describe the setting of this story?

Think How is setting important to the plot of this story?

Determined though I was, by Sunday I was out of ideas. I desperately wanted to communicate with the boy on the other hilltop, but nothing seemed to work. Irritated, frustrated, and lonelier than ever, I lay on my back watching the clouds float across the sky.

A sharp, crystal-clear sound traveled piercingly through the hot afternoon air. "U-pu-pu, u-pu-pu," it seemed to say. It was the song of the hoopoe bird. I listened intently as it mixed with the tinkling of goat bells down in the valley below. It was then that I remembered the whistling! When I was a very young child, my grandfather told me that the inhabitants of our island used to whistle to each other to communicate across the rugged landscape. I leaped to my feet and ran to my grandfather's house to find out exactly how the whistling language worked. He had known it once, and maybe he could teach me!

That evening, as the sun began to set, my friend and I took up our customary positions on our respective hilltops. I waved and he waved back. Then putting one finger to my mouth, as my grandfather had shown me, I whistled my first message: "Hello! What is your name?"

The whistle streamed out of my lungs and shot across the valley. I paused, waiting expectantly for a reply. Within seconds, my friend whistled back a message: "My name is Alejandro. Who are you?"

"I'm Francisco!" I whistled, overjoyed. For the next hour, even after the sun had gone down on the horizon, Alejandro and I practiced our new language.

Today, though Alejandro and I have never met, I'm never lonely. Just one quick whistle is all it takes to call my friend on the hilltop. Once my message has been sent, I know it'll only be a matter of minutes until I hear an answer.

There really is an island off the coast of Africa, called La Gomera, where people use a whistling language. It's been used there for centuries and is still taught in schools today.

100   101

Summary

Objectives: To read, understand, and discuss descriptive fiction; to apply a reading strategy to improve comprehension.

School subject: Social Studies: Culture

Text type: Descriptive fiction

Reading strategy: Setting

Big Question learning points: *People use language to communicate with each other. Language helps us to overcome obstacles. We use language to make friends and connect with others.*

Materials: Audio CD

Before Reading

- Read the title.
- Have students point to the picture and describe what they see.
- Ask students to predict what they think this story will be about.

- Tell students to read the box at the end of the story. Then ask *What do you think this story is about?*

During Reading 2·32

- Remind students to think about how the author describes the setting and why it is important to the story as they read.
- Play the audio. Students listen as they read along.
- Play the audio a second time if necessary.

Below level:

- Put students into small groups and have them read sections of the text after you. Elicit observations about the setting after the sections.
- Stop at the *Think* boxes and help the groups to answer them.

At level:

- Put students into pairs to read the text to each other. Pairs should stop and discuss the setting as they read.
- Ask them to stop at the *Think* boxes and answer them.

Above level:

- Have students read the text individually and make notes on the setting as they go.
- Put students into pairs to compare the notes they took and discuss why the setting is important.
- Have a few pairs tell the class their ideas.

Discussion questions:

- *Who are the main characters?*
- *What is the main feature of the setting in this story?*
- *Why do they have to whistle to communicate?*
- *Why do you think it is important for both boys to keep up with this communication?*
- *Could this story have taken place in a different setting? Explain.*
- *Can you think of times when it is easier to whistle than to yell?*
- *Can you think of any problems with this method of communication?*
- *Do you think it would be easy to learn?*

After Reading

- Put students into small groups to discuss what kinds of things you would need to communicate if you lived on the island in the story. How would a whistle language work to communicate?
- Then have groups share their ideas with the class.

CREATIVITY

- Put students into small groups of three or four.
- Tell them that they all live on an island which has big lakes. They all live across from each other, over the lakes. They can see each other on the opposite banks, but can't hear each other speak or shout.
- Have students think about how they could communicate with each other if they couldn't whistle. What other methods could they use?, e.g. making drums, smoke signals, animal noises.
- Have students decide how their method of communication would work – what would the different sounds or other things represent? How would it work?
- Have each group share their ideas with the class.
- Have the class vote on the most interesting method of communication.

CULTURE NOTE

The island of La Gomera is in the Atlantic Ocean off the coast of Africa. It is one of the Canary Islands that belong to Spain.

Because the island has been formed from a volcano, it has a steep peak and deep valleys. The exterior is rugged. Because of this geography, the people who originally lived on the island have used a whistling language, called *Silbo Gomera,* since Roman times.

When Spanish people came to live on the island in the 16th century, they adopted the language. The language nearly died out, but at the beginning of the 21st century, it became a required course in schools.

The language works by whistles that sound similar to the patterns of spoken Spanish. It is used in areas where people are far away or in mountainous regions and is more commonly used by shepherds to call their sheep or goats.

There are other whistling communities in Turkey, Greece, Mexico, and parts of Africa.

Further Practice
Workbook page 92
Online Practice Unit 10 • Read
Oxford iTools Unit 10 • Read

Understand

Comprehension

Think Have you ever felt lonely? What did you do about it?

A What is the setting like in "The Whistlers"? Fill in the organizer.

Setting: _____

How It's Described	Why It's Important
_____	_____
_____	_____

B Circle the correct answer.

1 People on the island used whistling _____.
  a to communicate with hoopoe birds
  b to communicate over long distances
  c because they liked the way it sounded
  d because they couldn't hear well

2 Francisco learned the whistling language from _____.
  a a hoopoe bird
  b his friend Alejandro
  c his grandfather
  d his grandmother

3 Francisco didn't try _____ to communicate.
  a gesturing
  b making loud noises
  c shouting
  d sending a letter

4 Francisco wanted to communicate with Alejandro because _____.
  a he was lonely
  b he was bored
  c he was lost
  d he wanted to practice whistling

C **Words in Context** Look at the words you circled in the story. Then use them to complete the sentences.

1 The beach was hot, so we stood in the shade of some _____.
2 After school, my friend and I went home to our _____ houses.
3 Jungles can be almost _____ when there are a lot of trees and plants.
4 I'm not an _____ child. I have a brother.
5 When I look at all the stars in the sky, I sometimes feel small and _____.
6 We saw _____ and other plants at the botanical garden.

102 Unit 10 *Comprehension*

Grammar in Use

Workbook Grammar pages 94–95

D Listen and read along. Then circle the correct answer. 2-33

> Hooray! The thief who stole my cookies has been arrested!
> I wonder if the thief has been locked up.
> Maybe he or she has been taken to the courthouse.
> Oh, it's you!
> I told you those cookies were good enough to steal!

1 Does April say who arrested the thief? **Yes** **No**
2 Do you know who arrested the thief? **Yes** **No**

You can use the passive voice when it's obvious who does the action.

E **Learn Grammar** Passive Statements (Present Perfect)

Use the **passive** voice when you don't say who does the action.

The object of an active sentence becomes the subject of a passive sentence.

Remember: You can use the passive voice in the **present** and the **past** tense. You can also use the passive voice in the **present perfect** tense.

Active	Passive
I've sent my message.	**My message has been sent.**
subject object	subject

Circle *active* or *passive*. If the sentence is active, underline who does the action.

1 The car has been repaired.   active   passive
2 An artist has created a mural.   active   passive
3 The fire has been put out.   active   passive
4 A package has been delivered.   active   passive
5 Janet has picked up the book.   active   passive

> The homework has been assigned.

F Make a chart like this one. Write your own active sentences. Then work with your partner to turn them into passive sentences.

Active	Passive
Our teacher has assigned the homework.	

Grammar: Passive Statements (Present Perfect) **Unit 10** **103**

Summary

Objectives: To demonstrate understanding of a descriptive fictional text; to understand the meaning and form of the grammar structure.

Reading: Comprehension

Grammar input: Passive statements (present perfect)

Grammar practice: Workbook exercises

Grammar production: Passive (present perfect)

Materials: Audio CD

Comprehension

Think

- Have students think about their answers individually first. Then hold a class discussion.
- Ask *Do you think you would get lonely living on an island? Why or why not?*

A What is the setting like in "The Whistlers"? Fill in the organizer.

- Read the instructions with the class.
- Tell the students to read the story again and then fill in the organizer on their own. Go around and help as needed.
- Elicit the information to complete them from the class.

ANSWERS

Setting: La Gomera island
How it's described: a radiant, almost perfectly circular island; warm blue sea; beaches; cloud forest; laurel forest; giant ferns; dense almost impenetrable

Why it's important: makes him feel insignificant; he feels lonely; he feels irritated, lonely, frustrated; he is overjoyed

DIFFERENTIATION

Below level:

- Help students to fill in the organizer. Refer back to the story on pages 100 and 101. Ask *What is the setting? Where will you write this on the organizer? How is the island described? Why is it important?*
- Put students into mixed-ability pairs to continue to fill in the organizer.

At level:

- Have students complete the organizer on their own and then compare with a partner.
- Check the answers with the class.

Above level:

- Have students complete the organizer on their own.
- Then put students into pairs to compare their answers. Ask pairs to discuss their reasons for their answers.
- Have pairs explain their organizers to the class.

B Circle the correct answer.

COLLABORATIVE LEARNING

- Put students into small mixed-ability groups.
- Have groups work together to answer the questions. Tell students to turn back to the story to find the answers.
- Check answers with the class.

ANSWERS
1 b 2 c 3 d 4 a

C Words in Context: Look at the words you circled in the story. Then use them to complete the sentences.

- Have students go back and find the words in the story.
- Tell them to use the context clues to guess at the meaning of each word.
- Ask students to complete the sentences.

CRITICAL THINKING

- Put students into pairs.
- Have pairs discuss the meaning of the words and then to write new sentences for the words in context.
- Tell pairs to write the sentences, but to leave a blank where the word in context goes. Allow students to use a dictionary.
- Then pairs trade papers with another pair and complete the sentences.
- Ask pairs to check each other's work.
- Have them share their sentences with the class.

Grammar in Use

D Listen and read along. Then circle the correct answer. 🎧 2·33

- Listen to the dialogue once and then read it together as a class.
- Play the audio again, if necessary.
- Have students circle the correct answers.

ANSWERS
1 No   2 Yes

E Learn Grammar: Passive Statements (Present Perfect)

- Read the *Learn Grammar* box together.
- Using the example in the book, ask *What is the difference between active and passive voice? Who did the action in the first example? Who did the action in the second example? Does the passive always have to be in the past tense? What other tenses can the passive be in?*

Circle *active* or *passive*. If the sentence is active, underline who does the action.

- Read the first sentence together. Ask the class to identify who did the action? (*We don't know.*) Elicit which tense it is (*passive*).
- Have students complete the rest on their own.
- Check answers with the class.

ANSWERS
1 passive   2 active (*an artist*)   3 passive
4 passive   5 active (*Janet*)

COLLABORATIVE LEARNING

- Put students into pairs.
- Have pairs think of four more sentences. Three should be passive and one should be active.
- Have pairs share their example sentences with the class.
- Ask the class to identify which sentence is active.

F Make a chart like this one. Write your own active sentences. Then work with your partner to turn them into passive sentences.

- Put students in pairs.
- Explain how to do the activity and then model the example dialogue with a volunteer.
- Have students take turns changing the sentences.

DIFFERENTIATION

Below level:

- Write four sentences on the board, as follows:
  The car ran out of gas.
  The boy lost his backpack.
  The artist won a prize.
  The girl baked cookies.
- Read the sentences with the class. Have the students work in pairs to rewrite the sentences as passive.
- Ask two volunteers to come to the board to write the passive sentences.

At level:

- Put students in a circle. One student says an active sentence, e.g. *The mouse ran under the chair.* The next student in the circle makes the sentence passive, e.g. *The chair has a mouse under it.*
- The next student in the circle takes the subject of the passive sentence and uses it in a new active sentence, e.g. *Someone broke the chair.* Continue in this way around the entire circle at least once.

Above level:

- Give students four words, e.g. *doctor, pilot, bicycle, city.*
- The students use the four words in eight sentences: four active and four passive.
- Have students trade papers with a partner to check each other's work.
- Ask students to share some pairs of sentences with the class.

Workbook Grammar

- Direct students to the Workbook for further practice.

Further practice
Workbook pages 93–95
Online Practice Unit 10 · Understand
Oxford iTools Unit 10 · Understand

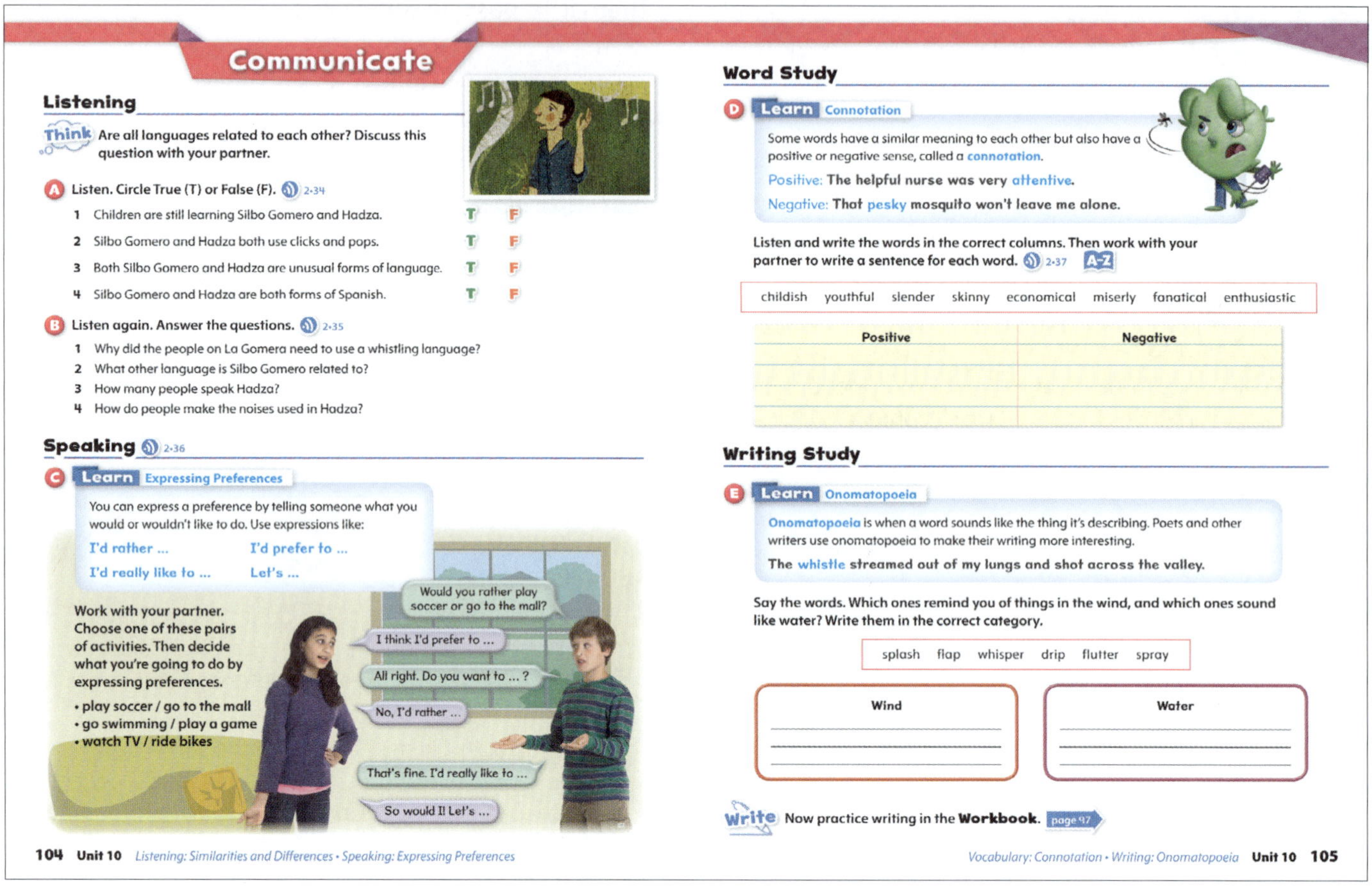

Communicate

Listening

Think Are all languages related to each other? Discuss this question with your partner.

A Listen. Circle True (T) or False (F). 2·34

1 Children are still learning Silbo Gomero and Hadza. T F
2 Silbo Gomero and Hadza both use clicks and pops. T F
3 Both Silbo Gomero and Hadza are unusual forms of language. T F
4 Silbo Gomero and Hadza are both forms of Spanish. T F

B Listen again. Answer the questions. 2·35

1 Why did the people on La Gomera need to use a whistling language?
2 What other language is Silbo Gomero related to?
3 How many people speak Hadza?
4 How do people make the noises used in Hadza?

Speaking 2·36

C **Learn** Expressing Preferences

You can express a preference by telling someone what you would or wouldn't like to do. Use expressions like:

I'd rather …   I'd prefer to …
I'd really like to …   Let's …

Work with your partner. Choose one of these pairs of activities. Then decide what you're going to do by expressing preferences.

• play soccer / go to the mall
• go swimming / play a game
• watch TV / ride bikes

Would you rather play soccer or go to the mall?
I think I'd prefer to …
All right. Do you want to … ?
No, I'd rather …
That's fine. I'd really like to …
So would I! Let's …

104 **Unit 10** *Listening: Similarities and Differences · Speaking: Expressing Preferences*

Word Study

D **Learn** Connotation

Some words have a similar meaning to each other but also have a positive or negative sense, called a **connotation**.

Positive: The helpful nurse was very **attentive**.
Negative: That **pesky** mosquito won't leave me alone.

Listen and write the words in the correct columns. Then work with your partner to write a sentence for each word. 2·37 **A-Z**

childish   youthful   slender   skinny   economical   miserly   fanatical   enthusiastic

Positive	Negative

Writing Study

E **Learn** Onomatopoeia

Onomatopoeia is when a word sounds like the thing it's describing. Poets and other writers use onomatopoeia to make their writing more interesting.
The **whistle** streamed out of my lungs and shot across the valley.

Say the words. Which ones remind you of things in the wind, and which ones sound like water? Write them in the correct category.

splash   flap   whisper   drip   flutter   spray

Wind	Water

Write Now practice writing in the **Workbook**. page 97

Vocabulary: Connotation · Writing: Onomatopoeia **Unit 10** 105

Summary

Objectives: To learn and practice listening, speaking, and writing strategies to facilitate effective communication.

Vocabulary: *childish, skinny, economical, fanatical, miserly, slender, youthful, enthusiastic*

Listening strategy: Listening for similarities and differences

Speaking: Expressing preferences

Word Study: Connotation

Writing Study: Onomatopoeia

Big Question learning points: *People use language to communicate with each other. We use language to make friends and connect with others.*

Materials: Audio CD

Listening

Think

• Have students discuss the question with a partner.
• Ask students to put up their hands to show who thinks languages are all related and who doesn't.
• Ask questions to get students to explain their position.

A Listen. Circle True (T) or False (F). 2·34

• Have students read the sentences. Ask *What will you listen for?*
• Play the audio once and have students listen.
• Tell students to circle the correct answer.
• Play the audio again so they can check their work.
• When checking the answers, have students correct the false answers.

ANSWERS
1 T   2 F (La Gomera is technically Spanish.)   3 T
4 F (Hadza is not related to Spanish, or any language.)

B Listen again. Answer the questions. 2·35

• Have students read the questions and think about the answers.
• Put students in pairs to discuss the answers.
• Play the audio so students can check their answers.

ANSWERS
1 To communicate across the steep ravines and valleys.
2 Silbo Gomera is related to Spanish.
3 Only a few thousand people speak Hadza.
4 People use their tongues to make the clicks and pops of Hadza.

Speaking 🔘 2·36

C Learn: Expressing Preferences
- Read the *Learn* box and the examples.
- Play the audio one time. Play the audio a second time for students to take parts and read along with it.
- Put students into pairs to do the dialogue.
- Ask a few volunteers to say their dialogue for the class.

Work with your partner. Choose one of these pairs of activities. Then decide what you're going to do by expressing preferences.

COMMUNICATION
- Have students think about one of the six things listed that they would like to do: play soccer, go to the mall, go swimming, play a game, watch TV, ride bikes.
- Give students a few minutes to circulate around the room expressing preferences according to the dialogue until they find a partner who wants to do the same things as they do.
- After everyone has found a partner, have a few students say their dialogue for the class.

Word Study

D Learn: Connotation
- Read the *Learn* box and examples together.
- Ask the class for definitions of the words. Ask *What does "attentive" mean? Is that a good thing for a nurse to be? What does "pesky" mean? Is being pesky a positive thing?*

Listen and write the words in the correct columns. Then work with your partner to write a sentence for each word. 🔘 2·37
- Say some of the words in random order and have students spell them.
- Ask students to write the words in the correct columns.
- Check answers with the class.

ANSWERS
Positive: youthful, slender, economical, enthusiastic
Negative: childish, skinny, miserly, fanatical

COLLABORATIVE LEARNING
- Put students into pairs. Have them write sentences for the words.
- Have pairs check each other's work.
- Invite some students to the board to write a sentence. Include one sentence for each word.

Writing Study

E Learn: Onomatopoeia
- Read the *Learn* box together. Have students repeat the word *o-no-ma-to-poe-ia* after you.
- Read the example with dramatic flair.

Say the words. Which ones remind you of things in the wind, and which ones sound like water? Write them in the correct category.
- Have students complete the exercise on their own.
- Then have them compare answers with a partner.
- Ask students to read the words aloud to resemble the different sounds.

ANSWERS
Wind: flap, whisper, flutter
Water: splash, drip, spray

DIFFERENTIATION
Below level:
- Put students into mixed-ability pairs.
- Have the more confident student help the other student choose the column each word goes in.
- Have pairs share their answers with another pair.

At level:
- Put students into pairs. Have them think of three more onomatopoetic words.
- Ask pairs to compare their words with a partner.
- Compile the list of words on the board.

Above level:
- Tell students to write sentences using the words.
- Students then swap papers to check each other's work.
- Have students write their sentences on the board.

Write
- Direct students to the Workbook for further writing practice.

Further practice
Workbook pages 96–97
Online Practice Unit 10 • Communicate
Oxford iTools Unit 10 • Communicate

Units 9 and 10 Wrap Up page 106

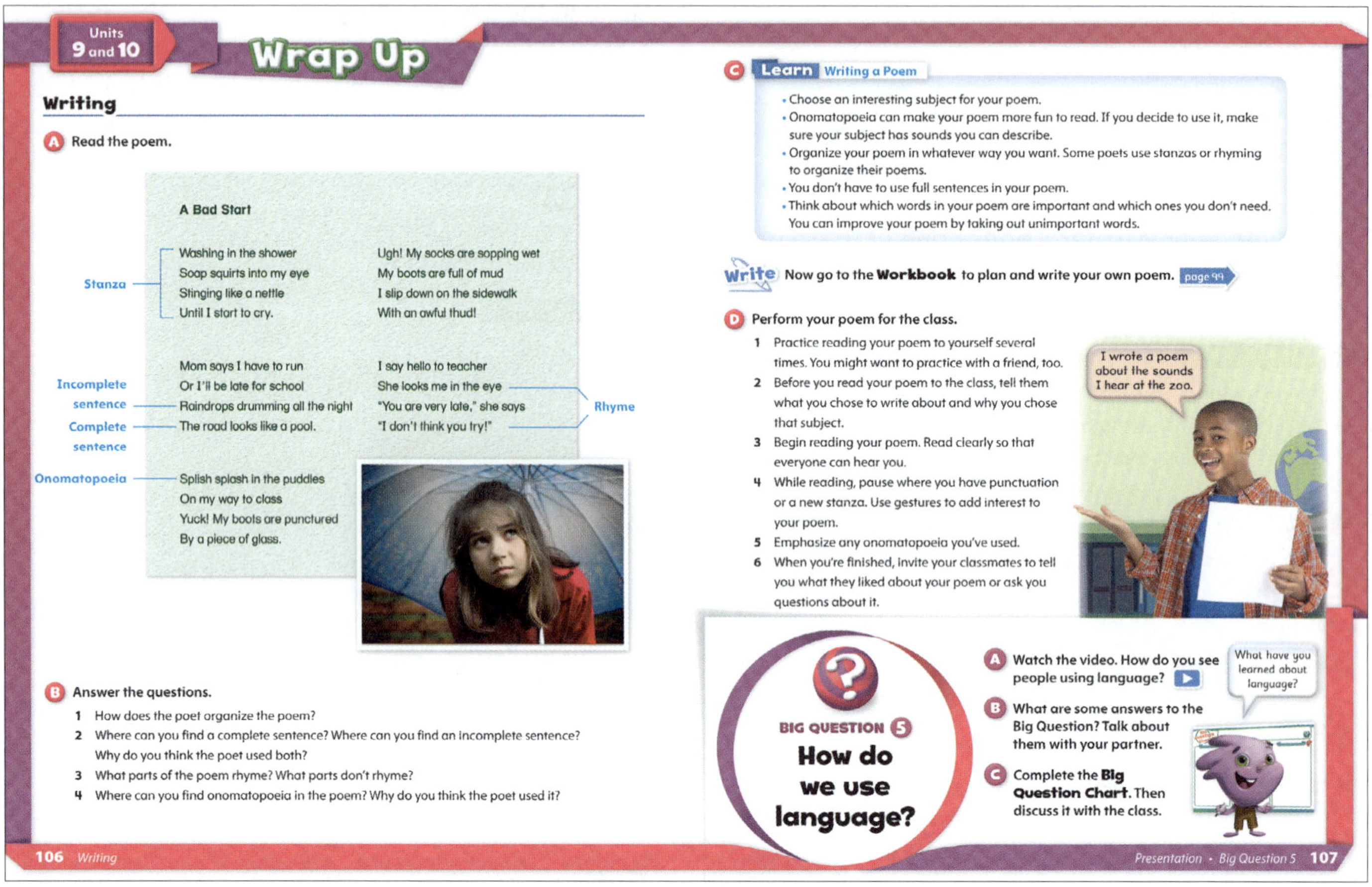
Units 9 and 10

Wrap Up

Writing

A Read the poem.

A Bad Start

Stanza
Washing in the shower
Soap squirts into my eye
Stinging like a nettle
Until I start to cry.

Ugh! My socks are sopping wet
My boots are full of mud
I slip down on the sidewalk
With an awful thud!

Incomplete sentence
Complete sentence
Mom says I have to run
Or I'll be late for school
Raindrops drumming all the night
The road looks like a pool.

I say hello to teacher
She looks me in the eye
"You are very late," she says
"I don't think you try!"

Rhyme

Onomatopoeia
Splish splash in the puddles
On my way to class
Yuck! My boots are punctured
By a piece of glass.

B Answer the questions.

1 How does the poet organize the poem?
2 Where can you find a complete sentence? Where can you find an incomplete sentence? Why do you think the poet used both?
3 What parts of the poem rhyme? What parts don't rhyme?
4 Where can you find onomatopoeia in the poem? Why do you think the poet used it?

C Learn Writing a Poem

- Choose an interesting subject for your poem.
- Onomatopoeia can make your poem more fun to read. If you decide to use it, make sure your subject has sounds you can describe.
- Organize your poem in whatever way you want. Some poets use stanzas or rhyming to organize their poems.
- You don't have to use full sentences in your poem.
- Think about which words in your poem are important and which ones you don't need. You can improve your poem by taking out unimportant words.

Write Now go to the **Workbook** to plan and write your own poem. page 99

D Perform your poem for the class.

1 Practice reading your poem to yourself several times. You might want to practice with a friend, too.
2 Before you read your poem to the class, tell them what you chose to write about and why you chose that subject.
3 Begin reading your poem. Read clearly so that everyone can hear you.
4 While reading, pause where you have punctuation or a new stanza. Use gestures to add interest to your poem.
5 Emphasize any onomatopoeia you've used.
6 When you're finished, invite your classmates to tell you what they liked about your poem or ask you questions about it.

I wrote a poem about the sounds I hear at the zoo.

BIG QUESTION 5
How do we use language?

A Watch the video. How do you see people using language?

B What are some answers to the Big Question? Talk about them with your partner.

C Complete the **Big Question Chart**. Then discuss it with the class.

What have you learned about language?

106 Writing

Presentation • Big Question 5 107

Summary
Objectives: To show what students have learned about the language and learning points of Units 9 and 10.
Reading: Reading a poem
Writing: Writing a poem
Speaking: Performing a poem
Big Question learning point: *Language gives us a way to describe the world around us.*
Materials: Big Question DVD, Discover Poster 5, Talk About It! Poster, Big Question Chart

Writing

A Read the poem.

- Read aloud the directions and explain that a poem is a literary art form that uses expressive and rhythmic qualities of language. Poems often create feelings, rather than tell about them. Ask if students have any favorite poems.
- Go over the structure of the poem before reading. Point out the labels and have the class say an example of one of them.
- Read the poem aloud one time for the class to listen.
- Have students read it with you one time. Encourage them to read dramatically to get the most out of the sounds of each word.

B Answer the questions.

- Have students work with a partner to answer the questions.
- Check the answers with the class.

ANSWERS

1 In stanzas.
2 Complete sentence: "The road looks like a pool." An incomplete sentence: "Raindrops drumming all the night."
3 Every other line rhymes, and the alternating lines don't rhyme.
4 Onomatopoeia is found throughout the poem. It contributes to the rhythm and to the sound of the poem, making it very lively. The poet uses onomatopoeia to underline the poem's meaning about sound.

C Learn: Writing a Poem

- Read the *Learn* box together.
- Explain that students should follow these guidelines when they plan and write their poems.

CRITICAL THINKING

- Have students go back to the model to see how the author addressed each requirement.
- Say *Point to the stanzas. How many lines are in each stanza? Why do the incomplete sentences work well? What are your favorite onomatopoeic words in the poem?*

Write

- Direct the students to the Workbook to plan and write their own poem.

CREATIVITY

- Brainstorm some ideas for a sound poem with the class.
- Write topics on the board. Then group students who choose similar topics together.

DIFFERENTIATION

Below level:

- Put students into small mixed-ability groups, preferably with the same topic, to discuss the Workbook activity.
- Have the more confident students help the other students to make a web to help write words, images, and ideas to include in the poem.
- After students write a draft, have the more confident students help to use the checklist to improve the poem.

At level:

- Have students complete their poems individually.
- Ask students to read their poems to a partner.
- The partner should use the checklist to check if the speech meets all of the requirements. If it doesn't, the partner should offer suggestions to do so.
- Then have students revise their poems.

Above level:

- Have students write their poems themselves, following the steps in the Workbook.
- Have a partner read the written poem aloud so the student can hear it. The partner should offer suggestions to improve the poem. Then they switch roles.
- Finally, both students revise their poems.

D Perform your poem for the class.

- Read the instruction list with the class. Model examples of the tips that could be useful.
- Give students time to practice reading their poems themselves. Encourage them to read dramatically and use gestures.
- Have students practice reading their poem to the class. The class responds with things they liked about it.

Units 9 and 10 Big Question Review

A Watch the video. How do you see people using language? ▷

- Play the video and when it is finished, ask students what they know about language now.
- Have students share ideas with the class.

B What are some answers to the Big Question? Talk about them with your partner.

COMMUNICATION

- Display **Discover Poster 5**. Point to familiar vocabulary items and elicit them from the class. Ask *What is this?*
- Ask students *What do you see?* Ask *What does that mean?*
- Refer to all of the learning points written on the poster and have students explain how they relate to the different pictures.
- Ask *What does this learning point mean*? Elicit answers from individual students.
- Display the **Talk About It! Poster** to help students with sentence frames for discussion of the learning points and for expressing their opinions.

C Complete the Big Question Chart. Then discuss it with the class.

- Ask students what they have learned about language while studying this unit.
- Put students into pairs or small groups to say two new things they have learned.
- Have students share their ideas with the class and add their ideas to the chart.
- Have students complete the chart in their Workbook.

Further practice
Workbook pages 98–101
Online Practice • Wrap Up 5
Oxford **iTools** • **Wrap Up 5**

In units 11 and 12 you will:

WATCH a video about history.

LEARN why recording history is important.

READ about Mount Everest and the life of a housemaid.

WRITE about a memory.

MAKE a memory wall.

BIG QUESTION 6

Why do we record history?

A Watch the video. Then talk about it with your partner.

B Look at the picture and discuss it with your class.

1 Why do you think someone took the old photo?

2 What can these pictures tell us about the past and the present?

C Think and answer the questions.

1 What is history?

2 How do people record history?

3 What kinds of events do people record?

4 Have you ever recorded your own history? How did you do it?

D Discuss this topic with your class. Fill out the **Big Question Chart**.

What do you know about recording history? What do you want to know?

108 Big Question 6

109

Reading Strategies

Students will practice:

- Corroborating
- Cause and effect

Vocabulary

Students will understand and use words about:

- Mountain climbing

Grammar

Students will understand and use:

- Passive questions (present perfect)
- Passive (past perfect)

Review

Students will review the language and Big Question learning points of Units 11 and 12 through:

- Writing about a memory

Units 11 and 12

Why do we record history?

Students will understand the Big Question learning points:

- People record history to make a record of important events.
- Recording history is a way for people to share their memories.
- People record history to remember their own lives.
- By recording their history, people can learn about themselves.
- People record history so that they don't forget things.

Listening Strategies

Students will practice:

- Listening for the main idea
- Listening for facts and opinions

Writing Study

Students will use and understand:

- Reflexive pronouns
- Titles in names

Students will:

- Write a memory

Word Study

Students will understand and use:

- Easily confused words
- Loan words

Speaking

Students will understand and use expressions for:

- Follow-up questions
- Telling a story about yourself

Units 11 and 12 Big Question page 108

Summary

Objectives: To activate students' existing knowledge of the topic and identify what they would like to learn about the topic.

Materials: Big Question DVD, Discover Poster 6, Big Question Chart

Introducing the topic

- Read out the Big Question. Ask *Why do we record history?*
- Write students' ideas on the board and discuss.

A Watch the video. Then talk about it with your partner.

- Play the video and when it is finished, ask students to answer the following questions in pairs:
  What do you see in the video?
  What is happening?
  Who do you think the people are?
  What do you like about the video?
- Have individual students share their answers with the class.

Below level:

- After watching, have students describe the historical things they saw in the video.
- Have students name events, situations, and people from history.

At level:

- After watching, have students list all of the historical references they saw in the video. Write the list on the board.
- Have the class say what they know about each item on the board.

Above level:

- After watching, have students write sentences to describe the historical references they saw in the video. For each reference they should write what they know about it.
- Have students share their writing with the class.

B Look at the picture and discuss it with your class.

- Students look at the big picture and talk about it. Ask *What do you see?*
- Ask additional questions:
  What do you notice about the photo?
  Do you think it is the same place in both photos?
  How old do you think the black and white photo is?
  Have you ever compared old and modern photos of the same place?

C Think and answer the questions.

- Have students discuss the questions in small groups, and then with the class.

- Ask students to think about the third question. Have students come to the board and write sentences.
- Ask students to think about the fourth question. Have students come to the board and write sentences.

Expanding the topic

- Display **Discover Poster 6** and give students enough time to look at the pictures.
- Get students to talk about familiar topics by pointing to different things in the pictures and asking *What's this? What is happening here?*
- Put students into small groups of three or four. Have each group choose a picture they find interesting.
- Ask each group to say five sentences about their picture.
- Have one person from each group stand up and read out the sentences they chose for their picture.
- Ask the class if they can add any more.

Below level:

- Encourage students to participate using short sentences.
- Point to details in the big picture and on the poster and ask *What's this?* Write the answers on the board.

At level:

- Elicit complete sentences on what students know about recorded history.
- Write their sentences on the board.

Above level:

- Elicit more detailed responses.
- Challenge students to write their own sentences on the board.

D Discuss this topic with your class. Fill out the Big Question Chart.

- Display the **Big Question Chart**.
- Ask the class *What do you know about recorded history? What do you want to know?*
- Ask students to write what they know and what they want to know in their Workbooks.
- Write a collection of ideas on the **Big Question Chart**.

Discover Poster 6

1 People greeting the famous pilot Amelia Earhart after one of her long solo flights; 2 A boy interviewing his grandfather about his life; 3 A girl writing in her journal; 4 A girl and her grandmother looking at a family photo album together; 5 A man filming his friends at a graduation ceremony

Further Practice

Workbook page 102
Online Practice · Big Question 6
Oxford iTools · Big Question 6

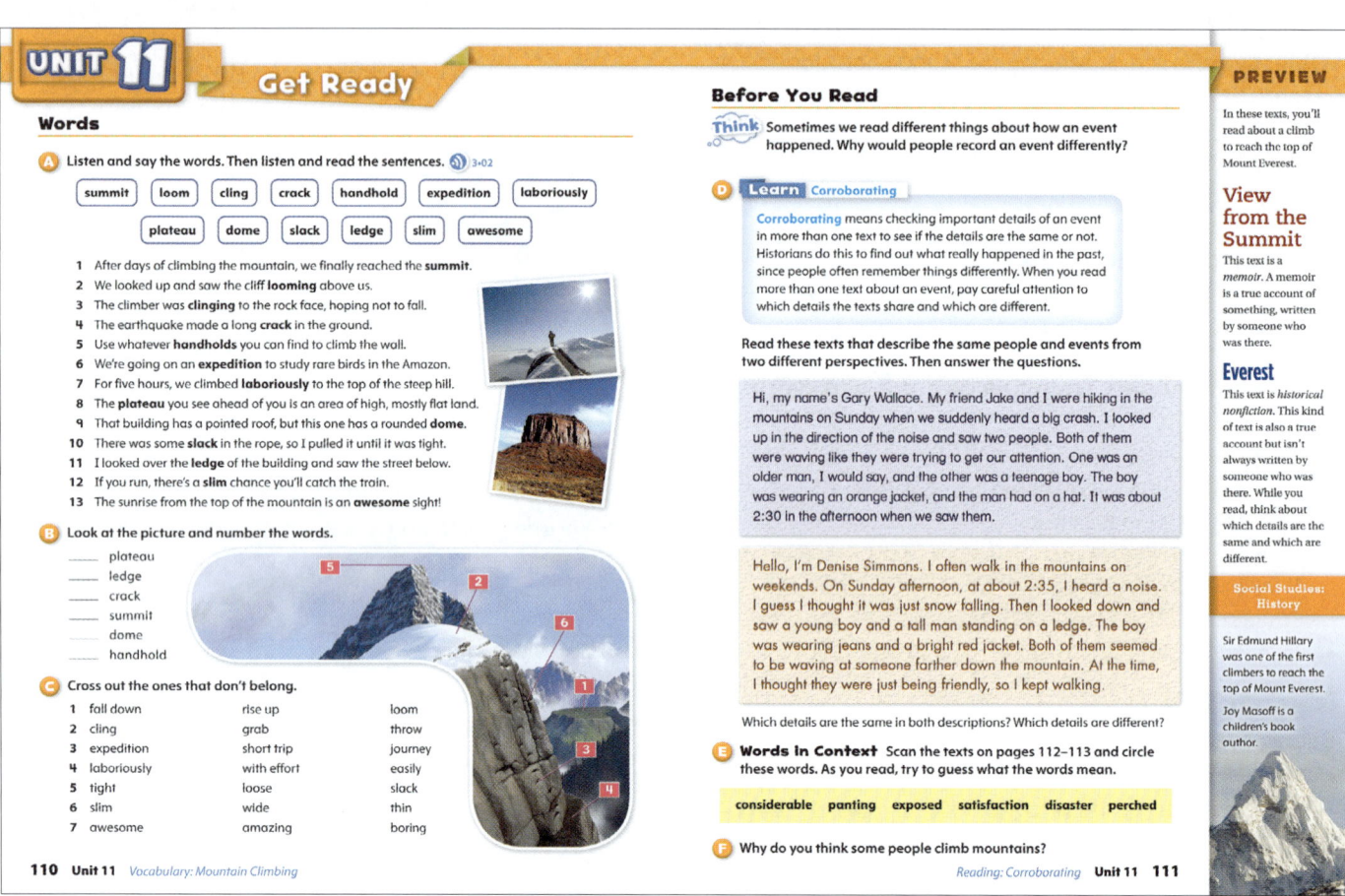

Summary

Objectives: To understand words about mountain climbing; to apply own experience and a reading strategy to help comprehension of a text.

Vocabulary: *summit, loom, cling, crack, handhold, expedition, laboriously, plateau, dome, slack, ledge, slim, awesome, considerable, panting, exposed, satisfaction, disaster, perched*

Reading strategy: Corroborating

Materials: Audio CD

Words

A Listen and say the words. Then listen and read the sentences. 3·02

- Play the audio. Ask students to point to the words and repeat the words when they hear them.
- Then have students listen and read the sentences as they hear them.
- Say the sentence numbers out of order and have the class read the sentences aloud.

B Look at the picture and number the words.

- Have students look at the picture and read the words.
- Tell students to write the correct number next to the word on the left side.
- Have students do the activity on their own.
- Ask students to compare their answers with a partner.
- Check answers with the class.

1 plateau   2 dome   3 handhold   4 ledge
5 summit   6 crack

COLLABORATIVE LEARNING

- Put students into pairs. Have them say sentences using the new words as they appear in the picture, e.g. *That ledge is too narrow to stand on.*
- Have pairs say some of their sentences to the class.

C Cross out the ones that don't belong.

- Have students do the activity on their own.
- Ask students to compare their answers with a partner.
- Check answers with the class.

ANSWERS

1 loom   2 throw   3 short trip   4 easily
5 tight   6 wide   7 boring

COLLABORATIVE LEARNING

- Put students into pairs. Have them write sentences for each of the new words in C, e.g. *He is so tall he looms over the other basketball players.* Pairs may use a dictionary.
- When they have finished, tell the pairs to swap their sentences with another pair.
- Pairs check their work with each other.
- Have pairs read some of their sentences to the class.

Before You Read

Think

- Put students into pairs to discuss the question.
- Have pairs share their answer with the class.
- Go over an example with the class. Choose something students would be familiar with, e.g. a school lunch. Say *One day the school served hamburgers for lunch. Half of the students don't like hamburgers. The other half love hamburgers. How do you think the first group, those who don't love hamburgers will describe the lunch? How would the second group, who love hamburgers, describe the lunch?*
- Elicit other examples from the class.

D Learn: Corroborating

- Read the *Learn* box together. Have a confident student read it for the class.
- Elicit examples from the class, e.g. *Do you have to use two or more sources when you write a paper? How about when a classmate tells you something and you don't think it's true. Do you ask a second person to check what they said?*

Read these texts that describe the same people and events from two different perspectives. Then answer the questions.

- Invite two confident students to read a text each aloud for the class.
- Have students answer the questions individually.
- Ask students to check their answers with a partner.
- Elicit answers from the class.

ANSWERS
Details that are the same: mountains; Sunday; heard a noise; saw a boy and a man; boy wearing a jacket; waving; afternoon
Details that are different: names (Gary / Denise); walking versus hiking; didn't know what noise was / thought maybe snow falling versus "a big crash"; looked up versus looked down; older versus tall man; teenage versus young boy; orange versus red jacket; man with hat versus didn't know what he was wearing; 2:30 versus 2:35 when they saw them.

CRITICAL THINKING

Ask the following questions to check understanding about corroboration:

- *How do you know which story has the correct facts? How could you find out? Who could you ask?*
- *How close was Gary to the noise? How do you know? How close was Denise to the noise? How do you know?*

E Words in Context: Scan the texts on pages 112–113 and circle these words. As you read, try to guess what the words mean.

- Read each word and have students follow your pronunciation.
- Have students scan the texts on pages 112 and 113 and circle the words. Tell them to guess what the words mean from the context.

DIFFERENTIATION
Below level:

- Give students some simple definitions for the words.
- Restate and / or explain the sentences from the story using the definitions, e.g. *I know "consider" means to think about something. So a "considerable challenge" might mean a challenge that really requires an effort. To put it simply, you could say, "To climb it directly, would be a big challenge."*
- Put students into mixed-ability pairs.
- Have students rephrase the sentences using the new definitions.
- For each word, the pair should look up the definition in the dictionary to check the meaning they worked out.

At level:

- Put students into pairs to figure out the meaning of the new words from context and to rephrase the sentences using their conceptions of the words.
- Tell pairs to look up any words they don't recognize in the dictionary.
- Have pairs share their answers with the class.

Above level:

- Put students into pairs to restate the sentences with alternate words in place of the words in context.
- Have pairs share their new sentences with the class.

F Why do you think some people climb mountains?

COMMUNICATION

- Put students into small groups to discuss the question.
- Tell groups to list the reasons that are their answers for the question.
- Go over the groups' answers and make notes on the board.

Reading Preview

- Read the title of the unit's reading text.
- Have students silently read the content of the preview bar.
- Ask *What type of text is the first text?* Ask *What is this type of text like?*
- Ask *What type of text is the second text?* Ask *What is this type of text like?*
- Tell students to think about which details are the same and which are different as they read.
- Read the Author Bio with the class.

Further Practice
Workbook pages 102–103
Online Practice Unit 11 · Get Ready
Oxford iTools Unit 11 · Get Ready

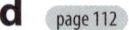

These two texts describe Edmund Hillary and Tenzing Norgay's historic climb to the top of Mount Everest on May 29, 1953. Before that year, no one had reached Mount Everest's summit. The first text is from Edmund Hillary's memoir about the climb. It's considered a *primary source*, since Edmund Hillary was there.

The second text is from a book about the climb, by author Joy Masoff. Since she didn't climb Mount Everest, her book is considered a *secondary source*. As you read, imagine the climbers' excitement. They're going where no person has ever gone. The summit of Mount Everest has never been reached!

View from the Summit:
The Remarkable Memoir by the First Person to Conquer Everest
By Sir Edmund Hillary

Ahead of me loomed the great rock step which we had observed from far below and which we knew might prove to be a major problem. I gazed up at the forty feet of rock with some concern. To climb it directly at nearly 29,000 feet would indeed be a considerable challenge. I looked to the right, there seemed a chance there. Clinging to the rock was a great ice cornice hanging over the mighty Kangshung Face. Under the effects of gravity, the ice had broken away from the rock and a narrow crack ran upward. Nervously, I wondered if the cornice might collapse under my pressure. There was only one way to find out!

Although it would be relatively useless, I got Tenzing to establish a belay[1]; then I eased my way into the crack, facing the rock. I jammed my crampons[2] into the ice behind me and then wriggled my way upward using every little handhold I could find. Puffing for breath, I made steady height—the ice was holding—and forty feet up I pulled myself out of the crack onto the top of the rock face. I had made it! For the first time on the whole expedition, I had a feeling of confidence that we were going to get to the top. I waved to Tenzing and brought in the rope as he, too, made his way laboriously up the crack and dragged himself out beside me, panting for breath.

We didn't waste any time. I started cutting steps again, seeking now rather anxiously for signs of the summit. We seemed to go on forever, tired now and moving rather slowly. In the distance I could see the barren plateau. I looked up to the right and there was a rounded snowy dome. It must be the summit! We drew closer together as Tenzing brought in the slack on the rope. I continued cutting a line of steps upward. Next moment I had moved onto a flattish exposed area of snow with nothing but space in every direction. Tenzing quickly joined me and we looked around in wonder. To our immense satisfaction, we realized we had reached the top of the world!

[1] **belay** *noun* an anchor for a person or rope

[2] **crampon** *noun* a plate with spikes that attaches to shoes to prevent slipping on ice or snow

Everest: Reaching for the Sky
By Joy Masoff

For the next few weeks, the team keeps moving higher up the mountain, setting up camp at greater altitudes. Finally, they reach Camp 8—the highest camp for the team. They are almost there!

John Hunt, the team leader, picks his two strongest climbers to try to reach the top of Everest first. Edmund Hillary and Tenzing Norgay are not chosen to go.

Then disaster strikes. The oxygen tanks don't work, and the first two climbers have to turn back. Hillary and Tenzing are told that they will have a chance to reach the summit after all!

Hillary and Tenzing feel excited, yet calm, as they begin their climb to the top. After spending the night perched on their little ledge, they are ready to make the final climb. It is minus 17°F (minus 27°C), and they have pulled on eight layers of clothing and three pairs of gloves. Their backpacks weigh 40 pounds (18 kilograms) each.

The two men move slowly, carefully hacking steps into the ice with their axes. Parts of the climb are really scary—ridges that are only as wide as a diving board. There are places where the mountain falls off 2 miles (3 kilometers) straight down. One wrong step could mean death.

Still, up they go, higher and higher, until they come to a rocky wall—40 feet (12 meters) high. Now what?

Hillary sees a slim crack in the rock. He jams a foot into it and begins to wiggle up, grabbing at any handhold he can find. Tenzing follows. They haven't come this far only to give up!

It takes almost half an hour to inch up using the crack. They can barely catch their breath. What else can happen?

The two men keep going up. They move from rock to snow, and soon they can climb no more because there is no more mountain left.

They have summitted—they have reached the top! Their tiredness quickly gives way to joy as they look out at the awesome sight all around them.

Think
What are some differences between this text and the first one?

Think
What are some similarities between this text and the first one?

112 · 113

Summary

Objectives: To read, understand, and discuss a memoir and historical nonfiction; to apply a reading strategy to improve comprehension.

School subject: Social Studies: History

Text type: Memoir and historical nonfiction

Reading strategy: Corroborating

Big Question learning points: *People record history to make a record of important events. Recording history is a way for people to share their memories.*

Materials: Talk About It! Poster, Audio CD

Before Reading

- Have students tell you what they see in the pictures.
- Ask students how they can tell one text is a memoir and the other is historical nonfiction?

During Reading 🔊 3·03

- Read the titles of the texts and opening notes together. Ask *What is a primary source? What is a secondary source?*
- Play the audio and have the class read along.

DIFFERENTIATION

Below level:

- Read chunks of the texts and have students repeat chunks of them after you.
- While reading, stop to discuss the *Think* boxes.

At level:

- Have students read in small groups, taking turns to read chunks of the texts, pausing at the *Think* boxes to discuss.

Above level:

- Have students read in pairs, taking turns to read chunks of the texts.
- Pairs should stop to talk about the *Think* boxes.
- Then the pairs discuss the differences between the two texts.

CRITICAL THINKING

Discussion questions:

- *What are some differences between the texts? Compare and give examples.*
- *Read the second* Think *box. What are some similarities between the two texts?*
- *Would you like to do something adventurous like this?*
- *What do you think the biggest dangers were during this climb?*
- *Why do you think they wanted to make such a dangerous climb in the first place?*

After Reading

CRITICAL THINKING

Put students into small groups to discuss the two texts. Have groups make notes to answer these questions:

- *What is the time frame for each text?*
- *Was Sir Edmund Hillary confident the whole time that he would reach the top?*
- *When did he know they would reach it? How do you know this?*
- *How did Masoff handle the same situation? What did she say?*
- *Do the two texts make you feel different when you read them? Explain.*

CREATIVITY

- Keep students in their small groups. Say *Imagine the memoir had been written by Tenzing Norgay, do you think it would be very different? Why or why not?*
- Have groups discuss the question.
- Ask groups to share their ideas with the class.

COLLABORATIVE LEARNING

- Display the **Talk About It! Poster** to help students with sentence frames for discussion and expressing personal opinions.
- Put students into pairs to discuss which part of the story is the most interesting.

CULTURE NOTE

Tenzing and Hillary reached the top of Mount Everest and stayed there for about 15 minutes. Hillary took a picture of Tenzing with his camera, but Hillary, it is reported, did not want his picture taken. The two men took several other pictures of the top of the mountain to prove they were there. When later asked who reached the top first, the men said that they reached the top together as a team.

For Tenzing, the climb meant that he had gone from being a poor mountain porter to receiving a medal from Queen Elizabeth II of England.

After the climb, Sir Edmund Hillary created a trust to help build schools and hospitals in Tenzing's native land of Nepal. He wrote his memoir of the climb in 1955.

Further Practice
Workbook page 104
Online Practice Unit 11 • Read
Oxford iTools Unit 11 • Read

Unit 11 Understand (page 114)

Understand

Comprehension

Think Which of the two texts felt more real to you? Why?

A Which important details do these texts share? Which details are different? Fill in the organizer and discuss it with your partner.

Text 1: View from the Summit
Text 2: Everest

Details That Are the Same	Details That Are Different

B Work with your partner to answer the questions.

1 Which text covers a longer period of time?
2 How do Edmund Hillary and Tenzing Norgay feel when they reach the top of Mount Everest?
3 If Tenzing Norgay had written about Mount Everest, would it be a primary or a secondary source?
4 If you wrote about Edmund Hillary and Tenzing Norgay's climb, which kind of source would it be?
5 Why do you think Edmund Hillary wrote about this climb?
6 Why do you think Joy Masoff wrote about this climb?

C **Words in Context** Look at the words you circled in the texts. Then use them to complete the short story.

Nancy and Mike had been following the trail all day and were _____ by the time they stopped. The top of the plateau, where they stood, was windy and _____. They looked down and saw the valley a _____ distance below them. "Be careful, Mike," said Nancy. "It would be a _____ if one of us fell." Then Nancy _____ on a large rock so that Mike could take her picture. They felt _____ at having reached the top, but it was getting dark, and they had a long walk ahead of them.

114 Unit 11 *Comprehension*

Grammar in Use

Workbook Grammar pages 106-107

D Listen and read along. Then circle the correct answer. 3•04

Who has delayed the flight?   a It's not important.   b April

You can use the passive voice when it's not important who does the action.

E **Learn Grammar** Passive Questions (Present Perfect)

Remember: You can use the passive voice in the present perfect tense.

Active	Passive
Has anyone ever **reached** the summit of Mount Everest?	**Has** the summit of Mount Everest **been reached**?

Check (✓) the passive sentence in each pair.

1 ☐ Has the janitor cleaned the classroom?
  ☐ Has the classroom been cleaned?

2 ☐ Has the meal been cooked?
  ☐ Has the chef cooked the meal?

3 ☐ Has the book been written?
  ☐ Has the author written the book?

4 ☐ Has your dad paid the bill?
  ☐ Has the bill been paid?

F Make a chart like this one. Write your own active questions. Then work with your partner to turn them into passive questions.

Has the project been started?

Active	Passive
Have you started the project?	
Has Jason returned your game?	

Grammar: Passive Questions (Present Perfect) Unit 11 115

Summary

Objectives: To demonstrate understanding of a memoir and historical nonfiction; to understand the meaning and form of the grammar structure.

Reading: Comprehension

Grammar input: Passive questions (present perfect)

Grammar practice: Workbook exercises

Grammar production: Passive questions

Materials: Audio CD

Comprehension

Think

- Read the questions with the class. Ask students to think about their answers.
- Put students into groups to discuss their answers.
- Have groups share their answers. Ask students to say which parts were most exciting.

A Which important details do these texts share? Which details are different? Fill in the organizer and discuss it with your partner.

- Ask students to reread the texts and then fill in the organizer. Check the answers with the class.

ANSWERS

Text 1: View from the Summit
Text 2: Everest: Reaching for the Sky
Details That Are the Same: 40-foot rock wall; a slim / narrow crack in the rock wall; wriggle / wiggle his way up crack; panting for breath after climbing up crack; wonder / immense satisfaction at top versus joy and awesome sights
Details That Are Different: EH – 29,000 feet; Kangshung Face; moving slowly; barren plateau of Tibet in distance; JM – Camp 8 and the rest of the team; John Hunt Team Leader; oxygen tanks don't work so first climbers have to turn back; spend night on ledge; 17°F (27°C); their backpacks weight 40 pounds; the mountain falls off 2 miles; takes almost half an hour to climb up crack

DIFFERENTIATION

Below level:
- Put students into mixed-ability pairs.
- Have the more confident student help the other student to fill out the organizer.
- The students should turn back to pages 112 and 113 where the more confident student helps the other student to find the answers.

At level:
- Have students fill in the organizer individually.
- Then put students into pairs to compare their organizers.

Above level:
- Have pairs of students each fill out one of the organizers.
- Ask students to trade papers to check each other's work on the other organizer.
- Students then discuss the organizers.

142 **Unit 11 • Understand**

B Work with your partner to answer the questions.

- Put students in pairs to answer the questions..
- Check answers with the class.

1 Joy Masoff's text does. (Weeks versus Edmund Hillary's single day)
2 They feel wonder and immense satisfaction.
3 Primary source
4 Secondary source
5 Because he knew it was an important and historic event and people would want to read about it later.
6 Joy Masoff may have written about the climb to provide a larger context, or to tell the full story, instead of just Edmund Hillary's perspective.

C Words in Context: Look at the words you circled in the texts. Then use them to complete the short story.

- Have students go back and find the circled words in the texts.
- Tell them to use the words and context clues to complete the blanks in the short story.
- Check the answers with the class.

ANSWERS

1 panting   2 exposed   3 considerable   4 disaster
5 perched   6 satisfaction

Grammar in Use

D Listen and read along. Then circle the correct answer. 3·04

- Listen to the dialogue once and have students read along.
- Then have students read the question and circle the correct answer.
- Play the dialogue again and have students check their answer. Check the answer with the class.

ANSWER

a It's not important.

E Learn Grammar: Passive Questions (Present Perfect)

- Read the *Learn Grammar* box together.
- Read the example sentences. Then ask questions to check understanding:
  What is the difference between active and passive tenses?
  Who is doing the thing in the active sentence?
  What is the subject in the active sentence?
  What is the subject in the passive sentence?

Check (✓) the passive sentence in each pair.

- Read the first pair together. Have the class identify the subject in each sentence.
- Ask students which sentence they will check.
- Then have students complete the rest on their own.
- Check the answers with the class.

ANSWERS

The following passive sentences should be checked:
1 Has the classroom been cleaned?
2 Has the meal been cooked?
3 Has the book been written?
4 Has the bill been paid?

CRITICAL THINKING

- In pairs, ask students to discuss when they would use the passive.
- Ask some pairs for their answers. If necessary, elicit answers such as: *When the thing doing the action isn't as important as the subject, e.g. In the example of the passive, "the summit of Mount Everest" is more important to us than who reached it.*

F Make a chart like this one. Write your own active questions. Then work with your partner to turn them into passive questions.

- Read the example questions and model the dialogue with a student. Remind students they only need to add an action.
- Put students into pairs to ask and answer questions.
- Have a few pairs say their questions and answers for the class.

COLLABORATIVE LEARNING

- In pairs, ask students to collaborate to write two new questions using the past perfect continuous.
- Then put students into small groups to ask and answer their questions to other members of the group.
- Be sure everyone has a chance to ask and answer.
- Have some students say their questions and answers for the class.

Workbook Grammar

- Direct students to the Workbook for further practice.

Further practice
Workbook pages 105–107
Online Practice Unit 11 · Understand
Oxford **iTools** Unit 11 · Understand

116   Unit 11   *Listening: Main Idea · Speaking: Follow-Up Questions*

Summary

Objectives: To learn and practice listening, speaking, and writing strategies to facilitate effective communication.

Vocabulary: *wander, wonder, course, coarse, advice, advise, affect, effect*

Listening strategy: Listening for the main idea

Speaking: Follow-up questions

Word Study: Easily confused words

Writing task: Reflexive pronouns

Big Question learning point: *Recording history is a way for people to share their memories.*

Materials: Discover Poster 6, Audio CD, Big Question Chart

Listening

Think

- Tell students to think about the question.
- After students have thought about the question on their own, put them into pairs to compare answers.
- Then hold a class discussion about recording history. Ask *What are some ways people recorded history in the past? What are some ways people record history now?*

A Listen. Check (✓) the main idea. 3·05

- Have students read the three sentences.
- Play the audio once and have students listen.
- Tell them to check the correct answer. Then play the audio again so they can check their work.
- Elicit answers from the class.

ANSWER

By recording someone, we can pass on their memories.

B Listen again. Circle True (T) or False (F). 3·06

- Play the audio and have students listen carefully without taking notes.
- Play the audio again if necessary.
- Have students complete the exercise and check answers with a partner before checking answers with the class.
- Play the audio again if necessary.

ANSWERS

1 T   2 F   3 F   4 T   5 T

Speaking 🔘 3·07

C Learn: Follow-Up Questions

- Read the *Learn* box and examples with the class.
- Play the audio one time as students listen.
- Model the dialogue with a confident student in front of the class.
- Say *To ask a follow-up question, you focus on something the person said and then ask a question about it.*
- Direct students' attention to the first sentence. Say *I used to go to a school on Kensington Street.* Explain how the follow-up question takes "Kensington Street" and uses it in the question, e.g. *Oh, really? Where's Kensington Street?*

Choose one of these topics and tell your partner something you remember about it. Use follow-up questions in your conversation.

COMMUNICATION

- Put students into pairs.
- Have them create short dialogues using the topics listed (a school you went to, a house you lived in, a friend or relative, a special day).
- Have a few pairs act out their dialogues for the class.

Word Study

D Learn: Easily Confused Words

- Read the *Learn* box together.
- Elicit the differences between the words. Ask *How do these words sound different? How are these words spelled differently? What does each word mean?*

Listen to the sentences and number the words. Then work with your partner to write a sentence for each word. 🔘 3·08

- Play the audio and have students individually number the words.
- Have students check their answers with a partner before checking with the class.
- Have students work with a partner to write sentences.
- Put one pair with another pair to compare sentences and to check accuracy.
- Ask some students to read one or two of their sentences to the class.

ANSWERS
1 coarse   2 course   3 wander   4 wonder   5 affect
6 effect   7 advise   8 advice

Writing Study

E Learn: Reflexive Pronouns

- Have a confident student read the *Learn* box to the class.
- Ask students *Who dragged himself? What is the subject in the sentence? What is the object?*

Use reflexive pronouns to complete the sentences.

- Ask the students to work individually to complete the sentences.
- Ask students to compare their answers with a partner before checking with the class.

ANSWERS
1 himself   2 yourself   3 herself   4 ourselves
5 themselves

DIFFERENTIATION

Below level:

- Write the following list of reflexive pronouns on the board: *myself, yourself, herself, himself, itself, ourselves, yourselves, themselves.*
- Say a number of different sentences that require reflexive pronouns, but pause before the reflexive pronoun and have students say the correct one, e.g. *We went to the shop _____ (ourselves). The book seemed to move by _____ (itself). I like to make dinner _____ (myself).*

At level:

- Dictate the same sentences as above and have students write the missing reflexive pronouns.
- Check answers with the class.

Above level:

- Have students write sentences that require reflexive pronouns, but leaving a gap where that word would be.
- Students trade papers with a partner and complete each other's sentences.
- Have some students read their sentences to the class.

Write

- Direct students to the Workbook for further writing practice.

Big Question 6 Review

Why do we record history?

- Display **Discover Poster 6**. Discuss what you see.
- Refer to the learning points covered in Unit 11 that are written on the poster and have students explain how they relate to the different pictures.
- Return to the **Big Question Chart**.
- Ask students what they have learned about recording history while studying this unit.

Further practice
Workbook pages 108–109
Online Practice Unit 11 · Communicate
Oxford **iTools** Unit 11 · Communicate

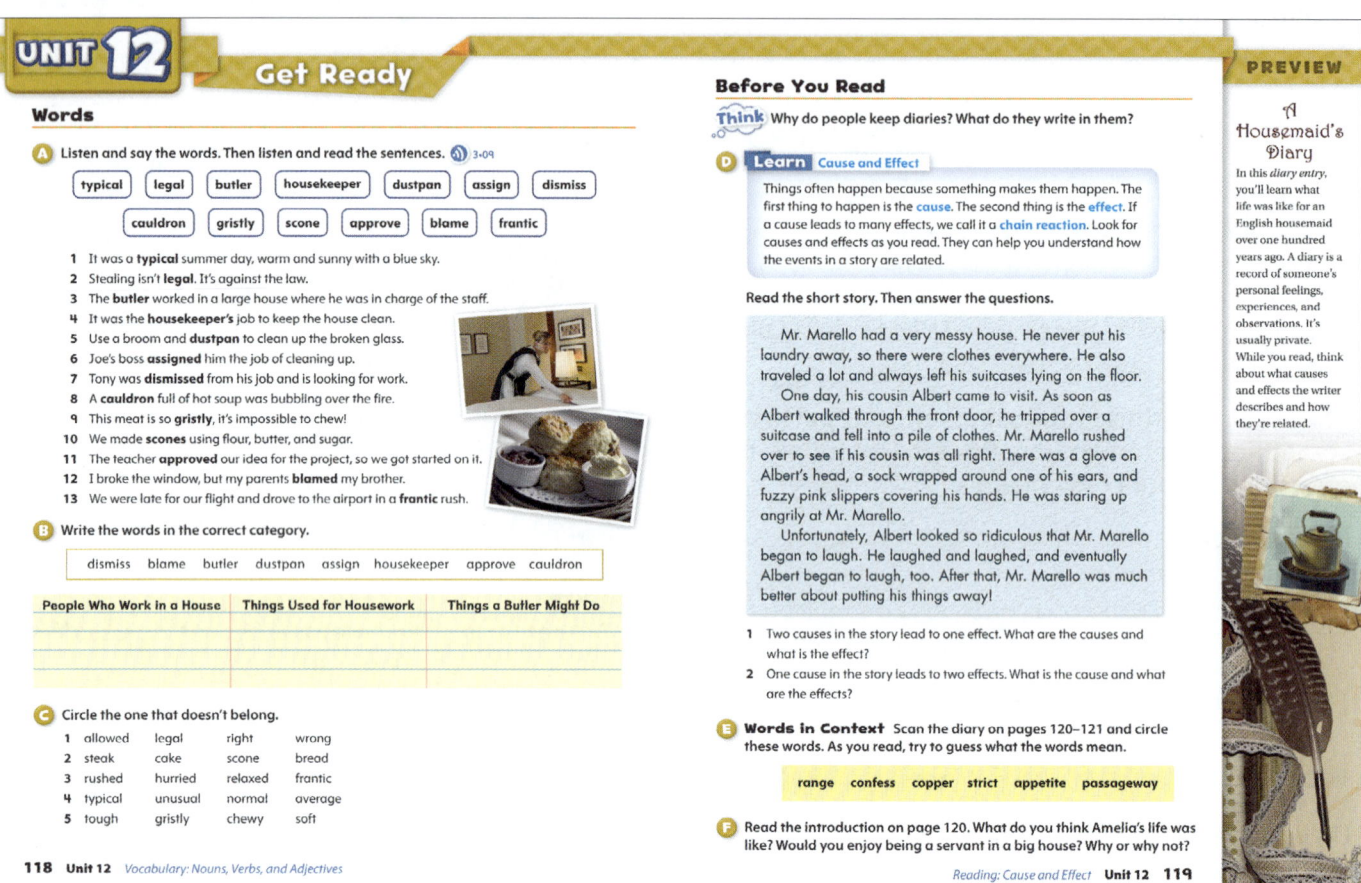

UNIT 12 — Get Ready

Words

A Listen and say the words. Then listen and read the sentences. 3·09

typical | legal | butler | housekeeper | dustpan | assign | dismiss

cauldron | gristly | scone | approve | blame | frantic

1 It was a **typical** summer day, warm and sunny with a blue sky.
2 Stealing isn't **legal**. It's against the law.
3 The **butler** worked in a large house where he was in charge of the staff.
4 It was the **housekeeper's** job to keep the house clean.
5 Use a broom and **dustpan** to clean up the broken glass.
6 Joe's boss **assigned** him the job of cleaning up.
7 Tony was **dismissed** from his job and is looking for work.
8 A **cauldron** full of hot soup was bubbling over the fire.
9 This meat is so **gristly**, it's impossible to chew!
10 We made **scones** using flour, butter, and sugar.
11 The teacher **approved** our idea for the project, so we got started on it.
12 I broke the window, but my parents **blamed** my brother.
13 We were late for our flight and drove to the airport in a **frantic** rush.

B Write the words in the correct category.

dismiss blame butler dustpan assign housekeeper approve cauldron

People Who Work in a House	Things Used for Housework	Things a Butler Might Do

C Circle the one that doesn't belong.

1 allowed | legal | right | wrong
2 steak | cake | scone | bread
3 rushed | hurried | relaxed | frantic
4 typical | unusual | normal | average
5 tough | gristly | chewy | soft

118 **Unit 12** *Vocabulary: Nouns, Verbs, and Adjectives*

Before You Read

Think Why do people keep diaries? What do they write in them?

D **Learn** Cause and Effect

Things often happen because something makes them happen. The first thing to happen is the **cause**. The second thing is the **effect**. If a cause leads to many effects, we call it a **chain reaction**. Look for causes and effects as you read. They can help you understand how the events in a story are related.

Read the short story. Then answer the questions.

Mr. Marello had a very messy house. He never put his laundry away, so there were clothes everywhere. He also traveled a lot and always left his suitcases lying on the floor.

One day, his cousin Albert came to visit. As soon as Albert walked through the front door, he tripped over a suitcase and fell into a pile of clothes. Mr. Marello rushed over to see if his cousin was all right. There was a glove on Albert's head, a sock wrapped around one of his ears, and fuzzy pink slippers covering his hands. He was staring up angrily at Mr. Marello.

Unfortunately, Albert looked so ridiculous that Mr. Marello began to laugh. He laughed and laughed, and eventually Albert began to laugh, too. After that, Mr. Marello was much better about putting his things away!

1 Two causes in the story lead to one effect. What are the causes and what is the effect?
2 One cause in the story leads to two effects. What is the cause and what are the effects?

E **Words in Context** Scan the diary on pages 120–121 and circle these words. As you read, try to guess what the words mean.

range confess copper strict appetite passageway

F Read the introduction on page 120. What do you think Amelia's life was like? Would you enjoy being a servant in a big house? Why or why not?

Reading: Cause and Effect **Unit 12** 119

PREVIEW

A Housemaid's Diary

In this *diary entry*, you'll learn what life was like for an English housemaid over one hundred years ago. A diary is a record of someone's personal feelings, experiences, and observations. It's usually private. While you read, think about what causes and effects the writer describes and how they're related.

Summary

Objectives: To understand about nouns, verbs, and adjectives; to apply own experience and a reading strategy to help comprehension of a text.

Vocabulary: *typical, legal, butler, housekeeper, dustpan, assign, dismiss, cauldron, gristly, scone, approve, blame, frantic, range, confess, copper, strict, appetite, passageway*

Reading strategy: Cause and effect

Materials: Audio CD

Words

A Listen and say the words. Then listen and read the sentences. 3·09

• Play the audio. Ask students to point to the words and repeat the words when they hear them.
• Then have students listen and read the sentences as they hear them.
• Say the sentence numbers out of order and have the class read the sentences aloud.

B Write the words in the correct category.

• Have students do the exercise on their own and then compare answers with a partner.
• Check answers with the class.

ANSWERS
People Who Work in a House: butler, housekeeper
Things Used for Housework: dustpan, cauldron
Things a Butler Might Do: dismiss, blame, assign, approve

• Put students into pairs and tell them to describe the meaning of the words to a partner. One student says, e.g. *This means something is "usual."* The partner guesses the word *typical*.
• Go around the room and have pairs say some of their sentences for the class.

C Circle the one that doesn't belong.

• Have students read the words and circle the one that doesn't belong.
• Check the answers with the class.

ANSWERS
1 wrong 2 steak 3 relaxed 4 unusual 5 soft

Before You Read

Think

• Have students read the questions and make notes about their answers individually.
• Students discuss their answers to the questions in small groups.
• Then share some of the answers with the class. Ask if anyone in the class keeps a diary.

D Learn: Cause and Effect

- Read the *Learn* box with the class.
- Ask questions to check for understanding:
  What is an event?
  What is a consequence?
  What is a chain reaction?

Read the short story. Then answer the questions.

- Have students read the text individually. Tell them to underline the causes and circle the effects, and draw lines connecting them.
- Have students answer the questions individually.
- Put students into pairs to talk about their answers.
- Check the answers with the class.

ANSWERS

1 Cause 1: Mr. Marello had a very messy house
  Cause 2: Left suitcases on floor
  Effect: Albert trips
2 Cause: Albert tripped and was covered in clothing
  Effect 1: Mr. Marello (and Albert) laugh
  Effect 2: Mr. Marello learns to put his things away

CRITICAL THINKING

Ask the following questions to discuss causes and effects.

- *One way you can tell the difference between a cause and effect, is to ask "What would the effect be if the cause was removed?" e.g. What if Mr. Marello put away both his clothes or suitcase? What would happen? What if he only did one of those things? How would that change the result?*

- *If you can't have an effect without a cause, is it possible for the effects to be different from the same cause? Could there be a different result for Albert than the one in the story even if the same causes happened?*

E Words in Context: Scan the diary on pages 120–121 and circle these words. As you read, try to guess what the words mean.

- Read each word and have students follow your pronunciation.
- Have students scan the texts on pages 120 and 121 and circle the words. Tell them to guess what the words mean from the context.

DIFFERENTIATION

Below level:

- Have mixed-ability pairs scan the text and find the words.
- For each word, the pair should discuss the meaning.
- Then they should check their guess using a dictionary. They should be sure to note the type of word it is.
- Have some pairs tell the class the meaning of the words.

At level:

- Have students do the activity on their own.
- Then put students into pairs. Pairs go over the words together and talk about what they think the words mean. Then they consult a dictionary to check their guesses.

Above level:

- Have students find the words on their own. Tell them to guess what they think the words mean.
- Put students into pairs. See if students can substitute the words in context for their own definitions of the words in context. They may use a dictionary to check the meanings.
- Students share some of their replacement sentences with the class.

F Read the introduction on page 120. What do you think Amelia's life was like? Would you enjoy being a servant in a big house? Why or why not?

COMMUNICATION

- Have students think about their answers to the questions on their own.
- Then have students discuss the questions with a partner.
- Ask students to talk about what they think Amelia's life was like and make notes on the board.

Reading Preview

- Read the title of the unit's reading text.
- Have students silently read the content of the preview bar.
- Ask *What type of text is it?* Ask *What is a diary?*
- Tell students to try to think about cause and effect as they read.

Further Practice
Workbook pages 110–111
Online Practice Unit 12 • Get Ready
Oxford iTools Unit 12 • Get Ready

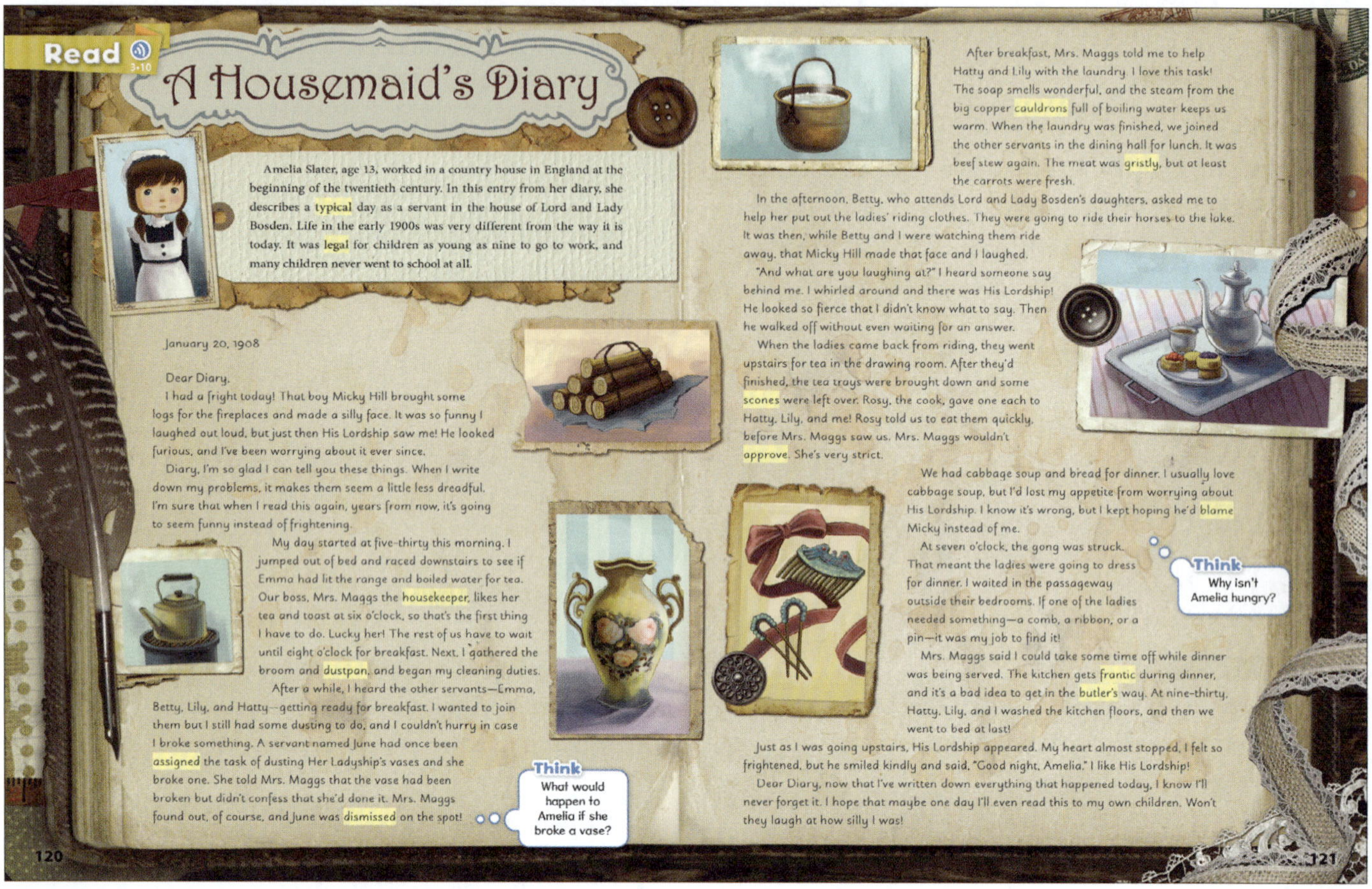

Read 3•10

A Housemaid's Diary

Amelia Slater, age 13, worked in a country house in England at the beginning of the twentieth century. In this entry from her diary, she describes a typical day as a servant in the house of Lord and Lady Bosden. Life in the early 1900s was very different from the way it is today. It was legal for children as young as nine to go to work, and many children never went to school at all.

January 20, 1908

Dear Diary,

I had a fright today! That boy Micky Hill brought some logs for the fireplaces and made a silly face. It was so funny I laughed out loud, but just then His Lordship saw me! He looked furious, and I've been worrying about it ever since.

Diary, I'm so glad I can tell you these things. When I write down my problems, it makes them seem a little less dreadful. I'm sure that when I read this again, years from now, it's going to seem funny instead of frightening.

My day started at five-thirty this morning. I jumped out of bed and raced downstairs to see if Emma had lit the range and boiled water for tea. Our boss, Mrs. Maggs the housekeeper, likes her tea and toast at six o'clock, so that's the first thing I have to do. Lucky her! The rest of us have to wait until eight o'clock for breakfast. Next, I gathered the broom and dustpan, and began my cleaning duties.

After a while, I heard the other servants—Emma, Betty, Lily, and Hatty—getting ready for breakfast. I wanted to join them but I still had some dusting to do, and I couldn't hurry in case I broke something. A servant named June had once been assigned the task of dusting Her Ladyship's vases and she broke one. She told Mrs. Maggs that the vase had been broken but didn't confess that she'd done it. Mrs. Maggs found out, of course, and June was dismissed on the spot!

Think What would happen to Amelia if she broke a vase?

After breakfast, Mrs. Maggs told me to help Hatty and Lily with the laundry. I love this task! The soap smells wonderful, and the steam from the big copper cauldrons full of boiling water keeps us warm. When the laundry was finished, we joined the other servants in the dining hall for lunch. It was beef stew again. The meat was gristly, but at least the carrots were fresh.

In the afternoon, Betty, who attends Lord and Lady Bosden's daughters, asked me to help her put out the ladies' riding clothes. They were going to ride their horses to the lake. It was then, while Betty and I were watching them ride away, that Micky Hill made that face and I laughed.

"And what are you laughing at?" I heard someone say behind me. I whirled around and there was His Lordship! He looked so fierce that I didn't know what to say. Then he walked off without even waiting for an answer.

When the ladies came back from riding, they went upstairs for tea in the drawing room. After they'd finished, the tea trays were brought down and some scones were left over. Rosy, the cook, gave one each to Hatty, Lily, and me! Rosy told us to eat them quickly, before Mrs. Maggs saw us. Mrs. Maggs wouldn't approve. She's very strict.

We had cabbage soup and bread for dinner. I usually love cabbage soup, but I'd lost my appetite from worrying about His Lordship. I know it's wrong, but I kept hoping he'd blame Micky instead of me.

At seven o'clock, the gong was struck. That meant the ladies were going to dress for dinner. I waited in the passageway outside their bedrooms. If one of the ladies needed something—a comb, a ribbon, or a pin—it was my job to find it!

Think Why isn't Amelia hungry?

Mrs. Maggs said I could take some time off while dinner was being served. The kitchen gets frantic during dinner, and it's a bad idea to get in the butler's way. At nine-thirty, Hatty, Lily, and I washed the kitchen floors, and then we went to bed at last!

Just as I was going upstairs, His Lordship appeared. My heart almost stopped. I felt so frightened, but he smiled kindly and said, "Good night, Amelia." I like His Lordship!

Dear Diary, now that I've written down everything that happened today, I know I'll never forget it. I hope that maybe one day I'll even read this to my own children. Won't they laugh at how silly I was!

120 121

Summary

Objectives: To read, understand, and discuss a diary entry; to apply a reading strategy to improve comprehension.

School subject: Social Studies: History

Text type: Diary entry (fiction)

Reading strategy: Cause and effect

Big Question learning points: *Recording history is a way for people to share their memories. People record history to remember their own lives. By recording their history, people can learn about themselves.*

Materials: Discover Poster 6, Audio CD

Before Reading

- Read the title.
- Have students point to the pictures and describe what they see.
- Read the date. Ask *How much time do you think this diary page will cover?*
- Preview the time the story takes place to activate what students know. Ask *When does the story take place?* (1900s) *Have you seen any movies or TV shows set around that time? What were people like back then?*

During Reading 3•10

- Read the first paragraph of the diary entry with the class. Ask some gist questions to check overall understanding, e.g. *What was the effect of her laughing? Why would the Lord of the house be furious if the housemaid laughed?*
- Allow students a few minutes to skim the text.
- Remind students that they should identify causes and effects while they read and think about the *Think* boxes.
- Play the audio. Students listen as they read along.
- Play the audio a second time, if necessary.

DIFFERENTIATION

Below level:

- Have students repeat after you as you read chunks of the diary aloud.
- Pause after each section to discuss the cause and effects.

At level:

- Have students read the diary entry silently to themselves one time.
- Then have pairs take turns to read aloud to each other, pausing to discuss the causes and effects.

Above level:

- Have students read the diary entry individually.
- Put students into pairs and have them summarize each section and name the causes and effects of each section.

Discussion questions about the diary entry:

- *Why did Amelia write about her encounter with His Lordship?*
- *What sort of things did Amelia write about?*
- *What was she hoping for that she knew was wrong?*
- *What is her opinion of the fact that she had been worried?*
- *Does Amelia believe that someone else may read her diary in the future?*
- *Is a diary an historical document?*
- *Is a diary important to anyone other than the author of the diary?*
- *What can a diary tell us about the time period when it was written?*

After Reading

- Go over the *Think* boxes with the class.
- For the first *Think* box, ask *What would happen to Amelia if she broke a vase?*
- For the second *Think* box, ask *Why isn't Amelia hungry at dinner?*

- Display **Discover Poster 6** to help students with sentence frames for discussion and expressing personal opinions.
- Put students into pairs to discuss what they find interesting about recorded history and the housemaid's diary.
- Ask students if they think differently about recorded history now. What did they think about recorded history before reading? What do they think now?

CULTURE NOTE

In England, at the end of the 19th century, being a housemaid was a common job for pre-teen and teenage women. There were approximately 1.25 million housemaids in 1881. But over the next thirty years, women began to stay in school later (until they were 14 years old).

By the time World War I began, more women entered the workforce, taking over jobs that were left by men who went off the fight in the war. This meant there were fewer maids.

Further Practice
Workbook page 112
Online Practice Unit 12 • Read
Oxford **iTools** Unit 12 • Read

Understand

Comprehension

Think Did you enjoy "A Housemaid's Diary"? What did you learn about what life was like in the early twentieth century?

A Look for a chain reaction in the story. Then fill in the organizer and discuss it with your partner.

Cause	Effect 1	Effect 2	Effect 3	Effect 4

B Circle the correct answer.

1 Amelia gets in trouble for laughing at _____.
   a Lord Bosden
   b Mrs. Maggs
   c the ladies
   d Micky Hill

2 Writing in her diary helps Amelia to _____.
   a forget things
   b remember things
   c make up stories
   d plan her future

3 When Amelia writes, her problems seem _____.
   a less serious
   b more serious
   c the same
   d unimportant

4 Amelia wrote this diary entry _____.
   a on September 5, 1910
   b at the beginning of her work day
   c at the end of her work day
   d when she was an adult

C **Words in Context** Look at the words you circled in the diary. Then match the words to their meanings.

1 confess — a a feeling of hunger
2 passageway — b something you cook on
3 range — c careful about following rules
4 copper — d to admit to something
5 strict — e a type of metal
6 appetite — f part of a building you pass through

122 **Unit 12** *Comprehension*

Grammar in Use

Workbook Grammar pages 114–115

D Listen and read along. Then circle the correct answer. 3•11

Help! When I got back to the kitchen, my cake had been stolen!

What did the cake look like?

This thief was very clever. By the time you got back, your cake had been eaten.

I'll solve this mystery.

It was chocolate with a cherry on top.

My cake had been eaten, huh? I wonder who did that!

Does Sonya want to say who stole the cake?   **Yes**   **No**
You can use the passive voice when you don't want to say who did the action.

E **Learn Grammar** Passive (Past Perfect)

You can use the passive voice in the past perfect tense.

Active	Passive
Mrs. Maggs **had assigned** June the task of dusting the vases.	June **had been assigned** the task of dusting the vases.

Circle *active* or *passive*. If the sentence is active, underline who did the action.

1 The window had been broken.   active   passive
2 Lucy had forgotten to water the plants.   active   passive
3 Jason had left the door unlocked.   active   passive
4 A mistake had been made.   active   passive
5 The teacher had forgotten our homework.   active   passive
6 The wrong ingredients had been used.   active   passive
7 All the pizza had been eaten.   active   passive
8 Someone had stolen my friend's bike.   active   passive

F You and your partner are detectives. Make a chart like this one and write your own passive sentences. Then take turns making active sentences to solve who did the action.

I know! Brandon used up all the supplies.

Passive	Active
All the supplies had been used up.	

Grammar: Passive (Past Perfect) **Unit 12** 123

Summary

Objectives: To demonstrate understanding of a diary; to understand the meaning and form of the grammar structure.

Reading: Comprehension

Grammar input: Passive (past perfect)

Grammar practice: Workbook exercises

Grammar production: Passive (past perfect)

Materials: Audio CD

Comprehension

Think

- Have students think about their answers individually first.
- Hold a class discussion. Ask students for examples to support their opinions.

COLLABORATIVE LEARNING

- Put students into small groups.
- Have groups make lists of all of the things they noticed about life in the early twentieth century, e.g. a maid would spend her whole day upset that her boss told her not to laugh. And that there were more and different types of servants in the house, too.
- Ask groups to share their lists with the class. Make notes on the board.

A Look for a chain reaction in the story. Then fill in the organizer and discuss it with your partner.

- Have students reread the diary and look for the chain reaction.

DIFFERENTIATION

Below level:

- Skim the text together and help students to identify the chain reaction. Tell them to underline these in their books.
- Put students into mixed-ability pairs to fill in the organizers.

At level:

- Have students fill in their organizers individually.
- Then have them discuss the organizers with a partner.
- Ask pairs to tell the class about their organizers.

Above level:

- Have students fill in their organizers individually.
- Then have them discuss them with a partner.
- Invite a few students to the board to complete the organizers for the class to check their work.
- As the class checks the work together, have the students explain the chain reaction.

B Circle the correct answer.

- Have students refer back to the text on pages 120 and 121 to answer the questions on their own.
- Have students compare answers with a partner.
- Check the answers with the class.

ANSWERS
1 d 2 b 3 a 4 c

C Words in Context: Look at the words you circled in the diary. Then match the words to their meanings.

- Read the instructions. Tell students to go back and find the words in the story and to use the context clues to help them figure out the answers.
- Students compare answers with a partner.
- Check the answers with the class.

ANSWERS
1 d 2 f 3 b 4 e 5 c 6 a

Grammar in Use

D Listen and read along. Then circle the correct answer. 🔊 3•11

- Listen to the dialogue once and then read it together as a class.
- Have students choose the correct answer.
- Check the answer with the class.

ANSWER
No

E Learn Grammar: Passive (Past Perfect)

- Read the *Learn Grammar* box together.
- Read the example sentences. Ask questions to check understanding, e.g. *What is the difference between the two example sentences?*

Circle *active* or *passive*. If the sentence is active, underline who did the action.

- Read the first sentence together. Ask the class how you can tell if the sentence is active or passive. Elicit *Active sentences say who or what does the action; passive ones don't.* Ask *Is number one active or passive?*
- Then have students complete the exercise on their own.
- Check the answers with the class.

ANSWERS
1 passive 2 active (*Lucy*) 3 active (*Jason*) 4 passive
5 active (*teacher*) 6 passive 7 passive
8 active (*someone*)

CRITICAL THINKING

- Put students into pairs.
- Tell pairs to rewrite sentences 2 and 3 to be passive.
- Explain that they may need to change the verb, but they should keep the meaning of the sentence the same or similar.

ANSWERS
2 The plants had not been watered. 3 The door had not been locked.

F You and your partner are detectives. Make a chart like this one and write your own passive sentences. Then take turns making active sentences to solve who did the action.

- Have students create the chart individually in their notebooks.
- Ask students to write three passive sentences. Remind them to look at the example for help.
- Have students take turns changing each other's sentences to make them active.

DIFFERENTIATION

Below level:

- Help students write the passive sentences. Brainstorm people they could write about and write ideas on the board.
- Put students into mixed-ability pairs to change the sentences to active and fill out the chart. Have students share their sentences with the class.

At level:

- Have students write their passive sentences.
- Ask students to tell their partner their passive sentences. Their partner says the active sentence version while the first student checks it against what they wrote.
- Then pairs check each other's work.

Above level:

- Have students write passive sentences on the board.
- Invite other students to come to the board and write the equivalent active sentence on the board below.
- Have the class correct any mistakes.

Workbook Grammar

- Direct students to the Workbook for further practice.

Further practice
Workbook pages 113–115
Online Practice Unit 12 • Understand
Oxford **iTools** Unit 12 • Understand

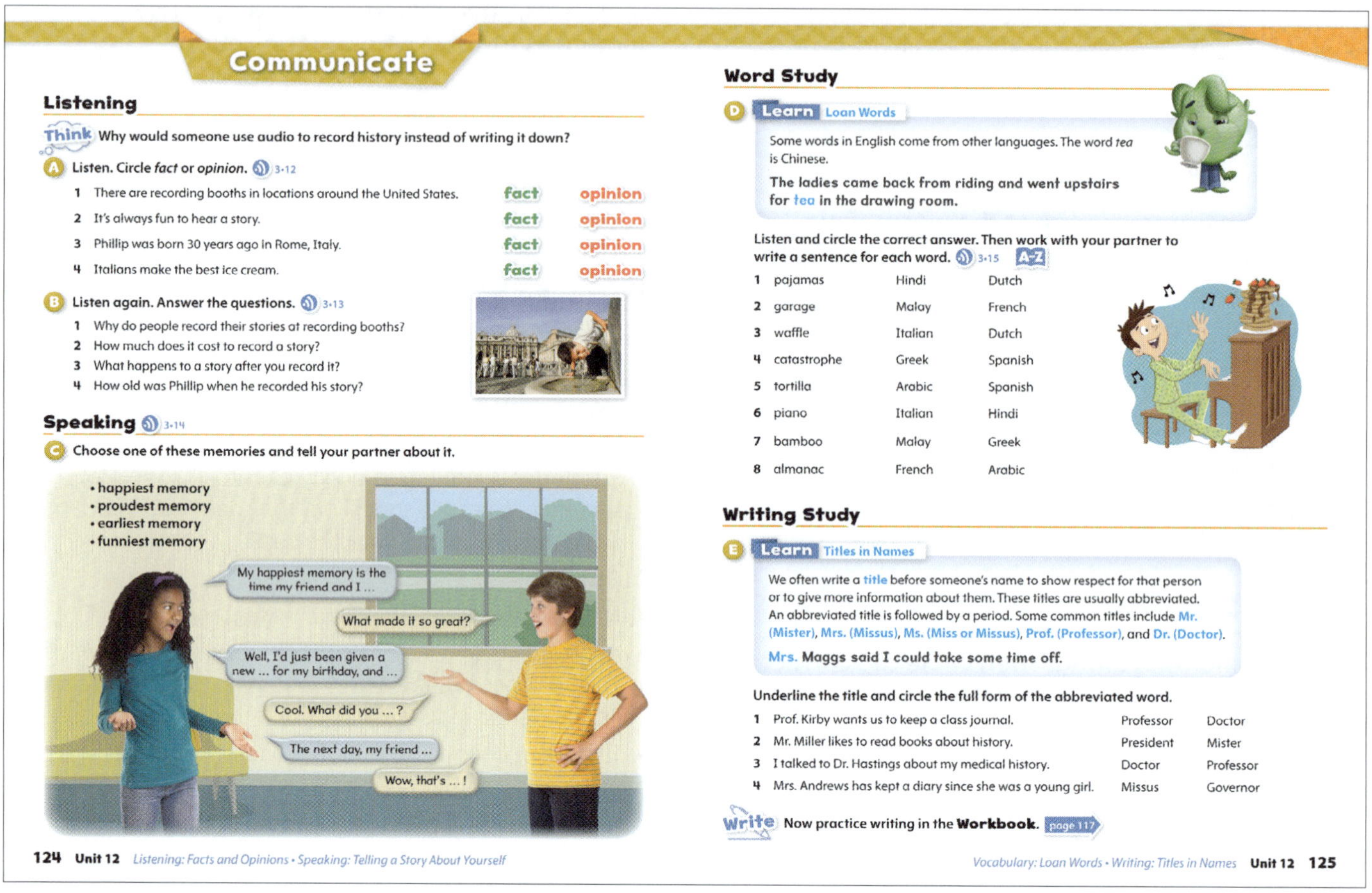

Communicate

Listening

Think Why would someone use audio to record history instead of writing it down?

A Listen. Circle *fact* or *opinion*. 3·12

1 There are recording booths in locations around the United States.   **fact** | opinion
2 It's always fun to hear a story.   fact | **opinion**
3 Phillip was born 30 years ago in Rome, Italy.   **fact** | opinion
4 Italians make the best ice cream.   fact | **opinion**

B Listen again. Answer the questions. 3·13

1 Why do people record their stories at recording booths?
2 How much does it cost to record a story?
3 What happens to a story after you record it?
4 How old was Phillip when he recorded his story?

Speaking 3·14

C Choose one of these memories and tell your partner about it.

- happiest memory
- proudest memory
- earliest memory
- funniest memory

My happiest memory is the time my friend and I ...

What made it so great?

Well, I'd just been given a new ... for my birthday, and ...

Cool. What did you ... ?

The next day, my friend ...

Wow, that's ... !

Word Study

D **Learn** Loan Words

Some words in English come from other languages. The word *tea* is Chinese.

The ladies came back from riding and went upstairs for *tea* in the drawing room.

Listen and circle the correct answer. Then work with your partner to write a sentence for each word. 3·15 A-Z

1	pajamas	Hindi	Dutch
2	garage	Malay	French
3	waffle	Italian	Dutch
4	catastrophe	Greek	Spanish
5	tortilla	Arabic	Spanish
6	piano	Italian	Hindi
7	bamboo	Malay	Greek
8	almanac	French	Arabic

Writing Study

E **Learn** Titles in Names

We often write a title before someone's name to show respect for that person or to give more information about them. These titles are usually abbreviated. An abbreviated title is followed by a period. Some common titles include Mr. (Mister), Mrs. (Missus), Ms. (Miss or Missus), Prof. (Professor), and Dr. (Doctor).

Mrs. Maggs said I could take some time off.

Underline the title and circle the full form of the abbreviated word.

1	Prof. Kirby wants us to keep a class journal.	Professor	Doctor
2	Mr. Miller likes to read books about history.	President	Mister
3	I talked to Dr. Hastings about my medical history.	Doctor	Professor
4	Mrs. Andrews has kept a diary since she was a young girl.	Missus	Governor

Write Now practice writing in the **Workbook.** page 117

124 **Unit 12**   *Listening: Facts and Opinions • Speaking: Telling a Story About Yourself*

Vocabulary: Loan Words • Writing: Titles in Names   **Unit 12   125**

Summary

Objectives: To learn and practice listening, speaking, and writing strategies to facilitate effective communication.

Vocabulary: *pajamas, garage, waffle, catastrophe, tortilla, piano, bamboo, almanac*

Listening strategy: Listening for facts and opinions

Speaking: Telling a story about yourself

Word Study: Loan words

Writing Study: Titles in names

Big Question learning points: *Recording history is a way for people to share their memories. People record history to remember their own lives.*

Materials: Audio CD

Listening

Think

- Tell students to think individually about why someone would use audio to record history instead of writing it down.
- Have students share their ideas with a partner.
- Ask students to tell the class their ideas and write them on the board.

A Listen. Circle *fact* or *opinion*. 3·12

- Have students read the statements and then listen for them.
- Play the audio once and have students listen. Ask *What will you listen for?*
- Have students complete the exercise.
- Play the audio again so they can check their work.

ANSWERS
1 fact   2 opinion   3 fact   4 opinion

B Listen again. Answer the questions. 3·13

- Play the audio. Have students answer the questions individually.
- Put students into pairs to check their answers.
- Elicit the answers from the class.

ANSWERS
1 They can record their history and their memories. They can also make connections and share stories with others.
2 It doesn't cost anything. It's free.
3 It is put on a CD and might be uploaded to the Internet.
4 30 years old.

Speaking 🔊 3·14

C Choose one of these memories and tell your partner about it.

COMMUNICATION

- Read the directions. Then play the audio and have students listen.
- Divide the class in half and assign a role to each half.
- Play the audio again and pause so students can repeat their parts. Then switch roles.
- Model an example with a volunteer. Then model it a second time using a different example and a different student.
- Put students into pairs to practice the dialogue. When they have completed the dialogue once, tell them to switch topics and roles. Go around and help as needed.
- Have a few pairs say their dialogues for the class.

Word Study

D Learn: Loan Words

- Read the *Learn* box together. Read the example.

Listen and circle the correct answer. Then work with your partner to write a sentence for each word. 🔊 3·15

- Play the audio and have students listen to the sentences.
- Play the audio again and have students match the words on the left with their language of origin on the right.
- Have students check their answers in pairs before checking with the class.
- Have students work in pairs to write a sentence for each word.
- Put two pairs together and ask them to trade papers so they are checking each other's sentences.
- Have some students read out one or more sentences to the class.

ANSWERS
1 Hindi 2 French 3 Dutch 4 Greek 5 Spanish
6 Italian 7 Malay 8 Arabic

COLLABORATIVE LEARNING

- Have partners work in pairs to write sentences for each word. Allow them to use a dictionary to help.
- Have pairs check each other's work.
- Then ask some pairs to say their sentences and write them on the board.

CRITICAL THINKING

After checking the answers, ask additional questions:
- *Are any English words commonly used when you speak your language?*
- *Are there any words in your language that you know that are loan words?*
- *How do you think loan words happen?*

Writing Study

E Learn: Titles in Names

- Read the *Learn* box and example together.

Underline the title and circle the full form of the abbreviated word.

- Go over the first one with the class. Read the sentence and ask *What does "Prof." mean? When reading aloud, do you read the abbreviation as it is written or do you read the word it stands for? How do abbreviations end?*
- Have students complete the exercise on their own.
- Go over the answers with the class and write examples on the board.

ANSWERS
1 Prof. = Professor
2 Mr. = Mister
3 Dr. = Doctor
4 Mrs. = Missus

DIFFERENTIATION
Below level:
- Have students practice saying and reading the abbreviations.
- Ask if there are any other abbreviations they know of and write them on the board.

At level:
- Write *Miss, Mrs,* and *Mr.* on the board.
- Have pairs talk about who would be called each, e.g. *Miss* is used for an unmarried women; *Mrs.* is for a married woman; *Mr.* is used for all men.
- Have pairs share their ideas with the class.

Above level:
- Write *B.A., M.A., P.H.d., J.D.,* and *C.E.O.* on the board.
- Ask pairs to figure out what each abbreviation stands for. They may use a dictionary if they wish.
- Have students write the meanings of each on the board.

Write
- Direct students to the Workbook for further writing practice.

Further practice
Workbook pages 116–117
Online Practice Unit 12 · Communicate
Oxford **iTools** Unit 12 · Communicate

Summary

Objectives: To show what students have learned about the language and learning points of Units 11 and 12.

Reading: Comprehension of a memoir

Writing: Writing about a memoir

Speaking: Talking about a memoir

Big Question learning point: *People record history so that they don't forget things.*

Materials: Big Question DVD, Discover Poster 6, Talk About It! Poster, Big Question Chart

Writing

A Read this memory.

- Ask *What is a memory?* Elicit answers, e.g. *It's a person's story.*
- Go over the structure of each section of the memory before reading by asking *What do we open with?*
- Read the memory with the class one time. Then have students read it one time on their own.

B Answer the questions.

- Have students find the answers to the questions in the text.
- Check the answers with the class.

POSSIBLE ANSWERS

1 The memory opens with the reason. The reason to write this memory is so the writer doesn't forget it.
2 Yes, the writer does include dialogue. Yes, I think it helps. In this case, to create suspense and to bring the story to life.
3 The conclusion includes details about the story, but also the writer's emotion and impact the story had. This helps to give the story a context / explain why the writer wrote it.

C Learn: Writing a Memory

- Read the *Learn* box together.
- Explain that students should follow these guidelines when they plan and write their memories.

CRITICAL THINKING

Have students go back to the model to see how the writer addressed each requirement. Ask:

- *Where do we find the reason for writing?*
- *What does dialogue do?*
- *Did the writer paraphrase? What is an example of it?*
- *What kind of language is used to paraphrase what someone said?*
- *What does a strong conclusion do?*

Write

- Direct the students to the Workbook to plan and write their own memory.

CREATIVITY

- Elicit some personal story ideas from the class for their memory. Remind students that this can be a happy or weird memory.
- Remind students it should be an event that felt significant. Write some examples on the board.

Below level:

- Go over the Workbook on page 119 with the students.
- Go around and help students work individually to complete parts A–C.
- Put students into mixed-ability pairs to go over their memories using the checklist in D before writing the final version in part E.
- Have the more confident partner help the less confident student to make revisions.

At level:

- Ask the students to go to page 119 of their Workbooks and work on their memories individually.
- Then have students discuss their memories with a partner using the checklist in part D. Partners should offer helpful suggestions to improve the story.
- Students then revise their organizers.
- Share a few memories with the class.

Above level:

- Have students complete their Workbook memory individually for parts A–C.
- Ask students to share their memories with a partner who gives suggestions.
- For part D, have students read each other's memory and apply the checklist. It might be helpful to have the partner read the memory aloud so the writer can hear his or her own writing clearly.

D Work with your classmates to make a memory wall.

- Read the directions with the class.
- Give students time to put up their memories. They may wish to draw a picture.
- Have students walk around and read all of the memories.
- After all have been read, ask students to retell a memory that they liked to the class.

- Put students into small groups.
- Explain that groups will discuss the memories and answer the following questions:
  What kinds of things did people write about?
  Categorize them.
  Which of the memory-writing tips were used successfully?
- Ask *Who plans to keep their memory for a long time?*

Units 11 and 12 Big Question Review

A Watch the video. What historical things do you see? ▷

- Play the video and when it is finished ask students what they know about recorded history now.
- Have students share ideas with the class.

B What are some answers to the Big Question? Talk about them with your partner.

- Display **Discover Poster 6**. Point to familiar vocabulary items and elicit them from the class. Ask *What is this?*
- Ask students *What do you see?* Ask *What does that mean?*
- Refer to all of the learning points written on the poster and have students explain how they relate to the different pictures.
- Ask *What does this learning point mean?* Elicit answers from individual students.
- Display the **Talk About It! Poster** to help students with sentence frames for discussion of the learning points and for expressing their opinions.

C Complete the Big Question Chart. Then discuss it with the class.

- Ask students what they have learned about recorded history while studying this unit.
- Put students into pairs or small groups to say two new things they have learned.
- Have students share their ideas with the class and add their ideas to the chart.
- Have students complete the chart in their Workbook.

> **Further practice**
> **Workbook pages 118–121**
> **Online Practice • Wrap Up 6**
> Oxford **iTools • Wrap Up 6**

Testing Practice

Testing Practice 2 (pages 128–129)

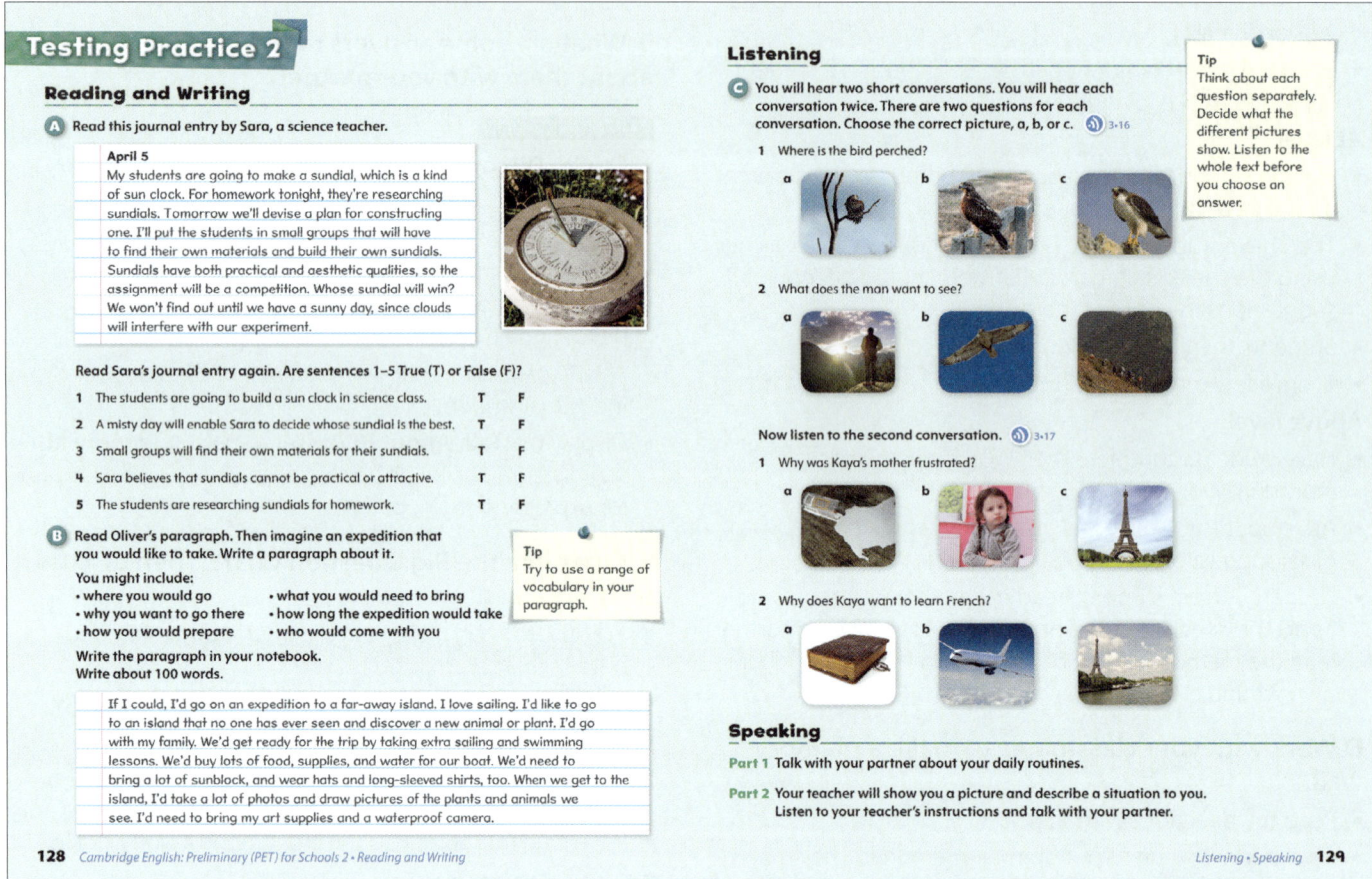

Reading and Writing

A Read this journal entry by Sara, a science teacher.

- Read the instructions with the class.
- Put students into mixed-ability pairs.
- Have students take turns to read a sentence out loud until they have completed the whole paragraph.
- Have the more confident student help the less confident student with pronunciation of unfamiliar or difficult words.

Read Sara's journal entry again. Are sentences 1–5 True (T) or False (F)?

- Read the instructions with the class.
- Have students do the activity.
- Check the answers with the class.

ANSWERS

1 T   2 F   3 T   4 F   5 T

B Read Oliver's paragraph. Then imagine an expedition that you would like to take. Write a paragraph about it.

- Read the instructions with the class.
- Have students read the paragraph.
- Explain that students will write a paragraph in their notebook. It should be about 100 words.
- Read the list of things they might include.
- Ask the class to come up with more ideas of what they could include in their paragraph.
- Read the *Tip* box to the class.
- Elicit what "a range of vocabulary" means. (Different and interesting words that are appropriate for their level.)
- Elicit some examples of interesting words and phrases that they could include in their paragraph. For example *adventure, supplies, mysterious, obstacles*.
- Ask *How should you start writing?* Elicit *make notes, make a list, make a mind map*. Explain that students should add vocabulary to their notes or graphic organizers.

Write the paragraph in your notebook. Write about 100 words.

SAMPLE ANSWER
I would like to go on a backpacking expedition somewhere with ancient ruins and maybe high mountains. I would like to climb high peaks. I would love to see mountains because I have never seen anything higher than a hill. My family and my best friend would come, too. We would prepare by climbing lots of stairs. We would need to bring warm clothes, food, and a map. A one-month trip would be nice. We would take photos of the rugged mountains. Maybe we would encounter a remote village and we could learn about different cultures.

Listening

C You will hear two short conversations. You will hear each conversation twice. There are two questions for each conversation. Choose the correct picture, a, b, or c. 3·16

- Read the instructions with the class.
- Read the *Tip* box with the class.
- Before (or after) students listen to the text, discuss what they can see in the pictures.

ANSWERS
1 c   2 a

Now listen to the second conversation. 3·17

- Have students work in pairs and discuss what they see in the pictures.
- Have students share their ideas with the class.

ANSWERS
1 b   2 a

Speaking

Part 1 Talk with your partner about your daily routines.

- Read the instructions with the class.
- Model a conversation using your own example, e.g. say *I wake up early. I always walk my dog. Then I usually eat toast for breakfast. I go to school in the morning. I arrive at seven fifteen. Sometimes I ride my bike. But if it's raining, I take the bus,* etc.
- Put students into pairs to do the activity.

DIFFERENTIATION

Below level:
- Write sentence frames on the board for students to use to do the activity, e.g. *I wake up at _____. I eat _____. I go to school at _____. I get home at _____. At night, I _____.*

At level:
- Have students do the activity.

Above level:
- Challenge students to compare their current routine to a routine they had when they were younger, e.g. *My brother used to walk me to school. But now he goes to a different school and I walk by myself.*

Part 2 Your teacher will show you a picture and describe a situation to you. Listen to your teacher's instructions and talk with your partner.

(Please refer to the the Assessment for Learning CD-ROM for the picture).

- Put students into pairs. Give each pair the photo.
- Explain that students will use the photo to discuss history and the importance of recording the past.
- Tell them that they will also talk about what they see in the photo.

DIFFERENTIATION

Below level:
- Elicit what students see in the photo.
- Write the words on the board as a mind map.
- Tell students that they can refer to this mind map and use the words as they do the activity.

At level:
- Have students do the activity

Above level:
- Have students discuss how the past is different to today.
- Have students tell if they would like to have lived in the past, and why or why not.
- Have students share their thought with the class.

In units **13** and **14** you will:

WATCH a video about birds.

LEARN about the beauty and intelligence of birds.

READ poems and a magazine article about birds.

WRITE an action plan.

PRESENT your action plan to the class.

BIG QUESTION 7

What makes birds special?

A Watch the video. Then talk about it with your partner. ▶

B Look at the picture and discuss it with your class.

1 What do you think is special about these birds?

2 How are these two types of birds different? How are they similar?

C Think and answer the questions.

1 What kinds of birds live in your area?

2 How are birds different from other animals?

3 Do you think birds are intelligent? Why?

4 Why do you think so many countries have a national bird?

D Discuss this topic with your class. Fill out the **Big Question Chart**.

What do you know about birds? What do you want to know?

130 *Big Question 7*

131

Reading Strategies
Students will practice:
- Visualizing
- Analyzing

Vocabulary
Students will understand and use words about:
- Bird behavior

Grammar
Students will understand and use:
- Passive (future)
- Passive review

Review
Students will review the language and Big Question learning points of Units 13 and 14 through:
- Writing an action plan

Units 13 and 14
What makes birds special?
Students will understand the Big Question learning points:
- People are inspired by birds.
- Birds can improve our well-being.
- Certain birds are highly intelligent.
- Some birds have amazing abilities, like flying in formation.
- Some birds can mimic things they hear.

Listening Strategies
Students will practice:
- Listening for reasons
- Listening for examples

Writing Study
Students will use and understand:
- Metaphor
- Simile

Students will:
- Write an action plan

Word Study
Students will understand and use:
- Alliteration
- Greek roots

Speaking
Students will understand and use expressions for:
- Expressing probability
- Talking about what you've learned

Units 13 and 14 Big Question page 130

Summary

Objectives: To activate students' existing knowledge of the topic and identify what they would like to learn about the topic.

Materials: Big Question DVD, Discover Poster 7, Big Question Chart

Introducing the topic

- Read out the Big Question. Ask *What makes birds special?*
- Write students' ideas on the board and discuss.

A Watch the video. Then talk about it with your partner. ▷

- Play the video and when it is finished, ask students to answer the following questions in pairs:
  What do you see in the video?
  What is happening?
  Who do you think the people are?
  What do you like about the video?
- Have individual students share their answers with the class.

B Look at the picture and discuss it with your class.

- Students look at the big picture and talk about it. Ask *What do you see?*
- Ask additional questions:
  Do you know the different types of birds in the photograph?
  Where do you think they are?
  Why does the flying bird have such a big beak?
  What are the other birds doing?

C Think and answer the questions.

- Have students discuss the questions in small groups, and then with the class.

DIFFERENTIATION

Below level:
- Put students into small mixed-ability groups. Have groups discuss each question and list their answers.

At level:
- Put students into pairs to answer the questions.
- Have pairs join another pair to discuss their answers.

Above level:
- Have students do the activity individually.
- Put students into small groups to share their answers and make a master list of answers.

Expanding the topic

COLLABORATIVE LEARNING

- Display **Discover Poster 7** and give students enough time to look at the pictures.
- Get students to talk about things you think they will know by pointing to different things in the pictures and asking *What's this? What do you know about this?*
- Put students into small groups of three or four. Have each group choose a picture that they find interesting.
- Ask each group to say five sentences to describe their picture without naming what it is.
- The rest of the class guesses which picture they are talking about.

CRITICAL THINKING

- Keep students in their groups. Ask each group to think about one question for each picture on the poster. Ask *What do you want to know about each picture? What are you curious about?*
- Have students say their questions and write them on the board.

D Discuss this topic with your class. Fill out the Big Question Chart.

- Display the **Big Question Chart**.
- Ask the class *What do you know about birds? What do you want to know about birds?*
- Ask students to write what they know and what they want to know in their Workbooks.
- Write a collection of ideas on the **Big Question Chart**.

Discover Poster 7

1 A hummingbird drinking nectar from a pink zinnia flower; 2 Two girls at a lake feeding bread to geese; 3 An African grey parrot solving a puzzle; 4 A flock of Canadian geese flying in formation

Further Practice
Workbook page 122
Online Practice · Big Question 7
Oxford **iTools** · **Big Question 7**

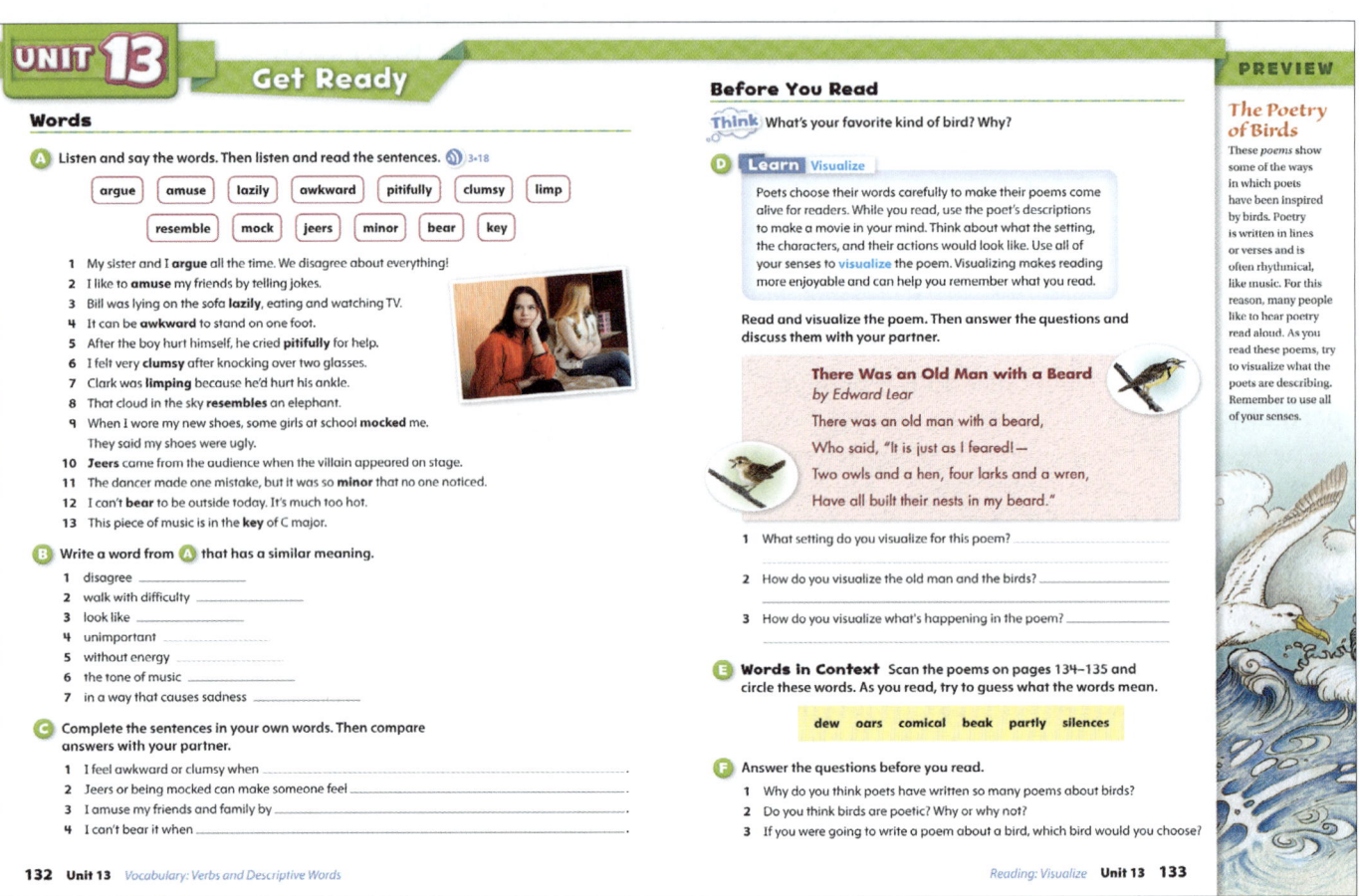

UNIT 13 Get Ready

Words

A Listen and say the words. Then listen and read the sentences. 3·18

argue · amuse · lazily · awkward · pitifully · clumsy · limp
resemble · mock · jeers · minor · bear · key

1 My sister and I **argue** all the time. We disagree about everything!
2 I like to **amuse** my friends by telling jokes.
3 Bill was lying on the sofa **lazily**, eating and watching TV.
4 It can be **awkward** to stand on one foot.
5 After the boy hurt himself, he cried **pitifully** for help.
6 I felt very **clumsy** after knocking over two glasses.
7 Clark was **limping** because he'd hurt his ankle.
8 That cloud in the sky **resembles** an elephant.
9 When I wore my new shoes, some girls at school **mocked** me. They said my shoes were ugly.
10 **Jeers** came from the audience when the villain appeared on stage.
11 The dancer made one mistake, but it was so **minor** that no one noticed.
12 I can't **bear** to be outside today. It's much too hot.
13 This piece of music is in the **key** of C major.

B Write a word from A that has a similar meaning.

1 disagree _____
2 walk with difficulty _____
3 look like _____
4 unimportant _____
5 without energy _____
6 the tone of music _____
7 in a way that causes sadness _____

C Complete the sentences in your own words. Then compare answers with your partner.

1 I feel awkward or clumsy when _____
2 Jeers or being mocked can make someone feel _____
3 I amuse my friends and family by _____
4 I can't bear it when _____

132 Unit 13 Vocabulary: Verbs and Descriptive Words

Before You Read

Think What's your favorite kind of bird? Why?

D Learn Visualize

Poets choose their words carefully to make their poems come alive for readers. While you read, use the poet's descriptions to make a movie in your mind. Think about what the setting, the characters, and their actions would look like. Use all of your senses to visualize the poem. Visualizing makes reading more enjoyable and can help you remember what you read.

Read and visualize the poem. Then answer the questions and discuss them with your partner.

There Was an Old Man with a Beard
by Edward Lear

There was an old man with a beard,
Who said, "It is just as I feared!—
Two owls and a hen, four larks and a wren,
Have all built their nests in my beard."

1 What setting do you visualize for this poem? _____
2 How do you visualize the old man and the birds? _____
3 How do you visualize what's happening in the poem? _____

E Words in Context Scan the poems on pages 134–135 and circle these words. As you read, try to guess what the words mean.

dew · oars · comical · beak · partly · silences

F Answer the questions before you read.

1 Why do you think poets have written so many poems about birds?
2 Do you think birds are poetic? Why or why not?
3 If you were going to write a poem about a bird, which bird would you choose?

Reading: Visualize Unit 13 133

PREVIEW

The Poetry of Birds

These poems show some of the ways in which poets have been inspired by birds. Poetry is written in lines or verses and is often rhythmical, like music. For this reason, many people like to hear poetry read aloud. As you read these poems, try to visualize what the poets are describing. Remember to use all of your senses.

Summary

Objectives: To understand about verbs and descriptive words; to apply own experience and a reading strategy to help comprehension of a text.

Vocabulary: *argue, amuse, lazily, awkward, pitifully, clumsy, limp, resemble, mock, jeers, minor, bear, key, dew, oars, comical, beak, partly, silences*

Reading strategy: Visualizing

Materials: Audio CD

Words

A Listen and say the words. Then listen and read the sentences. 3·18

- Play the audio. Ask students to point to the words and repeat the words when they hear them.
- Then have students listen and read the sentences as they hear them.
- Say the sentence numbers out of order and have the class read the sentences aloud.

CRITICAL THINKING

- Put students into pairs to classify the words. Tell them to use the context of the sentences to determine the classification. Ask *Which words are verbs? Nouns? Adverbs? Adjectives?*
- When they have finished listing the words, tell the pairs to swap their paper with another pair. Go over the answers with the class.

ANSWERS

Verbs: argue, amuse, limp, resemble, mock, bear
Nouns: jeers, key
Adverbs: lazily, pitifully
Adjectives: awkward, clumsy, minor

B Write a word from A that has a similar meaning.

- Have students do the activity on their own.
- Ask students to compare their answers with a partner.
- Check answers with the class.

ANSWERS

1 argue 2 limp 3 resemble 4 minor 5 lazily
6 key 7 pitifully

C Complete the sentences in your own words. Then compare answers with your partner.

- Have students do the activity on their own.
- Ask students to compare their answers with a partner.
- Check answers with the class.

COLLABORATIVE LEARNING

- Put students into pairs. Have pairs write sentences for all of the new words, e.g. *I only argue with my sister when we are in the car.*
- When they have finished, tell the pairs to swap their sentences with another pair.
- Pairs check their work with each other.
- Have pairs read some of their sentences to the class. Listen to at least two sentences for each new word.

Before You Read

Think

- Have students think about their answers.
- Have a class discussion. List the birds on the board which the students suggest, and total the number of birds to arrive at the most favorite bird of the class.

D Learn: Visualize

- Read the *Learn* box together.
- Ask *Have you ever read a book and pictured what the characters look like in your mind?* Then ask *Have you ever watched a movie that was based on a book? Did the characters look like you had imagined? Why or why not?*

Read and visualize the poem. Then answer the questions and discuss them with your partner.

- Read the poem with the class.
- Then have students answer the questions individually.
- Put students into pairs to check answers.
- Check answers with the class.

E Words in Context: Scan the poems on pages 134–135 and circle these words. As you read, try to guess what the words mean.

- Read each word and have students follow your pronunciation.
- Have students scan the poems on pages 134 and 135 and circle the words. Tell them to guess what the words mean from the context.
- Ask the students to share their ideas about the words' definitions.

Below level:

- Put students into mixed-ability pairs.
- Have the more confident student help the less confident student to figure out the meaning from context and take notes on a definition. Have the more confident student guide the less confident student in using the dictionary.
- Put pairs into groups to compare definitions. Share definitions with the class.

At level:

- Put students into pairs to figure out the meaning of the new words from context.
- Tell pairs to look up any words they don't recognize in the dictionary.
- Have pairs share their answers with the class.

Above level:

- Put students into pairs to work out each of the meanings together.
- Then give each pair a dictionary. One student reads a dictionary definition aloud, and the other student guesses which word it is.
- Then they reread the sentence in the poem and compare what they thought the word meant to the dictionary definition.
- Have pairs share some of their definitions with the class.

F Answer the questions before you read.

- Have students think individually about the questions first.
- Put students into pairs to discuss the questions. Tell students to explain their ideas.
- Go over the students' answers and make notes on the board.

Reading Preview

- Read the title of the unit's reading text.
- Have students silently read the content of the preview bar.
- Ask *What type of text is it?* Ask *What is typical of poetry? Why do poets have to choose their words carefully?*
- Tell students to visualize what the poet describes as they read.

Further Practice

Workbook pages 122–123
Online Practice Unit 13 · Get Ready
Oxford **iTools** Unit 13 · Get Ready

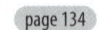

Read 3·19

The Poetry of Birds

FOR CENTURIES, POETS HAVE BEEN INSPIRED BY BIRDS. They've written about how birds sing and fly, hunt and nest, and their sometimes strange behavior. Although the poems here were written in different countries, during different time periods, and in different styles, they all reflect our fascination with the beauty and mystery of birds.

Emily Dickinson was an American poet, born in 1830. She was thought of as a minor poet in her lifetime, but many people read her poetry today.

A Bird Came Down the Walk
by Emily Dickinson

A bird came down the walk—
He did not know I saw—
He bit an angleworm in halves
And ate the fellow, raw,

And then he drank a dew
From a convenient grass—
And then hopped sidewise to the wall
To let a beetle pass—

He glanced with rapid eyes
That hurried all around—
They looked like frightened beads, I thought—
He stirred his velvet head

Like one in danger, cautious,
I offered him a crumb
And he unrolled his feathers
And rowed him softer home—

Than oars divide the ocean,
Too silver for a seam—
Or butterflies, off banks of noon
Leap, splashless as they swim

Masaoka Shiki, born in 1876, was a Japanese poet and author. He helped to develop modern haiku poetry.

On How to Sing
by Masaoka Shiki

On how to sing
the frog school and the skylark school
are arguing.

Du Fu is considered one of the greatest Chinese poets. He was born in 712.

A Pair of Yellow Warblers Sing in the Green Willow
by Du Fu

A pair of yellow warblers sing in the green willow,
a file of white herons climb the blue sky.
Framed in my window, the thousand autumn
snows of the western peaks;
tied by my gate, a boat to take me ten thousand
miles east to Wu.

> **Think**
> What do you see, hear, and feel when you read this poem?

Charles Baudelaire was a French poet, born in Paris in 1821. His most famous collection of poetry is *The Flowers of Evil*.

The Albatross
by Charles Baudelaire

Often, just to amuse themselves, sailors
Catch albatrosses, those huge sea birds
That lazily follow the ship
As it glides over the salty depths.

The moment they've been put on deck
These kings of the sky, now awkward and ashamed,
Let their great white wings hang pitifully
Like oars beside them.

The winged traveler looks weak and clumsy!
He who was once so beautiful is now comical and ugly!
A sailor taps its beak with a pipe,
Another, limping, mimics the disabled flier.

The poet resembles this prince of the clouds,
Fearlessly riding storms and mocking arrows.
When he's on the ground, surrounded by jeers,
His giant wings prevent him from walking.

> **Think**
> How did the albatross look in the air? How does it look when it's on the ground?

A Song For All Seasons
by Anonymous

In the lonely early morning
Very still and hard to bear
Suddenly come tiny voices
Breaking through the summer air.

Singing faintly, singing sweetly
In a soft melodic key
Partly hidden by the woodland
Yet they're very close to me.

As the sun begins to warm me
I gaze up from where I lie
Watching while the skylarks circle
Up into the summer sky.

Sad to think that winter's coming
Silences the skylarks' song
Cold creeps in and days are shorter
While the icy nights are long.

Yet without the sun there's birdsong
Even when the north winds blow
Sparrows, wrens, and blackbirds twitter
Robins sing amid the snow!

Kobayashi Issa was a Japanese poet known for his haiku poems. He lived from 1763–1827. His writing name, Issa, means "cup of tea."

The Tree Will Be Cut
by Kobayashi Issa

The tree will be cut
Not knowing the bird
Makes a nest

134 · 135

Summary

Objectives: To read, understand, and discuss poetry; to apply a reading strategy to improve comprehension.

School subject: Life Science

Text type: Poems

Reading strategy: Visualizing

Big Question learning point: *People are inspired by birds.*

Materials: Talk About It! Poster, Audio CD

Before Reading

- Have students tell you what they see in the pictures.
- Ask the students to read the introductory text. Ask *Why do you think we are reading so many poems from different times and places? What are you going to do as you read?*

During Reading 3·19

- Point out the *Think* boxes and explain that students should use these to think about the author's purpose.

DIFFERENTIATION

Below level:

- Have students read with you in small groups.
- During reading, pause and ask students questions such as: *What do you visualize for this word? What do you think the poet means by _____?*
- Stop and discuss the *Think* box questions when you come to them.

At level:

- Ask the students to take turns reading the poems with a partner.
- Have them stop at each *Think* box to discuss the questions.

Above level:

- Have students read the poems independently.
- Put students into pairs to discuss what they visualize and to discuss the *Think* boxes.

CRITICAL THINKING

- Discuss the *Think* boxes. Look at the first box. Ask *What do you visualize when you read "A Pair of Yellow Warblers Sing in the Green Willow?"*
- Have individual students share their visualizations. Ask questions for more information.
- Look at the second *Think* box. Ask *How does the albatross look in the air? How does it look when it's on the ground?*
- Have individual students share their visualizations. Ask questions for more information.

After Reading

CRITICAL THINKING

- Have students choose two poems (one short, one long).
- Ask them to underline the words and phrases that they find easiest to visualize. Have students do this individually.
- Put students into small groups. Have them compare their underlined words and phrases.
- Ask *Which poems did you find easiest to visualize? Which most difficult? Why do you think that is? Discuss with your group.* Go around and help as needed.
- Have groups share their ideas with the class.

CREATIVITY

- Put students into pairs.
- Explain that pairs will rewrite the poem, *"On How to Sing"*, by Masaoka Shiki. Tell them to change one or two of the animals on line two (frog, skylark), and the verb (arguing) on line three.
- It is optional, but they can change the verb *sing* in the first line if they wish. Students may find it easier to work within the parameters of *sing* and not change it.
- Then have pairs share their new poems with the class. For each poem, have other pairs describe what the poem made them visualize.

COLLABORATIVE LEARNING

- Display the **Talk About It! Poster** to help students with sentence frames for discussion and expressing personal opinions.
- Put students into pairs to discuss which part of the text is most interesting.

CULTURE NOTE

Birds have always fascinated humans – perhaps because they are found everywhere. Birds have been depicted since ancient time in cave paintings.

Perhaps because they have bright plumage and are very visible flying overhead, birds have appeared in art and design all over the world, such as in the peacock throne of the Persian / Mughal Empire.

Birds also have symbolic values in different cultures. In India, the peacock represents Mother Earth. In Europe, the owl is considered wise, but in Africa, it is associated with death.

Perhaps it is the bird's song that attracts poets. Poets, after all, have an ear for language and its rhythms. It may be that in a birdsong, a poet sees his or her own poem.

Further Practice
Workbook page 124
Online Practice Unit 13 · Read
Oxford **iTools** Unit 13 · Read

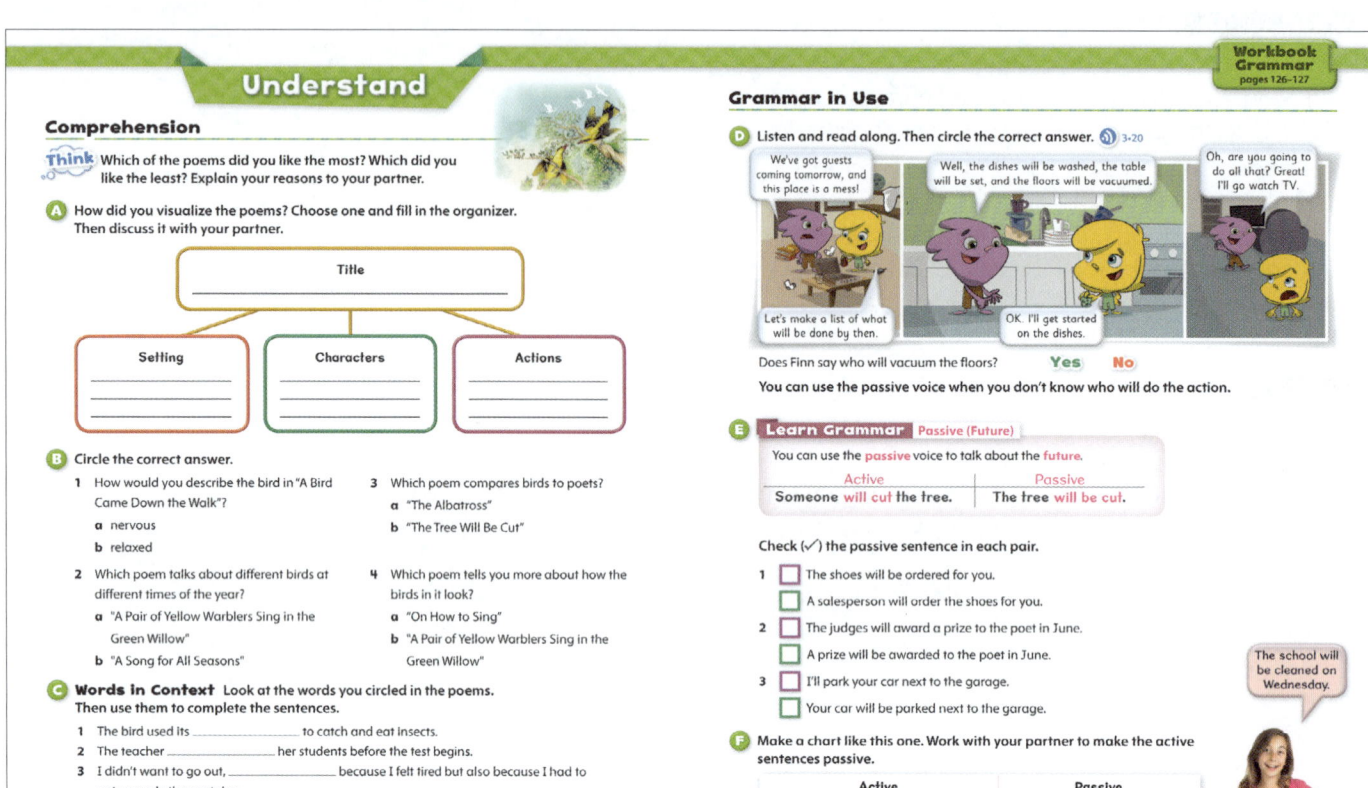

136 Unit 13 *Comprehension*

Grammar: Passive (Future) **Unit 13** **137**

Summary

Objectives: To demonstrate understanding of poetry; to understand the meaning and form of the grammar structure.

Reading: Comprehension

Grammar input: Passive (future)

Grammar practice: Workbook exercises

Grammar production: Using passive sentences in future tense

Materials: Audio CD

Comprehension

Think

- Read the questions with the class. Ask students to think about their answers.
- Put students into groups to discuss their answers.
- Have groups share their answers.

A How did you visualize the poems? Choose one and fill in the organizer. Then discuss it with your partner.

- Read the instructions with the class. Have students turn to the poems on pages 134 and 135. Ask them to choose a poem.
- Have students complete the organizer on their own. Go around and help as needed.
- Put students into pairs and tell them to compare their organizers.

- Complete the organizers on the board to check them.
- Elicit the information to complete them from the class.

POSSIBLE ANSWERS

Title: A Pair of Yellow Warblers Sing in the Green Willow
Setting: green willow trees; blue sky; window frame; a boat tied to a gate
Characters: pair of green warblers; white herons
Actions: herons flying by; the sound of the green warblers singing in the trees

DIFFERENTIATION

Below level:

- Put students into small mixed-ability groups.
- Assign a different poem to each of the groups.
- Have the groups reread the poem together, and then each student fills in the organizer individually. Go around and help as needed.
- Then have groups compare their organizers. Have all of the groups share a few of their organizers with the class.

At level:

- Students complete the organizers on their own.
- Put students into pairs who have chosen the same poem.
- Partners compare organizers to check each other's work.
- Have pairs share their organizers with the class.

Above level:
- Students complete the organizers on their own.
- Once complete, students can revise their organizer and add more details to explain their thoughts.
- Have students go through and embellish their organizers with full details of their visualization of the poem.
- Give students a few minutes to do the activity.
- Then have students compare their organizer with a partner. Have partners share their organizers with the class.

B Circle the correct answer.
- Have students do the activity on their own, looking back to pages 134–135 for answers.
- Have students compare their answers with a partner.
- Check the answers with the class.

POSSIBLE ANSWERS
1 a 2 b 3 a 4 b

C Words in Context: Look at the words you circled in the poems. Then use them to complete the sentences.
- Have students go back and find the words in the poems.
- Tell them to use the context clues to guess at the meaning of each word and then complete the sentences.
- Check answers with the class.

ANSWERS
1 beak 2 silences 3 partly 4 comical 5 dew
6 oars

COLLABORATIVE LEARNING
- In pairs, ask students to collaborate to write new sentences for the words in context.
- Tell groups to write the sentences, but to leave a blank where the word in context goes.
- As pairs write their sentences, encourage them to use the dictionary to help with definitions. Go around and help as necessary.
- Have pairs trade papers with another pair who fills in the blanks. Then they check each other's work.
- Have pairs share their sentences with the class.

Grammar in Use

D Listen and read along. Then circle the correct answer. 🔊 3·20
- Listen to the dialogue once and have students read along.
- Ask students to read the question and then circle the correct answer.
- Play the audio again and have students check their answer.
- Check the answer with the class.

ANSWER
No

E Learn Grammar: Passive (Future)
- Read the *Learn Grammar* box together.
- Ask *What is missing in the passive future sentence?*

Check (✓) the passive sentence in each pair.
- Have students complete the activity individually.
- Check answers with the class.

ANSWERS
The following sentences should be checked:
1 The shoes will be ordered for you.
2 A prize will be awarded to the poet in June.
3 Your car will be parked next to the garage.

F Make a chart like this one. Work with your partner to make the active sentences passive.
- Ask the students to individually create the chart in their notebooks.
- Tell them to write down three active sentences.
- Put students into pairs. Have them trade notebooks and write the passive equivalent of the active sentences.
- Ask them to hand their notebooks back and correct each other's work.
- Have some students read out their active and passive sentences to the class.

Workbook Grammar
- Direct students to the Workbook for further practice.

Further practice
Workbook pages 125–127
Online Practice Unit 13 · Understand
Oxford iTools Unit 13 · Understand

Communicate

Listening

Think What emotions do birds make you feel? Why?

A Listen. Circle the correct answer. 3·21

1 You have to believe in happiness or _____.
  a believe in the grass in days of snow
  b happiness never comes
2 What's the reason a bird can sing? _____.
  a On his darkest day, he believes in spring.
  b It isn't an outward thing.

B Listen again. Circle True (T) or False (F). 3·22

1 The poet says birds chirp even when they only find snow. T F
2 The poet says birds believe in spring. T F
3 This poem is about happiness and hope. T F
4 The poet is complaining in this poem. T F

Speaking 3·23

C **Learn** Expressing Probability

Use expressions of probability to talk about how likely you think something is.

I'll ...
I'll probably be ...
I might be ...
No way!

What will your life be like in five or ten years? Choose one of these questions or think of your own. Then discuss it with your partner.

• What university will you go to?
• What will you study?
• What kind of work will you do?
• Where will you live?

What will you be doing in five years?

I'll be ... I can't wait!

And what do you think you'll be ... ?

Well, I'll probably be ... I think it's really ...

Do you think you'll be living ... ?

No way! I might be ...

138 **Unit 13** *Listening: Reasons • Speaking: Expressing Probability*

Word Study

D **Learn** Alliteration

Alliteration is when two or more words that are close to each other begin with the same letter or sound. Poets often use alliteration to make their writing more fun and easier to remember.

The bird was not to blame.

Listen and complete the sentences. Then read them aloud to your partner. 3·24 A-Z

| always bower crow built albatross heard caterpillar have |

1 The _____ was too slow to catch the _____.
2 _____ you ever _____ of a hummingbird?
3 The busy bird _____ a _____.
4 Albert the _____ was almost _____ alert.

Writing Study

E **Learn** Metaphor

A metaphor compares two things without using the words *like* or *as*. Poets and other writers use metaphors to make their writing more expressive.

The albatross is the king of the sky.

Write a metaphor about each of these topics. Then share them with your partner.

• birds
• flight
• music
• happiness

Write Now practice writing in the **Workbook**. page 129

Vocabulary: Alliteration • Writing: Metaphor **Unit 13** **139**

BIG QUESTION 7

? What makes birds special?

Birds have inspired poets all over the world.

What kinds of things do poets say about birds?

Summary

Objectives: To learn and practice listening, speaking, and writing strategies to facilitate effective communication.

Vocabulary: *always, bower, crow, built, albatross, heard, caterpillar, have*

Listening strategy: Listening for reasons

Speaking: Expressing probability

Word Study: Alliteration

Writing Study: Metaphor

Big Question learning points: *People are inspired by birds. Birds can improve our well-being.*

Materials: Discover Poster 7, Audio CD, Big Question Chart

Listening

Think

• Tell students to think about the questions on their own.
• Ask students to think of examples of birds that illustrate their opinions. Model an example of your own: *Crows make me feel a menacing emotion, dark and sinister, like something bad is going to happen.*
• Put students into pairs to discuss the question.
• Have pairs share their ideas with the class.

A Listen. Circle the correct answer. 3·21

• Have students read the sentences first.
• Play the audio once and have students listen.
• Tell students to circle the correct answers.
• Play the audio again for students to check their work.

ANSWERS
1 b 2 a

B Listen again. Circle True (T) or False (F). 3·22

• Have students read the sentences first.
• Play the audio once and have students listen.
• Tell students to circle the correct answers.
• Play the audio again for students to check their work.

ANSWERS
1 F 2 T 3 T 4 F

Speaking 3·23

C Learn: Expressing Probability

• Read the *Learn* box with the class.
• Play the audio and have students listen.
• Model the dialogue and an example with a confident student in front of the class.
• Put students into pairs and tell them to practice the dialogue.

What will your life be like in five or ten years? Choose one of these questions or think of your own. Then discuss it with your partner.

- Put students into pairs. Each partner tells the other what he or she thinks they will be doing in five or ten years.
- Put students into small groups. Partners tell the group about what their partner will be doing in five or ten years' time, e.g. *She will probably be living in a big city…* Make sure each person in the group speaks.
- Have some partners tell the class about the person they spoke to.

Word Study

D Learn: Alliteration

- Read the *Learn* box together.
- Ask the class if any of the students have alliterative names, e.g. Keiko Kenobi.
- Write the names on the board and underline the alliterative letters and sounds.

Listen and complete the sentences. Then read them aloud to your partner. ⊙ 3·24

- Play the audio and have students write the words they hear.
- Play the audio again for students to check their answers.
- As a follow-up, put students into pairs. Have them look in a dictionary to find the meanings of any of the words they don't know. Have pairs share the definitions with the class.

ANSWERS
1 crow, caterpillar
2 have, heard
3 built, bower
4 albatross, always

CRITICAL THINKING

- Ask students to work in pairs.
- Each pair chooses four of the words from the Word Study and writes an alliterative sentence for each. They must choose a new alliterative word to match, instead of using the pairs in D.
- Invite a few pairs to say their sentences for the class.

Writing Study

E Learn: Metaphor

- Read the *Learn* box together.
- Ask *Does the example sentence say the albatross is similar to a king of the sky?* Confirm that it says he is the king of the sky. We understand that as an expression of what he is like.
- Ask students to look at page 135, the last stanza (paragraph) of *The Albatross* poem. Ask *Can you find the metaphor?* Give students time to look and raise their hands. Then check the answer.

Write a metaphor about each of these topics. Then share them with your partner.

- Have students write a metaphor about each of the words listed.
- Ask them to share their metaphors with a partner.

Below level:

- Do the first one with the students. Ask *What is a bird like? First, let's think of a specific bird.* Elicit a bird or use the word *seagull. What is a seagull like? I see them flying over water. I always see them stealing food when I eat outdoors. A-ha! What else steals things?* (A thief) *A seagull is a thief of French fries.*
- Continue with the next example, but this time eliciting ideas from the class.
- For the last two, have students work in mixed-ability pairs to think of metaphors.

At level:

- Have students write their metaphors individually.
- Ask them to compare their metaphors.
- Invite pairs to write their best two metaphors on the board. Then read over them with the class. Were any easier to think of than others?

Above level:

- Have students write their metaphors individually on small separate pieces of paper that they fold after writing.
- Put students into groups. They collect their papers so that no one can tell who wrote them. Put them in a hat or bag. Then the group pulls a paper and reads the metaphor.
- After all metaphors have been read, the group choose their favorite three metaphors and shares them with the class.
- Have the class choose their favorite metaphors.

Write

- Direct students to the Workbook for further writing practice.

Big Question 7 Review

What makes birds special?

- Display **Discover Poster 7**. Discuss what you see.
- Refer to the learning points covered in Unit 13 that are written on the poster and have students explain how they relate to the different pictures.
- Return to the **Big Question Chart**.
- Ask students what they have learned about birds while studying this unit.

Further practice
Workbook pages 128–129
Online Practice Unit 13 • Communicate
Oxford **iTools** Unit 13 • Communicate

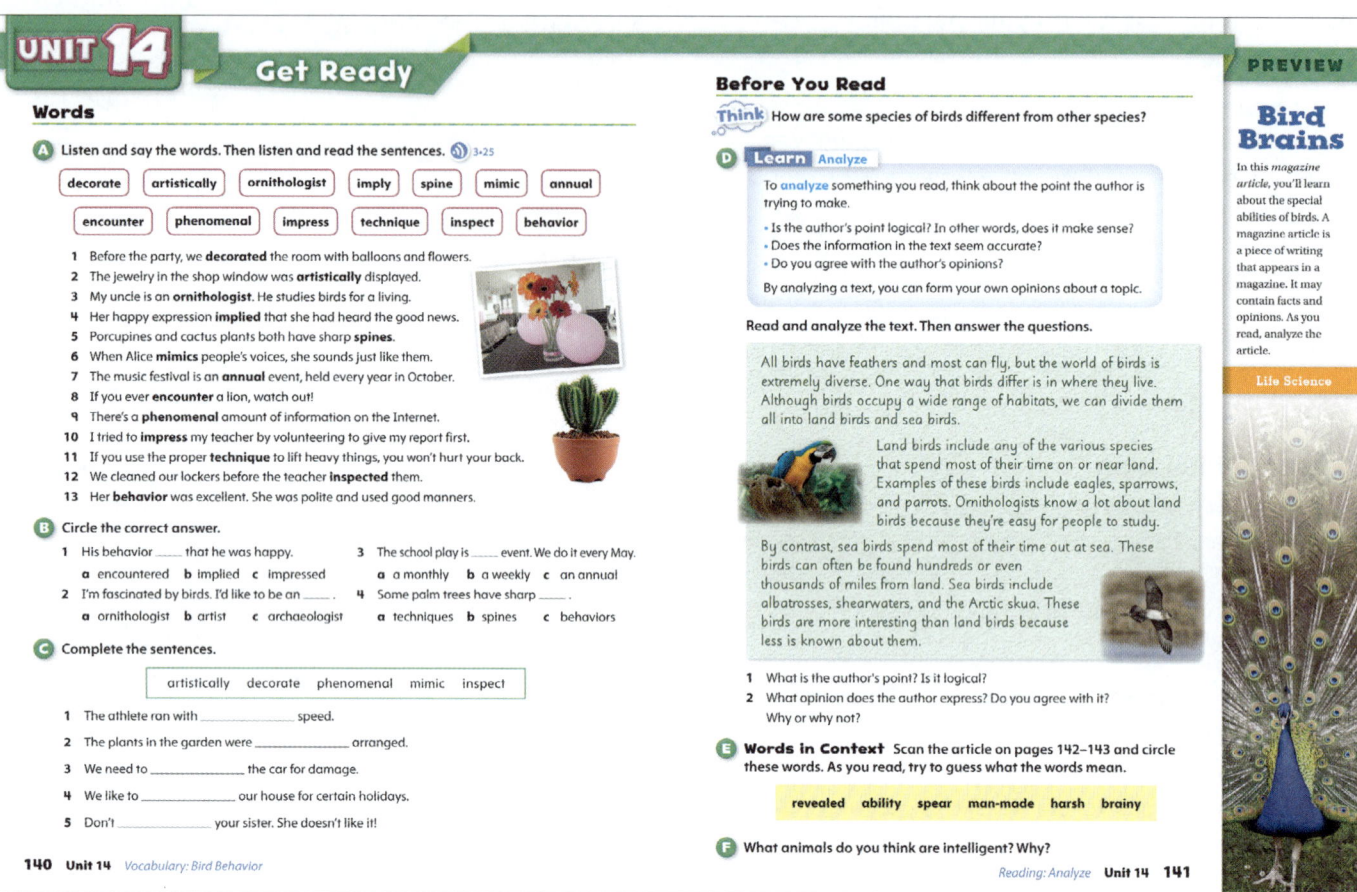

UNIT 14 — Get Ready

Words

A Listen and say the words. Then listen and read the sentences. 3·25

decorate | artistically | ornithologist | imply | spine | mimic | annual

encounter | phenomenal | impress | technique | inspect | behavior

1 Before the party, we **decorated** the room with balloons and flowers.
2 The jewelry in the shop window was **artistically** displayed.
3 My uncle is an **ornithologist**. He studies birds for a living.
4 Her happy expression **implied** that she had heard the good news.
5 Porcupines and cactus plants both have sharp **spines**.
6 When Alice **mimics** people's voices, she sounds just like them.
7 The music festival is an **annual** event, held every year in October.
8 If you ever **encounter** a lion, watch out!
9 There's a **phenomenal** amount of information on the Internet.
10 I tried to **impress** my teacher by volunteering to give my report first.
11 If you use the proper **technique** to lift heavy things, you won't hurt your back.
12 We cleaned our lockers before the teacher **inspected** them.
13 Her **behavior** was excellent. She was polite and used good manners.

B Circle the correct answer.

1 His behavior _____ that he was happy.
   a encountered   b implied   c impressed
2 I'm fascinated by birds. I'd like to be an _____.
   a ornithologist   b artist   c archaeologist
3 The school play is _____ event. We do it every May.
   a a monthly   b a weekly   c an annual
4 Some palm trees have sharp _____ .
   a techniques   b spines   c behaviors

C Complete the sentences.

artistically   decorate   phenomenal   mimic   inspect

1 The athlete ran with _____ speed.
2 The plants in the garden were _____ arranged.
3 We need to _____ the car for damage.
4 We like to _____ our house for certain holidays.
5 Don't _____ your sister. She doesn't like it!

140   Unit 14   Vocabulary: Bird Behavior

Before You Read

Think How are some species of birds different from other species?

D Learn Analyze

To **analyze** something you read, think about the point the author is trying to make.

• Is the author's point logical? In other words, does it make sense?
• Does the information in the text seem accurate?
• Do you agree with the author's opinions?

By analyzing a text, you can form your own opinions about a topic.

Read and analyze the text. Then answer the questions.

All birds have feathers and most can fly, but the world of birds is extremely diverse. One way that birds differ is in where they live. Although birds occupy a wide range of habitats, we can divide them all into land birds and sea birds.

Land birds include any of the various species that spend most of their time on or near land. Examples of these birds include eagles, sparrows, and parrots. Ornithologists know a lot about land birds because they're easy for people to study.

By contrast, sea birds spend most of their time out at sea. These birds can often be found hundreds or even thousands of miles from land. Sea birds include albatrosses, shearwaters, and the Arctic skua. These birds are more interesting than land birds because less is known about them.

1 What is the author's point? Is it logical?
2 What opinion does the author express? Do you agree with it? Why or why not?

E Words in Context Scan the article on pages 142–143 and circle these words. As you read, try to guess what the words mean.

revealed   ability   spear   man-made   harsh   brainy

F What animals do you think are intelligent? Why?

Reading: Analyze   Unit 14   141

PREVIEW

Bird Brains

In this *magazine article*, you'll learn about the special abilities of birds. A magazine article is a piece of writing that appears in a magazine. It may contain facts and opinions. As you read, analyze the article.

Life Science

Summary

Objectives: To understand words about bird behavior; to apply own experience and a reading strategy to help comprehension of a text.

Vocabulary: *decorate, artistically, ornithologist, imply, spine, mimic, annual, encounter, phenomenal, impress, technique, inspect, behavior, revealed, ability, spear, man-made, harsh, brainy*

Reading strategy: Analyzing

Materials: Audio CD

Words

A Listen and say the words. Then listen and read the sentences. 3·25

• Play the audio. Ask students to point to the words and repeat the words when they hear them.
• Then have students listen and read the sentences as they hear them.
• Say the sentence numbers out of order and have the class read the sentences aloud.

CRITICAL THINKING

Ask the following questions to check understanding:

• *What kinds of things can you use to decorate your room?*
• *If someone is interested in studying birds, what would their title be?*
• *If you mimic your favorite celebrity's behavior, what does that imply?*
• *What do you call an event that you do every year?*

B Circle the correct answer.

• Have students do the activity on their own and then compare answers with a partner.
• Check answers with the class.

ANSWERS
1 b   2 a   3 c   4 b

COLLABORATIVE LEARNING

• Put students into pairs. Say one of the words.
• Ask each pair to think of a sentence to say and then raise their hand.
• Call on the first few hands up and have those pairs say their sentence for the class.

C Complete the sentences.

• Have students do the activity on their own.
• Check the answers with the class.

ANSWERS
1 phenomenal   2 artistically   3 inspect
4 decorate   5 mimic

Before You Read

Think

- Have students read the question and make notes about their answers individually.
- Students discuss their answers to the questions in small groups.
- Ask them to share some of the answers with the class. List the answers on the board. If necessary, ask questions to get students to name different kinds of birds, talk about appearance, birdsong, where they live, what they eat, how they fly, etc.

D Learn: Analyze

- Read the *Learn* box with the class.
- Ask this question to check understanding: *When you read a text, do you accept what the author has to say? Or do you question it and think about it?*

Read and analyze the text. Then answer the questions.

- Have students read the text individually and answer the questions.
- Put students into pairs to check their answers and analyze the text together. Explain that partners should explain their opinions to their partner.
- Then check answers with the class.

POSSIBLE ANSWERS

1 Birds are very diverse. Yes, it is logical.
2 Sea birds are more interesting than land birds.

CRITICAL THINKING

Ask the following questions to check understanding about the text:

- *What are the three types of land birds mentioned?*
- *Can you name any other types of land birds?*
- *Where can you find land birds?*
- *What are the three types of sea birds mentioned?*
- *Can you name any other types of sea birds?*
- *Do sea birds often fly near land or far from land?*
- *How does analyzing help you to understand the text?*
- *The author says you can divide birds by where they live. Can you think of some other ways you could divide birds into different categories?*

DIFFERENTIATION

Below level:

- Put students into mixed-ability pairs to read the text and complete the questions.
- Tell them to underline the opinions. Go around and help as needed.

At level:

- After students have answered the questions, put them into small groups.
- Have groups discuss if they agree with the writer's opinions or not.
- Have some groups share their ideas with the class.

Above level:

- Have students do the activity individually.
- Then put students into small groups. Tell groups to think about penguins. Are they land birds or sea birds? What about ducks?
- Have groups share their discussions with the class.

E Words in Context: Scan the article on pages 142–143 and circle these words. As you read, try to guess what the words mean.

- Read each word and have students follow your pronunciation.
- Have students do the activity on their own. Then ask them to discuss the words with a partner.
- Have a few pairs share their meanings with the class.

F What animals do you think are intelligent? Why?

COMMUNICATION

- Have students answer the questions individually.
- Put students into small groups to discuss the answers. Have each group list the animals they talked about.
- Have a class discussion about each question. Elicit examples to support the students' ideas and write them on the board.

Reading Preview

- Read the title of the unit's reading text.
- Have students silently read the content of the preview bar.
- Ask *What type of text is it?* Ask *What does this type of text do?*
- Tell students to analyze as they read.

Further Practice
Workbook pages 130–131
Online Practice Unit 14 • Get Ready
Oxford iTools Unit 14 • Get Ready

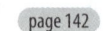

The following is a reproduction of the student book pages 142–143:

Read 3·26

Bird Brains

Have you ever heard the expression "birdbrain"? It's used to say that a person isn't very smart and **implies** that birds aren't smart, either. We all know that birds have remarkable gifts, from the peregrine falcon's incredible speed to the peacock's amazing display of plumage, but what about their intelligence? In fact, **ornithologists** have revealed that some birds are among the smartest creatures on Earth. Parrots can learn hundreds of words, pigeons use complex math, and scrub jays are great at remembering where to find things. Birds have also shown the ability to make tools, navigate huge distances, and construct elaborate nests. Maybe they're not so "birdbrained" after all!

Tool-Making Birds

Tools have been essential in the development of human civilization. People used to think that only humans had the ability to make tools. Then scientists discovered that some apes, like chimpanzees, also make tools. And guess what? Some birds can make tools, too!

The woodpecker finch is a bird that's native to the Galápagos Islands. It displays remarkable intelligence by using the **spine** from a cactus as a tool.

Think
What is the author's point? Is it logical? Why or why not?

The finch uses this spine to spear insects and remove them from their hiding places. A different type of finch, called a cactus finch, has also learned this skill by watching and **mimicking** the woodpecker finch. How's that for smart?

Occasionally, birds even use humans to help them. Carrion crows in Japan have been seen placing walnuts on busy highways. Why would they do this? These crows have figured out that it's simpler to have a car smash a nut for them than to open it using their beaks. The crow first drops the nut on the highway and then flies to a safe place. Next, it patiently waits for a car to run over the nut. Once the nut is smashed, the crow watches for the traffic lights to change and the cars to stop. It then flies down to eat its freshly opened treat!

The woodpecker finch and carrion crow both use tools to get food.

Willow warblers migrate from Africa to Europe and back again.

breeding
feeding/wintering
0   1,000 mi
0   2,000 km

Long-Distance Travelers

Birds like to be warm and have abundant supplies of food. They also need a place to breed. As the weather grows colder in one part of the world, many birds will fly vast distances to find new homes and sources of food. These **annual** journeys, called migrations, can be dangerous. The birds may **encounter** man-made hazards, like power lines and skyscrapers, or dangerous weather, such as high winds that can push them out to sea.

In the spring of every year, a tiny bird called the willow warbler flies from Africa to the UK. During this flight, it travels a **phenomenal** distance of several thousand kilometers, crossing deserts, mountains, and oceans. Then, in the fall, it returns to Africa to avoid the harsh winter and the absence of the insects it feeds on in Europe.

Show-offs!

Like us, birds occasionally want to **impress** each other. They do this in a variety of ways, including singing and showing off their colorful feathers. These displays are usually meant to attract a mate.

The bowerbird has an interesting **technique** for impressing others. It builds its nest, or bower, on the ground, not up in a tree like most other birds. The bower

This bowerbird has been decorating his nest.

itself is made of twigs, leaves, and a plant called moss. Like an artist, the bowerbird then **decorates** its nest with bright objects in matching colors! These might include feathers, shells, small stones, and even man-made objects, such as bottle caps, that the bowerbird collects and **artistically** arranges. After the bower is completed, the male bowerbird's design will be **inspected** by a female bowerbird.

Birds make and use tools, travel great distances, and decorate their homes like artists. Far from being "birdbrained," they're very brainy creatures indeed! As ornithologists continue to study and learn more about our feathered friends, they anticipate discovering even more amazing bird **behaviors**.

Think
What opinion does the author express? Do you agree with the author? Why or why not?

Some birds use colorful displays to attract a mate.

142   143

Summary

Objectives: To read, understand, and discuss a magazine article; to apply a reading strategy to improve comprehension.

School subject: Life Science

Text type: Magazine article (nonfiction)

Reading strategy: Analyzing

Big Question learning points: *Certain birds are highly intelligent. Some birds have amazing abilities, like flying in formation.*

Materials: Talk About It! Poster, Audio CD

Before Reading

- Read the title.
- Have students point to the photos and describe what they see.
- Ask the class to read the headings. Ask *What do you want to find out about the article?*

During Reading 3·26

- Remind students that they should analyze as they read. Ask *Is this logical? Is it a fact? Is this an opinion?*
- Play the audio. Students listen as they read along.
- Play the audio a second time if necessary.

Below level:

- Have students read with you in small groups, repeating chunks of text after you.
- Then pause to analyze each section of text.

At level:

- Have students read the text silently to themselves one time.
- Put students into pairs to take turns analyzing chunks of the text. Move throughout the room and provide help as necessary.

Above level:

- Have students read the text individually.
- Put students into pairs and have them analyze the text.

Discussion questions:

- *What are some things birds do that ornithologists say are smart?*
- *Which birds use cactus pines as spears?*
- *What do carrion crows eat?*
- *What is the annual journey of a bird called?*
- *What are some man-made hazards on the journey?*
- *How far does the willow warbler migrate?*
- *What are some ways birds impress a mate?*

After Reading

COLLABORATIVE LEARNING

- Put students into pairs.
- Have them discuss which of the birds mentioned they think is the smartest and why.
- Then have a class discussion to determine the smartest bird. Monitor the discussion and help students by asking questions that analyze their own arguments and ideas for logic, fact, and opinion.

COLLABORATIVE LEARNING

- Display **Talk About It! Poster** to help students with sentence frames for discussion and expressing personal opinions.
- Put students into pairs to discuss what they find interesting about the story.

CULTURE NOTE

Finch

Finches are a family of seed-eating songbirds. Most species live in the Northern Hemisphere. Finches often live in woods or areas with lots of trees, but can also occasionally be found in deserts or on mountains. Finches are common cage birds because most of them sing so well. In the wild they build basket-shaped nests between rocks or in trees.

Carrion Crow

Carrion crows are members of the crow family. They mostly live in Western Europe and East Asia. They are completely black in color, and often have a purple or green sheen on the feathers. They usually nest in very tall trees, but in cities or towns they can be found on old buildings or even electricity pylons.

Willow Warbler

Willow warblers are quite common birds and are often found in Northern Europe and Asia. They are very migratory and spend their winters in sub-Saharan Africa. They like to live in open woodland and build their nests in trees or shrubs close to the ground.

Bowerbird

There are 20 species in the bowerbird family, and they are found in the tropical regions of Australia and Papua New Guinea. They eat mostly fruit, but also insects, flowers, leaves, and nectar. Bowerbirds are very good vocal mimics. Macgregor's Bowerbird is well known for imitating other animal noises, including people speaking, and natural sounds such as a waterfall.

Further Practice
Workbook page 132
Online Practice Unit 14 • Read
Oxford **iTools** Unit 14 • Read

Understand

Comprehension

Think Did reading "Bird Brains" change your opinion of birds? How did you feel about birds before and how do you feel now?

A Analyze "Birds Brains" and answer the questions. Discuss your answers with your partner.

1 What is the author's point? Is it logical? Why or why not? _____

2 What are the author's opinions? Do you agree with them? Why or why not? _____

3 Does the text seem accurate? Give examples. _____

B Circle True (T) or False (F).

1 Calling someone a "birdbrain" implies that birds aren't smart.	T	F
2 A peregrine falcon's speed is an example of its intelligence.	T	F
3 The cactus finch learned to use a tool by watching the woodpecker finch.	T	F
4 Carrion crows use cars as tools.	T	F
5 In the spring, the willow warbler migrates from the UK to Africa.	T	F
6 The bowerbird decorates its nest to impress people.	T	F

C **Words In Context** Look at the words you circled in the article. Then match the words to their meanings.

1 harsh — — a made by humans
2 spear — — b showed something that was hidden
3 brainy — — c to strike and pierce something
4 revealed — — d showing intelligence
5 ability — — e irritating or uncomfortable
6 man-made — — f the power to do something

144 Unit 14 *Comprehension*

Grammar in Use

Workbook Grammar pages 134–135

D Listen and read along. Then circle the correct answer. 3-27

What's wrong? / I got a zero on my test! / That's because you didn't study. / No, it's because people don't realize I'm a genius! / You're a genius? / Of course! One day, I'll be admired by other geniuses! / Really? What will you be admired for? / Well, not for my schoolwork!

Who does Charlie think will admire him one day? **a** Sonya **b** other geniuses

E **Learn Grammar** Passive Review

Remember: You can use the **passive** voice in the **present perfect** tense, the **past perfect** tense, and the **future**.

Sometimes when you're using the passive voice, you want to say who does the action. In that case, you can use **by + person**.

Present Perfect	The design **has been inspected** by a female bowerbird.
Past Perfect	The design **had been inspected** by a female bowerbird.
Future	The design **will be inspected** by a female bowerbird.

Change the sentences from active to passive. Use *by* + person.

1 The head teacher will give a prize.
2 Coach Miller has chosen the players.
3 Our class had designed the school newsletter.
4 A famous composer will conduct the orchestra.

F Write a list of passive sentences with *by* + person. Use the present perfect, past perfect, and future. Then work with your partner to say each sentence in a different tense.

The comic will be drawn by my favorite artist.
My bike has been repaired by the mechanic.

The comic has been drawn by my favorite artist.

Grammar: Passive Review Unit 14 145

Summary

Objectives: To demonstrate understanding of a magazine article; to understand the meaning and form of the grammar structure.

Reading: Comprehension

Grammar input: Passive review

Grammar practice: Workbook exercises

Grammar production: Passive

Materials: Audio CD

Comprehension

Think

• Have students think about their answers individually first.
• Then hold a class discussion.

A Analyze "Bird Brains" and the answer the questions. Discuss your answers with your partner.

• Have students reread the magazine article on pages 142 and 143, and then answer the questions.
• Put students into pairs to discuss their answers.

DIFFERENTIATION

Below level:

• Read parts of the text aloud and give clues to help students answer the questions:
The author's point is in the first paragraph. (*Ornithologists say some birds are among the smartest creatures on Earth.*) Is it a logical point? How do you know? (*The author uses facts to support it, e.g. pigeons can use math.*)

What are the author's opinions? (*The author says the bower bird "artistically arranges" its nest and "decorate their nests like artists." We can't really know that.*)
Do you agree with the author's opinions? (*I don't agree that birds are artistic. I think the author is giving them too much credit.*)
Does the text seem accurate? (*Yes, the willow warbler returns to Africa (from Europe) in fall to avoid the harsh winter. That would be correct because when it is winter in Europe, it would be summer in Africa.*)

At level:

• Have students answer the questions in pairs.
• Then students compare their answers with another pair.

Above level:

• Students do the activity individually.
• Put students into pairs to compare answers and analyze the text together.

B Circle True (T) or False (F).

• Have students do the activity on their own, looking back to pages 142–143 for answers.
• Have students compare their answers with a partner. Ask them to correct the false answers.
• Check the answers with the class.

ANSWERS

1 T 2 F 3 T 4 T 5 F 6 F

C Words in Context: Look at the words you circled in the article. Then match the words to their meanings.

- Have students go back and find the words in the article.
- Tell them to use the context clues to guess at the meaning of each word.
- Ask students to match the words on the left to the descriptions on the right.
- Check answers with the class.

ANSWERS
1 e 2 c 3 d 4 b 5 f 6 a

COLLABORATIVE LEARNING

- Put students into pairs. Have pairs think of sentences for each of the words in context.
- Have pairs share their sentences with the class.

Grammar in Use

D Listen and read along. Then circle the correct answer. 🔊 3·27

- Listen to the dialogue once and then read it together as a class.
- Play the audio again if necessary.
- Then have students answer the question.

ANSWER
b other geniuses

E Learn Grammar: Passive Review

- Read the *Learn Grammar* box together.
- Write the example sentences on the board and then read them aloud. Underline *by + a*.
- Say *In these passive sentences, we do say who does the action. So why would we use a passive sentence instead of an active sentence in these examples?* (Because the main point of the sentence is the design and not the bird. It's not important who does the action in these sentences.)

Change the sentences from active to passive. Use *by* + person.

- Have students do the activity individually. Then check the answers.

ANSWERS
1 A prize will be given by the head teacher.
2 The players have been chosen by Coach Miller.
3 The school newsletter has been designed by our class.
4 The orchestra will be conducted by a famous composer.

CRITICAL THINKING

- Put students into small groups.
- Have groups discuss the question: *Active sentences are about doing. What are passive sentences about?*
- Ask the groups to discuss the question. Have them look up the word "passive" in the dictionary.
- Ask groups to share their idea of passive sentences and definitions with the class.

F Write a list of passive sentences with *by* + person. Use the present perfect, past perfect, and future. Then work with your partner to say each sentence in a different tense.

- Have students create the chart individually in their notebooks.
- Ask students to make a list of passive sentences with *by* + person. Get them to look at the example.
- In pairs, ask students to write more passive sentences.
- Have a few students say their sentences to the class.

Workbook Grammar

- Direct students to the Workbook for further practice.

Further practice
Workbook pages 133–135
Online Practice Unit 14 · Understand
Oxford iTools Unit 14 · Understand

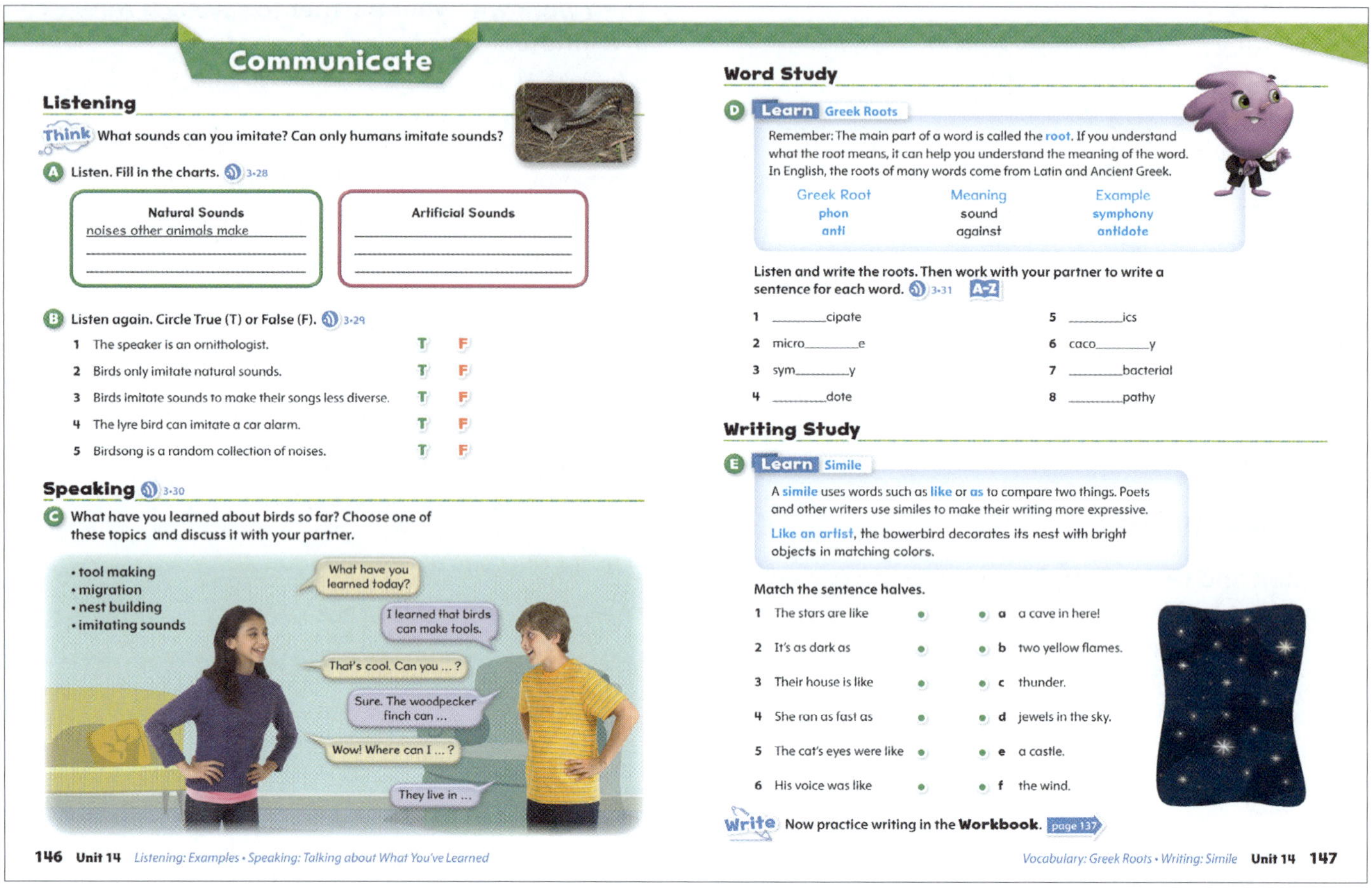

Communicate

Listening

Think What sounds can you imitate? Can only humans imitate sounds?

A Listen. Fill in the charts. 3·28

Natural Sounds	Artificial Sounds
noises other animals make	

B Listen again. Circle True (T) or False (F). 3·29

1 The speaker is an ornithologist. T F
2 Birds only imitate natural sounds. T F
3 Birds imitate sounds to make their songs less diverse. T F
4 The lyre bird can imitate a car alarm. T F
5 Birdsong is a random collection of noises. T F

Speaking 3·30

C What have you learned about birds so far? Choose one of these topics and discuss it with your partner.

- tool making
- migration
- nest building
- imitating sounds

What have you learned today?

I learned that birds can make tools.

That's cool. Can you ... ?

Sure. The woodpecker finch can ...

Wow! Where can I ... ?

They live in ...

146 Unit 14 *Listening: Examples • Speaking: Talking about What You've Learned*

Word Study

D Learn Greek Roots

Remember: The main part of a word is called the root. If you understand what the root means, it can help you understand the meaning of the word. In English, the roots of many words come from Latin and Ancient Greek.

Greek Root	Meaning	Example
phon	sound	symphony
anti	against	antidote

Listen and write the roots. Then work with your partner to write a sentence for each word. 3·31 A-Z

1 _____cipate
2 micro_____e
3 sym_____y
4 _____dote
5 _____ics
6 caco_____y
7 _____bacterial
8 _____pathy

Writing Study

E Learn Simile

A simile uses words such as **like** or **as** to compare two things. Poets and other writers use similes to make their writing more expressive.

Like an artist, the bowerbird decorates its nest with bright objects in matching colors.

Match the sentence halves.

1 The stars are like •   • a a cave in here!
2 It's as dark as •   • b two yellow flames.
3 Their house is like •   • c thunder.
4 She ran as fast as •   • d jewels in the sky.
5 The cat's eyes were like •   • e a castle.
6 His voice was like •   • f the wind.

Write Now practice writing in the **Workbook**. page 137

Vocabulary: Greek Roots • Writing: Simile Unit 14 147

Summary

Objectives: To learn and practice listening, speaking, and writing strategies to facilitate effective communication.

Vocabulary: *anticipate, microphone, symphony, antidote, phonics, cacophony, antibacterial, antipathy*

Listening strategy: Listening for examples

Speaking: Talking about what you've learned

Word Study: Greek roots

Writing Study: Simile

Big Question learning points: *Some birds have amazing abilities like flying in formation. Some birds can mimic things they hear.*

Materials: Audio CD

Listening

Think

- Have students think about the questions.
- Get students to tell a partner their ideas and imitate sounds. Encourage them to have fun with it.
- Demonstrate some silly sounds yourself, such as a car honking or a dog barking.
- Go around the room and have students make sounds and ask the class to guess what they are.

A Listen. Fill in the charts. 3·28

- Play the audio once and have students listen.
- Tell students to write their answers in the charts.
- Play the audio again so they can check their work.

ANSWERS

Natural Sounds: animal noises, bird songs, tree falling
Artificial Sounds: car alarm, camera shutter, phone ringing

B Listen again. Circle True (T) or False (F). 3·29

- Play the audio and have students complete the activity.
- Tell students to correct the false answers.
- Check the answers with the class.

ANSWERS
1 T 2 F 3 F 4 T 5 F

CRITICAL THINKING

- After checking the answers, put students into small groups.
- Have groups analyze the listening text.
- Questions to discuss:
  Is it logical?
  Is it fact or opinion?
  Does it seem accurate?
- Have groups share their analysis and discussion with the class.

Speaking ◎ 3·30

C What have you learned about birds so far? Choose one of these topics and discuss it with your partner.

COMMUNICATION

- Read the examples with the class. Remind students to ask follow-up questions.
- Play the audio and have students listen.
- Model the dialogue using one of the examples from the list with a confident student in front of the class.
- Put students into pairs and tell them to practice the dialogue.

DIFFERENTIATION

Below level:

- Put students into mixed-ability pairs.
- Have the more confident student help the less confident student to write out the dialogue using one of the topics from the list. Tell them they can refer back to the article for information if necessary.
- Once dialogues are written, the pair can read from it to practice.
- Have pairs share their dialogues with another pair.

At level:

- Have pairs choose one of the topics to practice.
- Then they find a new partner and practice using a new topic.
- Continue until students have practiced all topics.

Above level:

- Put students into small groups to practice talking about what they've learned about birds.
- Tell groups that they can talk about any of the topics. Remind them to ask follow-up questions and to politely agree or disagree.
- They should monitor the conversation so that everyone has a chance to speak.
- Have the group tell the class how their group conversation went.

Word Study

D Learn: Greek Roots

- Read the *Learn* box together.
- Have students' dictionaries ready. Ask *What is a "symphony" and an "antidote"?*
- Have students raise their hands once they have found the definitions in the dictionary. Call on one or two students to say the definitions.

Listen and write the roots. Then work with your partner to write a sentence for each word. ◎ 3·31

- Play the audio one time and have students repeat.
- Play the audio a second time and have students write the words.
- Check the spelling when checking the answers.

ANSWERS

1 anticipate   2 microphone   3 symphony
4 antidote   5 phonics   6 cacophony
7 antibacterial   8 antipathy

Writing Study

E Learn: Simile

- Read the *Learn* box together.
- Read the example sentence. Ask the following:
  What is the simile in the sentence?
  What does a simile do?
  If the sentence was, "The bowerbird is an artist, it decorates its nest colorfully." What would that be?
  What words do similes use?

Match the sentence halves.

- Have students complete the activity individually.
- Check the answers with the class.

ANSWERS

1 d   2 a   3 e   4 f   5 b   6 c

COLLABORATIVE LEARNING

- Put students into pairs to write new similes for the six phrases in E, e.g. *The stars are like sequins in the sky.*
- Tell students that they can use any common similes that they know of if they match, e.g. *It's as dark as night.*
- Go around and help as needed.
- Have pairs share their new similes with the class.

Write

- Direct students to the Workbook for further writing practice.

Further practice
Workbook pages 136–137
Online Practice Unit 14 · Communicate
Oxford iTools Unit 14 · Communicate

Units 13 and 14 — Wrap Up

Writing

A Read this action plan.

Bird Conservation Plan

Wh-questions

What?
We want to help bird populations survive and even increase by improving local bird habitats.

Why?
Birds' habitats are disappearing. Birds need places to nest and raise their young. They also need places to spend the winter and rest during their long migrations.

Who?
Adults and kids of all ages! We think everyone can play an important part in bird conservation.

Details about how

How?
We'll put up birdhouses in our yards and make sure there's fresh water for birds all year round. In winter, birds will be provided with feeders and bird food to help them get through the cold weather. We'll also remember to turn off lights at night. Birds are attracted to the lights and are sometimes killed by flying into buildings. We plan to plant bushes and fruit trees to make it easier for birds to find food.

Wh-questions

Where?
In our backyards and at school.

When?
Right away! It's cheap and easy to do something now.

B Answer the questions.
1 What kinds of questions does the writer use to organize the action plan?
2 Which questions does the writer start and end with?
3 Which part of the plan is the most detailed?
4 Is the order of the questions important? Why?

C Learn *Writing an Action Plan*
- To choose a topic for your action plan, think about something you want to change or accomplish.
- Choose a clear title for your plan so people will know what it's about.
- Use your plan to answer the questions *who, what, when, where, why,* and *how*.
- Think carefully about the order of your questions. Start by answering the ones that will help people understand your plan. End by answering the ones that will tell them how to take action.
- Include details of how your plan will work. Spend more time thinking about the *how* question than the others.

Write Now go to the **Workbook** to plan and write your own action plan. page 139

D Present your action plan to the class.
1 Practice reading your plan aloud a few times.
2 Read your action plan to the class.
3 Remember to read carefully and loudly enough for everyone to hear.
4 Show enthusiasm for your plan. Remember, you want other people to care about it.
5 After you've read your action plan, ask the class if they have any questions. Make sure you have good answers!
6 Listen carefully while your classmates are reading their plans.
7 Take a vote on who has the best plan.

What can I do to help?
That's a good question. Let's meet after school.

BIG QUESTION 7
What makes birds special?

A Watch the video. What do you see birds doing?
B What are some answers to the Big Question? Talk about them with your partner.
C Complete the **Big Question Chart**. Then discuss it with the class.

What have you learned about birds?

Summary

Objectives: To show what students have learned about the language and learning points of Units 13 and 14.

Reading: Reading an action plan

Writing: Writing an action plan

Speaking: Sharing an action plan

Materials: Big Question DVD, Discover Poster 7, Talk About It! Poster, Big Question Chart

Writing

A Read this action plan.

- Read aloud the directions and explain that an action plan is an individual's or a group's plan to do something and the steps involved to do it.
- Go over the structure of each section of the plan before reading. Ask *How does the plan start? What details are included? How does it end?* Then read the action plan.
- After reading the plan with the class, have students read it one time on their own.

B Answer the questions.

- Have students find the answers in the text.

POSSIBLE ANSWERS
1 Wh-questions
2 "What?" and "When?"
3 The "How?" section.
4 Yes, the order of the plan is important. It uses the Wh-questions in a clear order to say what the action plan is about.

CRITICAL THINKING

Discussion questions:
- *Which question introduces the problem?*
- *Which question explains the reason the action is needed?*
- *Why do the "Where?" and "When?" questions come last?*

C Learn: Writing an Action Plan

- Read the directions in the *Learn* box together.
- Explain that students should follow these guidelines when they plan and write their action plan.

Write

- Direct the students to the Workbook to plan and write their own action plan.

CREATIVITY

- Brainstorm with the class some ideas to write an action plan about.
- Tell students it should be something they are concerned about, e.g. a beach clean up or a campaign to help stray dogs and cats.
- Take suggestions and ideas from the class and write them on the board.

Below level:

- Ask students to go to page 139 of their Workbooks. Go over the Action Plan with them.
- Put students into mixed-ability pairs, preferably with the same topic interest, to discuss their ideas and opinions.
- Explain that students should use the structure in the *Learn* box and the model plan.
- Have the more confident student help the less confident student to complete steps A through D.

At level:

- Ask students to go to page 139 of their Workbooks.
- Have students complete steps A through C individually. Then have students trade papers with a partner for step D to check the action plan against the Writing Checklist and offer feedback.

Above level:

- Ask students to go to page 139 of their Workbooks.
- Have students discuss the initial ideas for their action plan with a partner and then do the activity individually A through C.
- Then put students into pairs for step D. Have them read each other's action plan and give feedback. If students have chosen the same topic, have them work together.

D Present your action plan to the class.

- Read the list with the class.
- Give students time to practice reading their action plans aloud.
- Have students take turns reading their action plans to the class. Ensure they follow the steps in the direction list.
- After all plans have been read, the class votes on who has the best plan.

- Put students into small groups.
- Tell groups to choose an action that they would like to do.
- They may want to revise an existing plan of one of the group members or do a new plan for the plan voted best.
- Have groups write a new action plan and read it aloud to the class.

Units 13 and 14 Big Question Review

A Watch the video. What do you see birds doing?

- Play the video and when it is finished, ask students what they know about birds now.
- Have students share ideas with the class.

B What are some answers to the Big Question? Talk about them with your partner.

- Display **Discover Poster 7**. Point to familiar vocabulary items and elicit them from the class. Ask *What is this?*
- Ask students *What do you see?* Ask *What does that mean?*
- Refer to all of the learning points written on the poster and have students explain how they relate to the different pictures.
- Ask *What does this learning point mean?* Elicit answers from individual students.
- Display the **Talk About It! Poster** to help students with sentence frames for discussion of the learning points and for expressing their opinions.

C Complete the Big Question Chart. Then discuss it with the class.

- Ask students what they have learned about birds while studying this unit.
- Put students into pairs or small groups to say two new things they have learned.
- Have students share their ideas with the class and add their ideas to the chart.
- Have students complete the chart in their Workbook.

Further practice
Workbook pages 138–141
Online Practice • Wrap Up 7
Oxford **iTools** • Wrap Up 7

In units 15 and 16 you will:

WATCH a video about fear.

LEARN what people fear and why.

READ about where fear comes from and a boy's fear of the dark.

WRITE an instructional guide.

PRESENT your guide to the class.

BIG QUESTION 8

What are we afraid of?

A Watch the video. Then talk about it with your partner.

B Look at the picture and discuss it with your class.
1 What do you think these people are afraid of?
2 How are they reacting to fear?

C Think and answer the questions.
1 Do you have any fears? What are they?
2 What were you afraid of when you were younger?
3 What kinds of things are other people afraid of?
4 Is fear a useful emotion? Why or why not?

D Discuss this topic with your class. Fill out the **Big Question Chart.**

What do you know about fear? What do you want to know?

150 Big Question 8

151

Reading Strategies
Students will practice:
- Intensive reading
- Character analysis

Vocabulary
Students will understand and use words about:
- Fight or flight

Grammar
Students will understand and use:
- Past unreal conditional
- *If only* and *I wish*

Review
Students will review the language and Big Question learning points of Units 15 and 16 through:
- Writing an instructional guide

Units 15 and 16
What are we afraid of?
Students will understand the Big Question learning points:
- People fear dangerous or threatening situations.
- Some people are afraid of specific things, like crowds.
- Strange or unfamiliar things are sometimes frightening.
- Some activities, like skydiving, can be scary, but fun.
- Many people fear going to the doctor.

Listening Strategies
Students will practice:
- Listening for clues
- Listening for reactions

Writing Study
Students will use and understand:
- Connectors to show condition
- Avoiding generalizations
Students will:
- Write an instructional text

Word Study
Students will understand and use:
- Suffix *-ic*
- Connotation

Speaking
Students will understand and use expressions for:
- Suggesting solutions
- Talking about things that are scary but fun

Units 15 and 16 Big Question page 150

Summary
Objectives: To activate students' existing knowledge of the topic and identify what they would like to learn about the topic.

Materials: Big Question DVD, Discover Poster 8, Big Question Chart

Introducing the topic
- Read out the Big Question. Ask *What are we afraid of?*
- Write students' ideas on the board and discuss.

A Watch the video. Then talk about it with your partner.
- Play the video and when it is finished ask students to answer the following questions in pairs:
  What do you see in the video?
  What is happening?
  How is fear used in the video?
  What do you like about the video?
- Have individual students share their answers with the class.

B Look at the picture and discuss it with your class.
- Students look at the big picture and talk about it. Ask *What do you see?*
- Ask additional questions:
  Where do you think the people are?
  How do you know?
  Why are they wearing the strange glasses?
  Have you ever been somewhere like this?

- Ask students to think individually about the following:
  What is most interesting to you in the picture?
  What is most frightening? Why do you think so?
  Do you think other people are afraid of the same things?
- Put students into pairs to discuss the questions.
- Have pairs share their ideas with the class.

C Think and answer the questions.
- Have students discuss the questions in small groups, and then with the class.

Below level:
- Put students into mixed-ability groups.
- Have the more confident students help the less confident students to answer the questions.
- Go around and help as needed. Then have groups tell the class about their discussion.

At level:
- Have pairs make notes together on their answers.
- Then have them compare their answers with another pair.
- Finally, discuss the questions with the class and write notes about their answers on the board.

Above level:
- Have students circulate and ask the questions to their classmates. Tell them to interview three people.
- Then have students report on their findings to the class.

Expanding the topic

- Display **Discover Poster 8** and give students enough time to look at the pictures.
- Get students to talk about things you think they will know by pointing to different things in the pictures and asking *What's this? What is happening here?*
- Put students into small groups of three or four. Have each group choose a picture that they find interesting.
- Ask each group to say five sentences about their picture.
- Have one person from each group stand up and read out the sentences they chose for their picture.
- Ask the class if they can add any more.

Below level:
- Encourage students to participate using short sentences.
- Point to details in the big picture and on the poster and ask *What is this?* Write the answers on the board.

At level:
- Elicit complete sentences about what students know about fear.
- Write their sentences on the board.

Above level:
- Elicit more detailed responses.
- Ask students to write their own sentences on the board

D Discuss this topic with your class. Fill out the Big Question Chart.
- Display the **Big Question Chart**.
- Ask the class *What do you know about fear? What do you want to know about fear?*
- Ask students to write what they know and what they want to know in their Workbooks.
- Write a collection of ideas on the **Big Question Chart**.

Discover Poster 8
1 A woman climbing a mountainside; 2 A crowded commuter train in Beijing, China; 3 A dentist explaining a dental drill to a child; 4 Two people skydiving over California

Further Practice
Workbook page 142
Online Practice • Big Question 8
Oxford **iTools** • Big Question 8

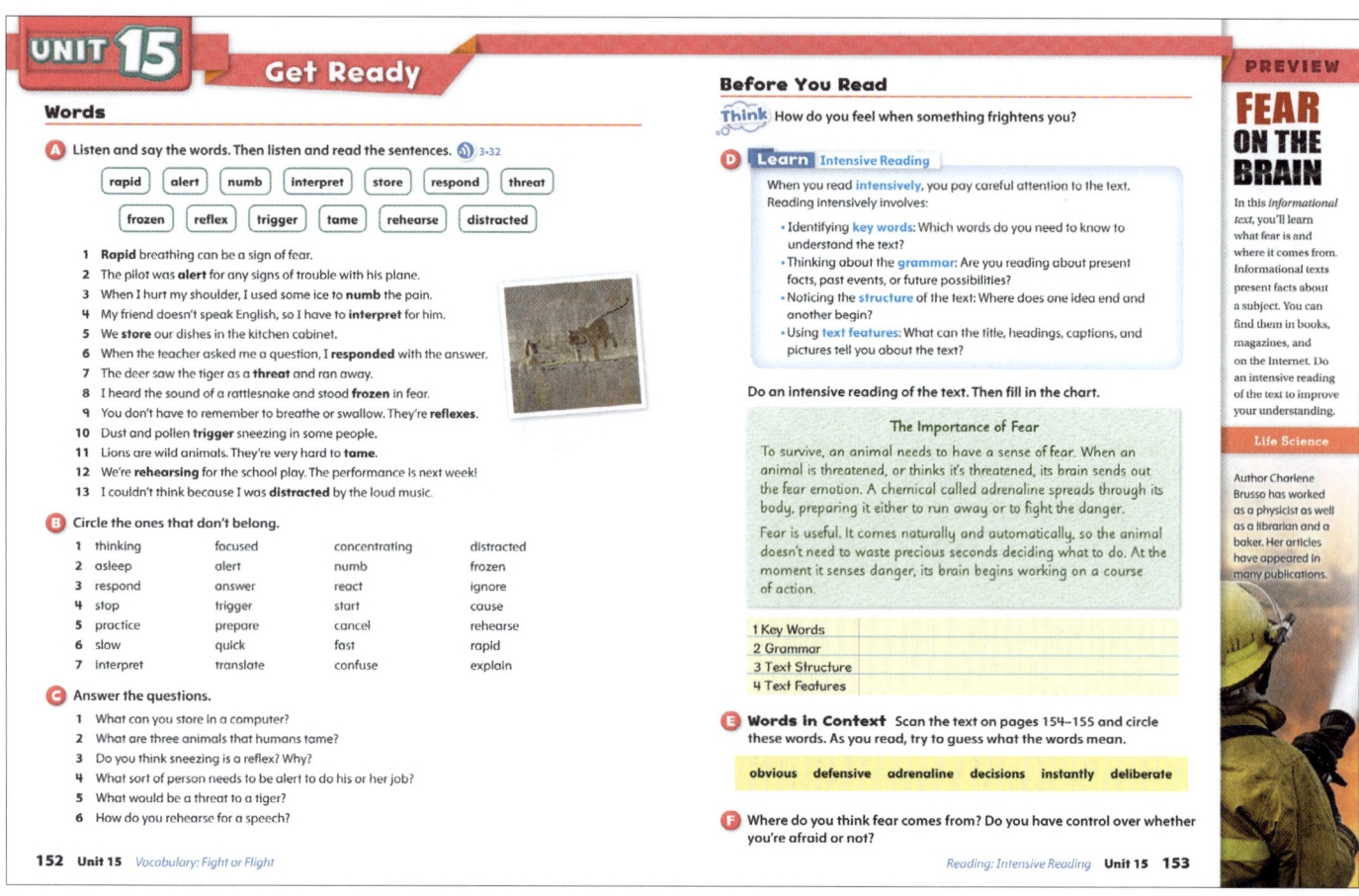

UNIT 15   Get Ready

Words

A Listen and say the words. Then listen and read the sentences. 3·32

| rapid | alert | numb | interpret | store | respond | threat |

| frozen | reflex | trigger | tame | rehearse | distracted |

1 **Rapid** breathing can be a sign of fear.
2 The pilot was **alert** for any signs of trouble with his plane.
3 When I hurt my shoulder, I used some ice to **numb** the pain.
4 My friend doesn't speak English, so I have to **interpret** for him.
5 We **store** our dishes in the kitchen cabinet.
6 When the teacher asked me a question, I **responded** with the answer.
7 The deer saw the tiger as a **threat** and ran away.
8 I heard the sound of a rattlesnake and stood **frozen** in fear.
9 You don't have to remember to breathe or swallow. They're **reflexes**.
10 Dust and pollen **trigger** sneezing in some people.
11 Lions are wild animals. They're very hard to **tame**.
12 We're **rehearsing** for the school play. The performance is next week!
13 I couldn't think because I was **distracted** by the loud music.

B Circle the ones that don't belong.

1 thinking	focused	concentrating	distracted
2 asleep	alert	numb	frozen
3 respond	answer	react	ignore
4 stop	trigger	start	cause
5 practice	prepare	cancel	rehearse
6 slow	quick	fast	rapid
7 interpret	translate	confuse	explain

C Answer the questions.

1 What can you store in a computer?
2 What are three animals that humans tame?
3 Do you think sneezing is a reflex? Why?
4 What sort of person needs to be alert to do his or her job?
5 What would be a threat to a tiger?
6 How do you rehearse for a speech?

152 Unit 15 Vocabulary: Fight or Flight

Before You Read

Think How do you feel when something frightens you?

D **Learn** Intensive Reading

When you read **intensively**, you pay careful attention to the text. Reading intensively involves:

• Identifying **key words**: Which words do you need to know to understand the text?
• Thinking about the **grammar**: Are you reading about present facts, past events, or future possibilities?
• Noticing the **structure** of the text: Where does one idea end and another begin?
• Using **text features**: What can the title, headings, captions, and pictures tell you about the text?

Do an intensive reading of the text. Then fill in the chart.

The Importance of Fear

To survive, an animal needs to have a sense of fear. When an animal is threatened, or thinks it's threatened, its brain sends out the fear emotion. A chemical called adrenaline spreads through its body, preparing it either to run away or to fight the danger.

Fear is useful. It comes naturally and automatically, so the animal doesn't need to waste precious seconds deciding what to do. At the moment it senses danger, its brain begins working on a course of action.

1 Key Words	
2 Grammar	
3 Text Structure	
4 Text Features	

E **Words in Context** Scan the text on pages 154–155 and circle these words. As you read, try to guess what the words mean.

obvious   defensive   adrenaline   decisions   instantly   deliberate

F Where do you think fear comes from? Do you have control over whether you're afraid or not?

Reading: Intensive Reading Unit 15 153

PREVIEW

FEAR ON THE BRAIN

In this *informational text*, you'll learn what fear is and where it comes from. Informational texts present facts about a subject. You can find them in books, magazines, and on the Internet. Do an intensive reading of the text to improve your understanding.

Life Science

Author Charlene Brusso has worked as a physicist as well as a librarian and a baker. Her articles have appeared in many publications.

Summary

Objectives: To understand words about fight or flight; to apply own experience and a reading strategy to help comprehension of a text.

Vocabulary: *rapid, alert, numb, interpret, store, respond, threat, frozen, reflex, trigger, tame, rehearse, distracted, obvious, defensive, adrenaline, decisions, instantly, deliberate*

Reading strategy: Intensive reading

Materials: Audio CD

Words

A Listen and say the words. Then listen and read the sentences. 3·32

• Play the audio. Ask students to point to the words and repeat the words when they hear them.
• Then have students listen and read the sentences as they hear them.
• Say the sentence numbers out of order and have the class read the sentences aloud.

B Circle the ones that don't belong.

• Have students do the activity on their own.
• Ask students to compare their answers with a partner.
• Check answers with the class.

ANSWERS

1 distracted   2 alert   3 ignore   4 stop   5 cancel
6 slow   7 confuse

CRITICAL THINKING

• Put students into pairs. Have pairs revise the sentences in A to replace the new words.
• Tell them that the opposite words in B can help, e.g. replace *rapid* with *fast* in *Fast breathing can be a sign of fear.* They can also use a dictionary.
• Have pairs share their sentences with the class.

C Answer the questions.

• Put students into pairs to answer the questions.
• Have them compare their answers with another pair.
• Check answers with the class.

POSSIBLE ANSWERS

1 A computer can store files, documents, photos, music, and other things.
2 Humans tame dogs, horses, cats, guinea pigs, camels, ferrets, some rabbits, and mice.
3 I do think sneezing is a reflex because some people sneeze when they first go into sunlight.
4 A race car driver needs to be alert to do his or her job.
5 A human is a threat to a tiger. An angry elephant or a lion could be a threat to a tiger.
6 To rehearse for a speech, I would say my words over and over again to myself and to a partner.

- Put students into mixed-ability pairs.
- Have them think of three more questions using the new words. Suggest, e.g. *What kind of food do you eat frozen?*
- Then ask pairs to join another pair and take turns asking questions.
- Share some questions with the class.

Before You Read

Think

- Have students think about their answer individually.
- Put students into pairs to discuss their answer. Hold a class discussion and list possible answers on the board.

D Learn: Intensive Reading

- Read the *Learn* box together.
- Ask questions to check understanding:
  What do key words do?
  What does grammar tell you about a text?
  What is it called when you notice where one idea begins and the other ends?
  What are examples of text features?
  What is helpful to do to understand a text?

Do an intensive reading of the text. Then fill in the chart.

- Read the directions and then read the text one time with the class.
- Have students reread the text individually.
- Then ask students to write examples in the chart individually before comparing with partner.

ANSWERS

1 Key Words: adrenaline (a chemical that spreads upon fear)
2 Grammar: present tense (for facts)
3 Text Structure: two paragraphs: first one is about the fear response; second one is about usefulness of fear
4 Text Features: heading

CRITICAL THINKING

Ask questions to check understanding:

- *What does an animal need to survive?*
- *What does adrenaline do?*
- *Why would we use the present tense to talk about facts?*
- *What tense would you use for things that haven't happened, but are possible?*
- *How do headings, pictures, and captions help improve your understanding?*

E Words in Context: Scan the text on pages 154–155 and circle these words. As you read, try to guess what the words mean.

- Read the instructions with the class.
- Read each word and have students follow your pronunciation.
- Ask students to scan the article on pages 154 and 155 and circle the words. Tell them to guess what the words mean from the context.

- Ask the students to share their ideas about the words' definitions.

DIFFERENTIATION

Below level:

- Put students into pairs. Have one student look for the first three words and the second student looks for the second three words.
- Ask students to tell each other about their words and show where they found the word in the text. Together, the pair discusses what the words mean.

At level:

- Put students into pairs to figure out the meaning of the new words from context.
- Tell pairs to underline clues in the text that indicate the meaning of the words.
- Have pairs share their answers with the class.

Above level:

- Put students into pairs to use the context to provide a definition of each word.
- Have pairs share their definitions with the class.
- Ask them to paraphrase the sentences using their definitions.

F Where do you think fear comes from? Do you have control over whether you're afraid or not?

COMMUNICATION

- Put students into small groups to discuss the questions.
- Tell groups to give examples that support their answers.
- Go over the groups' answers.

Reading Preview

- Read the title of the unit's reading text.
- Have students silently read the content of the preview bar.
- Ask *What type of text is it?* Ask *What does this type of text do?*
- Tell students to practice intensive reading as they read the text.

Further Practice

Workbook page 142–143
Online Practice Unit 15 • Get Ready
Oxford iTools Unit 15 • Get Ready

Read 3·33 FEAR ON THE BRAIN

Your heart is racing, your hands feel like ice, and your skin is clammy with sweat. Butterflies swarm in your stomach, and it's impossible to think straight. You're scared. That's obvious. But what makes your body react this way?

It's all your brain's fault. Fear is an emotion, and all emotions, including fear, are made in your brain. Fear is your brain's defensive response to danger. You might be thinking that sweaty hands and a stomachache are not helping much.

But these are all part of your brain getting your body ready for rapid action. You breathe faster to feed more oxygen to busy cells. Your racing heart pumps more blood around your body, so muscles are set for fast action. Down in your middle, your adrenal glands flood your body with adrenaline, a chemical that gives you a burst of strength and energy, makes you extra alert, and even numbs pain. Adrenaline also makes you sweat and can give you an upset stomach. And if you can't think clearly, it's because your brain wants to focus on only one thing: the danger in front of you.

WHERE DOES FEAR COME FROM?

Fear starts in a very old part of the brain called the limbic system. Scientists think the limbic system first evolved in early animal brains about 220 million years ago. Even the dinosaurs probably had a limbic system pretty similar to ours. The limbic system does two things very well. First, it interprets information from your senses—the things you see, hear, and feel—and decides how you should react emotionally to that information. The limbic system also stores memories of danger and whether what you did (say, running away) helped or made things worse. These memories help the brain make very fast decisions about how to respond to threats.

Think
We usually use the present tense for facts. What does that tell you about this paragraph?

limbic system

adrenal glands

Fear affects many parts of the body, including the heart, brain, and muscles.

This gazelle chose *flight* instead of *fight*. If it hadn't been afraid, it wouldn't have run away.

FIGHT OR FLIGHT

Fear is automatic and happens instantly when your brain sees trouble—you don't have to "decide" to be afraid. And the fear response is very similar in most animals, including humans. First, the animal freezes for a split second, focusing all of its attention on the threat. If it decides the threat is not serious, the animal calms down. If the danger is real, the animal might stay frozen, hoping to hide. Or it makes a quick choice to defend itself or run away, a reflex called "fight or flight."

You can't get rid of fear entirely—fear is built into your brain and is a basic part of human and animal nature. But you can learn to control what triggers fear, what your brain sees as dangerous. And understanding fear can help you choose to react in other ways besides running or fighting.

Think
Which words do you need to know to understand these paragraphs? Use the dictionary to look up any you don't know.

GETTING FEAR UNDER CONTROL

When fear strikes, it can be hard to think clearly and not panic. But with practice, you can tame fear.

No one is actually fearless. Brave people still feel fear like everyone else—the difference is in how they respond to it. People who work in dangerous jobs, like police officers, firefighters, and airplane pilots, learn to manage their fear by practicing for emergencies so they'll be prepared if the worst happens. They learn to focus on what needs to be done.

Then they practice it over and over so that in a real emergency they can act quickly and without thinking, even if they're really scared. Planning and rehearsing help them learn not to be distracted by fear. They also learn to balance their fear with the knowledge that they can solve the problem. Pilots sometimes call this skill "deliberate calm."

Practicing for scary situations can help even for less dangerous moments. If you are nervous about having to give a speech in front of a class or assembly, rehearsing can keep your fear in check and help you focus on doing a good job. Fear is an automatic reflex, thanks to the brain's limbic system—but the way we deal with it is not. It takes practice to learn to stay calm in scary situations, but it can be done. After all, learning is what the brain does best.

154 / 155

Summary

Objectives: To read, understand, and discuss an informational text; to apply a reading strategy to improve comprehension.

School subject: Life Science

Text type: Informational text (nonfiction)

Reading strategy: Intensive reading

Big Question learning point: *People fear dangerous or threatening situations.*

Materials: Talk About It! Poster, Audio CD

Before Reading

- Have students tell you what they see in the photos.
- Ask them to read the headings.
- Have students say what they already know about fear.
- Remind them to practice intensive reading as they read. That means: underlining key words to look up after words paying attention to grammar, pausing to notice structure, and changes in ideas. Using text features such as subheads, photos, and captions.
- Tell them to look up any key words or other unknown words before rereading.

During Reading 3·33

- Have students read along with the audio one time.
- Ask them to read one time individually.
- Then have students skim the reading again practicing intensive reading.
- Remind them to stop and answer the *Think* boxes.

DIFFERENTIATION

Below level:

- Have students take turns to read the text to each other in small groups.
- As they read, have them stop after each section and practice intensive reading.
- Then, after looking up any key words or other unknown words in a dictionary, have them read a second time fluently, taking turns to read sections.

At level:

- Ask students to read with a partner, taking turns to read the sections of the text.
- Have them stop to evaluate each section as they read, practicing intensive reading.
- For the second reading, have each student take a turn. This time, they work to improve fluency by reading aloud as quickly and accurately as possible.

Above level:

- Have students read the text individually one time, reading intensively.
- Then put students into pairs to summarize the text for each other. They should make note of any sections or concepts they are unclear on, and then go back and discuss them.
- Ask students to take turns reading fluently to each other, as quickly and accurately as possible.

After Reading

- Put students into pairs. Have them discuss the *Think* boxes.
- For the first *Think* box, say *Think about the tense the paragraph is written in and how it helps to understand the paragraph. Now imagine the paragraph is written in the past tense or future tense and think how different that would be to read. Discuss with your partner.*
- For the second *Think* box, have pairs use a dictionary to look up the key words that they need to know.
- Go over the *Think* box answers with the class, having pairs share their discussions.

COLLABORATIVE LEARNING

- Put the pairs into small groups.
- Have groups discuss the text and anything else they didn't understand in it.
- Tell each group to think of at least two questions about the text, e.g. *What does "clammy" mean in the first paragraph?*
- Then take groups' questions for the whole class and help students to find or understand the answers.

COLLABORATIVE LEARNING

- Display the **Talk About It! Poster** to help students with sentence frames for discussion and expressing personal opinions.
- Put students into pairs to discuss which part of the text is most interesting and what new things they've learned.

CULTURE NOTE

The brain is made up of different parts. While they all work together, they are each responsible for different functions. The brain consists of three main parts, plus the limbic system: the cerebrum, the cerebellum, and the brainstem.

Outside, we have the wrinkled cerebrum that is the largest part of the human brain. It accounts for our cognitive abilities, such as problem solving and thinking. This is believed to be the most recently evolved part of the brain.

An older part of the brain is the cerebellum, which is found under the cerebrum at the rear. It controls balance and movement.

The limbic system or the "emotional brain" is found within the cerebellum. This is our center for emotions, learning, and memory.

The oldest part of the brain is the brainstem, which is responsible for automatic functions, such as breathing and controlling the heartbeat.

Human brain size, relative to body size, is the largest of all the mammals, followed by the bottlenose dolphin and the chimpanzee.

Further Practice
Workbook page 144
Online Practice Unit 15 • Read
Oxford iTools Unit 15 • Read

Understand

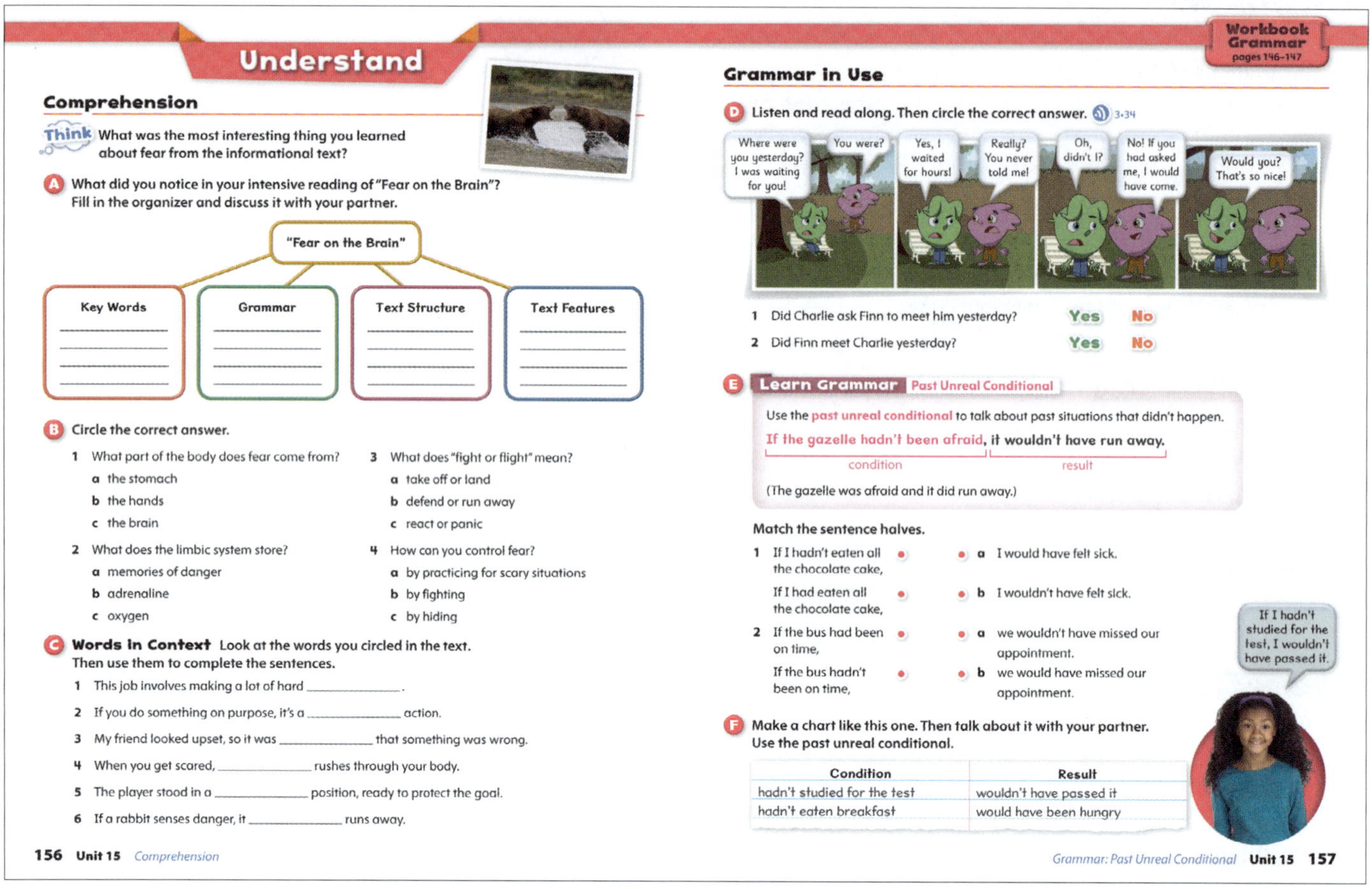

Comprehension

Think What was the most interesting thing you learned about fear from the informational text?

A What did you notice in your intensive reading of "Fear on the Brain"? Fill in the organizer and discuss it with your partner.

"Fear on the Brain"
- Key Words
- Grammar
- Text Structure
- Text Features

B Circle the correct answer.

1 What part of the body does fear come from?
a the stomach
b the hands
c the brain

2 What does the limbic system store?
a memories of danger
b adrenaline
c oxygen

3 What does "fight or flight" mean?
a take off or land
b defend or run away
c react or panic

4 How can you control fear?
a by practicing for scary situations
b by fighting
c by hiding

C **Words In Context** Look at the words you circled in the text. Then use them to complete the sentences.

1 This job involves making a lot of hard _____.
2 If you do something on purpose, it's a _____ action.
3 My friend looked upset, so it was _____ that something was wrong.
4 When you get scared, _____ rushes through your body.
5 The player stood in a _____ position, ready to protect the goal.
6 If a rabbit senses danger, it _____ runs away.

156 Unit 15 Comprehension

Grammar in Use

D Listen and read along. Then circle the correct answer. 3·34

Where were you yesterday? I was waiting for you! / You were? / Yes, I waited for hours! / Really? You never told me! / Oh, didn't I? / No! If you had asked me, I would have come. / Would you? That's so nice!

1 Did Charlie ask Finn to meet him yesterday? Yes No
2 Did Finn meet Charlie yesterday? Yes No

E **Learn Grammar** Past Unreal Conditional

Use the past unreal conditional to talk about past situations that didn't happen.

If the gazelle hadn't been afraid, it wouldn't have run away.
  condition   result

(The gazelle was afraid and it did run away.)

Match the sentence halves.

1 If I hadn't eaten all the chocolate cake, •
  If I had eaten all the chocolate cake, •
  • a I would have felt sick.
  • b I wouldn't have felt sick.

2 If the bus had been on time, •
  If the bus hadn't been on time, •
  • a we wouldn't have missed our appointment.
  • b we would have missed our appointment.

If I hadn't studied for the test, I wouldn't have passed it.

F Make a chart like this one. Then talk about it with your partner. Use the past unreal conditional.

Condition	Result
hadn't studied for the test	wouldn't have passed it
hadn't eaten breakfast	would have been hungry

Grammar: Past Unreal Conditional Unit 15 157

Comprehension

Think

- Read the question with the class. Ask students to think about their answer individually.
- Put students into pairs to discuss their answers.
- Have pairs share their discussions with the class. Take notes on students' responses on the board and classify them as *the brain*, *fight or flight*, or *controlling fear*.

A What did you notice in your intensive reading of "Fear on the Brain"? Fill in the organizer and discuss it with your partner.

- Read the instructions with the class.
- For all levels of students, have them reread the text individually. Remind them to read intensively.
- Review the organizer with the class. Ask *What are key words? What will you write in the grammar box? What is text structure? What are text features?*
- Ask students to fill out the organizer according to level.

Above level:

- After students have completed the organizers, put them into pairs.
- Have pairs compare their organizers.
- Have them explain the organizers to the class.

B Circle the correct answer.

- Students do the activity individually.
- Check the answers with the class.

CRITICAL THINKING

Ask students additional questions to check understanding:

- *What is fear a response to?*
- *What is adrenaline? What effect does it have on the body?*
- *What else does it do?*
- *What are two things the limbic system does well?*
- *Why do animals need a fight or flight response?*
- *Planning and rehearsing doesn't stop fear. So why do it?*

C Words in Context: Look at the words you circled in the text. Then use them to complete the sentences.

- Have students go back and find the words in the text.
- Tell them to use the context clues to guess at the meaning of each word. Then use these words to complete the sentences.
- Check the answers with the class.

ANSWERS
1 decisions 2 deliberate 3 obvious 4 adrenaline
5 defensive 6 instantly

Grammar in Use

D Listen and read along. Then circle the correct answer. 🔊 3•34

- Listen to the dialogue once and have students read along.
- Then have students read the question and then circle the correct answer.
- Play the audio again and have students check their answers.
- Check the answers with the class.

ANSWERS
1 No 2 No

E Learn Grammar: Past Unreal Conditional

- Read the *Learn Grammar* box together. Then read the example.
- Ask questions to check understanding:
  What is the condition?
  Is the condition something that did or didn't happen?
  What was the result of the condition?
  Did the result happen?

Match the sentences halves.

- Have students complete the activity on their own.
- Check answers with the class.

ANSWERS
1 b If I hadn't eaten all the chocolate cake, I wouldn't have felt sick.
  a If I had eaten all the chocolate cake, I would have felt sick.
2 a If the bus had been on time, we wouldn't have missed our appointment.
  b If the bus hadn't been on time, we would have missed our appointment.

COLLABORATIVE LEARNING

- In pairs, have students rephrase the four sentences without using the conditionals.
- Share their answers with the class, e.g. *I ate all the chocolate cake and I feel sick.*

F Make a chart like this one. Then talk about it with your partner. Use the past unreal conditional.

- Read the conditions and the results to the class.
- Have students create the chart in their notebooks.
- Ask students to fill in the chart with three conditions and three results.

DIFFERENTIATION

Below level:

- Put students into mixed-ability pairs to do the activity.

At level:

- Put students into pairs to do the activity.
- After pairs have said sentences for all the phrases, have them share some sentences with the class.

Above level:

- Have students write the conditions and results. Tell them to make one sentence negative and two sentences positive.
- Then have students circulate around the room and talk to other students, saying one of their conditions. The other student must give a result.
- Ask them to note down how many students gave the same result as they wrote down themselves.

Workbook Grammar

- Direct students to the Workbook for further practice.

Further practice
Workbook pages 145–147
Online Practice Unit 15 • Understand
Oxford **iTools** Unit 15 • Understand

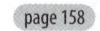

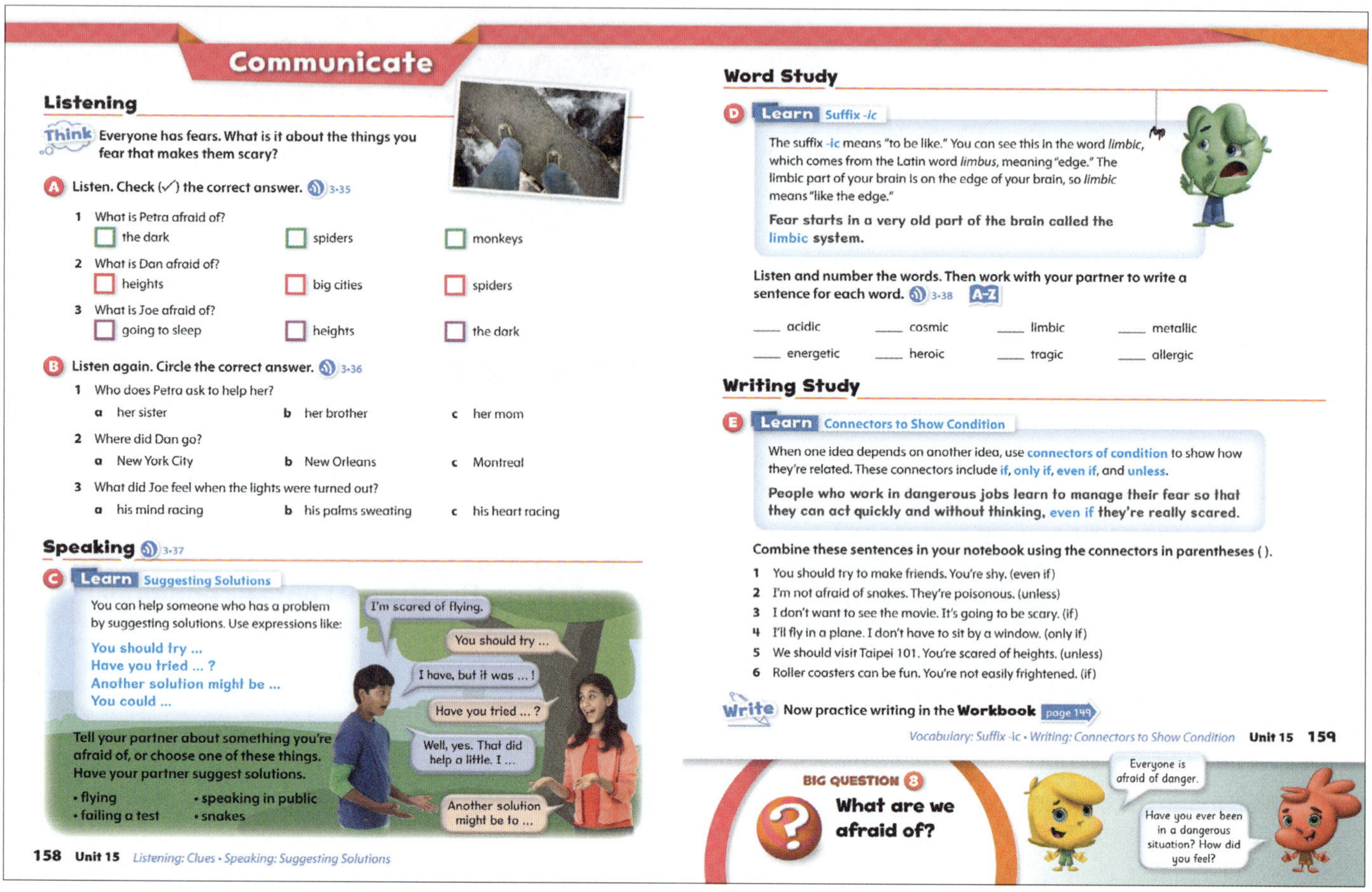

Communicate

Listening

Think Everyone has fears. What is it about the things you fear that makes them scary?

A Listen. Check (✓) the correct answer. 3·35

1 What is Petra afraid of?
☐ the dark ☐ spiders ☐ monkeys

2 What is Dan afraid of?
☐ heights ☐ big cities ☐ spiders

3 What is Joe afraid of?
☐ going to sleep ☐ heights ☐ the dark

B Listen again. Circle the correct answer. 3·36

1 Who does Petra ask to help her?
a her sister b her brother c her mom

2 Where did Dan go?
a New York City b New Orleans c Montreal

3 What did Joe feel when the lights were turned out?
a his mind racing b his palms sweating c his heart racing

Speaking 3·37

C **Learn** Suggesting Solutions

You can help someone who has a problem by suggesting solutions. Use expressions like:

You should try ...
Have you tried ... ?
Another solution might be ...
You could ...

Tell your partner about something you're afraid of, or choose one of these things. Have your partner suggest solutions.
- flying
- speaking in public
- failing a test
- snakes

Speech bubbles:
I'm scared of flying.
You should try ...
I have, but it was ...!
Have you tried ... ?
Well, yes. That did help a little. I ...
Another solution might be to ...

158 Unit 15 Listening: Clues · Speaking: Suggesting Solutions

Word Study

D **Learn** Suffix -ic

The suffix -ic means "to be like." You can see this in the word limbic, which comes from the Latin word limbus, meaning "edge." The limbic part of your brain is on the edge of your brain, so limbic means "like the edge."

Fear starts in a very old part of the brain called the limbic system.

Listen and number the words. Then work with your partner to write a sentence for each word. 3·38 **A-Z**

____ acidic ____ cosmic ____ limbic ____ metallic
____ energetic ____ heroic ____ tragic ____ allergic

Writing Study

E **Learn** Connectors to Show Condition

When one idea depends on another idea, use connectors of condition to show how they're related. These connectors include if, only if, even if, and unless.

People who work in dangerous jobs learn to manage their fear so that they can act quickly and without thinking, even if they're really scared.

Combine these sentences in your notebook using the connectors in parentheses ( ).

1 You should try to make friends. You're shy. (even if)
2 I'm not afraid of snakes. They're poisonous. (unless)
3 I don't want to see the movie. It's going to be scary. (if)
4 I'll fly in a plane. I don't have to sit by a window. (only if)
5 We should visit Taipei 101. You're scared of heights. (unless)
6 Roller coasters can be fun. You're not easily frightened. (if)

Write Now practice writing in the **Workbook** page 149

Vocabulary: Suffix -ic · Writing: Connectors to Show Condition Unit 15 **159**

BIG QUESTION 8
? What are we afraid of?

Speech bubbles:
Everyone is afraid of danger.
Have you ever been in a dangerous situation? How did you feel?

Summary

Objectives: To learn and practice listening, speaking, and writing strategies to facilitate effective communication.

Vocabulary: *acidic, cosmic, limbic, metallic, energetic, heroic, tragic, allergic*

Listening strategy: Listening for clues

Speaking: Suggesting solutions

Word Study: Suffix -ic

Writing Study: Connectors to show condition

Big Question learning point: *Some people are afraid of specific things, like crowds.*

Materials: Discover Poster 8, Audio CD, Big Question Chart

Listening

Think

- Tell students to think about the questions individually.
- Explain that they should think of an example of a thing they are afraid of, e.g. snakes. Ask *What is it about snakes that makes them scary? Most of them aren't that big. And most of them won't hurt you. Is it the way they move? Is it because they move quickly? Does that make them seem sneaky and out of your control? Is it because they could bite you? Analyze the elements of the things that scare you to explain why you are afraid.*
- Have students discuss their answers with a partner.
- Share the discussions with the class. Ask questions to get students to hone in on what exactly makes them scared.

A Listen. Check (✓) the correct answer. 3·35

- Have students read the questions and the answers.
- Play the audio so students can complete the activity.
- Have students check their answers in small groups.
- Check all answers with the class.

ANSWERS
The following should be checked:
1 spiders 2 heights 3 the dark

B Listen again. Circle the correct answer. 3·36

- Have students read the questions.
- Play the audio so students can complete the exercise.

ANSWERS
1 b 2 a 3 c

Speaking 3·37

C Learn: Suggesting Solutions

- Read the *Learn* box with the class.
- Have students listen to the audio and read along.
- Say each of the expressions with students echoing as they hear each line.
- Put students into pairs and tell them to practice the dialogue and suggest solutions.
- Have pairs say their dialogue for the class.

Tell your partner about something you're afraid of, or choose one of these things. Have your partner suggest solutions.

- Put students into pairs. Tell them to choose one of the fears from the list: (flying, failing a test, speaking in public, snakes).
- Have students conduct the conversation with one person talking about their fear, and the other offering solutions to help them overcome that fear.
- Have a few pairs demonstrate their conversation for the class.

Word Study

D Learn: Suffix -ic

- Read the *Learn* box and example together.

Listen and number the words. Then work with your partner to write a sentence for each word. 🎧 3•38

- Play the audio and have students number the words in the order they hear them.
- Check answers with the class.

1 cosmic   2 energetic   3 acidic   4 metallic   5 tragic
6 allergic   7 heroic   8 limbic

- Put students into pairs. Have them discuss the meanings of the words and then check their guesses by looking up the definitions in the dictionary.
- Ask pairs to write the words in sentences.
- Have them read their sentences to the class.

Writing Study

E Learn: Connectors to Show Condition

- Read the *Learn* box and example together.
- Ask a question to check understanding, e.g. *What do connector words do?*
- Explain that *even if* in the example sentence means approximately *in the case that*.
- Ask *What comes before the phrase?*

Combine these sentences in your notebook using the connectors in parentheses ( ).

- Have students do the activity individually.
- Then put them into pairs to check each other's work before checking answers with the class.

1 You should try to make friends, even if you're shy.
2 I'm not afraid of snakes, unless they're poisonous.
3 I don't want to see the movie if it's going to be scary.
4 I'll fly in a plane, only if I don't have to sit by a window.
5 We should visit Taipei 101, unless you're scared of heights.
6 Roller coasters can be fun, if you're not easily frightened.

Below level:

- Put students into pairs to do the Workbook. Have them choose a topic.
- Tell them to list about three to five pieces of advice, e.g. *You only need to bathe your dog once every month or two.*
- For each piece of advice, have them try to add a conditional, e.g. *You only need to bathe your dog once every month or two, unless he's encountered a skunk.*

At level:

- Tell students to list their advice first and then add connectors to show condition. They should change some of their expressions to the past unreal conditional.

Above level:

- Have students write their advice.
- Then have students trade papers with a partner to check.
- Have the partner suggest two more pieces of advice and look for places where conditionals can be used or if sentences can be turned into the past unreal conditional.

Write

- Direct students to the Workbook for further writing practice.

Big Question 8 Review

What are we afraid of?

- Display **Discover Poster 8**. Discuss what you see.
- Refer to the learning points covered in Unit 15 that are written on the poster and have students explain how they relate to the different pictures.
- Return to the **Big Question Chart**.
- Ask students what they have learned about fear while studying this unit.

Further practice
Workbook pages 148–149
Online Practice Unit 15 • Communicate
Oxford **iTools** Unit 15 • Communicate

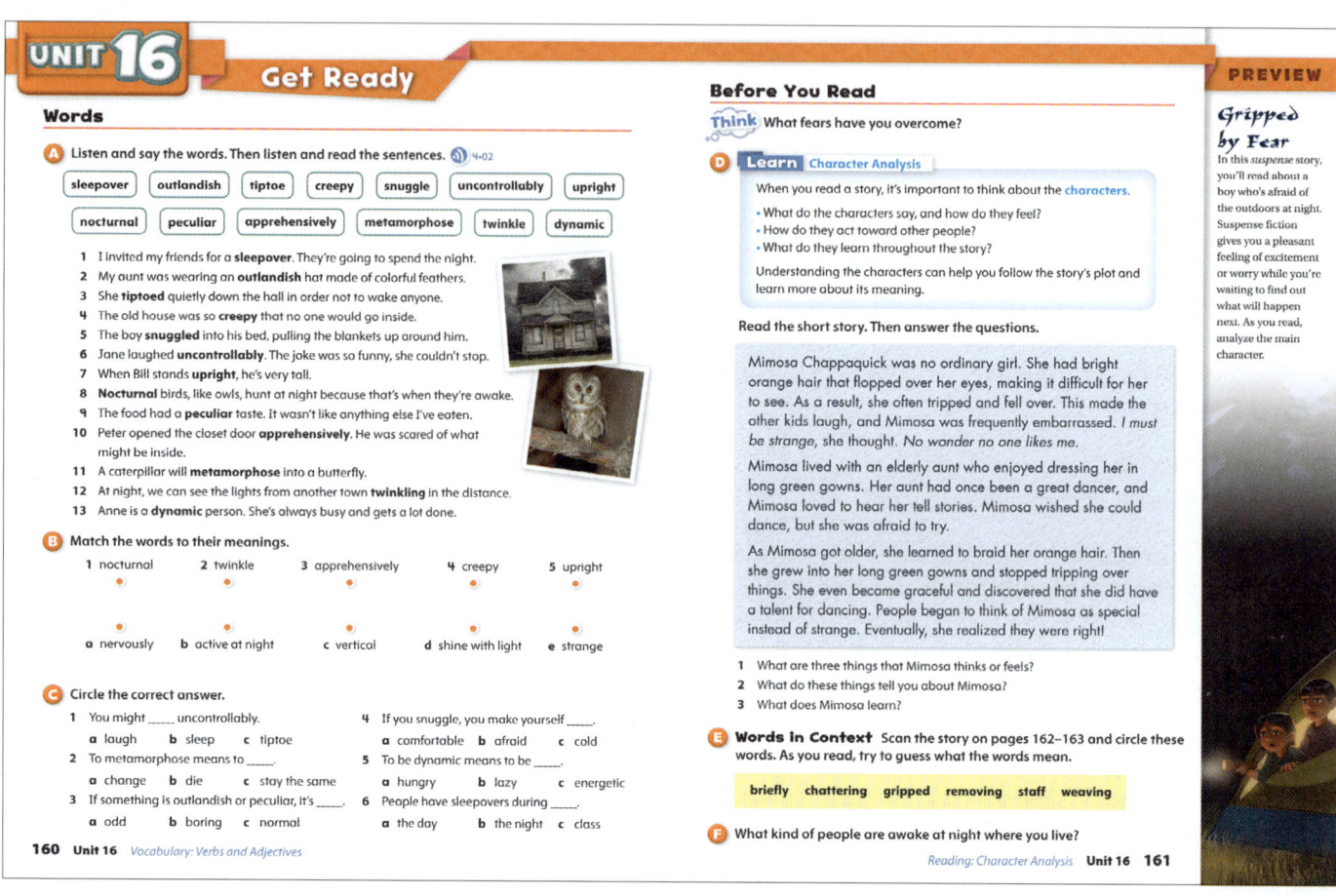

Summary

Objectives: To understand about verbs and adjectives; to apply own experience and a reading strategy to help comprehension of a text.

Vocabulary: *sleepover, outlandish, tiptoe, creepy, snuggle, uncontrollably, upright, nocturnal, peculiar, apprehensively, metamorphose, twinkle, dynamic, briefly, chattering, gripped, removing, staff, weaving*

Reading strategy: Character analysis

Materials: Audio CD

Words

A Listen and say the words. Then listen and read the sentences. 🔊 4•02

- Play the audio. Ask students to point to the words and repeat the words when they hear them.
- Then have students listen and read the sentences as they hear them. Say the sentence numbers out of order and have the class read the sentences aloud.

B Match the words to their meanings.

- Have students do the activity on their own and then compare answers with a partner.
- Check answers with the class.

ANSWERS
1 b 2 d 3 a 4 e 5 c

CRITICAL THINKING

- Tell students to find the words in the sentences in A and replace them with the definitions in B. Explain that they should modify whatever is needed with the phrase or in the sentence so it is grammatically correct.

C Circle the correct answer.

- Have students do the activity on their own and then compare answers with a partner.
- Check answers with the class.

ANSWERS
1 a 2 a 3 a 4 a 5 c 6 b

COLLABORATIVE LEARNING

- Put students into pairs and have them write sentences for the new words, but tell them to leave a blank where the word goes.
- Have pairs trade papers with another pair to complete the sentences.
- Pairs then correct each other's work and discuss any meanings they are not clear about.
- Share some sentences with the class by having pairs write them on the board.

Before You Read

Think

- Have students read the question and make notes about their ideas and answers individually.
- Students discuss their ideas to the question in small groups.
- Then share some of the ideas with the class. List the ideas on the board.

D Learn: Character Analysis

- Read the *Learn* box with the class.
- Ask questions:
  Name a character in a story, book, or movie. Is that a main character?
  Do stories usually revolve around a main character?
  How does understanding the character help you understand the story?

Read the short story. Then answer the questions.

- Students read the short story individually.
- Ask them to answer the questions about the main character, Mimosa.
- Put students into pairs to compare their answers.
- Then go over the answers with the class.

POSSIBLE ANSWERS

1 Embarrassed, strange, that no one liked her, clumsy, special.
2 They tell you that she worried about how she appeared to others and felt different. When she was young she didn't relate to people easily. She was shy.
3 She learns that being different isn't a bad thing and to be confident in who she was.

DIFFERENTIATION

Below level:

- Put students into mixed-ability pairs.
- Have pairs discuss and answer to the questions together.
- Ask them to share their ideas with the class.

At level:

- Have pairs answer the questions individually before comparing them with a partner.
- Have them share their ideas with the class.

Above level:

- Have students answer the questions in pairs.
- Ask them to answer the same questions about themselves.
- Put students into small groups.
- Have them share their personal answers with the other members of the group.

CRITICAL THINKING

Ask the following questions to check understanding about the text:

- *How does Mimosa change over the time of the story?*
- *What is the role of Mimosa's aunt in the story? (What purpose does her character serve in relation to Mimosa?)*

E Words in Context: Scan the story on pages 162–163 and circle these words. As you read, try to guess what the words mean.

- Read each word and have students follow your pronunciation.
- Elicit meanings for the words to check if students know them. Then ask questions to help students guess what they think the words could mean before they do the activity.
- Tell students to think about the words as they read the story.

F What kind of people are awake at night where you live?

COMMUNICATION

- Put students into pairs to discuss the question.
- Put one pair with another pair to share their ideas.
- Elicit ideas from the whole class.

Reading Preview

- Read the title of the unit's reading text.
- Have students silently read the content of the preview bar.
- Ask *What type of text is it?* Ask *What does this type of text do?*
- Tell students to analyze the main character as they read.

Further Practice
Workbook pages 150–151
Online Practice Unit 16 • Get Ready
Oxford iTools Unit 16 • Get Ready

Unit 16 Read · page 162

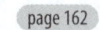

Gripped by Fear

It was Friday afternoon, and Aroon had just gotten home from school. When the phone rang, he sprang up to answer it. It was his friend, Deepak.

"Don't forget the sleepover," said Deepak. "Bring a sleeping bag and a flashlight, OK?"

Aroon loved sleepovers. Maybe he, Deepak, and Deepak's brother Salim would play video games or watch a movie! He briefly wondered why he might need a flashlight, but he was too excited to think about it for long. Aroon's dad packed him a snack, and his mom helped him find the bus that would take him to Deepak and Salim's house, far out in the country. He was excited to be taking such a long journey by himself and smiled the entire way.

When Aroon arrived, Deepak and Salim's mom had prepared his favorite dinner of curry and chappatis. The boys ate happily, chattering about their upcoming vacation. Then Deepak and Salim's dad came in from the yard.

"The tent's up!" he said.

"The tent?" Aroon asked.

"Yes, we're sleeping outdoors tonight," replied Salim. "It'll be great!"

"Oh," said Aroon in a small voice. He was gripped by fear but didn't want to show it. *I wish we could play video games, instead,* he thought. Where Aroon lived in the city, it never truly got dark, and people were always busy at night. Here in the countryside, the nights were black and silent, except for the outlandish noises that wild animals made. Aroon had always been terrified of the outdoors at night.

When they went outside, there was no moon visible. All Aroon could see, as he tiptoed into the darkness, was an ink-black sky and some tall, creepy objects swaying in the breeze. The boys got into the tent, zipped up the door, and snuggled into their sleeping bags. "Turn out your flashlight, Aroon," said Salim. "Then we can tell scary stories!"

At that moment, Aroon heard a noise. *Whuk, whuk, whuk,* it went. It seemed to be right outside the tent!

"What's that?" he asked apprehensively, sitting upright, his hair standing on end.

"It's a scops owl," replied Salim. "They're nocturnal."

"Oh, right. An owl," said Aroon.

Then a peculiar quacking noise made him jump. He crawled deeper into his sleeping bag and began to shake uncontrollably. "And what's that?" he squeaked.

"It's just a frog," said Deepak.

"Really? That's a frog?" asked Aroon. Salim pointed the flashlight at him.

"What's up, Aroon? Are you afraid of the dark?"

Think How does Aroon feel? Why does he feel this way?

"Outdoors ... yes!" replied Aroon. "Very!"

"No problem," said Deepak. "Salim and I used to be afraid of the dark, but our dad taught us to see things differently." Deepak and Salim's dad was a biologist, and they often went on camping trips with him. Deepak unzipped the door of the tent, and they looked outside. "There are three things you need to do, Aroon," said Salim. "See, listen, and imagine. Look around you. What can you see?"

Aroon's eyes gradually adjusted to the darkness, and to his immense surprise, he discovered that he *could* see. The tall, creepy objects were trees! The ink-black sky had metamorphosed as the moon appeared from behind the clouds. Now there were millions of twinkling stars.

"Listen," said Salim. "You heard the scops owl and the frog. What else do you hear?"

"A weird scratching noise," said Aroon.

"Yes! That's a porcupine looking for food," said Deepak.

"If only I'd known that!" said Aroon. Suddenly, he didn't feel so afraid. "What did your dad mean when he said you had to imagine?"

"Imagine the city at night," said Deepak. "Imagine the thousands of people working, talking, laughing, drinking tea. There are dustcarts removing the garbage and staff cleaning the offices. There are doctors and nurses in hospitals. Taxi drivers are moving people from place to place. Well, just like those people, animals are busy at night, too. There are bats catching insects and spiders weaving webs."

"I get it!" Aroon interrupted. "There are owls flying and hyenas hunting."

"Right!" said Salim. "So, you see, the dark in the countryside is nothing to be afraid of. Just like in the city, it's as dynamic at night as it is by day!"

"Thanks!" said Aroon, smiling broadly. "If we hadn't camped outside tonight, I wouldn't have thought about any of that. Can I sleep over again tomorrow night? And can we sleep out here, where it's fun?"

Think What does Aroon learn?

162 · 163

Summary

Objectives: To read, understand, and discuss suspense fiction; to apply a reading strategy to improve comprehension.

School subject: Life Science

Text type: Suspense (fiction)

Reading strategy: Character analysis

Big Question learning point: *Strange or unfamiliar things are sometimes frightening.*

Materials: Audio CD

Before Reading

- Read the title of the story.
- Have students point to the pictures and describe what they see.
- Ask them to predict what they think this story will be about.

- Tell students to skim read the story. Then ask *What do you think this story is about? What information on the page helped you decide this?*

During Reading 4·03

- Remind students to think about the main character as they read.
- Play the audio. Students listen as they read along.
- Play the audio a second time if necessary.

Below level:

- Put students into a circle and have them take turns reading sections.
- Help them pronounce any unfamiliar or difficult words and phrases.
- Pause to answer the *Think* boxes.

At level:

- Put students into mixed-ability pairs.
- Have students take turns reading paragraphs.
- Have the more confident student help the less confident student pronounce unfamiliar or difficult words and phrases.
- Have pairs stop at the *Think* boxes and answer them.

Above level:

- Put students into small groups to read, with one or two students as narrators, and other students to read the parts of Aroon, Salim, and Deepak.
- Tell the characters that they will read only their lines in quotes; the narrator will read the "he said" parts.
- Have groups perform part of the text for the class.

Discussion questions:

- *Who is the main character?*
- *What is the main problem the character is having?*
- *Who are Deepak and Salim?*
- *Why aren't Deepak and Salim afraid?*
- *What do you think Aroon thought the strange sounds were from inside the tent?*
- *Why do you think Deepak and Salim's dad was so helpful about what to do with their fears of the dark?*
- *Are you scared of the dark?*
- *Have you ever been on a camping trip like the one described in this story?*
- *Would you like to go on a camping trip like this? Why or why not?*

After Reading

- Put students into pairs.
- Have pairs find the words in context again and discuss their meaning.

COLLABORATIVE LEARNING

Discussion questions:

- *Have you ever slept outside? If so, what was it like? If not, what do you think it would be like? Would you like to do so?*
- Then have groups share their ideas with the class.

CULTURE NOTE

Nocturnal animals are especially adapted to the night. They have large eyes to see in the dark and excellent hearing and sense of smell.

Some nocturnal animals, like bats, use echolocation, in which the animal gives out a high-pitched sound which bounces off objects. The sound then comes back to the animal, giving it information about the object's shape, direction, distance, and texture.

Some nocturnal animals also come out in the daytime, but hunt at night, whereas others sleep or rest during the day.

Plenty of animals are nocturnal. Animals that live in warm climates need to avoid the heat of the day. For some animals, sleeping during the day is useful to avoid diurnal (active in daytime) predators. For others, it's to avoid competition from diurnal animals that eat the same food.

Some common nocturnal animals are gray wolves, mice, coyotes, cats, possums, spiders, and bats.

Further Practice
Workbook page 152
Online Practice Unit 16 • Read
Oxford iTools Unit 16 • Read

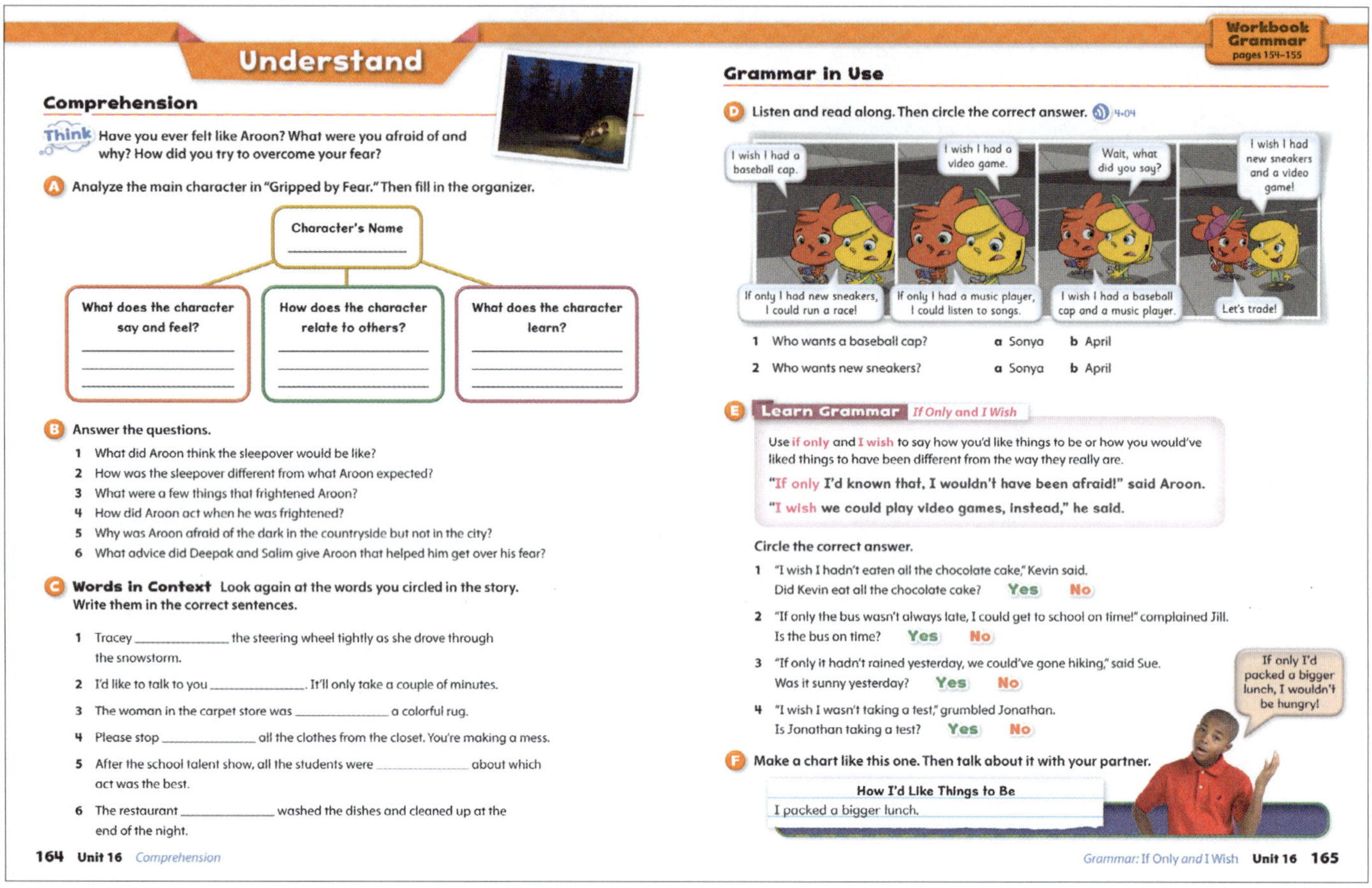

Understand

Comprehension

Think Have you ever felt like Aroon? What were you afraid of and why? How did you try to overcome your fear?

A Analyze the main character in "Gripped by Fear." Then fill in the organizer.

Character's Name
_____

What does the character say and feel?	How does the character relate to others?	What does the character learn?
_____	_____	_____
_____	_____	_____
_____	_____	_____

B Answer the questions.

1 What did Aroon think the sleepover would be like?
2 How was the sleepover different from what Aroon expected?
3 What were a few things that frightened Aroon?
4 How did Aroon act when he was frightened?
5 Why was Aroon afraid of the dark in the countryside but not in the city?
6 What advice did Deepak and Salim give Aroon that helped him get over his fear?

C **Words in Context** Look again at the words you circled in the story. Write them in the correct sentences.

1 Tracey _____ the steering wheel tightly as she drove through the snowstorm.
2 I'd like to talk to you _____. It'll only take a couple of minutes.
3 The woman in the carpet store was _____ a colorful rug.
4 Please stop _____ all the clothes from the closet. You're making a mess.
5 After the school talent show, all the students were _____ about which act was the best.
6 The restaurant _____ washed the dishes and cleaned up at the end of the night.

164 Unit 16 *Comprehension*

Grammar in Use

Workbook Grammar pages 154–155

D Listen and read along. Then circle the correct answer. 4-04

1 Who wants a baseball cap? a Sonya b April
2 Who wants new sneakers? a Sonya b April

E **Learn Grammar** *If Only and I Wish*

Use **if only** and **I wish** to say how you'd like things to be or how you would've liked things to have been different from the way they really are.

"**If only** I'd known that, I wouldn't have been afraid!" said Aroon.
"**I wish** we could play video games, instead," he said.

Circle the correct answer.

1 "I wish I hadn't eaten all the chocolate cake," Kevin said.
Did Kevin eat all the chocolate cake? **Yes** **No**

2 "If only the bus wasn't always late, I could get to school on time!" complained Jill.
Is the bus on time? **Yes** **No**

3 "If only it hadn't rained yesterday, we could've gone hiking," said Sue.
Was it sunny yesterday? **Yes** **No**

4 "I wish I wasn't taking a test," grumbled Jonathan.
Is Jonathan taking a test? **Yes** **No**

If only I'd packed a bigger lunch, I wouldn't be hungry!

F Make a chart like this one. Then talk about it with your partner.

How I'd Like Things to Be
I packed a bigger lunch.

Grammar: If Only and I Wish Unit 16 165

Summary

Objectives: To demonstrate understanding of suspense fiction; to understand the meaning and form of the grammar structure.

Reading: Character analysis
Grammar input: *If only* and *I wish*
Grammar practice: Workbook exercises
Grammar production: *If only* and *I wish*
Materials: Audio CD

Comprehension

Think

- Have students think about their answers individually first. Then hold a class discussion.

A Analyze the main character in "Gripped by Fear." Then fill in the organizer.

- Have students reread the story before filling in the organizer.

DIFFERENTIATION

Below level:

- Refer students back to the story on pages 162 and 163.
- Scan the text and show students where to find one example for each box of the organizer. Say *What does the character say and feel?* Then point to the first column of the story and read *Aaron loved sleepovers … he was too excited to think about it. How does Aaron feel?*

- Continue in this way with the class to find an example for each box. Then put students into mixed-ability pairs to continue to fill out the organizer.

At level:

- Have students complete the organizer in pairs.
- Then check the answers with the class.

Above level:

- Have students complete the organizer individually.
- Put students into pairs to compare their answers. Have pairs discuss "How do Aroon's emotions relate to the plot?"
- Have pairs explain their organizers to the class and talk about the questions.

ANSWERS

Character's Name: Aroon
What does the character say and feel?: Excited for the sleepover, gripped by fear / scared to sleep outdoors, then appreciative (thanks)
How does the character relate to others?: He hides his fear at first; then he listens to their advice
What does the character learn?: He learns how to think about the outdoors at night differently.

B Answer the questions.

COLLABORATIVE LEARNING

- Put students into small mixed-ability groups.
- Ask groups to work together to answer the questions.
- Tell students to turn back to the story to find the answers.

ANSWERS

1 He thought they would play video games or watch a movie.
2 They were sleeping outdoors in a tent.
3 An owl, a frog, and a porcupine.
4 His hair stood on end, he began to shake uncontrollably, and his voice was a squeak.
5 He was afraid of the dark in the countryside because it was unfamiliar to him. He did not know how to look or listen.
6 The advice they gave to Aroon to get over his fear was to imagine the animals busy like people are in the city at night.

C Words in Context: Look again at the words you circled in the story. Write them in the correct sentences.

- Have students go back and find the words in the story.
- Tell them to use the context clues to guess at the meaning of each word.
- Ask students to complete the sentences.

ANSWERS

1 gripped   2 briefly   3 weaving   4 removing
5 chattering   6 staff

COMMUNICATION

- Put students into pairs.
- Have them say sentences that use the words in context.
- Have pairs share their sentences with the class.

Grammar in Use

D Listen and read along. Then circle the correct answer. 🔘 4•04

- Listen to the dialogue once and then read it together as a class.
- Play the audio again if necessary.
- Check the answers with the class.

ANSWERS

1 Sonya   2 April

E Learn Grammar: *If Only* and *I Wish*

- Read the *Learn Grammar* box and examples together.
- Give an example. Say *If only I had a million dollars. Does that mean that I have a million dollars?*

Circle the correct answer.

- Have students complete the activity individually and then check answers with a partner.
- Check answers with the class. Explain any sentences they may be confused about.

ANSWERS

1 Yes   2 No   3 No   4 Yes

CRITICAL THINKING

- Put students into pairs.
- Have pairs change all four sentences in E to be *No* answers, e.g. *I wish I had eaten all of the chocolate cake,* would mean that Kevin had not eaten all of the cake.
- Have pairs change number 4 and then check answers with the class.

ANSWERS

4 I wish I was taking a test.

F Make a chart like this one. Then talk about it with your partner.

- Have students create the chart in their notebooks.
- Ask them to write three more sentences.
- Put students into pairs.
- Have students take turns saying their sentences.
- Ask some students to share their sentences with the class.

Workbook Grammar

- Direct students to the Workbook for further practice.

Further practice
Workbook pages 153–155
Online Practice Unit 16 • Understand
Oxford **iTools** Unit 16 • Understand

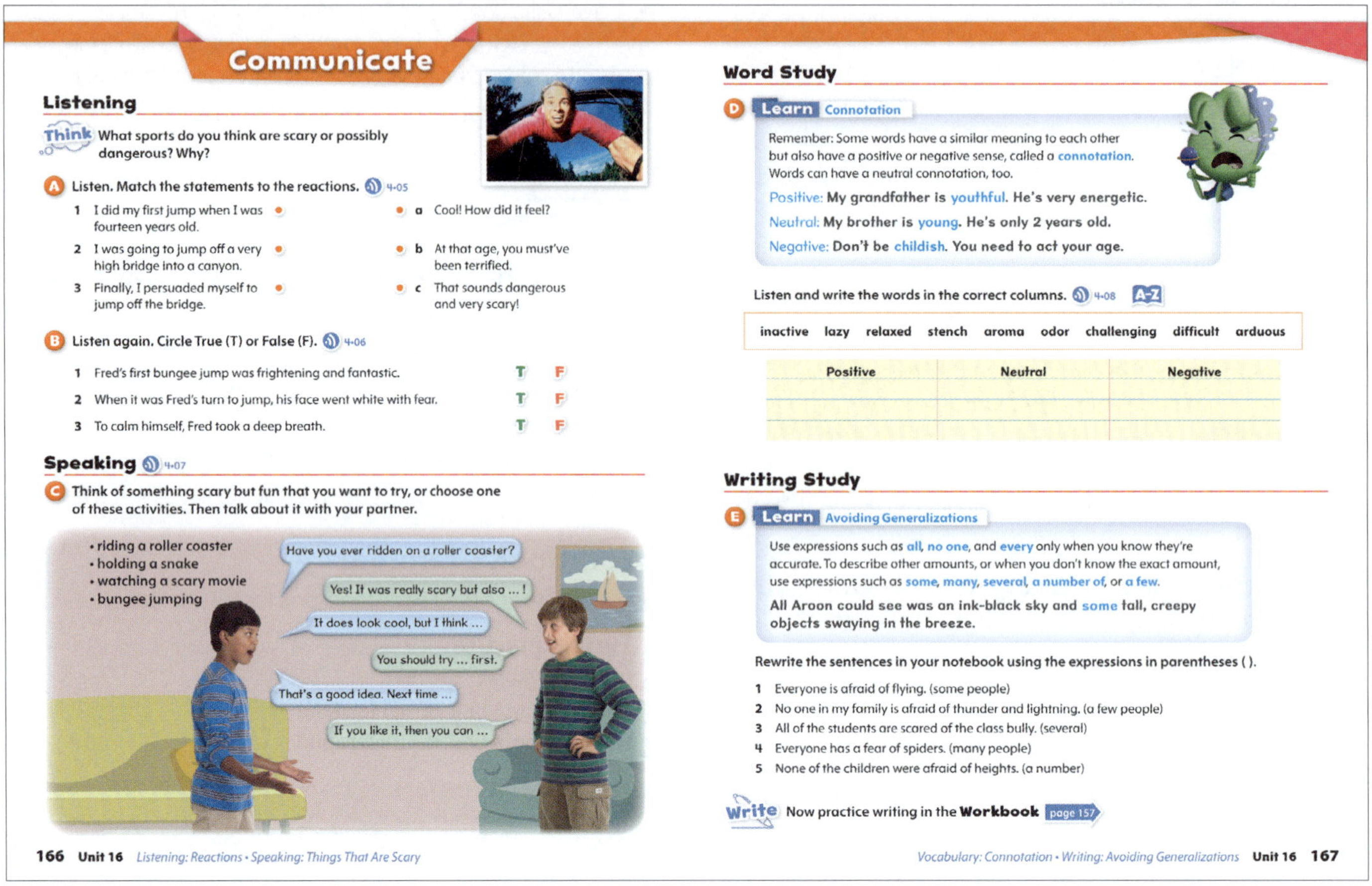

Communicate

Listening

Think What sports do you think are scary or possibly dangerous? Why?

A Listen. Match the statements to the reactions. 4·05

1 I did my first jump when I was fourteen years old. •
2 I was going to jump off a very high bridge into a canyon. •
3 Finally, I persuaded myself to jump off the bridge. •

• a Cool! How did it feel?
• b At that age, you must've been terrified.
• c That sounds dangerous and very scary!

B Listen again. Circle True (T) or False (F). 4·06

1 Fred's first bungee jump was frightening and fantastic.   T   F
2 When it was Fred's turn to jump, his face went white with fear.   T   F
3 To calm himself, Fred took a deep breath.   T   F

Speaking 4·07

C Think of something scary but fun that you want to try, or choose one of these activities. Then talk about it with your partner.

- riding a roller coaster
- holding a snake
- watching a scary movie
- bungee jumping

Have you ever ridden on a roller coaster?
Yes! It was really scary but also ... !
It does look cool, but I think ...
You should try ... first.
That's a good idea. Next time ...
If you like it, then you can ...

Word Study

D **Learn** Connotation

Remember: Some words have a similar meaning to each other but also have a positive or negative sense, called a connotation. Words can have a neutral connotation, too.

Positive: My grandfather is youthful. He's very energetic.
Neutral: My brother is young. He's only 2 years old.
Negative: Don't be childish. You need to act your age.

Listen and write the words in the correct columns. 4·08 A-Z

inactive	lazy	relaxed	stench	aroma	odor	challenging	difficult	arduous

Positive	Neutral	Negative

Writing Study

E **Learn** Avoiding Generalizations

Use expressions such as all, no one, and every only when you know they're accurate. To describe other amounts, or when you don't know the exact amount, use expressions such as some, many, several, a number of, or a few.

All Aroon could see was an ink-black sky and some tall, creepy objects swaying in the breeze.

Rewrite the sentences in your notebook using the expressions in parentheses ( ).

1 Everyone is afraid of flying. (some people)
2 No one in my family is afraid of thunder and lightning. (a few people)
3 All of the students are scared of the class bully. (several)
4 Everyone has a fear of spiders. (many people)
5 None of the children were afraid of heights. (a number)

Write Now practice writing in the **Workbook** page 157

Summary

Objectives: To learn and practice listening, speaking, and writing strategies to facilitate effective communication.

Vocabulary: *lazy, stench, arduous, aroma, challenging, relaxed, inactive, odor, difficult*

Listening strategy: Listening for reactions

Speaking: Talking about things that are scary but fun

Word Study: Connotation

Writing Study: Avoiding generalizations

Big Question learning point: *Some activities, like skydiving, can be scary but fun.*

Materials: Audio CD

Listening

Think

- Tell students to think about their answers to the questions and the reasons.
- Have students discuss the questions with a partner.
- Have pairs share their ideas. Elicit names of extreme sports, if necessary.
- Take notes on the students' answers and leave them on the board for the Speaking activity.

A Listen. Match the statements to the reactions. 4·05

- Have students read the sentences.
- Play the audio once and tell students to listen.
- Ask students to match the correct answer.
- Play the audio again so they can check their work.

ANSWERS
1 b   2 c   3 a

B Listen again. Circle True (T) or False (F). 4·06

- Play the audio again. Ask the students to do the activity individually.
- Put students into pairs to compare answers. Tell students to correct the false statements.
- Play the audio again so students can check their answers.

ANSWERS
1 T   2 F   3 T

Speaking 4·07

C Think of something scary but fun that you want to try, or choose one of these activities. Then talk about it with your partner.

- Read the presentation box and the examples.
- Play the audio one time. Play the audio a second time for students to take parts and read along with it.
- Model the dialogue with a volunteer.
- Put students into pairs and ask them to do the dialogue.
- Have a few volunteers say their dialogue for the class.

- Have students think of one of the sports from the *Think* activity on top of the page.
- Then give students a few minutes to circulate around the room talking about their extreme sport with a classmate.
- Have a few students say their dialogue for the class.

Word Study

D Learn: Connotation

- Read the *Learn* box and examples together.
- Ask *Why is "young" neutral?*

Listen and write the words in the correct columns. 🎧 4·08

- Read the words to the class and have them follow your pronunciation.
- Ask them to list the words under the correct headings.
- Check the answers with the class.
- As a follow-up, have students close their books. Say the words in random order and have students take turns coming up to the board to spell them.

- Put students into pairs. Have them write sentences for the words.
- Invite some students to the board to write a sentence.
- Ask the class to determine if the words have been used in the sentences with the correct connotation, e.g. *She plugged her nose at the aroma of the skunk,* is incorrect. *She plugged her nose at the stench of the skunk,* is correct.

Writing Study

E Learn: Avoiding Generalizations

- Read the *Learn* box and example together.

Rewrite the sentences in your notebook using the expressions in parentheses ( ).

- Have students complete the activity on their own.
- Ask them to compare answers with a partner.

ANSWERS
1 Some people are afraid of flying.
2 A few people in my family are afraid of thunder and lightning.
3 Several of the students are scared of the class bully.
4 Many people have a fear of spiders.
5 A number of the children were afraid of heights.

Below level:

- Put students into mixed-ability pairs.
- Have pairs write three sentences that make general statements that are accurate, e.g. *A number of students in our class bring lunch.*
- Have pairs share their answers with another pair.

At level:

- Have students write five sentences that make general statements that are accurate.
- Ask them to share their answers with a partner.

Above level:

- Say a sentence starter using one of the accurate expressions, e.g. *A few of my friends … .*
- Have students take it down as dictation and then complete the sentence on their own.
- Ask students to check their sentences with a partner.
- Have them write some sentences on the board.

Write

- Direct students to the Workbook for further writing practice.

Further practice
Workbook pages 156–157
Online Practice Unit 16 · Communicate
Oxford iTools Unit 16 · Communicate

Summary

Objectives: To show what students have learned about fear and the learning points of Units 15 and 16.

Reading: Reading an instructional text

Writing: Writing an instructional text

Speaking: Sharing an instructional text

Big Question learning point: *Many people fear going to the doctor.*

Materials: Big Question DVD , Discover Poster 8, Talk About It! Poster, Big Question Chart

Writing

A Read this instructional guide.

- Read aloud the directions to the class. Elicit *What is an instructional guide?*
- Go over the structure of the instructional guide before reading. Ask *Why does this guide have numbers?* Elicit the answer.
- Read the guide aloud one time for the class to listen. Then have students read it with you one time.

B Answer the questions.

- Have students work with a partner to answer the questions.
- Check the answers with the class.

ANSWERS

1 The title tells you what the guide is about.
2 They are numbered.
3 The reader directly, using "you" and "your"
4 Advice about overcoming a fear.

CRITICAL THINKING

Ask these questions to check understanding:
- *Why is it a good idea to number the tips?*
- *How can friends help you overcome your fear?*
- *Which tip is most like the advice from the reading, which deals with fear, on page 155?*

C Learn: Writing an Instructional Guide

- Read the *Learn* box together.
- Explain that students should follow these guidelines when they plan and write their instructional guides.

CREATIVITY

- Brainstorm some ideas for an instructional guide with the class, e.g. *How to overcome your fear of bees. How to draw a realistic picture. How to take a good photo.*
- Write topics on the board. Then group students who choose similar topics together.

DIFFERENTIATION

Below level:
- Put students into small mixed-ability groups, preferably with the same topic, to discuss the Workbook activity on page 159.
- Have the more confident student help the less confident student to list and organize the points to cover.
- After students write a draft, have the more confident student help to use the checklist to improve the text.

At level:

- Have students complete their first draft individually.
- Then have students read aloud their text to a partner. (This will help them to identify anything that needs improving.)
- The partner should use the checklist to check if the text meets all of the requirements. If it doesn't, the partner should offer suggestions to do so. Then they switch roles.
- Ask all students to revise their texts.

Above level:

- Have students write their instructional guide individually, following the steps in the Workbook on page 159.
- Put them into pairs, and ask a partner to read the instructional guide aloud so the student can hear it fresh when someone else is reading it. The partner should then offer suggestions to improve the text. Then they switch roles.
- Finally, all students should revise their text.

Write

- Direct students to the Workbook to plan and write their own instructional guide.

D Present your instructional guide to the class.

- Read the list with the class.
- Give students time to practice reading their texts themselves.
- Encourage them to read carefully, with a good pace.
- Have students practice reading their instructional guide to the class. The class responds with feedback.

Units 15 and 16 Big Question Review

A Watch the video. What things do you see that people are afraid of? ▷

- Play the video and when it is finished ask students what they know about fear now.
- Have students share ideas with the class.

B What are some answers to the Big Question? Talk about them with your partner.

COMMUNICATION

- Display **Discover Poster 8**. Point to familiar vocabulary items and elicit them from the class. Ask *What is this?*
- Ask students *What do you see?* Ask *What does that mean?*
- Refer to all of the learning points written on the poster and have students explain how they relate to the different pictures.
- Ask *What does this learning point mean*? Elicit answers from individual students.
- Display the **Talk About It! Poster** to help students with sentence frames for discussion of the learning points and for expressing their opinions.

C Complete the Big Question Chart. Then discuss it with the class.

- Ask students what they have learned about fear while studying this unit.
- Put students into pairs or small groups to say two new things they have learned.
- Have students share their ideas with the class and add their ideas to the chart.
- Have students complete the chart in their Workbook.

Further practice
Workbook pages 158–161
Online Practice • Wrap Up 8
Oxford **iTools** • Wrap Up 8

In units 17 and 18 you will:

WATCH a video about stories.

LEARN how we use stories to inform and entertain.

READ about different types of stories and a girl's adventure.

WRITE your own story.

PRESENT your story to the class.

BIG QUESTION 9

Why are stories important?

A Watch the video. Then talk about it with your partner.

B Look at the picture and discuss it with your class.
1 What are the girls doing?
2 What kind of book do you think they're reading?

C Think and answer the questions.
1 What is a story?
2 How do people share stories?
3 What's your favorite story?
4 How many types of stories can you think of?

D Discuss this topic with your class. Fill out the **Big Question Chart**.

What do you know about stories? What do you want to know?

170 Big Question 9

171

Reading Strategies
Students will learn about:
- Theme
- Persuasion

Vocabulary
Students will understand and use words about:
- Storytelling

Grammar
Students will review:
- Present and past tenses
- Future forms

Review
Students will review the language and Big Question learning points of Units 17 and 18 through:
- Writing a story

Units 17 and 18
Why are stories important?
Students will understand the Big Question learning points:
- Stories entertain us.
- We use stories to teach valuable lessons.
- Stories give people a way to share their experiences.
- Through stories, we learn about different times and places.
- Stories let us explore imaginary worlds.

Listening Strategies
Students will practice:
- Listening for the main idea
- Listening for gist

Writing Study
Students will use and understand:
- Reporting verbs
- Using numerals
Students will:
- Write a story

Word Study
Students will understand and use:
- Suffix -less
- Heteronyms

Speaking
Students will understand and use expressions for:
- Clarifying what you've said
- Talking about opinions

Units 17 and 18 Big Question page 170

Summary

Objectives: To activate students' existing knowledge of the topic and identify what they would like to learn about the topic.

Materials: Big Question DVD, Discover Poster 9, Big Question Chart

Introducing the topic

- Read out the Big Question. Ask *Why are stories important?*
- Write students' ideas on the board and discuss.

A Watch the video. Then talk about it with your partner.

- Play the video and when it is finished ask students to answer the following questions in pairs:
  What do you see in the video?
  What is happening?
  Who do you think the people are?
  What do you like about the video?
- Have individual students share their answers with the class.

DIFFERENTIATION

Below level:

- After watching, put students into small groups. Have groups discuss and summarize what they saw in the video. Go around and help as needed.
- Then have groups share their summaries with the class. Ask questions to get students to add details to their summaries.

At level:

- After watching, have pairs summarize the video together.
- Then create a class summary of the video, in which all pairs contribute to the summary. Take notes on the board. Ask for details.
- After the summary is complete, have a class discussion

Above level:

- After watching, have pairs summarize the video together.
- Tell them to discuss how the video relates to the unit question *Why are stories important?*
- Have the pairs tell the class their summary and explain how it relates to the unit question.

B Look at the picture and discuss it with your class.

- Students look at the big picture and talk about it. Ask *What do you see?*
- Ask additional questions:
  Where are the girls?
  Why do you think they are there?
  Have you ever been camping?
  What do you do when you go camping? Do you read or tell stories?

C Think and answer the questions.

- Have students discuss the questions in small groups, and then with the class.

CRITICAL THINKING

- Ask students to think about the first question. Ask *Is a fiction novel a story? What about a nonfiction novel? Is a movie a story? Is a newspaper article about a house that caught on fire a story? Is a newspaper article about a political election a story?*
- Ask students to think about the their answer to question three in relation to question four. Ask *What kind of story is your favorite story? Do you have a favorite kind of story?*
- Have students tell their opinions.

Expanding the topic

COLLABORATIVE LEARNING

- Display **Discover Poster 9** and give students enough time to look at the pictures.
- Get students to talk about things you think they will know by pointing to different things in the pictures and asking *What's this? What is happening here?*
- Put students into small groups of three or four. Have each group choose a picture that they find interesting.
- Ask each group to say five sentences about their picture.
- Have one person from each group stand up and read out the sentences they chose for their picture.
- Ask the class if they can add any more.

DIFFERENTIATION

Below level:

- Encourage students to participate using short sentences.
- Point to details in the big picture and on the poster and ask *What's this?* Write the answers on the board.

At level:

- Elicit complete sentences on what students know about why stories are important.
- Write their sentences on the board.

Above level:

- Elicit more detailed responses.
- Have students write their own sentences on the board.

D Discuss this topic with your class. Fill out the Big Question Chart.

- Display the **Big Question Chart**.
- Ask the class *What do you know about why stories are important? What do you want to know?*
- Ask students to write what they know and what they want to know in their Workbooks.
- Write a collection of ideas on the **Big Question Chart**.

Discover Poster 9

1 A grandmother and granddaughter reading together; 2 A teacher explaining a lesson to his students; 3 A girl reading a biography of Albert Einstein; 4 A boy reading a book about Mayan civilization; 5 A boy imagining a furturistic world

Further Practice

Workbook page 162
Online Practice · Big Question 9
Oxford iTools · Big Question 9

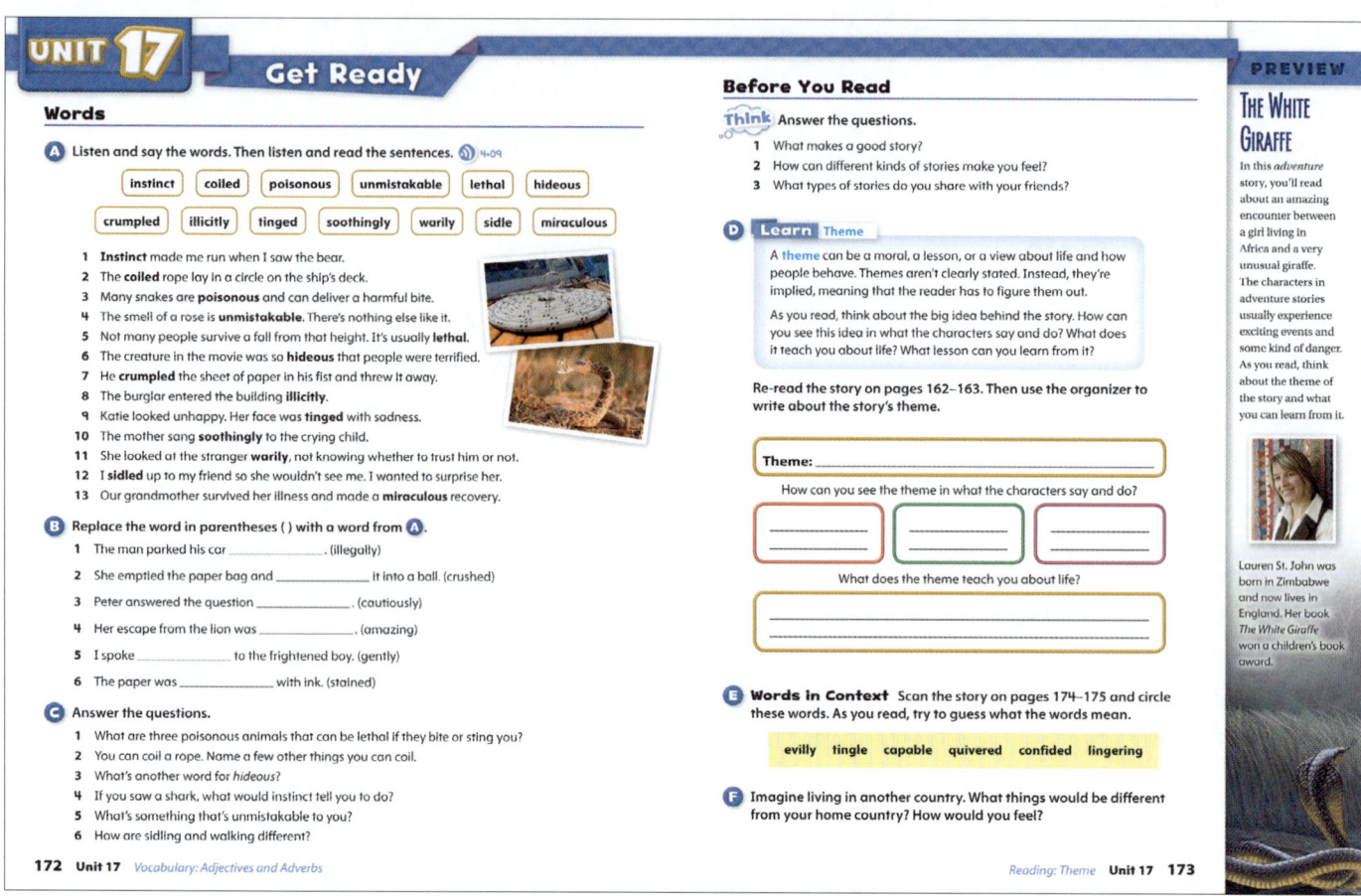

Summary

Objectives: To understand about adjectives and adverbs; to apply own experience and a reading strategy to help comprehension of a text.

Vocabulary: *instinct, coiled, poisonous, unmistakable, lethal, hideous, crumpled, illicitly, tinged, soothingly, warily, sidle, miraculous, evilly, tingle, capable, quivered, confided, lingering*

Reading strategy: Theme

Materials: Audio CD

Words

A Listen and say the words. Then listen and read the sentences. ● 4•09

- Play the audio. Ask students to point to the words and repeat the words when they hear them.
- Have them listen and read the sentences as they hear them. Say the sentence numbers out of order and have the class read the sentences aloud.

CRITICAL THINKING

- Put students into pairs. Have pairs read through the sentences and classify the words according to type: noun, verb, adjective, and adverb.

ANSWERS

Noun: instinct
Verb: crumpled, tinged, sidled
Adjective: coiled, poisonous, unmistakable, lethal, hideous, miraculous
Adverb: illicitly, soothingly, warily

CRITICAL THINKING

- Ask students to guess which adjective could also be used as it is, as a verb.
- Say *Look as the new words.* Ask *What do some of these words make you think of? Guess what you think this story might be about.*
- Write the students' answers on the board.

B Replace the word in parentheses ( ) with a word from A.

- Tell students that the words in parentheses have a similar meaning to one of the words in A.
- Remind them that identifying the type of word (noun, adverb, etc.) can be a clue to the answer. Have students do the activity on their own.
- Ask students to compare their answers with a partner.
- Check answers with the class.

ANSWERS

1 illicitly **2** crumpled **3** warily **4** miraculous
5 soothingly **6** tinged

C Answer the questions.

COLLABORATIVE LEARNING

- Put students into pairs. Have pairs do the activity together.
- Tell them to use a dictionary to help answer the questions.
- For question three, ask students to write a sentence using the word replacement they found for *hideous*.
- For question five, be sure partners each write their own answer.

- For question six, tell students to name an animal that *sidles*.
- Check the answer with the class.

1 snake, bee, spider, shark, scorpion
2 string, wire, hair, yarn, paper
3 ugly, revolting, repulsive, gruesome
4 to swim away, to punch it in the nose, to scream, to freeze with fear
5 my friend's laugh, my mom's voice when she's mad, a song by my favorite singer
6 Sidling is like shuffling sideways, sneaky; walking is moving two feet. A snake or a crab sidles.

Before You Read

Think

- Put students into pairs to discuss the questions.
- Have pairs share their answers with the class. Make notes on the board.

D Learn: Theme

- Read the *Learn* box together.
- Elicit examples from the class. Ask *Are you familiar with any stories that have a theme?*
- If you are familiar with any thematic, popular stories, or movies the class may know, explain as a reference.

Reread the story on pages 162–163. Then use the organizer to write about the story's theme.

- Read the organizer with students. Have them reread the text.
- Then follow one of the approaches below.

Below level:

- Complete the organizer with students by writing it on the board.
- For each box, ask *What can we fill in here?* Have the students raise their hand to offer answers.
- Provide guiding questions for each of the boxes: *What is the theme of the story?* If students can't answer this box, continue to the next four boxes and return to the theme at the end.
- Ask *What did Aroon expect of the sleepover? What happened during the sleepover? What did Aroon learn? What is the lesson of the story?*

At level:

- Put students into pairs to complete the organizer.
- Have pairs compare their organizers in small groups.
- Then have a class discussion and complete an organizer with the entire class.

Above level:

- Have students complete the organizer on their own.
- Have students compare their organizer with a partner.

Theme: Conquering fear / Learning from new experiences
How can you see the theme in what the characters say and do: 1) Aroon is disappointed / scared when sleepover isn't what he expected; 2) Aroon is scared of noises outside; 3) the brothers show him how to experience the country night differently.
What does the theme teach you about life?: To be open to new experiences; to try to look at the world differently

E Words in Context: Scan the story on pages 174–175 and circle these words. As you read, try to guess what the words mean.

- Read each word and have students follow your pronunciation.
- Have students scan the story on pages 174 and 175 and circle the words. Tell them to guess what the words mean from the context.
- Ask the students to share their ideas about the words' definitions.

F Imagine living in another country. What things would be different from your home country? How would you feel?

- Put students into small groups to discuss the questions.
- Go over the groups' answers and make notes on the board.
- Ask students about language, knowing their city, friends, weather, etc.

Reading Preview

- Read the title of the unit's reading text.
- Have students silently read the content of the preview bar.
- Ask *What type of text is this?* Ask *What is this type of text like?* Say *Remember when we learned about fear in Unit 8? Why do you think people like to read about risk or danger?*
- Tell students to think about the theme of the story and what they can learn from it as they read.
- Read the Author Bio with the class. Ask *Where is Zimbabwe located?* If possible, have students identify the country on a map of Africa.

| Further Practice
Workbook pages 162–163
Online Practice Unit 17 • Get Ready
Oxford iTools Unit 17 • Get Ready

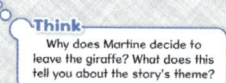

The White Giraffe (story spread, pages 174–175)

Summary

Objectives: To read, understand, and discuss an adventure story (fiction); to apply a reading strategy to improve comprehension.

School subject: Social Studies: Culture

Text type: Adventure (fiction)

Reading strategy: Theme

Big Question learning points: *Stories entertain us. We use stories to teach valuable lessons. Through stories, we learn about different times and places.*

Materials: Talk About It! Poster, Audio CD

Before Reading

- Have students tell you what they see in the picture.
- Have students explain who they think the characters are and what they think will happen. Ask *What do you think the theme will be about?*

During Reading   4·10

- Play the audio one time and have the class read along.

DIFFERENTIATION

Below level:

- Read chunks of the story and have students repeat chunks of it after you.
- While reading, stop to discuss the *Think* boxes.

At level:

- Have students read in small groups, taking turns to read chunks of the story, pausing at the *Think* boxes to discuss.

Above level:

- Put students into pairs. Have them take turns to practice reading fluently.
- One partner reads the story aloud as quickly and fluently as possible, while the other partner marks any words or phrases that were troublesome.
- The first student repeats the phrases he or she had difficulty with. Then they switch turns.

CRITICAL THINKING

- Discuss the *Think* boxes. Read the first *Think* box. Ask *How does Martine feel she and the giraffe are alike?*
- Have students explain and give examples from the story. Say *Read the second* Think *box. Why does Martine decide to leave the giraffe?*

After Reading

CRITICAL THINKING

- Put students into mixed-ability pairs. Have each pair write a summary for the story.
- Explain that the summary should be about five sentences long. One sentence for the intro, three sentences for the action, and one sentence for the closing.
- Have pairs compare their summary with another pair.

- Then work together on a class summary, having the class offer suggestions and agree upon the five-line summary as you take notes on the board.

COMMUNICATION

- Display the **Talk About It! Poster** to help students with sentence frames for discussion and expressing personal opinions.
- Put students into pairs to discuss which part of the story is most interesting.

DIFFERENTIATION

Below level:

- Put students into mixed-ability pairs.
- Have them talk about the parts of the story that were the most interesting, most exciting, and most emotional.
- Have pairs write one sentence for each of those topics.

At level:

- Put students into pairs. Explain that they should discuss what they liked most about the story, liked least, and how they felt about it as an adventure story.

Above level:

- Have students think about these questions:
  What may have happened to Martine's parents?
  Why might she have snuck into the game reserve?
  What is your opinion of Martine's feeling that she understood what Jemmy was thinking?
- Put students into pairs to compare their answers.
- Have pairs share their ideas with the class.

CULTURE NOTE

This episode from the novel, *The White Giraffe,* occurs early in the story, after Martine is getting settled into her new home. On this night, she sneaks into the game reserve to find the white giraffe that is rumored to exist.

After this initial encounter with the giraffe, Martine meets Jemmy again at night. They overhear poachers talking about Jemmy, and Martine rides him to escape.

A few nights later, she meets a local medicine woman who gives her healing herbs.

Next, the medicine woman tells her that the poachers took Jemmy. From a classmate, Martine learns that Jemmy may be in a ship that belongs to the classmate's father.

They sneak in and find an injured Jemmy. Martine uses the healing herbs she got from the medicine woman to heal Jemmy. Then they ride back to the game reserve and police capture the poachers.

Further Practice
Workbook page 164
Online Practice Unit 17 • Read
Oxford **iTools Unit 17 • Read**

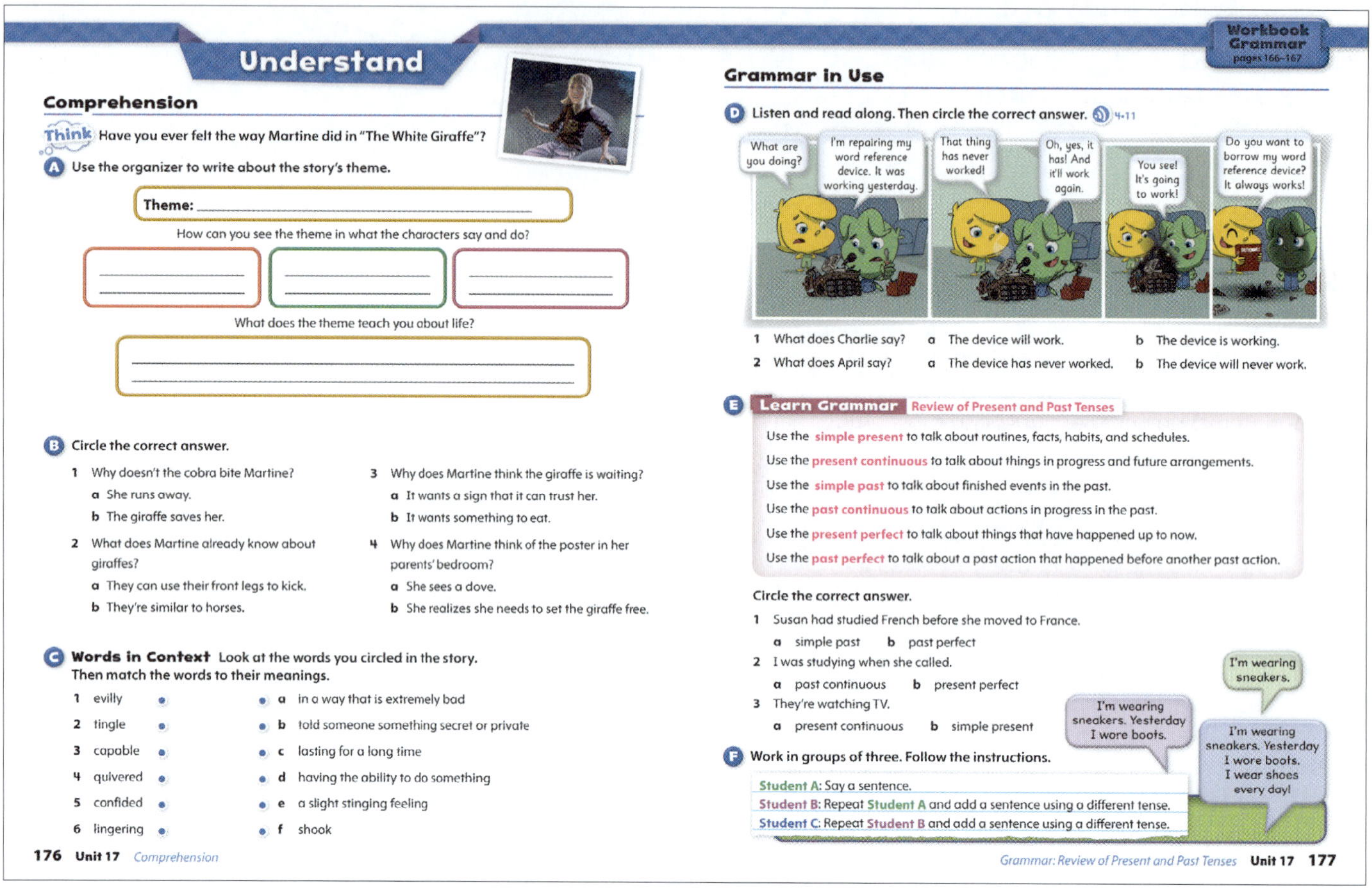

Understand

Comprehension

Think Have you ever felt the way Martine did in "The White Giraffe"?

A Use the organizer to write about the story's theme.

Theme: _____

How can you see the theme in what the characters say and do?

_____ _____ _____

What does the theme teach you about life?

_____

B Circle the correct answer.

1 Why doesn't the cobra bite Martine?
   a She runs away.
   b The giraffe saves her.

2 What does Martine already know about giraffes?
   a They can use their front legs to kick.
   b They're similar to horses.

3 Why does Martine think the giraffe is waiting?
   a It wants a sign that it can trust her.
   b It wants something to eat.

4 Why does Martine think of the poster in her parents' bedroom?
   a She sees a dove.
   b She realizes she needs to set the giraffe free.

C **Words in Context** Look at the words you circled in the story. Then match the words to their meanings.

1 evilly • • a in a way that is extremely bad
2 tingle • • b told someone something secret or private
3 capable • • c lasting for a long time
4 quivered • • d having the ability to do something
5 confided • • e a slight stinging feeling
6 lingering • • f shook

176 **Unit 17** *Comprehension*

Grammar in Use

D Listen and read along. Then circle the correct answer. 4-11

What are you doing? | I'm repairing my word reference device. It was working yesterday. | That thing has never worked! | Oh, yes, it has! And it'll work again. | You see! It's going to work! | Do you want to borrow my word reference device? It always works!

1 What does Charlie say?   a The device will work.   b The device is working.
2 What does April say?   a The device has never worked.   b The device will never work.

E **Learn Grammar** Review of Present and Past Tenses

Use the **simple present** to talk about routines, facts, habits, and schedules.
Use the **present continuous** to talk about things in progress and future arrangements.
Use the **simple past** to talk about finished events in the past.
Use the **past continuous** to talk about actions in progress in the past.
Use the **present perfect** to talk about things that have happened up to now.
Use the **past perfect** to talk about a past action that happened before another past action.

Circle the correct answer.

1 Susan had studied French before she moved to France.
   a simple past   b past perfect
2 I was studying when she called.
   a past continuous   b present perfect
3 They're watching TV.
   a present continuous   b simple present

F Work in groups of three. Follow the instructions.

Student A: Say a sentence.
Student B: Repeat Student A and add a sentence using a different tense.
Student C: Repeat Student B and add a sentence using a different tense.

I'm wearing sneakers.

I'm wearing sneakers. Yesterday I wore boots.

I'm wearing sneakers. Yesterday I wore boots. I wear shoes every day!

Grammar: Review of Present and Past Tenses **Unit 17** 177

Summary

Objectives: To demonstrate understanding of an adventure story; to understand the meaning and form of the grammar structure.

Reading: Comprehension

Grammar input: Review of present and past tenses

Grammar practice: Workbook exercises

Grammar production: Using different tenses

Materials: Audio CD

Comprehension

Think

- Read the question with the class. Ask students to think about their answer.
- Put students into groups to discuss their answers.
- Have groups share their answers.

A Use the organizer to write about the story's theme.

- Have students reread the adventure story. Ask them to fill in the organizer.

ANSWERS

Theme: Love / friendship / loneliness

How can you see the theme in what the characters say and do? giraffe saves Martine; Martine feels she understands the giraffe; Martine must leave the giraffe to earn his friendship

What does the theme teach you about life?: If you love something, set it free

DIFFERENTIATION

Below level:

- Put students into mixed-ability pairs.
- Have the more confident student help the less confident student to fill out the organizer.
- The students should turn back to pages 174 and 175 where the more confident student helps the less confident student find the answers. Remind them they can refer to the five-line summaries they made to help complete the three boxes about the characters' actions.

At level:

- Have students fill in the organizer individually.
- Remind students they can refer to the five-line summaries they made to help complete the three boxes about the characters' actions.
- Then put students into small groups to compare their organizers.

Above level:

- Have students fill in the organizer individually.
- Students then compare their organizers in small groups.
- Then each group comes to the board to write their best version of the organizer.
- Have the class discuss and choose the best organizer.

B Circle the correct answer.

- Have students answer the questions individually.
- Ask them to compare their answers with a partner.
- Then check answers with the class.

ANSWERS
1 b   2 a   3 a   4 b

C Words in Context: Look at the words you circled in the story. Then match the words to their meanings.

- Have students go back and find the circled words in the story.
- Tell them to use the words and context clues to match the words to the meanings.
- Check answers with the class.

ANSWERS
1 a   2 e   3 d   4 f   5 b   6 c

COLLABORATIVE LEARNING

- In pairs, ask students to collaborate to write new sentences for the words in context. Tell them to leave a blank where the word goes.
- Ask pairs to switch papers with another pair to complete each other's sentences. Then they check each other's work.
- Have some pairs say their sentences for the class.

Grammar in Use

D Listen and read along. Then circle the correct answer. 🎧 4•11

- Listen to the dialogue once and have students read along.
- Then have students read the questions and circle the correct answers.
- Play the audio again and have students check their answers.
- Check the answers with the class.

ANSWERS
1 a   2 a

E Learn Grammar: Review of Present and Past Tenses

- Read the *Learn Grammar* box together.

Circle the correct answer.

- Have students complete the activity individually.
- Then have students compare answers with a partner.

ANSWERS
1 b   2 a   3 a

CRITICAL THINKING

- Put students into pairs. Have each pair write one sentence for each verb tense. Tell them to refer to the *Learn Grammar* box, but ask them not to write the sentences in the same order as the box.
- Have pairs switch papers with another pair. They underline the verbs, and identify and write the verb tense for each sentence.
- The original pair then checks that the work is correct.
- Ask some pairs for their sentence examples.

F Work in groups of three. Follow the instructions.

- Read the chart and model the dialogue with two students.
- Put students into groups of three to do the activity.
- Have a few groups say their sentences for the class.
- Ask the class to identify each verb tense when the group has finished speaking.

Workbook

- Direct students to the Workbook for further practice.

Further practice
Workbook pages 165–167
Online Practice Unit 17 • Understand
Oxford **iTools** Unit 17 • Understand

Summary

Objectives: To learn and practice listening, speaking, and writing strategies to facilitate effective communication.

Vocabulary: *hopeless, weightless, airless, restless, toothless, meaningless, helpless, thoughtless*

Listening strategy: Listening for the main idea

Speaking: Clarifying what you've said

Word Study: Suffix *-less*

Writing Study: Reporting verbs

Big Question learning points: *Stories entertain us. We use stories to teach valuable lessons. Through stories, we learn about different times and places.*

Materials: Discover Poster 9, Audio CD, Big Question Chart

Listening

Think

• Tell students to think about the question. Explain that they should also think of other stories that teach lessons, e.g. fables they may know *The Tortoise and the Hare*. The lesson is: slow and steady wins the race.

• After students have thought about the question on their own, put them into pairs to compare answers.

• Then hold a class discussion about lessons that stories teach us. Ask *What are some ways stories teach us lessons? What are some examples of stories with lessons? What are the lessons?*

A Listen. Check (✓) the main idea. ⊙ 4•12

• Have students read the sentences first. Then ask *What are you listening for in this activity?*

• Play the audio once and have students listen.

• Tell students to check the correct answer. Then play the audio again so they can check their work.

ANSWERS

If you lie then no one will believe you, even when you tell the truth.

B Listen again. Answer the questions. ⊙ 4•13

• Have students read the questions first to preview them.

• Play the audio so students can complete the activity.

• Have students compare answers with a partner before checking answers with the class.

ANSWERS

1 Ahmed lives in the mountains in Jordan.
2 People are afraid of the lynx.
3 People run away.
4 People are furious.
5 Ahmed's father tells him never to do it again.
6 People never believed Ahmed once they found out he was lying.

Speaking 🔊 4·14

C Learn: Clarifying What You've Said

- Read the *Learn* box and the dialogue.

Choose one of these topics or think of your own. Then discuss it with your partner. Clarify anything you've said that your partner doesn't understand.

- Play the audio one time as students listen.
- Model the dialogue with a confident student in front of the class.
- Explain *To clarify what you've said, you rephrase it, which means to say it again in a different way or explain it further.* Ask *What are some situations in which you might need to clarify what you've said?*
- Put students into pairs and tell them to use one of the topics in the book and have a conversation that includes clarifying what you've said.
- Then have students find a new partner and talk about a different topic from the list. Switch until everyone has conversed on several different topics.

COMMUNICATION

- Put students into pairs. Tell them to choose one of the topics from the list. Tell them to choose a position: They either like, e.g. the movie, or they don't like the movie.
- Have students repeat the conversation, this time approaching the same subject from two different viewpoints.
- Ask a few pairs to demonstrate their conversation for the class.

Word Study

D Learn: Suffix *-less*

- Read the *Learn* box together.
- Ask *How was she waiting? What does that mean?*

Listen and write to make each noun an adjective. Then work with your partner to write a sentence for each adjective. 🔊 4·15

- Play the audio and ask students to listen to the words.
- Have them make each noun into an adjective.
- Put students into pairs and ask them to write a sentence for each adjective.
- Check answers with the class.

ANSWERS

1 hopeless 2 weightless 3 airless 4 restless
5 toothless 6 meaningless 7 helpless 8 thoughtless

DIFFERENTIATION

Below level:

- Say the words and have students repeat them.
- Have students find the meanings of the words in a dictionary. Go over the meanings.
- Use the words in a sentence and have students spell the correct word.

At level:

- Put students into pairs. Have them write sentences for each of the words.
- Then pairs check another pair's work.

Above level:

- Have students write sentences using the words, but leaving a blank where the word goes.
- Students trade papers with a partner and complete each other's sentences.

Writing Study

E Learn: Reporting Words

- Read the *Learn* box together.
- Ask questions to check understanding:
  What is an example of a more common word that "confided" is replacing?
  Which of the other example words in the box could we use instead of "confided?"

Use the reporting verbs in the box to complete the sentences.

- Have students do the activity individually.
- Check the answers with the class.

ANSWERS

1 reminded 2 agreed 3 offered
4 suggested 5 explained

CRITICAL THINKING

- Hold a class discussion about reporting verbs.
- Say *Look at the example in the presentation box. "I'm alone too, Martine confided to the giraffe." Why is "confided" a better word choice than "said?"*
- Prompt *How does that word change the relationship of Martine to the giraffe?*

Write

- Direct students to the Workbook for further practice.

Big Question 9 Review

Why are stories important?

- Display **Discover Poster 9**. Discuss what you see.
- Refer to the learning points covered in Unit 17 that are written on the poster and have students explain how they relate to the different pictures.
- Return to the **Big Question Chart**.
- Ask students what they have learned about stories while studying this unit.

Further practice
Workbook pages 168–169
Online Practice Unit 17 • Communicate
Oxford **iTools** Unit 17 • Communicate

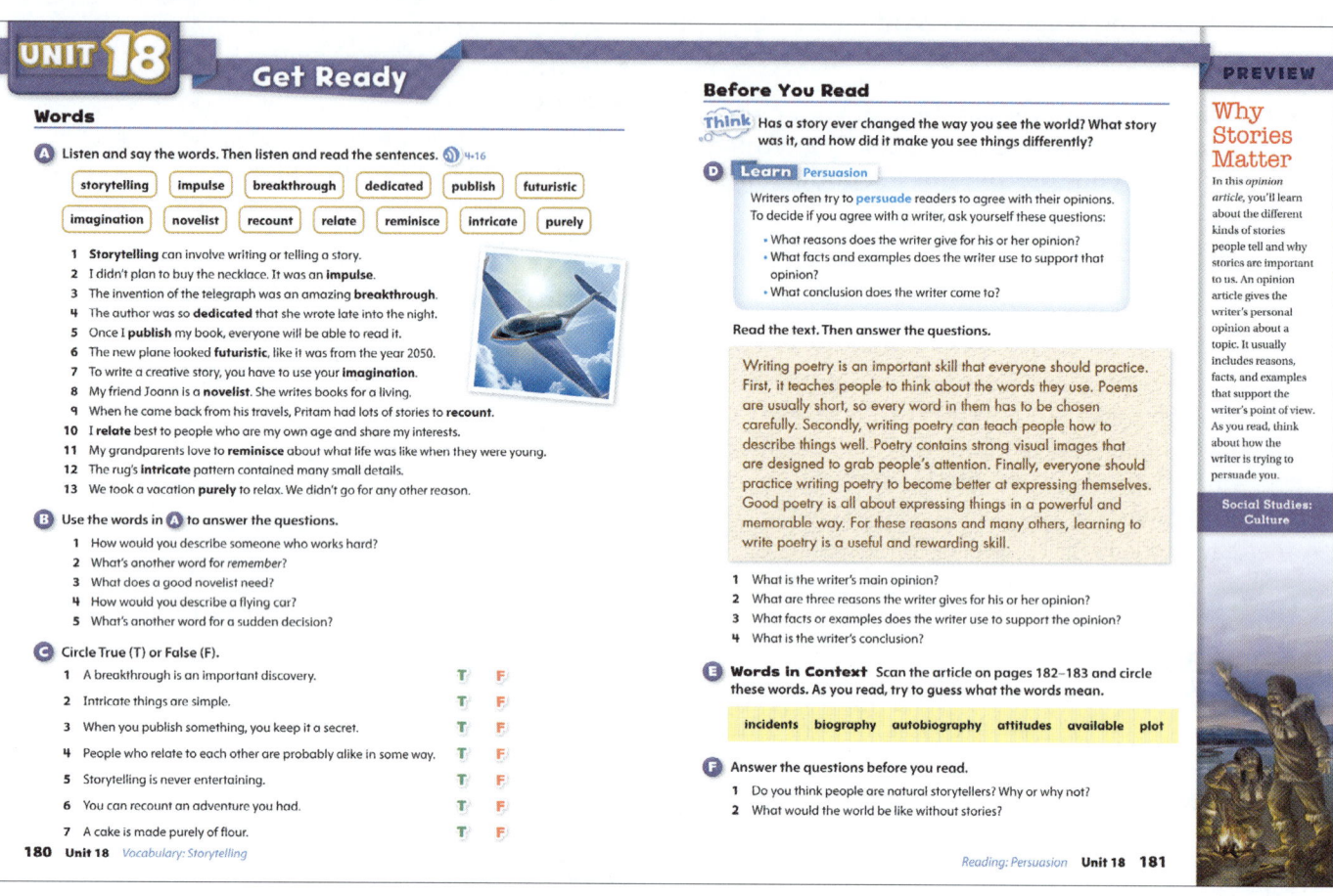

Summary

Objectives: To understand words about storytelling; to apply own experience and a reading strategy to help comprehension of a text.

Vocabulary: *storytelling, impulse, breakthrough, dedicated, publish, futuristic, imagination, novelist, recount, relate, reminisce, intricate, purely, incidents, biography, autobiography, attitudes, available, plot*

Reading strategy: Persuasion

Materials: Audio CD

Words

A Listen and say the words. Then listen and read the sentences. 4•16

- Play the audio. Ask students to point to the words and repeat the words when they hear them.
- Then have students listen and read the sentences as they hear them.
- Say the sentence numbers out of order and have the class read the sentences aloud.

B Use the words in A to answer the questions.

- Have students do the activity on their own and then compare answers with a partner.
- Check answers with the class.

ANSWERS

1 dedicated   2 reminisce   3 imagination
4 futuristic   5 impulse

COLLABORATIVE LEARNING

- Put students into small groups and tell them to discuss the meaning of the words. Any words the group doesn't understand or can't approximate a definition of, they should look up in a dictionary and then use in a sentence.
- Have a group discussion of the words.
- Call on groups to say definitions and to use the words in sentences to check understanding.

C Circle True (T) or False (F).

- Have students read the words and circle T for true or F for false.
- After students have completed the activity, they check answers with a partner and then correct the false sentences.
- Check the answers with the class.

ANSWERS

1 T   2 F (intricate things are detailed / complex.)
3 F (you tell people about it / broadcast it)   4 T
5 F (often / usually)   6 T   7 F (There are many ingredients in cake, not just flour.)

Before You Read

Think

- Have students read the questions and make notes about their answers individually. Provide an example from your own life, e.g. *When I read the (name of novel), it made me aware of (issue / theme).*
- Students discuss their answers to the questions in small groups. Go around and help.
- Then share some of the answers with the class. If students don't offer any examples, then ask about familiar and popular stories or movies and elicit information using those examples.

D Learn: Persuasion

- Read the *Learn* box with the class.
- Ask questions check understanding:
  What does it mean to persuade someone?
  What does an opinion need to support it?

Read the text. Then answer the questions.

Below level:

- Put students into mixed-ability pairs.
- Ask them to read the paragraph.
- Have them underline the reasons and circle the facts or examples. Tell them to draw a box around the opinion and conclusion.
- Ask the pairs to answer the questions.
- Have the pairs talk about their answers.

At level:

- Have students read the text individually.
- Tell them to underline the reasons and circle the facts or examples. Tell them to draw a box around the opinion and conclusion.
- Ask the students to answer the questions individually.
- Put students into pairs to talk about their answers.

Above level:

- Have students read the text individually.
- Ask them to answer the questions.
- Then put students into pairs to compare their work.
- Have a student write some of the answers on the board for the class to compare to their own.

1 Writer's opinion: Everyone should practice writing poetry.
2 Reason 1: It teaches people to think about words they use; Reason 2: It can teach people to describe things well; Reason 3: You can become better at expressing yourself
3 Fact 1: Every word must be carefully chosen because poems are short; Fact 2: visual images; Fact 3: expressing in a powerful and memorable way
4 Writer's conclusion: for these reasons and others, writing poetry is a useful and rewarding skill

Ask the following questions to discuss persuasion:

- *Do the facts or examples support the reasons?*
- *Do you agree that writing poetry is a useful and rewarding skill? Why or why not? Support your opinion with facts and reasons.*

E Words in Context: Scan the article on pages 182–183 and circle these words. As you read, try to guess what the words mean.

- Read each word and have students follow your pronunciation.
- Put students into pairs to go over the words in context together.
- Discuss the meanings of the words with the class.

F Answer the questions before you read.

- Have students think about their answers to the questions on their own.
- Then have students discuss the questions in small groups.
- Remind them to use facts and reasons to support their ideas and opinions.
- Hold a class discussion. Ask students for facts and reasons to support their ideas and opinions if they don't offer them.

Reading Preview

- Read the title of the unit's reading text.
- Have students silently read the content of the preview bar.
- Ask *What type of text is it?* Ask *What do you find in an opinion essay?*
- Tell students to try to think about how the writer is trying to persuade them as they read.

Further Practice
Workbook pages 170–171
Online Practice Unit 18 • Get Ready
Oxford iTools Unit 18 • Get Ready

The reading article "Why Stories Matter" appears on pages 182–183 of the student book.

Summary

Objectives: To read, understand, and discuss an opinion article; to apply a reading strategy to improve comprehension.

School subject: Social Studies: Culture

Text type: Opinion article (nonfiction)

Reading strategy: Persuasion

Big Question learning points: *Stories entertain us. We use stories to teach valuable lessons. Stories give people a way to share their experiences. Through stories, we learn about different times and places. Stories let us explore imaginary worlds.*

Materials: Talk About It! Poster, Audio CD

Before Reading

- Read the title.
- Have students point to the pictures and describe what they see. Have students read the subheads.
- Ask students to try to predict how the text will explain why stories matter. Take notes on their answers on the board.

During Reading ⊚ 4·17

- With the class, read the first paragraph and discuss the *Think* box. Say *What is the writer trying to persuade you to think or feel?*
- Remind students that they should think about the writer's facts, reasons, and examples to support this opinion.
- Play the audio. Students listen as they read along.
- Play the audio a second time if necessary.

Below level:

- Have students repeat after you as you read chunks of the article aloud.
- Have them read as a group, aiming for a fast, fluent speed.
- Read along with them softly to set the pace.

At level:

- Have students read the article silently to themselves one time.
- Put students into pairs and ask them to read aloud in unison.

Above level:

- Have students read the article individually.
- Put students into pairs and have them take turns reading sections to each other.

Discussion questions about the article:

- *Consider the structure of the essay: Where do we find the opinion?*
- *Where do we find the facts that support the opinion?*
- *Why do you think "Other Ways to Share Stories" comes close to the end?*

After Reading

- Go over the second *Think* box with the class. Ask *What facts or opinions does the writer use to support his or her opinion?*

CRITICAL THINKING

Put students into small groups to discuss the following:

- *Which of the mentioned examples of storytelling impulse do you think are the strongest? For instance, is a comic book as much of a story as a blog? How about an autobiography? Support your opinion with examples.*

COLLABORATIVE LEARNING

- Display the **Talk About It! Poster** to help students with sentence frames for discussion and expressing personal opinions.

- Put students into pairs to discuss what they find interesting about why stories are important.

- Ask students if they think differently about why stories are important now. What did they think about why stories are important before reading? What do they think now?

CULTURE NOTE

Oral storytelling is an ancient tradition, which existed in most cultures. It was a more intimate way of sharing stories because the storyteller and the listeners were physically close.

In many cultures, stories were treasured and kept by the elders in each tribe or group. The elders would pass the stories down to the next generation and this would continue, year after year.

The Australian Aboriginal people have a long tradition of oral storytelling, which forms a strong basis for their culture. They share Dreamtime Stories. These stories use myths to explain the origin of nature and encourage a close relationship and appreciation of the land.

Oral storytelling not only passes on important cultural truths down through the generations, but also transmits information about the people and landscape as they existed thousands and thousands of years ago. Since no books or written documents date back that long ago, oral storytelling was the primary way to share and teach. There are Australian Aboriginal stories, which describe whole rivers or lakes as being dry land, for example, and geological research has shown that this would have been true 10,000 years ago.

Further Practice
Workbook page 172
Online Practice Unit 18 • Read
Oxford iTools Unit 18 • Read

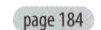

The reproduced student-book spread:

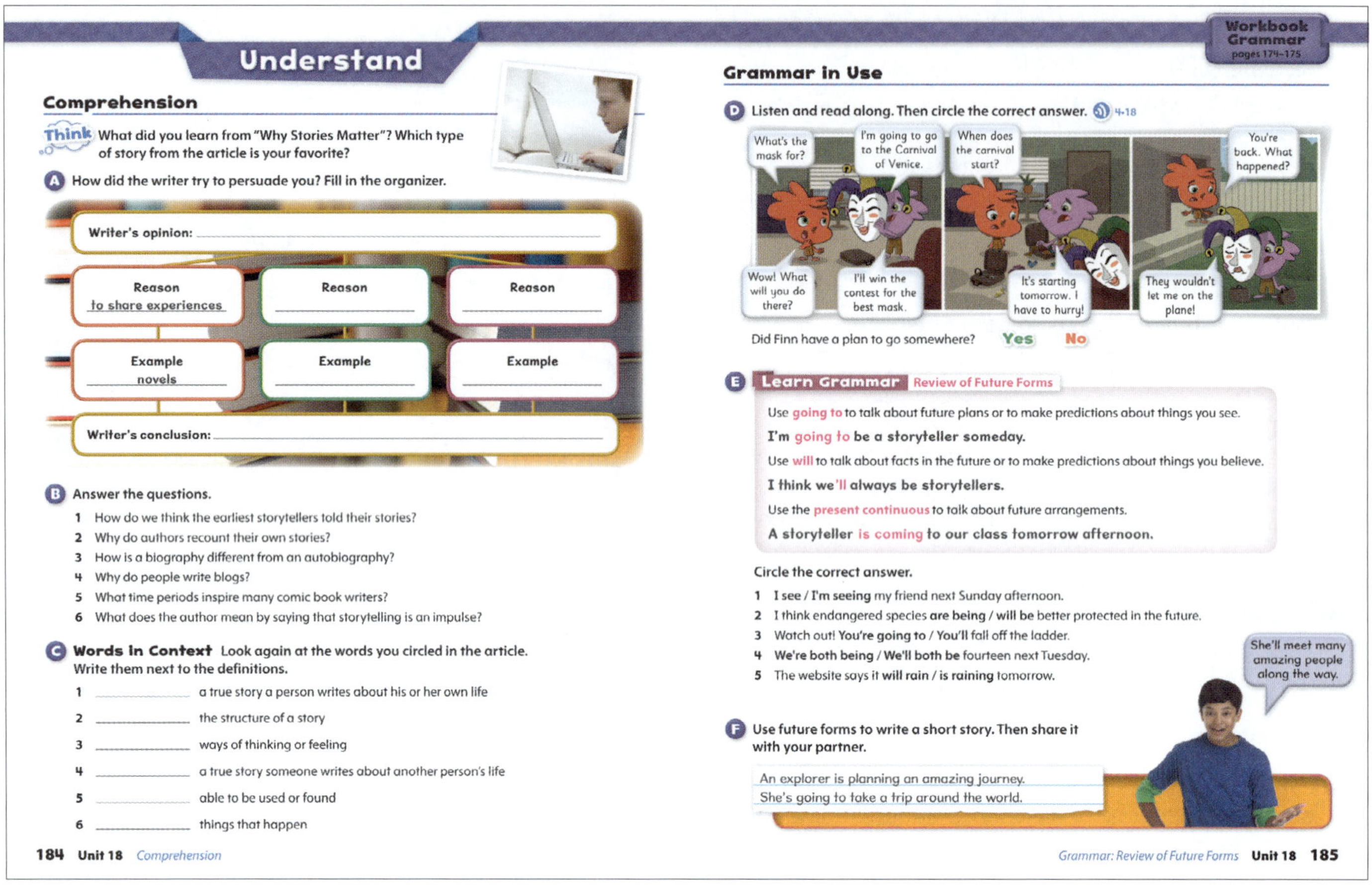

Understand

Comprehension

Think What did you learn from "Why Stories Matter"? Which type of story from the article is your favorite?

A How did the writer try to persuade you? Fill in the organizer.

Writer's opinion: _____

| Reason to share experiences | Reason _____ | Reason _____ |
| Example novels | Example _____ | Example _____ |

Writer's conclusion: _____

B Answer the questions.
1 How do we think the earliest storytellers told their stories?
2 Why do authors recount their own stories?
3 How is a biography different from an autobiography?
4 Why do people write blogs?
5 What time periods inspire many comic book writers?
6 What does the author mean by saying that storytelling is an impulse?

C **Words in Context** Look again at the words you circled in the article. Write them next to the definitions.
1 _____ a true story a person writes about his or her own life
2 _____ the structure of a story
3 _____ ways of thinking or feeling
4 _____ a true story someone writes about another person's life
5 _____ able to be used or found
6 _____ things that happen

184 Unit 18 *Comprehension*

Grammar in Use

Workbook Grammar pages 174–175

D Listen and read along. Then circle the correct answer. 4-18

What's the mask for? / I'm going to go to the Carnival of Venice. / When does the carnival start? / You're back. What happened?
Wow! What will you do there? / I'll win the contest for the best mask. / It's starting tomorrow. I have to hurry! / They wouldn't let me on the plane!

Did Finn have a plan to go somewhere? **Yes** **No**

E **Learn Grammar** Review of Future Forms

Use **going to** to talk about future plans or to make predictions about things you see.
I'm going to be a storyteller someday.
Use **will** to talk about facts in the future or to make predictions about things you believe.
I think we'll always be storytellers.
Use the **present continuous** to talk about future arrangements.
A storyteller **is coming** to our class tomorrow afternoon.

Circle the correct answer.
1 I see / I'm seeing my friend next Sunday afternoon.
2 I think endangered species **are being / will be** better protected in the future.
3 Watch out! You're going to / You'll fall off the ladder.
4 We're both being / We'll both be fourteen next Tuesday.
5 The website says it will rain / is raining tomorrow.

She'll meet many amazing people along the way.

F Use future forms to write a short story. Then share it with your partner.

An explorer is planning an amazing journey.
She's going to take a trip around the world.

Grammar: Review of Future Forms Unit 18 185

Summary

Objectives: To demonstrate understanding of an opinion article; to understand the meaning and form of the grammar structure.

Reading: Comprehension

Grammar input: Review of future forms

Grammar practice: Workbook exercises

Grammar production: Future forms

Materials: Audio CD

Comprehension

Think
- Model your own example, e.g. *I think that biographies are my favorite type of story. I like when another writer can bring a new perspective to the person the biography was written about.*
- Have students think about their answers individually first.
- Hold a class discussion. Ask students for examples to support their opinions.

A How did the writer try to persuade you? Fill in the organizer.
- Have students reread the essay on pages 182–183. Ask them to fill in the organizer.
- Check answers with the class.

POSSIBLE ANSWERS
Writer's opinion: Humans are natural storytellers.
Reason 1: People want to share their experience, e.g. novels

Reason 2: People are helping others to learn about cultures, attitudes, thoughts, feelings, e.g. blogs
Reason 3: People want to connect with each other, e.g. news
Example 1: novels
Example 2: biographies / autobiographies
Example 3: blogs / comic books
Writer's conclusion: Humans will always be natural storytellers.

DIFFERENTIATION

Below level:
- Skim the text together and help students to identify the reasons and examples. Tell them to underline the reasons in their books.
- Put students into mixed-ability pairs to complete the organizers.

At level:
- Have students fill in their organizers individually.
- Then have them discuss the organizers with a partner.
- Have pairs tell the class about their organizers.

Above level:
- Have students fill in their organizers individually.
- Then have them discuss their organizer with a partner.
- Invite a few students to the board to complete the organizers for the class to check their work.
- As the class checks the work together, have the students explain their organizer to the class.

B Answer the questions.

- Have students refer back to the article on pages 182 and 183 to answer the questions on their own.
- Then have students compare answers with a partner.
- Check the answers with the class.

1 The earliest storytellers probably used music, dance, and other art forms.
2 Because they want to share their experiences.
3 A biography is written about someone else; an autobiography is written by the author about himself / herself.
4 Because they have an impulse to share their stories.
5 Historical or futuristic time periods.
6 By saying it is an impulse, the author means that we are compelled to do it.

C Words in Context: Look again at the words you circled in the article. Write them next to the definitions.

- Read the instructions. Tell students to go back and find the words in the article and to use the context clues to help them figure out the answers.
- Students compare answers with a partner.
- Check the answers with the class.

ANSWERS

1 autobiography 2 plot 3 attitudes 4 biography
5 available 6 incidents

Grammar in Use

D Listen and read along. Then circle the correct answer. 🔊 4•18

- Listen to the dialogue once and then read it together as a class.
- Check the answer with the class.

ANSWER
Yes

COLLABORATIVE LEARNING

- Put students into pairs.
- Have pairs underline the verbs in the dialogue and identify if they are future or past.
- Then have pairs write the sentences on the board, underlining the verbs and writing the verb tense for the class to check.

E Learn Grammar: Review of Future Forms

- Read the *Learn Grammar* box together.
- Read the example sentences. Ask this question to check understanding: *What is the difference between a future prediction and a future arrangement?*

Circle the correct answer.

- Have students complete the activity on their own.
- Check the answers with the class.

ANSWERS

1 I'm seeing 2 will be 3 You're going to
4 We'll both be 5 will rain

CRITICAL THINKING

- Put students into pairs.
- Tell them to rewrite sentences one and two so that they are correct for the incorrect words choices. This will change the meaning of the sentences. They may need to modify other words in the sentence for it to be correct, e.g. *I see my friend every Sunday afternoon.*
- Check answers with the class.

ANSWERS

1 I see my friend every Sunday afternoon.
2 I think endangered species are being better protected now (than they were in the past).

F Use future forms to write a short story. Then share it with your partner.

CREATIVITY

- Have students write sentences using future forms in their notebooks, as in the example.
- Have students join the sentences together to make a short story.
- Put students into small groups and have them take turns to share their stories with each other.
- Have one or two students share their stories with the class.

DIFFERENTIATION

Below level:

- Put students into mixed-ability pairs.
- Have pairs first make a list of topics in the future to discuss, e.g. *Next year, next summer, when you're older…,* etc.
- Then have the more confident student help the less confident student to ask questions. Go around and help.
- Have students share their sentences with the class.

At level:

- Have students practice future conversations with three partners.

Above level:

- Have students each think of their answers to the questions: *What are you going to do next weekend? Where are you going to be next summer? What do you want to do when you are older?*
- Students then circulate and talk to at least three people about their future plans using the questions above.
- After all students have had a chance to ask and answer questions, they return to their seats.
- Ask the class for answers about the students, e.g. *What is Asha going to do next weekend?* Students who've spoken to Asha put up their hands to answer.

Workbook Grammar

- Direct students to the Workbook for further practice.

Further practice
Workbook pages 173–175
Online Practice Unit 18 • Understand
Oxford iTools Unit 18 • Understand

Communicate

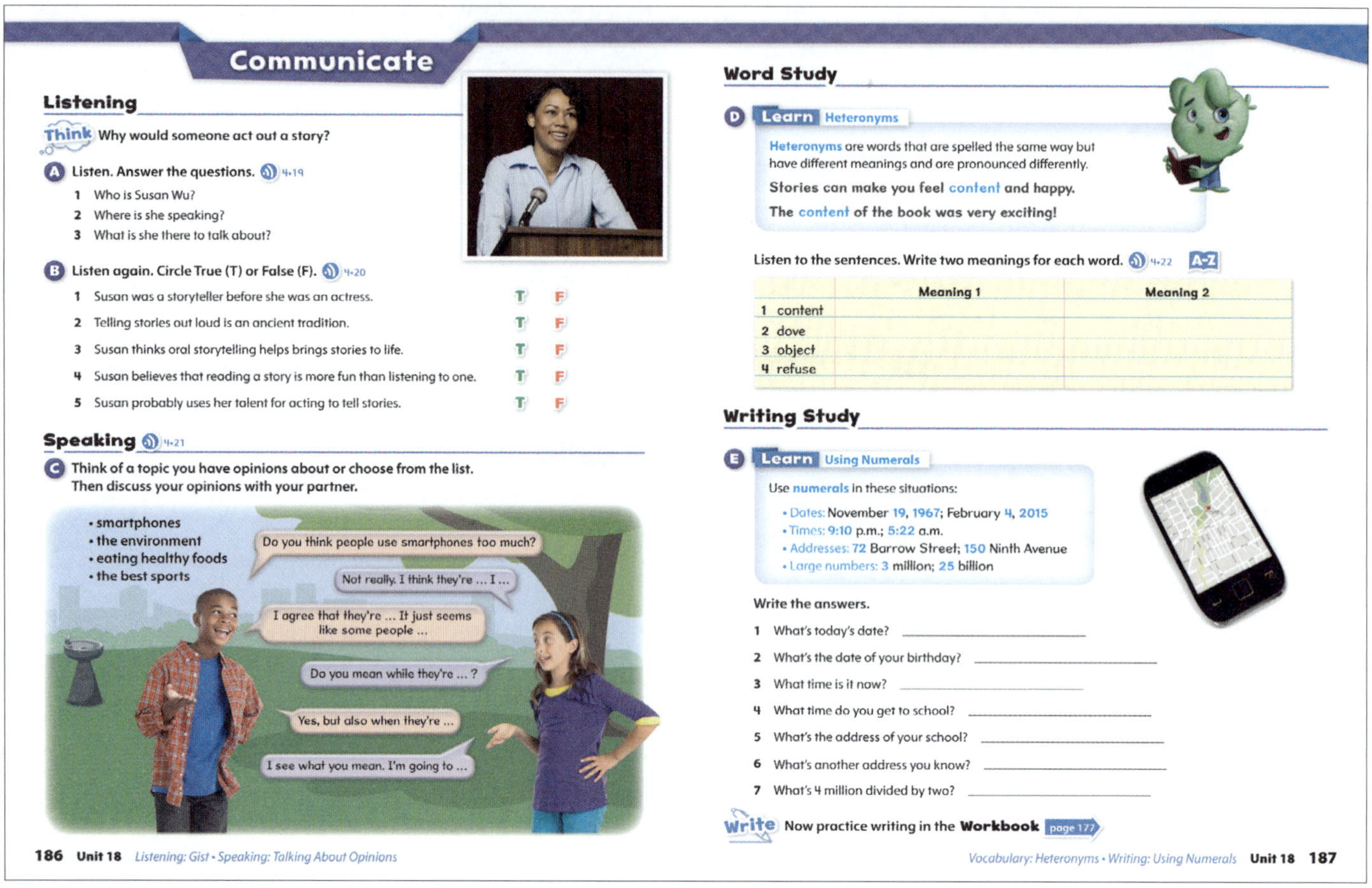

Listening

Think Why would someone act out a story?

A Listen. Answer the questions. 🔊 4•19
1 Who is Susan Wu?
2 Where is she speaking?
3 What is she there to talk about?

B Listen again. Circle True (T) or False (F). 🔊 4•20
1 Susan was a storyteller before she was an actress.   T   F
2 Telling stories out loud is an ancient tradition.   T   F
3 Susan thinks oral storytelling helps brings stories to life.   T   F
4 Susan believes that reading a story is more fun than listening to one.   T   F
5 Susan probably uses her talent for acting to tell stories.   T   F

Speaking 🔊 4•21

C Think of a topic you have opinions about or choose from the list. Then discuss your opinions with your partner.

- smartphones
- the environment
- eating healthy foods
- the best sports

Do you think people use smartphones too much?

Not really. I think they're … I …

I agree that they're … It just seems like some people …

Do you mean while they're … ?

Yes, but also when they're …

I see what you mean. I'm going to …

Word Study

D **Learn** Heteronyms

Heteronyms are words that are spelled the same way but have different meanings and are pronounced differently.
Stories can make you feel content and happy.
The content of the book was very exciting!

Listen to the sentences. Write two meanings for each word. 🔊 4•22   A-Z

	Meaning 1	Meaning 2
1 content		
2 dove		
3 object		
4 refuse		

Writing Study

E **Learn** Using Numerals

Use numerals in these situations:
- Dates: November 19, 1967; February 4, 2015
- Times: 9:10 p.m.; 5:22 a.m.
- Addresses: 72 Barrow Street; 150 Ninth Avenue
- Large numbers: 3 million; 25 billion

Write the answers.
1 What's today's date? _____
2 What's the date of your birthday? _____
3 What time is it now? _____
4 What time do you get to school? _____
5 What's the address of your school? _____
6 What's another address you know? _____
7 What's 4 million divided by two? _____

Write Now practice writing in the **Workbook** page 177

Summary

Objectives: To learn and practice listening, speaking, and writing strategies to facilitate effective communication.

Vocabulary: *content, dove, object, refuse*

Listening strategy: Listening for gist

Speaking: Talking about opinions

Word Study: Heteronyms

Writing Study: Using numerals

Big Question learning point: *Stories entertain us.*

Materials: Audio CD

Listening

Think

- Tell students to think individually about why someone would act out a story.
- Additionally ask *Have you ever acted out a story? Did you enjoy it? Why or why not?*
- Have students share their ideas with a partner.
- Ask students to tell the class their ideas and write them on the board.

A Listen. Answer the questions. 🔊 4•19

- Have students read the questions and then listen for the answers.
- Play the audio once and have students listen. Ask *What will you listen for?*
- Have students complete the activity.
- Play the audio again so they can check their work.

ANSWERS
1 A professional storyteller   2 at a school   3 She is there to talk about how she got into storytelling.

B Listen again. Circle True (T) or False (F). 🔊 4•20

- Play the audio so students can complete the activity.
- Have them check their answers in pairs before checking answers with the class.

ANSWERS
1 F   2 T   3 T   4 F   5 T

CRITICAL THINKING

After checking the answers, ask additional questions:
- *What kind of school did Susan go to?*
- *What can you do when you act out a story?*
- *What does that mean?*
- *Why do people pay more attention when watching a storyteller?*

Speaking 💿 4•21

C Think of a topic you have opinions about or choose from the list. Then discuss your opinions with your partner.

- Read the directions. Then play the audio and have students listen.
- Model an example with a volunteer. Then model it a second time using a different example and a different student.
- Put students into pairs to practice the dialogue. When they have completed the dialogue once, tell them to switch topics and roles. Go around and help as needed.
- Have a few pairs say their dialogues for the class.

Word Study

D Learn: Heteronyms

- Read the *Learn* box together. Read the examples.
- Write two sentences on the board: *The dog stares at the stairs. He is not close enough to close the door.* Underline *stare / stair* and *close / close*.
- Ask the class which pair is the heteronym. (*close / close*) *Why? Because they are spelled the same, but have different meanings.*
- Elicit the meanings as they are in the example sentences from the class.

Listen to the sentences. Write two meanings for each word. 💿 4•22

- Play the audio and have students listen. Then play the audio again and have students write the answers.

1 content: happy and comfortable; what something consists of
2 dove: a bird; the past tense of "dive"
3 object: an item; refuse or say no
4 refuse: trash; say no

- Put students into pairs to write sentences for each word. Allow them to use a dictionary to help.
- Have pairs check each other's work.
- Then have some pairs say their sentences and write them on the board.

Writing Study

E Learn: Using Numerals

- Read the *Learn* box and examples together.
- Then ask students to read the examples again.

Write the answers.

- Go over the first one with the class. Ask *What's today's date?* Invite several students to the board write it. Ask *What is your birth date?* Invite more students to write their birth date on the board.
- If the class needs extra practice, dictate a few addresses and numbers to the class for them to write.

- Have individuals come to the board to write the answers to check them.
- Ask students to complete the activity on their own. Then go over answers with the class and write examples on the board.

Below level:

- Have students practice saying and writing their own birth dates and addresses.
- Ask some students to write them on the board.

At level:

- Put students into pairs. They take turns to tell each other their birth date and addresses while the partner writes them down. Then they check each other's work.

Above level:

- Have pairs circulate to tell each other their birth date and addresses while the partner writes them down. Then they check each other's work.

Write

- Direct students to the Workbook for further practice.

Further practice
Workbook pages 176–177
Online Practice Unit 18 • Communicate
Oxford **iTools** Unit 18 • Communicate

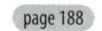

Units 17 and 18 Wrap Up page 188

Units 17 and 18 Wrap Up

Writing

A Read the story.

The Mystery of Ursus Arctos

Setting — As night fell once more over the frozen landscape,

Problem — Sid and Nadia began to despair. They were detectives on a mission to solve an ancient legend, but it was beginning to feel like a bad idea.

The legend claimed that long ago, King Olaf of Scandinavia had taken a journey through the north of his country. The brown bear, known as *ursus arctos*, was the sign of Olaf's kingdom, and he had worn a necklace with a golden pendant in the shape of a bear's tooth. Then King Olaf had disappeared, along with the pendant. Historians had been searching for it ever since, to prove that the legend was true.

Internal conflict — "Maybe we can't solve this mystery," said Nadia. "We've been hiking for days with no sign of a clue!"

"Of course we can!" replied her brother. "We know King Olaf came this way."

External conflict — The next morning, Sid and Nadia awoke to a snowstorm. As they continued their hike, struggling forward in the freezing wind, they came across a strange house. It was made entirely of ice! Nadia peered inside."It doesn't look like anyone's been here for a long time," she said.

Resolution — Cautiously, they tiptoed into the house. It was dark inside but surprisingly warm. In one corner was a pile of reindeer skins, and near it a small table with two chairs. Sid and Nadia sat down, feeling disappointed. There was no sign of the pendant. Then Sid leaned back and noticed a hook on the wall above him. There was something bright and golden hanging from the hook.

"There it is!" he said excitedly. "We did it, Nadia! We found King Olaf's pendant!"

B Answer the questions.

1 How does the writer describe the setting?
2 How does the writer introduce a problem to create conflict in the story?
3 Does the problem lead to an internal or external conflict?
4 How does the writer resolve the conflict?

C Learn Writing a Story

- Describe the setting of your story. Think about whether the setting contributes to the problems your characters face.
- Think of a problem or a challenge for your characters. What do they want? Why? This is the conflict in your story.
- Consider whether the conflict should be internal (from inside the characters) or external (from someone else or from nature).
- Present a solution to your characters' problems or challenges. This is the resolution in your story.

Write Now go to the **Workbook** to plan and write your own story. page 179

D Present your story to the class.

1 Practice reading your story aloud.
2 Take note of places in your story where you can gesture, use different voices, or put more excitement into your voice.
3 Act out your story. Sit in a chair or stand at the front of the class. Use tone and gestures to bring your story to life.
4 After you've finished your story, ask the class what they think about it.
5 Listen carefully while your classmates are acting out their stories.

"There it is!" she said excitedly.

BIG QUESTION 9 Why are stories important?

A Watch the video. What kinds of stories do you see?

B What are some answers to the Big Question? Talk about them with your partner.

C Complete the **Big Question Chart**. Then discuss it with the class.

What have you learned about stories?

188 Writing

Presentation • Big Question 9 189

Summary

Objectives: To show what students have learned about the language and learning points of Units 17 and 18.

Reading: Comprehension of a story

Writing: Writing a story

Speaking: Sharing a story

Materials: Big Question DVD, Discover Poster 9, Talk About It! Poster, Big Question Chart

Writing

A Read the story.

- Go over the structure of each section of the story before reading. Ask the following:
  What is a setting?
  What is internal conflict?
  What is external conflict?
- Read the story with the class one time. Then have students read it one time on their own.

B Answer the questions.

- Have students find the answers in the story.
- Check the answers with the class.

POSSIBLE ANSWERS

1 The writer describes the setting as frozen and at night.
2 The writer introduces problems that are in conflict with what the character wants.
3 The conflict is internal: dealing with emotions like despair and giving up.
4 The writer resolves the conflict by having the characters find what they were looking for.

C Learn: Writing a Story

- Read the *Learn* box together.
- Explain that students should follow these guidelines when they plan and write their stories.

CRITICAL THINKING

Have students go back to the model to see how the writer addressed each requirement. Ask:

- *How does the opening setting contribute to the characters' problems?*
- *How does the setting change at the end when the conflict is resolved?*
- *What do the characters want?*
- *What is the challenge?*
- *Is the internal conflict used well in this story?* Elicit opinions and reasons to support this.
- *What is the solution to the problem?*

Write

- Direct the students to the Workbook to plan and write their own story.

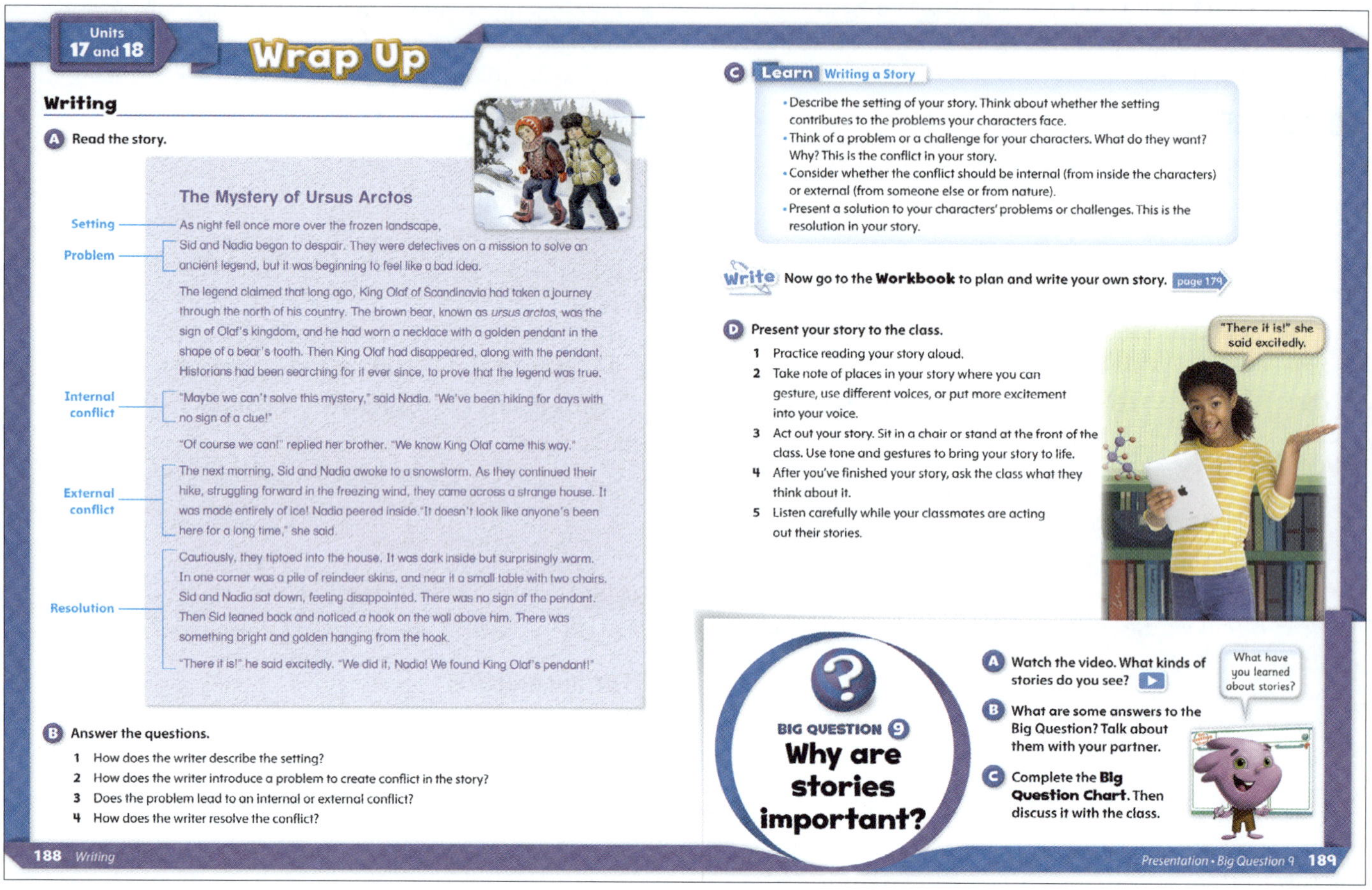

- Go over the Workbook page 179 with the students.
- Read through all of the steps and instructions with the class.
- Brainstorm some story ideas on the board. Ask *What kinds of stories do you like to read?* List students' answers on the board, e.g. *mysteries*.
- Then say *It is a good idea to write the kinds of stories you enjoy reading and are interested in. For each of these types / genres of stories, give me some examples of things you'd like to read about or write about.*
- List them on the board, e.g. mysteries – with kid detectives or set in international settings.
- Then proceed as below to complete the writing.

Below level:

- Put students into mixed-ability pairs to write a story together. Have pairs choose a genre and topic. (Or pair students based on this choice.)
- Go over an example of a web using one of the brainstorming examples or a pair's choice on the board.
- Have students continue through the rest of the steps together.
- If it is appropriate for his or her abilities, have each student develop the story individually at step C, the first draft.

At level:

- Have students work on their Workbook stories individually.
- Then have students discuss their stories with a partner using the Writing Checklist in step D. Partners should offer helpful suggestions to improve the story.
- Have students then revise their stories.

Above level:

- Have students complete their Workbook story individually.
- For step D, have students read each other's story and apply the Writing Checklist. It might be helpful to have the partner read the story aloud so the writer can hear his or her own writing a fresh.

D Present your story to the class.

- Read the directions with the class.
- Give students time to practice reading their stories aloud. Encourage them to use gestures.
- Have students discuss the stories after reading them. Ask questions such as: *What did this story remind you of? Did you feel connected to the character? Could you relate? What was the theme? What was the conflict?*

- Put students into small groups.
- Explain that groups will choose one or two of their stories to act out for the class.
- Students will take roles, one or two narrators can fill in. Groups may wish to write additional dialogue.
- Give groups time to practice their story.
- Encourage dramatic acting and full participation in the role-play. Remind the class to listen carefully.

Units 17 and 18 Big Question Review

A Watch the video. What kinds of stories do you see? ▷

- Play the video and when it is finished ask students what they know about why stories are important now.
- Have students share ideas with the class.

B What are some answers to the Big Question? Talk about them with your partner.

- Display **Discover Poster 9**. Point to familiar vocabulary items and elicit them from the class. Ask *What is this?*
- Ask students *What do you see?* Ask *What does that mean?*
- Refer to all of the learning points written on the poster and have students explain how they relate to the different pictures.
- Ask *What does this learning point mean?* Elicit answers from individual students.
- Display the **Talk About It! Poster** to help students with sentence frames for discussion of the learning points and for expressing their opinions.

C Complete the Big Question Chart. Then discuss it with the class.

- Ask students what they have learned about why stories are important while studying this unit.
- Put students into pairs or small groups to say two new things they have learned.
- Have students share their ideas with the class and add their ideas to the chart.
- Have students complete the chart in their Workbook.

Further practice
Workbook pages 178–181
Online Practice • Wrap Up 9
Oxford iTools • Wrap Up 9

Testing Practice

Testing Practice 3 pages 190–191

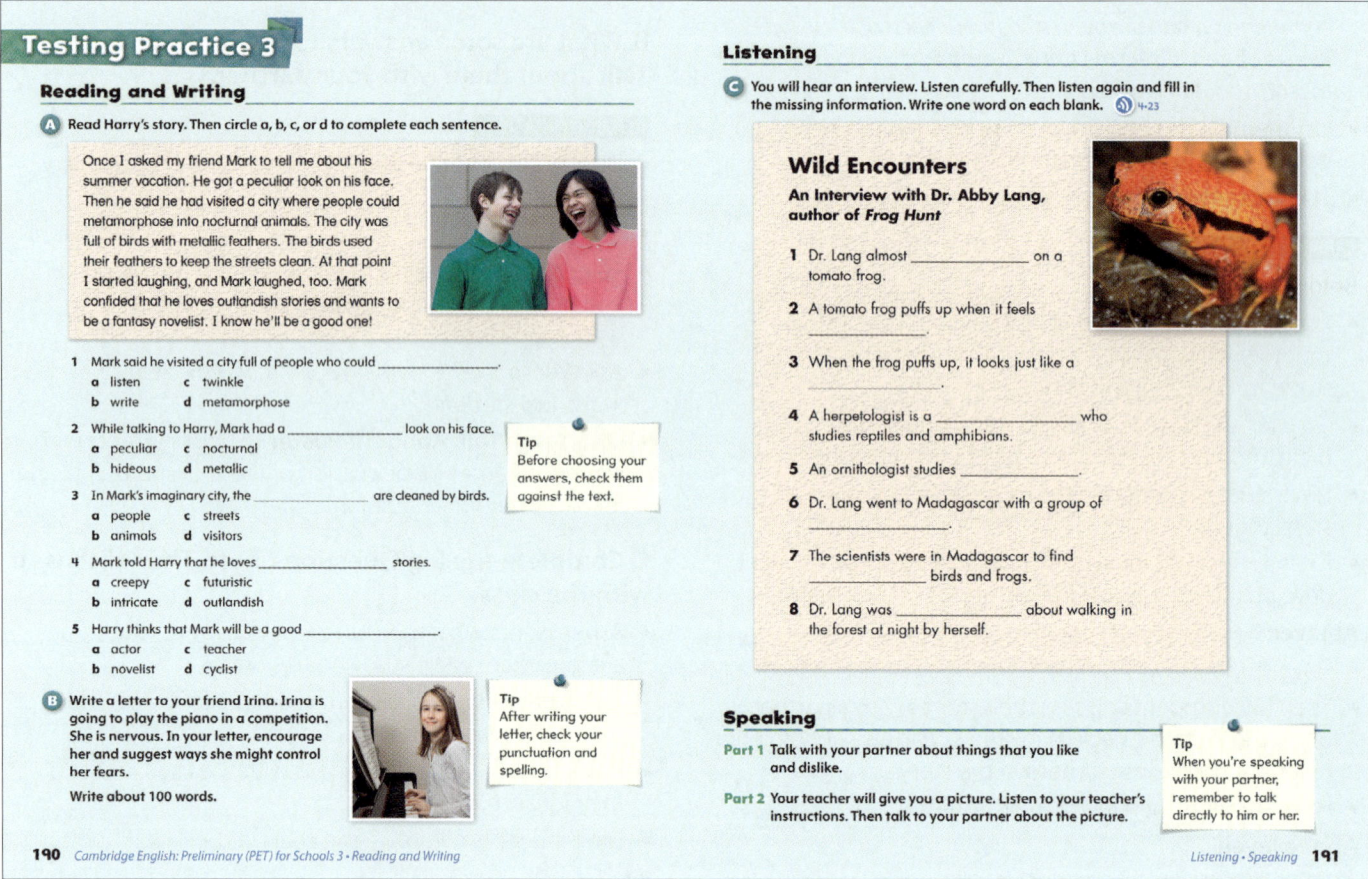

Reading and Writing

A Read Harry's story. Then circle a, b, c, or d to complete each sentence.

- Read the instructions with the class.
- Put students into mixed-ability pairs.
- Have students take turns reading a sentence each until each pair has completed reading the entire paragraph.
- Read the *Tip* box with the class.
- Have students do the activity.
- Check the answers with the class.

ANSWERS

1 d   2 a   3 c   4 d   5 b

B Write a letter to your friend Irina. Irina is going to play the piano in a competition. She is nervous. In your letter, encourage her and suggest ways she might control her fears.

Write about 100 words.

- Read the instructions with the class.
- Have students write the letter individually.
- Read the *Tip* box with the class.
- Ask *How should you start writing?* Elicit (*make notes, make a list, make a web*).

SAMPLE ANSWER

Dear Irina,
Your piano competition is coming up. Try not to be too nervous. I know you will play beautifully. If you do get nervous, here are some things you can do. First, practice the piece over and over, so you can play it even if you are scared. In your mind, imagine going to the competition and playing in front of people. Think about this while practicing at home. Then when you play at the competition, you won't be distracted by fear. You will be calm.
This is how pilots train for emergencies! It really works.
Good luck!
(Name)

Listening

C You will hear an interview. Listen carefully. Then listen again and fill in the missing information. Write one word on each blank. 🔊 4•23

- Read the instructions with the class.
- Have students read the title and look at the picture. Ask *What do you think this interview is about?*
- Give students at least five minutes to read the sentences, so they are prepared for the listening text.
- Tell students they can guess some of the missing words from context, and then use the listening to check their answer, changing them as necessary.
- Read the *Tip* box with the class.
- Check the answers with the class.

ANSWERS
1 stepped 2 threatened 3 tomato 4 scientist
5 birds 6 ornithologists 7 nocturnal 8 apprehensive

Speaking

Part 1 Talk with your partner about things that you like and dislike.

- Read the instructions with the class.
- Model a conversation with a confident student. Say:
  T: *I really like movies about animals. How about you?*
  S: *I like movies about superheroes.*
  T: *You do? Why?*
  S: *I like the setting of the movies. They're are usually in the future. Why do you like movies about animals?*
- Put students into pairs to talk about things they like and dislike.

DIFFERENTIATION

Below level:

- Write sentence frames on the board for students to use to do the activity. A: *I like _____.* B: *Why do you like _____?* A: *Because it's / they're _____. Don't you like _____?* B: *Yes, / No, I think they're _____. I like _____.*

At level:

- Have students do the activity.

Above level:

- Tell students to ask follow-up questions about their partners preferences.
- Have student report back to the class about their partner.

Part 2 Your teacher will give you a picture. Listen to your teacher's instructions. Then talk to your partner about the picture.

(Please refer to the the Assessment for Learning CD-ROM for the pictures).

- Put students into pairs. Give each student a picture. One student in the pair will receive one image, and the other student the other image.
- Explain that students will use the picture to make up a story.
- Tell students to think about the setting, name the characters, and explain how they feel.
- Tell students to take turns talking about their picture.
- They should talk about what happened right before the picture and what will happen right after it.

Audio Script

Listening Transcripts

Here are the listening transcripts from all the listening, speaking, and word study sections of the Student Book. It can be useful to ask students to read along as they listen to the audio CD, as it provides support for listening skills.

Unit 1

Page 14 Listening

🎵 1.05A 🎵 1.06B

For me, the subway is fantastic. I live in Manhattan, but in the summer I use the subway to go to the beach at Coney Island. It's a great journey because the train goes through a tunnel under the East River. It takes about 40 minutes to get to the beach from where I live. When I'm ready to go back home, I take a different train. That one goes over the Mahattan Bridge, and you get to see some really impressive views of the city!

My friends and I use the subway a lot, especially on the weekends. For example, we like to go to the movies, so we might take the subway to the theater in Times Square. And in summer, we enjoy going to Central Park. The subway is so fast! Of course, that's because it goes through tunnels underground, so it avoids all the city traffic. It's much cheaper than taking a taxi. Often, we ride the subway all the way down to lower Manhattan so we can walk along the river.

I live in New Jersey. Every morning I take a bus over the George Washington Bridge. I love it because I can see all the way up and down the Hudson River. I'm a journalist and my offices are near Lincoln Center, so when I get off the bus I switch to the subway train that goes down to Lincoln Center. I find it the fastest way to get to work on time. I'm usually up at 5:00 and on the subway by 6:30, just a little before the rush hour. It's great because I get to read the news, listen to music, and plan my busy day ahead.

Page 14 Speaking

🎵 1.07

That bridge is probably used for freight trains.
Are you sure?
Yes, because it has train tracks on it.
Actually, I think it's for people trains.
Don't you mean passenger trains?
Oh, right. Thanks!

Unit 2

Page 22 Listening

🎵 1.12A 🎵 1.13B

Hello, this is Cheryl Jackson with Channel 4 news. I'm here with David King, the Chief Engineer behind our amazing new bridge on Dolphin Bay. David, could you please describe the steps you went through from the very beginning?

Sure! It was pretty complicated but I'll try to keep it simple. First, we looked carefully at the site to determine what kind of bridge we needed. In this case, it was a suspension bridge because we needed to get across the bay.

Is that a very expensive type of bridge?

It is expensive, but when we considered the width of the bay and the amount of traffic that would be crossing the bridge we knew a suspension bridge was the best choice. We identified the correct place to build the bridge, and then calculated the length of the bridge. After that, we designed the bridge itself, using a computer program.

OK, what did you do then?

We started digging to place the supports, and then we began to build the bridge. Finally, we opened it to the public and here it is! It took us 6 years in total.

Page 22 Speaking

🎵 1.14

The first step to making a greeting card is choosing some art supplies.
What do you do after that?
Next, I draw something I like.
Cool. And then what?
Well, then I add a message. Finally, I mail the card.
That sounds like fun!

Unit 3

Page 34 Listening

🎵 1.19A 🎵 1.20B

I'm a journalist for the magazine Science Now, and I'm researching information to write an article. To get this information, I'm about to call Dr. Kuznetsov, a scientist.

Hello?

Hello, Dr. Kuznetsov? This is Alex. Can you hear me OK?

Yes, Alex, I can hear you perfectly! Thanks for the questions you emailed me this morning. I'm talking to you from one of the coldest places on Earth: Antarctica. I'm here with a team of scientists and we're carrying out important research. We've found a lake, called Lake Vostok, deep under the ice. The lake has been hidden for 20 million years! That's longer than there have been human beings on the planet! As I said in my last email, we hope to explore the lake. We are looking for ancient bacteria that might still be living there. One day, it's possible we'll be able to send a robot down to explore the lake in more detail, but for now we're drilling to remove water samples. Lake Vostok is one of about 400 underground lakes in Antarctica, and is one of the largest lakes on Earth. We estimate that it's 257 kilometers long and about 48 kilometers wide. I'll report more discoveries next week! Bye for now!

Page 34 Speaking

🎵 1.21

What can you tell us about the new cave you discovered?

Well, it could be hundreds of kilometers long.

I see. Do you think it might be the largest cave on Earth?

We can't be sure, but we think it must be one of the largest.

That's amazing! Would you mind telling us how you discovered it?

Sure. I'd be happy to!

🔊 1.22

1 I used a match to light the candle.
   There was a great tennis match on TV.
2 The sky is clear. There are no clouds.
   My friend smiled, so it was clear that he was happy.
3 The archer used a bow to shoot the arrow.
   She likes to wear a bow in her hair.
4 The game was a tie. Both teams scored three points.
   My dad wears a suit and tie to work.

Unit 4

Page 42 Listening

🔊 1.26A 🔊 1.27B

Today we're giving our presentations on what Earth is made of. Who wants to go first?

I will!

OK, Amanda. What's the title of your presentation?

I called it, What Happens When a Volcano Erupts.

Excellent! OK, please start.

OK, so ... below a volcano, gas builds up in the Earth's crust, creating pressure. This powerful pressure forces a kind of liquid rock, called magma, to rise and burst out of the volcano! It's at that point, after it comes out of the volcano, that we call it lava. Some of the magma starts to cool and solidify on its way upwards. When that happens, it's sometimes blasted out of the volcano as huge chunks of hot rock or as volcanic dust and ash.

All volcanoes are dangerous because even volcanoes that haven't erupted for many years can suddenly erupt. There are three types of volcano: active, dormant, and extinct. Active volcanoes are ones that have erupted in the last 10,000 years. Dormant volcanoes are "sleeping." They haven't erupted in at least 10,000 years. And extinct volcanoes haven't erupted for even longer than that, but they still might!

Thank you, Amanda. That was an excellent presentation! Now ... who's next?

Page 42 Speaking

🔊 1.28

We could make a collage for our presentation.

That sounds good, but aren't we supposed to include some writing?

Oh, right. How about we do a report then?

Well, what if we made a poster? That way we could include pictures and writing.

That's a great idea! I've got some magazines at home with pictures we could use.

This is going to be an awesome project!

Page 43 Word Study

🔊 1.29

1 This candy is very sweet.
2 If you work hard, you can achieve anything.
3 There was a fleet of ships in the harbor.
4 Do you agree with his opinion?
5 I believe that friendship is important.
6 You have something on the sleeve of your shirt.
7 The chief of the village was old and wise.
8 My brother earned a degree in science.

Unit 5

Page 54 Listening

🔊 1.33A 🔊 1.34B

My name's Mitch and I'm an actor with the West City Theater Group. It's a great place to work. At the moment, we're rehearsing for a new play that I absolutely love. This play is a masked play so all the main actors wear masks. It's interesting because there are several rules about wearing masks and you have to follow them. First, and maybe most important, is that actors must always put the mask on facing *away* from the audience. This helps the audience believe in your character – the character that you become when you put on the mask. It's the same when you take the mask off. You should never be facing the audience. You need to make sure the mask is firmly in place and that it feels comfortable on your face before you turn around on stage. Next, you must never touch the mask while you're wearing it. You have to pretend it's your own face, not a mask. And finally, never, ever talk or act as yourself while you're wearing the mask. You have to act and speak as the character that you're playing. Every time you put the mask on, you change into the character. It's great fun. Everyone should try it!

Page 54 Speaking

🔊 1.35

What is this thing called? It's used to play a role.

Oh, is it a script?

No, that's not it. It's something you wear.

Hmm, it must be a costume.

Sorry, that's not it either. It's one of those things that an actor puts over his or her face.

Ah-hah! I know. It's a mask!

Unit 6

Page 62 Listening

🔊 2.05A 🔊 2.06B

Today we're talking to an Olympic fencing champion, Tanya Galluzzo. Tanya, welcome! Tell us how you first got started in fencing.

It's a funny story, really. I wasn't that great at sports in school, and especially not at soccer! Then one day, when I was in seventh grade, I saw a sign on the school noticeboard. It said "Join the fencing team!", so I did! Now I travel all over the world taking part in competitions.

Cool! Were you good at fencing right away?

Actually, no. At first I thought it was awesome to play with a sword, but one day this older kid on the team beat me in match after match and showed me just how hard fencing can be. After that, I became very serious about the sport. To be good, you need to be quick on your feet and have good reflexes. It takes a lot of training. You train and train and train until you're exhausted!

Is fencing dangerous? Does it hurt when you get hit by a sword?

It can be, but of course safety is crucial. You wear protective clothing and a mask. You learn all about safety at the start. The most common injuries are things like twisted ankles and muscle strains. The sword bends, so when it touches you it's like getting poked with someone's finger.

Page 62 Speaking

🔊 2.07

I think surgeons should have to wear masks.

Why do you think so?

Because a surgeon is someone who works with sick people.

I see your point, but I disagree. I think surgeons are probably careful not to get people sick.

Well, a mask is also important because it protects the surgeon.

Oh, that's true. I think you're right.

Page 67 Listening

🔊 2.09

Hello, my name is Theo Jones. I'm a counselor. People come to me to talk. Some people are skeptical about counseling. However, I believe that counseling can help people to overcome obstacles and change problematic situations in their lives. For example, many people feel a lot of pressure at their jobs. Too much pressure can make a person unhappy or ill. Sometimes, people who feel isolated – such as elderly people, or young parents at home – become unhappy. No matter their situation, it's normal for all kinds of people to feel discouraged or unhappy at one time or another. With all of my patients, I spend most of my time listening and asking questions. I try to help them understand their problems by talking about them. I insist that my patients come once a week. I have a full schedule, but I like to keep busy, so I like it. In fact, I enjoy my work.

Unit 7

Page 76 Listening

🔊 2.13A 🔊 2.14B

Hi, Uncle George. Can I interview you for my school assignment? Our teacher asked us to interview someone about their job.

Sure, Joey. What do you want to know?

Well, you're a carpenter, right? Can you make anything anyone wants?

Sure, I can make just about anything: tables, chairs, beds, shelves. You name it!

Cool. And what do you make this stuff out of?

All kinds of wood. I use oak, beech, cherry, teak. There are so many types.

Carpentry's difficult, isn't it?

Well, you need to choose the wood carefully, of course. It has to be good quality. But I guess the most important thing is making the furniture symmetrical. Otherwise it just doesn't work!

Really? What do you mean it doesn't work?

Well, imagine if you had a table that wasn't symmetrical. Things would fall off it and it would be difficult to eat at it.

Yes, I guess you're right! My salad would slide right off!

And the table wouldn't look right in any case. Nobody wants a table that isn't symmetrical! They really need four legs and equal proportions.

I hadn't thought of that. It would look weird. Does it take you long to make a table?

Not really, but of course I trained as a carpenter for many years and I've made a lot of furniture! I've been doing this job for 22 years now.

That's a lot of tables and chairs!

Page 76 Speaking

🔊 2.15

Look! These pictures are identical.

I don't know the word "identical." How do you spell it?

Like this, I D E N T I C A L. It's an adjective.

Could you give me another example?

Sure. These pictures are exactly the same. They're identical.

Oh, I understand now. Thanks!

Unit 8

Page 84 Listening

🔊 2.20A 🔊 2.21B

Hi, everyone. I'm here to speak to you today about the fascinating world of fractals. So what are fractals? A fractal is a never-ending pattern that repeats itself. A fractal is also an example of symmetry. Fractal patterns look the same from close up as they do from very far away. Think of the veins in a leaf. If you looked at one of those veins under a microscope, you would see the same pattern that you saw on the leaf.

Fractals can most easily be found in nature. In nature, we see fractals in lightning bolts, seashells, clouds, trees, rivers, and even things like vegetables. One type of vegetable in which you can see fractals is called a Romanesco. It looks similar to broccoli and cauliflower.

The really cool thing about fractals is that the pattern you see remains the same no matter how much you magnify the object. This is because fractals have a special kind of symmetry called symmetry of scale. This means that they look the same from any distance. A coast is an example of this. It's hard to believe, but the coast of a country looks the same from an airplane as the beach would look if you saw it under a microscope!

I look forward to seeing you all again next week, when I'll be telling you about how we see fractals in Math.

Page 84 Speaking

🔊 2.22

My favorite example of symmetry is a race car.

Cool. What made you choose that?

I like it because it has an interesting shape.

Do you like because it's the same on both sides?

Yes, and that also helps it to go faster.

That's a great choice!

Unit 9

Page 96 Listening

🔊 2.27A 🔊 2.28B

This movie isn't very interesting. Would you mind if we changed channel?

Oh, you don't like it? I was really enjoying it. Let's just see what happens next. If you still don't like it we can watch something else.

Oh, look, it's Jane Burgess! She's my favorite actress!

I didn't know she was in this movie. She's amazin.

But why is her character helping the bank robber? That guy's such a jerk!

I'm not sure. Do you think they're both criminals?

I feel so sorry for that little girl. She's sick and no one is helping her.

Now they're in trouble! The police are on the way! They'll catch those crooks and help that poor girl.

Wow, I'm glad we kept watching this. It's actually a really great movie.

Page 96 Speaking

 2.29

Let's go to the museum this weekend!

No, thanks. I don't feel like going to the museum.

But you said you wanted to go!

I'm sorry. What if we went to beach instead?

Actually, that sounds like fun.

Cool! I'll get my towel and flip flops!

Unit 10

Page 104 Listening

 2.34A 2.35B

On the tiny island of La Gomera, off the coast of Africa, a new lesson is being taught in schools.

Children across the island are learning "Silbo Gomero," the ancient whistling language that has been used on the island for centuries. It's a type of whistled Spanish and can be heard up to three kilometers away! There used to be no telephones on La Gomera, so communicating was hard. Whistling allowed the people living there to communicate across the valleys and ravines of their rugged island.

In Tanzania, Africa, there's another unusual form of language. It's called Hadza. Only a few thousand people speak it, but children still learn it. Hadza sounds like a series of clicks and pops.

The Hadza people make these noises using their tongues. Hadza is a unique language. There's no other language that's anything like it.

Page 104 Speaking

 2.36

Would you rather play soccer or go to the mall?

I think I'd prefer to play soccer.

All right. Do you want to go to the field near our school?

No, I'd rather go to the one near my house.

That's fine. I'd really like to get something to eat first.

So would I! Let's do that.

Page 105 Word Study

 2.37

1 Don't be childish. You need to act your age.

2 My grandfather is youthful. He's very energetic.

3 That gazelle is a beautiful animal. It's so slender.

4 I lost a lot of weight when I was sick. I was much too skinny!

5 She's economical with her money. She doesn't waste it.

6 My aunt is so miserly, she won't spend money on anything.

7 That guy is fanatical about soccer. He ignores everything else in his life.

8 I'm enthusiastic about this new project. I can't wait to get started!

Unit 11

Page 116 Listening

 3.05A 3.06B

Today, I am interviewing my mother, Sylvia, so that I can pass her story on to my kids and grandkids. Mom was born in 1924 and she's 89 years old. She lives in New York City.

Mom, tell us a little about where your parents came from and why they moved to New York City.

My mom and dad came from the Ukraine, in Russia. In the 1920s things were very bad there so they decided to seek a new life in America. They wanted to escape from being poor. In Russia, Mom was a dentist and Dad was an accountant, but when they came to New York, Dad started selling insurance. Unfortunately, he died when I was just four years old so Mom had to raise me alone.

That must have been very hard for her.

Oh, yes, it was! She didn't speak much English and she had to take over Dad's business. We were quite poor when I was a child. Mom and I stayed in rooms with different families around the city. I went to 12 different elementary schools!

Wow! How were things different in the city back then?

Well, there weren't many cars or taxis. I remember once I was given a taxi ride as a birthday present. It was so exciting! The subway and bus rides cost 5 cents each and there weren't any fast food restaurants!

What did you do for fun?

You know … I used to collect milk bottles and return them to the store. For every empty milk bottle, I got 2 cents. By the end of each week, I had 14 cents. Then I spent 10 cents on seeing a movie and the rest on candy. I also used to go to Central Park a lot and watch the clouds. I love clouds even now that I'm 89 years old.

What's your happiest memory?

Oh, Phil … that's easy! Marrying your father! And I was very happy when you and your sister were born. I always wanted children.

Page 116 Speaking

 3.07

I used to go to a school on Kensington Street.

Oh, really? Where's Kensington Street?

It's on the west side of town.

How old were you then?

I was about five. I went there for kindergarten.

I went to school on the west side, too. I like it over there.

Page 117 Word Study

 3.08

1 This fabric is very coarse. It's not comfortable to wear.

2 My sister is taking an English course at the university.

3 I like to wander through the woods.

4 I wonder if our team will win the championship.

5 Were you affected by the big storm?

6 More people went swimming as an effect of the hot weather.

7 I advise you to get plenty of rest before the race.

8 My friend gave me advice about how to solve my problem.

Unit 12

Page 124 Listening

 3.12A 3.13B

In various locations around the United States, there are StoryCorps recording booths. StoryCorps is this very cool organization that allows anyone to go into a recording booth and record their story, completely free. You get a free CD and some of the stories are uploaded to the Internet, so that anyone can listen to them. The idea is that you're recording a little bit of your own history – your memories. It's a way of preserving history, just like we preserve it in history books. It's also a way of making connections between people and sharing stories with others. It's always fun to hear a story, right? Now let's listen to a man named Philip recording his own story.

Hi, my name's Philip and this is my story. I was born 30 years ago in Rome, Italy. My dad was a teacher – a history teacher, in fact. He taught at an English school not far from the apartment my mom and dad lived in. So anyway, I was born in June and I spent the first two years of my life in Rome. I learned to walk by holding on to the railings around the fountain in one of the squares and I went to kindergarten. I grew up speaking a kind of strange mix of Italian and English. Oh yeah! And I loved ice cream! Italians make the best ice cream you ever tasted. Then, when I was about two and a half, my parents moved to …

Page 124 Speaking

3.14

My happiest memory is the time my friend and I went camping last summer.

What made it so great?

Well, I'd just been given a new tent for my birthday and we used it for the first time. We stayed out all night!

Cool. What did you do then?

The next day, my friend invited me over to her house. She lives near some woods, so we camped out there.

Wow, that's neat!

Page 125 Word Study

3.15

1 I wear my pajamas to bed. The word pajamas comes from Hindi.
2 We park our car in the garage. The word garage comes from French.
3 I like to eat waffles for breakfast. The word waffle comes from Dutch.
4 The forest fire was a catastrophe. The word catastrophe comes from Greek.
5 I ate a tortilla for lunch. The word tortilla comes from Spanish.
6 My sister knows how to play the piano. The word piano comes from Italian.
7 Pandas like to eat bamboo. The word bamboo comes from Malay.
8 An almanac is a very useful book. The word almanac comes from Arabic.

Page 129 Listening

3.16

Wow, look at that mountain!

Do you see where that bird is perched? On the ledge by those pine trees?

Yeah. I bet it would take a day to walk there.

Do you want to try it? There is a hiking group we could join.

Oh, I don't know. The trail looks pretty rugged. And look, that gust of wind nearly blew the bird off the ledge!

Well, I think it could be fun to try mountain climbing. I'd like to see the view from the summit!

Page 129 Listening

3.17

Lianne, were you raised in France?

That's right, Kaya. Why do you ask?

I desperately want to learn French!

But isn't your mother French?

Yes, she is, but I refused to learn French as a child. My poor mother was so frustrated.

So why do you want to learn it now?

I'd like to be able to read about my ancestors. I'd like to see my mother's astonishment, too. She'd be so happy.

Unit 13

Page 138 Listening

3.21A 3.22B

You Have to Believe by Douglas Malloch

You have to believe in happiness, or happiness never comes.

I know that a bird chirps none the less, when all he finds is crumbs.

You have to believe the buds will blow, believe in the grass in days of snow.

That's the reason a bird can sing, on his darkest day, he believes in spring.

You have to believe in happiness, it isn't an outward thing.

The spring never makes the song, I guess. As much as the song the spring.

Aye, many a heart could find content, if it saw the joy on the road it went.

The joy ahead when it had to grieve.

For the joy is there – but, you have to believe.

Page 138 Speaking

3.23

What will you be doing in five years?

I'll be in college. I can't wait!

And what do you think you'll be studying there?

Well, I'll probably be studying medicine. I think it's really interesting.

Do you think you'll be living with your parents?

No way! I might be living in an apartment.

Page 139 Word Study

3.24

1 The crow was too slow to catch the caterpillar.
2 Have you ever heard of a hummingbird?
3 The busy bird built a bower.
4 Albert the albatross was almost always alert.

Unit 14

Page 146 Listening

3.28A 3.29B

Hi, my name's Mark and I'm an ornithologist. Today, I'll be taking you into the wonderful world of birds that imitate, or mimic, sounds. Imitating sounds is something birds do to add to the diversity of their songs. They pick up the natural sounds around them, like the noises that other animals make or the songs of other birds, and repeat them back, almost like a recording. But now that human sounds are everywhere, birds have started to imitate those, too. Listen. What do you think this is?

It might sound like a car alarm, but it's actually a lyre bird! Now how about this noise?

That, too, is a lyre bird. Bet you thought it was a camera, didn't you? For a bird it makes no difference whether a sound is a natural one, like a tree falling, or an artificial one, like a car alarm. It's just a sound. It's how birds acquire their songs. To you and me, birdsong might sound like a random collection of noises, but in the case of birds that mimic sound it's actually a composition made up of things the bird has heard. Starlings are especially good mimics. Here's one. What noise is it making?

That's right! This starling is imitating a phone!

Page 146 Speaking

🔘 3.30

What have you learned today?

I learned that birds can make tools.

That's cool. Can you give me an example?

Sure. The woodpecker finch can use the spine of a cactus to catch bugs.

Wow! Where can I see one of those?

They live in the Galapagos Islands.

Unit 15

Page 158 Listening

🔘 3.35A 🔘 3.36B

My name's Petra and I have a serious fear of them. I think I get it from my mom. I'm terrified of them because they look hairy and I don't like the way they run around. I know they're harmless but they have eight legs and sometimes they're really big. Every time I see one, my hands start to shake. I usually call my brother to catch them and take them outside.

Hi, I'm Dan. I'm from Montreal, Canada. Every time I go in an elevator, my legs get weak. Once, my mom and dad took me to the top of the Empire State Building in New York City. I was so scared! We reached the 86th floor and I went completely white with fear. I didn't dare look down to the street below. I'll never go there again!

My friends call me JJ but my real name's Joe. It doesn't bother me at all now, but when I was younger I was terrified of it. Every night, I used to climb into bed and I could feel my heart racing when it was time to turn out the light. I don't really know why it scared me so much. Maybe because I couldn't see what was around me, so I began to imagine things that weren't really there.

Page 158 Speaking

🔘 3.37

I'm scared of flying.

You should try taking a short flight.

I have, but it was terrifying! The plane was so small.

Have you tried reading about it?

Well, yes. That did help a little. I know it's actually very safe.

Another solution might be to pretend you're on a bus.

Unit 16

Page 166 Listening

🔘 4.05A 🔘 4.06B

Today we have the great privilege of talking to Fearless Fred, the world famous sportsman. Fred, welcome, and thanks for taking the time to come and talk to us.

Oh, you're welcome! Delighted to be here.

So, to kick us off, tell us how old you were when you started bungee jumping and what first made you want to do it.

Hmm, let's see. I did my first jump when I was fourteen years old. It's a day I'll never forget. It was frightening but absolutely fantastic at the same time.

At that age, you must've been terrified. Tell us what happened.

Well I was going to jump off a very high bridge into a canyon. That means throwing yourself off a bridge and free-falling 45 meters with your feet tied to a strong elastic rope.

That sounds dangerous and very scary! How did you feel at the time?

I thought it was going to be easy but then I saw the girl in line ahead of me and her face was completely white with fear. I started to shake uncontrollably, but there was no turning back. I took a deep breath to calm myself, but I was so scared that I couldn't move. Finally, I persuaded myself to jump off the bridge.

Cool! How did it feel?

It was just amazing. I was screaming and laughing at the same time. From that moment on, I was hooked on bungee jumping.

Page 166 Speaking

🔘 4.07

Have you ever ridden on a roller coaster?

Yes! It was really scary but also very exciting!

It does look cool, but I think I'd be too scared to try it.

You should try going on a slower ride first.

That's a good idea. Next time I go to the amusement park I'll try one of the slower rides.

If you like it, then you can go on the roller coaster.

Page 167 Word Study

🔘 4.08

1 That machine is inactive. It's not running right now.

2 I was so lazy yesterday, all I did was watch TV.

3 When I went on vacation I felt happy and relaxed.

4 Please take out the garbage! That stench is terrible.

5 I love the aroma of fresh flowers.

6 I smelled the shirt but it didn't really have any odor.

7 I like my job because it's challenging.

8 It's difficult to run a race.

9 Working outside in the hot sun can be arduous.

Unit 17

Page 178 Listening

🔘 4.12A 🔘 4.13B

Ahmed lived in the mountains in Jordan. His dad had a farm where he kept some goats. There were wild animals where Ahmed lived, and the one everybody was scared of was a wild cat called a Lynx. One morning, Ahmed was walking in the hills near his house when he saw a shepherd taking care of some sheep. He crept up behind the shepherd and hollered: "Lynx! Lynx!" The shepherd ran away and Ahmed laughed because there wasn't a Lynx there. Later that day, Ahmed went to the village. He saw a lot of people chatting in the square. Hiding behind a monument, Ahmed yelled "Lynx, Lynx!" and laughed as all the people ran to their houses. When the people found out that Ahmed hadn't seen a Lynx, they were furious.

The following day, Ahmed saw a girl at the market. She was busy choosing fruits and vegetables. Ahmed sidled up to her and whispered "Lynx, Lynx" in her ear. The girl ran away, dropping her basket as she ran. Ahmed's father discovered that Ahmed was teasing people about a Lynx and he was very annoyed. He told him never to do it again. No one believed Ahmed anymore.

That night, Ahmed was walking home. As he walked through the yard, he saw big yellow eyes glowing in the darkness. Then he saw a Lynx chasing one of his dad's goats. "Lynx, Lynx!" Ahmed shouted. But no one would listen to him and the Lynx ate all the goats.

Page 178 Speaking

 4.14

That movie wasn't very good.

Oh, you didn't like it?

What I mean is, it was kind of boring.

Really? So you didn't think it had enough action?

Well, not exactly. In other words, I thought it needed a better plot.

Got it! I'll go see something else.

Unit 18

Page 186 Listening

 4.19A  4.20B

Please welcome Susan Wu, a professional storyteller who travels all over the world telling stories in schools. She's going to tell us a little about how she got into storytelling. Susan, thank you for coming to our school. Please start whenever you're ready.

Thank you for having me! It's wonderful to be here. Well, where do I start? At first, it wasn't storytelling. I was about 13, I guess. I was in school and I realized I had a talent for acting. I was in every school play and I just loved it, so I decided to go to acting school. I trained for several years to become an actress because I wanted to be really good at it, but then I realized I wanted to tell my own stories, too.

I think oral storytelling – you know, telling stories out loud – is very important. It's an ancient tradition and it's an important one because it helps bring stories to life. When you act out a story, you can develop the characters really well and the audience loves it. They're engaged and involved in the story. You're taking them on a journey.

Also, I think listening to a story is even more fun than reading one. People pay more attention when they're watching a storyteller. They're always wondering what'll happen next. Now, let me see. Does anyone have any questions so far? Yes, you in the red sweater at the back. What's your question?

Page 186 Speaking

4.21

Do you think people use smartphones too much?

Not really. I think they're great. I use mine for everything.

I agree that they're useful. It just seems like some people get distracted by them.

Do you mean while they're driving?

Yes, but also when they're in class or having a conversation with someone.

I see what you mean. I'm going to be more careful about that from now on.

Page 187 Word Study

4.22

1 I feel content in my new house. It's very cozy.
  The content of this article is surprising.

2 Is that a dove flying in the sky?
  I dove into the pool and began swimming.

3 What's that object you're holding? Is it some kind of tool?
  I wouldn't object to another slice of cake.

4 Please throw that refuse away.
  When they asked me to work late I had to refuse.

Page 191 Listening

4.23

Today on "Wild Encounters," Gerald Kim interviews Dr. Abby Lang, author of the newly published book, *Frog Hunt*.

Dr. Lang, tell us about your first encounter with a tomato frog.

Well, I almost stepped on one! The poor frog was all puffed up – that's what tomato frogs do when they feel threatened. I'm glad it did that, because it would have been tragic if I hadn't seen it. It looked just like its name – like a big tomato!

Where were you?

I was in Madagascar with a group of ornithologists. I was the only herpetologist in the group. A "herpetologist" is a scientist who studies reptiles and amphibians.

Ornithologists study birds, don't they? Why were you with them if you study frogs?

I was looking for nocturnal frogs and they were looking for nocturnal birds, like the Red Owl. I was apprehensive about tiptoeing through the forest by myself at night, so when I heard about their group trip, I asked if I could come along.

I see. Did you encounter anything scary while you there?

I did, but you'll have to read my book to find out!

Workbook Answer Key

Unit 1

Page 2

A

1 f   2 a   3 e   4 d   5 b   6 c

Page 3

B

1 c   2 a   3 b   4 b   5 d   6 c

C

1 b   2 a   3 b   4 a   5 a

Page 4

A

An ecoduct is a crossing for wildlife.

B

The article informs.

Page 5

A

Answers will vary. 'Inform' is the most important of the author's purposes.
Example sentences:
The French designed these structures to protect animals from the hazardous roads and traffic.
Since then, many other countries have also built wildlife crossings.
In fact, in the Netherlands there are over 600 special bridges and tunnels, called ecoducts.
Ecoducts, also called "green bridges," are structures that engineers build over big roads and freeways.
Most ecoducts have soil and plants on them, which provide a good habitat for wildlife and encourage animals to use the structures.

B

1 T   2 F   3 F   4 F   5 F   6 F

C

1 Some ecoducts are called overpasses. They go over a road.
2 Some ecoducts are called underpasses. They go under a road.

D

1 base   2 fade   3 gratefully
4 unseen   5 shone   6 herds

Page 6

B

Sentences 1, 3, 4, 5

C

1 They aren't going to be building any tunnels.
2 Will they be drawing a map of the site next week?
3 The engineers will be digging for three months.
4 Trains won't be crossing the bridge.

5 Cars and buses will be using the bridge.
6 People aren't going to be walking across the bridge.

Page 7

D

1 We won't be using the Mont Blanc tunnel on our trip.
2 You aren't going to be traveling in June.
3 Sam isn't going to be researching ecoducts.
4 I won't be learning about bridges.
5 She won't be visiting the park next week.

E

1 will they be designing
2 is going to be managing
3 will they be putting
4 are they going to be starting

Page 8

A

1 bisect   2 tricolor   3 binoculars
4 tricycle   5 bilingual   6 biceps
7 triangular   8 triplets

B

1 biceps   2 binoculars   3 tricolor
4 bilingual   5 triangular   6 bisect
7 triplets   8 tricycle

Page 9

A

New paragraph should begin:
Work has begun …

B

1 b   2 d   3 a   4 c

Unit 2

Page 10

A

1 obstacle   2 waterway
3 explosives   4 span   5 cables
6 beam

B

Page 11

C

1 overcome   2 problematic
3 varied   4 link   5 situation
6 waterway   7 span   8 Explosives

D

1 b   2 a   3 c   4 b   5 c   6 a

Page 12

A

Because they want to go swimming off Breezy island.

Page 13

B

1 d   2 a   3 c   4 b   5 b   6 c

D

1 d   2 c   3 b   4 a   5 f   6 e

Page 14

B

1 going to go   2 I wasn't   3 we'll be
4 were   5 He's   6 are
7 Have you been   8 aren't

C

1 will / be doing   2 not working
3 have been living   4 was watching
5 'm not eating   6 haven't been
taking   7 were / playing   8 are /
laughing

Page 15

E

Examples:
1 The man is carrying the logs.
2 A boy is building the bridge.
3 The girl is measuring the wood.
4 They're digging a hole.
5 The woman is helping the boy.

Page 16

A

1 site   2 dessert   3 accept
4 new   5 lose   6 desert
7 except   8 knew   9 sight
10 loose

B

Across
3 desert   4 lose   5 site   8 new
9 accept
Down
6 except   7 knew

Page 17

A

1 I like tigers. In fact, I like all big cats.
2 Many bridges are in need of repair. Similarly, many tunnels require repairs as they get older.

3 Many animals are dangerous. For example, some caterpillars and jellyfish contain poison.

4 We learned about extinct animals. In particular, we learned about dodos.

5 Cell phones are getting smaller. Likewise, computers are getting smaller.

Page 18

A

date
salutation
purpose statement
argument for
argument against
action statement
closing
signature

B

1 should   2 good   3 Always
4 polite   5 should

Page 20

A

1 suspended   2 strand
3 waterway   4 binoculars
5 triplets   6 sapphire
7 hazardous   8 obstacle
9 desert   10 span

Page 21

B

1 isolated   2 problematic
3 bilingual   4 admire

C

1 present continuous
2 present perfect continuous
3 future continuous
4 past continuous

D

1 learning
2 were you doing
3 has been raining
4 haven't been working
5 were studying
6 isn't coming

E

The break should occur before "Later, the Romans …"
Examples of connectors include: In fact (line 1), For example (line 1–2), Similarly (line 4), and Later (line 5)

Unit 3

Page 22

A

1 geologist   2 sphere   3 collide
4 chunk   5 element   6 pressure
7 crust   8 chamber

Page 23

B

1 c   2 d   3 b   4 a   5 b   6 d

C

Nouns	Verbs	Adverbs
mass	comprise	gradually
crust	collide	chemically
sphere	erode	
chamber		
chunk		
geologist		
pressure		
element		

Page 24

A

Hot water and steam come out of a geyser.

Page 25

B

1 T   2 F   3 F   4 T   5 T   6 F

C

Examples: Geysers and volcanoes both erupt.
Geysers and volcanoes occur in the same parts of the world.
Geysers send jets of hot water and steam into the air. Volcanoes send lava and rock into the air.

D

1 enormous   2 sections
3 intense   4 continental
5 erupt   6 mantle

Page 26

B

1 e   2 a   3 f   4 d   5 c   6 b

C

1 must   2 Could   3 weren't able to   4 can't   5 Can   6 might
7 Could   8 need to

Page 27

D

1 Geysers can send jets of hot water into the air.

2 In the future many of Iceland's volcanoes could erupt.

3 Can I help you find some information about Earth's mantle?

4 That man must be a geologist because he knows so much.

5 People had to study geology without modern technology a hundred years ago.

6 Geologists need to handle fossils with special care because fossils are so old.

E

1 must / have to
2 didn't have to

3 couldn't / wasn't able to
4 could
5 can't
6 could / was able to
7 Can / Could
8 could / might

Page 28

A

1 match   2 bow   3 tie   4 clear
5 bow   6 rock   7 clear   8 tie
9 rock   10 match

B

1 match   2 rock   3 tie   4 bow
5 tie   6 match   7 clear   8 bow
9 rock   10 clear

Page 29

A

1 Some jobs (such as being a surgeon) are difficult.

2 The water (which takes a long time to reach the deepest part of the Earth) rises to the surface as steam.

3 Many animals (including tigers and pandas) are severely endangered.

4 Old Faithful (a geyser in Yellowstone National Park) is famous all over the world.

5 Geologists (like many other types of scientists) are interesting people to talk to.

6 Brussels (which is the capital of Belgium) is known for having great food.

7 Certain vegetables (including mushrooms and broccoli) are called superfoods.

8 Some games (like this one on my phone) are free to download.

B

T

Unit 4

Page 30

A

Across
3 gasp   6 wheeze   8 boiling
10 charred   12 pumice   13 debris
Down
1 spatter   2 flutter   4 shower
5 flaming   7 cough   9 gravel
11 boulder

Page 31

B

1 b   2 a   3 b   4 a   5 a   6 a
7 a   8 b   9 b   10 b

C

Things you can do
1 gasp   2 cough   3 wheeze

Things you can touch
1 gravel **2** pumice **3** boulder
4 debris
Things you can watch happening
1 flutter **2** boiling **3** flaming
4 spatter

Page 32

A
A volcano erupting.

Page 33

B
1 They were told to leave.
2 She felt frightened.
3 They breathed the gray powder.
4 geysers, glaciers, ash

D
1 shore **2** scribe **3** deftly
4 observations **5** shifted
6 retreat

Page 34

B
1 (Had) anyone (been) in the house before you arrived?
2 When (I'd finished) my swimming lesson, I realized my sister had left.
3 We (hadn't traveled) far when the sun began to shine.
4 As soon as (I'd eaten) lunch, I started to feel hungry again!
5 (Had the) movie (started) before they bought the tickets?
6 Before the scientists found the fossil, they (hadn't discovered) anything at the site.

C
1 had formed
2 had heard
3 hadn't erupted
4 hadn't seen
5 had learned
6 had found
7 hadn't gone
8 had / done
9 had started
10 had melted

Page 35

D
1 c **2** b **3** a
E
1 Had you ever seen a volcano before?
2 Had the volcano had erupted before?
3 Had there been a warning?
4 Had you packed a bag?
5 Had the mayor told you where to go?
6 Had you seen your neighbors?

Page 36

A
1 believe **2** sleeve **3** achieve
4 chief **5** sweet **6** agree
7 degree **8** fleet

B

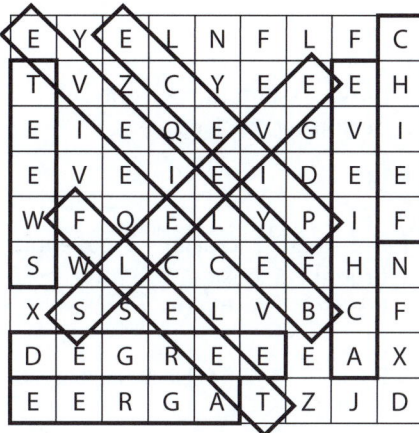

E	Y	E	L	N	F	L	F	C
T	V	Z	C	Y	E	E	E	H
E	I	E	Q	E	V	G	V	I
E	V	E	I	E	I	D	E	E
W	F	Q	E	L	Y	P	I	F
S	W	L	C	C	E	F	H	N
X	S	S	E	L	V	B	C	F
D	E	G	R	E	E	E	A	X
E	E	R	G	A	T	Z	J	D

C
1 piece **2** chief **3** sweet
4 agree **5** fleet **6** achieve
7 degree **8** believe **9** sleeve

Page 37

A
1 "Don't get too close to the geyser," the guide said.
2 "And," he added, "make sure that you're wearing suitable clothing."
3 "Everyone must leave home immediately," announced the mayor.
4 "The volcano has started to erupt," he continued. "You will be safer in the shelter."
5 "Is it already erupting?" asked my friend.
6 "Wow!" said Katy. "That's amazing."
7 "Hot water erupts from the geyser," he explained.
8 "Hurry up!" yelled the officer. "You must get to safety immediately."

B
1 "Please don't run in the corridors," said the teacher.
2 "What time does the movie start?" asked Tom.
3 "Watch out!" yelled Mina. "There's a car coming."
4 "Next," continued the guide, "we'll learn about these fossils."

Page 38

A
Opening statements
Body
Conclusion

B
1 c **2** b **3** d **4** a

Page 40

A
1 match **2** charred **3** boiling
4 enormous **5** agree **6** tie
7 sweet **8** shore **9** geologist
10 continental

Page 41

B
1 b **2** b **3** a **4** a **5** a **6** b
C
1 c **2** b **3** a **4** e **5** d
D
1 had researched
2 hadn't started
3 Had … erupted
4 hadn't found
5 Had … thrown
E
"Can you please explain what this piece of rock is?" asked Tommy.
"Yes, of course," replied the teacher, (Mr. Santos.)
(Mr. Santos, (like many of Tommy's other teachers,) was a kind and patient man. He gently took the piece of rock from Tommy's hand.
"This rock, (which is, in fact, a fossil,) is about 50,000 years old," he said.
"That's very old!" exclaimed Tommy.

Unit 5

Page 42

A
1 h **2** g **3** i **4** b **5** j **6** f
7 d **8** c **9** e **10** a

Page 43

B
1 b **2** c **3** d **4** c **5** b **6** a
C
1 decay **2** withers
3 tempestuous **4** Eternity
5 consistently **6** transition
7 schedule **8** spectacular
D

Nouns	Verbs	Adverbs	Adjectives
schedule	decay	consistently	tempestuous
eternity	withers		spectacular
transition			

Page 44

A
The Masked Man has good intentions.

B
They're internal and external conflicts.

Page 45

A

Conflict with self and conflict with characters are checked.
The Masked Man faces conflict with McSweeny and McBride. He also faces conflict when he has to choose between helping the little girl or McSweeny.

B

1 supermarket
2 journalist
3 taking a picture of the Masked Man
4 the little girl
5 Answers will vary

D

1 doubt   2 mood   3 adapt
4 control   5 accurately   6 decent

Page 46

B

1 b   2 a   3 b   4 b   5 b   6 a

C

1 had been studying
2 hadn't been swimming
3 hadn't been correcting
4 had been waiting

Page 47

D

1 had been working
2 hadn't been waiting
3 had been living
4 had been learning
5 had been driving
6 hadn't been paying

E

1 was / had been working
2 failed / hadn't been studying
3 had been waiting / felt
4 came / had been exercising
5 had been saving / bought
6 hadn't been playing / started

Page 48

A

1 plumber   2 actor   3 surveyor
4 counselor   5 trainer   6 inventor
7 painter   8 builder

B

1 inventor   2 counselor
3 plumber   4 painter   5 actor
6 builder   7 surveyor   8 trainer

C

1 trainer   2 surveyor   3 plumber
4 counselor   5 inventor   6 painter

Page 49

A

it catches the reader's attention and it makes the reader want to keep reading are checked.

B

1 a   2 b

Unit 6

Page 50

A

Across
2 disguise   6 covering   8 shield
9 entertainment   10 elaborate
11 safeguard
Down
1 basic   3 urgent   4 central
5 performer   7 lifesaver

Page 51

B

1 essential   2 crucial   3 covering
4 urgent   5 basic   6 central
7 lifesaver   8 shield

C

1 F   2 F   3 T   4 F   5 T   6 F
7 T   8 F

Page 52

A

To be able to see underwater.

Page 53

B

1 b   2 b   3 d   4 a   5 c   6 b

D

1 enthusiasm   2 individual
3 germs   4 ridiculous
5 operations   6 antiquity

Page 54

B

1 A fencer is an (athlete) who uses a mask and a sword.
2 On the Ivory Coast there are (people) that use masks in ceremonial costumes.
3 Is that the (girl) who doesn't like hip hop?
4 Welders are (workers) that join pieces of metal together.
5 Football players are (athletes) that wear masks to play football.
6 Captain Davies is the (pilot) that doesn't like flying!

C

1 Tom's teacher is the lady who / that lives next door.
2 Which man is the writer who / that writes science fiction?
3 Is there anyone who / that doesn't like chocolate?
4 I don't know anyone who / that doesn't like movies.
5 What's the name of the singer who / that was on TV last night?
6 I felt bad for the girl who / that lost her book bag.

Page 55

D

1 A nurse is a person who / that works in a hospital.
2 These are the people who / that celebrate the carnival in Venice.
3 A mask maker is a professional who / that makes masks.
4 A baseball player is an athlete who / that doesn't wear a mask.
5 Mr. Kamal is the man who / that teaches music.

E

1 They're both people that / who play sports.
2 They're both people that / who work with animals.
3 They're both people that / who look after your health.
4 They're both people that / who deal with emergencies.
5 They're both people that / who entertain.
6 They're both people that / who work in a restaurant.
7 They're both people that / who work in a law court.
8 They're both people that / who work in fashion.
9 They're both people that / who are artists.
10 They're both people that / who know about the stars.

Page 56

A

1 happiness   2 tiredness
3 softness   4 illness   5 ugliness
6 hopefulness   7 laziness
8 weakness

B

1 illness   2 ugliness   3 softness
4 tiredness   5 weakness
6 laziness

C

1 happiness   2 weakness
3 illness   4 ugliness   5 softness
6 laziness   7 Tiredness
8 Hopefulness

Page 57

A

1 T   2 F   3 T   4 F   5 F   6 T

B

1 Masks Around the World
2 Practical Masks
3 Masks for Entertainment

Page 58

A

The hook
Scene setting
Details
Conclusion

B

1 The author starts with a hook to get the reader's attention.
2 The author talks about the scene in the first paragraph.
3 The author gives details in the second paragraph.
4 The narrative ends with a conclusion.

Page 60

A

1 a 2 b 3 a 4 b 5 a 6 a
7 b 8 b 9 b 10 a

B

1 disguise   2 elaborate   3 germs
4 performer   5 accurately
6 eternity

Page 61

C

1 c 2 e 3 d 4 b 5 a

D

1 had been training
2 had been categorizing
3 had been providing
4 had been responding
5 had been drawing

E

1 Fencers are athletes who / that use a mask for their face.
4 A surgeon is a type of doctor who / that does operations.
6 A pilot is someone who / that needs to look at a schedule
8 A chemist is someone who / that can mix chemicals accurately.
2 Welders are workers who / that need to shield their face with a mask.

F

1 tiredness   2 actor   3 happiness
4 laziness   5 painter   6 plumber
7 inventor   8 illness

Unit 7

Page 62

A

1 h 2 c 3 a 4 d 5 g 6 f
7 b 8 e

Page 63

B

1 b 2 a 3 b 4 a 5 b 6 b

C

1 shorten   2 external   3 different
4 limited   5 separate

D

1 an artist   2 a butterfly
3 when you're learning
4 endless   5 builders

Page 64

A

His wife's death.

Page 65

A

Symmetry
You can see the symmetry in the pool.
There is reflection symmetry in the decorations.
Repetition
The main building is cube-shaped with four identical sides.
There are four minarets.
The garden is divided into four sections.

B

1 c 2 b 3 a 4 d

D

1 employ   2 hesitate   3 practical
4 approximately   5 constituent
6 experiment

Page 66

B

1 Marble is a ⟨rock⟩ that people used to build palaces.
2 The Taj Mahal is a ⟨palace⟩ that is famous all over the world.
3 Construction workers are ⟨people⟩ who build structures.
4 Vikram Singh is the ⟨man⟩ who wrote the travel guide.
5 This is the ⟨place⟩ where you can take great pictures of the Taj Mahal.
6 The Taj Café is a ⟨restaurant⟩ which is famous for making good meals.
7 This is a nice ⟨hotel⟩ where you can stay in when you visit Agra.
8 The ⟨tile⟩ that is used in the Taj Mahal is completely symmetrical.

C

1 that   2 who / that   3 that
4 where   5 which   6 that

Page 67

D

1 Minarets are tall structures that look like towers.
2 An emperor is someone who is the ruler of a country.
3 Repetition is a principle which is used in the design of buildings.
4 India is a country where elephants live.
5 Agra is a place that people like to visit.

E

1 A butterfly is an insect that has mirror symmetry.
2 This is a pattern that / which has an interlocking design.
3 Mumtaz Mahal was the woman who / that married Shah Jahan.

4 A cloud is something that / which isn't symmetrical.
5 This is the pool of water that / which reflects the Taj Mahal.
6 This is the entrance where tourists enter the Taj Mahal.
7 In the 1600s, elephants were the animals that / which carried building materials.
8 This is a drawing of a lighthouse that / which was at Alexandria.

Page 68

A

1 i 2 e 3 f 4 a 5 d 6 c
7 g 8 h 9 b

B

1 intermission   2 transport
3 intersection   4 translate
5 interfere   6 transient
7 translation   8 interlocking
9 transatlantic

Page 69

A

1 fifteen   2 thirty-two   3 sixteen
4 ninety-seven   5 forty-two   6 Five

B

1 a three-minute song
2 ten insects
3 twenty-two years ago
4 fifty-nine dollars

Unit 8

Page 70

A

B

1 fragment   2 dazzling
3 eyepiece   4 laboratory
5 minute   6 image
7 astonishment   8 triumphantly

Page 71

C

1 panic   2 triumphantly
3 astonishment   4 dazzling
5 minute   6 laboratory
7 eyepiece   8 fragment   9 image
10 copious   11 examination
12 surpass   13 stare

D

Adjectives	Nouns	Verbs	Adverbs
dazzling	panic	stare	triumphantly
minute	astonishment	surpass	
copious	laboratory		
	eyepiece		
	fragment		
	image		
	examination		

Page 72

A

He doesn't paint symmetrically.

Page 73

B

1 he's in a panic
2 their idea of happiness
3 He splashes paint all over the paper.
4 He's happy and proud.

D

1 bothered   2 piles   3 flickered
4 forecast   5 gust   6 scrambled

Page 74

B

1 Dr. Baskerville is the (doctor) whose office is on the second floor.
2 There's the (man) whose son plays the drums.
3 Molly is the (girl) whose brother is in sixth grade.
4 That's the (neighbor) whose house has a blue roof.
5 Is that the (girl) whose mom is a doctor?
6 Which is the (painter) whose painting is the Mona Lisa?
7 That's the (actor) whose real name is Bill Smith.
8 My (cousin), whose name is Sammy, is a great dancer.

C

1 Shakespeare is the playwright whose plays are famous all over the world.
2 Which is the boy whose sister plays in the school band?
3 What's the name of the teacher whose hair is red?
4 Where is the man whose daughter won first prize?

Page 75

D

1 Mark is the friend whose dog performs tricks.
2 Mrs. Baggini is the woman whose daughter won a prize.
3 That's the athlete whose running speed broke all records.

4 Do you know the teacher whose car is bright red?
5 There's the man whose wallet was stolen.
6 That's the singer whose song went to number 1.
7 She's the author whose books are famous.
8 Mr. Marielos is the man whose house is by the ocean.
9 That's the police officer whose car broke down.
10 You're the artist whose paintings are in the art gallery.

E

1 whose   2 who / that   3 that / which   4 whose   5 that / which
6 whose   7 that / which   8 who
9 whose   10 that / which

Page 76

A

	-ing form	*-ed* form
chill	chilling	chilled
trouble	troubling	troubled
pierce	piercing	pierced
intrigue	intriguing	intrigued

B

1 chilling   2 intriguing   3 piercing
4 pierced   5 chilled   6 troubling
7 intrigued   8 troubled

C

1 piercing   2 troubled   3 intrigued
4 intriguing   5 chilling

Page 77

A

1 We ate lunch in the dining room.
2 Can you play volleyball on the lawn?
3 I took my little sister to school.
4 Sometimes we watch a video at school.
5 I bought some peaches at the market.
6 They are building a gym downtown.

Page 78

A

story summary
comparisons
likes
dislikes
final thoughts

B

1 c   2 a   3 b

Page 80

A

1 troubled   2 stare   3 laboratory
4 extend   5 translation   6 hesitate
7 minute   8 identical

B

1 triumphantly   2 forecast
3 interlocking   4 dimensions
5 repetition   6 experiment
7 approximately

Page 81

C

1 whose   2 which   3 whose
4 where   5 whose   6 that
7 who   8 which

Unit 9

Page 82

A

1 d   2 b   3 g   4 f   5 a   6 c
7 h   8 e

Page 83

B

1 distress   2 invaluable   3 enable
4 consists   5 lack

C

1 lack   2 disapproval   3 concealed
4 distress   5 raised   6 transmit

D

1 send away   2 comfort   3 show
4 separate   5 compliment
6 forbid   7 cheap   8 own

Page 84

A

We no longer use typewriters.

Page 85

A

Technology can help people who can't talk.
Details will vary.

B

1 Most people can't remember the first words they said.
2 Some people are born unable to speak.
3 Illness or injury can take away a person's speech.
4 In the 1960s some people had typewriters but few people had computers.
5 Reg Malin made a machine called a POSSUM that helped people communicate.

C

We use technology.

D

1 brand-new   2 ancestors
3 widely   4 estimate   5 allies
6 ingenious

Page 86

B

1 Ulan Bator, <u>which is the capital of Outer Mongolia</u>, is a place I'd like to visit.
2 My teacher, <u>whose name is Mrs. Anders</u>, is extremely intelligent.
3 This machine, <u>which someone invented a long time ago</u>, looks old-fashioned.
4 A scanner, <u>which copies documents</u>, is useful to have.
5 Beethoven, <u>whose compositions are beautiful</u>, is famous worldwide.
6 Many people eat fast food, <u>which isn't very healthy</u>.
7 Woolly mammoths, <u>whose close relatives are elephants</u>, died out millions of years ago.
8 Astrophysics, <u>which I know very little about</u>, sounds very interesting.
9 That boy, <u>whose name is Timothy</u>, was my partner in gym class.
10 Baseball, <u>which is a very popular sport</u>, isn't one that I enjoy.

C

1, 3, 5, 6

Page 87

D

1 My cousin, whose pen pal lives in New York, loves emailing.
2 Cairo, which the capital of Egypt, is a large, exciting place.
3 Astronomy, which I'm interested in, is the study of stars, planets, and the universe.
4 Chocolate, which everyone in my class likes, originated in South America.
5 Grey catbirds, whose nests are built in woodlands, often live near coasts and lakes.
6 A rainbow, which you can only see when there's rain and sun, is multicolored.

Page 88

A

Across
2 astronomer   6 confident
8 conclude
Down
1 astrophysics   3 asterisk
4 connect   5 astrobiology
6 concept   7 concur

B

1 a   2 a

C

1 astrophysics   2 concur
3 conclude   4 asterisk
5 concept   6 confident

Page 89

A

1, 3, 4, 6, and 8

B

1 Running can be good for you. On the other hand, you have to be careful of injury.
2 My friend Cristina loves singing. However, she's not very good at it!
3 Eagles are skilled flyers. Unlike eagles, chickens aren't good at flying.

C

My mom and dad, who are both teachers, are really good at science. (Unlike) them, I'm not very good at it because I find the concepts hard. (However) I'm very skilled at learning languages. When I was very young, I learned Spanish and then Italian. I like to practice speaking languages with other people. Sometimes I make mistakes, but that's OK because you can learn from mistakes. (On the other hand), you do need to be careful to correct the mistakes you make.

Unit 10

Page 90

A

1 pesky
2 piercingly
3 customary
4 intently
5 shimmer
6 rugged
7 circular
8 devise

B

1 In class last week, we devised a plan for our research.
   The silvery water shimmered in the morning sun.
2 I looked intently at the shell, trying to figure out what it was.
   My mom looked radiant in her new dress.
3 We were both tired and desperately wanted to go to sleep.
   "Don't do that!" he said, irritated by my actions.
4 Sue loves it when it's misty outside.
   He waved at me with his customary smile on his face.

Page 91

C

1 T   2 F   3 F   4 T   5 F   6 T
7 T   8 T   9 T   10 T

D

1 an object   2 a person
3 a person   4 the weather
5 mountains   6 an insect
7 a plan   8 a person

Page 92

A

They're looking for the Hillbury Shield.

Page 93

A

Story setting	How it is described
The town of Hillbury	There was a famous battle there.
Bakele in Africa	It's very hot there and Johnson feels uncomfortable.

B

1 a   2 b   3 a   4 b   5 b   6 a

D

1 Only children have no brothers or sisters.
2 The impenetrable forest was too thick to hike through.
3 Both palms and ferns grow in my country.
4 At the end of the mystery story, the candle is an insignificant object.
5 Please put each book back on its respective shelf.

Page 94

B

1 P   2 P   3 A   4 A   5 P   6 A
7 P   8 P   9 A   10 P

C

1 police officer / police
2 teacher
3 pilot

Page 95

D

When the story begins, the main character has just left on a plane because some important papers <u>have been stolen</u>. The character thinks <u>they've been taken</u> to Mexico City but he doesn't know why. He decides to investigate. Over the previous few weeks, a number of letters and messages <u>have been received</u> at the police station. These messages show pictures of an old building, but the detective doesn't see what the connection is at first. After the detective receives a map, he gets more curious. When all the preparations <u>have been made</u> and the tickets <u>have been bought</u>, the detective and his colleague board a plane to Mexico.

E
1 My sandwich has been eaten!
2 The train tickets have been booked.
3 The case has been investigated.
4 The door has been opened.
5 Has the letter been read?
6 The phone has been answered.

F
1 The books have been stacked.
2 The board has been cleaned.
3 The window has been shut.
4 The computer has been restarted.
5 The homework has been corrected.
6 The trash has been emptied.
7 The desks have been straightened.
8 The floor has been swept.
9 The supplies have been put away.
10 The lights have been switched off.

Page 96

A

E	C	O	N	O	M	I	C	A	L	U	W	M	F
Y	T	E	N	T	H	U	S	I	A	S	T	I	C
L	L	G	C	H	I	L	D	I	S	H	Q	D	O
R	E	S	I	Y	N	N	I	K	S	T	V	T	G
E	S	A	K	J	I	L	U	F	H	T	U	O	Y
S	K	C	F	A	N	A	T	I	C	A	L	I	L
I	R	C	E	I	L	P	N	E	V	E	N	Y	Q
M	P	E	V	I	T	N	E	T	T	A	J	L	J
H	D	W	C	C	R	E	D	N	E	L	S	M	M

B
1 skinny NG   slender P
2 childish NG   youthful P
3 enthusiastic P   fanatical NG
4 economical P   miserly NG

C
1 enthusiastic   2 childish
3 youthful   5 fanatical   6 miserly
7 attentive

Page 97

A
1 flap   wind
2 splash   water
3 whisper   wind
4 drip   water
5 spray   water
6 flutter   wind

B
1 a   2 b   3 a   4 b   5 a   6 b

C
Crunch an apple
Munch on pizza
Glug milk into a glass
Listen to the fizz of soda water
Sip, slurp…
That tastes good!
Flip-flops off
Splash in the pool
Flags flutter in the breeze

A tennis ball has been bounced!
Ha, ha, ha …
Life is cool!

Page 98

A
onomatopoeia
rhyme
incomplete sentence
complete sentence
stanza

B
1 a   2 b   3 a   4 a

Page 100

A
1 d   2 e   3 b   4 h   5 f   6 c
7 g   8 a

B
1 a   2 b   3 b   4 b   5 a   6 b
7 b   8 a

Page 101

C
1 The message has been transmited by e-mail.
2 The code has been cracked.
3 The thief has been arrested.
4 The game has been won.
5 The tire has been changed.
6 The house has been built.

D
1 Sherlock Holmes, who was a famous fictional detective, was very clever.
2 Morse Code, which is still used today, was invented in the nineteenth century.
3 Silbo Gomera, which is a whistling language, comes from an island in near Africa.
4 The POSSUM, which was adapted from a typewriter, had a mouthpiece.
5 Reg Malin, who was British, was interested in helping people.

E
1 Unlike my sister, my brother does silly things.
2 We watched the flags fluttering.
3 The water whooshed down the mountainside.
4 I'm very artistic. On the other hand, I'm not at all musical.
5 The faucet dripped a slow, steady drip.
6 It's going to rain. However, we can still go out.

Unit 11

Page 102

A
1 h   2 e   3 f   4 c   5 g   6 a
7 b   8 d

Page 103

B
1 b   2 d   3 b   4 a   5 d   6 b

C
1 summit   2 awesome
3 laboriously   4 handholds
5 cling   6 plateau

Page 104

A
The writer is in the mountains. He is on a climb.

Page 105

B
1 T   2 F   3 T   4 F   5 F   6 T
7 T   8 T

D
1 considerable   2 exposed
3 satisfaction   4 disaster
5 panting   6 perched

Page 106

B
1 A   2 P   3 P   4 A   5 A   6 A
7 P   8 P

C
1 Have the climbers been prepared for the arsh conditions?
2 Has a safety code been devised?
3 A route hasn't been selected.
4 Haven't the ropes been checked?
5 Blankets have been packed.
6 The flashlights have been found.
7 Has a rest site been chosen?
8 The expedition has been planned carefully.

Page 107

D
1 Our tickets haven't been booked yet.
2 The guidebook hasn't been packed.
3 Our parents haven't been told.
4 The school hasn't been informed.
5 Haven't rooms been reserved?
6 The maps have been read.

E
1 What type of equipment has been chosen?
2 Who has been selected to lead the expedition?
3 Where have the tents been put up?
4 What food has been prepared?
5 Which route has been planned?

F
1 The theater hasn't been cleaned yet?
2 The lines haven't been learned yet.
3 The stage hasn't been decorated yet.
4 The costumes haven't been finished yet.
5 The last tickets haven't been sold yet.

Page 108

A

1 g 2 a 3 h 4 b 5 f 6 e
7 c 8 d

B

1 advice 2 effect 3 wander
4 coarse

Page 109

A

	Subject pronoun	Reflexive pronoun
1	I	myself
2	you (singular)	yourself
3	he	himself
4	she	herself
5	it	itself
6	we	ourselves
7	you (plural)	yourselves
8	they	themselves

B

1 Be careful with that knife! You might cut yourself.
2 We congratulated ourselves for winning the match.
3 Serena is vain. She is always looking at herself in the mirror.
4 Joey, Nick, and Sam, please get yourselves a soda and a snack from the fridge.
5 Their parents were out, so they had to make lunch for themselves.
6 I love painting! I painted this picture myself.

Unit 12

Page 110

A

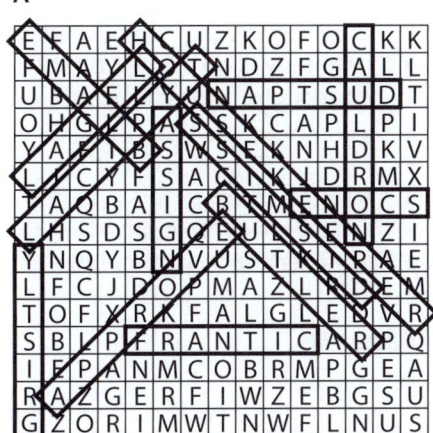

B

1 butler 2 housekeeper
3 dustpan 4 cauldron 5 scones

Page 111

C

1 assigns 2 gristly 3 dismiss
4 legal 5 frantic 6 blame

D

1 c 2 b 3 a 4 b 5 c 6 a

Page 112

A

Because he wants to share memories of living in Istanbul with his childen and grandchildren.

Page 113

A

	Cause	Effect
1	Gilbert's father moved to Istanbul for a job in 1961.	Gilbert was born in Istanbul.
2	Gilbert and his friends could smell fish grilling.	Gilbert and his friends felt hungry as they came down the hill.
3	Friends of Gilbert's parents came to visit.	Gilbert took them to buy Turkish Delight.

B

1 c 2 b 3 c 4 b

D

1 f 2 d 3 a 4 c 5 e 6 b

Page 114

B

2, 4, 5, 8, and 9

C

1 Marcus 2 We don't know.
3 Billy 4 We don't know.
5 We don't know. 6 Danny

Page 115

D

1 had been 2 hadn't been 3 had been 4 had been 5 hadn't been
6 had been 7 had been
8 had been

E

1 My video game hadn't been played.
2 My bedroom hadn't been cleaned.
3 The dog hadn't been fed.
4 The front door hadn't been locked.
5 My bed hadn't been made.
6 Dinner hadn't been made.

Page 116

A

1 pajamas 2 tortilla 3 piano
4 waffle 5 catastrophe 6 garage
7 bamboo 8 almanac

B

1 almanac 2 Bamboo 3 garage
4 waffle 5 pajamas 6 piano
7 catastrophe 8 tortilla

Page 117

A

For a man: Mr.
For a woman: Mrs, Ms.
For a man or woman: Dr., Prof.

B

Receptionist Hello, this is Mrs. / (Dr.) Katz's office. How may I help you?
Ginny Oh, hello. This is Mr. / (Mrs.) Karras. I'd like to make an appointment for my husband, (Mr.) / Ms. John Karras.
Receptionist Certainly, Dr. / (Mrs.) Karras. Does your husband want to see Prof. / (Dr.) Katz or the nurse?
Ginny He'd like to see (Dr.) / Mr. Katz, please.
Jack Hi there, could you put me through to Ms. / (Prof.) Alberto Quinto, please?
College secretary Yes, of course. Who shall I say is calling?
Jack It's Jack. I'm in (Prof.) / Mrs. Quinto's math class.

Page 118

A

Reason for writing
Dialogue
Final thought

B

1 should 2 can 3 don't have to
4 good

Page 120

A

1 ledge 2 typical 3 legal
4 appetite 5 catastrophe 6 slim
7 confessed 8 loom 9 wonder
10 tortillas

B

1 domes 2 butler 3 dismiss
4 cauldron 5 perched

Page 121

C

1 Has the expedition been organized?
2 The bags haven't been packed.
3 Has the map been checked?
4 The top of this mountain hasn't been climbed.
5 Have the tents been put up?

D

When we arrived at base camp, we had already been instructed by the team leaders which route to take. The guides had unpacked our equipment and a fire had been lit. Then we noticed that some food had been cooked. Since we had been informed about bad weather in the mountains, we decided to wait two days before setting off.

F
1 Mrs.　2 yourself　3 Dr.
4 myself　5 Prof.　6 ourselves

Unit 13

Page 122

A
3 clumsy　2 lazily　5 amuse
1 argue　4 resemble　6 limp

B
1 awkward　2 lazily　3 mock
4 resembles　5 Jeers　6 bear
7 a minor　8 clumsy　9 amused

Page 123

C
1 argue　2 minor　3 amuse
4 lazily　5 mocks　6 key
7 resemble　8 pitifully　9 bear
10 clumsy

D

Verbs	Nouns	Adjectives	Adverbs
resemble	jeers	clumsy	pitifully
bear	key	awkward	lazily
argue		minor	
limp			
mock			

Page 124

A
They use echolocation.

Page 125

B
1 a　2 d　3 c　4 b　5 b　6 d

D
1 c　2 e　3 f　4 d　5 b　6 a

Page 126

B
Paul and Sam are going on a trip to a bird sanctuary in India. <u>They will be picked up</u> at their hotel at 6:00 a.m. <u>They'll be taken by bus</u> to a place called Bharatpur where there are many different species of birds. On the journey to Bharatpur, <u>they'll be told</u> what types of birds they can expect to see. On arrival, <u>they'll be introduced</u> to their guide. Paul and Sam <u>will be driven</u> through the sanctuary in a rickshaw, which is a type of bicycle with space for passengers. <u>They'll be asked</u> to keep quiet because it's important not to frighten the birds. At the end of the day, Paul and Sam <u>will be escorted</u> back to their hotel in Fatehpur Sikri where <u>they'll be given</u> a delicious Indian curry.

C
1 will pick up　2 will take　3 will tell　4 will introduce　5 will drive　6 will ask　7 will escort
8 will give

Page 127

D
1 The suitcases will be
2 The refrigerator will be emptied.
3 The guidebooks will be read.
4 The windows will be locked.
5 The tickets will be bought.
6 The luggage tags will be completed.

E
1 will be held
2 will be invited
3 will be given
4 will be organized
5 will be read
6 will be shown
7 will be asked
8 will be announced

F
1 Will a cake be baked?
2 Decorations will be put up.
3 Games will be brought.

Page 128

A
2, 3, 5, 7, and 8

B
1 fight　2 crash　3 munch
4 taste　5 grows　6 chatter
7 run　8 bounce

Page 129

A
The world is a stage.
The men and women of the world are actors.

B
1 c　2 f　3 a　4 d　5 b　6 e

Unit 14

Page 130

A
1 h　2 i　3 e　4 d　5 g　6 b
7 c　8 a　9 j　10 f

B
1 decorate　2 encounter　3 imply
4 inspect　5 behavior
6 phenomenal　7 technique
8 mimic

Page 131

C
1 c　2 d　3 b　4 d　5 c　6 c

D
1 inspect　2 mimic　3 decorated
4 Phenomenal　5 Spines
6 ornithologist　7 technique
8 implied

Page 132

A
It's a domesticated rock pigeon.

Page 133

B
1 It comes from Latin.
2 They're trained by putting food in one place and the pigeons' homes in another.
3 A pigeon can be a lifesaver by recognizing objects or people in the ocean.
4 Answers will vary.

D
1 brainy　2 man-made　3 spear
4 Harsh　5 ability　6 reveals

Page 134

B
1 A　2 P　3 A　4 P　5 P　6 A
7 P　8 P

C
1 This piece of music was composed by Mozart.
2 The compass was invented by the Chinese.
3 My homework hadn't been corrected by my teacher.
4 A pizza is to be made by the chef.

Page 135

D
1 The lake will be drained by Saryi.
2 An office will be built by Milo.
3 Fences will be put up by Kamal.
4 Bird boxes will be installed by Tino.
5 Feeding stations will be set up by Boris.
6 The water quality will be tested by Jan.
7 The paths will be cleaned by Siridej.
8 Flowers will be planted by Maria.
9 The gates will be painted by Katy.
10 Information sheets will be printed by Michel.

E
1 had been asked　2 by
3 had agreed　4 be built
5 assembled　6 was completed
7 will be admired　8 by

Page 136

A

Root: *anti*	Root: *phon*
1 anticipate	1 microphone
2 antidote	2 phonics
3 antibacterial	3 cacophony
4 antipathy	4 symphony

B

1 Symphony   2 antidote
3 cacophony   4 antibacterial
5 anticipate   6 Phonics
7 microphone   8 Antipathy

Page 137

A

1, 3, 4, 7

B

1 M   2 S   3 M   4 S   5 M   6 S

Page 138

A

Wh-questions
Details about how

B

1 The author has organized the action plan with wh-questions.
2 The longest part of the action plan is the 'how' part.
3 It's the longest part because it explains how the plan will be successful.

Page 140

A

1 resemble   2 mimicking
3 artistically   4 ornithologist
5 limping

B

1 a   2 b   3 a   4 b   5 a   6 b
7 b

Page 141

C

1, 3, 4, 5, 7, and 10

D

1 M   2 A   3 A   4 M   5 A   6 A
7 A   8 M

E

1 A lot of money has been raised for charity.
2 A cure was found for the disease.
3 Plans have been made to sell the medicine.
4 Doctors are told about new medicines.
5 The medicine will be sent all over the world.
6 The charity has been discussed on TV.

Unit 15

Page 142

A

1 e   2 c   3 a   4 d   5 b   6 f

Page 143

B

1 a   2 c   3 d   4 a   5 b   6 b

C

1 threat   2 triggered   3 store
4 numbs   5 reflex   6 respond

Page 144

A

He's a naturalist. / He's the star of TV shows.

Page 145

B

1 T   2 F   3 F   4 T   5 T   6 F
7 T   8 F

D

1 instantly   2 defensive
3 decisions   4 deliberate
5 obvious   6 Adrenaline

Page 146

B

2, 4, 5, 7, and 8

C

1 Y   2 Y   3 N   4 N   5 Y

Page 147

D

1 If it had been hot and sunny, we would have gone to the beach.
2 If Mom had had the time, she would have made homemade ice cream.
3 If his car hadn't run out of gas, Dad would have made it the meeting on time.
4 If I hadn't forgotten her birthday, my friend wouldn't have gotten mad.
5 If it hadn't been dark, we wouldn't have gotten lost.
6 If I had studied for the test, I would have got a good grade.

E

1 hadn't   2 would   3 been
4 wouldn't   5 hadn't   6 have
7 hadn't   8 have   9 hadn't
10 would

Page 148

A

1 acidic   2 cosmic   3 limbic
4 metallic   5 energetic   6 heroic
7 tragic   8 allergic

B

1 energetic   2 limbic   3 tragic
4 allergic   5 acidic   6 cosmic
7 heroic   8 metallic

Page 149

A

If you're out on a hike and you see a wild animal, you shouldn't approach it, unless you're an experienced naturalist! Animals in the wild aren't used to people and may react defensively even if you don't intend to harm them.

Our advice is to stay calm and walk quietly in a different direction so you don't risk being hurt. You should stay around only if you're absolutely sure the animal is harmless. We all have a "fight or flight" instinct.
Either be ready to fight if the animal attacks you, or run away!

B

1 if   2 Unless   3 Even if   4 If
5 even if   6 Unless

Unit 16

Page 150

A

```
D S E N P B R A X J E B K L T
I E S O H P R O M A T E M V N
B D R S N U G G L E S X L T M
F C I M A N Y D D K U K H H O
C A P P R E H E N S I V E L Y
R P T I P T O E E G D S C D I
E Q D H J S P E C U L I A R Z
E G N U V P W X W N A T Q J H
P O U T L A N D I S H M C H V
Y F R E V O P E E L S Y R D E
```

B

1 uncontrollably   2 nocturnal
3 upright   4 twinkle

Page 151

C

1 snuggle   2 apprehensively
3 metamorphose   4 peculiar
5 dynamic   6 tiptoe

D

1 c   2 a   3 c   4 c   5 b   6 a

Page 152

A

She's afraid of riding in elevators.

Page 153

A

How does she feel?	She's scared and nervous.
How does she act toward others?	She relates well to her friends.
What does she learn?	She learns that you can overcome a fear.

B

1 d   2 d   3 b   4 d   5 c   6 d

D

1 f   2 e   3 c   4 a   5 d   6 b

Page 154

B

1 F   2 F   3 T   4 T   5 T   6 F

C

1 didn't   2 would   3 could
4 called   5 didn't   6 hadn't

Page 155

D

1 I wish I hadn't gone to bed so late. I wouldn't be tired.
2 If only I hadn't forgotten to eat breakfast, I wouldn't be hungry.
3 I wish I hadn't kicked a football and broken the neighbor's window.
4 If only I hadn't been late, I wouldn't have missed the start of the movie.
5 I wish I'd studied for the test. I wouldn't have failed it.
6 If only I hadn't gone out in the rain without a jacket, I wouldn't have gotten wet.
7 I wish I'd remembered my grandfather's birthday.
8 If only I'd taken care of my teeth, I wouldn't have a cavity.
9 I wish I hadn't put salt in the cake instead of sugar. It wouldn't have been disgusting!
10 If only I hadn't recorded the wrong show on TV, I wouldn't have missed my favorite program.

Page 156

A

	P	N	N
childish		✗	
young			✗
youthful	✗		✗
aroma	✗		
stench		✗	
odor			✗
inactive			✗
relaxed	✗		
lazy		✗	
arduous		✗	
challenging	✗		
difficult			✗

B

1 stench 2 aroma 3 challenging
4 difficult 5 arduous 6 odor

Page 157

A

1, 3, 5, 7, and 8

Page 158

A

Title
Numbered instructions

B

1 Yes, the author uses a title. It explains what the text is about.
2 The author organizes the tips with numbered instructions.
3 The author is addressing the reader.

Page 160

A

1 g 2 h 3 a 4 j 5 b 6 i
7 d 8 e 9 f 10 c

B

1 b 2 a 3 b 4 a 5 b 6 a
7 b 8 b 9 a 10 a

Page 161

C

1 had gone / wouldn't have overslept
2 wouldn't have gone / had seen
3 would have seen / hadn't been
4 would have invited / had known
5 would have sent / had had
6 wouldn't have bought / had known

D

1 I wish I hadn't lost my backpack. If only I hadn't lost my backpack, I wouldn't have gotten into trouble.
2 I wish I hadn't missed the bus. If only I hadn't missed the bus, I wouldn't have been late.
3 I wish I hadn't eaten so much cake. If only I hadn't eaten so much cake, I wouldn't have felt sick.
4 I wish I hadn't forgotten my umbrella. If only I hadn't forgotten my umbrella, I wouldn't have gotten wet.

E

1 If 2 unless 3 only if 4 Even if

Unit 17

Page 162

A

1 g 2 h 3 b 4 d 5 a 6 e
7 c 8 f

Page 163

B

1 c 2 b 3 a 4 d 5 b 6 a

C

1 instinct 2 poisonous 3 coiled
4 Hideous 5 illicitly 6 lethal
7 unmistakable 8 soothingly

D

Nouns	Adjectives	Verbs	Adverbs
instinct	coiled	sidle	illicitly
	poisonous		warily
	unmistakable		soothingly
	lethal		
	hideous		
	crumpled		
	tinged		
	miraculous		

Page 164

A

Felipe likes to take risks.

Page 165

B

1 rainforest 2 hot and humid
3 head home 4 Jorge
5 cute 6 it's poisonous
7 Listen to other people and respect nature.

D

1 tingle 2 capable 3 quivered
4 confided 5 evilly 6 lingering

Page 166

B

1 b 2 a 3 b 4 a 5 b 6 a

C

1 b 2 b 3 b 4 b 5 c

Page 167

D

1 had started 2 get up
3 were researching 4 haven't tasted
5 are doing 6 didn't know

E

1 had been watching, remembered
2 had been jogging, wanted
3 hadn't been waiting, arrived
4 achieved, had been studying
5 had been learning, lived
6 hadn't been playing, weren't

Page 168

A

1 airless 2 weightless
3 meaningless 4 helpless
5 toothless 6 hopeless
7 restless 8 thoughtless

B

1 hopeless 2 thoughtless
3 airless 4 meaningless
5 weightless 6 restless

Page 169

A

1 asked / explained
2 suggested / agreed
3 reminded / said
4 confided / offered

B

1 agreed   2 suggested   3 argued
4 confided   5 offered

C

Harry looked down at the dark underwater cave.
"I want to dive down there," he explained.
"But you can't. It's too deep," argued Justin.
"No, it isn't," argued Harry. Lowering his voice, he confided, "It might be a little dangerous, but I'm a good swimmer."
"Maybe we should both go in. suggested Justin. "Shall I dive with you?" he offered.
"OK," agreed Harry. "Let's do it."
Answers will vary.

Unit 18

Page 170

A

Across
2 intricate   4 purely   7 recount
9 novelist   10 storytelling
12 relate
Down
1 futuristic   2 imagination
3 dedicated   5 breakthrough
6 publish   8 reminisce
11 impulse

Page 171

B

1 publish   2 breakthrough
3 futuristic   4 imagination
5 dedicated   6 reminisce
7 recounted   8 an impulse

C

1 T   2 F   3 T   4 T   5 F   6 F
7 F   8 T

Page 172

A

She was a mystery writer.

Page 173

A

Writer's opinion: Agatha Christie was the most famous mystery writer of all time.
Possible examples: Her abilities are unmatched. She wrote 66 detective novels.
She's the best-selling novelist of all time. Approximately 4 billion copies of her books have been sold.
She wrote a play. It's still on stage after 60 years.

B

1 d   2 c   3 d   4 a   5 d   6 c

D

1 incidents   2 available
3 autobiography   4 attitudes
5 plot   6 biography

Page 174

B

1 going to   2 will   3 present
continuous   4 will

C

1 going to go on vacation
2 going to be a hot day
3 going to go on a picnic
4 going to fall

Page 175

E

1 They're leaving for the airport on Sunday.
2 They're flying to Cancún on Monday.
3 They're visiting Mérida on Tuesday.
4 They're snorkeling in Cozumel on Wednesday.
5 They're exploring the ancient city of Tulum on Thursday.
6 They're learning to cook Mexican food on Friday.

Page 176

A

1 dove   2 object   3 content
4 content   5 refuse   6 dove
7 refuse   8 object

B

1 content   2 refuse   3 dove
4 Refuse   5 object   6 refuse
7 content   8 dove

Page 177

A

1 57   2 1922   3 9:32   4 60
5 22   6 1987   7 14 / 15   8 1.5

B

1 Philip's birthday is August 12.
2 My mother was born in 1986.
3 Our school's address is 162 Main Street.
4 More than 3 million people visit the city every year.
5 The plane took off at 11:15. It's going to land at 4:30.

Page 178

A

Setting
Problem
Internal conflict
External conflict

B

1 The author describes the setting by writing about the library that Sid and Nadia are in.
2 The author introduces a conflict between Sid and Nadia through dialogue.

Page 180

A

1 b   2 b   3 a   4 a   5 a   6 b
7 a   8 b   9 b   10 a

Page 181

C

1 restless   2 warily   3 capable
4 available   5 meaningless
6 miraculous   7 autobiography
8 refuse

D

1 reminded   2 confided
3 15 / asked   4 16 / explained

E

1 am reading; is; travels; sees
2 was; decided; started; was walking; saw
3 Have; wanted; have dreamed; haven't traveled; have made

Word List

Unit 1

base
fade
gratefully
herds
shone
unseen
admire
depart
discouraged
exquisite
hazardous
insist
isolated
labor
sapphire
skeptical
strand
suspicious
wriggle
biceps
bilingual
binoculars
bisect
triangular
tricolor
tricycle
triplets

Unit 2

aqueducts
commonly
factors
load bearing
stacks
suspension
beam
cable
explosive
link
obstacle
overcome
problematic
situation
span
support
suspended
varied
waterway

accept
dessert
except
knew
loose
sight
site
desert
new
lose

Unit 3

continental
enormous
erupt
intense
mantle
sections
chamber
chemically
chunk
collide
comprise
crust
element
erode
geologist
gradually
mass
pressure
sphere
bow
clear
match
tie

Unit 4

deftly
observations
retreat
scribe
shifted
shore
boiling
boulder
charred
coughing
debris
flaming

flutter
gasp
gravel
pumice
shower
spatter
wheeze
achieve
agree
believe
chief
degree
fleet
sleeve
sweet

Unit 5

accurately
adapt
control
decent
doubt
mood
categorize
consistently
decay
eternity
frost
irritating
literally
predictable
schedule
spectacular
tempestuous
transition
wither
actor
builder
counselor
inventor
painter
plumber
surveyor
trainer

Unit 6

antiquity
enthusiasm
germs

individual
operations
ridiculous
basic
central
covering
crucial
disguise
elaborate
entertainment
essential
lifesaver
performer
safeguard
shield
urgent
happiness
hopefulness
illness
laziness
softness
tiredness
ugliness
weakness

Unit 7
approximately
constituent
employ
experiment
hesitate
practical
aesthetic
arrangement
dimensions
equilateral
extend
identical
infinite
interlocking
internal
repetition
reproduce
structure
symmetrical
interfere
intermission
intersection
transatlantic
transient
translation
translate
transport

Unit 8
bothered
flickered
forecast
gust
piles
scrambled
astonishment
copious
dazzling
examination
eyepiece
fragment
image
laboratory
minute
panic
stare
surpass
triumphantly
chilling
chilled
intrigued
intriguing
pierced
piercing
troubled
troubling

Unit 9
allies
ancestor
brand new
estimate
ingenious
widely
beckon
conceal
consist
disapproval
distress
enable
gesture
group
invaluable
lack
raised
refusal
transmit
asterisk
astrobiology
astrophysics
astronomer
concept

conclude
concur
confident

Unit 10
ferns
impenetrable
insignificant
only
palms
respective
circular
customary
desperately
devise
frustrated
intently
irritated
misty
pesky
piercingly
radiant
rugged
shimmer
childish
enthusiastic
fanatical
skinny
slender
economical
miserly
youthful

Unit 11
considerable
disaster
exposed
panting
perched
satisfaction
awesome
cling
crack
dome
expedition
handhold
laboriously
ledge
loom
plateau
slack
slim
summit

advice
advise
affect
coarse
course
effect
wander
wonder

Unit 12
appetite
confess
copper
passageway
range
strict
approve
assign
blame
butler
cauldron
dismiss
dustpan
frantic
gristly
housekeeper
legal
scone
typical
almanac
bamboo
catastrophe
garage
pajamas
piano
tortilla
waffle

Unit 13
beak
comical
dew
oars
partly
silences
amuse
argue
awkward
bear
clumsy
jeers
key
lazily

limp
minor
mock
pitifully
resemble
albatross
always
bower
built
caterpillar
crow
have
heard

Unit 14
ability
brainy
harsh
man-made
revealed
spear
annual
artistically
behavior
decorate
encounter
imply
impress
inspect
mimic
ornithologist
phenomenal
spine
technique
antibacterial
anticipate
antidote
antipathy
cacophony
microphone
phonics
symphony

Unit 15
adrenaline
decisions
defensive
deliberate
instantly
obvious
alert
distracted
frozen

interpret
numb
rapid
reflex
rehearse
respond
store
tame
threat
trigger
acidic
allergic
cosmic
energetic
heroic
limbic
metallic
tragic

Unit 16
briefly
chattering
gripped
removing
staff
weaving
apprehensively
creepy
dynamic
metamorphose
nocturnal
outlandish
peculiar
sleepover
snuggle
tiptoe
twinkle
uncontrollably
upright
arduous
aroma
lazy
odor
relaxed
challenging
inactive
stench
difficult

Unit 17
capable
confided
evilly

lingering
quivered
tingle
coiled
crumpled
hideous
illicitly
instinct
lethal
miraculous
poisonous
sidle
soothingly
tinged
unmistakable
warily
airless
helpless
hopeless
meaningless
restless
thoughtless
toothless
weightless

Unit 18
attitudes
autobiography
available
biography
incidents
plot
breakthrough
dedicated
futuristic
imagination
impulse
intricate
novelist
publish
purely
recount
relate
reminisce
storytelling
content
dove
object
refuse

OXFORD
UNIVERSITY PRESS

Great Clarendon Street, Oxford, OX2 6DP, United Kingdom

Oxford University Press is a department of the University of Oxford.
It furthers the University's objective of excellence in research, scholarship,
and education by publishing worldwide. Oxford is a registered trade
mark of Oxford University Press in the UK and in certain other countries

ISBN: 978 0 19 427824 9   Integrated Teacher's Toolkit 6
ISBN: 978 0 19 427851 5   Teacher's book with online practice
ISBN: 978 0 19 427852 2   Teacher's access card
ISBN: 978 0 19 427928 4   Assessment CD-ROM
ISBN: 978 0 19 427934 5   Big Question DVD

Printed in China

This book is printed on paper from certified and well-managed sources

ACKNOWLEDGEMENTS

Assessment illustration

Illustrations by: Constanza Basaluzzo; Mike Dammer; George Hamblin;
Jannie Ho; Ian Joven; Anthony Lewis; Margeaux Lucas; Q2A Media Services;
Jomike Tejido.

Photo stock credits, Assessment Worksheets: Olga Danylenko/shutterstock; Ocean/
Corbis; FOTOSEARCH RM - www.agefotostock.com; Erik Tham/Demotix/
Corbis.

Photo stock credits, Testing Practice 2 and 3: Paul Martin/Hulton Archive/Getty
Images; Oleg Zabielin/shutterstock; Sabphoto/shutterstock.

Discover Posters photo credits

Illustrations by: POSTER 2: Stephen Durke (cutaway earth and world map);
POSTER 4: Stephen Durker (sugar crystals inset).

*We would also like to thank the following for permission to reproduce the following
photographs:* POSTER 1: Andreas Strauss/LOOK/Getty Images; David Wall
Photo/Lonely Planet Images/Getty Images; Rolf Adlercreutz/Alamy; Walter
Geiersperger/Corbis; Tim Brakemeier/dpa/picture-alliance/Newscom.
POSTER 2: Ruud de Man/E+/Getty Images; Bjorn Holland/The Image Bank/
Getty Images; LianeM/Alamy; Sebastián Crespo Photography/Flickr/Getty
Images; LOWELL GEORGIA/National Geographic Creative. POSTER 3: Gunter
Marx/Alamy; altrendo images/Altrendo/Getty Images; Chen Hang/Xinhua
Press/Corbis; Simon Balson/Alamy; Ball Miwako/Alamy. POSTER 4: Daniel
Stein/E+/Getty Images; Erik Isakson/Getty Images; Roderick Chen/All Canada
Photos/Getty Images; KidStock/Blend Images/Corbis. POSTER 5: Jade/Blend
Images/Corbis; Chung Sung-Jun/Staff/Getty Images Sport/Getty Images; David
Burton/Alamy; Jetta Productions/Walter Hodges/Getty Images; Ocean/Corbis.
POSTER 6: Keystone Pictures USA/Alamy; Phillip Jarrell Photographer/The
Image Bank/Getty Images; Fotosearch/Getty Images; Maria Pavlova/Vetta/
Getty Images; Barry Austin Photography/Iconica/Getty Images. POSTER 7: Jody
Trappe Photography/Flickr Open/Getty Images; Marcos Welsh/Design Pics/
Design Pics/Corbis; Juniors Bildarchiv GmbH/Alamy; Chase Swift/CORBIS.
POSTER 8: Thorsten Henn/Cultúra RM/Age Fotostock; Caro/Alamy; Izabela
Habur/E+/Getty Images; Joe McBride/The Image Bank/Getty Images. POSTER
9: Eric Audras/Onoky/Corbis; Marc Romanelli/Blend Images/Corbis; Africa
Studio/Shutterstock; The Gallery Collection/Corbis; Jacek Chabraszewski/
Shutterstock; Travel Ink/Getty Images; Mel Yates/Taxi/Getty Images; Corey
Ford/Stocktrek Images/Getty Images.